D1276985

The Child

Infants and Children

Nancy J. Cobb
California State University, Los Angeles

Mayfield Publishing Company
Mountain View, California
London • Toronto

Copyright © 2001 by Mayfield Publishing Company

All rights reserved. No portion of this book may be reproduced in any form or by any means without written permission of the publisher.

Library of Congress Cataloging-in-Publication Data

Cobb, Nancy J.
 The Child: infants and children / Nancy J. Cobb.
  p.   cm.
 Includes bibliographical references and indexes.
 ISBN 0-7674-2339-9
 1. Child psychology 2. Child development. I. Title.
 BF721.C5622000
 305.231—dc21   00-053292

Manufactured in the United States of America
10   9   8   7   6   5   4   3   2

Sponsoring editor, Franklin C. Graham; developmental editor, Barbara Armentrout;
production editor, Melissa Williams Kreischer; manuscript editor, Margaret Moore;
design manager and cover designer, Susan Breitbard; text designer, Ellen Pettengell;
art editor, Robin Mouat; illustrators, Lineworks and John and Judy Waller; manufacturing
manager, Randy Hurst; permissions editor, Marty Granahan. Cover photo © Martin
Klimek/Jeroboam, Inc. The text was set in 10.5/12 Legacy Serif Book by GTS Graphics,
Inc., and printed on acid-free 45# Somerset Matte by R. R. Donnelley and Sons Company.

Photo, text, and illustration credits appear following the References on pages C-1–C-4,
which constitute an extension of the copyright page.

Brief Contents

Contents

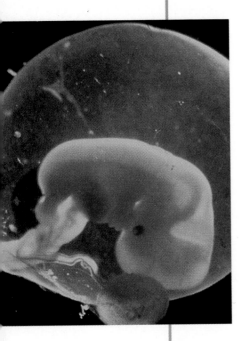

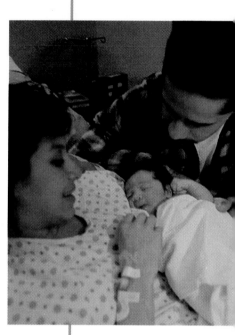

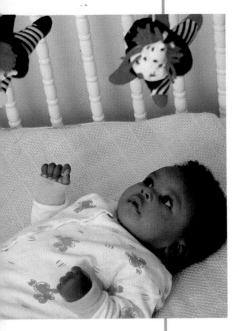

chaptereight Early Childhood
Cognitive Development   295

chaptertwelve Middle Childhood
Psychosocial Development 447

Narratives

Preface

What do you remember of your own childhood or the games you played? Imagine yourself sitting on a park bench watching children at play. Over next to the trees, you notice a few school-age children taking turns on the swings. Close by, you can make out four young children playing contentedly by themselves in a sandpit, one with a shovel and the others with various toys. In the distance is a skateboard park seemingly used only by boys, each doing their own thing on the ramps or clustered in small knots around the perimeter. A number of girls their age are walking through the park by two's and three's, involved intensely in conversation. You continue watching. Have you ever really looked at children playing before? Is there more than meets the eye in the way children of different ages play?

What is play, you wonder? Do toddlers usually play alone, even if they are right next to each other? When do children learn to take turns? Why were only boys at the skateboard park? Is the scene at this park typical for children of these ages? You were a child once, presumably much like these children. But, you're surprised to find you don't have answers to these questions. And then you wonder what makes some children aggressive and others shy? What brought aggression to mind? You remember seeing a news story on TV only this morning about a school shooting. Several experts in child development talked about possible signs of disturbance that could have told the parents or teachers that something was going wrong, or already had gone wrong, in the lives of those children. Others commented that many times there are no reliable signs to distinguish children who are truly troubled from those who are not. They also said that troubled children can come from homes that are just as loving and supportive as those of other children.

Last Sunday's newspaper profiled a very different child. The Teen Life section described the day-to-day life of a teenage boy—active in 4-H, a merit scholar bound for the university next fall—whose favorite activity is serving as a volunteer at an after-school day care center near his home. Three days a week, for 3 years now, he has helped children with their homework, played games with them, and just kept them company. What makes children so different? How much of a difference is there to begin with from one child to the next? How do circumstances change life outcomes, you wonder? As a casual observer you may never discover the answers to these questions. But, as a student of child development, some questions may be answered and others that you never imagined may come to mind.

This book introduces you to ordinary children, such as those in the park, with the hope that you will see things about them that you previously never noticed or thought about. Instead of simply talking about children, as many textbooks do, this book will let children talk to you as well. This textbook relies on the use of narrative, using children's own words as well as stories about children and their families, to help you understand developmental concepts. In addition, three features distinguish this textbook's approach: This book will emphasize a constructive perspective to development, it will highlight ethnic and gender diversity, and it will stress continuity of development.

A Narrative Approach

As you read this text, you will be invited to see things from the perspective of the children as well as from that of the researchers who study them. The things children say and do, as well as narrative accounts of their experiences by others, provide a rich database from which to study development. You will be encouraged to analyze and make sense of children, as developmentalists do, by observing them and their families firsthand through these narrative accounts. Instead of simply presenting you with various theories or research findings, you will be included in the process of discovery itself by being introduced to the developmental issues, in the form of narrative accounts, that research and theory were designed to address.

A Constructive Perspective

As you begin to look at things from the vantage point of children, you will see that they frequently see things differently than do adults. The constructive perspective assumes that individuals actively "construct" reality rather than passively react to events. In doing so, they organize experience in meaningful ways that change predictably with age. Individuals continually interpret the events they experience. As a consequence, a single event can mean different things to different people. Perceiving the world, whether listening to someone talk or making sense of what we are seeing, is an active process. Reality does not come at us packaged for passive absorption. In order to experience a coherent, meaningful world, a person must construct or assemble it from the moment, from less coherent raw material. This view of perception as an active, constructive process is termed the constructive perspective and will inform the pages of this text.

Gender and Ethnic Diversity

In reading this book, you will discover how differences of gender and ethnicity contribute to the way children construct their reality. Few differences are as important to children, or to individuals of any age, for that matter, as those associated with their gender. Some differences are biologically based, whereas others are socially determined and reflect what a particular culture expects of children depending on gender. Culture contributes to development in even more general ways, affecting everything from which foods children like (preferences that may be established even before birth) to which language they use when talking to a grandparent. The very rituals, beliefs, and rhythms to life that a culture provides furnish the perspective from which children learn to view the world. Culture, whether this is provided by children's sex or their ethnicity, provides the interpretive lens through which they look when constructing the events they experience.

Continuity of Development

You may be surprised to discover yourself in the experiences of the children you are reading about. Development brings many changes—in size, skills, maturity and understanding—but each of us still carries within us the self we were at different points in our lives. Continuity of development assumes that within every adult there lurks an adolescent and an even younger child. Issues of intimacy, for instance, are salient not only in early adulthood but also in infancy. A concern with autonomy is central not only to adolescence, but also to toddlerhood, and emerges again as an issue in later adulthood. As you discover how children at different ages deal with various issues, you may discover new things about yourself as well.

Continuity exists in yet another way. Despite obvious differences between groups of children defined by factors such as ethnicity or gender, the differences *among* children within any group are greater than the differences *between* those groups. Underlying commonalities may suggest ways of conceptualizing solutions to some of the social ills that affect children's lives. With respect to this point, each chapter contains a social policy box that highlights a policy related to some aspect of children's well-being. Issues covered in these policy boxes include substance abuse in pregnancy and how to balance the rights and responsibilities of the individual with those of the community, genetic testing and the human genome project, and how best to teach schoolchildren who are not proficient in English.

Additional Features

What else distinguishes this book? One of the most important features of this text is one that you may *not* notice at first. The writing style of this book is designed to be "reader friendly" and conversational. The text is intended to read much the way someone would sound when speaking to you—informal and personal. When this approach is successful, you, the reader, become aware only of the concepts you are asked to think about and not the process of reading about them. Don't be misled by the informal tone to the text; you will be getting a sophisticated analysis of developmental concepts, research, and theory.

In addition to boxes highlighting social policy, this book contains boxes highlighting research. The study of child development involves two quite different types of knowledge. One of these describes *what* we know about children's development, the ways they change with age and the factors that are responsible for those changes. The other describes *how* we know what we know, the research methods that generate the findings you'll be reading about. The Research Focus boxes introduce you to this second type of knowledge: the basic methods of developmental research. These boxes are important because they provide you with the tools you will need to actively analyze what you're reading rather than simply taking in the facts. Each box begins with a practical problem and then illustrates how researchers used a particular approach to solve it. Some examples are "Descriptive Statistics: How harmful *Is* Secondhand Smoke?" "Ethics: Kangaroo Care for Low-Birthweight Infants," and "Internal and External Validity: 'Tuning Out' Powerless Adults." All together, the boxes cover all of the basic topics important for understanding the methodologies used by developmental researchers.

Organization of This Text

The book is divided into five parts: Foundations, Infancy and Toddlerhood, Early Childhood, Middle Childhood, and Adolescence. Each part contains three chapters: physical development, cognitive development, and psychosocial development. All chapters begin with an outline of the material that is to be covered. Each chapter begins with a brief vignette or opening section designed to draw you into the chapter, and ends with a summary that describes the major points of the chapter. Key terms appear in a running glossary in the margins of the text, to highlight developmental concepts as you read. Also, each chapter contains Stop-and-Think questions that are designed to engage you with the material as you read.

Teaching and Learning Tools

- *Instructor's Manual and Test Bank.* This is a comprehensive resource for instructors. Part One of the manual includes, for each chapter: chapter outlines, summaries, and learning objectives; lecture organizers (the text of the PowerPoint slides available on the Instructor's CD and *The Child* Web site); lecture suggestions; discussion and critical thinking questions; suggested answers to the text's Stop-and-Think questions; activities; and student worksheets. Part Two offers Internet Resources, with suggested Web sites and worksheets to guide students through Internet-related assignments. Part Three, Video Resources, gives detailed descriptions and reviews of suggested videos for each chapter. The Test Bank contains over 1,500 questions in multiple choice, true-false, short answer, and essay formats. Answers with page references and topic identification are provided.

- *Computerized Test Bank.* MicroTest III, developed by Chariot Software Group, contains the complete test bank, including answers, topic identification and page references. MicroTest allows you to design tests using the questions included with *The Child* and/or to incorporate your own questions. The testing program is available in both Windows and Macintosh formats.

- *Transparency Acetates.* Provided to enhance lectures, the 50 acetates, many in full-color, include selected art and other images from the text. They are also available on the Instructor's CD and the Web site.

- The Child *Web Site (http://www.mayfieldpub.com/cobb).* Instructor's resources on the site include a syllabus builder (which allows instructors to customize a syllabus and post it at a unique Web address), the Instructor's Resource Guide, PowerPoint slides, an image bank, electronic transparencies, and Internet links. The entire instructor's section is password-protected. Student's resources on the site include an interactive study guide, Internet activities, and a Web tutorial.

- *The Mayfield Child and Adolescent Development Custom Video.* This video, developed to accompany *The Child*, contains more than 15 video clips ranging from 5 to 10 minutes in length. With at least one clip per chapter, the video is a valuable resource for encouraging class discussion. Topics include classical and operant conditioning, pediatric brain development, the diagnosis and treatment of Attention Deficit Disorder, differences between the sexes, memory, and depression in children and adolescents.

- *Instructor's CD-ROM.* This CD contains PowerPoint slides, electronic transparencies, an image bank of images from the text, and the Instructor's Resource Guide. The PowerPoint slides, as shown in the lecture organizers section of the Instructor's Manual, provide a lecture outline for each chapter and can be combined with the electronic transparencies for an integrated classroom presentation. The Instructor's Manual can be downloaded from the CD and materials customized to fit any course organization. This complete package of presentation resources can be used with both IBM-compatible and Macintosh computers.

- *Study Guide.* Written to coordinate with the materials found in the Instructor's Manual and Test Bank, this guide uses the SQ4R method and offers for each chapter: chapter outline, summary, and learning objectives; flash cards; questions for reflection and application; activities and observations; worksheets; and practice quizzes.

Acknowledgments

I would like to thank all of those who have helped with the writing of this book. To all of you at Mayfield who have been involved in this project, my sincerest thanks. This book would not have come into being without the work that you have contributed to it. I am deeply thankful for this, as I am for the opportunity to have worked with you. My sincere thanks go to Barbara Armentrout, the developmental editor for this project, who helped to flesh out and develop the manuscript at every stage of the writing. Your contributions have enriched this text in ways that are too numerous to mention. To Melissa Williams, the production editor, many thanks for your creative touch and your attentiveness to detail as you shepherded this project through to completion. Your efforts in its production have resulted in a beautiful book. Thanks also go to Joan Pendleton for your expert and careful reading and copyediting of the manuscript. Finally, I am especially thankful for the opportunity of working once again with Frank Graham, the sponsoring editor for this project. For your vision for this project, your integrity as an editor and a person, for your good spirits, and for being a friend, Frank, I thank you.

Thanks also to talented and creative students past and present, and to their supportive spouses, to Jennie Euler, who found references when I could not, and to Larry Albinski, who dropped these off at all hours of the day and night. Thank you, thank you! To Anita Rosenfield and Andrea Weyermann, for doing an outstanding job on the ancillaries, my sincere thanks for making this book a more meaningful experience for those who will use it.

To my prayer partners, Roberta Veit, Monteene Ivey, and Holly Tone, my deepest thanks for your friendship, prayers, and encouragement. To Bill Cobb, for your humor, CDs, and nostalgia, thank you; these made writing, not to mention my life, so much easier. To Joshua and Jenny, I thank you for the brave way you live your lives; you have been my tie to what is real as a parent and as a person. To Michael, if one can thank another for wisdom and love, I thank you for these, and for your courageous honesty and generosity of spirit, for always taking the time to listen to ideas and read pages of manuscript, even when this was time that you took from your writing. I could not have written this, nor done much else, without you—nor would I want to.

My thanks also go to those colleagues who have reviewed the manuscript and offered both helpful suggestions and informed criticism: Nancy Ahlander, Ricks College; Eric Ansel, Weber State University; Daniel R. Bellack, Trident Technical College; Kenneth S. Bordens, Indiana University, Purdue University at Fort Wayne; Kathleen W. Brown, California State University, Fullerton; Joan B. Cannon, University of Massachusetts–Lowell; Elaine Cassel, Marymount University; Melonye Curtis, Amarillo College; Denise Davidson, Loyola University of Chicago; Deborah Davis, Chaffey College; Nancy E. Dye, Humboldt State University; Diane Widmeyer Eyer, Cañada College; William J. Gnagey, Illinois State University; Dale Goldhaber, University of Vermont; Janet Gonzalez-Mena, Napa Valley College; Mary Jo Graham, Marshall University; Allen Keniston, University of Wisconsin–

Eau Claire; Kina Leitner, New York University; Terry F. McNabb, Coe College; Philip J. Mohan, University of Idaho; Linda C. Monahon, Simmons College; Marilyn Moore, Illinois State University; David L. Morgan, Spalding University; Peggy Perkins, University of Nevada, Las Vegas; Jay B. Pozner, Jackson Community College; Joe Price, San Diego State University; Wanda L. Ruffin, Hood College; Jane A. Rysberg, California State University, Chico; Marie Saracino, Stephen F. Austin State University; Rochelle Robinson Warm, Palm Beach Community College; and Valjean Whitlow, Belmont University.

*For I know the thoughts I think concerning you,
says the Lord, thoughts of peace and not of hurt,
to give you a future and a hope.*

Jeremiah 29:11

chapterone

Introduction and Theories of Development

The French call memories *souvenirs*—a part of the past we take with us. Impossible? Time, after all, can't be put in a pocket, to be carried off for another day. Just as with sand, by which it's been measured, time slips through fingers like water and light. "Souvenirs" exist nonetheless. But how? How does one hold on to a moment? Remember a childhood? The answer, I believe, is that *we* become the souvenirs. The souvenirs we carry are *ourselves,* changed by the act of collecting them.

In *Salt Dancers,* Ursula Hegi describes a scene from childhood:

> When I turned four, my father taught me the salt dance: he sprinkled a line of salt on the living room floor, positioned my bare feet on top of his shoes, and told me to leave everything I feared or no longer wanted behind that line. His gold-flecked eyes high above me, he walked me across that salt border into my brand-new year—he backward, I forward—my chin tilted against the buttons of his silk vest. . . . Though I no longer recall what I left behind the salt line that day or chose to take with me, I can still evoke the tingling in my arms as they encircled my father's lanky waist. Below his right eyebrow curved the moon-sliver scar where a dog had bitten him when he was a boy. Rooted to his feet, I didn't slip off as we danced, careful at first—"Two steps to the right, Julia, one to the left"—then spinning through the rooms, past the radiant faces of my mother and brother. (p. 11) ◄

In a sense, all children dance into the future on the feet of their parents. We carry the past within us, measuring our steps to its rhythms. The cadence of the

familiar provides us with footholds to the present—the past and the present meeting in the assembling of the moment. Listen for such a "meeting" in this young boy's account of his first day at school, as he makes sense of his experiences in the only way he can, in terms of what he brings with him, the "souvenirs" of experience:

> I spent that first day picking holes in paper, then went home in a smoldering temper.
>
> "What's the matter, Love? Didn't he like it at school then?"
>
> "They never gave me the present."
>
> "Present? What present?"
>
> "They said they'd give me a present."
>
> "Well, now, I'm sure they didn't."
>
> "They did! They said: 'You're Laurie Lee, aren't you? Well just you sit there for the present.' I sat there all day but I never got it. I ain't going back there again." (Donaldson, 1978, p. 9) ◄

Laurie Lee's misunderstanding of what the teacher said illustrates the way his expectations colored his experiences (in Scotland, Laurie Lee is a common name for boys). But the "present" is not a simple reality. Events are not necessarily perceived in the same way by each of the persons experiencing them. There are, in fact, as many realities—presents—as there are people to experience them. In order for any one of these realities to emerge for a person, the person must construct, or "assemble," that particular reality and not any of the others. This understanding of human activity, referred to as a **constructive approach,** will inform the pages of this text.

Children and adults alike continually put together the events to which they respond, doing so effortlessly, imbuing these with meaning. This activity is so centrally human that Robert Kegan (1982), a psychologist at Harvard, calls us "meaning makers."

In *Sula*, Toni Morrison (1973) describes the reactions of two girls, Sula and Nell, who are responsible for the accidental drowning of a young boy. Each has constructed the event in a different way. Sula is from "a household of throbbing disorder constantly awry with things, people, voices and the slamming of doors," whereas Nell is daily "surrounded by the high silence of her mother's incredibly orderly house, feeling the neatness pointing at her back." The two friends have spent the hot afternoon by the bank of a river, lying in the grass, wordlessly sharing the day. Chicken, a small boy whom they know, appears and Sula invites him over to play. Nell is put off by the child, who is dressed in clothes too large and is digging his finger in his nose, but Sula playfully grasps the boy's hands and, to his terror and delight, swings him in circles by the river's edge. Sula's grasp slips and Chicken sails out over the river, disappears beneath the water, and drowns. Nell calms the distraught Sula and makes sure they leave no trace of their presence by the river's bank. The girls are silent about their part in the death; and, as Sula cries at the boy's funeral, Nell assures herself she has done nothing wrong. Years later, Nell is stunned when Sula's grandmother interrupts the polite chatter of Nell's social call by asking her how she had killed that little boy. Nell assures the grandmother that it had been Sula, not she. But the grandmother responds, "You. Sula. What's the difference? You was there. You watched, didn't you?" (p. 168). ◄

Despite its terrible finality, the child's death is no more a simple reality than was Laurie Lee's misunderstanding of the teacher's remark. Chicken's death meant different things to those involved—sorrow to one girl, self-protective concern to the other, and grief to still others. The "real" meaning of the story is made

constructive approach The theoretical perspective that individuals' expectations color their experiences of the world; that each individual constructs a particular reality from experience.

**FIGURE 1.1 The Process of
Constructing Meaning**

no clearer by examining the objective event—the drowning—to which each character responds. Instead, it is the grandmother's remark that focuses our attention on what Kegan (1982) calls "that most human of 'regions' *between* an event and a reaction to it . . . the place where the event is privately composed, made sense of, the place where it actually *becomes* an event for that person . . . this zone of mediation where meaning is made" (p. 2). This process is schematically represented in Figure 1.1.

In this zone, Nell had composed a reality in which she had no responsibility for the drowning. Chicken's death carried no meaning of loss or guilt for her as it did for Sula. However, in making sense of the grandmother's question, she is surprised by another reality—that she shares responsibility for the drowning with Sula, that the "neatness pointing at her back" is not a salt line behind which she can leave what she has feared all her life—death and loss, and the impotence of an orderly life to change either.

You will meet many children in the pages of this text, children like Laurie Lee, Sula, and Nell. Each has a story to tell, and each will bring to life the developmental themes and concepts of the book. The book itself has three organizing themes: it adopts a constructive perspective on development, it focuses on issues of diversity, and it stresses the continuity of development.

The Constructive Perspective on Development

Children do not necessarily see things the way adults see them, nor even the way children a bit older or younger do. The Swiss developmentalist, Jean Piaget, has given us a powerful way of understanding these differences; his approach illustrates the constructive developmental perspective. Piaget was fascinated by differences in the way children and adults understood their world. By simply talking with children, he discovered, for instance, that they believed that dreams came

Differences in cognitive development at different ages affect how children make sense of the world. This small child doesn't understand why he can't always have the ball whenever he wants it.

in through the window at night, that taller people had to be older than shorter ones, or that how much there was to something had more to do with how many pieces there were than with the size of the pieces. Observations such as these convinced Piaget that what we call knowledge is more than a simple copy of reality. Piaget assumed, instead, that we actively construct what we know of the world and that we organize this understanding in qualitatively different ways with age, each new organization resulting in a distinctly different stage of thought.

Robert Kegan (1982) illustrates one such stage difference humorously with the following story in which a mother of two young sons had just about "had it" with their continual squabbling. They had bickered their way through the day, and her patience was nearing its end as she watched them quarrel over the dessert she had just given them—little pastries of different sizes filled with assorted jams. She had given her 4-year-old the biggest of three pastries and her 10-year-old the two smaller ones. The 4-year-old was tearfully complaining that his brother had "more," and that he wanted two pieces as well. His mother and his brother assured him that his one piece was just as big as the two smaller ones put together, but he was unmoved by the logic of their argument. Kegan describes the situation as the mother, now well beyond the limits of her patience:

> "in a fit of sarcasm . . . swept down on his plate with a knife, saying, 'You want two pieces? Okay, I'll give you two pieces. Here!'—whereupon she neatly cut the younger boy's pastry in half. Immediately, all the tension

What might Piaget suggest as a way to help children sleep through the night when they are scared of bad dreams?

FIGURE 1.2 Letter Recognition

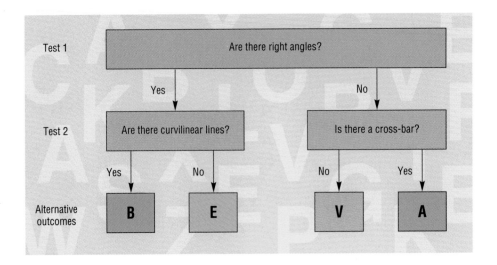

went out of him; he thanked his mother sincerely, and contentedly set upon his dessert. The mother and the older son were both astonished. They looked at the boy the way you would look at something stirring in a waste-basket. Then they looked at each other; and in that moment they shared a mutually discovered insight into the reality of their son and brother, a reality quite different from their own" (pp. 27–28). ◄

The constructive perspective maintains that a child's reality is not *of necessity* one that is shared by others, as this mother and older brother discovered. However, instead of then dismissing children's reality as bizarre or simply "mistaken," the constructive perspective assumes that their reality reflects a logic of its own, one that is internally consistent and through which they make sense of their world.

Assuming that individuals *do* continually interpret their experience, composing or making sense of the events to which they react, how, you might ask, do they do this? How, in other words, are we to understand such a constructive process?

We can begin an explanation by examining the activity you are engaging in at this very moment—reading. The constructive approach assumes that perception is an active process. To perceive the letters that make up a sentence, in other words, one must do something other than simply keep one's eyes open and on the page. The nature of this perceptual activity takes the form of scanning the lines that form the letters to determine which features are present. Features are the characteristics of letters that enable us to distinguish one letter from another, such as whether the lines are straight or curved, open or closed, form angles, and so on. Perceptual scanning is directed by expectations of what a letter *might* be, based on what has preceded it. Given the number of letters that are possible, each of which is distinguished by multiple features, such expectations play a major role in perception.

Look at Figure 1.2. Are there right angles? Could that letter be a B? An E? An E has the same number of right angles as a B, but lacks curvilinear lines. Are there curvilinear lines? Research on letter recognition lends substantial support to this type of analysis. Confusion errors in tasks calling for individuals to quickly identify letters flashed on a screen confirm that the more features two letters have in common, the more likely they are to be confused with each other (Neisser, 1967).

Given the explanation of the constructivist theory of reading, why is it so difficult to proof your own written work?

FIGURE 1.3 *The same physical arrangement of lines that forms the letter B also forms the number 13.*

If you are still not convinced that we actively "construct" the events to which we respond, take a moment to look at Figure 1.3. Notice that the very same lines that form the letter B in the top row also form the number 13 in the bottom row. What determines whether you will see these lines as a letter or as a number? The answer, obviously, is not in the physical arrangement of the lines themselves, since this arrangement is the same in either case. Rather, it is your, the reader's, expectation of seeing one or the other figure that determines how the arrangement of lines will be read. This expectation, in turn, is derived from the context in which the lines appear—that context being either a row of letters or a row of numbers. Whether you eventually perceive a letter or a number, the event itself will be assembled in Kegan's "zone of mediation where meaning is made," constructed in the process of perceiving it.

This same active, constructive process occurs at each of many levels of human functioning, from the relatively molecular level of perceptual processing that we have just examined to the molar level of social interactions. An experiment by Condry and Ross (1985) illustrates how the same constructive process occurs in the perception of social behavior. The investigators showed college students a videotape of two children rough-and-tumbling in the snow. The actual sex of the children couldn't be determined because of their bulky snowsuits; some viewers were told the children were boys and others that they were girls. Viewers who believed the children to be boys perceived the children's behavior as playful. However, those who thought they were looking at girls perceived the identical behavior (remember, they all viewed the same videotape) as aggressive. Boys' play, you see, is expected to be rough; and actions such as wrestling or pummeling someone with snowballs fit the viewers' expectations of how boys play. In other words, it was easy for them to "read" such actions as playful. Conversely, girls' play is expected to be quiet. Given that expectation, wrestling and pummeling could only be perceived as aggressive.

What determined what each viewer saw? Just as in the previous example, the answer is not to be found in the videotape of the two children. The same videotape was seen by all subjects. Rather, it is to be found in the expectations of the viewers. What they saw is what they constructed, guided by their expectations, as these gave meaning to the activity they were viewing. See the Research

An Experiment: "Who You Pushin', Buddy!"— Perceptions of Aggressiveness BY MICHAEL WAPNER

People interpret experience by literally constructing or piecing together the events to which they respond. One of the most important manifestations of this interpretive construction occurs in determining the intentions of others. Even when an action is so obvious that it leaves little to interpretation, the motives behind the action still need to be understood, and this usually requires a good deal of cognitive construction. Observers may all agree that George bumped into Ira. But what the observers feel and do about it depends more on why they think George did it than the mere fact that he did. If George stumbled and could not keep from bumping Ira, that's one thing. But if George bumped Ira to get ahead of him in line, that's entirely different.

What determines how observers interpret the intentions behind an act? Mary Lynne Courtney and Robert Cohen (1996) designed an experiment to investigate this question. In particular, they looked at the contribution of two variables to the interpretation of intention: (1) prior information and (2) the personality of the observer. These two variables, in addition to influencing an observer's interpretation of the intentions behind an action, illustrate, by their difference, something fundamental about the design of experiments in general.

Briefly, boys between 8 and 12 were shown a videotape of two boys playing tag on a playground. At a critical point in the middle of the tape, the boy being chased falls down after being tagged by the other boy. The fallen boy slowly gets up and resumes the game. The variables were introduced as follows:

1. Prior Information: An Independent Variable Previous research, and common sense, would suggest that observers' interpretation of the intention behind an act should depend on what else they know about the actors. Thus, one would guess that the subjects would more likely attribute hostile intent to the tag that caused the fall if they were told beforehand that the two boys were enemies and had just recently been fighting. Conversely, the likelihood of seeing the tag as accidental should increase if the observers believed the boys to be good friends. But what if the observers knew nothing about the boys? These three conditions— let us call them hostile, benign, and ambiguous—constitute the independent variable in the experiment.

In an *experiment*, each group of subjects is treated differently than the others. In all other respects the groups are equivalent. If the groups differ afterward, we can assume the difference is due to the way they were treated. In order to be confident about this assumption, however, we must be sure that the groups are the same at the outset. The simplest way to ensure this would be to start with identical groups. But because no two individuals are ever the same in all respects, such a tactic is impossible. An equally good approach is to make sure the groups don't differ in any *systematic* way. We can accomplish this by assigning individuals at random to each condition. If each person has the same chance of being assigned to each group, and if we assign enough people to each, the differences among the people would balance out among the groups. *Random assignment* will distrib-

Focus, "An Experiment: 'Who You Pushin,' Buddy!—Perceptions of Aggressiveness," for more information on how individuals might construct the meaning of aggressiveness.

Diversity

A second theme to the book is its emphasis on diversity. The proportion of children born to cultural and ethnic minorities has increased steadily in the United States over the past 50 years. Estimates based on the latest U.S. Census data project that by 2050, one out of four individuals in our society will belong to an ethnic minority (Day, 1996). There is a pressing need to understand the effects of such diversity on the lives of children and on the society in which they live.

Individuals reflect their cultural heritages, and the meaning that events have for them—that is, the sense they make of their experiences—will vary with differences in their cultural backgrounds. Meaning, in other words, is relative. This text will highlight the cultural diversity that increasingly distinguishes our society. Laurie Lee's frustration with school arose because, in an important sense, he and the teacher did not speak the same language. Yet his difficulties are magnified tenfold in the hundreds of thousands of children for whom not only their language but also their customs differ from the ones they encounter at school. In this

ute any initial differences more or less evenly among the groups. Contrast this type of independent variable with a second variable these investigators studied.

2. Aggressiveness of the Observer: A Classification Variable Aggressive boys have been found to attribute hostile intentions to the actions of others more frequently than less aggressive boys. Courtney and Cohen incorporated the variable of aggressiveness by having classmates rate each boy for aggressiveness. Notice that, unlike assignment to the prior knowledge variable, aggressiveness scores could not be assigned randomly. Rather, subjects were *classified* based on judgments of a preexisting characteristic—that is, aggressiveness. Thus, if we find a difference between aggressive and unaggressive boys, we cannot be sure that the difference is not due to something else that might be correlated with aggressiveness.

Now let's look at the results of the study. The subjects (randomly assigned and classified as described above) were shown the videotape and asked to "segment" the action by pressing a button whenever one action stopped and another began. These points of segmentation are labeled "breakpoints." Of course, most natural behavior does not have discrete breakpoints. Rather, one activity flows into another. Thus, segmenting the flow of action is not simply marking what already objectively exists; rather, it is an act of cognitive construction and will vary from observer to observer.

A dramatic example of segmentation as a cognitive construction lies in the fact that we hear our native language spoken in discrete word segments although the sound issuing from the speaker's mouth is continuous, as can be demonstrated by visualizing normal speech on the screen of an oscilloscope. It is our knowledge of the rhythms and sounds of our native language, as well as familiarity with the vocabulary and current context, that allows us to segment accurately. You can test this proposition. Rent a film in an unfamiliar foreign language. Then gather a few friends who are equally ignorant of the language and all try to count the number of words spoken in two minutes of dialogue. You will be surprised at the wildly different counts.

Segmenting the action in Courtney and Cohen's videotape is roughly the same kind of cognitive task. But unlike speech, there is no cultural consensus as to where the breakpoints belong. Because the number of breakpoints should increase when an individual is seeking more information, it was expected that identifying breakpoints would be a function of how much information the boys had about the action. Recall, each boy got information from two sources: (1) from what he was told about the boys' friendship (the condition of prior information to which he had been assigned) and (2) from what he assumed (based on his level of aggressiveness). When subjects were given information that the boys were enemies, aggressiveness did not predict the amount of segmentation. Everyone "knew," in other words, what was going on and didn't have to look for it. When subjects were told the boys were friends, or were told nothing at all, subjects who were more aggressive identified more breakpoints than less aggressive ones, suggesting that their perception of ongoing behavior differed from that of less aggressive boys. Aggressiveness relates not only to the motives one attributes to others, but also to the ways in which one organizes one's perception of ongoing events.

text, we will frequently look at the families of children and often at their cultural and ethnic backgrounds as well. Each of these affects the lives of children in intimate and pervasive ways.

Sex, as well as culture, contributes to diversity. Another important theme of this text is the impact of differences related to sex on children's development. All cultures hold up one set of expectations for females and a different set for males. These expectations powerfully influence our perceptions of children even when we are not aware of their doing so. At no age are children immune from such expectations. For instance, when first-time parents were interviewed about their infants, who were by this time only hours old, the parents had already started to perceive their infants in terms of existing stereotypes for children of either sex. Thus, parents of females saw their infants as softer and having finer, more delicate features than did parents of males. In contrast, the latter saw their infants as hardier, stronger, and more coordinated than did parents of females. It should be pointed out that measures of such characteristics as alertness, coordination, or physical appearance revealed no differences between infants of either sex (Rubin, Provenzano, & Luria, 1974).

Because of expectations based on sex, females and males are likely to follow different developmental paths. These paths give rise to important differences in personality development, as well as different definitions of maturity. As we trace

Q Can parents' expectations of their children influence development of preference, such as favorite color or most-played-with toy? Why or why not?

9

Cultural background and gender affect how we make sense of our experiences.

these differences through the chapters of this text, we will question prevailing definitions of maturity. It is important to keep in mind, however, that differences *within* groups defined by culture and gender are larger than the differences that exist *between* these groups.

Continuity

As a final theme, this text will emphasize the continuities that are present in development as well as the more obvious changes that occur with age. A day in the life of a toddler, a teenager, and a grandparent are very different. And yet each may be coping with many of the same issues: closeness and separation, competence and autonomy, dependence and independence. The toddler and grandparent, for example, may face problems in dressing themselves—the one due to fingers not yet under fine motor control and the other to fingers immobilized by arthritis. The teenager's problem, on the other hand, may arise from restrictions on what clothes she can get away with wearing. Yet each is struggling with an issue of independence versus dependence.

Not only do individuals face many of the same issues at different points in their lives, but, in addition, the way they cope with these bears the particular

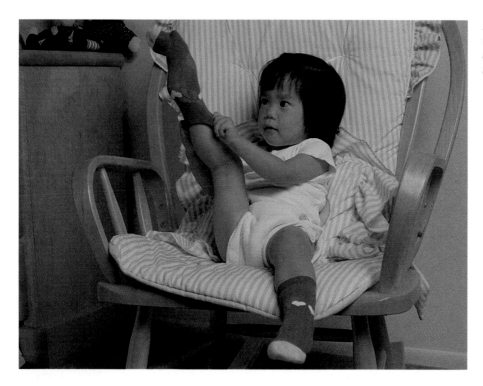

How we resolve issues such as independence/dependence may be determined by our personality and shows some continuity over time.

stamp of their personalities. How people resolve issues such as these affects their sense of self and gives their behavior over time a certain continuity.

Defining Development

How are we to define *development*? Briefly, we can say that **development** is the orderly set of changes that occur over time as individuals move from conception to death. Three features characterize these changes: growth, differentiation, and complexity. Although each of these aspects of development is most apparent in the very young, development itself is a lifelong process.

Growth is the result of metabolic processes in which proteins are broken down and used to make new cells. In a process called *mitosis*, cells divide to produce new cells, eventually producing the trillions of cells that form the adult body. Although growth at certain points in development can be very rapid, it is always an orderly process.

Growth progresses from the general to the specific. This aspect of development is known as **differentiation.** During prenatal development, for example, a single cell, the zygote, develops into the many different types of cells that will form the liver, the eyes, the fingernails, and the eyelashes of the fetus. Differentiation characterizes behavioral as well as physical development. Toddlers, for example, catch a ball with their whole bodies, clasping it to themselves; preschoolers can catch it with two hands; and, somewhere in middle childhood, children learn to catch with a single hand.

Differentiation brings new *complexity*, and with it comes a need to organize cells into a functioning whole. The nervous system and endocrine system accomplish this integration. As the central nervous system assumes control over activity, for example, the jerky reflexes of the fetus give way to fluid movements.

development The orderly set of changes that occur over the life span.

growth The result of metabolic processes in which proteins are broken down and used to make new cells.

differentiation A developmental trend characterized by a progression from the general to the specific.

Development is the result of growth, differentiation, and complexity.

Similarly, in adolescence, the endocrine system integrates much of the body's functioning through the action of hormones, although adolescents will attest that the integration achieved is less than perfect. A girl can have the figure of a woman before she ever begins to menstruate, and a boy can be inches taller than his father and have not a wisp of hair on his chin.

Describing Development

Do you remember as a child riding a merry-go-round and trying to grab the brass ring as you passed by? Remember having to lean out over the horse, straining to reach the ring, balancing all the while as your horse moved up and down? It wasn't easy. That was probably what made it so much fun. Studying human development is a bit like riding a carousel—reaching for the brass ring on a moving horse. So much is changing in children at any given moment that it is hard to get a fix on any one thing. Just as they begin to walk, they are also speaking their first words and charming those around them with new social skills. All this in one who has tripled in size from birth! In order to simplify our study of development, we will consider separately three aspects that make up the whole of development (Figure 1.4). *Physical development* covers such things as growth of the brain and body and can be seen in such "simple" activities as being able to pick up a crayon, use scissors, or kick a ball. *Intellectual development* covers perceiving, remembering, thinking, and language and includes developments such as, in the example of the two brothers, the understanding that two pastries are not necessarily more than one if they also differ in size. Finally, *psychosocial development* covers the development of emotions, personality, and relationships with others.

These three aspects of development will be covered in separate chapters at each of the four ages covered in this text: infancy and toddlerhood, early child-

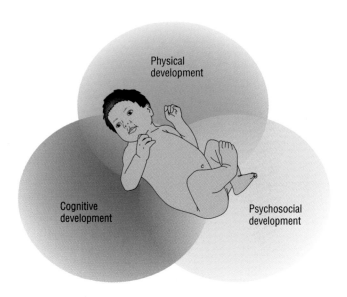

FIGURE 1.4 The Three Domains of Development

hood, middle childhood, and adolescence. As you read these chapters, however, keep in mind that this division is simply heuristic; it works because it simplifies our view of development, reducing it to manageable proportions. In actuality, changes in any of these areas of development affect each of the others.

The constructive perspective adopted in this text is not new. It derives from a set of assumptions, known as the organismic model, that have appeared in one form or another in the writings of many developmentalists. An alternative set of assumptions influencing developmental thought, known as the environmental model, can be seen in the work of early and contemporary behaviorists. We turn now to an examination of these models, or ways of looking at development, and to some of the theories they have spawned.

Models and Theories

Beneath the surface of every scientific theory are the beliefs we hold about the world we live in. We believe, for instance, that boys and girls *are* different. Many of us believe that there *has to be* a difference. Many of us believe that without differences the human species would be less viable than it is. These assumptions can be so fundamental that they go unnoticed, yet they exert powerful influences on the theories they generate.

A Model Defined

The assumptions we make about the world determine which questions appear reasonable and which seem foolish. If a developmentalist assumes that children's behaviors are primarily reactions to events in the environment, then it makes sense to inquire what is different about the events that precede their different behaviors. If another developmentalist assumes that behavior reflects goal-directed decisions, then it is reasonable to ask children about their goals and how they make their decisions. Notice that the first developmentalist is likely to observe what children do and what's going on around them when they do it. The second is likely to ask children *why* they do what they do. In each case, the beliefs that direct

Is nature or nurture most responsible for how similar or different twins turn out to be?

scientific investigation are collectively called a **model.** It is important to know just what a model is and how it serves our understanding of development.

You might think that only scientists have models of human behavior. Actually, we all do. Do you think behavior is intentional and goal-directed, or does it simply reflect past reinforcements? What motivates us? A succession of rewards and punishments? Inner goals? How much are we influenced by our biology? Does our genetic inheritance shape our interests and drives? Or do our interests and drives reflect acquired tastes and passions?

Not all of us share the same model. Models are easiest to see when the differences between them are extreme. Consider a teenage baby-sitter putting a young child to bed. The child lost a tooth that day and insists on placing it under his pillow. The child's belief system (model) includes tooth fairies. The baby-sitter's does not. What would the baby-sitter think if the child were to run up to her later with money in his hand and explain that he found it under the pillow? The teenager would question her sanity before admitting to anything like the tooth fairy—and with good reason. Scientists and teenagers alike base their theories on assumptions about what is real and what is not, and most adolescents assume that fairies are not real (Kuhn, 1962; Reese & Overton, 1970).

Models are useful because they generate theories. But models themselves are too general and often too vague to test. Theories, on the other hand, are specific explanations of particular phenomena that can be confirmed or disconfirmed. The baby-sitter dismisses the child's explanation because she assumes that a person, not a fairy, must have put the money under the pillow. We can even imagine her reviewing each alternative: "The money was there all along . . . I put it there and forgot . . . His mom or dad put it under the pillow before leaving . . . He took the money from his piggy bank just to put one over on me?" Each possibility reflects

model A set of assumptions about reality and human nature from which theories proceed.

a model in which *people* put money under pillows, a model that bestows reality on some events—whether they be people, quarks, or electromagnetic fields—and nonreality on others.

A Theory Defined

Theories reflect the models from which they derive. A look at our example shows us why. A **theory** consists of statements arranged from the very general to the very specific. The most general statements derive directly from the model and are called **axioms;** they are the assumptions one never thinks to question. An axiom that might be derived from the teenager's belief system would be that only things occupying space and existing in time are real. This axiom would exclude all but the most substantial of fairies. A **law** is at the next level. Derived from axioms, laws state relationships that are either true or false. Careful observations inform us of the validity of laws. A law from the preceding example might be that inanimate objects (such as teeth) remain stationary unless moved by some external force. Laws make it possible to predict specific events. We might predict that a tooth placed under a pillow would be there the next morning unless someone moved it.

All developmental theories have one thing in common: Each is an attempt to explain the constancies and changes in functioning that occur throughout the life course. Rather than embrace all aspects of functioning, developmental theories have limited themselves to particular aspects. Some, for instance, are concerned with personality development, others with social or intellectual development, still others with moral and ethical development. Whatever their focus, each theory looks at the similarities and differences that occur with age and attempts to explain them in terms of their sources or causes (Lerner, 1986).

Developmental Questions

Questions concerning the source of development have traditionally divided theorists into two camps. The division reflects their position on the **nature-nurture controversy:** Is nature—that is, heredity—primarily responsible for development, or is nurture—that is, the environment—responsible? Those who view nature as organizing developmental variables emphasize the importance of factors such as genetic inheritance and maturation. Developmentalists who look to nurture for explanations emphasize conditions such as the home environment and learning.

A second question, following from the first, also distinguishes developmental theories. This question concerns the form of the developmental laws that relate behavior to either source: the **continuity-discontinuity issue.** Can one explain behavior at any, and every, point in the life cycle without formulating new sets of laws? Do the same laws apply to other species as well (continuity)? Or do lawful relationships change with age and across species (discontinuity)? Figure 1.5 illustrates the contrasting concepts. Developmentalists who stress the importance of genetic inheritance and maturation typically assume that different sets of laws are needed for species with different genetic endowments and, within a species, at different points in development due to maturation. These theorists see development as occurring in discrete stages. Conversely, those who trace development to environmental sources are more likely to see these forces as exerting the same influence independent of age or species (Lerner, 1986).

Finally, developmentalists differ in the assumptions they make when explaining the occurrence of new behavior. Those who assume that the same set of laws

theory A set of testable statements derived from the axioms of a model.

axioms The unquestioned assumptions that form the basis of a theory.

laws Relationships that are derived from axioms and that can be proven to be true or false.

nature-nurture controversy The controversy concerning whether heredity (nature) or the environment (nurture) is primarily responsible for development.

continuity-discontinuity issue The question of whether the same set of developmental laws applies to all stages of the life cycle and to all species (continuity assumption) or whether different laws apply to different stages and different species (discontinuity assumption).

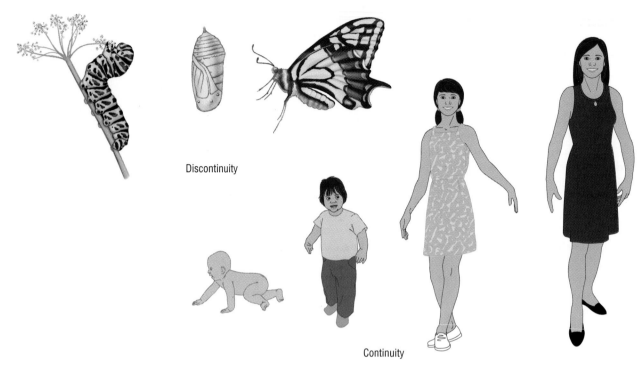

Discontinuity

Continuity

FIGURE 1.5 Continuity Versus Discontinuity of Development

Would a researcher who assumes that toddlers and middle adults experience disappointment for the same reasons be a reductionist or an epigenesist?

reductionism The explanation of complex behaviors by reducing them to their simpler components.

epigenesis At each stage of development, the emergence of new complexities that cannot be predicted from, or reduced to, earlier forms.

is sufficient to describe behavior at all points in the life cycle believe in **reductionism,** which is an attempt to explain complex behavior by reducing it to its simpler components. Developmentalists who assume that new laws are needed at different ages argue from the standpoint of **epigenesis,** holding that new complexities in development emerge that cannot be predicted from earlier forms (Lerner, 1986).

Differences in these sets of assumptions characterize different models of behavior: the environmental and the organismic. The first considers the environment to be the primary source of behavior, assumes continuity in developmental laws, and is reductionist in nature. The second looks to genetic or maturational forces—that is, nature—to explain development, assumes a noncontinuity position, and views development as epigenetic. All the theories deriving from a model bear a strong "family resemblance." Even so, you will find that the degree to which they reflect the assumptions characterizing the model will vary. Some theories reflect each of the model's assumptions perfectly; others are only a good approximation.

One organismic theory, the psychodynamic theory of Freud, is sufficiently broad in scope and has spawned enough offshoots that it is given separate treatment as a model. The psychodynamic approach gives importance to environmental as well as biological forces. This model adopts a compromise position with respect to continuity of developmental laws and assumes certain relationships to hold at all developmental periods and others to be specific to each particular period (Lerner, 1976).

Of the three models we will consider, the organismic model most directly represents the constructive approach adopted in this text, catching the dynamic interplay between the child's expectations and its experiences. Since the environmental model puts least emphasis on this active, constructive process, I have chosen to begin with that model and move to the one that best captures this dynamic developmental process.

The Environmental Model

The environmental model traces development to environmental forces. These forces affect behavior in lawful ways; the laws are assumed to apply at all levels of development. The assumption of continuity to behavioral laws underlies a strong reductionist approach in environmental theories. Since everything from silicon chips to bones and brain tissue is made of atoms and molecules, the laws that describe their actions should describe the functioning of humans as well as the workings of a computer. To explain vision, an environmentalist would speak of the amount of light necessary to stimulate receptors in the retina or of the exchange of sodium and potassium ions across the membrane of a neuron as the impulse is propagated along the neural fiber. Everything from a toddler taking first steps to the virtuosity of a concert cellist playing a Bach fugue is understood as a sequence of simple reactions, each prompted by the completion of the last and all traceable to an external force. In other words, "there is nothing special about the complex pattern of events we call psychological function. In the final analysis these events involve the functioning of the very same atoms and molecules that are involved in the workings of a liver, a kidney, or a shooting star" (Lerner, 1986, p. 45).

Reductionism reduces psychological phenomena to simple components that operate, in principle, no differently than do those in a machine. The metaphor of a machine is helpful in understanding the environmental model, because it translates otherwise abstract assumptions into an everyday example. Based on what we know about the example, we can predict certain outcomes and events that otherwise might remain unclear.

In order to get a machine to work, you have to start it; a machine does not start on its own. You have to plug it in, push a button, or whatever. This sets off a chained sequence of events that takes the same form each time it unfolds. As long as the parts bear the same relationship to each other, tripping one will set the next in motion. Machines do only what they are constructed to do. Vacuum cleaners do not give off light, and refrigerators don't suck up dirt. But, if you know what kind of machine you have and just what point in the sequence is unfolding, you should be able to predict what it will do next.

Is human behavior this predictable? The environmental model assumes it is—ideally. In actuality, it is difficult, if not impossible, to specify the myriad parts that make up the human machine. Even if one could, must our actions be started by something external to ourselves, or are we capable of self-initiated behavior? The environmental and organismic models give us different answers (Reese & Overton, 1970).

If the model of the machine is correct, behavior is always a response to an external event. Actions are *re*actions to forces external to us. The environment becomes the source of our behavior. We, like machines, remain quiescent until something stimulates us to act. Does an engine fail to start because it doesn't "want" to? Intention and desire are reduced by the environmentalist to links in the chain of human behavior. The burden for explaining and changing behavior remains with the environment. Is a first-grader disruptive in school? Look for the events in the classroom that cause this behavior. Is a child anxious in new situations? Have that child list situations from the most to the least anxiety-producing, and then tackle the easiest. Success will make the next situation more

Is it events (environmental) that explain this child's precocity, or is it how the child made sense of and reacted to those events?

approachable. While it is often difficult to trace behaviors to the events that occasion them, it is infinitely easier than it would be if organisms could, at any moment, choose to alter what they were doing just because they felt like it. Human behavior is, at least in the abstract, predictable for those who hold to this model.

Notice that, in this model, there is no reference to what takes place *"between an event and a reaction to it . . . the place where the event is privately composed, made sense of . . . where it actually becomes an event for that person,"* as Kegan (1982) would say. Such a constructive process is not thought to be a necessary precursor to one's response to events. However, just such a process does characterize the organismic model.

The Organismic Model

The organismic model, from which the constructive perspective derives, takes the living, biological system as its metaphor for human behavior. This model explains human development in terms of variables closely tied to the nature of the organism and governing its growth. Organismic theorists differ sharply from environmentalists, practically point by point, in their views of human nature (Table 1.1).

Q One method used to train pre-school children to stop wetting the bed is an alarm installed under the sheets that sounds when the child has wet the bed. What would organismic theorists probably think about this technique?

Three points summarize these differences. Organismic theorists view the human organism as active rather than passive. They believe this activity to be internally organized, and not just a reaction to external events. Finally, they understand behavior as the unfolding of genetically programmed processes, which produce discontinuous development, marked by qualitatively different stages. Environmentalists, on the other hand, view developmental change as continuous, with ever-more-complex behaviors being formed from the same simple building blocks (Lerner, 1986; Reese & Overton, 1970).

TABLE 1.1 Comparison of Developmental Models

	Environmental Model	Organismic Model
Organism Is	Reactive	Active
Behavior Is	Structured by environment	Internally organized
Development Is Due to	Behavioral conditioning	Environmental-genetic interactions
Focus Is on	Behavior	Cognition, perception, motivation
Developmental Stages?	No	Yes

The Active Organism   Organismic theorists point out that environmental events become clear only when we respond to them. It takes an action from us to define the conditions that will then be perceived as events. Noam Chomsky (1957), a psycholinguist at MIT, has pressed this argument effectively (John Dewey made the same argument in 1896). Chomsky argues that many sentences appearing to have a single meaning actually have many. They appear clear because we have *already* assumed a context in which they are unambiguous. Consider the sentence, "They are eating apples." Seems clear enough. What are they doing? They are eating apples. Yet if the sentence is a response to the question "What kind of apples are those?" its meaning changes. There are different kinds of apples. Some are for cooking and others for eating. And what are those? They are eating apples.

Organized Activity   Let's look at a simple experiment to illustrate the point: Individuals heard a click every 20 seconds for several minutes. With the first click, heart rate, brain-wave activity, sensory receptivity, and electrical conductance of the skin changed. These changes make up the *orienting response,* a general reaction to novel events. With each recurrence of the click, the orienting response decreased until it barely occurred at all (Sokolov, 1963). When **habituation,** or decreased response, had been pretty well established, the click was stopped, and everyone reacted with a full-scale orienting response. What was the stimulus for their reaction? Could it have been the *absence* of sound? The same silence, however, did not produce a reaction before the procedure began.

The phenomenon of habituation tells us that organisms detect regularities in their surroundings and anticipate them. Events that match, or confirm, their anticipations provoke no further reaction. Those that do not conform prompt a reaction. Notice that our definition of a stimulus has changed. The stimulus is no longer an external event. Nor is it simply an internal event. It is a product of both. The stimulus is the match, or mismatch, of input with what is anticipated. As such, the original meaning of stimulus, as a goad or prod to action, is lost (Miller, Galanter, & Pribram, 1960).

Developmental Stages   Organismic theorists argue that as children age, they organize experience in different ways than they did during the preceding period of development. Each period is a separate **stage** with its own characteristics. For example, Jean Piaget, a Swiss developmentalist, described several stages in the development of thought, the last of which begins in adolescence. In the first stage, infants do not have symbols through which they can represent their experiences, and thought in the absence of symbols is very different from the symbolic thought of adults, or even of slightly older children. When language first develops, young children organize their experience in personal ways, not according to the linguistic categories used by older children or adults (Piaget, 1952, 1954).

habituation Decreased responsiveness to a stimulus with repeated exposure to it.

stage A level of development that is assumed to be qualitatively different from the earlier level from which it evolves. Stages are assumed to occur in a fixed sequence and to occur universally within a species.

You can see this difference for yourself with a simple procedure. Just ask a preschooler and an adolescent to say the first word that comes to mind after you say each of two words. To "fork" the preschooler is likely to say "eat"; the adolescent will most likely say "spoon." To "chair" the preschooler will likely respond "sit"; the adolescent, "table." Preschoolers organize experience in terms of what they do with things. They answer with functional categories: One eats with a fork and sits on a chair. Adolescents organize experience in terms of linguistic categories: "Fork" and "spoon" are both utensils, and "chair" and "table" are furniture.

A final point before leaving our discussion of this model concerns the way we know our world. Recall that the environmental model views perception as a passive copy of reality. The organismic model maintains, predictably enough, just the opposite—that perception is an active, constructive process. The example given earlier in the chapter, of the way we recognize words by actively scanning the features of letters when we read, illustrates this position.

These two models have generated a lively debate in the scientific community. The third model offers yet another perspective and, along with it, fuel for more debate.

The Psychodynamic Model

Psychodynamic theories, like many other organismic theories and some environmental ones such as social-cognitive theory, combine elements of both approaches. They hold that development is organized around stages that take form as maturation enables the organism to interact with its surroundings in new ways. Like environmentalists, they emphasize the way the environment contributes to the personal experiences that focus inner organization. Freud, for example, assumed that young boys experience horror when they first see a little girl naked, believing that she has been castrated. Their reaction to this experience both reflects and redirects inner psychic forces. Freud (1925b/1961) would argue that maturation has brought them to a stage in which sexual tensions receive genital focus and also involve them in a dangerous rivalry with their fathers. To protect themselves from a fate similar to the girls', boys must repress their sexual fantasies, thus resolving the Oedipal complex and moving them into the next stage of development.

For psychodynamic theorists, life is a battle, and we are all on the front lines. Two opposing forces, one within us and the other outside, fight for control. Since each is an integral aspect of our personalities, the victory of either one means a sure defeat to the individual. This model emphasizes both inner processes and external events.

The psychodynamic model stresses a balance between strong biological instincts and social constraints. We achieve this balance only with time and at some personal cost. As in any war, there are casualties. True spontaneity may be the first to go. The second takes the form of compromise: We learn to make do with lesser delights to avoid the anxiety provoked by indulging our first instincts. There are victories as well. We gain control over instinctual urges that otherwise, these theorists say, could destroy us and our civilization (Hall, 1954).

Like organismic theorists, psychodynamic theorists believe that development occurs over distinct stages that unfold in different zones of the body, focusing the expression of psychic energy. This energy, which Freud termed **libido**, takes different forms depending on the body zone through which it is channeled. Expression of the libido moves from the region of the mouth in infancy (*oral stage*), to

libido In psychoanalytic theory, the psychic energy that is expressed through different zones of the body and motivates much of behavior.

the sphincters in toddlerhood (*anal stage*), to the genital region in early childhood (*phallic stage*). Because genital expression of the libido in early childhood is associated with tremendous anxiety, it goes underground (*latency stage*), so to speak, and does not arise again until it emerges full-force with puberty (*genital stage*), once again pressing for genital expression (Freud, 1961).

Different aspects of the personality express or inhibit these instincts. The **id** demands immediate gratification of the biological impulses which it houses. It operates according to the pleasure principle. The **ego** attempts to satisfy impulses in the most diplomatic way without getting the organism into really deep trouble. It operates according to the reality principle. Even so, Freud assumed that reality for most of early childhood does not include issues of right and wrong, only what one can get away with without getting punished. Moral concerns arise when the **superego** emerges, and with it the conscience. This part of the personality internalizes social standards and comes about when the child identifies with the parent of its own sex. (The emergence of the superego is discussed later in this chapter.)

Although Freud included both biological and environmental forces in his theory, he embodied each in a separate aspect of the personality: biological forces in the id and social standards in the superego. The ego, like a clever general, is given the job of leading the weary troops between these warring factions. The functions of the ego—such as planning, comparing, and evaluating—emphasize the active role we take in structuring our experiences, an assumption shared with organismic theorists. Perhaps because the psychodynamic model does not require us to choose between environmental and biological influences, by relegating each to different aspects of personality functioning, it has remained immensely popular. And, since it is willing to address unconscious motives and thoughts, it permits us to explain much of human behavior that otherwise would remain obscure (Hall, 1954).

Is the psychodynamic model better than the others for these reasons? Or perhaps the environmental model is more "scientific," because it focuses on behaviors that can be observed and precisely measured? Comparisons all too frequently lead to evaluations, and someone ends up holding the short end of the theoretical stick. Comparisons can also be misleading. Each model addresses different aspects of human function. We need all three to begin unraveling the knotty problems of development. The psychodynamic model helps us understand motives and feelings that otherwise would never see the light of day. The environmental model gives us objective and easily testable theories of behavior. The organismic model offers sophisticated approaches to cognition and perception. Unless we are willing to settle for theories about children who act but don't think and feel, or children who think and feel but can't act, we need the insights each model offers.

But what about the developmental theories spawned by these models? Remember, a single model can parent many theories. We will look at several theories for each. Examining more than one theory should help distinguish the assumptions of the model from the particular form they take in a theory.

Environmental Theories

Environmental theories, recall, look to forces outside the individual to explain development. These theories assume that behavior is essentially a reaction to surrounding events. As a consequence, these theories attempt to describe development in terms of lawful changes that relate behavior to external events.

id In psychoanalytic theory, the aspect of the personality that demands immediate gratification of biological impulses; operates according to the pleasure principle.

ego In psychoanalytic theory, the executive aspect of the personality that attempts to satisfy impulses in socially acceptable ways.

superego In psychoanalytic theory, the aspect of the personality that represents the internalized standards and values of society and emerges when the child identifies with the parent of its own sex.

FIGURE 1.6 Pavlov's Conditioning Apparatus

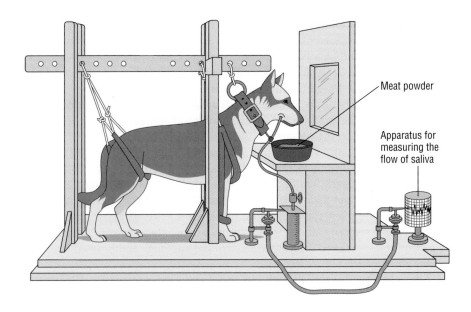

Meat powder

Apparatus for measuring the flow of saliva

Ivan Pavlov

How might Pavlov explain the response we have to familiar smells like Mom's pancakes or the smell of a family barbeque?

Ivan Pavlov, a Russian physiologist, noticed that his laboratory animals began salivating at the sounds of their evening meal being prepared. Many of us have probably noticed the same thing when feeding a pet. To a physiologist, salivation in response to a *sound* is highly unusual—and requires explaining. Salivation, you see, is a reflex that should occur only when triggered by its own stimulus. The trigger is a chemical reaction caused by food touching the membranes lining the mouth. Pavlov's dogs were salivating *before* food ever reached their mouths (Pavlov, 1927). His conditioning apparatus is shown in Figure 1.6.

Pavlov had identified a simple form of learning, which he termed **respondent conditioning.** Respondents are reflexes that occur involuntarily, in response to particular stimuli, such as salivation in response to food in one's mouth or the knee jerk in response to a sharp tap beneath the knee. Respondents can be brought under the control of other environmental stimuli through respondent conditioning, also known as classical conditioning.

Pavlov identified four elements in respondent conditioning. The food that triggers the salivation is the **unconditional stimulus (UCS),** and reflexive salivation to the food is the **unconditional response (UCR).** The food-preparation sounds are the **conditional stimulus (CS),** and salivation in response to the sounds is the **conditional response (CR).** To make sure you have the components of respondent conditioning down pat, try analyzing the following example for the UCS, UCR, CS, and CR.

A 10-year-old who had difficulty waking for school in the morning solved his problem by placing an alarm clock inches away from his pillow. Each morning, as the first rays of light appeared through the blinds, the alarm went off and he was startled awake. He was especially annoyed during spring vacation to find that he continued to awaken at the first rays of light, even though he had not set the alarm. What are the UCS and the UCR in this example? Can you identify the CS? The CR? (The answers appear at the end of the chapter.)

B. F. Skinner

Most human behavior is not reflexive. B. F. Skinner, an American psychologist, referred to voluntary, or nonreflexive, actions as *operants,* to distinguish them from

respondent conditioning A simple form of learning in which an involuntary reflex is brought under the control of another environmental stimulus.

unconditional stimulus (UCS) In respondent conditioning, the stimulus that triggers a reflexive, or unconditional, response.

unconditional response (UCR) In respondent conditioning, the reflexive response to a particular stimulus.

conditional stimulus (CS) In respondent conditioning, the new environmental stimulus used to elicit a reflexive, or conditional, response.

conditional response (CR) In respondent conditioning, the reflex learned in response to a new stimulus.

respondents. He pointed out that operants frequently do not have identifiable stimuli to elicit them. Instead, Skinner reduced the nuances and complexities of human behavior to the events that follow it rather than to what might have preceded it. His approach is a radical departure from the way most people understand their behavior. Most of us think that what we do is a response to inner states, to our feelings and thoughts. Skinner told us our behavior is under the control of external events. He called his approach radical behaviorism.

Skinner said it is senseless to talk about inner states such as motives and intentions. We can't measure or observe them. He believed we can only understand behavior by describing the conditions under which it occurs. When antecedent conditions cannot be identified, he suggested looking at what follows the behavior. When we do, lawful relationships emerge. Operants, just like respondents, can be brought under the control of environmental events. Skinner studied this simple form of learning—operant conditioning—extensively (Skinner, 1938, 1953, 1961).

Skinner successfully used operant conditioning in laboratories, classrooms, and mental hospitals. The breadth of his successes supports his conviction that the environment exerts a pervasive influence on human behavior. Together, these two forms of learning, respondent and operant, tie many aspects of behavior to environmental sources. Reflexive responses ranging from behavioral reflexes to emotional responses (the involuntary nervous system is involved in emotional expression) can be respondently conditioned, and nonreflexive actions, whether a simple tap of a toe or the double axel of an Olympic skating champion like Kristi Yamaguchi, can be explained in terms of operant conditioning (Skinner, 1953).

Skinner's (1938) first subjects were rats. He constructed a small box with a metal lever protruding from one wall and selected a simple behavior—pressing the lever—for study. Since there was little for an animal to do in such a small space, its explorations soon brought it near the lever. Skinner waited until the animal touched the lever and then dropped a food pellet into a chute that ended in a dish beneath the lever. Each time the rat pressed the lever, a pellet of food dropped into the dish. In no time the rat began to steadily press the lever. Skinner had brought a voluntary behavior—putting a paw on a metal lever and depressing it—under the control of its consequences. By making food contingent on lever pressing, he controlled the frequency with which the rat pressed the lever.

Critics reacted by saying that humans are different from animals or, at the very least, different from rats. Our behavior reflects motives and intentions, not contingencies. Skinner's reply to these objections was that our intentions reflect our reinforcement histories. Consider a teenager who has a favorite color—purple, for instance—and buys many of her clothes in that color. Skinner would explain this preference for purple in terms of past reinforcements when wearing purple. She may have worn a purple skirt one day and received several compliments. When next shopping for clothes, she tried on several items that were purple, finally buying one. She spent a few extra minutes with her appearance the day she wore her new clothes and once again received several compliments. Skinner would suggest that this history of reinforcements shaped her preference for purple.

Some reinforcements are pleasant. When they follow a behavior, the behavior becomes more frequent; this procedure is called **positive reinforcement.** Other reinforcements can be unpleasant, and behavior that *removes* them becomes more frequent; this procedure is called **negative reinforcement.** Positive and negative reinforcement have powerful and pervasive effects on behavior.

We can analyze many social interactions in terms of positive and negative reinforcement. Sometimes such an analysis seems especially appropriate with children and their parents. Let's look at an exchange between a 5-year-old and

Q How might Skinner describe a room full of people gambling on slot machines?

positive reinforcement An event that increases the frequency of the behavior on which its occurrence is made contingent.

negative reinforcement An event that increases the frequency of the behavior on which its removal is made contingent.

his mother. The mother has just told him to pick his clothes up from the living room floor. "Awhh," he whines. She reacts quickly and sharply, with more animation than he has seen all morning. He picks up his clothes and carries them off to his room.

Now take a closer look at what has just taken place. The mother reinforced her son when she allowed herself to become "engaged" by his whining. She paid more attention to him than she had all morning. Attention is a powerful reinforcer. Even though this may not be the kind of attention the child, or anyone, seeks, if it is more than he usually gets and if he frequently whines when his mother scolds, she is very likely reinforcing a behavior that in fact annoys her.

Also notice that *he* reinforced *her* scolding. By picking his clothes up when she scolded (removing something that displeased her), he negatively reinforced her scolding—the very behavior that maintains his whining. We can analyze many parent-child interactions in terms of the reciprocal effects of positive and negative reinforcement. Children frequently develop the very behaviors their parents find most objectionable. According to behaviorists such as Skinner, this is no accident. Those are the very behaviors parents are most likely to notice.

Reinforcement is a powerful force in shaping and maintaining behavior. But must we actually do something or receive reinforcement in order to learn? Critics of radical behaviorism point out that we can know *what* to do before we ever do it. Many actions are novel, yet they unfold in smooth, successful sequences, not in the on-again, off-again manner one would expect if trial and error governed their performance. Language itself is perhaps the most intricate of all human activities and the most difficult for Skinner to explain. We produce endless numbers of novel sentences each day. Has each been shaped through reinforcement? How is radical behaviorism to account for each of these?

Albert Bandura

Albert Bandura, a psychologist at Stanford University, stresses the social nature of learning; his approach is called social-cognitive theory. Bandura believes that most human learning is **observational learning,** not conditioning, and occurs by *observing* what others do and *imitating* what one sees. One need not actually perform the behavior oneself. Inner processes such as attention and memory focus behavior. This theory departs from strict environmentalist assumptions by emphasizing inner, cognitive processes by which individuals interpret their experiences. Bandura supported his position in a dramatic study of aggression in children.

Children at play watched a model punch and kick a large inflated doll in unusual ways (Bandura, Ross, & Ross, 1963). The model sat on it, shouted "Sock him in the nose," punched the doll, and then hit it with a hammer and yelled "Pow!" Later, when the children were left alone with the doll and other toys, they imitated the same unusual sequences, often copying exactly what they had seen. Other children who had watched a model play with Tinkertoys showed none of the same aggressive behaviors. Numerous studies support the importance of observation and imitation in human learning (Bandura, 1977, 1980).

Social-cognitive theorists are willing to talk about many of the same processes as organismic theorists, such as thoughts and motives. Many of these processes suggest that the learner actively use information instead of being a passive receiver of input. Yet social-cognitive theorists, just like other environmentalists, assume that developmental changes are continuous. Unlike organismic theorists, they do not explain change as a succession of stages distinguished by qualitatively different features. Psychodynamic theorists give us a very different view of things.

observational learning In social-cognitive theory, learning by observing what others do and imitating what one sees.

How important are observation and information in human learning? Bandura's bobo doll experiment supports the idea that aggression is learned through imitation.

Psychodynamic Theories

Psychodynamic theories, like environmental ones, assume that environmental forces significantly contribute to development. However, these theories also assume there are powerful forces within each of us that interact with environmental ones in giving shape to development.

Sigmund Freud

As a young physician with a private practice in neurology, Sigmund Freud might have been more surprised than anyone else at the direction his career would take. Were it not for some of his patients who complained of mysterious ailments, he might have remained an obscure but successful Viennese doctor.

The mysterious symptoms were no different from those he saw daily, such as numbness and paralysis from damaged nerves. But the nerves in these patients were unaffected; he found only healthy neural tissue when he examined them. How could patients suffer neurological symptoms with no physical damage? Fortunately, a Frenchman named Jean Charcot had just concluded a series of studies in which healthy people were told under hypnosis that they would awake with physical symptoms (among those suggested were numbness and paralysis). When they awoke, they had no memory of the suggestion, yet they exhibited the symptoms, just as Freud's patients did (Thomas, 1979).

The Unconscious Freud (1961) eventually solved the mystery, but only by tossing aside current notions about the mind. He asserted that we have an active mental life of which we remain completely unaware, an unconscious that affects our actions in direct ways. Thoughts, feelings, or problems that are too disturbing to face or that cannot be solved immediately are pushed out of the conscious mind, repressed to the unconscious realm of thought. Although **repression**

repression A defense mechanism that operates by relegating distressful thoughts and feelings to the unconscious.

Sigmund Freud

momentarily reduces the distress, it does not get rid of the problem. The thoughts and feelings continue to exist and continue to push for expression, like a teapot that has been brought to a boil: If you cover the spout, the pressure within continues to build until the steam is released through some other opening, perhaps by blowing off the lid. The repressed ideas and feelings escape in many ways—in dreams, actions, or even physical symptoms, as with Freud's patients. The only requirement limiting their expression is that the person remain unaware of their true meaning, thereby protected from the distress they occasion. The treatment that Freud eventually devised involved discovering the unconscious source of the patient's distress and bringing it to light in the safe atmosphere of therapy.

Freud formulated his theory of personality development while treating these unusual symptoms. He believed that they resulted from an inner war between conflicting aspects of the personality. Although Freud first noticed these aspects of personality in his patients, he believed them to be present in all of us.

Three Facets of the Personality   For Freud, all thought and action are motivated. He termed the life force that motivates these the *libido* (see "The Psychodynamic Model," earlier in the chapter). Different aspects of the personality control the expression or inhibition of libido. Its expression is highly pleasurable (assuming a sexual nature even in infancy), and the pressure resulting from its blockage is painful. The facet of the personality that seeks immediately to satisfy the libido's expression is the *id*. Present from birth, the id has limited means for gratifying libidinal impulses. The infant can only cry its displeasure or fantasize about the food and comfort it desires.

The *ego* soon emerges as a means of realistically satisfying these instinctual impulses. The ego can distinguish the id's fantasies from actual goals and can negotiate the realities of the environment. It also realizes that while some forms of expression will be tolerated, others will bring more pain than they're worth. The ego seeks to gratify as many of the id's demands as possible without bringing on the wrath of parents, peers, and society. It operates according to the reality principle, both facilitating and blocking the expression of the libido.

A final aspect of the personality, emerging from the ego when the child is about 4 or 5, contains the moral values acquired from our culture and dictates what we should and should not do. Freud called this the *superego*. It has two aspects, the conscience and the ego-ideal. The conscience embodies the "should-nots," those thoughts and actions for which we have been punished in the past; the ego-ideal represents the "shoulds," the positive values we have learned as children. These two aspects of the superego gradually assume the controls that once had to be exercised by parents and others, so that, with the ego and superego working in concert, behavior becomes self-regulated (Hall, 1954).

The baton Freud carried was passed to a successor who also viewed development as unfolding in a single, universal sequence for females and males alike—a sequence that again takes a male perspective.

Q According to Freud, is it reasonable to expect a 3-year-old to know the difference between "good" and "bad" behavior?

Erik Erikson

As a restless young man, Erik Erikson traveled about Europe, earning a living as an artist and eventually teaching art in a school for young children. The position at the school proved to be a turning point in his life, for the school had been founded by Freud's daughter Anna, who herself was an analyst and involved in establishing the new discipline of child analysis. Erikson became part of the intimate circle of associates and friends of the Freuds, eventually entering into analysis with Anna Freud and completing his training as a psychoanalyst (Coles, 1970).

Erikson built on Freud's analysis of the personality as id, ego, and superego and on his stages of psychosexual development. Yet he differed from Freud in several important respects. Perhaps the most significant is Erikson's emphasis on the healthy personality. Freud regarded health as the *absence* of something—neurosis. Erikson regarded it as the *presence* of something—vitality. Erikson (1968) cites Marie Jahoda's definition of a healthy personality in enumerating three things essential to vitality: *mastery* of one's surroundings, *unity* of the personality, and *accuracy* in perceiving one's world and oneself. See the Research Focus, "Erikson's Psychohistorical Approach: A Clinician's Notebook from the Dakota Prairies," for a discussion of Erikson's view of development within a social community.

Erik Erikson

Psychosocial Stages of Development   Erikson (1963) believed that new aspects of the person emerge through inner growth, making new types of social encounters possible. As with other stage theorists, he assumed that development occurs in the same set sequence for all, reflecting an internal ground plan in which each stage has its own period of ascendance, a time in which the individual is especially vulnerable to certain influences and insensitive to others. (This assumption is known as Erikson's **epigenetic principle.**) Society challenges us with new demands as we age. We experience these as crises. Each takes a slightly different form and gives each age its unique characteristics. Table 1.2 describes each of Erikson's life stages.

Each of the first four crises equips individuals to meet the central challenge of achieving an ego identity. Trust establishes the confidence in themselves and in

TABLE 1.2 Erikson's Developmental Stages	
Stage	**Psychosocial Crisis**
Birth to Adolescence	
Infancy	Trust versus mistrust. Realization that needs will be met leads to trust in others and self.
Toddlerhood	Autonomy versus shame and doubt. Physical maturation gives sense of being able to do things for self.
Early childhood	Initiative versus guilt. Increasing abilities promote exploration and expand experience.
Middle childhood	Industry versus inferiority. Accomplishments and skills provide basis for self-esteem.
Adolescence to Old Age	
Adolescence	Identity versus identity diffusion. Biological and social changes of adolescence occasion a search for continuity of self.
Early adulthood	Intimacy versus isolation. Sense of self provides the basis for sexual and emotional intimacy with another adult.
Middle adulthood	Generativity versus stagnation. Concern for children and future generations reflects need to leave something of oneself.
Late adulthood	Integrity versus despair. Acceptance of one's life as having meaning gives one a sense of dignity.

Source: E. Erikson. (1963). *Childhood and society.* New York: Norton.

epigenetic principle Erikson's assumption that an internal plan governs the timing or period of ascendance for each new development.

Erikson's Psychohistorical Approach: A Clinician's Notebook from the Dakota Prairies WITH MICHAEL WAPNER

When we neared the simple, clean homestead, the little sons were playing the small Indian boy's favorite game, roping a tree stump, while a little girl was lazily sitting on her father's knees, playing with his patient hands. Jim's wife was working in the house. We had brought some additional supplies, knowing that with Indians nothing can be settled in a few hours; our conversation would have to proceed in the slow, thoughtful, shy manner of the hosts. Jim's wife had asked some women relatives to attend our session. From time to time she went to the door to look out over the prairie which rolled away on every side, merging in the distance with the white processions of slow-moving clouds. As we sat and said little, I had time to consider what Jim's place among the living generations of his people might be. (Erikson, 1963, pp. 120–121)

So begins Erikson's description of the conversations that contributed to his understanding of the Sioux's early childhood experiences and their difficulty as adults in finding meaning to life. More generally, these observations led to his understanding of the ways in which one's society influences the course of each person's development.

Erik Erikson developed a unique style of research that combined the tools of clinical analysis with those of fieldwork. His insights into human development reflected the same psychoanalytic training that Freud and others practiced in urban European offices. Erikson took these skills to the rolling plains of the Dakotas, and later to the forested dwellings of the Yurok in the Northwest, and, in doing so, opened new vistas in our understanding of human development.

His observations made him keenly aware that human development takes place within a social community. Each community raises its children to participate in the world as adults—but there are as many worlds as there are communities. Children are indulged or controlled, taught to give away or to hoard, and so on, depending on the wisdom of their group—a wisdom that reflects the peace their group has made with the realities of geography and the historical moment. The area in which one lives determines the form life takes, whether in the specifics of what one eats or wears or in abstractions such as notions of goodness and propriety (Coles, 1970).

The Sioux, for instance, value generosity and regard the accumulation of wealth as tantamount to evil. Erikson traces these attitudes to a nomadic life in which they followed the buffalo across the plains. The buffalo existed in great numbers and the Sioux rarely experienced need. As nomads, the Sioux learned to live lightly, without the encumbrances of possessions. Generosity, because it reflected a more basic harmony with their surroundings, was a virtue. Conversely, the Yurok value thrift and a meticulous management of resources. They live in settlements along the Klamath River. Once a year, when the salmon return to breed, they experience the abundance that the Sioux lived with in every season. For the rest of the year, they must cautiously manage that brief harvest to avoid hunger and need.

These particular differences are less important than the common function served by the communal practices of either group. Ritual ways of living provided each with a group identity. It is from this group identity that members of the community derived a sense of their own identity. Erikson arrived at this observation after noting what he referred to as a "cultural pathology" among the present-day Sioux. He traced this problem to their inability to find "fitting images to connect the past with the future" (Erikson, 1963, p. 117). The Sioux's lifestyle had been tied to the buffalo, the provider of meat for food; pelts for clothing and shelter; bones for needles, ornaments, and toys; and even dried droppings for fuel. The destruction of the buffalo herds by White settlers resulted in the destruction of the Sioux's way of life—and the group identity from which new generations could derive a sense of themselves. Speaking of the present generation of Sioux, Erikson (1963) noted that

the majority of them have as little concept of the future as they are beginning to have of the past. This youngest generation, then, finds itself between the impressive dignity of its grandparents, who honestly refuse to believe that the white man is here to stay, and the white man himself, who feels that the Indian persists in being a rather impractical relic of a dead past. (p. 121)

If Erikson's theory is correct, that without "fitting images to connect the past with the future" young people are lost, what are the images that performed this function for you? Is there any single or even small set of recurrent experiences that anchor you in your community and physical environment the way the buffalo anchored the Sioux? Is it possible that our present society in the United States has no such single image? Perhaps these images belong to subgroups rather than the culture as a whole. For instance, is the gang for the East Los Angeles gang member in any way analogous to the buffalo for the Sioux? What functions would the gang have to fulfill for its members to qualify as an image? If it is an image in the Eriksonian sense, then what will it take to discourage gang membership in East Los Angeles and similar urban communities?

others that is needed to begin the task. Autonomy gives self-direction and purpose, the ability to follow goals that one sets for oneself rather than those set by others. Initiative allows individuals to explore options as these open up, and industry allows them to realistically evaluate these options and select the ones they will commit themselves to (Erikson, 1963, 1968).

The establishment of identity involves the individual in a succession of commitments to life goals that serve to define the self. The young adult faces the crisis of sharing that self with another—of intimacy, first with a mate and then, for most, with children. Middle adulthood extends the adult's concerns beyond this intimate group to others in the community. Older adults face a final crisis of reviewing their lives and accepting the decisions they have made. Erikson calls this last crisis one of personal integrity.

Like Freud's, Erikson's theory reflects a male bias. Erikson considers the achievement of identity to be the central crisis of adolescence, even though he asserts that a different sequence exists for females. Most females resolve the crisis of intimacy, which Erikson places in early adulthood, *before* they complete identity issues. Their sense of themselves derives more from their relationships than from commitments to work and ideology. Although Erikson notes these differences, he does not change his sequence of life stages; that is, he equates the male experience with development in general (Bardwick & Douvan, 1971; Josselson, 1988).

Nancy Chodorow

Nancy Chodorow

Another theorist, also influenced by Freud, gives us a different view of development. Nancy Chodorow offers an alternative to the universal developmental sequence charted by Freud and Erikson. Chodorow (1978) attributes psychological differences in the makeup of females and males to the social fact that for most children the first intimate relationship is with a woman—their mother. This initial relationship has different consequences for girls than it does for boys.

Chodorow (1978) asserts that infants experience themselves as continuous with the mother. They live within the boundless security of her presence, little caring which smile is theirs or whose hand reaches out to the other, all of it part of the same encircling awareness. Mothers, too, empathically relate to their infants and experience a continuity with them:

> In a society where mothers provide nearly exclusive care and certainly the most meaningful relationship to the infant, the infant develops its sense of self mainly in relation to her. Insofar as the relationship with its mother has continuity, the infant comes to define aspects of its self . . . in relation to internalized representations of aspects of its mother. (p. 78)

Important to Chodorow are the necessary differences in the way children of either sex develop beyond this point. Girls can continue to define themselves within the context of this first relationship. Mothers, as well, can see their daughters as extensions of themselves. Girls can experience a continuing attachment to the mother while still defining themselves as females. None of this is possible for boys. They must separate themselves from the mother much earlier than girls do in order to develop as males. Mothers, too, experience their sons as separate and different from themselves, unlike their daughters. Thus, boys embark on a developmental path marked not by attachment but by separation and increasing individuation.

Chodorow argues that since the primary caregiver is the same sex for girls, there is less need for the girl to differentiate herself in terms of ego boundaries.

The Declining Fortunes of Children: How Best to Help? BY ANDREA HAYES

Historically, attitudes toward the poor in this nation have vacillated between believing that their poverty was due to undisciplined behavior and believing them to be truly disadvantaged through no fault of their own. Consequently, assistance has been divided into "workfare" and "welfare" approaches. August 1996 brought one of the most radical pieces of legislation regarding public assistance since the 1930s, shifting the swing of the legislative pendulum in the direction of "workfare" rather than "welfare." The Personal Responsibility Work Opportunity and Reconciliation Act (PRWORA), or welfare reform law of 1996, indicated that legislators no longer saw welfare as helpful assistance to the disadvantaged, but rather as a handout that fostered continued dependence.

The 1996 welfare reform law replaces the former Aid to Families with Dependent Children (AFDC), a program that offered guaranteed federal income support to economically disadvantaged families, with a new program, Temporary Assistance to Needy Families (TANF), in which individual states determine assistance eligibility. TANF represents a significant departure from AFDC in several important respects. The new bill imposes a lifetime limit on public assistance of no more than 5 years, introduces work requirements, and ties support to limitations on the size of families.

Will requirements and limitations such as these prompt the parents of children living in poverty to find jobs and limit the size of their families? Or do they impose additional hardships on children by failing to take child welfare issues into consideration (Wise, Chavkin, & Romero, 1999)?

Mothers complying with the "workfare" requirements of TANF are most likely to find work in physically demanding, entry-level jobs that allow little flexibility for attending to family responsibilities. Typically, employment does not include leave time to attend to children's health care, nor is it likely to include paid vacation leave. Factors such as these can significantly affect children's welfare in that mothers previously on AFDC are significantly more likely than those never receiving welfare to have a child with some type of chronic health condition. They are also more likely to be single parents, with all the additional demands on their time that single parenthood places (Heymann & Earle, 1999).

PRWORA addresses some of these potential hardships by adding certain provisions to the bill. The State Child Health Insurance Plan of 1997, for instance, ensures that children can have health coverage even if their parents do not. Additionally, certain states have passed legislation exempting women who are victims of domestic violence from TANF's time limit requirements through the Family Violence Option. In this way victims of violence can receive support while both learning new job skills and ensuring their child's safety (Wise et al., 1999). Communities have also stepped in, developing special programs to foster the health and cognitive development of children living in poverty (see Chapter 5, the Social Policy Focus on early intervention programs).

Social problems are multifaceted and complex. As a consequence, social policy introduces a host of questions, all addressing the issue of "how best to help."

Chodorow brings us to a point made earlier by Freud: The personalities of women are frequently less differentiated than those of men and are more closely tied to their relationships. But she sees this difference as an asset, as a strength rather than a weakness. Girls can experience continuity with others and relate to their feelings. Chodorow points to the heavy costs males pay for their greater individuation. In curtailing their emotional attachment to the mother, they also limit their ability in general to relate empathically to others. Thus, differences in ego boundaries lay the foundation for a greater capacity for empathy in females. In fact, Chodorow sees the capacity for empathy to be a core part of the feminine personality, giving women a sense of connectedness with others (Chodorow, 1978; Gilligan, 1982). See the Social Policy Focus, "The Declining Fortunes of Children: How Best to Help?"

Organismic Theories

Organismic theories share with psychodynamic ones the assumptions that forces within the organism give shape to development and that development progresses through a succession of qualitatively different stages. Individuals are seen as actively interpreting the events to which they respond, imbuing these with meaning in the process of doing so.

Jean Piaget

By training, Jean Piaget was a biologist. However, his first job, after getting his degree in biology, was in the new field of intelligence testing. Piaget left his native Switzerland and went to Paris to work with Alfred Binet, standardizing questions for Binet's scales of intelligence. Perhaps because Piaget was first interested in biology, he approached human intelligence with questions a biologist might ask if discovering a new organism. How does a creature adapt to its surroundings? What does it do that allows it to survive? How is it changed by the processes that maintain it? For Piaget, intelligence was a means of adapting to one's environment, and only those forms of thought that promoted adaptation survived with increasing age.

Jean Piaget

Piaget regarded intelligence as an adaptive process through which we maintain an equilibrium with our environment. Adaptation takes place through two related processes, assimilation and accommodation. **Assimilation** is the process by which individuals fit new information into their present ways of understanding, as when they act on a new object in a way that is similar to previous actions on other objects. Quite often—but not always—we can understand new experiences in terms of what we already know. And sometimes the actions by which we attempt to gain understanding are modified by the process of gaining it. **Accommodation** is the process by which cognitive structures are altered to fit new experiences.

A closer look at children's behavior reveals these two processes frequently to be at work. For instance, consider a young child who has spent the day at the beach, learning to build sand castles by first shoveling wet sand into a bucket, inverting the bucket, and then pulling it off to make a castle. Several days later at the park, the child may spot a play area filled with sand and attempt to make more castles. This sand, however, is dry; and when the child inverts the bucket, it all runs out. The child has attempted to assimilate this new situation into her understanding of sand castles. That is, she has acted here just as she did with the sand at the beach. In order to be successful, she would need to revise this understanding to include an awareness that the sand must be wet. Such a revision illustrates accommodation.

The processes of assimilation and accommodation must be complementary for us to remain in equilibrium with the environment. If assimilation predominates, the organism imposes its own order on the environment; and, if accommodation predominates, the converse occurs. Neither one by itself represents the homeostatic state of balance between organism and environment that characterizes adaptation. Thus with each assimilation, accommodation must occur. Piaget referred to the balance thus achieved as **equilibration:** the process responsible for the growth of thought.

Not surprisingly, given his background, Piaget (1971) viewed intellectual development as biologically based: He assumed that differences in intellectual functioning with age reflected an underlying maturation of the nervous system. This emphasis did not prevent him from giving equal importance to environmental contributions. In fact, a singularly distinctive feature of his theory is the manner in which it accounts for intellectual development through the interaction of environmental and biological forces. Rather than viewing maturation as providing "ready-made knowledge" or "pre-formed structures," Piaget viewed it as

assimilation Piaget's term for the process by which individuals fit new information into their present ways of understanding.

accommodation Piaget's term for the process by which individuals alter cognitive structures to fit new experiences or events.

equilibration Piaget's term for the balance between assimilation and accommodation that is responsible for the growth of thought.

TABLE 1.3 Piaget's Four Stages of Cognitive Development	
Stage	**Description**
Sensorimotor (birth–2 years)	Infants' awareness of their world is limited to their senses and their reactions to general action patterns (such as sucking, grasping) through which they incorporate their experiences.
Preoperational (2–7 years)	Children can use symbols such as words and images to think about things, but confuse the way things appear with the way they must be.
Concrete operational (7–11 years)	Thinking becomes more flexible, allowing children to consider several dimensions to things simultaneously, to realize that though an object may look different, it has not necessarily changed.
Formal operational (11 years–adulthood)	Thinking becomes abstract, embracing thought itself; adolescents can consider things that are only possible, as well as those that are real.

"open[ing] up new possibilities . . . which still have to be actualized by collaboration with the environment" (p. 21).

Piaget's theory of intelligence illustrates the central assumptions of the organismic model, and of the constructivist approach taken in this text, perhaps better than any other. Piaget believed knowledge to be more than a copy of reality, as it might be if all it reflected were a faithful detecting and recording by an ever-more-mature nervous system. On the contrary, Piaget assumed that we actively construct what we know of the world—that we are active, not passive, organisms. He also assumed that we organize our experiences in qualitatively different ways with age, leading to distinctly different apprehensions of reality or stages of intellectual development.

Piaget (1954) assumed that all knowledge is based initially on actions. Actions are transformed into thought through a process of **reflective abstraction,** in which features of the actions become abstracted so that they can be applied in other contexts. The way we interact with our environment changes with age; and, as a result, our experience also changes. Initially, infants have no way of holding experience in mind, and their awareness is limited to immediate sensations. Through repeatedly interacting with things around them, infants develop ways of representing these experiences, though at first the objects they recall are not distinguished from the activities leading to their discovery. For example, an infant who delights in a game of finding a toy hidden under a pillow may again look under the pillow even thought she has just watched her parent hide the toy in a new place. Why? Because seeing the toy is part of the same experience as pulling away the pillow. With time, children separate the way they have come to represent their world from the way they act on it. As adolescents, once they can free their ideas from objects, they can relate these ideas to other ideas, and thought becomes abstract. Each form of knowledge evolves from the preceding one. In all, Piaget argued that we progress through four stages. Table 1.3 presents the major characteristics of each of Piaget's four stages.

Piaget studied many aspects of cognitive development, from understanding time and space to the use of rules in children's games. He regarded the latter as important because he believed they provided the foundation for later social and moral development. His approach was always the same, whether studying children's concept of number or of social justice: He watched children and asked them questions about what they were doing. In the matter of moral development, Piaget

reflective abstraction Piaget's term for the process in which features of actions become abstracted, turning the actions into thought.

watched children play marbles, a game common at the time. When he questioned them about the rules of the game, he began to construct a view of the stages of cognitive and moral thinking.

Younger and older children answered his questions in different ways. The youngest boys (the players were rarely girls) regarded the rules as absolute and didn't think they could be changed. When asked where the rules came from, they assumed they had always existed in their present form. They didn't realize that rules are important only for the purpose they serve, making it possible to continue with the game when disagreements arise. Older boys knew that rules are a matter of convenience and are worked out by the players. They also knew rules can be changed if all agree (Piaget, 1965).

Piaget (1965) found that girls and boys approached rules differently. Girls were more lax, more pragmatic, and willing to break the rules as the need arose. Piaget believed the girls' approach was not as well developed as that of boys, who had a better sense of the legal function of rules. Since Piaget is one of the most influential theorists in child development, his belief that this sense of rules is critical for moral development has important implications for our view of the sexes.

Piaget is not the only theorist to measure females against a yardstick developed with males (marbles is a boys' game) and find them lacking. Freud and Erikson did the same. Harvard psychologist Carol Gilligan (1982), commenting on psychological theorists in general, writes

> Implicitly adopting the male life as the norm, they have tried to fashion women out of a masculine cloth. It all goes back, of course, to Adam and Eve—a story which shows, among other things, that if you make a woman out of a man, you are bound to get into trouble. In the life cycle, as in the Garden of Eden, the woman has been the deviant. (p. 6)

Lev Vygotsky

Just like Piaget, Lev Vygotsky believed that individuals acquire knowledge of their world simply in the course of doing whatever they happen to be doing, without having to be formally instructed. But Vygotsky differed from Piaget in an important respect. For Vygotsky (1978), acquisition of this knowledge is fundamentally a social process, taking place under the tutelage of another simply as a natural consequence of working alongside someone who has already discovered a better way of doing things. Vygotsky pointed out that for much of the time children and adolescents play or engage in the tasks they must do in the presence of someone who is older—and more skilled at the very activity in which they are engaged. The discoveries of others, what Vygotsky refers to as cultural tools, get passed on to children in this social context, without ever breaking the flow of the activity itself or being labeled "learning" as such.

Take, as an example, a weekend project—painting a room. Everyone pitches in, the room gets painted, and the furniture is moved back into place. Mom, a veteran of many painted rooms, heads over to the window with a razor blade, handing another to her son on the way. He watches her slide the blade under the dried paint on the pane and does the same until they have cleaned paint off all the panes. The use of a tool—not the razor blade, but the wisdom that it is easier to scrape paint *off* than to put masking tape *on*—has been acquired in a social context, without the need for direct instruction.

Both Piaget and Vygotsky analyze, or view, the course of cognitive development in terms of progressive adaptations to one's environment. But they differ in what they take as the proper unit of analysis (Rogoff, 1990). Piaget takes as this

This girl is able to benefit from her older sister's help using the computer because she has reached a zone of proximal development where she is close to being able to grasp the skills needed.

How might Vygotsky have regarded questions on intelligence tests about the best or right way to complete tasks or think through problems?

zone of proximal development Vygotsky's term for the closeness between a person's current performance and what it might optimally be; readiness to learn something new.

unit the solitary individual, gaining a sense of his or her world through inspecting the objects that make it up. By observing what a person does and says, Piaget "enters" the mind of the individual and examines the processes by which that person grasps hold of his or her reality. Thinking, for Piaget, is a mental activity taking place *in the mind* of a person as that person adapts to his or her environment. As such, thinking is a *property* of the individual (Rogoff, 1990).

Vygotsky takes as his unit of analysis not the solitary individual, but a social person playing or working alongside others, engaging in activities that are characteristic of the group, whether these be learning the best way to remove paint from window panes or to program the VCR. By observing people as they acquire the skills of those they live with—that is, of their culture—Vygotsky identifies thought in terms of the "tools" that have enabled the members of the culture to "grasp" things more easily than they might otherwise have done. Thinking, for Vygotsky, develops as a person internalizes these tools through interacting with those who already use them. As such, thinking is a *process*, one that is fundamentally social in nature, that occurs as a result of living within a social group. The "mind" that Piaget observed within the individual (that is, the individual's grasp on reality) exists, for Vygotsky, in the society in which that person lives, in the form of the cultural wisdoms which the child internalizes through its interactions with those who are already skilled in their use. Thinking takes the form of the person's internalization of these cultural "tools." It is no accident that Vygotsky (1978) titled the book in which he set forth this theory *Mind in Society* (emphasis added).

Vygotsky believed that, just as with tools, the mind of the apprentice learner "grasps" these cultural wisdoms. He believed, as did Piaget, that their acquisition changes the way the mind apprehends reality; but, unlike Piaget, he did not regard them as being forged anew by the individual, through her or his own interaction with the physical world. Instead, he saw them as handed down from those who are more skilled to those who are less skilled in their use.

For something to be passed on in this manner, the learner must be close enough to reach out for it. Vygotsky termed this closeness the **zone of proximal development.** This zone is the distance separating a person's current performance from what it optimally might be. *Proximal* means "near" or "close to." Thus, in order for people to profit from working alongside those who are more skilled, their own performance must come close to, or approximate, the behavior of the other person. The zone represents the range of skills that individuals must possess in order to profit from exposure to those who are more skilled. We see this zone illustrated in the example of removing paint from the windows. This boy was able to internalize the cultural wisdom that it's easier to scrape the paint off than to put something else on only because his own behavior was sufficiently close to the behavior he eventually acquired; in other words, he was already skilled in using tools such as the one his mother handed him.

Barbara Rogoff

Regarding the expertise of a culture as tools to be used by its members has implications for the way one thinks of intellectual development. Barbara Rogoff, a psychologist at Stanford, speaks of this development as an "apprenticeship" in thinking.

The term *apprenticeship* suggests that development is fundamentally a social process and that thinking, rather than a private event occurring within a person's head, is an activity that is shared with others. Thinking, in other words, is not so much a process by which we "produce thoughts" as one that guides "practical action" (Rogoff, 1990). This action can be as playful as it is practical when it involves children and caregivers. Rogoff describes a scene in which 9-month-old twins, who were eating dry Cheerios in their high chairs, were surprised when their mother walked by and popped some of their cereal in her mouth. How silly for Mom to be eating their food! Each time the mother snatched some cereal, the twins would laugh. The mother then put a Cheerio in one twin's fingers and, opening her mouth, bent down close to her: "Valerie began putting the Cheerio in her own mouth reflexively but stopped abruptly when her mother opened her mouth. Valerie looked at her mother's open mouth and began laughing hilariously with her hand poised in midair" (p. 17). This child's thought (I could pop this in *Mom's* mouth!) arises out of the shared activity of their game.

For Rogoff, as for Vygotsky, the unit of analysis is the activity in which the child is engaged. For Vygotsky, however, this activity is initially only a social activity, taking part "outside" the child, and must be internalized in order to regulate behavior as thought. Rogoff does not make such a distinction. Rogoff's focus on the *shared* activity as the crucible of development avoids the age-old developmental question of what is on the "outside" and what on the "inside" of the child. Rogoff does not regard the child, the mother, or the social context (the game) as separable elements, but sees each as a part of the other. Instead of thinking of context as an influence *on* behavior, Rogoff sees behavior as embedded *in* context, taking its particular shape and direction from context. The activity (popping Cheerios into mouths) is the unit of analysis—not the child, not the Cheerio, and not the child *and* the Cheerio. By focusing on the activity and not the Cheerio (or Mom's mouth) for instance, we can predict that once the child knows that the Cheerio can be popped into Mom's mouth, the child also knows that she can pop it into her brother's mouth—and she knows that other digestibles (and indigestibles) can be similarly "popped."

Rogoff does not need to explain how this knowledge is internalized—that is, to explain how it moves from a social realm that is "outside" the child to a realm of thought that is "inside." Such a distinction would suggest a barrier of some kind across which the activity must pass, changing form in the process. Instead, Rogoff sees children as appropriating features of an activity in which they are already engaged with another. What they have practiced with the other is not on the "outside," nor does it need to be brought "inside," or internalized. "The

Carol Gilligan

'boundaries' between people who are in communication are already permeated; it is impossible to say . . . 'whose' a collaborative idea is" (Rogoff, 1990, p. 195). Valerie was already putting *her* Cheerios into her own mouth—as was her mother. Popping a Cheerio into her mother's mouth was "appropriated from," or fit into, this activity. Both activities, in other words, were on the same side of the "barrier."

Valerie's discovery illustrates Rogoff's concept of **guided participation.** This concept extends Vygotsky's concept of the zone of proximal development. Guided participation captures the notion that the child shares with an adult an activity in which both participate to decrease the distance between their respective contributions to the activity in which they are engaged. Rogoff (1990) focuses more than Vygotsky on the ways in which children actively participate in their development: "Children see, structure, and even demand the assistance of those around them in learning how to solve problems of all kinds" (p. 16). She also places greater emphasis than Vygotsky on the importance of tacit, or unspoken, forms of communication, as in the example of Valerie and the Cheerio.

Rogoff points out that the child's strategies for learning its culture are the same one would recommend to any visitor to a foreign culture: Stay close to your guide, watch what the guide does, get involved whenever you can, and pay attention to what the guide may tell or show you. The "guide" complements the child's activity by adjusting the difficulty of the activity to match the child's abilities, modeling the behavior that is sought while the child is watching, and accommodating his or her own behavior to what the child can grasp.

Rogoff views development as multidirectional. Unlike Piaget, for instance, she does not see development as moving toward a single "end point," toward a universal set of achievements, such as Piaget's formal thought. Instead, the course of development can take any of a number of forms, depending on the types of skills that are valued in the child's culture. These skills, whether they be literacy or goat herding, establish the developmental goals that are local to each culture. Thus, Piaget's developmental end point of logical, abstract thought reflects the value placed in our society on scientific reasoning. Formal thought, in other words, represents the "local" goals of Western societies.

Another theorist also views development as progressing toward more than a single end point. Carol Gilligan argues that children of either sex are likely to follow quite different developmental paths.

Carol Gilligan

Carol Gilligan notes striking differences in the ways males and females think of themselves. These differences extend to the ways they resolve issues involving others. Gilligan (1982) finds that males tend to see themselves as separate from others; females describe themselves in terms of their relationships with others. These themes of separation and connectedness appear over and over again in her research, whether she is studying morality and choice, descriptions of the self, or interpersonal dynamics.

Notice the way two children interviewed by Gilligan, an 11-year-old boy and an 11-year-old girl, describe themselves (their descriptions are in Box 1.1).

Jake describes himself at length. He first identifies himself by his age and name and then his status within his community. We never know what his mother does, but we know that her job doesn't contribute to his sense of position the way his father's occupation does. He then identifies his abilities and interests. He ends with a description of an important physical characteristic. We get the impression of a distinct personality from this description. Gilligan agrees. Jake has described himself in terms of the things that distinguish him from others. His self-description emphasizes his uniqueness and separateness.

guided participation Rogoff's term for the shared activity of a novice and one who is more skilled, in which both participate to decrease the distance between their respective contributions to the activity; an extension of Vygotsky's zone of proximal development that assumes a more active role for the learner.

Psychodynamic Theories

Freud assumed that all thoughts and actions are motivated; he termed the life force motivating these the libido. Different aspects of the personality control the expression of the libido. The id, present from birth, has limited means for gratifying libidinal impulses. The ego, next to develop, seeks to gratify as many libidinal impulses as possible within social constraints. The last aspect of the personality to develop, the superego, contains the moral values of one's culture and dictates what one should and should not do.

Erik Erikson assumed, as did Freud, that personality develops through a sequence of stages, but he carried these through the life span. He assumed that society challenges us with new demands as we age and that we experience these as crises. Each crisis takes a slightly different form and gives each stage its unique characteristics. Achievement of a personal identity is the central crisis of adolescence; this involves adolescents in a set of commitments to life goals that give definition to the self.

Nancy Chodorow builds on a foundation provided by Freud but attributes gender differences to the social fact that for almost all children the first intimate relationship is with a female—the mother. Girls can continue to define themselves within the context of this first relationship, but boys must separate themselves in order to develop as males. As a consequence, girls' development is characterized by attachment, and boys' by separation and individuation.

Organismic Theories

Jean Piaget viewed intelligence as a means of adapting to one's environment, with only those forms of thought that promote adaptation surviving over the years. Piaget viewed intelligence as biologically based. He assumed that knowledge, rather than being a simple copy of reality, is an active construction of what we know of the world. He also assumed that our experiences are organized in qualitatively different stages with age.

Like Piaget, Lev Vygotsky believed that events do not have meaning until people actively interpret and internalize them. He differs from Piaget, however, in his notion that thinking and learning are fundamentally social in nature, rather than the result of individual experience. For Vygotsky, cognitive development is the internalization of the tools of cultural wisdom.

Barbara Rogoff extends Vygotsky's concept of the zone of proximal development with her concept of guided participation; the child doesn't simply copy the adult's behavior but actively participates in the activity. Rogoff, unlike Piaget, sees development as multidirectional, depending on the goals and values of the particular culture.

Carol Gilligan focuses on the interpersonal aspects of development. She notes striking gender differences in the ways individuals of either sex define themselves. Males tend to view themselves as separate from others; females typically describe themselves in terms of their relationships with others.

Robert Kegan has built on the constructive process described by Piaget. Kegan argues that the most central human activity is meaning making, or constructing a reality that corresponds to our sense of self in relation to events and other people. Development, for Kegan, is a cumulative process of differentiating the "me" from the "not-me." As our sense of "me" changes, so do our ways of relating to others and responding to events—and those changes lead to further changes in our sense of self.

Key Terms

accommodation (p. 31)
assimilation (p. 31)
axioms (p. 15)
conditional response (CR) (p. 22)
conditional stimulus (CS) (p. 22)
constructive approach (p. 3)
continuity-discontinuity issue (p. 15)
development (p. 11)
differentiation (p. 11)
ego (p. 21)
epigenesis (p. 16)
epigenetic principle (p. 22)

equilibration (p. 31)
growth (p. 11)
guided participation (p. 36)
habituation (p. 19)
id (p. 21)
laws (p. 15)
libido (p. 20)
model (p. 14)
nature-nurture controversy (p. 15)
negative reinforcement (p. 23)
observational learning (p. 24)
positive reinforcement (p. 23)

reductionism (p. 16)
reflective abstraction (p. 32)
repression (p. 25)
respondent conditioning (p. 22)
stage (p. 19)
superego (p. 21)
theory (p. 15)
unconditional response (UCR) (p. 22)
unconditional stimulus (UCS) (p. 22)
zone of proximal development (p. 34)

chaptertwo

The Context of Development
Genetic Action and Environmental Influences

This time the sea of waters pressed too forcefully against the straining membrane. It burst and the massive body within rode the exploding corona of fluids toward freedom and the beginnings of life. This drama repeats itself monthly within the body of every sexually mature female as an egg ripens and breaks its protective covering within one of the ovaries. It is the first leg of the long journey into life. This chapter charts the beginnings of this journey, examining genetic and environmental influences on the developing organism.

The Beginnings: DNA and Life

They worked quickly. Pacing, talking, they went over it once again. The solution was so close, and yet it eluded them. They knew that any moment another team might break the code. Like many codes, it was simple. Just a handful of elements made up the ancient alphabet. Millions of years old, the alphabet disclosed how life reproduced itself.

James Watson, an American geneticist, and Francis Crick, an English biologist, broke the code when they arrived at the structure of deoxyribonucleic acid (DNA). **DNA** is the tightly coiled molecule of which chromosomes are formed (represented schematically in Figure 2.1). Not until 1944 was it known that DNA was the material in chromosomes responsible for genetic transmission. Nine years later Crick and Watson, working with Rosalind Franklin, whose crystallography data confirmed their model, discovered how it provided the genetic blueprint for all living things (Watson, 1968).

Traits are passed on from one generation to the next through **genes,** short segments of the DNA strand. Thousands of genes are carried within each of the chromosomes making up the 23 pairs found in every cell in the body. In a remarkable excess of nature, each cell, with the exception of mature sex cells, contains all the genetic information needed to replicate the entire organism, some 150,000 genes in all (Tjian, 1995).

DNA is composed of units called **nucleotides,** which, in different combinations, spell out the plans for everything from eyelashes to elbows. Since each nucleotide is made of just three elements—a sugar, a phosphate, and one of four nitrogenous bases—the genetic code looks deceptively simple. And yet, the number of combinations of these elements is myriad, just as is the number of words and sentences that can be formed from our alphabet of 26 letters.

One can think of DNA as a zipper. As Figure 2.1 illustrates, the nucleotides form two twisted strands of genetic material held loosely together in the middle. The edges of the zipper are sugars and phosphates. Attached to each sugar and phosphate is a nitrogenous base: adenine, thymine, cytosine, or guanine. The bases form the teeth of the zipper. And just as with a zipper, the teeth "fit" each other. Whenever adenine is a tooth on one side of the zipper, thymine must be the tooth corresponding to it on the other side. The same is true of cytosine and guanine. When DNA unzips, as it does in cell division, enzymes attract free-floating nucleotides to form complementary halves. The sequence of sugars and phosphates making up the side of the zipper remains unchanged by division as does the ascending sequence of "teeth" attached to either half. Since each tooth can fit, or bond with, only one of the three remaining possible types, the new strand becomes a mirror likeness of the old, reproducing itself.

The blueprint for the construction of new cells is provided by the order of the bases, or the teeth, in the chain. On average, each gene is "spelled out" by anywhere from 900 to 1,500 such pairs of bases. The order of these pairs determines which proteins, the building blocks of the body, will be manufactured. Just as in

Q Does a strand of DNA duplicate through growth or by each enzyme finding a perfect match?

DNA Deoxyribonucleic acid, the double-stranded molecule in chromosomes that encodes genetic information.

genes Short segments of the DNA strand, responsible for transmission of particular traits; thousands of genes are carried within each chromosome.

nucleotides Subunits of DNA consisting of a sugar molecule, a phosphate molecule, and a nitrogenous base.

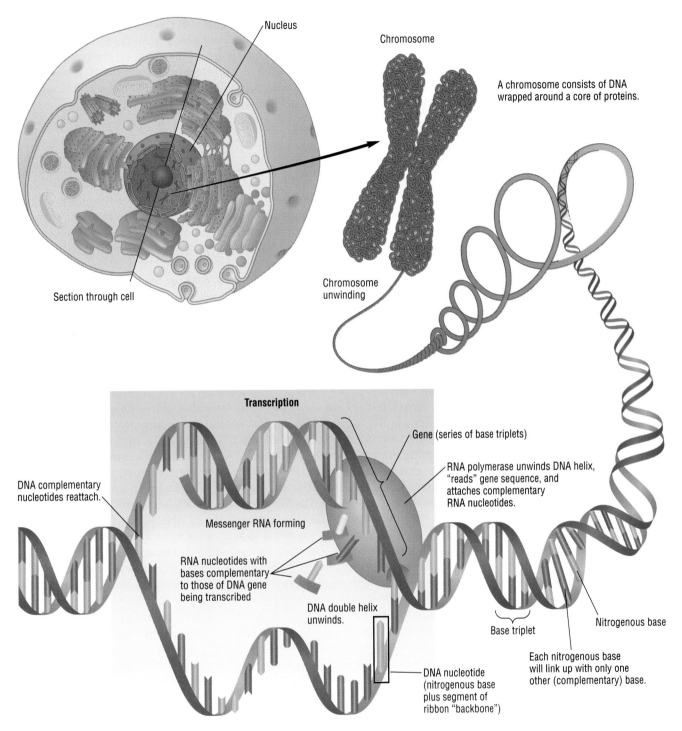

FIGURE 2.1 **Cell Structure and the Transcription Process**

the spelling of a word, changing a single letter can change the entire meaning, as in "si*t*" versus "si*p*". So, too, changing a single base pair in the hundreds of bases spelling out a trait can change the "meaning" of that trait. Of the more than 400 base pairs that form the gene related to red blood cells, for instance, a single base pair makes the difference between the production of normal blood and blood with the distorted cells known as sickle-cell anemia (Meryash, 1995).

Genes

DNA directs the manufacture of proteins with the aid of two related substances, messenger RNA (m-RNA) and transfer RNA (t-RNA). **Messenger RNA** is a copy of DNA, in much the same way a photograph is of a negative; m-RNA serves as the model for the new construction (see Figure 2.1). **Transfer RNA,** a smaller copy which matches only short segments of the model, picks up molecules from the surrounding cytoplasm and carries these "piggyback" to the chain under construction.

Two functionally distinct types of genes make up the DNA strand. **Structural genes** provide the actual codes for the construction of new proteins, the biological building blocks that make up the various cells of the body. **Regulatory genes** control which genes are copied. The transcription, or copying, process involves a number of steps. Initially, many different proteins converge on the DNA molecule, forming what Robert Tjian (1995), a biochemist and molecular biologist at Berkeley, calls a "transcription engine." Tjian likens the DNA molecule itself to a track. Certain stretches of the track provide the code for the construction of new proteins; these stretches are made up of the structural genes. Other stretches of the track contain the regulatory genes that control the coding process.

The transcription engine enters the DNA track on a stretch of the molecule containing the regulatory genes, usually just preceding the stretch to be copied. The engine rides along the DNA, sliding over the coding region containing the structural genes. The actual work of copying is done by an enzyme, **RNA polymerase,** which copies the DNA into messenger RNA as it rolls along the track. Since RNA polymerase will copy anything it rolls over, additional regulatory elements are involved that program it to copy only certain segments of the DNA. These regulatory genes are often located some distance either up or down the track from the segment that is being copied. Certain regulatory genes facilitate the copying and are known as *enhancers.* Others, called *silencers,* work to inhibit copying (Tjian, 1995).

How do regulatory genes influence an activity taking place sometimes at a great distance from them? Tjian and his co-workers found the existence of other proteins, **activators** and **repressors,** that "dock" at these regulatory sites along the DNA track, picking up their messages to copy or to inhibit copying, and relaying them on to other molecules, **coactivators,** which integrate signals from many such proteins before sending the product on to **basal factors,** which communicate directly with RNA polymerase. These different regulatory elements work together to influence the rate at which genes are copied (Tjian, 1995).

Although identical enhancers and silencers can be shared by several genes, no two genes have exactly the same combination of these, thus making it possible for each cell to control the transcription of genes individually. Because each cell in the body contains all the genetic information needed to replicate the entire organism, regulatory genes serve an important function by suppressing genes that are unrelated to the replication of a particular cell, thereby enabling that cell to replicate only itself. Thus, liver cells, for instance, are able to produce additional

messenger RNA (mRNA) The form of ribonucleic acid (RNA) that carries genetic codes from the DNA in the cell nucleus to the sites of protein synthesis in the cytoplasm.

transfer RNA (tRNA) The form of ribonucleic acid (RNA) that carries amino acids to the cytoplasm, where proteins are assembled according to the genetic code carried by the messenger RNA.

structural genes Genes in the DNA strand that provide the codes for the construction of new proteins.

regulatory genes Genes in the DNA strand that regulate which genes are copied.

RNA polymerase An enzyme that copies DNA into messenger RNA during the transcription process.

activators Proteins that facilitate the copying of DNA segments by picking up messages at regulatory sites along the DNA track and relaying them to coactivators.

repressors Proteins that inhibit the copying of DNA segments by picking up messages at regulatory sites along the DNA track and relaying them to coactivators.

coactivators Molecules that integrate signals from activators and repressors and send them on to basal factors.

basal factors Factors that communicate directly with RNA polymerase.

Nettie Stevens discovered XX and XY chromosomes when she was a postdoctoral student with Theodor Boveri.

liver cells, and not bone or kidney cells, because the genes for the latter, also contained within the cell nucleus, are suppressed.

How do the regulatory genes distinguish which genes in the cell nucleus to turn off and which to turn on? Definitive answers await further research. However, we do know that cells are sensitive to their environments, just as individuals are. For instance, up to a certain point in development, if cells from the brain region of a developing newt, or salamander, are transplanted to another part of the body, such as its back, they develop into skin cells and not brain cells. Depending on where a cell is and what is taking place around it, the cell will behave in quite different ways (Gilbert, 1994).

Chromosomes

Thousands of genes, segments of coiled DNA, make up a single chromosome. **Chromosomes** are microscopic filaments within the nucleus of a cell. Each cell contains 23 pairs of chromosomes, one member of the pair coming from the mother and the other from the father. Twenty-two of these are matching pairs, called **autosomes.** Research at the turn of the century by Nettie Stevens (as cited in Gilbert, 1994), however, revealed that the 23rd pair, which determines the sex of the child, matches for females but not for males. As Figure 2.2 shows, in females, both **sex chromosomes** are relatively long and X-shaped (XX), whereas in males one is considerably shorter and Y-shaped (XY). The sex chromosome received from the mother is always an X (females do not have a Y chromosome

Q Why can't cells from different parts of the body, such as neurons, bone cells, and heart cells, replicate into other kinds of cells?

chromosomes Microscopic filaments within a cell nucleus carrying genetic information and composed of DNA and protein.

autosomes The 22 matching pairs of chromosomes that, together with the sex chromosomes of the 23rd pair, are found in the cell nucleus.

sex chromosomes The 23rd pair of chromosomes that determine the sex of the child; females have two X chromosomes, and males have one X and one Y chromosome.

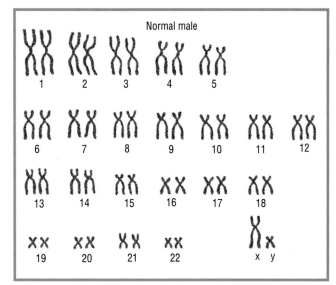

FIGURE 2.2 *The 23 pairs of chromosomes in the normal male and normal female human being. The sex chromosomes are the 23rd pair.*

to pass on); that from the father can be either an X or a Y. The sex of a child is determined by one or more genes located along the Y chromosome, which trigger the production of androgens, male sex hormones that masculinize the developing organism. Without the presence of these hormones, the organism would develop as a female (Page, Fisher, McGillivray, & Brown, 1990; Sinclair et al., 1990).

Gametes: The Ovum and Sperm

The sex cells that unite at conception are known as **gametes.** Within the nucleus of each gamete are the chromosomes containing the genetic material that will direct the formation of the developing organism. However, before the gametes can ever serve their reproductive function, they themselves must develop. Immature sex cells, just like all other cells within the body, contain 23 pairs of chromosomes. Sex cells mature through a series of cell divisions, termed **meiosis,** which leaves them with half the number of chromosomes. Like strangers bearing an important message, each gamete carries half a torn ticket to identify itself.

Were it not for meiosis, the union of ovum and sperm would result in a cell containing twice the normal number of chromosomes, instead of the 46 per cell that characterize humans—and the number would double with each generation. All other body cells divide through a process of **mitosis,** in which the resulting cells each end up with 23 pairs of chromosomes. Meiosis progresses in similar ways in ova and sperm, but with important differences (Figure 2.3). We will consider this process first in ova.

Each infant girl is born with several million ova, contained within the ovaries that flank the uterus. Only about 400 of these will mature in her lifetime (Gilbert, 1994). At puberty, increases in follicle stimulating hormone (FSH) and luteinizing hormone (LH) stimulate the ovaries to begin producing **estrogens,** female sex hormones. Each month an ovum in one of the ovaries matures through two cell divisions. The first division results in two "daughter" cells, each still with 23 pairs of chromosomes. With the second cell division, the chromosomes forming each pair separate, migrating to opposite sides of the nucleus as it pulls apart, resulting in cells that contain only half of each pair, or 23 *single* chromosomes. Meiosis produces only a single mature ovum, instead of the four that one might expect from

gametes Sperm and ova, which, when mature, have 23 individual instead of 23 pairs of chromosomes.

meiosis The process of cell division in which sex cells mature, reducing the number of chromosomes from 23 pairs to 23 individual chromosomes.

mitosis The process of cell division in which body cells replicate; the chromosomes of each new cell are identical to those of the parent cell.

estrogens Sex hormones produced primarily by the ovaries.

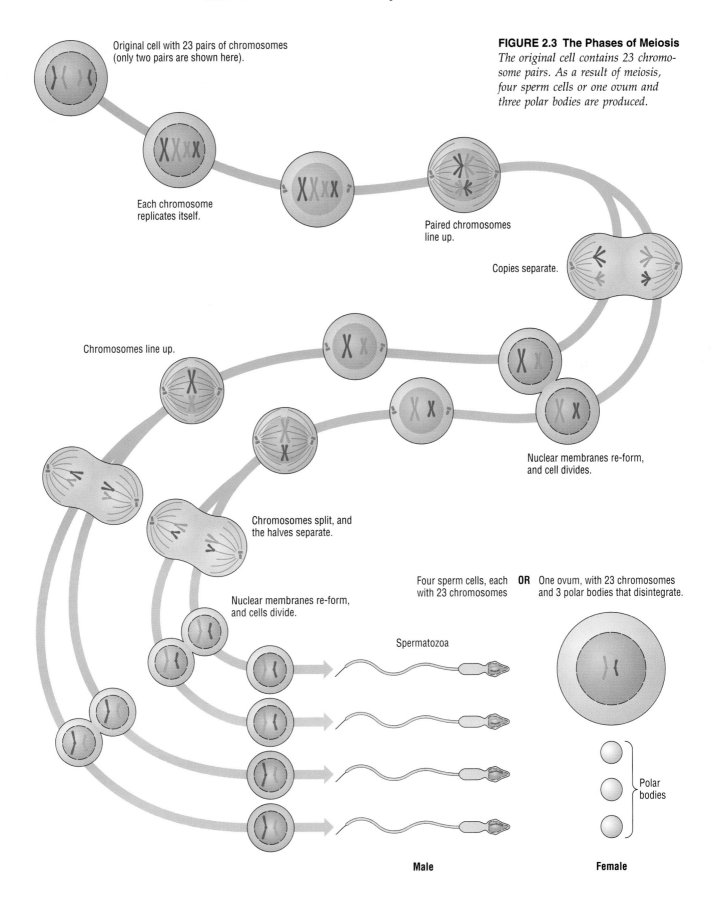

Original cell with 23 pairs of chromosomes (only two pairs are shown here).

Each chromosome replicates itself.

Paired chromosomes line up.

Copies separate.

Chromosomes line up.

Nuclear membranes re-form, and cell divides.

Chromosomes split, and the halves separate.

Nuclear membranes re-form, and cells divide.

Four sperm cells, each with 23 chromosomes **OR** One ovum, with 23 chromosomes and 3 polar bodies that disintegrate.

Spermatozoa

Polar bodies

Male

Female

FIGURE 2.3 The Phases of Meiosis
The original cell contains 23 chromosome pairs. As a result of meiosis, four sperm cells or one ovum and three polar bodies are produced.

There are approximately 200 million sperm produced in a single ejaculation. Typically, following ejaculation during intercourse, fewer than 100 will reach a fallopian tube where an ovulated oocyte may be present.

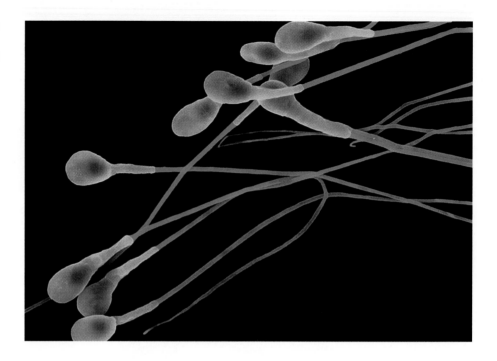

Q What would be the possible consequence for a man who does not have the ability to produce Sertoli cells?

Q Which parent is responsible for the sex of a child?

two cell divisions, since three of the cells receive very little cytoplasm and eventually disintegrate (Gilbert, 1994).

In contrast to the single ovum that matures in the female each month, a mature male produces several hundred million sperm each hour, and in any ejaculate there are approximately 200 million mature sperm (Harper 1988). Sperm develop in tubules in the testes, which are contained within the scrotal sac hanging beneath the penis. Here they are maintained at a temperature ideal for their breeding, several degrees less than that found inside the body. At puberty, increases in FSH and LH, the same hormones that stimulate the ovaries, stimulate the testes to secrete **testosterone**, a male sex hormone, which is involved in the production of sperm.

Two types of cells line the tubes in which sperm develop: sperm-producing cells (germinal epithelial cells) and nurse cells (Sertoli cells). Division of the germinal cells produces sperm. One part remains for later cell divisions (unlike the female, the male will continue to produce sex cells throughout his life); the other will mature as sperm. Sertoli cells function as "nurses" for the immature sperm, which nestle among them to receive nourishment while they develop. As with the ovum, the first cell division produces two cells, each still with 23 pairs of chromosomes. The members of all 23 pairs are similar, with the exception of the two chromosomes making up the 23rd pair. A close inspection shows that one of these is X-shaped and the other is shaped like a Y. With the last cell division, one sperm receives the X chromosome and the other the Y. These chromosomes determine the sex of the child. If an X-bearing sperm fertilizes the ovum, the child will be a female; a Y-bearing sperm produces a male. Thus, which type of sperm fertilizes the ovum will determine the sex of the child.

One might almost say that "sex differences" are apparent right from the start. Y-bearing sperm, called androsperm, have sleeker, narrower bodies and swim faster than the more rounded and heavier X-bearing spermatids, or gynosperm. The X chromosome carried by the latter is 5 times the size of the Y carried by the androsperm, and differences in the size and weight of their genetic cargo slow the

testosterone A sex hormone produced by the testes.

X-bearing sperm. As a consequence of the greater speed of the androsperm, it is estimated that 400 to 500 males are conceived for every 100 females. Were it not for the fact that androsperm are also more vulnerable to "environmental" stresses once within the vagina and uterus, there would be a very real imbalance in the sexes. As it is, for every 100 females born, there are 105 males (Lips, 1997).

Increasingly, parents are turning to technology to select the sex of their child, some because they carry genes for disorders affecting one sex but not the other and others to add a child of one sex to a household where children are exclusively of the other sex. In interviews with women considering such procedures, Lisa Belkin (1999), a contributing writer for the *New York Times Magazine,* writes, "We care about the sex of our children. Some of us care more than others, but we all care. It is the first question asked about a baby, almost from conception, certainly at the moment of birth" (p. 27).

Genetic Diversity

Recall that in the fertilized ovum, or **zygote,** one chromosome in each pair comes from the mother and the other from the father. The combination of these chromosomes results in an individual who is distinct from either parent. The process of meiosis itself, by which these two sex cells have matured, has further contributed to diversity. Meiosis reduces the number of chromosomes in the mature sex cell by half, shuffling the members of each pair into either one gamete or the other as the cell divides. The number of possible different combinations of chromosomes making up the two mature gametes that result from the shuffling of 23 pairs is 2 to the 23rd power, or about 8 million different possible gametes from the maturation of a single sex cell. A similar number of gametes results from cell division in the other parent. Since any one of these gametes can fertilize, or be fertilized by, any of the others, the number of chromosomally different zygotes that could result is very large—64 trillion (Plomin, DeFries, & McClearn, 1990).

Geneticists note that this figure is only the beginning of diversity. Additional genetic diversity occurs through a process of **crossing over,** which takes place during cell division. During meiosis, the members of each pair line up, and segments of the chromosomes making up each pair break off and cross over to corresponding positions along the other chromosome, resulting in two different chromosomes, neither of which resembles the ones that were inherited from either parent.

Twins

Some of you at this point might be thinking of individuals you know who have a twin sibling. Wouldn't such twin pairs prove the exception to nature's rule of diversity? Although at first glance the answer might appear to be yes, such is not always the case. Identical twins are individuals who share identical genetic makeups. The technical term for identical twins is **monozygotic,** referring to the fact that each twin originates from the same fertilized ovum, or zygote (Figure 2.4). The diversity resulting from the combination of each parent's chromosomes, as well as from meiosis and crossing over, virtually guarantees that each and every *zygote* will be different from the next. However, since identical twins originate from the same zygote, they will have identical genes (100% genetic relatedness). Identical twins are formed when a single zygote separates into two clusters of cells, instead of continuing as a single cluster, during initial cell division. The frequency of monozygotic twins is approximately 4 of every 1,000 births and is unrelated to any known factors.

zygote A single cell resulting from the union of the ovum and sperm at conception.

crossing over During meiosis, the exchange of corresponding genes in homologous chromosomes; one of the sources of genetic diversity.

monozygotic twins Twins who develop from the same fertilized ovum, or zygote.

Identical (Monozygotic) Twins

It yields one zygote.

The zygote divides, and the
two new zygotes separate.

Sperm
Ovum

Follicle

One ovum is
available for
fertilization.

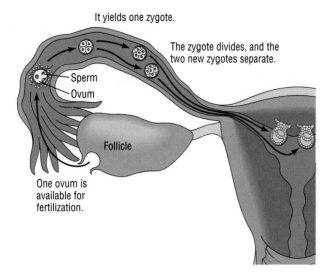

Two genetically identical embryos develop.

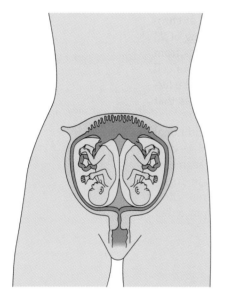

Fraternal (Dizygotic) Twins

They yield two zygotes.

Sperm
Ovum

Follicles

Two ova are
available for
fertilization.

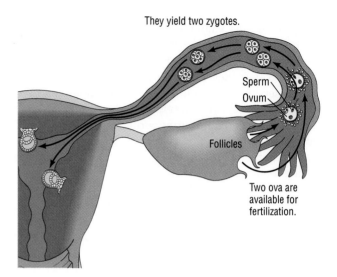

Two genetically different embryos develop.

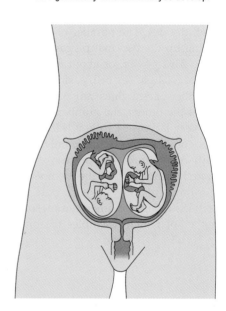

FIGURE 2.4 The Genetics of Identical and Fraternal Twins

 Can a boy and a girl be
monozygotic twins?

dizygotic twins Twins who develop
from two separate ova, fertilized at
the same time by different sperm.

Twins can also be fraternal, or **dizygotic.** Fraternal twins originate when two
ova are released during ovulation, and each is fertilized (see Figure 2.4). Dizygotic
twins, although born at the same time, are no more alike genetically than any
other two siblings with the same parents (50% genetic relatedness). The frequency
of dizygotic twins has been found to vary with a number of factors, such as ethnicity, the mother's age, and the use of fertility drugs. Fraternal twins occur twice
as frequently among Whites (8 per 1,000 births) as among Asians (4 per 1,000).
Among African Americans, fraternal twins are even more frequent, 12 to 16 for
every 1,000 births. The incidence of fraternal twins increases with the mother's

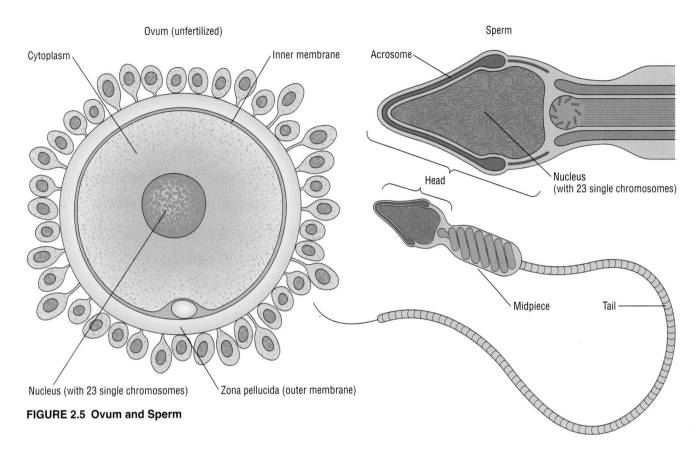

FIGURE 2.5 Ovum and Sperm

age and with the number of children she has already had. The use of fertility drugs also increases the likelihood of multiple births (Keith & Luke, 1993).

Fertilization

The ovum is one of the largest cells in the body, just large enough to be seen without magnification. Its size reflects the nutrients it stores, not the size of the organism it will produce. Human ova are about the same size as those of mice—and whales (Phillips & Dryden, 1991). When fertilized, elements in the cytoplasm will provide a biochemical support system to the developing organism (Wasserman, 1988). The ovum is covered with a tough outer membrane, the zona pellucida (Figure 2.5). Under this thick outer coat, a second membrane encases the cell nucleus and the surrounding cytoplasm, the rich storehouse of nutrients on which the dividing cells, should fertilization occur, must rely before they receive nourishment from the mother's body. The latter is possible only when implantation occurs, nearly a week away. Until then, the long journey down the Fallopian tubes is, at the cellular level at least, the equivalent of "backpacking."

It has been estimated that all of the eggs necessary to reproduce the population of North America could be placed in a 3-inch cube. All the sperm needed for this could be put on the head of a pin (Arey, 1954). These cells are quite obviously different, each uniquely specialized for the function it will serve—ova for providing life-sustaining nourishment and sperm for delivering a genetic cargo. Sperm are composed of a compact head carrying the nucleus with its genetic message; a short neck, or midpiece; and a long lashing tail that propels it forcefully in a swimming motion (see Figure 2.5). The head of the sperm is covered with a

Only a single sperm completely fuses with the membrane of the ovum to achieve fertilization. All other sperm trying to fuse are shed from the surface of the ovum.

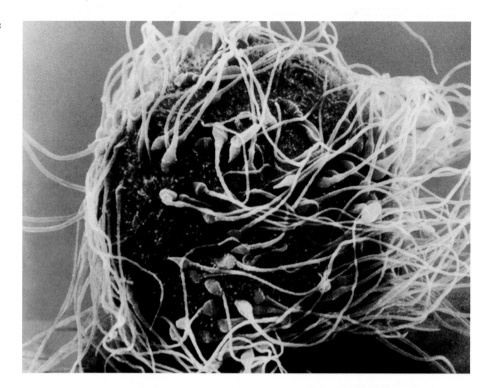

acrosome The cap on the head of the sperm containing enzymes that digest the outer surface of the ovum.

capacitation A change in the outer membrane of the sperm, triggered by chemicals in the female reproductive tract, that allows the acrosome's enzymes to be released.

acrosomal reaction The release of the enzymes by the acrosome as a result of capacitation.

cap, termed the **acrosome,** that is filled with enzymes. In contrast to ova, which contain much cytoplasm, the sperm has almost none. Its structure reflects its function: Everything has been given over to motility.

Fertilization occurs near the top of the Fallopian tube. Unlike sperm, the ovum has no movement of its own. Instead, it must depend on muscular contractions of the Fallopian tube and on tiny hairlike cilia that line the walls of the tube to sweep it along its course. The Fallopian tube, or oviduct, is a tight fit for the ovum. Cilial action forceful enough to move the inert ovum would be too great a force for sperm to swim against. Secretory cells lining the oviduct may play a part in sperm transport. During ovulation, a tide of mucus rises from the cells lining the Fallopian tubes, impeding the action of the cilia; this subsides only after ovulation. These secretory tides, controlled by hormones, may help the microscopic sperm to reach the ovum lodged at the top of the Fallopian tube. At present, however, there is no conclusive evidence implicating one mechanism as more important than any other (Harper, 1988; Jansen, 1984).

Of the millions of sperm present in an ejaculate, only several hundred reach the ovum; and, of these, only a single sperm will get through the protective layers of the ovum to have its nucleus unite with that of the ovum. Because sperm are highly motile, there is a tendency to think of them as playing a more active rule than the ovum in the fertilization process. Such is not the case. Some evidence suggests that the ovum may actually signal the sperm by secreting a chemical signal and, when the sperm get within reach, anchoring them to its surface with tiny hairlike filaments (Roberts, 1991). Even before this, however, chemicals in the female reproductive tract trigger a process known as **capacitation** in sperm. In capacitation, the outer membrane of the sperm fuses with the membrane of the acrosome. This fusion allows the enzymes contained within the acrosome to be released, a process known as the **acrosomal reaction.**

A complex molecular mechanism allows the sperm and the ovum to recognize each other. On the membrane of the ovum are "docking sites" to which the

Ernest Just was the first to identify membrane depolarization and zona reaction.

sperm binds. Once the sperm reaches a docking site, microvilli on the ovum's surface tether the sperm in place; at this time the enzymes covering the surface of the sperm soften the tough outer membrane of the ovum. Only a single sperm fuses with the membrane of the ovum (Gilbert, 1994). What prevents more than one sperm from doing so?

Ernest Just (1919) identified two distinct gating mechanisms that are precipitated by this fusion. Fusion with the ovum's membrane triggers an action potential, a change in the surface polarization that radiates across the membrane. Much like an electric gate that swings shut, this **membrane depolarization** bars entrance by other sperm. Like a toppled row of dominoes collapsing the spaces between, a change in voltage makes substances within the ovum's membrane unavailable for further fusion with other sperm. The sperm's fusion with the ovum's membrane triggers a second, slower reaction known as the **zona reaction.** Sacs that lie just below the membrane release granular particles and enzymes that affect the membrane's ability to bind with sperm. Thus sperm that may have begun this process at other binding sites can no longer maintain it and are shed from the ovum's surface (Gilbert, 1994).

The nuclei of the sperm and ovum have yet to exchange their genetic contents, however. The sperm's nucleus is still near the outer perimeter of the egg, which in volume is 85,000 times that of the sperm. Further, only wreckage remains of the capsule that crashed against the egg's surface before depositing its cargo safely inside. Now, it is the nucleus of the ovum that migrates toward that of the sperm. The two nuclei meet and, migrating to the center of the zygote, combine genetic materials, forming a single cell with 23 pairs of chromosomes. One member of each pair has been contributed by the mother and the other by the father (Longo, 1987).

A woman is fertile for approximately 6 days each month, for approximately 5 days preceding ovulation and on the day of ovulation itself. The sooner intercourse occurs before ovulation, the greater the chance of conceiving. Investigators using daily urine samples to estimate time of ovulation, have found the likelihood of conception to increase from 8% on the 5th day preceding ovulation to 36% on

membrane depolarization The neutralization of the surface polarity of the ovum after a sperm succeeds in fusing with the ovum's membrane; this change bars entrance by other sperm.

zona reaction A release of granular particles and enzymes beneath the ovum's outer membrane, triggered by the sperm's fusion with the ovum's membrane, that affects the membrane's ability to bind with sperm.

When during her menstrual cycle is a woman most likely to become pregnant if she has intercourse?

the day of ovulation. No conceptions occurred for intercourse on days following ovulation or when intercourse preceded ovulation by more than 6 days (Wilcox, Weinberg, & Baird, 1995).

How long the ovum remains viable and capable of fertilization cannot be said with certainty. It is not known, for instance, whether the sudden drop in the probability of conceiving immediately following ovulation reflects the viability of the ovum itself or the inability of any additional sperm to reach the ovum due to cervical mucus. The fact that intercourse 5 days prior to ovulation can result in conception indicates that sperm are viable for at least that long. Some research has found live sperm even after 7 days (Glezerman, 1993). How old the sperm is does not appear to be related to the viability of the embryo, given conception, since differences in live births were not found for infants conceived at different days within the 6-day interval. However, relatively few (6%) infants were conceived with sperm 3 or more days old. Given conception, the same has been found for ova. Simpson (1995) reports no difference in live births for the few conceptions he observed to occur following ovulation than for those preceding it. Additionally, no relationship was observed between the timing of intercourse and the sex of the infant (Wilcox, Weinberg, & Baird, 1995).

Most women are unaware of the time at which they ovulate. Few symptoms accompany its occurrence, and it rarely occurs at exactly the same time in the cycle from month to month. On the average, ovulation occurs about 10 days prior to the start of the next period.

Patterns of Genetic Action

Genes at corresponding positions along the lengths of a pair carry related information. We know much of the functioning of these gene pairs, or **alleles,** from the work of an obscure 19th-century Augustinian monk, Gregor Mendel, whose study of the ordinary garden pea become the basis for the science of genetics.

Mendel noticed that many characteristics of the pea appeared in either of two forms. Their flowers, for example, were either white or red, their pods yellow or green, and the seeds within either wrinkled or smooth. He thought that each characteristic must be controlled by a pair of factors. Exactly how these factors passed their characteristics from one generation to the next was not so obvious, however. For one thing, plants of the next generation did not always show the same characteristics as the parent generation. Were the factors controlling those characteristics lost? Did they merge with other, more dominant, factors, or did they pass hidden but unchanged to the next generation?

What would happen, Mendel asked, if the pollen from white flowering plants were used to fertilize red flowering plants? Would some of the seedlings mature into white flowering plants and others into red flowering plants? Would they all be red? Or all be white? With hoe in hand, Mendel set about to get an answer and, in spring, neat rows of plants all blossomed in red. Since all the plants had red flowers, Mendel reasoned that the factor controlling this characteristic must be **dominant.** Whenever it is present, the trait it carries will occur.

But what of the other factor, that for white flowers? Was it lost? Mendel bred the second generation of red flowering plants with each other and found that, though most of the following generation had red flowers, some bloomed in white. The other factor, which he called **recessive,** had been masked by the first but was passed to the next generation. In order for the trait carried by the recessive gene to occur, *both* members of the allele pair had to be recessive.

alleles The complementary forms of a gene located at the same site on the autosomes that determine the expression of a particular trait.

dominant allele The gene of an allele pair that produces a particular trait.

recessive allele The gene of an allele pair that governs the expression of a trait only in the presence of another recessive allele.

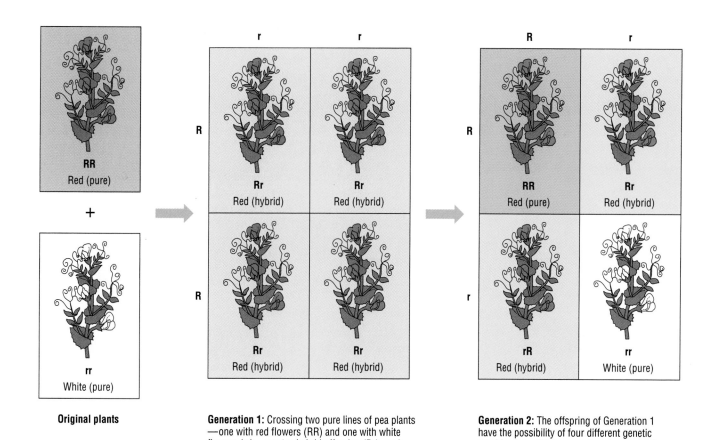

Original plants

Generation 1: Crossing two pure lines of pea plants
—one with red flowers (RR) and one with white
flowers (rr)—creates hybrid offspring (Rr), each
with one red gene and one white gene. Because red
is dominant, all the flowers appear red.

Generation 2: The offspring of Generation 1
have the possibility of four different genetic
combinations: RR (pure red), rr (pure white),
Rr (hybrid red), and rR (hybrid red).

FIGURE 2.6 Mendel's Pea Plants

If there were an equal likelihood of receiving either a dominant or a recessive
gene from either parent, there should be approximately equal numbers of plants
in which both genes are dominant (AA), one gene is dominant and one is recessive (Aa and aA), and both genes are recessive (aa). Only in the last group of
plants will the recessive trait appear. A count of the blossoms in Mendel's garden
showed that just one fourth of the plants flowered in white—as one would expect.
Figure 2.6 diagrams this process.

What holds for peas holds for people—in many respects. As with peas,
human genes function in pairs and the members of a pair can be dominant or
recessive. Because some genes are recessive, it is not always possible to know
whether a person carries the genes for certain traits. The observable or measurable characteristics displayed by a person make up that person's **phenotype.** These
traits reflect the action of dominant genes, either paired or singly, or of pairs of
recessive genes. However, many hidden recessive genes are carried in the **genotype,** the set of genes acquired at conception that constitutes each person's genetic
makeup. Box 2.1 lists some traits inherited by humans.

Most traits result from the combination of many gene pairs working together
in complex ways to produce the trait. In some cases, the action of one pair adds
to that of other pairs, each contributing something to the final result. In others,
genes may contribute only a "go ahead" for the action of other pairs or, conversely,

phenotype The observable or
measurable characteristics of an
organism, resulting from the interaction between the genotype and
the environment.

genotype The total set of genes
inherited at conception.

Box 2.1 *Some Inherited Traits*

Allergic reactions

- Asthma—recessive trait
- Allergic sensitivity to ragweed pollen—dominant trait
- Hypersensitivity to insect stings—may be dominant trait

Ears

- Earlobes may be present or absent, free or attached—probably dominant trait
- Ability to wiggle ears without touching them—probably dominant trait
- Earwax may be dry (as in about 85% of Japanese) or wet (as in most Caucasians and Blacks)—dominant traits

Eyes

- Earlier idea that blue eye color is a simple autosomal recessive trait is no longer accepted
- Unusually long eyelashes—probably dominantly inherited

Facial features

- Cheek dimples—dominant trait
- Chin dimple (cleft chin)—dominant trait

Gastrointestinal tract

- Celiac disease (a failure to absorb foods normally, especially fats)—polygenic; risk to child of affected person is about 3%
- Crohn disease (an autoimmune inflammation of the bowel)—polygenic; risk to child of affected person is probably 0.4%–1%
- Peptic ulcer—may be polygenic or autosomal dominant; risk to child of affected person is probably 5–10%

Hair

- Male-pattern baldness—recessive trait
- Curly hair—probably dominant trait
- Hair on middle segments of fingers—dominant trait
- Very blond hair—may be recessive trait
- Very red hair—may be recessive trait (however, red pigment in hair is dominantly inherited)

Joints

- Dislocation of hips—polygenic, but dominant inheritance may also be responsible
- Rheumatoid arthritis—polygenic, more frequent in females than in males; risk to child of affected person is 3–5%

Skin

- Painful calluses over pressure points in hands and feet—dominant trait
- Susceptibility to chilblain—dominant trait that especially affects young women
- Pigmented moles—probably dominant trait
- Psoriasis—polygenic; risk to child of affected person is about 1%

Smell

- Absent or deficient sense of smell—usually dominant trait, but sex-linked forms also occur
- Inability to smell cyanide—may be sex-linked
- Inability to smell musk—recessive trait affecting about 7% of Caucasians but no Blacks
- Inability to smell skunk—probably recessive trait

Speech

- Stammering (stuttering)—dominant trait that is unusually frequent in Japanese, very infrequent in Polynesians, and almost completely absent in American Indians

Teeth

- Peg-shaped, conical, variably sized, or pitted teeth—dominant trait
- Overbite due to upper front teeth that jut out too far—dominant trait
- Impacted teeth—may be sex-linked trait

Toes

- First toe (big toe) longer than the second—probably recessive trait
- Second toe longer than the first—probably dominant trait

Tongue

- Ability to roll or curl sides of tongue and form trough down center—probably dominant trait
- Ability to fold up tip of tongue—probably recessive trait

Vision

- Difficulty seeing blue and yellow but not red and green—may be dominant or sex-linked trait
- Severe myopia—can be dominant, recessive, or sex-linked trait

Other traits

- Achoo syndrome (sneezing stimulated by sudden exposure to sunlight or other intense light)—dominant trait
- Aspirin intolerance—recessive trait
- Hypersensitivity to cold (resulting in skin wheals and possibly pain, swelling of joints, chills, fever)—dominant trait
- Double groin hernia—probably dominant trait
- Apnea (periods of not breathing during sleep)—dominant trait
- Abundant sweating, especially on forehead, tip of the nose, and upper lip, while eating spicy or sour foods—dominant trait
- Tone deafness—probably dominant trait
- Varicose veins—may be due to both autosomal and sex-linked inheritance

Source: From Aubrey Milunsky; *Choices, Not Chances.* Copyright © 1977, 1989 by Aubrey Milunsky, MD.

Multiple Determinancy: Personality Traits

BY MICHAEL WAPNER

Yes or no, is intelligence inherited? Yes or no, does being raised in a poor neighborhood lead to delinquency? Yes or no, does watching violence on TV lead to aggressive behavior? How often have we all heard these kinds of questions? How often have we witnessed arguments about whether some such life circumstance does or does not lead to a particular consequence? Life certainly would be simpler, although probably not as interesting, if things like emotional adjustment, delinquency, intelligence, and aggression each were determined by a single variable. Certainly it would make it easier to predict later behavior from childhood experience. Did you watch violent programs on TV when you were a kid? Then you will be violent. Were you raised in poverty? Then you will be delinquent. Did your parents score low on intelligence tests? Then you will score low also.

While each of these statements is false as presented, each may contain a grain of truth. There *is* a relationship between the intelligence of parents and their children, between socioeconomic status and delinquency, between exposure to TV violence and aggressive behavior. So what's wrong with these statements?

What is wrong is that characteristics such as violence, intelligence, and delinquency are **multiply determined.** Each is the result of *many contributing factors* that combine in complex ways to produce the final behavior, and it is grossly misleading to single out only one factor as the "cause." When the behavior or condition under consideration is undesirable, these contributing factors are termed **risk factors.** As the number of risk factors that are present increases, the likelihood of the behavior occurring also increases. Thus, for instance, while poverty is not "the cause" of delinquency in boys, it is a risk factor. So is growing up in a single-parent family. And when both are present, the probability of a boy becoming a delinquent is greater than when only one is present. However, there are generally also factors that oppose risk factors and reduce the probability of the undesirable result. These are termed **protective factors.** The presence of involved men in the community is a protective factor. Thus, a behavior as complex as delinquency is the net result of both risk and protective factors. You can see how ignoring all but one of them can lead to misunderstanding.

Of course, multiple determinacy also presents problems for research. How do we investigate the way many risk and protective factors combine? Happily, a number of research techniques have been developed for this purpose. One of them is a statistical technique called **multiple regression.** While the details are more technical than we need go into here, we can illustrate its use. Greenberg, Coie, Lengua, and Pinderhughes (1999) were interested in the relationship between a number of risk factors in the preschool years and social competence, as evaluated by the teacher, in first-grade children. (Actually, the study by Greenberg et al. was extensive, investigating the relationship between the listed risk factors and a number of different

multiply determined Of characteristics that are the result of many contributing factors.

risk factors Factors associated with an increased rate of undesirable behavior or disease.

protective factors Factors that counter risk factors and reduce the probability of undesirable developmental results.

multiple regression A statistical technique designed to investigate the relationship between a set of predictor variables and an outcome variable.

may inhibit their action. In other cases, single genes result in the expression of different traits depending on the presence or absence of other genes. And in yet other cases, genes require certain environmental conditions to be present for their expression. The fur of the Himalayan rabbit, for instance, is white, although its ears, feet, and tail are black. The genes governing the expression of fur color are sensitive to temperature, "turning on" only when the body temperature is low, as it is in the extremities. The action of this gene only in low temperatures becomes apparent if one shaves a patch of fur off the rabbit's back and straps on a cold pack, making that part of the back as cold as the animal's ears, feet, or tail: The fur that previously had grown in white will grow in black. The complexity of attributing cause to either genetic or environmental factors is discussed in the Research Focus, "Multiple Determinacy: Personality Traits."

Sex-Linked Inheritance

In some cases, genes are not paired. When this occurs, even recessive genes will determine the presence of a trait. Sex-linked traits, such as color blindness, illustrate the operation of unpaired recessive genes. Males are more likely to be affected by these genes than are females. Recall that in males, the Y chromosome of the 23rd pair is substantially shorter than the X chromosome, leaving many of the genes along the X chromosome with no matching allele. All of the traits influ-

outcome variables. We have chosen to look at only one.) The risk factors they investigated are listed below, organized in categories.

1. Specific demographics	2. SES–Race	3. Family risk
No. of siblings	Education	Life stress
Mother's age	Occupation	Family expressiveness
Single parenthood	Race	Social support
Marital stress		
Home environment		

4. Mother's depression

5. Neighborhood risk

Each of these factors has been shown, in one context or another, to be associated with emotional and/or academic problems in school. Each risk factor was assigned a value, with the higher scores reflecting greater risk. Thus, for instance, a child who lived with both parents might be given a 0, while a child living with only its mother would be given a 1 on the *single parenthood* risk factor. Similarly, on the *neighborhood* risk factor, a child living in a high-crime neighborhood might be given a 3, while a child living in a more law-abiding community might be given a 1. Thus, each child was assigned a score on each risk factor—the higher the score, the greater the risk. Similarly, each child was rated on social competence by the first-grade teacher and given an *outcome* score.

Basically, multiple correlation allows us to determine what proportion of the differences among the outcome scores (referred to as outcome variance) can be attributed to each risk factor. In the study by Greenberg et al., all of the risk factors taken together accounted for 24% of the outcome variance. That means that 24% of the differences among all the children with respect to social competence could be related to the 13 risk factors selected. Seventy-six percent of the differences in social competence must have been due to something else or, more likely, *a number of other things*. Of the 24% of the outcome variance accounted for, *demographic factors* (number of siblings, mother's age at time of child's birth, one- or two-parent household) accounted for 7%. *Socioeconomic status and race* (parents' occupation, level of education, and race) accounted for another 7%, and *family risk* (levels of stress and support within the family) accounted for 6%. All the remaining factors together accounted for only 4% of the outcome variance.

With these results in mind, consider how complex is the mix of factors underlying the social competence of first-graders. Consider what a small part of the differences among children can be attributed to any single variable (risk or protective factor) and how an accurate picture begins to emerge only when we recognize the *multiplicity of contributing factors*.

So, yes or no, does being raised by a single parent make a child less socially competent? If you are less comfortable now than you would have been a little while ago with that question, phrased exactly that way, then you have grasped the point of this box.

enced by these unpaired genes will be expressed in males, even when these genes are recessive. Females, who have two chromosomes of equal length, are less likely to be affected by a recessive gene, since all alleles are paired, and the other member of any pair may be dominant. Since these females still carry the recessive gene, however, they can pass it on to their children.

Exceptions to Mendel's Laws

Mendel's laws specified patterns of genetic action solely in terms of dominant and recessive genes. As long as a pair contained a dominant gene, the trait would be expressed. It was not supposed to matter *which* parent contributed that gene; alleles of either the form Aa or aA should be functionally equivalent. Recent gene research shows that this assumption doesn't always hold. It appears that some genes, at least, are marked for parentage, for whether they are received from the mother or from the father. When such a gene is inherited from one parent, it will have one effect; and it will have a different effect when inherited from the other parent. For instance, if a particular segment of genetic material along the 15th chromosome is missing, it will result in a form of mental retardation. The particular type of retardation, however, will depend on whether the child receives that chromosome from the father or from the mother (Nicholls, 1993). In other cases, inheriting a gene from the father can result in a genetic disorder that will *not*

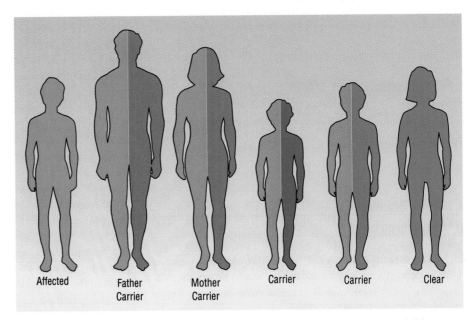

Affected   Father   Mother   Carrier   Carrier   Clear
                Carrier   Carrier

FIGURE 2.7 The Inheritance of Cystic Fibrosis *The gene for the disease is carried by symptomless individuals. A child will be affected only if he or she inherits a copy of the cystic fibrosis gene from both parents. On average, one child in every four born in such a family will be affected by the disease; two out of four will be symptomless carriers; and one will be entirely free of the gene. This pattern follows the rules laid down by Gregor Mendel.*

appear if that same gene is inherited from the mother. Thus a father can pass the gene in question on to both a son and a daughter, both of whom will develop the disorder. The son and daughter, in turn, can pass the gene on to their children. The son's children, because they receive the gene from their father, will develop the disorder. Their cousins, who receive the same gene, but from their mother, will not (Hoffman, 1991).

Other exceptions to Mendel's laws exist. Among each pair of alleles, one member of the pair was always thought to be inherited from the mother and the other from the father. However, recent research shows that, on occasion, both members of a pair can come from the same parent. This exception to the rules happens when the nucleus of a gamete contains more than its share of genetic material. When this nucleus unites with the other, any excess DNA is "shed." If the DNA that is shed is from the nucleus of the *other* gamete, the one parent will have supplied all, as opposed to half, the DNA along those segments of that chromosome.

In the case of certain recessive disorders, the consequences for parents and child can be disastrous. Cystic fibrosis, for instance, is a genetic disease characterized by the accumulation of excessive mucus in the lungs. Because this is a recessive disorder, it occurs only when both parents carry the recessive gene and pass it on to the child (Figure 2.7). When one parent has two dominant normal genes, the child will not inherit the disorder. If tested for cystic fibrosis, a couple like this would be told that none of their children could inherit the disorder even though one parent carried the recessive gene. However, if excess genetic material from the carrier parent were to cause "shedding" of the dominant genes from the other parent, and if the excess material consisted of copies of the recessive gene, a child could be born with cystic fibrosis. As more and more parents go for genetic

TABLE 2.1 Frequency of Selected Genetic Disorders

Disease	Description	Genetic Transmission	Incidence
(Cooley's anemia (thalassemia)	Abnormal blood cells, resulting in lethargy and listlessness, reduced populations resistance to infection, and retarded growth	Recessive	1 in 100 (can be higher) among Mediterranean, some Asian, and African
Cystic fibrosis	Secretion of excessive mucus, resulting in breathing and digestive problems	Recessive	Most common among Caucasians, affecting 1 in 2,000
Hemophilia	Failure of blood to clot, resulting in excessive bleeding	Recessive, sex-linked	Occurs in males, affecting 1 in 10,000
Huntington's disease	Progressive degeneration of central in nervous system, resulting in difficulties movement and breathing; symptoms appear in mid-30s	Dominant	1 in 20,000
Muscular dystrophy	Wasting of muscles, resulting in difficulties in motor coordination, inability to walk	Recessive; some forms are sex-linked	Incidence varies widely with type of disorder
Phenylketonuria (PKU)	Inability to metabolize certain proteins, resulting in severe mental retardation, but treatable with special diet	Recessive	1 in 15,000
Sickle-cell anemia	Abnormal red blood cells, resulting in swelling and pain, reduced resistance to infection, and retarded growth	Recessive	Among African Americans, 1 in 500
Tay-Sachs disease	Inability to metabolize fatty substances, resulting in neurological degeneration, blindness, deafness, and death before the age of 5	Recessive	1 in 3,500 Eastern European Jews

screening, geneticists are discovering that such exceptions to Mendel's laws, though rare, can occur. A small number of children, for instance, whose parents were told they could not *possibly* inherit cystic fibrosis have been identified (Dahl, Tybjaerg-Hansen, Wittrup, Lange, & Nordestgaard, 1998).

Genetic and Chromosomal Disorders

Genetic Disorders

As noted, Mendel's work has special significance for humans in cases of genetic disorders, many of which are carried by a single pair of genes. In all but the most unusual of cases, in recessive single-gene disorders, both parents must be carriers of the disorder for any of their children to be affected. The chances that a child will receive the recessive gene from each parent and inherit the disorder are one in four. There is a 50% chance, though, of receiving the gene from only one parent and being a carrier of the disorder, even though not actually affected by it. Cystic fibrosis, Cooley's anemia, Tay-Sachs disease, and sickle-cell anemia are all carried by a single pair of recessive genes (Table 2.1).

Some genetic disorders are carried by a single dominant gene. In these, a gene from just one parent can result in the disorder. Each conception carries with it a 50% risk if only one parent carries the gene. Huntington's disease, a neurological disorder, is carried by a single dominant gene. This disease, like so many others, would have remained obscure were it not for the personal bravery of individuals whose lives have been affected. In the case of Huntington's disease, Marjorie Guthrie, the wife of the folk singer Woody Guthrie, who succumbed to the disease, was largely responsible for establishing a committee to support research and to help affected families.

Chromosomal Disorders

Some developmental disorders can be traced to irregularities affecting the chromosomes during meiosis. During cell division, chromosomes can fail to separate, or part of a chromosome can break off, leaving either too much or too little genetic material. Since these irregularities involve stretches of DNA and not single genes, they frequently affect a broader range of behaviors than do genetic disorders.

Down syndrome is one of the more common chromosomal disorders, increasing in frequency with the mother's age. For women under 30, the risk of giving birth to a child with Down syndrome is 1 in 1,000 births, but increases to 1 in 20 for women over 45. Down syndrome results when the 21st pair of chromosomes fails to separate during meiosis, resulting in 47 rather than the normal 46 chromosomes. Children with Down syndrome share a number of physical and psychological characteristics. They tend to be shorter than average, with a stocky build. Certain facial features are present, such as almond-shaped eyes resulting from a fold along the eyelid, a slightly pug nose and flattened face, and a thick tongue. Motor development tends to be slower in these children, and mental retardation is present in almost all cases, but varies in severity, differing with the particular nature of the disorder and with the amount of stimulation and support in the child's environment. In some, retardation is severe; others learn to read and write and live semi-independent lives. Down syndrome children characteristically have a sweet disposition and a mischievous humor. These children are more likely to experience a number of physical problems, such as congenital heart defects and certain visual and hearing problems; are more subject to certain types of cancer; and have a reduced life expectancy.

Sex Chromosome Disorders

Instead of inheriting the normal pair of sex chromosomes, either two X chromosomes or an X and a Y for females and males, respectively, children with sex chromosome disorders have either a single X chromosome or an additional X or Y chromosome.

Approximately 1 in 2,000 females have a single X chromosome, or **Turner's syndrome.** A number of irregularities characterize their development. In terms of their physical appearance, these females tend to be short, have a broad chest, and a characteristic webbing on the neck. The ovaries fail to develop, resulting in infertility. Secondary sex characteristics fail to develop at puberty unless estrogen replacement therapy is given. Even though intelligence is normal, deficiencies in spatial perception are characteristic.

Approximately 1 in 1,000 males have an extra Y chromosome, or **XYY syndrome.** These males tend to be somewhat taller than average, with large body builds, and they may have severe acne. They are of normal intelligence, develop normal secondary sex characteristics, and are fertile. With respect to personality characteristics, their parents report somewhat higher activity levels and more impulsiveness than for XY males (Thompson & Thompson, 1986).

Anywhere from 1 in 400 to 1 in 1,000 males have an extra X chromosome, or **Klinefelter's syndrome.** These males, though taller than normal, may have a somewhat feminized body build and incomplete development of secondary sex

Q Why is Down syndrome a chromosomal, rather than a genetic, disorder?

Down syndrome A chromosomal disorder caused by an extra 21st chromosome (trisomy 21); characterized by distinctive facial features, slow motor development, and some degree of mental retardation.

Turner's syndrome A rare genetic disorder in females caused by the absence of one X chromosome; characterized by a distinctive physical appearance (such as webbing of the neck and drooping eyelids) and failure of the ovaries to develop.

XYY syndrome A genetic disorder in males caused by an extra Y chromosome; symptoms may include above-average stature, speech delays, learning disabilities, some degree of mental retardation, and behavior disturbance. Also known as polysome Y syndrome.

Klinefelter's syndrome A genetic disorder in males caused by an extra X chromosome; symptoms include small testes, insufficient production of testosterone, and infertility.

Down syndrome is a common chromosomal disorder with characteristic features.

characteristics at puberty. Most report problems of sterility in adulthood. Intelligence is normal, although verbal skills are frequently affected.

Detecting Birth Defects

Most conceptions in which the fetus is severely compromised spontaneously abort early in pregnancy, usually before the mother even realizes she has been pregnant. Genetic and chromosomal disorders vary widely in the extent to which they can compromise the quality of a child's life. Some disorders, such as Down syndrome, even though affecting both mental and physical functioning, do not always prevent children from living meaningful lives, with supportive family environments. Other diseases do; for example, Tay-Sachs disease, which results in a progressive deterioration of the nervous system, causes profound mental retardation and leads to a painful early death, usually by the age of 2.

Prospective parents can receive genetic counseling, in which they go over their family histories with someone who can help them interpret patterns in family illnesses that suggest an inherited disease. Even though most prospective parents do not receive such counseling, it is especially recommended for couples who have a family member with a genetic disease, either a child who has already been born or a relative in one or the other's family. Also, those who have had difficulty conceiving or carrying a pregnancy to term should receive such counseling, since many such difficulties actually represent spontaneous abortions of compromised conceptions. Genetic counseling is usually offered to prospective parents who are older, since a number of chromosomal abnormalities are associated with parental age, especially that of the mother. Couples who receive genetic counseling are in a better position to weigh the risks of having a child with a birth defect and to consider the alternatives. The Social Policy Focus, "Genetic Testing and the Human Genome Project," explores some of the complications of deciding to get genetic testing.

A number of tests enable prospective parents to determine whether they might pass a disorder on to their children. A simple blood test can be used to detect whether the genes for a number of the more common genetic disorders are carried by one or both prospective parents, who can then make informed decisions about parenting, knowing the potential risks of giving birth to a child with a disorder. Other tests can reveal, once pregnancy has occurred, whether a fetus

Genetic Testing and the Human Genome Project

BY MICHAEL WAPNER

More information is not always better, especially when it's about things over which we have no control. Until fairly recently, screening for health problems has been accompanied by available treatments should the tests bring bad news. For instance, early detection of cancer (mammograms, pap smears, and the like) allowed earlier treatment and a better prognosis. However, the incredible advances in medical technology triggered by the Human Genome Project are increasingly making possible prediction of health threats for which no treatment yet exists. For some people with a family history of hereditary disease, genetic testing may bring reassurance that they have been spared. But for others the results of testing will be ominous. What do you do with the news that you, your child, the fetus that you are carrying, or your yet-to-be-conceived offspring do, or will likely, carry the genes for eventual schizophrenia, Alzheimer's disease, some form of cancer, or depression?

A number of questions regarding the psychological problems produced by genetic testing need to be answered, but health professionals have just recently begun to investigate them:

1. What determines the decision to seek genetic testing? Early results already suggest that fewer people than expected take advantage of the opportunity when it is available (Codori, Hanson, & Brandt, 1994; Lannfelt, Axelman, Lilius, & Basun, 1995).

2. What sorts of response can we expect from those for whom screening brings bad news? Will shock and worry outweigh the benefits of early knowledge? A few studies have already been published—with inconsistent results. Some studies report few or no negative reactions. Other studies report stronger emotional responses. However, these studies did not use the same methods to assess emotional reactions. Some only asked the patient general questions and did not follow up after the initial meeting. Other studies used more probing assessments, followed the patient for a longer period of time, or did both. Some published accounts of individual cases report quite serious reactions. In one case, an individual who was told that he carried the gene for Alzheimer's disease reacted with "anxiety, sorrow, . . . depression, and . . . suicidal thoughts" lasting 6 months. In another case, being told that she carried the genes for Huntington's disease brought a woman to the brink of suicide (Salkovskis & Rimes, 1997). Are these last examples extreme cases? Or, with deeper assessment and longer follow-ups, will they turn out to be fairly typical?

3. Given the likelihood of strong emotional reactions in some cases of genetic screening, can mental health professionals provide counseling and other psychological support to mitigate this distress? And if so, what kind? Should it be provided before the patient takes the test? Or should it be on receiving the results? Or both? Should everyone receive counseling, or only those with obvious negative reactions?

An article prepared for the World Health Organization (Wertz, Fletcher, & Borg, 1995) focuses on pretest genetic counseling and warns that the supportive aspects are at least as important as the informational aspects. The article goes on to suggest nondirective counseling except where there is "high risk of serious harm." (Nondirective counseling emphasizes active listening, empathy, and reflecting back to the patient what seem to the counselor to be the patient's own feelings. There is an avoidance of behavioral or medicinal prescriptions, interpretations, or advice.) However, a review article by Salkovskis and Rimes (1997) is critical of the use of nondirective counseling. These authors, along with calling for much more research, suggest the use of a cognitive-behavioral approach both to assessing the individuals' reaction to screening and to treatment should the reaction be problematic. The cognitive-behavioral approach emphasizes the importance of the way people think about the information they receive. Individuals who habitually interpret ambiguous information in a pessimistic way, who quickly feel hopeless and helpless in the face of threats, are more likely to have serious negative reactions to the results of genetic screening. Thus, by evaluating an individual's beliefs and attitudes toward health and illness, predictions might be made about that person's reaction to the results of genetic tests. The cognitive-behavioral approach also has developed various techniques and exercises for changing beliefs and attitudes and hence one's emotional reactions. Thus, this model provides an approach for both assessment and treatment. Whether it is as good or better than a nondirective approach remains to be seen.

As you can see, there is still a lot to be learned about the emotional impact of genetic screening and how to deal with it. But there is something we can say about this problem now. History tells us that whatever we can do, we do. There is no undoing of our knowledge about the human genome. It will be used to predict our future, whether those predictions are happy or frightening. Thus, the only intelligent response to the negative effects of this new knowledge is still more knowledge. It is important, therefore, that along with support for the Genome Project itself, there be adequate financing for research into coping with the emotional consequences.

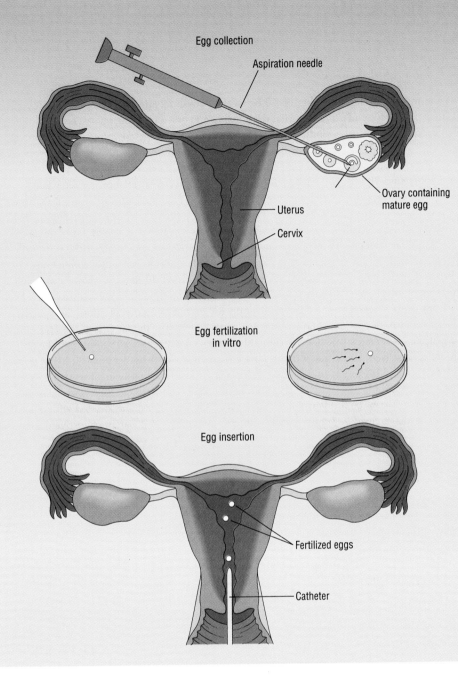

Egg collection

Aspiration needle

Ovary containing mature egg

Uterus

Cervix

Egg fertilization in vitro

Egg insertion

Fertilized eggs

Catheter

In Vitro Fertilization

The woman receives hormone injections to stimulate production of ova. Additional hormones are given to stimulate ovulation and to prepare the uterus to receive the fertilized ovum. The follicles are viewed through a laparoscope inserted through an incision at the navel. The ova are retrieved by being drawn into a long, hollow needle. (The ovary may also be viewed and the ova extracted through the vagina.) Each ovum, or egg cell, is placed in a laboratory dish containing a culture that is chemically similar to the uterine environment. Sperm are added. Two days later, the fertilized ova (usually no more than three) are injected into the uterus.

ing and soothing them. One of the greatest mysteries, though, is that of conceiving them. Of this she writes, "We conceive our children in deepest night, in blazing sun, outdoors, in barns and alleys and minivans. We have no rules, no ceremonies, we don't even need a driver's license. Conception is often something of a by-product of sex, a candle in a one-room studio, pure brute chance, a wonder. To make love with the desire for a child is to move the act out of its singularity, to make the need of the moment an eternal wish. But of all passing notions, that of a human being for a child is perhaps the purest in the abstract, and the most complicated in reality" (p. 3). ◄

For some couples, that reality is complicated from the very beginning. The Research Focus, "Factor Analysis: Fertility Procedures," discusses the psychological consequences of reproductive technologies.

donor insemination A fertility procedure in which sperm from a donor are injected into the birth mother's uterus at the time of ovulation.

egg and sperm donation A fertility procedure in which donor sperm are used to fertilize donor ova, and the resulting embryo is inserted into the birth mother's uterus.

Factor Analysis: Fertility Procedures *(continued)*

hundreds of questions were obtained. How, you might wonder, could these researchers make sense of all that data? How, in other words, does one go about looking for, and finding, meaningful patterns?

Factor analysis is a statistical procedure designed to do just that. Using this procedure, researchers can identify underlying dimensions or *factors* that account for the ways in which individuals respond to different measures such as the ones mentioned above. Several steps are involved in factor analysis. The first step, already described, consists in choosing a set of measures that are conceptually related to each other. For instance, Golombok and her associates used a number of questionnaires as well as data gathered from interviews to assess parental attitudes and practices. In the second step, each measure is correlated with each of the other measures to yield a matrix of correlation coefficients (see the table). Correlation coefficients indicate the degree to which two variables are related (see the Research Focus, "Bias and Blind Controls" in Chapter 13) or both measure the same thing. An index of the proportion of variance that is shared by each of these measures can be obtained by squaring this correlation coefficient. Thus, a corre-

lation of .70 between a questionnaire measuring the quality of the marital relationship and one measuring mental health would indicate that 49% of what was being measured by the marital relationship questionnaire was also being measured by the questionnaire on mental health.

Let's take a look at a matrix of correlations to see what it is that factor analysis needs to accomplish (keep in mind that the data are fictitious). Looking at these correlations, we can see that parental warmth is highly correlated with emotional involvement, but not with parental stress. Looking over the rest of the table, can you see a pattern to any of the other correlations?

One of the first things you might notice is that warmth and emotional involvement are highly correlated with each other, and the correlation for each with parental stress and parent-child dysfunction is low. Similarly, the latter two measures are themselves highly correlated. Mental health appears to be only moderately correlated with any of the other items. Judging from this matrix, then, we might say that there are two factors accounting for the relationships among these five measures. Warmth and emotional involvement are associated with one of these factors, and parental stress and parent-child dysfunction

Infertility

Just as with high-performance cars and toys on Christmas morning, reproductive systems do not always function according to the manual. Approximately 15% of couples in the United States are infertile, incapable of becoming pregnant within a year of trying. Infertility has risen over the decades. We live with increasing numbers of environmental toxins and occupational hazards that can affect the production of gametes. A rise in sexually transmitted diseases is also implicated. These are infections of the reproductive tract that, when healed, leave scar tissue that can block the passage of gametes. Also, a trend toward postponing childbearing contributes to increased infertility rates. For instance, infertility affects approximately 5% of women in their early 20s, but nearly 3 times that number of women in their early 30s (Menken, Trussell, & Larsen, 1986).

It comes as a surprise to most individuals that, when contraceptives are finally put aside, conception does not occur. They have been worrying about finding a convenient and safe way to prevent pregnancy, having assumed that unless precautions were taken, pregnancy would ensue. This assumption underlies basic attitudes most adults hold about themselves. Fertility and potency are central to what it means to be female and male. Infertility challenges these assumptions and, with these, one's sense of self.

Infertility also transforms the sexual encounter. For infertile couples sex is easily stripped of romance and passion and becomes scheduled by the calendar, visits to the doctor, and morning basal temperature charts (indicating time of ovulation) rather than by desire. The American Fertility Society estimates that 70% of infertile couples can be helped. However, treatment is costly, frequently lengthy, sometimes painful, and always emotionally intrusive.

surrogate birth mother A woman who becomes pregnant usually by artificial insemination or surgical implantation of a fertilized egg for the purpose of carrying the fetus for another woman.

factor analysis A statistical procedure designed to identify underlying dimensions, or factors, that account for the relationship among several variables.

Table of Matrix of Correlations

	1	2	3	4	5
1. Parental warmth	1.00	.25	.75	.22	.55
2. Parental stress	.25	1.00	.19	.70	.51
3. Emotional involvement	.75	.19	1.00	.26	.49
4. Parent-child dysfunction	.22	.70	.26	1.00	.50
5. Mental health	.55	.51	.49	.50	1.00

with the other factor. Mental health appears to be associated to some degree with both of these factors.

With only a few measures, such as in the example here, it is not that difficult to see patterns as they arise. However, when many measures are involved, a statistical procedure must be used to identify the underlying factors. These procedures enable researchers not only to identify factors, but also to estimate the importance of each in accounting for the overall variability of scores.

And what did Golombok and her associates discover about parent-child relationships in families created by new reproductive technologies?

The quality of parenting was actually superior in assisted reproduction families, irrespective of whether the children were genetically related to one or both of the parents. Assisted reproduction mothers showed more warmth and more emotional involvement (the latter was also true for adoptive mothers) toward their children than did those who naturally conceived their children. Additionally, mothers and fathers of assisted reproduction children, as well as adoptive parents, interacted more with their children than did parents who naturally conceived their children. Factor analysis of the parenting variables identified from the interview data (warmth, emotional involvement, mother-child interaction, and father-child interaction) and of the parental stress index yielded a single factor that accounted for 43% of the variance. Overall, these findings suggest that how well a family functions is affected less by the genetic similarity among family members than by the parents' desire to have a child. Furthermore, fathers who were genetically unrelated to their children, as in the case of donor insemination and adoption, did not have difficulty relating to their children.

In about 40% of the cases, infertility can be traced to the woman. Another 40% can be traced to the man, and in many couples the problem lies with both partners. Dramatic advances in science and medicine now make it possible to treat many causes of infertility. Synthetic hormones, microsurgery, in vitro fertilization, and donor procedures offer new hope to childless couples.

Among women, failure to ovulate is a frequent cause of infertility. Synthetic hormones can stimulate the hypothalamus, a brain center that regulates bodily functions, to release hormones that in turn stimulate the pituitary to release FSH and LH, thus starting the ovulatory cycle. These hormones, however, lack the delicate touch of nature and may cause several follicles to ripen at the same time, thus increasing the chance of multiple births.

Another common cause of infertility among women is endometriosis, a disorder in which the tissues lining the uterus grow within the abdominal cavity, enveloping the ovaries and Fallopian tubes and blocking the passage of gametes. This condition can be treated with drugs that shrink the abnormal tissue or by surgical removal of the tissue. Blocked Fallopian tubes resulting from adhesions and scar tissue are another common cause of infertility in women. Microsurgery can often be used to open the blocked tubes.

In men, an inadequate sperm count is a frequent cause of infertility. Sperm are either too few, not sufficiently motile, or insufficiently developed. Many factors can be responsible. Childhood diseases such as mumps can damage the cells that produce sperm; infections can leave scar tissue blocking the passageways the sperm must travel; and occupational hazards such as chemicals, radiation, or excessive heat can permanently or temporarily alter sperm production (see Chapter 3).

Summary

Genes and Chromosomes

Traits are passed from one generation to the next through genes, segments of the DNA strand making up a chromosome. DNA provides the blueprint for the construction of new cells by directing the manufacture of proteins with the aid of messenger RNA and transfer RNA. Two distinct types of genes are involved. Structural genes provide the actual codes for the construction of new proteins, whereas regulatory genes determine which genes are copied.

Twenty-three pairs of chromosomes are contained within the nucleus of each body cell; one member of each pair comes from the mother and the other from the father. Twenty-two of these are matching pairs called autosomes. The 23rd pair, which determines the sex of the child, contains two matching X chromosomes in females and an X and a Y chromosome in males. Since a Y chromosome can be received only from the father, it is the father that determines the sex of the child.

Gametes: Ovum and Sperm

The chromosomes making up the 23rd pair are known as gametes. Gametes mature through a process of cell division termed meiosis, in which the number of chromosomes is reduced to 23 single chromosomes. In comparison, cell division in body cells, termed mitosis, maintains 23 pairs of chromosomes in each of the resulting cells. Females are born with all of the ova they will ever produce, with generally only one of these maturing each month. Males continue to produce sperm throughout their lives, and as many as 200 million may be contained in a single ejaculate.

Genetic Diversity

With the exception of identical twins, each individual is genetically distinct from every other individual. Genetic diversity is achieved in a number of ways. Individuals are distinct from either of their parents since one chromosome of each pair is from one parent and the second from the other. Meiosis further contributes to diversity by shuffling the members of each pair into either one gamete or the other as cell division occurs. Additional diversity occurs through crossing over, a process occurring during cell division in which segments of the chromosomes making up each pair break off and cross over to corresponding positions along the other chromosome.

Twins

Identical, or monozygotic, twins share identical genetic makeups since they result from the same fertilized ovum, or zygote, which then separates into two clusters of cells during initial cell division. Fraternal, or dizygotic, twins originate when two ova are released during ovulation and each is fertilized by a separate sperm.

Fertilization

Fertilization occurs near the top of the Fallopian tube. Once inside the female reproductive tract, sperm undergo a process known as capacitation, which allows the release of enzymes that enable the sperm to fuse with the membrane of the ovum. Only a single sperm can fertilize an ovum due to a dual-action gating mechanism triggered by this fusion. A woman is fertile for approximately 6 days each month, approximately 5 days preceding ovulation and on the day of ovulation itself.

Patterns of Genetic Action

Genes at corresponding positions along the lengths of paired chromosomes carry related information. These gene pairs, or alleles, can contain two types of genes: Members of a pair can be dominant or recessive. When a dominant gene is present, the trait that it determines will be expressed. In order for a trait carried by a recessive gene to occur, both members of the allele pair must be recessive. The observable or measurable characteristics displayed by a person make up that person's phenotype. These traits reflect the action of dominant genes, either paired or singly, or of pairs of recessive genes. Additionally, many recessive genes are carried in a person's genotype, or the set of genes acquired at conception that constitutes each person's genetic makeup.

Genetic and Chromosomal Disorders

Most genetic disorders are caused by a single recessive gene; children must receive the recessive gene from each parent to be affected. Chromosomal disorders can be traced to irregularities affecting the chromosomes during meiosis that result in either extra or insufficient genetic material. Down syndrome is one of the more common chromosomal disorders and results from the 21st pair of chromosomes failing to separate during meiosis. Sex chromosome disorders result from inheriting either a single X chromosome or an additional X or Y chromosome rather than two X chromosomes or an X and a Y for females and males, respectively.

Detecting Birth Defects

A number of tests enable prospective parents to determine whether they might pass a disorder on to their children. Ultrasound imaging is useful in detecting abnormalities in head growth and organ or limb development, but does not reveal some of the genetic and chromosomal disorders that can be detected through other procedures. Both amniocentesis and chorionic villus sampling obtain cells, either from the amniotic fluid or from the placenta, which can be tested to detect genetic and chromosomal disorders, whereas alpha-fetoprotein screening utilizes a blood test to screen for certain specific disorders.

The Contexts of Genetic Action

Depending on the presence of other factors, genes can have different effects; their final expression will depend on the environment in which the genes are present. This environment can be intracellular, involving the presence of other genes, or it can be the surroundings provided by a family or community.

Infertility

Infertility affects approximately 15% of couples within the United States. In 40% of these the problem can be traced to the woman, and in another 40% the problem lies with the man. New techniques such as microsurgery, the use of synthetic hormones, and donor gametes allow the successful treatment of infertility in approximately 70% of affected couples.

Key Terms

acrosomal reaction (p. 56)
acrosome (p. 56)
activators (p. 48)
alleles (p. 58)
autosomes (p. 49)
basal factors (p. 48)
capacitation (p. 56)
chromosomes (p. 49)
coactivators (p. 48)
crossing over (p. 53)
dizygotic twins (p. 54)
DNA (p. 46)
dominant allele (p. 58)
donor insemination (p. 75)
Down syndrome (p. 66)
egg and sperm donation (p. 75)

egg donation (p. 74)
estrogens (p. 50)
factor analysis (p. 76)
gametes (p. 50)
genes (p. 46)
genotype (p. 59)
in vitro fertilization (p. 74)
Klinefelter's syndrome (p. 66)
meiosis (p. 50)
membrane depolarization (57)
messenger RNA (mRNA) (p. 48)
mitosis (p. 50)
monozygotic twins (p. 53)
multiple regression (p. 62)
multiply determined (p. 62)
nucleotides (p. 46)

phenotype (p. 59)
protective factors (p. 62)
recessive allele (p. 58)
regulatory genes (p. 48)
repressors (p. 48)
risk factors (p. 62)
RNA polymerase (p. 48)
sex chromosomes (p. 48)
structural genes (p. 48)
surrogate birth mother (p. 76)
testosterone (p. 52)
transfer RNA (tRNA) (p. 48)
Turner's syndrome (p. 66)
XYY syndrome (p. 66)
zona reaction (p. 57)
zygotes (p. 53)

chapterthree
Prenatal Development

Time plays on itself fast or slow, depending on the measure of change. Suspended between worlds the fertilized ovum marks the passage of time to its own rhythms. Within its gated perimeter, the two nuclei combine their genetic contents while on its surface the beating tails of remaining sperm cause the giant body beneath to rotate with their movement. Like an expanding universe, the timeless capsule divides, first once, then twice, increasing exponentially in number with each division, drawing the spinning sphere into the pull of time.

Stages of Prenatal Development

The course of development can be charted according to the inner world of the developing organism or the calendar months of the world it has yet to enter. The first alternative chronicles development in terms of gestational age, measured from conception, and divides prenatal development into three stages: the germinal stage, the embryonic stage, and the fetal stage. The second alternative, that of the calendar, divides pregnancy into three trimesters, each approximately 13 weeks long. The germinal and embryonic stages together correspond roughly to the first trimester. The fetal stage, lasting from the 9th week to birth, encompasses the second and third trimesters. Since most women are unaware of the time of conception, the first trimester is measured from the beginning of the last monthly period, adding 2 weeks for a 38-week gestation period (Singer, 1995).

Development in the Germinal Stage
(Conception Through the 2nd Week)

The germinal stage begins with fertilization and ends when the organism becomes attached to the uterine wall. Fertilization, you may recall, is the process by which the nuclei of the two gametes fuse, combining their genetic contents as the chromosomes within each of the two nuclei arrange themselves into corresponding pairs. Fertilization initiates a number of processes, not only restoring the number of chromosomes to 23 pairs, but also determining the sex of the child and initiating **cleavage,** or cell division (Sadler, 1990) (Figure 3.1).

Cleavage is a unique form of cell division that differs from mitosis in an important respect. In mitosis, each cell division is preceded by a period of growth in which the cell doubles in size before dividing. Such growth does not precede cleavage. As a consequence, each new generation of cells is smaller than the last. Since only the nuclear contents are replicated, whereas the cytoplasm is not, the size of the cell nucleus changes in respect to that of the rest of the cell, which must do with an ever-diminishing amount of cytoplasm. A change in this ratio, in fact, may trigger the activation of genes that begin the transcription process in which cell differentiation begins to take place (Gilbert, 1994).

The first cell division occurs approximately 24 hours after the two nuclei merge. In this division, as in all later ones, each pair of chromosomes replicates before the cell pulls apart. Each new cell again divides, with subsequent divisions occurring at about 12-hour intervals. The resulting cluster of cells is termed a **morula,** deriving its name from the Latin word for a mulberry, which it resembles slightly in appearance (Singer, 1995). As the morula divides, it moves down the Fallopian tube, propelled by repeated contractions of the tube and by the beating fingers of millions of cilia, tiny hairlike filaments lining the tube, which set up powerful currents within the fluid interior of the oviduct. Approximately a week

cleavage The form of cell division initiated by fertilization; unlike ordinary mitosis, the cells do not double in size before dividing.

morula A solid cluster of cells resulting from the cleavage of a fertilized ovum.

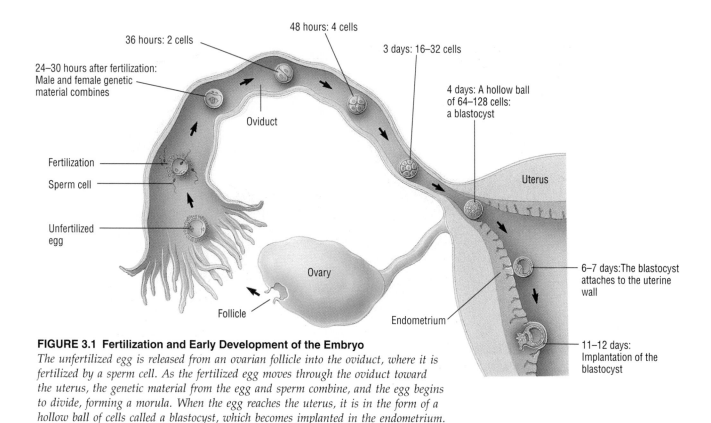

FIGURE 3.1 Fertilization and Early Development of the Embryo
*The unfertilized egg is released from an ovarian follicle into the oviduct, where it is
fertilized by a sperm cell. As the fertilized egg moves through the oviduct toward
the uterus, the genetic material from the egg and sperm combine, and the egg begins
to divide, forming a morula. When the egg reaches the uterus, it is in the form of a
hollow ball of cells called a blastocyst, which becomes implanted in the endometrium.*

after conception, the tiny cluster of cells, now termed a **blastocyst,** reaches the
entrance to the uterus.

Just as news of a distant event often spreads by word of mouth before any of
the characters themselves arrive, news of fertilization reaches the uterine environment before the tiny organism does. Hormones, the body's chemical messengers, have signaled its imminent arrival. Immediately following ovulation, cells
lining the ruptured follicle from which the ovum was released begin secreting
progesterone, which, in combination with several other hormones, causes the lining of the uterus to become thick and spongy and rich with blood vessels. The
journey down the Fallopian tube provides just enough time for the lining of the
uterus, the **endometrium,** to become sufficiently thick to be hospitable to the tiny
organism. Were it to arrive any sooner, or much later, the organism could not
embed itself within the endometrium.

The ruptured follicle, now known as the **corpus luteum,** plays a critical role
in the pregnancy for the next several months. The follicle increases in size until it
becomes nearly half as large as the ovary itself. Its secretion of progesterone prevents the uterus from shedding the lining in which the organism is embedded.
Not until the end of the 4th month does the placenta become capable of producing
enough progesterone to maintain the pregnancy (Sadler, 1990).

At first only individual cells are recognizable as the zygote, encased within
its transparent membrane, moves down the Fallopian tube to the uterus. Once the
zygote sheds its protective covering within the uterine cavity, however, one can
discern the emergence of *structure* in the arrangement of its cells: An outer layer

blastocyst A thin-walled hollow
sphere resulting from the differentiation of morula cells into the trophoblast and the inner cell mass.

endometrium The inner lining of
the uterus.

corpus luteum The ruptured ovarian follicle formed by the release of
an ovum; important source of progesterone early in pregnancy.

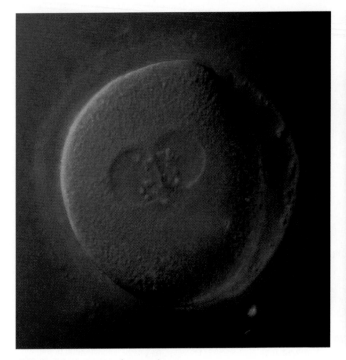 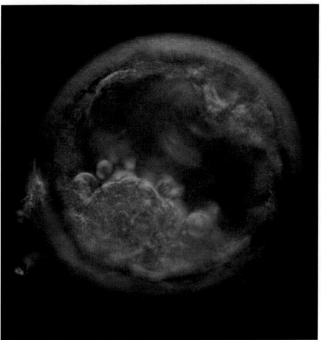

Cell division creates changes in a cell's environment as dramatic as those within the cell itself. Shown are the first cell division at about 24 hours—the morula (left) and a cluster of cells at about 4 days—the blastocyst (right).

surrounds an inner mass. On the one hand, the emergence of distinct structures is what development is all about. On the other hand, this poses an interesting question. Each cell, you may recall, contains all of the genetic instructions necessary to reproduce the entire organism, yet only certain of these instructions will be used as the cell divides; the remaining instructions will not be, resulting in the many different types of cells that eventually make up the human body. Cell differentiation remains one of the most intriguing aspects of development. How do different types of cells emerge if each cell contains the same genetic information as all other cells? How does a cell "know," in other words, whether it is to be a bone cell, a blood cell, or a heart cell?

Cell Differentiation Very early in development, specialized regions in the embryo organize the way cells will develop. These regions are set up, much like coordinating "headquarters," to direct the differentiation of cells under their command. As different parts of the body develop, activity in these regions switches on or off. For instance, research with chicks has identified a region located in the posterior limb bud, called the zone of polarizing activity, which organizes the development of the limb bud into a jointed leg and foot. This region switches on when the limb is developing and turns off once development of the limb is completed (Tickle, Summerbell, & Wolpert, 1975).

These organizer regions contain something akin to "genetic generals," genes that operate by sending out signals to cells, telling them which part of the body they will become (Johnson, Laufer, Riddle, & Tabin, 1994). These genes, referred to as **hedgehog genes,** operate by directing the manufacture of molecules called **morphogens,** literally "form-givers." Morphogens are proteins that diffuse across the cells, tagging different cells for the functions they will assume, telling them where to go and what they are to become (Smith, 1994).

You might be saying at this point, "Wait a minute, how does the *hedgehog gene* know whether a cell is to be a bone cell, a blood cell, or a heart cell?" Luckily, it

hedgehog genes Genes that direct the manufacture of morphogens.

morphogens Proteins that tag different embryonic cells for different functions.

doesn't have to. Jill Heemskerk and Stephen DiNardo (1994), at Columbia University, found that the particular message that a cell receives is determined by a gradient of dispersion. The signal is encoded, in other words, by the concentration of the protein reaching it. Cells that are closest to the hedgehog gene get more of the protein and so receive one message, whereas those that are further away get less of the protein and receive a different message. As a limb bud develops into a leg and foot, for instance, those cells that receive the heaviest concentration of the morphogen develop as the big toe and those receiving the lightest develop as the little toe (Smith, 1994).

Precisely how the proteins communicate their instructions to the genes within a cell remains unclear. We do know that the cells they reach contain two types of genes: regulatory genes and structural genes (see Chapter 2). The regulatory genes, called "smart genes" by Eric Davidson (1990), an embryologist at California Institute of Technology, control the transcription of DNA, selecting which structural genes are to be copied. Only those structural genes that are copied will direct protein growth in the new cell (see Chapter 2). These smart genes function like computers, arriving at decisions based on information as to what is taking place in other parts of the cell, as well as acting on information from outside the cell (Beardsley, 1991). Not only the genes themselves, but also the larger cellular environment in which they operate, then, determine the unfolding developmental process. The same cell, in other words, would develop in different ways if placed in a different environment.

The environment of the cell, as well as the cell itself, changes with cell division. With the first division, for instance, each new cell becomes part of the other's chemical and structural surround. The metabolism of one cell creates by-products that, passing through its membrane, affect the neighboring cell. Similarly, each cell is bounded on one side by a second cell instead of the medium in which it previously existed. Cell division, in other words, creates changes in a cell's environment as dramatic as those within the cell itself, changes that in turn affect subsequent developments within the cell, supporting the copying of only those genetic instructions that are appropriate to that environment. An infant need not yet be born, in other words, for environmental influences to be present. Environments exist at all levels, whether in the form of neighboring cells or the welcoming arms of a parent. An environment is simply whatever surrounds something else, the medium in which the other exists.

As cells multiply, they surround other cells, forming a cellular environment. Cells in the center of the developing mass of cells encounter a different environment that do those on the perimeter; the former are bounded by other cells within the mass, while the latter come into contact with the cells of the outer membrane.

Implantation   As the blastocyst divides and cells differentiate, two distinct groups of cells appear. One group of cells, bunched up together at one end of the sphere (the **inner cell mass**), will develop into the embryo. A second group of cells (the **outer cell mass**) forms a surrounding layer, the **trophoblast,** from which the placenta will develop. The blastocyst has remained encased within the outer shell of the zona pellucida during its journey to the uterus. However, it must shed this shell before implantation can occur within the uterine wall. As the blastocyst enters the uterus, the zona pellucida begins to disintegrate, allowing fluids to seep in and fill the space within, forming an inner cavity. The outer cell mass flattens out, forming an outer wall. Together, the cluster of cells now numbers more than 100.

The blastocyst is now ready for the final, and somewhat perilous, leg of its journey—implantation in the lining of the uterus. The trophoblast sends out tiny

inner cell mass The group of cells in the blastocyst from which the embryo is formed.

outer cell mass The outer layer of cells (the trophoblast) of the blastocyst that will develop into tissues supporting the developing organism.

trophoblast The outer layer of blastocyst cells from which develop the tissues that support the developing organism.

A fertilized ovum at about 11 days burrows completely beneath the surface of the endometrium, thus becoming the blastocyst. Secreting a hormone, the new blastocyst helps to keep the uterine lining "friendly" to the organism.

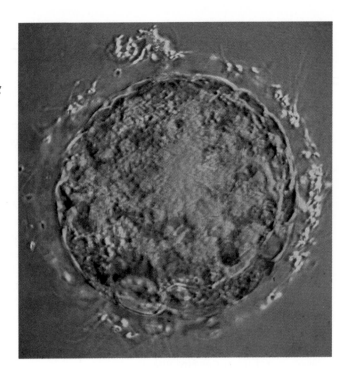

fingerlike filaments that reach within the cells making up the endometrium, breaking a few blood vessels as they do. These villi anchor the blastocyst and supply nutrients for its growth. Viewed under magnification, it looks like a tiny blister with a crimson halo (the broken vessels) on the pale lavender lining of the uterus. Implantation begins by the end of the 1st week. It will take another week for the process to be completed, during which time the blastocyst burrows completely beneath the surface of the endometrium (Sadler, 1990).

Implantation is not without its risks. It is estimated that more than 50% of conceptions spontaneously abort without the mother ever realizing that she has been pregnant (Sadler, 1990). A number of hazards attend the process. One is the possibility that the blastocyst will be rejected by the mother's immune system. Because the blastocyst is genetically distinct from other tissues within the mother's body, it could be treated as a foreign body. A hormone secreted by the blastocyst, human chorionic gonadotrophin (HCG), helps to keep the uterine lining "friendly" to the tiny organism. The uterine lining, in turn, produces substances that promote the activity of the blastocyst. Implantation is thus mutually regulated by an exchange of hormones between the tiny organism and the mother's body (Sadler, 1990; Strong & DeVault, 1999).

The flurry of hormonal messages and directions by which the organism and its host interact prompts changes not only within the uterus, but also throughout the woman's body. These produce, in many women, the first signs of pregnancy: tiredness, tender breasts, a slight queasiness, and sometimes a change in the way things taste and smell. Some of these changes offer important protections for the developing organism. For instance, a glass of wine or a cigarette—for some women a means of relaxing—may occasion feelings of nausea early in pregnancy. Thus, even before they know they should be avoiding substances like alcohol or cigarettes, many women are prompted to change habits that could otherwise endanger the new organism.

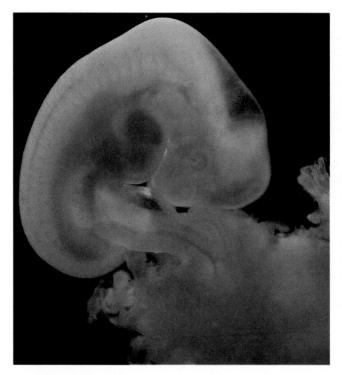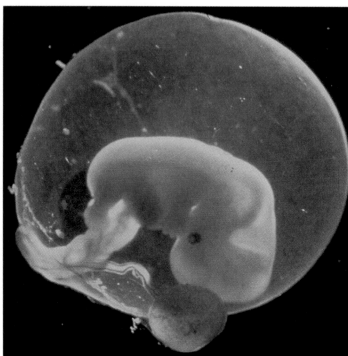

By the 5th week, the embryo has developed a rudimentary brain, spinal cord, and heart (left). At 6 weeks (right), you can also see the development of fingers and eyes.

Development in the Embryonic Stage (3rd Through the 8th Week)

The embryonic stage begins with implantation and ends with the appearance of true bone cells by the end of the 7th week. These signal the end of this stage and the beginning of the fetal stage since they also coincide with the completion of all the body parts. Prior to the appearance of bone cells, the embryo develops a complete skeleton of cartilage, as in the tip of one's nose, rather than of bone.

One of the first events in the embryonic stage is **gastrulation,** the formation of three distinct layers of cells from the inner cell mass; all parts of the body will be formed from these layers. The outer layer **(ectoderm)** will develop into those parts that bring the organism into contact with its environment: the outer layer of skin, the nervous system, and sensory organs. The middle layer **(mesoderm)** gives rise to the muscles and bones forming the skeletal structure, the inner layers of skin, and the circulatory, excretory, and reproductive systems. The innermost layer **(endoderm)** gives rise to the digestive and respiratory tracts and to internal glands and organs.

The outer cell mass, the trophoblast, develops into structures that will nourish and support the growth of the embryo: the amniotic sac, the placenta, the umbilical cord, and the yolk sac. The **amniotic sac** is a transparent, watertight membrane that develops around the embryo. Filled with amniotic fluid, it provides support for the developing organism by permitting the movement of limbs that otherwise would be too heavy to lift and offering protection from sharp edges and jarring.

The **placenta** is a spongy mass of tissue attached to the uterine lining and connected to the embryo by the umbilical cord. It is the embryo's life-support

gastrulation The formation of three layers of embryonic cells: the ectoderm, the mesoderm, and the endoderm.

ectoderm The outer layer of the inner cell mass, which will develop into the outer layer of skin, the nervous system, and the sensory organs.

mesoderm The middle layer of the inner cell mass; it will develop into the muscles, bones, and circulatory, excretory, and reproductive systems.

endoderm The inner layer of the inner cell mass, which will develop into the digestive and respiratory tracts and internal glands and organs.

amniotic sac A transparent, watertight membrane that develops around the embryo and is filled with amniotic fluid.

placenta A spongy mass of tissue attached to the uterine lining and connected to the embryo by the umbilical cord from which the fetus receives oxygen and nutrients and through which waste products are excreted.

system, supplying oxygen-rich blood and nutrients to the embryo and removing waste products from the embryo's blood. The exchange of these materials takes place in tiny villi that reach, like the roots of a tree, deep within the uterine lining where they come into contact with the mother's blood supply. The walls of the villi are semipermeable, allowing some molecules to pass through but not others. Smaller molecules carried in the blood, such as oxygen, carbon dioxide, some proteins and sugars, can pass through the membranes; but larger molecules, such as the blood cells themselves, cannot. The placenta thus keeps the two blood systems separate.

The placenta serves other functions as well. It produces hormones that initiate and orchestrate the transactions taking place between the developing organism and the mother's body. For instance, just prior to birth, the placenta, together with the fetus, produces enormous amounts of estrogens each day, generating as much as normally would be produced by the woman's ovaries over a 3-year period. These hormones prepare the mother's body for birth, causing the cervix to soften prior to labor and readying the breasts for lactation. The placenta will also supply maternal antibodies, which provide immunity against a number of infectious diseases (Coustan, 1995a).

The **umbilical cord,** through which oxygenated blood is carried to the fetus and waste products are removed, is about 2 feet long and carries 300 quarts of liquid a day. Blood travels at 4 miles an hour through the cord. This force gives the cord the properties of a garden hose filled with water, making it rigid and resistant to knotting that might otherwise cut off vital supplies of oxygen and nutrients (Coustan, 1995a).

A **yolk sac,** external to the body, produces blood cells until the organism's liver, spleen, and bone marrow are sufficiently developed to take over this function.

The embryo changes dramatically from day to day. By the end of the 1st month, the embryo is only ½-inch long. Yet a rudimentary brain and spinal cord are visible, and the heart, which is disproportionately large in comparison to the rest of the body, has begun to beat and pump blood. On closer inspection, the embryo also has what looks like a tail as well as ridges on either side of the head that resemble gill slits. The "tail" is actually the end of the spine. It covers the spinal cord, which is oversized at first, anticipating the complex nervous system that will develop, and is temporarily longer than the body. The "gills" are folds of tissue for the chin, cheeks, jaw, and ears.

By the end of the 2nd month, the embryo has more than doubled in size, measuring over an inch in length. Limb buds, which were just visible at the end of the 5th week, have developed into long, thin arms and legs, and movements appear from 7 weeks on (Nijhuis, 1995). Delicate fingers and toes have formed on the tiny hands and feet, and the rims of ears appear on either side of the oversized head. The face is distinctly human, with eyes, ears, nose, lips, and tongue. There are even milk teeth buds within the gums.

Brain growth has progressed at a phenomenal pace, with 100,000 neurons, or brain cells, appearing every minute. Subdivisions of the central nervous system are apparent by the 2nd month, in the form of two zones from which new neurons are created. One zone is associated with the part of the brain that regulates basic bodily functioning and the other with the cortex, which is responsible for intentional, conscious action (Nowakowski, 1987). The cortex itself is divided, left to right, into two cerebral hemispheres, which begin to emerge as early as the 5th week (Sadler, 1990).

The brain sends out signals to the functioning organs, the heart beats, the stomach secretes digestive fluids, the liver produces blood cells, and the kidneys take uric acid from the blood. Sensitivity to touch begins to develop, first in the region of the head, and then, over the next few weeks, over the rest of the body.

umbilical cord The cord connecting the embryo to the placenta through which oxygenated blood and nutrients are carried to the organism, and waste products are removed.

yolk sac A sac outside the body of the embryo that produces blood cells until the embryo's liver, spleen, and bone marrow are sufficiently developed to take over this function.

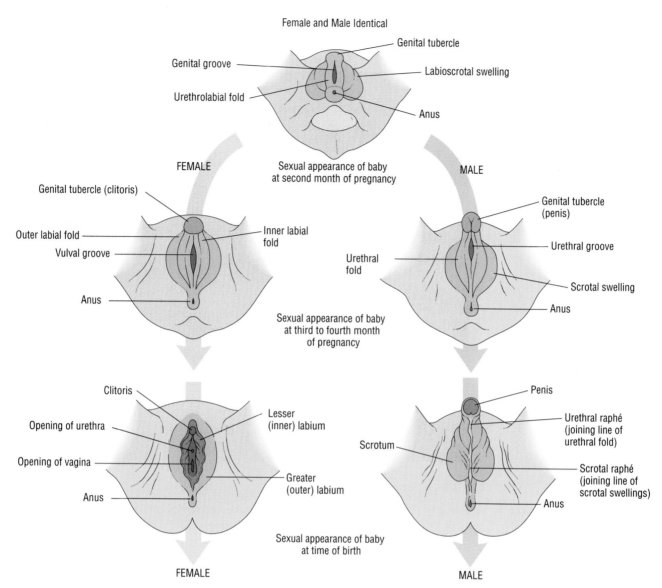

Female and Male Identical

Genital groove

Genital tubercle

Urethrolabial fold

Labioscrotal swelling

Anus

FEMALE

MALE

Sexual appearance of baby
at second month of pregnancy

Genital tubercle (clitoris)

Outer labial fold

Vulval groove

Inner labial
fold

Anus

Genital tubercle
(penis)

Urethral
fold

Urethral groove

Scrotal swelling

Anus

Sexual appearance of baby
at third to fourth month
of pregnancy

Clitoris

Opening of urethra

Opening of vagina

Anus

Lesser
(inner) labium

Greater
(outer) labium

Penis

Scrotum

Urethral raphé
(joining line of
urethral fold)

Scrotal raphé
(joining line of
scrotal swellings)

Anus

Sexual appearance of baby
at time of birth

FEMALE

MALE

FIGURE 3.2 Three Stages of
External Genital Differentiation in
the Human Fetus *Source:* J. Money &
A. A. Ehrhardt. (1972). *Man and woman, boy
and girl* (p. 44). Baltimore: Johns Hopkins
University Press.

Perhaps most surprising of all, the tiny organism can react to things. If the lip is brushed with a hair, a global, reflexive reaction occurs, the head pulling back and turning to the side and arms and legs moving in synchrony (Hooker, 1952; Nilsson & Hamberger, 1990).

Development follows two predictable patterns. The first of these is the **cephalocaudal trend,** growth proceeding from the region of the head downward. This pattern is illustrated in the growth of the arms and legs, in which the arms form several days before the legs, just as do the fingers before the toes. It is the size of the head in relation to the rest of the body, however, that best illustrates this trend. The head makes up nearly half of the entire body length at the end of the embryonic period (at birth, it is one fourth the body's length and, in adults, about one eighth). The second pattern to growth is the **proximodistal trend,** development proceeding from the center of the body outward to the extremities. Illustrating this trend, first the shoulder, then the arm, and last the hand develops. Only then do fingers begin to form. A similar progression occurs with the legs, feet, and toes.

In the 8th week the external genitals begin to differentiate into those of a male or a female. The genitals of either sex develop from the same structures (Figure 3.2), the genital tubercle becoming either a penis or a clitoris, and the labioscrotal swelling

Q What will develop first, the shoulders or the hands and fingers?

cephalocaudal trend The tendency of physical development to proceed from the region of the head downward.

proximodistal trend The tendency of physical development to proceed from the center of the body outward to the extremities.

By the 15th week, the face of the fetus looks like that of a baby. The whole body is sensitive to touch and most of the movements that can be seen in the third trimester and even after birth, have already emerged.

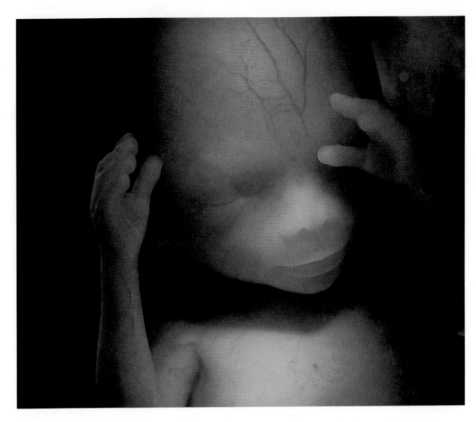

At what point in development might the sex of the baby be detected by ultrasound picture?

either closing to form the scrotal sac in males or remaining open to form the labia in females. By the 12th week, these developments are clearly visible (Lips, 1997).

At the end of the embryonic period, all of the body parts have been formed and are in place. The tiny organism has a complete skeleton, the organs have begun to function, and the embryo can react reflexively to events in its surround if stimulated.

Development in the Fetal Stage (9th Week to Birth)

The fetal stage includes the second and third trimesters and ends with the birth of the baby.

Second Trimester   The physical structures that were largely complete by the end of the embryonic period are refined in the fetal period. The bone cells that appeared by the end of the 7th to the 8th week have begun to replace the cartilage cells forming the skeleton. In the 3rd month, the eyes move from the sides of the face closer to the nose, eyelids form and close over the eyes, and ears that were low on the sides of the head move up to the level of the eyes. The result is a face that is more distinctly that of a baby. By the end of the 2nd month, the fetus has begun to move on its own, moving its arms and legs, stretching, kicking, sucking, and swallowing (Table 3.1). By the middle of the 3rd month (14 weeks), the whole body is sensitive to touch (Hepper, 1992), and most of the movements that can be seen in the third trimester, and even after birth, have already emerged (de Vries, 1992).

Even though all of the body parts were formed in the embryonic stage, finishing touches have yet to be added. The fetus develops eyelashes, eyebrows, baby

TABLE 3.1 First Appearance of Movement Patterns During the First Trimester in 12 Fetuses	
Movement Patterns	First Appearance: Range in Weeks Postmenstrual Age
Startle	8.0–9.5
General body movements	8.5–9.5
Stretch	10.0–15.5
Turning of the body	10.0
Hiccups	8.5–10.5
Breathing movements	10.0–11.5
Arm and leg movements	9.0–10.5
Finger movements	12.0
Head movements	
backward	9.5–12.5
turning	9.5–12.5
forward	10.5–14.5
Mouth opens	10.5–12.5
Sucking and swallowing	12.5–14.5
Tongue movements	11.0
Hand-face contact	10.0–12.5
Yawn	11.5–15.5
Eye movements	
slow	16.0
rapid	23.0

Source: Adapted from J. I. P. de Vries. (1992). The first trimester. In J. I. P. de Vries (Ed.), *Fetal behavior: Developmental and perinatal aspects* (pp. 3–16). New York: Oxford University Press.

hair, fingernails, and toenails. The familiar lines forming handprints and footprints appear, forever sealing its individuality. Bodily organs grow in size and begin to function more efficiently. The fetus adds inches and ounces, growing to half its birth size in the 4th month (Figure 3.3).

The brain continues to develop at a rapid pace. By the end of the second trimester, all of the neurons—some 100 billion—have formed. Glial cells, which surround and nourish the neurons, continue to develop throughout pregnancy. Once formed, neurons must migrate to their final destinations, following paths laid down by the glial cells, before undergoing the special developments that make it possible for them to communicate with other nerve cells. The neuron develops an **axon**, a long filament extending out from the cell body, enabling one neuron to reach another, even across great distances (Figure 3.4). **Dendrites**, looking like the branches of a tree, extend from the other end of the cell, making connections with many different neurons possible. Neurons also develop **neurotransmitters**, chemicals by which they communicate with neighboring neurons. Connections between neurons begin to be established as soon as the cells migrate to their proper locations. Bundles of fibers connecting the two hemispheres begin to form in the 10th week (Sadler, 1990). Electrical impulses, which signal the activity of the brain, take the characteristic form of brain-wave patterns by the end of the second trimester (Goldman-Rakic, 1987; Nowakowski, 1987).

With the development of the brain, the activity of the fetus changes and behaviors emerge. By the 7th month, characteristic cycles of sleeping and waking and even positions for sleeping appear. For instance, the fetus typically assumes the same position each time it sleeps. Many fetuses even suck their thumbs

axon A long filament extending from the cell body of a neuron along which neural impulses are conducted, enabling it to communicate with other nerve cells.

dendrites Fibers extending from a neuron that receive input from neighboring neurons.

neurotransmitters Chemicals released into the synapse that mediate the transmission of impulses.

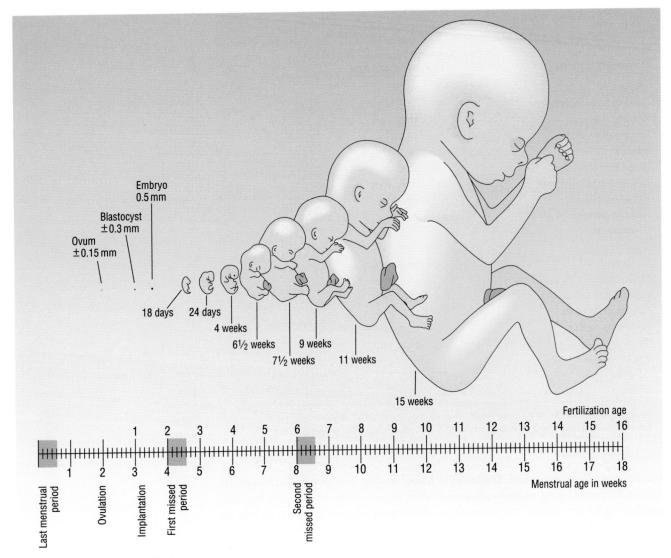

Ovum
±0.15 mm

Blastocyst
±0.3 mm

Embryo
0.5 mm

18 days   24 days

4 weeks

6½ weeks

7½ weeks

9 weeks

11 weeks

15 weeks

Fertilization age

| | | | | | | | | | | | | | | | |
1   2   3   4   5   6   7   8   9   10   11   12   13   14   15   16

1   2   3   4   5   6   7   8   9   10   11   12   13   14   15   16   17   18

Menstrual age in weeks

Last menstrual period

Ovulation

Implantation

First missed period

Second missed period

FIGURE 3.3 Growth of the Embryo and Fetus *The actual sizes of the developing embryo and fetus are shown here, from conception through the first 15 weeks.*

quiet sleep A sleep state characterized by relative inactivity except for brief startles; rapid eye movements (REM) are absent in quiet sleep.

active sleep A sleep state characterized by frequent body movement; also known as REM sleep because of the presence of rapid eye movements.

(Hepper, 1992). Patterns of sleeping and waking become more regular with passing weeks, until behavioral states indistinguishable from those of the newborn can be detected just prior to birth. Two of these states describe types of sleep, and two describe waking states.

The fetus spends most of its time, by far, asleep. About 30% of the time it is asleep, it is in a state of **quiet sleep,** not moving its body except for brief startles. Rapid eye movements (REM) also are absent in quiet sleep. The remaining time the fetus is sleeping, nearly 60%, it is in a state of **active sleep,** in which it frequently stretches its body and moves its arms and legs (Groome, Bentz, & Singh, 1995). This state is also known as REM sleep because of the presence of rapid eye movements. REM sleep is intriguing since, metabolically, it is an expensive state to maintain, using much more oxygen and glucose (about 30% more) than quiet sleep, suggesting that it benefits the organism in some way. One possible way would be in cortical development. We know, for instance, that the proportion of time spent in REM sleep declines rapidly with age, dropping from 60%, or approximately 14 hours a day, in the newborn, to 10% in late adulthood, and that sup-

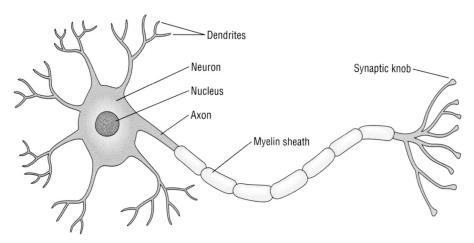

FIGURE 3.4 Neuron

Dendrites

Neuron

Nucleus

Axon

Myelin sheath

Synaptic knob

pression of REM sleep in fetal rats reduces the size of their cortex, as well as affecting their behavior (Mirmiran, 1995).

In the remaining two states, the fetus is awake. When the fetus is **quietly awake,** it moves its eyes about, but is otherwise still, not moving its body as much as in active sleep. When **actively awake,** the fetus frequently and vigorously moves its body, as well as moving its eyes. Characteristic changes in heart rate also accompany changes in each of these states (Nijhuis, 1995). Just how active or quiet a particular fetus is varies considerably (Nijhuis, 1995).

The fetus also develops a biological clock that regulates periods of activity and inactivity. This diurnal, or daily, 24-hour cycle develops several months earlier (at 20 weeks) than the cycle of sleeping and waking, and is independent of the latter. The cycle is interesting in that it is a reversal of the adult's daily cycle, the fetus being most active in the evening and least active in the morning. Unlike the sleep-wake cycles that are regulated by cortical development, the diurnal cycle appears to be regulated by maternal hormones (Arduini, Rizzo, & Romanini, 1995).

The senses have also begun to develop, enabling the fetus to react to its surroundings. The fetus, in fact, is surrounded by a kaleidoscopically changing world of sense impressions. It experiences the gentle jostlings of its mother's movements as well as the ripple of its own, hears the sounds unique to its uterine life and those reaching it from the outside world. Sensitivity to touch, first seen as early as 7 weeks, develops over the entire body by the 14th week. The fetus experiences a variety of tastes, since the sense of taste is well developed before birth. Taste buds appear by the 4th month and the fetus has been shown to have taste "preferences." When the amniotic fluid is sweetened, for instance, through injections of a saccharin solution, the fetus swallows more. Similarly, when an unpleasant-tasting substance is injected, sucking movements decrease (Hepper, 1992).

The sense of smell is also well developed before birth. Although odors can be sensed better when carried in the air, they are nonetheless discernible when dissolved in a liquid such as the liquid environment of the fetus. The amniotic fluid takes on various odors, reflecting the maternal diet. Obstetricians, for instance, have reported being able to smell spices such as curry and cumin in the amniotic fluid when assisting at the birth of infants delivered shortly after their mothers had eaten food strongly flavored with these spices (Schaal, Orgeur, & Rognon, 1995). We know, in addition, that preterm infants as young as 28 weeks react to strong smells, just as do full-term infants 3 months later.

> Q Why do mothers in the second half of pregnancy often report that their baby won't "let" them get any sleep?

quietly awake A waking state characterized by quiet wakefulness.

actively awake A waking state characterized by frequent and vigorous movements.

Vision and hearing also develop relatively early. The fetus reacts to external sounds by 4 months, blinking, moving, and showing changes in its heart rate (Hepper, 1992). In addition, the fetus is surrounded by the sounds and movements of its internal world: the rhythmic beating of the mother's heart, the pulsing of her blood, even the sounds of her voice as she talks. The latter reaches its watery world as a muffled, but nevertheless distinctive, voice (Hepper, 1992). One team of investigators asked prospective mothers to read *The Cat in the Hat* out loud each day during the last 6 weeks of pregnancy. Following the birth, their infants were given an electronic nipple to suck that "switched on" either *The Cat in the Hat* or another, unfamiliar story, depending on the frequency with which they sucked. Infants changed their sucking to hear the story they had heard in the womb (DeCasper & Spence, 1986). Of course, other sounds reach the fetus from the outside world as well, and most prospective mothers will tell you that, just like a newborn, the fetus can be wakened by loud sounds. Also, by about 6½ months, the fetus can respond to light. However, little patterned stimulation is available in the dark uterine interior.

By the 6th month the fetus can open and close its eyes, and buds for the permanent teeth have appeared in the gums above the milk teeth. The amniotic fluid that cushions and protects the fetus maintains it at a constant temperature; this feature of the amniotic environment is important since the fetus has yet to develop the layer of subcutaneous fat that insulates the newborn from temperature changes. The fluid surroundings of the fetus also free it from the force of gravity. Like an astronaut, the fetus floats weightlessly, moving arms and legs and a head that will be too heavy to lift for months after birth. Its skin is covered with a greaselike coating, called **vernix,** and a fine downy hair, **lanugo.** The fetus could not survive on its own if born now, since its lungs, digestive system, and the neural centers regulating its breathing are still immature.

Third Trimester   In the 7th month, the fetus sheds its covering of lanugo and gains weight, 1 pound in the 7th month and another 4 pounds in the next 6 weeks. The once-roomy uterus starts to become a tight fit by the 8th month, and activity is restricted by the cramped quarters. The fetus usually settles into a head-down position by the 9th month. Its quarters are so close that its movements can be seen as ripples on the mother's swollen abdomen, and a good kick can upset something in her lap.

The fetus becomes viable by the 7th month, although it weighs a mere 2–2½ pounds and lacks the layer of fat that holds in heat in full-term infants. Infants born at this age require special postnatal care, needing to be maintained on a respirator while their lungs develop. Before 6½ months, the tiny air pockets in the lungs have not developed sufficiently to permit the absorption of adequate amounts of oxygen or to get rid of carbon monoxide. In adults and children, a layer of fat containing the protein **surfactant** lines these air pockets and keeps them from collapsing when air is breathed out. Surfactant is absent before 6½ months and does not begin to be produced in any quantity until 7½ or 8 months. In addition to respiratory problems, preterm infants also experience digestive problems. Their digestive systems are not sufficiently developed to permit an adequate absorption of nutrients. Also, sucking and swallowing are not coordinated prior to about 34 weeks (Ensher & Clark, 1994). Most premature infants lose weight initially as a result. They are also more susceptible than full-term infants to infection since they have not received the immunities to many diseases that are transmitted as antibodies in the mother's blood during these last important months (Ensher & Clark, 1994).

Q If a father wants to increase his ability to soothe his newborn and foster a stronger connection to him or her before birth, what might he do?

vernix A protective white, greasy coating that covers the skin of the fetus.

lanugo Fine, downy hair that covers the skin of the fetus.

surfactant A substance that lines the air pockets in the lungs.

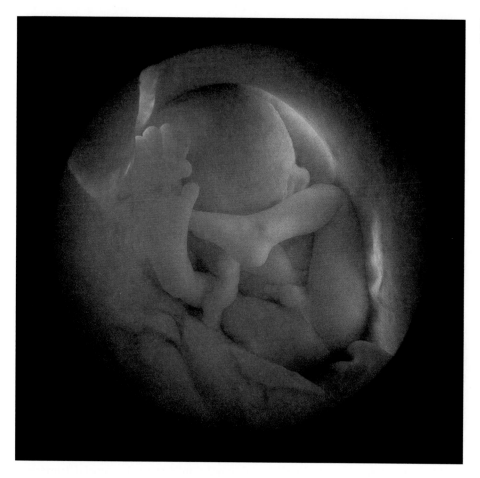

By the 8th month, the uterus starts to become a tight fit for the fetus.

By the end of the 9th month, the fetus has been readied for life outside the uterus as much as possible. The first preparation for birth is the "lightening"; the uterus drops slightly, and the fetus's head (or buttocks if a breech birth) fits snugly into the pelvic area, wedged in place. The fetus stops growing about a week before birth. The placenta is now aging and less able to supply nutrients and manage the by-products of metabolism. The fetus participates actively in the changes in the mother's body that trigger labor, communicating with the maternal system through chemical messages that modify the tone of the uterus and the activities of the placenta (Menticoglou, Manning, Harmon, & Morrison, 1995). A final change in hormone levels will trigger the birth process, ending one of the most intimate of human relationships—and beginning another.

Maternal Changes

One of the most common first signs of pregnancy is missing a monthly period, since the uterine lining is not sloughed off in the form of a menstrual flow if conception has occurred. However, monthly cycles are not a reliable index. Many women have highly variable cycles. Stress, tension, diet, activity, and body weight can all affect the menstrual cycle. Many women experience some nausea, frequently referred to as morning sickness, early in pregnancy. Despite its name, "morning sickness" is no more likely to occur in the morning than at any other time throughout the day. The hormonal changes contributing to nausea can also cause sleepiness and emotional ups and downs. These mood changes can be heightened by how a woman feels toward the pregnancy. Even pregnancies that are planned can be greeted with some ambivalence (Coustan, 1995b).

Numerous physical changes occur throughout the mother's body during pregnancy. One of the most noticeable of these is weight gain, anywhere from 20 to 30 pounds being typical. Most women gain from 2 to 6 pounds during the first trimester, adding another 10 to 12 pounds in each of the remaining trimesters (Coustan, 1995b). Only about 11 pounds is contributed by the infant (7.5 pounds) and its support system, the placenta, the amniotic sac and its fluid (3.5 pounds). The remaining weight is gained by the mother. Increases in fluids and fat are responsible for about 10 pounds of this gain. The remainder is due to the increased weight of the uterus (about 2.5 lbs), the breasts (1 lb), and the increased volume of circulating blood (3.5 lbs) (Coustan, 1995b). Of course, gaining more than 20–30 pounds is not unusual either. Apart from changes due to the pregnancy itself, simply gaining weight can cause women to feel uncomfortable, lethargic, or otherwise different from usual.

Thyroid activity increases after the first 8 weeks of pregnancy, sometimes causing more than the usual amount of sweating. Even though the uterus is still quite small, it presses against the bladder, and so women often need to urinate frequently during the first trimester. The uterus rises in the second trimester, relieving the pressure. The rapidly growing fetus again crowds the bladder in the third trimester.

Other changes are less noticeable to the mother. Her rib cage expands, and muscles and ligaments soften and stretch throughout the body, including the joints between the pelvic bones, making the birth of the baby easier. Metabolism becomes more efficient; blood volume increases, lungs take in more air, and kidneys function more efficiently.

Many women report feeling in peak condition during the second trimester. Their bodies have adjusted to the additional demands made by pregnancy, and the fetus has not yet grown to a size where it is a source of discomfort. By the third trimester, with a larger and more active fetus, the prospective mother may have difficulty sleeping and may also experience backaches and some swelling of hands and ankles. Swelling sometimes signals a condition called toxemia and should always be reported immediately to one's doctor.

In the 9th month, just when it seems that pregnancy has become a permanent condition, the "lightening" occurs. The uterus drops about 2 inches, relieving pressure on the rib cage and making it possible to breathe more comfortably, and the fetus's head slips into the pelvic region. With the fetus again pressing against the bladder, there is a need to urinate more frequently. Toward the end of pregnancy, the prospective mother will experience some contractions. These are short and irregular. Unlike labor, they do not increase in intensity; and after an hour or so they stop.

The Prenatal Environment

The fetus becomes a part of the family long before it is born, contributing to the plans of the parents and sharing in their pastimes. "Having a baby" frequently means changes in work schedules and living arrangements for parents. Also, parents' routines and habits can affect the fetus just as they affect other siblings in the family. Eating habits, such as the mother's diet, are obviously important. So,

Q What are some of the earliest signs of pregnancy, and how early in pregnancy are they experienced?

too, are other habits that may introduce substances into the maternal bloodstream. It was once thought that the placenta acted as a barrier protecting the fetus against harmful substances; however, any substance that can enter the mother's bloodstream, whether vitamins and minerals or nicotine and other drugs, can affect the fetus. Infectious diseases are no exception. Surprisingly, even the *father's* health habits and type of work can affect the health of the fetus.

Health Factors and Health Hazards

Factors that interfere with normal development are called **teratogens.** Teratogens can interfere with development at any point in pregnancy. They can prevent ovulation, damage sperm, diminish chances of fertilization, interfere with implantation, or do direct or indirect damage to the embryo or fetus. Not all of their effects may be apparent at birth as, for instance, those affecting neural development. Some teratogens have sweeping effects, and others produce very specific effects. The effect of a teratogen will vary with its timing, the amount of exposure, and individual differences in susceptibility to it.

The average infant will be exposed to approximately 20 drugs from the moment of conception through the first several days of life. Most pregnant women know better than to take pills indiscriminately, but most women do not know initially when they are pregnant. Furthermore, medicine cabinets are chock-full of things that many Americans fail to think of as drugs—aspirin, laxatives, cold pills, antihistamines, cough medicines, and tablets for upset stomachs, to mention just a few; and many of these can affect the fetus. More potential teratogens can usually be found in the kitchen in the form of megavitamins and alcoholic beverages.

Research on teratogens reveals that their effects are rarely simple. Whether a substance will harm the fetus or leave it unaffected, in other words, depends on more than whether the fetus has been exposed to the teratogen. One of the most important factors contributing to a substance's effect is *when* the fetus is exposed—its timing, in other words. Not all parts of the body are vulnerable at the same time. An organ is most vulnerable during the time of its most rapid growth, when it is being formed (Figure 3.5). Since different parts of the body develop at different times, a substance can affect one organ or body part and leave others unaffected. Also, some teratogens affect specific parts of the body, leaving others untouched. The antibiotic tetracycline, for instance, can create staining in the teeth and affect bone growth, but does not affect other parts of the body, such as the central nervous system or organ development.

The *amount* of a teratogen the fetus is exposed to also determines its effect. Some teratogens have simple cumulative effects: The more the fetus is exposed to the substance, the greater the effect. With cigarettes, for instance, each one that is smoked is associated statistically with a reduction in the birthweight of the fetus by a certain average amount. Other teratogens must reach a critical level before they have an effect, affecting the fetus only once a threshold has been passed. The danger with any potential teratogen, however, is that its effect frequently depends on what other substances are present. Alcohol taken in combination with a barbiturate, for instance, can affect the fetus in ways that cannot be predicted by knowing the effect of either the alcohol or the barbiturate alone.

The manner in which any of the potential disabilities resulting from a teratogen will affect an infant depends to a great extent on the larger developmental context for that infant. An infant born with a disability, for instance, with parents who provide a warm, loving, and stimulating environment, who encourage independence, and who can afford corrective medical intervention will develop in

teratogens Agents that interfere with normal prenatal development.

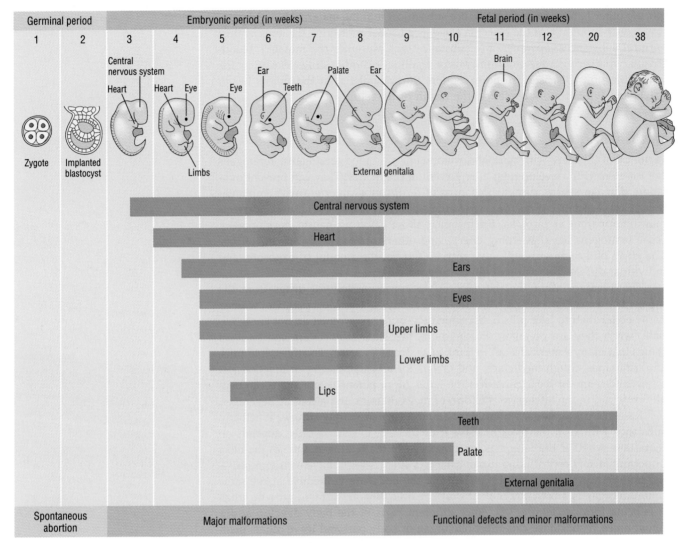

Germinal period		Embryonic period (in weeks)						Fetal period (in weeks)					
1	2	3	4	5	6	7	8	9	10	11	12	20	38

FIGURE 3.5 Susceptibility to Teratogenesis for Organ Systems

Solid bar denotes highly sensitive periods. Source: T. W. Sadler. (1990). *Langman's medical embryo* (6th ed.). Baltimore: Williams & Wilkins.

different ways than will an infant with the same impairments and equally loving parents, but ones who may be fearfully overprotective, limit the child's independence, and fail to take advantage of available interventions.

Maternal Nutrition

Maternal nutrition is one of the most important factors affecting prenatal development. The mother's diet supplies not only the nutrients she needs but all of those needed by the fetus as well. In addition to meeting the specific nutritional needs of the fetus, an adequate diet protects against low birthweight, a general index associated with health complications. Eating a variety of foods, including fresh vegetables and fruits, will supply most of the minerals and vitamins needed. There are, of course, some exceptions. One is the need for iron, which is typically not met by diet alone. Daily supplements of iron, especially for the last two trimesters, are recommended (Lynch, 2000). Calcium, another important mineral, may also need to be supplemented, especially in younger women (under 25). The best sources of calcium, however, remain the dairy products consumed in one's

Q Why are women encouraged to have regular prenatal visits during their entire pregnancy, even if they "feel" healthy and the pregnancy appears to be going well?

Adequate maternal nutrition protects against low birthweight, a general index associated with health complications.

diet, such as milk, cottage cheese, yogurt, eggs, and cheese. Pregnant women also need somewhat greater amounts of protein.

Additionally, if women of childbearing age—whether they knew themselves to be pregnant or not—simply took a multivitamin containing folic acid each day, the number of children born with a variety of birth defects could be significantly reduced (Shaw, O'Malley, Wasserman, Tolarova, & Lammer, 1995). Additional vitamin and mineral supplements need to be taken with caution. Too much can cause harm as well as too little. For instance, excessive amounts of iron can result in a zinc deficiency, which can cause birth complications. Similarly, megadoses of vitamin A, which are involved in some treatments of severe acne, can produce a variety of birth defects, ranging from cleft lip to heart problems, when such use occurs early in pregnancy (Rosa, Wilk, & Kelsey, 1986).

It is also important to eat enough of the right things. And this, of course, means that the woman is going to gain weight. How much is enough? The weight a woman needs to gain during pregnancy will depend, for the most part, on how much she weighed prior to getting pregnant. A woman who is of normal weight for her height should expect to gain from 25 to 34 pounds, gaining about 1 pound a week in the last two trimesters. Women who were underweight may need to gain as much as 40 pounds, depending on their initial weight and height. Over-weight women, conversely, need to gain considerably less, from 15 to 24 pounds (Cogswell, Scanlon, Fein, & Schieve, 1999).

Much of what we know concerning the importance of nutrition comes from the experiences of pregnant women who have been malnourished. One of the most severe "natural experiments" on the effects of malnutrition comes from a famine imposed on certain parts of the Netherlands during the last 7 months of World War II, in which many pregnant women lived on a diet of 400 calories a day (Stein, Susser, Saenger, & Marolla, 1975).

As might be expected, the famine affected not only birthweight, but also infant survival. Infants who experienced the famine during the last trimester, the time of most rapid weight gain, weighed almost a pound less and were more likely to die in the first several months following birth than were those born to well-nourished mothers. However, even infants who were well nourished for the last two trimesters and experienced malnutrition only during the first trimester were less likely to survive infancy. These infants were also more likely to have birth defects affecting the central nervous system, which undergoes rapid development in the first trimester.

Malnutrition need not be this severe to affect the developing fetus. Similar defects, including spina bifida and anencephaly, have been found to occur in infants born in the United States to women with inadequate amounts of folic acid in their diets. Folic acid is a vitamin B compound found in green leafy vegetables and some fruits, such as bananas. Dietary supplements of folic acid taken during pregnancy dramatically reduce the number of infants with birth defects involving the central nervous system (T. K. Estes, 1998; Oakley, 1997; Shaw, O'Malley, Wasserman, Tolarova, & Lammer, 1995). Since most pregnancies are not planned and many women are not aware initially that they are pregnant, daily use of a multivitamin that contains folic acid is important for all women of child-bearing age.

One of the most surprising findings to emerge from the study of the Dutch victims of famine concerns not the children, or even their mothers, but the grand-children of the mothers who experienced famine during pregnancy. Adult daughters who were malnourished as fetuses in the first or second trimester were more likely to give birth to low-birthweight babies themselves than were their well-nourished counterparts, even though these infants received adequate nutrition throughout their prenatal development. The severe malnourishment of their mothers, when they themselves were fetuses, is likely to have affected the course of oogenesis, or the formation of ova in these females. Immature ova begin to form as early as the 3rd week, migrating to the ovaries by the 5th week, where they begin cell division, replicating their DNA. The maximum number of ova is not reached until the 5th month, in the second trimester (Sadler, 1990). Findings such as these demonstrate the far-ranging effects of developmental experiences and the difficulties, as a result, in anticipating their consequences. They also underscore the importance of social programs, such as supplemental food programs for preg-nant women and infants, and free prenatal care, including advice on nutrition.

Such programs can benefit a society for generations to come. Nutrition, like most factors that either safeguard the health or present hazards to the developing fetus, does not work in isolation. The ameliorating effects of supportive programs are evidence of this.

Maternal Stress

It has long been suspected that a mother's emotional state can affect fetal development. A recent study of pregnant women, comparing those who were severely stressed with those who were not, provides support for the adverse effects of maternal stress on fetal development. Women who were severely stressed during pregnancy, because of divorce, a death in the family, or a physical attack, for instance, gave birth to infants with lower birthweights. The infants also had smaller head circumferences, even when corrected for their smaller size, suggesting that severe stress may affect brain growth. Responses to a neurological inventory, given several days after birth, supported the notion that, at least initially, cognitive functioning as well as head size was affected (Lou et al., 1994).

It is always difficult for research such as this to rule out alternative explanations. For instance, women who were stressed drank and smoked more, as might be expected, than did those who were not stressed. However, when these differences were corrected for statistically, the results remained unchanged (Lou et al., 1994). Of course, other differences might still exist. Women under stress might fail to eat and sleep as regularly, or otherwise not take as good care of their health, as do women whose pregnancies were free of stress.

Clearly, though, physical mechanisms exist by which stress can affect the developing fetus. When stressed, the body releases corticoids that stimulate the cardiovascular system and increase available sources of energy, enabling the body to cope better with the stressor. However, by redirecting the body's available resources, these hormones also inhibit cell division. If chronically present, they could well affect fetal growth. Typically, the placenta secretes an enzyme that protects the fetus from excessive levels of such hormones; however, inordinate amounts of these hormones will inhibit the enzyme.

A certain amount of stress is to be expected. After all, pregnancy itself is a major life transition, and transitions bring their own stresses, even when they are positive. Is divorce stressful? Yes; however, so is marriage. Similarly, a promotion is stressful, just as is losing a job, and birth as well as death is stressful. In addition to bringing physical and psychosocial changes, pregnancy involves a number of life adjustments. Work and living arrangements may change. Some women may decide to cut back on their work schedules while others may increase their work hours to pay for the additional expenses of a baby. An apartment that was just the right size for two might soon become too small. Relationships, also, can change in subtle or not-so-subtle ways.

The effects that these or other stresses will have depend on the larger context of the pregnancy. Women who can count on the supporting presence of others find stress more manageable. What constitutes support? Support can be simply having someone to talk to or just relaxing with friends. At other times, it may take the form of someone else's taking over household responsibilities, such as grocery shopping or child care.

Not only pregnancy, but also the anticipation of labor can be a source of stress for some women. In *The Blue Jay's Dance,* Louise Erdrich (1996) writes, "I look down into my smooth, huge lap, feel my baby twist, and I can't figure out how I'll ever stretch wide enough. I fear I've made a ship inside a bottle. I'll have to break. I'm not me. I feel myself becoming less a person than a place, inhabited, a foreign land"(p. 9). ◄

TABLE 3.2 Some Maternal Conditions Associated with Problems in a Fetus or Infant

Condition	Potential Effects
Chlamydia	Eye infections, pneumonia
Cytomegalovirus (CMV)	Small head, mental retardation, blindness
Diabetes (insulin-dependent)	Malformations of the brain, spine, and heart
Gonorrhea	Eye infection leading to blindness if untreated
Hepatitis B	Liver failure, hepatitis infection, jaundice, fever
Herpes	Brain damage, death
HIV infection	Impaired immunity, death
Rubella (German measles)	Malformation of eyes or ears causing deafness or blindness; small head; mental retardation
Syphilis	Fetal death and miscarriage, prematurity, physical deformities
Toxoplasmosis	Small head, mental retardation, blindness, hearing impairments, seizures, learning disorders

Source: P. M. Insel & W. T. Roth. (2000). *Core concepts in health* (8th ed.). Mountain View, CA: Mayfield.

Infections

Infections that initially affect the mother can cross the placenta to infect the fetus which can also be infected during birth itself by coming into contact with organisms in the birth canal. The first type of infection, known as **transplacental infections,** most commonly includes a number of viruses—rubella, cytomegalovirus, HIV, and hepatitis B, as well as syphilis, a bacterial infection, and toxoplasmosis, a parasitic infection. The most common infections transmitted during birth, known as **ascending infections,** are the herpesvirus and gonorrhea, a bacterial infection. Infants can be infected with HIV during delivery as well as during the pregnancy. Breast-feeding can also lead to infection with HIV. Table 3.2 compares these infections and their potential effects.

Rubella (German measles) was once a common cause of birth defects in the United States. Currently, an aggressive national immunization program targeting children under the age of 3 has resulted in over 90% of young children being immunized for measles; this program has virtually eliminated congenital rubella in the United States, with only five cases reported in 1997 (National Center for Health Statistics, 1999).

The importance of immunization programs such as this cannot be overemphasized. Rubella can severely affect the fetus, causing partial deafness (about 87% of infected infants), blindness (about 34%), heart disease (about 46%), and mental retardation (about 40%). The likelihood and severity of damage depend on when the mother contracts the disease and are greatest if she is infected in the first trimester. Women who are not sure whether they possess immunity to rubella can get a blood test and, if they are not already immune, can be immunized before getting pregnant (Ensher & Clark, 1994).

Cytomegalovirus, a member of the herpes family, has become the most common form of fetal viral infection now that rubella has been controlled through immunization. This virus has effects similar to those of rubella and, just as with rubella, the timing of the infection determines the way in which the fetus is likely to be affected, with infections occurring in the first trimester having more serious consequences than those occurring later. At present, no immunization against this virus exists; and, once acquired, the infection remains throughout life (Ensher & Clark, 1994).

transplacental infections Infections of the fetus due to organisms that initially infect the mother and then cross the placenta.

ascending infections Infections transmitted during birth; the most common are the herpesvirus and gonorrhea.

rubella German measles; once a common cause of birth defects in the United States.

cytomegalovirus A member of the herpes family that has become the most common form of fetal viral infection.

The **human immunodeficiency virus (HIV),** attacks the immune system, making the infant vulnerable to infections and eventually leading to death. Approximately 2% of women of childbearing age in the United States are HIV-positive; and, of these, anywhere from 15 to 30% will transmit the virus to the fetus. Translated into numbers, these percentages mean that about 7,000 infants are born each year to HIV-positive women; and, of these, 1,000 to 2,000 are infected with the virus (CDC, 1995c). The incubation period for the disease is shorter in infants than in adults, perhaps because their immune systems are less well developed. Most infected infants are healthy at birth, but show symptoms of severe immunodeficiency by 5 to 10 months. Seventy-five percent die within the first year after AIDS symptoms appear. Since recent advances in drug therapy have made it possible to reduce the risk of transmitting HIV to the infant, pregnant women who are at risk for infection should know their HIV status (CDC, 1995c; Ensher & Clark, 1994).

Hepatitis B is a virus that can cause liver failure and less-severe symptoms of jaundice and fever in infants infected with it, even though it is symptomless in 40% of adult carriers. This virus poses an increasing risk to infants born in the United States due to large numbers of immigrants from countries in which it is prevalent. An infant born to an infected mother has a 50% risk of being infected. Since the incubation period is from 1½ to 6 months, infants born to infected mothers need to be followed closely and treated with protective immunoglobulins (Ensher & Clark, 1994). A vaccine is available, and the percentage of preschool children vaccinated against hepatitis B has increased significantly in recent years (National Center for Health Statistics, 1999).

Toxoplasmosis results from a parasite transmitted by the mother, who usually has no symptoms. The parasite can be acquired by eating undercooked meat or contaminated foods or by inhaling the eggs when emptying out cat litter. The parasite develops in the intestinal tract and is carried in the blood to organs in the body, where it forms cysts. Infection in the first trimester can produce a range of birth defects, from auditory and visual problems to impairments in brain growth and the development of body organs.

Syphilis and **gonorrhea** are sexually transmitted bacterial infections. Syphilis can cause damage to the central nervous system as well as to developing organs and bones. It may go unnoticed at birth, however, if the mother's symptoms are subtle; and infants may receive medical attention for it only when they develop swelling in the joints or difficulty moving their limbs. Syphilis is easily treated with antibiotics. Gonorrhea is more frequently transmitted to the infant during birth. If not treated with antibiotics, the infection can lead to blindness. Almost all newborns are given antibiotic ointment or drops of silver nitrate in the eyes at birth to prevent damage to the eyes.

Herpes is a viral infection that is most frequently transmitted during birth. The most common symptom is lethargy. Many infants also experience respiratory problems. The virus targets the central nervous system and can cause blindness, seizures, and mental retardation. Even mothers who have no symptoms at the time of birth can transmit the disease to the fetus; cesarean delivery reduces the infant's risk of infection. Once acquired, the infection remains throughout life and can be reactivated when resistance is low (Ensher & Clark, 1994).

Legal Drugs

The most commonly used drugs with the potential to harm the fetus are not "street drugs," such as cocaine, heroin, or marijuana, but legal ones—cigarettes and alcohol. The risks to the fetus from smoking and drinking during pregnancy have been

human immunodeficiency virus (HIV) Can be transmitted by an infected mother to her fetus; the risk of transmission can be reduced with drug therapy.

hepatitis B A virus that can cause liver failure, jaundice, and fever in infected infants.

toxoplasmosis A parasitic disease, often transmitted in cat feces, that can cause birth defects if the mother is infected during the first trimester.

syphilis A sexually transmitted bacterial infection that can cause damage to the central nervous system and to developing organs and bones; easily treated with antibiotics.

gonorrhea A sexually transmitted bacterial infection that can be transmitted to an infant during birth and can lead to blindness; damage can be averted with preventive measures at birth.

herpes A viral infection that can be transmitted during birth; can damage the central nervous system.

FIGURE 3.6 Percentage of Low-Birthweight Infants Born to Women As a Function of Number of Cigarettes Smoked *Source:* B. Zuckerman. (1988). Marijuana and cigarette smoking during pregnancy. In I. J. Chasnoff (Ed.), *Drugs, alcohol, pregnancy, and parenting* (pp. 73–89). Hingham, MA: Kluwer Academic.

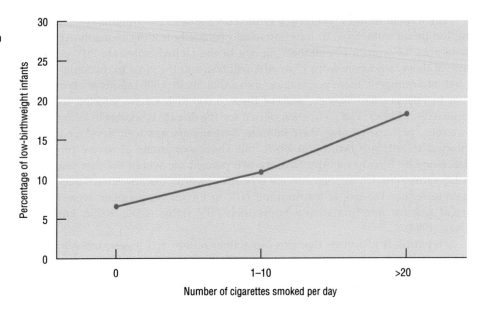

extensively studied. This body of research unequivocally documents the risks to the fetus that attend the use of cigarettes and alcohol during pregnancy and, with cigarettes, the risks associated with their use subsequent to birth (Ensher & Clark, 1994; Klonoff-Cohen et al., 1995; Zhang, Savitz, Schwingl, & Cai, 1992).

Cigarettes Smoking when pregnant poses a significant and serious risk to the fetus. Women who smoke have smaller babies (Dejin-Karlsson, Hanson, Oestergren, Sjoberg, & Marsal, 1998; Horta, Victora, Menezes, Halpern, & Barros, 1997), have more miscarriages and stillbirths (Ness et al., 1999), and give birth to infants with more health complications (Hanna, Faden, & Dufour, 1997). They are also more likely to have an infant die of sudden infant death syndrome during the 1st year of life (Guntheroth, 1995; Mitchell et al., 1997).

The association between smoking and low birthweight is well established (Muscati, Koski, & Gray-Donald, 1996; Nieto, Matorras, Serra, Valenzuela, & Molero, 1994; Olsen, 1992). As can be seen in Figure 3.6, the likelihood of giving birth to a low-birthweight infant increases with the number of cigarettes a woman smokes (Horta et al., 1997; Roquer, Figueras, Botet, & Jimenez, 1995; Zuckerman, 1988). Additionally, the nicotine content of the cigarettes a woman smokes has been found to be related to retarded fetal growth (Olsen, 1992). Not only is maternal smoking associated with reduced birthweight, but so is passive exposure from partners who smoke (Dejin-Karlsson et al., 1998; Horta et al., 1997; Roquer, Figueras, Botet, & Jimenez, 1995). Birthweight can be reduced by approximately 4 ounces for each pack of cigarettes smoked a day by a partner (Rubin, Krasnilikkoff, Leventhal, Weile, & Berget, 1986). Finally, infants born to mothers who smoke may also be somewhat shorter as toddlers (Eskenazi & Bergmann, 1995; Fried & Watkinson, 1990; Leger, Limoni, & Czernichow, 1997).

Several nutrients important to fetal development have been found to differ in smoking and nonsmoking women. Levels of vitamins A, B_{12}, and C as well as of zinc and folate and of several amino acids are lower in those who smoke. These nutritional differences are likely to play a role in the greater number of premature births to women who smoke during pregnancy, as well as in fetal growth retardation (Witter & Keith, 1993). Smoking can also affect the ratio of blood gases reaching the fetus, reducing oxygenation by affecting the efficiency of the placenta

Q Why is it important that a woman stop smoking during pregnancy as well as stay away from secondhand smoke from her mate and others?

in exchanging blood gases. In addition, blood levels of hemoglobin and hematocrit differ between women who do and do not smoke during pregnancy (Witter & Keith, 1993).

Maternal smoking is implicated in a host of health complications in infancy—from lower Apgar scores to congenital heart problems (Malloy, Kleinman, Land, & Schramm, 1988). Some of the most serious findings implicate cigarette smoking in **sudden infant death syndrome (SIDS).** SIDS, commonly known as crib death, is the principal cause of death in infants from the 1st month to the 1st year of life. These deaths are sudden and unexpected, striking infants with no discernible health problems. Smoking during pregnancy increases the risk of SIDS. The increase is dose-dependent, with even half a pack of cigarettes a day significantly affecting the risk (Mitchell et al., 1991). Smoking habits of the fathers, as well as those of the mothers, were associated with greater risk of infant death. Infants whose fathers smoked throughout the pregnancy, even when the mother did not smoke, were 3 times more likely to die from SIDS than were those whose fathers did not smoke.

Paternal smoking has also been found to be associated with slight increases in the risk of birth defects, such as anencephaly, cleft palate, and peculiarities in skin pigmentation. These risks increase with the number of cigarettes smoked by fathers. It cannot be said with any certainty at this point whether smoking has an effect on sperm or whether it exerts its effect in other ways, such as by changing the uterine environment through passive maternal smoking (Zhang et al., 1992).

According to the National Center for Health Statistics (1999), one quarter of women who are of childbearing age smoke. Although many women attempt to quit during pregnancy, doing so is difficult, since cigarette smoking is highly addictive (CDC, 1995b). A national household survey on drug use, for instance, found that cigarette smokers were more likely than those using alcohol, marijuana, or cocaine to say they had tried to cut back, but were twice as likely to have failed. In fact, only 2.5% of cigarette smokers each year are successful in kicking the habit, even though most smokers say they want to quit (CDC, 1995b). Cigarette smokers who decide to quit during pregnancy, even if they have smoked for part of the pregnancy, immediately reduce the risk of health complications to their infants (Ahlsten, Cnattinguis, & Lindmark, 1993).

Alcohol Alcohol is a powerful teratogen that can affect many aspects of fetal development. The particular damage that is done will depend on when the fetus is exposed to alcohol and how much it is exposed to. Women who are heavy drinkers during pregnancy are more likely to give birth to infants with a pattern of deficits that include mental retardation, low birthweight, heart defects, and atypical facial features. However, even women who do not consider themselves to be drinkers, but who may have a number of drinks over a short period of time expose the fetus to increased risk because of the threshold-dependent effects of alcohol (Rosenthal, 1990).

It is difficult to predict how much alcohol is dangerous since the level of alcohol in the blood must reach a certain level, or threshold, before it becomes dangerous to the fetus. This threshold varies from individual to individual and differs as well for different organs within the body. The use of alcohol carries a special risk for brain development, since the brain develops throughout pregnancy and since the threshold for damage to the brain may be lower than that for other organs. Because of the difficulty in predicting when this threshold is reached for any individual, the safest course to follow during pregnancy is abstinence.

Secondhand smoke from fathers has been associated with birth defects.

sudden infant death syndrome (SIDS) Also called crib death, the principal cause of death in infants from the 1st month to the 1st year of life; smoking during pregnancy increases the risk.

Fetal alcohol syndrome is a pattern of disabilities affecting children whose mothers drank during pregnancy.

The risk to the fetus is significantly increased among women who drink heavily. The pattern of deficits mentioned earlier, known as **fetal alcohol syndrome (FAS),** affects all aspects of development. FAS children have smaller heads, retarded physical growth, and characteristic facial features, such as flat, upturned noses and widely spaced eyes with droopy lids. In addition, mental retardation is typical, as are problems with attention and judgment. FAS children also are likely to have poor social skills and behavior problems (Miller et al., 1995).

In *The Broken Cord* (1989), Michael Dorris describes the moment he realized his teenage son Adam, adopted as a toddler, suffered from this syndrome. Until this moment, he had assumed that his son's problems reflected the quirks of his own personality rather than a profile of damage wrought by alcohol. As he stands talking to the director of Project Phoenix, a Native American treatment center for teenagers, several boys suffering from FAS enter the room:

There was a noise behind us, and I moved to make room for three young boys, "clients" the director called them, to enter. Ignoring our presence, they turned on the TV, dropped onto chairs and couches, and stared straight ahead.

I stared too. They could have been Adam's twin brothers. They resembled him in every facial feature, in every gesture, in body type. They came from a living situation as different as possible from an eighteenth-century farmhouse in rural New Hampshire; they were bare survivors of family cri-

fetal alcohol syndrome (FAS) A pattern of disabilities, including mental retardation, low birthweight, heart defects, and atypical facial features, resulting from consumption of alcohol during pregnancy.

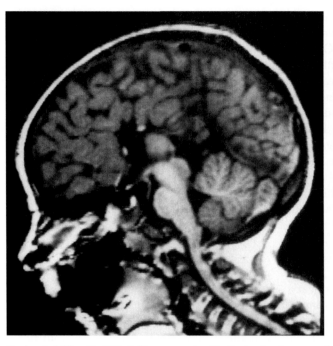 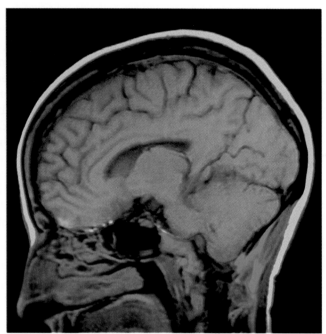

Brain of child with FAS (left) compared with the brain of a normal child (right).

sis, of violence, of abuse—otherwise they wouldn't be at Project Phoenix—and Adam, after the dislocations of his first three years, had been protected, defined as "special," monitored in his every phase of development. Yet there was something so uncannily familiar to me about these boys, about their facial expressions and posture, their choice of television program, their screening out of all but a few elements in the environment that surrounded them. The correspondences seemed too great for mere coinci-dence; they were not superficial either. The fact that these boys and Adam shared the same ethnic group was far less central to their similarities than was the unmistakable set of fine tunings that transformed disparate individuals into the same general category. Some common denominator was obvious—clear as it would have been if in a gathering of people only a few had blue skin, were seven feet tall, spoke a language no one else understood. (p. 137) ◄

A related pattern, which is less severe than FAS, is that of **fetal alcohol effects (FAE).** These infants are not retarded and do not have the distinguishing facial features characteristic of FAS. However, they share a pattern of disabilities that implicate involvement of the central nervous system, including impulsivity, difficulty in initiating and carrying through with actions, problems with attention and memory, and hyperactivity. Many of these children also experience problems in their relationships with others and have difficulty maintaining friendships. Because of the absence of distinguishing features at birth, most are not diagnosed until childhood (Streissguth, 1994).

Approximately 20% of women drink during pregnancy. Most of these women have at most three, or fewer, drinks a month (National Center for Health Statistics, 1999). Is this a "safe" amount, or is it harmful? How much alcohol is dangerous to the developing infant? What effect will a glass of wine or a toast to one's health have on the developing fetus? As with other teratogens, the effect that

fetal alcohol effects (FAE) A pattern of disabilities related to, but less severe than, fetal alcohol syndrome.

drinking will have on any particular pregnancy cannot be predicted. Even among heavy drinkers, not every fetus chronically exposed to alcohol develops fetal alcohol syndrome (Fried, O'Connell, & Watkinson, 1992). On the other hand, a woman who drinks infrequently but has more than a few drinks at any one time can risk harming the fetus because the threshold for toxicity is more easily reached with "binge" drinking. Something to keep in mind while awaiting a definitive answer is that alcohol distributes evenly throughout all the tissues of the body—which means that the blood level of the mother and the fetus will be the same after a drink. Until data indicate just how much is too much, or whether any amount at all is safe, the most prudent course of action is to refrain from having *any* alcohol during pregnancy. Just as with cigarettes, the use of alcohol carries risks to the infant that can last a lifetime. The Social Policy Focus, "Drinking While Pregnant: Who Should Protect the Unborn?," looks at the question of whether society has a role in protecting embryos and fetuses from the mother's use of alcohol.

Illegal Drugs

Estimates of cocaine use vary widely with age and geographic area, ranging from 3% to nearly 50% of women of childbearing age. Over 15% of women receiving routine prenatal care, in one study, admitted to having used cocaine at least once while pregnant. Across all socioeconomic groups, it is estimated that from 10% to 20% of infants are exposed to cocaine during pregnancy. However, this figure can approach 50% for inner-city populations (Lester, Freier, & LaGasse, 1995, Mayes & Bornstein, 1995).

Cocaine is a central nervous system stimulant that inhibits the uptake of certain neurotransmitters, chemicals that facilitate the passage of impulses from one neuron to that next, thereby producing a state of arousal. It can have both direct and indirect effects on the fetus. Cocaine freely crosses the placenta and can directly affect brain development. It is also a vasoconstrictor, indirectly affecting the fetus by restricting the supply of maternal blood to the fetus. Even more indirectly, frequent cocaine use is associated with a host of health hazards, such as poor nutrition, environmental stress, lack of social supports, and multidrug abuse.

Infants born to mothers who have a history of cocaine use during pregnancy have a greater risk of weighing less at birth and having smaller head sizes. Behaviorally, these infants can be more excitable and irritable or, paradoxically, more lethargic, more difficult to wake or to keep alert (Lester, Freier, & LaGasse, 1995). It is important to note that these infants are not a homogeneous group, and not all infants born to women who have used cocaine during pregnancy have symptoms. At present we know little about the long-term effects of cocaine use, in part because longitudinal studies have only recently begun to follow infants exposed prenatally to cocaine into childhood (Olson, Grant, Martin, & Streissguth, 1995) and in part because of the welter of methodological complexities involved in separating out the effects of cocaine from the host of other risk factors that are frequently present. For instance, not only is exposure to cocaine frequently confounded with the use of other drugs, but also what we know is based on the study of low-income children, where the effects of cocaine are inextricably mixed with those of poverty. (Table 3.3 summarizes the effects of various drugs and environmental contaminants on fetuses and infants.) Comparable studies of middle- and upper-income children do not exist. Finally, most research has focused on potential cognitive and intellectual effects, with the result that we know little about other areas of functioning, such as its social-emotional consequences (Lester, Freier, & LaGasse, 1995).

Social Policy Focus

Drinking While Pregnant: Who Should Protect the Unborn? WITH MICHAEL WAPNER

Michael Dorris (1989), whose oldest adopted son was identified as having fetal alcohol syndrome (FAS), writes of his reaction one day at overhearing a pregnant woman at a nearby table in a restaurant order a martini:

> "Excuse me," I said. "But it's really not safe to drink when you're pregnant. I'm working on a book, and . . ."
>
> "Mind your own business," she snapped back, then turned to her friend and loudly complained about how typical it was for a man to think he knew more than she about her own body. When her drink arrived, she caught my eye and held up the glass in my direction. "Cheers," she said, and took her first sip.

Dorris recounts his feelings at this point:

> There was a part of me that wanted to whip out my wallet, show her Adam's picture, tell her his story. There was a part of me that wanted to make a citizen's arrest or to plead for her baby's brain cells. There was a part of me that wanted to ask her if she intended to fill a formula bottle with gin and vermouth, to feed that to her child when it was born—since there would probably be less harm done at that stage than what she was doing today. But I kept silent, turned away in embarrassment. (p. 199)

No one knew better than this father the developmental implications of consuming alcohol during pregnancy. At the age of 5, his son Adam suffered from seizures, was still not toilet-trained, and hadn't yet learned to count to 5 or name the basic colors. Nor did he seem to connect to his world in the way most children do, imaginatively and inquisitively. Dorris recalls one of the many small behaviors that bespoke the enormity of his son's problems:

> Every morning and late afternoon, as I drove him to and from his school, I talked a steady stream, pointing out interesting sights, asking about his activities, recounting tales of my adventures at work. At its midpoint our route traversed a railroad track. . . .
>
> "Choo choo train!" he sang the first time.
>
> . . . He did the same the next morning and the next evening, and the next and the next. For the two years he attended his day care, he never once failed to chime in, but he rarely said anything else. . . .
>
> It was a small thing, a silly thing to have been upset about. Now that I don't drive that way anymore and that Adam thinks about some other things, those trips can even be fashioned into a funny story of parental overreaction. But at the time, after the first month, there was nothing

humorous about it to me. Adam always crossed those tracks in the same way, as if he had never done so before. . . . He had grasped a single connection in the universe that resonated to him, and it was enough, it was sufficient, it obscured from his view everything behind it. He lacked the quality so celebrated in our species: the desire to see over the top of the next hill. (pp. 43–44)

Adam's mother had been an alcoholic, who drank heavily throughout her pregnancy and who died several years after Adam's birth from acute alcohol poisoning. For many of us, it is all too easy to think of the potential abuse of substances as limited to chemically dependent women living in desperate circumstances. But in an upscale restaurant? With crisp white tablecloths and the sounds of conversation mingled with those of ice clinking softly in water goblets? How many women continue to drink, smoke, or use other dangerous substances during pregnancy? And how many of them are aware of the potential consequences to the fetus of the substances they are using?

Was Michael Dorris's response to this woman out of line? Was her reaction irresponsible and uncaring? More generally, what is the role of society, if any, in protecting the fetus from potential harm? And, conversely, what is the point beyond which society's interest would constitute an intolerable encroachment on personal privacy? *Roe v. Wade* (1973), by legalizing abortion up to a certain point in pregnancy, established that up to that point the embryo or fetus is a part of the mother's body and hence its welfare is the mother's, and not society's, concern. On the other hand, that same Supreme Court decision, by fixing a point beyond which a pregnancy cannot be terminated, also implicated society in protecting the fetus (Cohen, 1995). Does that protection include monitoring the mother's intake of alcohol? If it does, then is the point of transition from personal privacy to public concern the same as for abortion—even though the vulnerability of the unborn begins much earlier? And if the public is given the right to involve itself in a pregnant woman's alcohol intake, what about smoking? What about diet? What about vitamins or regular visits to the doctor? On the other hand, if the conduct of pregnancy is totally the mother's business, then do we imply that society has nothing to say about the willful or ignorant behavior that results in tragedies such as those recounted by Michael Dorris?

Simple answers are not forthcoming. However, a combination of education, social policy, and the funding of supportive structured environments for pregnant women with substance abuse problems is urgently needed.

TABLE 3.3 Some Drugs and Other Substances Associated with Problems in a Fetus or Infant

Drug or Substance	Potential Effects
Accutane (acne medication)	Small head, mental retardation, deformed or absent ears, heart defects, cleft lip and palate
Alcohol	Fetal alcohol syndrome (FAS) or fetal alcohol effect (FAE): unusual facial characteristics, small head, heart defects, mental impairment, defective joints
Antiseizure medications	Small head and possible mental retardation, cleft lip and palate, genital and kidney abnormalities, spina bifida
Cigarette smoking	Miscarriage, stillbirth, low birthweight, increased risk of respiratory problems and sudden infant death (SIDS)
Cocaine	Miscarriage, stillbirth, low birthweight, small head, defects of genital and urinary tract
Lead	Reduced IQ, learning disorder
Lithium	Heart defects
Marijuana	Impaired fetal growth; increase in alcohol-related fetal damage
Mercury	Brain damage
Radiation (high dose)	Small head, growth and mental retardation, multiple birth defects
Streptomycin	Deafness
Tetracycline	Pigmentation of teeth, underdevelopment of enamel
Vitamin A (excess)	Miscarriage; defects of the head, brain, spine, and urinary tract

Source: P. M. Insel & W. T. Roth. (2000). *Core concepts in health* (8th ed.). Mountain View, CA: Mayfield.

Paternal Factors

The father's occupation and lifestyle have come under increasing scrutiny as potential sources of toxicity that might affect fetal development. It can't be said with any certainty whether such exposure brings about genetic changes in the sperm or affects other factors such as the seminal fluid—or whether potentially harmful substances contaminate the home, thereby entering the maternal system and crossing the placenta (Friedler, 1996). Research on the effects of any particular toxin is complicated by numerous difficulties. Even ascertaining exposure is problematic. Some toxins, for instance, can accumulate in parental tissues and not be released until pregnancy, years after the initial exposure occurred (Marcus, Silbergeld, Mattison, & the Research Needs Working Group, 1993). In any case, certain occupations are associated with increased risks to the fetus.

Women whose husbands are agricultural workers or who work in petroleum refineries, rubber manufacturing plants, and operating rooms, for instance, are more likely to spontaneously abort (Olshan & Faustman, 1993). Fathers who are exposed to X-rays and certain chemicals, such as benzene, run a greater risk of having their wives deliver preterm (Savitz, Whelan, & Kleckner, 1989). Also, fathers who work in petroleum and chemical industries and those exposed to paint have a somewhat greater risk of their children having certain types of cancer (Savitz & Chen, 1990; Savitz, Whelan, & Kleckner, 1989). Similarly, male firefighters, who risk exposure to toxic elements in smoke, have a greater risk of birth defects in their children (Olshan, Teschke, & Baird, 1990). Even excessive heat may pose a problem, such as with factory workers who must work close to furnaces. Since researchers have just begun to investigate the potential ways in which men's reproductive capacities can be affected by workplace hazards, we know relatively little about the dangers of different substances. In the absence of clear research findings and because clear guidelines do not exist, industries usually do not alert their male workers to the danger of potential reproductive hazards (Kenen, 1993).

The father's lifestyle can also affect the fetus. There is a modest association, for instance, between paternal smoking and increased risk of stillbirth, preterm deliveries, birth defects, and childhood cancers (as there is for maternal smoking). For instance, Esther John, David Savitz, and Dale Sandler (1991) found that males who were smokers when their infants were conceived had a somewhat greater chance of having their child develop certain childhood cancers than did those who did not smoke, even when the mother was not a smoker. The Research Focus, "Descriptive Statistics: How Harmful *Is* Secondhand Smoke?" considers the effects of passive smoking on birthweight.

The father's use of alcohol prior to conception has also been implicated in fetal development, although not consistently. One study of over 350 fathers found that men who were regular drinkers—that is, who had 1 or more ounces of alcohol a day or one binge (five or more drinks at a time) during the month prior to conception—had infants who weighed 137 g (nearly 5 ounces) less at birth, even when corrections were made for differences in other factors such as paternal smoking and drug use and maternal drinking (Little & Sing, 1987). A larger epidemiological study of over 10,000 births, however, found no relationship between paternal use of alcohol and birthweight (Savitz, Zhang, Schwingl, & John, 1992). These latter researchers point out, however, that most of the fathers in their study drank considerably less than those in the study reporting an effect for alcohol. In other respects, the samples were similar, both being primarily middle-class and healthy. It appears that modest use of alcohol by fathers carries little or no risk to the fetus; however, heavier use may pose a risk. Further research is needed before we can say whether there actually is a risk or just how great that might be.

Older fathers (over 35) are somewhat more likely to have children born with certain types of birth defects, such as cleft palate, heart defects, and hydrocephalus than are younger fathers (Savitz, Schwingl, & Keels, 1991). Most of the previous research has looked only at the effects of the mother's age on birth defects, such as the increase in the frequency of Down syndrome with advanced maternal age (see Chapter 2).

Q Are there any negative effects to the baby from prenatal paternal behaviors? If so, what are they?

How might factors such as the father's use of alcohol prior to conception or exposure to chemicals on the job affect an infant that has not as yet even been conceived? Gladys Friedler (1988, 1996), a researcher at Boston University School of Medicine who has investigated male-mediated effects of toxicity, suggests that more than one mechanism is likely, given the diverse effects that have been observed and the variety of toxins that are involved. It is possible, for instance, for toxins to directly affect sperm, altering the genetic code. Toxins need not cause genetic mutations to be damaging, however, and can affect other factors, such as the motility of sperm or even the rate at which they mature. Conversely, toxins might leave sperm unaffected, but change the composition of the semen in which they are carried, introducing elements that could then be absorbed into the maternal system and affect the developing organism once conception has occurred.

Just how much risk any particular teratogen poses to the fetus or the infant cannot be said in any absolute sense. The risk varies with the presence of other factors. Infants born to very young and older mothers, for instance, are more vulnerable, as are those whose mothers' health and diet are poor. Potential teratogens such as cigarettes, alcohol, or other drugs are capable of exerting both direct and indirect effects. For each of these substances, clearly established physical pathways exist through which development can be affected. For instance, smoking can

Descriptive Statistics: How Harmful *Is* Secondhand Smoke?

Wally left the others in the living room and stepped out onto the front porch, reaching in his shirt pocket and drawing out a cigarette as he did so. Shivering a bit in the crisp night air, he stared off at the surrounding mountains, listening to the coyotes in the distance. When had it become customary, he wondered, for members of his family to not smoke in the house? Thinking back, he couldn't really remember. At this point, he and all the others automatically headed for the door whenever they wanted a cigarette. At times he felt resentful. After all, just how bad could it be for someone to breathe in a little cigarette smoke? It wasn't like actually smoking a cigarette, was it? What was all the fuss about?

Wally, like so many smokers, didn't know just how much of a problem his cigarette smoke could pose for others. He also didn't realize that for infants problems could start well before birth. But how can one link such problems to secondhand cigarette smoke?

Elizabeth Dejin-Karlsson and her associates (1998) in the Department of Community Medicine at Malmoe University Hospital in Sweden asked the same question. They wanted to know whether women who were exposed to the cigarette smoke of others, sometimes referred to as passive smoking, were more likely to give birth to infants who suffered problems as a result of this exposure. They used birthweight as their measure of well-being, with low birthweight signaling problems.

It turns out that one of the best predictors of well-being in infants is how much they weigh at birth, with infants whose weight is below the range of what is considered to be normal being more likely to experience problems. Infants can be low birthweight for a number of reasons. One group of low-birthweight infants that experiences more than its share of problems consists of those who are small for gestational age, weighing less than would be expected for their gestational age even when born full-term.

Dejin-Karlsson and her associates obtained information from nearly 900 women early in their pregnancies concerning a number of lifestyle variables, including the presence of passive smoking ("Do other people smoke near you at home or at work?"). They also obtained information concerning the weight of their infants at birth. They defined low-birthweight infants as those whose weight fell below the range of what is considered to be normal. But how, precisely, is one to say what constitutes a normal range? Weight in newborns, after all, can differ widely and still be considered normal, ranging anywhere from 5½ pounds to 9½ pounds. Who is to say what is "normal" and what is not?

These investigators used a statistical approach in defining a normal range for birthweight. They knew that weight, just like height or intelligence, is **normally distributed.** That is, given a

relatively large sample, such as the one they were studying, if one were to plot the frequency with which each possible birthweight occurred, the resulting distribution would be shaped like a bell (see figure). In addition to their shape, normal distributions are defined by the percentages of cases that fall different distances from the mean. These distances are measured in standardized units that express the average variability among the scores. Just as one can compute the average score for a set of scores, one can also compute the average variability among that set of scores. One such measure of variability is termed the **standard deviation.** In a normal distribution, 66.7% of the cases fall within +1 and −1 standard deviations on either side of the mean, 95% of all the cases fall within +2 and −2 standard deviations, and 99% fall within +3 and −3 standard deviations.

These investigators defined normal birthweight as anything falling within two standard deviations from the mean in either direction. Thus, infants who were small for gestational age were defined as those whose weight was *more* than two standard deviations below the mean. Using this criterion, 6.7% of the infants born to women in this sample were identified as small for gestational age. Of greater importance, however, Dejin-Karlsson and her associates found that passive smoking during early pregnancy was significantly linked to an infant being small for gestational age. In fact, exposure to the cigarette smoke of others *doubled* the chances that a woman would give birth to a small-for-gestational-age infant.

These investigators concluded that the prevalence of small-for-gestational-age infants could be substantially reduced if women were not exposed to others' smoke during pregnancy. This fact, together with the fact that maternal smoking has been identified as a major risk factor for sudden infant death syndrome (Mitchell et al., 1997), should be enough to keep pregnant women a healthy distance from shivering souls such as Wally, as well as to alert them to the very real dangers of smoking cigarettes themselves.

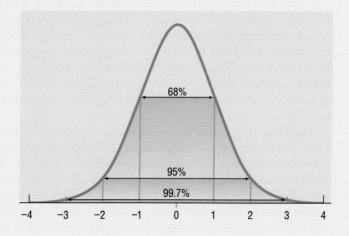

directly affect fetal growth and development by reducing oxygenation in the maternal blood supply. Cigarettes also can indirectly affect development to the extent that smoking affects eating habits; a woman might choose to have a cigarette, for example, instead of a snack, reducing her intake of essential nutrients. Similar examples exist for alcohol and other drugs.

In addition to either the direct or indirect effects of a substance are the broader effects of the physical and social environment into which the child is born. The use of substances such as cigarettes, alcohol, marijuana, and cocaine cuts across all socioeconomic levels. One study found that approximately 15% of pregnant women use alcohol or one or more illegal drugs during pregnancy. The incidence of use differs little between women who go to public clinics (16.3%) or to private physicians (13.1%) or between White women (15.4%) and Black women (14.1%). Despite these similarities in use across socioeconomic and racial lines, however, low-income women are more likely to be studied than middle- or upper-income women, and Black women are 10 times more likely to be studied than are White women (Chasnoff, Landress, & Barrett, 1990). Most of our information about the effects of various substances, in other words, comes from studying children in low-income homes. We do not know whether the same findings would be seen in children raised in middle- or upper-income families. Does this larger developmental context mediate the effects of drug exposure? Factors such as the quality of prenatal care, the number of books in the home, and the caliber of schooling, to mention just a few, have been found to have a developmental impact; and each of these also vary with income level (Ensher & Clark, 1994).

Our understanding of the effects of most teratogens has been guided by an "insult" model. Such models outline the ways in which a substance can alter normal development. However, little is known of how the body or brain compensates for exposure to a substance. Such "recovery" models incorporate protective as well as risk factors in predicting outcomes of exposure, such as differences in the supportiveness of the environment into which exposed infants are born (Lester, Freier, & LaGasse, 1995). In fact, research on newborns with medical complications has found that the quality of the home into which infants are born, rather than their initial condition at birth, is the best predictor of their eventual outcome (Werner, 1994). Margaret Bendersky and her colleagues (1995), examining a variety of predictors of eventual outcome, similarly find that, even with brain insults such as those arising from intraventricular hemorrhage (IVH), environmental factors account for significantly more of the outcome. Both children's language development and their understanding of number, although not their motor development, were affected more by environmental conditions than medical ones (Figure 3.7).

Birth

In the weeks preceding labor, the cervix, the muscular opening to the uterus, begins to soften and dilate, so that with the first gentle contractions, the mucous plug that has sealed off the entrance to the uterus, protecting the fetus from infection, becomes dislodged and is expelled (called the "showing"). Labor involves the work of the uterus, which must accomplish two things. The contractions of the uterus cause the cervix to dilate, or open, enough for the infant to pass through, and they expel the infant. By far the longest part of labor is taken up with dilation of the cervix, in the first stage of labor. The second stage, expulsion of the infant, moves the infant through the birth canal and is much shorter, usually lasting under an hour. In the third stage, the placenta is expelled, taking only a matter of minutes (Figure 3.8).

normally distributed Frequency distributions in which most scores cluster around the middle, or the mean, in the shape of a bell curve.

standard deviation A standardized unit that expresses the average variability among scores.

FIGURE 3.7 Three-Year Outcome Measures *Environmental factors account for more of the outcome in language development and understanding of number than do intraventricular hemorrhage or medical condition at birth.* Source: Adapted from M. Bendersky, S. M. Alessandri, M. W. Sullivan, & M. Lewis (1995). Measuring the effects of prenatal cocaine exposure. In M. Lewis & M. Bendersky (Eds.), *Mothers, babies, and cocaine: The role of toxins in development* (pp. 163–178). Hillsdale, NJ: Erlbaum.

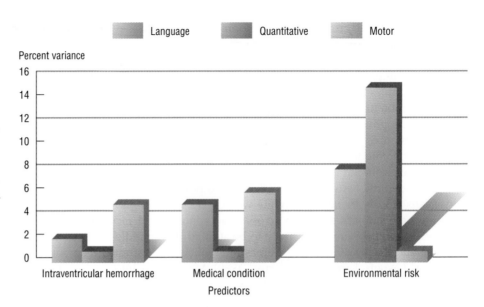

The uterus contracts at the top, where it bunches up and thickens, pulling itself thin at the bottom. With each contraction, the muscle shortens ever so slightly, gradually pulling the cervix open. Contractions are mild at first, increasing in intensity only as labor progresses. The pain of labor comes when the infant's head is forced against the cervix and pelvis. Tightening and tensing the muscles, an involuntary response to pain, works against the uterus. Courses in prepared childbirth teach ways of relaxing during contractions to minimize the pain and speed the course of labor.

The first stage begins with the onset of regular contractions and ends when the cervix has dilated enough to allow passage of the infant's head, approximately 4 inches (10 cm). Contractions initially are brief and spaced far apart, occurring every 15 to 20 minutes. This stage of labor usually takes from 8 to 12 hours for first births and from 6 to 8 hours for subsequent births, although the duration of labor varies considerably. Some of this time will be spent at home. Depending on the hours of the day or night, it is possible to catnap, talk with friends, sit in the sun, count the stars, watch the snow fall, practice one's breathing, repack the bag for the hospital, or wonder about the infant soon to arrive.

The course of labor, once the mother arrives at the hospital, is carefully monitored. Monitoring can be done at regular intervals by a nurse or physician who checks the fetal heartbeat and the dilation of the cervix, or an instrument can be used to continuously monitor the fetus's heart rate and the frequency of contractions. Ultrasound can also be used to determine the position of the infant, so that decisions can be made as to whether to intervene when the infant is in a breech, or feet first, position. For high-risk mothers, the availability of technological support, such as monitoring and surgical intervention, saves lives. However, the use of sensitive monitors may cause physicians to intervene too quickly, interrupting a labor that would otherwise progress safely. For instance, roughly 21% of all births in the United States are by cesarean (National Center for Health Statistics, 1999).

Uterine contractions increase in frequency and intensity with time. When the cervix is nearly completely dilated, contractions reach a peak, coming every 2 to 3 minutes and lasting for as long as a minute apiece. This phase of labor, known as **transition,** is the most difficult for the mother. It is also the shortest part of the first stage and usually lasts under an hour. The presence of a "labor coach," such as the father or a close friend, can help the mother to relax and shortens the actual duration of labor.

transition The phase of labor when uterine contractions reach a peak and the cervix is nearly completely dilated.

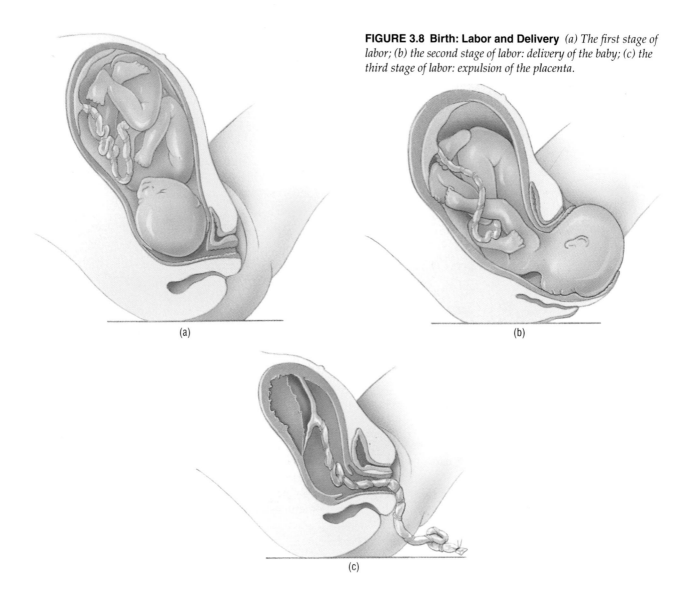

FIGURE 3.8 Birth: Labor and Delivery *(a) The first stage of labor; (b) the second stage of labor: delivery of the baby; (c) the third stage of labor: expulsion of the placenta.*

(a)

(b)

(c)

Louise Erdrich (1996) in *The Blue Jay's Dance,* describes her experience of labor. Though each birth is uniquely personal, her description has a universal quality to it:

> The first part of labor feels, to me anyway, like dance exercises—slow stretches that become only slightly painful as a muscle is pulled to its limit. After each contraction, the feeling subsides. The contractions move in longer waves, one after another, closer and closer together until a sea of physical sensation washes and then crashes over. In the beginning I breathe in concentration, watching Michael's eyes. I feel myself slip beneath the waves as they roar over, cresting just above my head. I duck every time the contraction peaks. As the hours pass and one wave builds on another there are times the undertow grabs me. I struggle, slammed to the bottom, unable to gather the force of nerve for the next. Thrown down, I rely on animal fierceness, swim back, surface, breathe, and try to stay open, willing. Staying *open and willing* is difficult. Very often in labor one must fight the instinct to resist pain and instead embrace it, move toward it, work with what hurts the most.

Lamaze classes teach the mother breathing and relaxation techniques and the father how to be supportive and help her use them.

The waves come faster. Charlotte asks me to keep breathing *yes, yes.* To say yes instead of shuddering in refusal. Whether I am standing on the earth or not, whether I am moored to the dock, whether I remember who I am, whether I am mentally prepared, whether I am going to float beneath or ride above, the waves pound in. At shorter intervals, crazy now, electric, in storms, they wash. Sometimes I'm gone. I've poured myself into some deeper fissure below the sea only to be dragged forth, hair streaming. (pp. 45–46)◄

Labor is difficult for the infant as well. Contractions reduce the amount of oxygen reaching the infant, by constricting the placenta and the umbilical cord. In response, the infant's adrenal glands secrete stress hormones, adrenaline and nor-adrenaline, which increase its heart rate and redirect more blood to the brain, the part of the body that is most sensitive to a reduction in oxygen. These same hormones also ready the respiratory system for breathing.

Grantly Dick-Read, an English physician, argued that the pain of labor could be greatly minimized by reducing the mother's fear, which causes her to tense her muscles, making the work of the uterus more difficult and even prolonging labor. Elizabeth Bing and Rosemary Carmel promoted a similar approach, known as the Lamaze method, in the United States. Each of these approaches encourages an attitude of active work, rather than an attitude in which suffering is anticipated. Couples attend classes where they learn about childbirth. The father is encouraged to take an active, supportive role in the birth process, serving as the mother's labor "coach," assisting her throughout labor and delivery.

In childbirth classes, couples learn breathing techniques that help the woman relax during contractions, thereby lessening pain. Even without these techniques, simply having a supportive companion present can cut the number of hours of labor significantly (Kennell, Klaus, McGrath, Robertson, & Hinkley, 1991). The presence of a labor companion also leads to fewer birth complications for mother

This is termed *informed consent*. In this study, informed consent was requested only after patients were randomly assigned to one group or the other, and then it was requested only of parents assigned to the experimental (KMC) condition. The investigators explain this unusual procedure in the following way. Because mothers in the KMC group are able to leave the hospital with the infants much earlier than mothers in the control group, the KMC group is much more appealing. It was very likely that a majority of the parents would have asked to be in the KMC group. (Indeed, the researchers report a situation in Guatemala where research on KMC had to be terminated because overwhelming parental desire to be in the KMC group disrupted the study.) Consultation with the Ethics Committee of the University to which the hospital belonged led the researchers to conclude that since the control group was receiving the usual care provided in these cases there was no ethical problem in not informing them. In support of this conclusion, it should be noted that this study is different from medical studies in which the experimental group is selected for possibly effective treatment from among sufferers of a condition for which no other adequate treatment is available. In such cases, *untreated controls* are without benefit of any treatment except possible *placebo effects*.

In general, the overriding principle governing any research with humans is to protect the *dignity and welfare* of the subjects who participate in the research. Investigators must inform *all* prospective subjects that their participation is *voluntary* and can be discontinued at any point—assuming that the nature of the research is such that sudden or unscheduled withdrawal is not itself harmful, as might be the case in certain drug studies, a situation of which the subjects must, of course, also be informed. Once individuals agree to serve as subjects, investigators assume responsibility for protecting them from *physical or psychological distress*. Avoidance of "psychological distress" to the subjects is particularly important in psychological or behavioral research where physical dangers are fewer than in medical research, but the possibility of emotional discomfort is still present.

After the data have been collected, it is important for the investigator to *debrief* the subjects, informing them about the nature of the study and removing any misconceptions that may have arisen. If the investigators suspect any undesirable consequences, they have the responsibility to correct them. Any information gained about the participants is, of course, confidential. And should the results of the research be made public, then the *anonymity* of the participants must be maintained.

As it turned out, kangaroo mothering care does seem promising. Growth and body weight were essentially the same among both groups of infants. The number and proportion of deaths were lower among the KMC infants, although not significantly so. The occurrence of serious infections was the same in both groups. But while the frequency of mild-to-moderate infections was higher among KMC infants, the total number of infectious episodes was lower among KMC babies. However, the data gathered do not mention what must have been the enormous psychological and emotional benefits which accrued to both mothers and children in the kangaroo care group.

tion—a frequent predictor of distractibility and attentional problems later in infancy.

Findings such as these perhaps are not that surprising. Most parents of a preterm infant have been warned that their infant will experience somewhat more difficulty falling asleep, waking up, or attending to what is going on. Parents are also told that their child will catch up. And these children do. But not in any simple fashion. Als and her co-workers followed the preterm infants and tested them for various aspects of cognitive functioning 8 years later. These children displayed tremendous variability in their performance on the various measures of intellectual functioning, a child placing as high as three standard deviations above the mean on some subtests (in the very superior range of intellectual functioning) and falling more than a standard deviation below the mean on other measures (in the dull normal to borderline range) (see the Research Focus, "Descriptive Statistics" for an explanation of standard deviation). Figure 3.11 illustrates such variability for one child across the various subscales of the Wechsler Intelligence Scale for Children. Thus, these children will have trouble with some things and be very good at others. Als speculates that the sensory experiences of these children, occurring as they did at a time when their brains were still developing, may have reorganized the normal course of cortical development, accounting for "peaks of excellence" alongside "valleys of disability."

FIGURE 3.11 Test Profile of Early-Born, Medically Healthy Preterm Child *Source:* H. Als. (1995). The preterm infant: A model for the study of fetal brain expectation. In J. P. Lecanuet, W. P. Fifer, N. A. Krasnegor, & W. P. Smotherman (Eds.), *Fetal development: A psychobiological per-spective* (pp. 439–471). Hillsdale, NJ: Erlbaum.

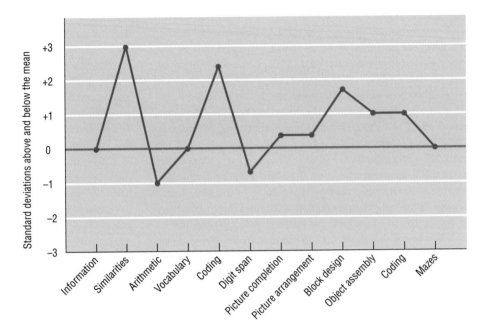

Als (1995) recommends that the experiences of the intensive-care nursery be brought more closely in line with the expected intrauterine experiences for sensory input, with the best index of what is expected being the infant's own behavior. Excessive stimulation, such as loud noises and bright fluorescent lighting is reduced, and nurses are trained to give individualized care, being sensitive to the infant's reactions and guided by the way the infant contributes to its care. Infants assigned at random to individualized care do significantly better than those randomly assigned to traditional care, spending less time on the ventilator, gaining more weight, and leaving the hospital earlier.

Infants also benefit from gentle touch. Tiffany Field and her colleagues investigated the effects of touch by stroking and moving the limbs of preterm infants for 15 minutes, 3 times a day. These investigators have found that infants who are touched gain weight faster than those who are maintained solely in incubators. They also have shorter stays in the hospital before going home (Field et al., 1986; Dawson & Fischer, 1994). A number of studies also have examined the effects of placing preterm infants on waterbeds, since these more closely approximate intrauterine life by moving with the infant's own movements. These infants have been found to have fewer breathing problems than do those on regular mattresses (Dawson & Fischer, 1994).

In many neonatal intensive-care units, preterm infants are benefiting from KMC, "kangaroo mother care," an approach in which the infant is removed from its incubator for several hours each day and placed directly on the mother's or father's chest, skin-to-skin, where it is warmed by the parent's body and soothed by the familiar sounds of a heartbeat. Parents also have a chance to gently touch and stroke the infant. The contact helps regulate the infant's body temperature and breathing. These infants also put on weight faster and show more organized body states, falling asleep better and being more attentive when awake (Dawson & Fischer, 1994). The Research Focus, "Ethics: Kangaroo Mother Care for Low-Birthweight Infants," discusses a study that compared KMC to traditional neonatal intensive care.

What are some of the ways parents and nursing staff can improve the health of and decrease hospital stay time for preterm infants?

Summary

Stages of Prenatal Development

The three stages of prenatal development can be measured from conception, termed gestational age, or from the beginning of the last monthly period. This chapter charts development according to gestational age.

Germinal Stage

The germinal stage begins with fertilization and ends with implantation, approximately 1 week later. Fertilization accomplishes three things: it restores the number of chromosomes to 23 pairs, determines the sex of the child, and initiates cleavage.

Cell Differentiation

Specialized regions in the embryo organize the way cells will develop when they divide. These regions contain hedgehog genes that operate by directing the manufacture of proteins known as morphogens, which tag different cells for the functions they will assume. The tag, or message, is communicated to cells by a gradient of dispersion. Within each cell, regulatory genes control the transcription of DNA, selecting which structural genes will be copied.

Implantation

The cluster of cells, termed a blastocyst, that implants within the lining of the uterus contains two distinct groups of cells, an inner cell mass that will develop into the embryo and an outer cell mass that will develop into the placenta.

Embryonic Stage

The embryonic stage begins with implantation and ends with the appearance of true bone cells, by the 7th or 8th weeks. One of the first events in this stage is gastrulation, in which three distinct layers of cells form from the inner cell mass. Structures that will nourish and support the growth of the embryo—the amniotic sac, the placenta, the umbilical cord, and the yolk sac—develop from the outer cell mass. Two trends characterize development during this and all subsequent stages of development. Development proceeds according to cephalocaudal trend in which growth proceeds from the region of the head downward. A second pattern of growth is the proximodistal trend in which development proceeds from the center of the body outward to the extremities. At the end of the embryonic period, all of the body parts have been formed. The tiny organism has a complete skeleton, the organs have begun to function, and the embryo can react reflexively to events in its surround if stimulated.

Fetal Stage

The physical structures that were largely complete by the end of the embryonic period are refined in the fetal period. By the end of the 2nd month, the fetus has begun to move on its own and by the middle of the 3rd month the whole body is sensitive to touch. Brain growth continues at a rapid pace throughout this stage. With the development of the brain, the activity of the fetus changes and behaviors emerge, such as characteristic cycles of sleeping and waking. The senses have also begun to develop, enabling the fetus to react to its surroundings. The fetus becomes viable by the 7th month, although infants born at this age require special postnatal care.

Maternal Changes

Many women experience some nausea early in pregnancy. The hormonal changes contributing to nausea can also cause sleepiness and emotional lability. Many women report feeling in peak condition during the second trimester. Their bodies have adjusted to the additional demands made by pregnancy, and the fetus has not yet grown to a size where it is a source of discomfort. By the third trimester, because of the increasing size of the fetus, women may again experience some discomfort and have difficulty sleeping.

Health Factors and Health Hazards

Substances that interfere with normal development are called teratogens. The extent to which any particular teratogen will affect a fetus depends on the timing and the amount of exposure. An organ is most vulnerable during the time of its most rapid growth. Since different parts of the body develop at different times, a substance can affect one organ and leave others unaffected. The amount of a teratogen the fetus is exposed to also determines its effect. Some teratogens have cumulative effects; the more the fetus is exposed to the substance, the greater the effect. Other teratogens must reach a critical level before they have an effect.

Maternal Nutrition and Stress

Maternal nutrition is an important factor affecting prenatal development. Eating a variety of foods supplies most of the minerals and vitamins needed; however, some supplements, such as of iron, calcium, and folic acid, are recommended. Supplements need to be taken with caution, as too much can cause as much harm as too little. There is also some evidence that maternal stress can adversely affect fetal development.

Infections

The fetus can be infected by exposure to organisms that initially infect the mother and then cross the placenta to infect the fetus, or it can be infected during birth by coming into contact with organisms in the birth canal.

Cigarettes

Smoking during pregnancy poses a significant and serious risk to the fetus. Women who smoke have smaller babies, more miscarriages and stillbirths; give birth to infants with more health complications; and are more likely to have an infant die of sudden infant death syndrome during the 1st year of life. Secondhand smoke has also been associated with increased risks to the fetus.

Alcohol

Alcohol is a powerful teratogen that can affect many aspects of fetal development. Women who are heavy drinkers during pregnancy are more likely to give birth to infants with a pattern of deficits that includes mental retardation, low birthweight, heart defects, and atypical facial features. However, because alcohol's effects are threshold-dependent, even women who do not consider themselves to be drinkers, but who may have a number of drinks over a short period of time, expose the fetus to increased risk.

Paternal Factors

Occupations in which men are exposed to certain chemicals, X-rays, or excessive heat have been found to affect men's reproductive capacities, and fetal development. Leisure activities, such as smoking and use of alcohol, have also been associated with effects on fetal development.

Birth

The first stage of labor takes from 8 to 12 hours for first births and begins with the onset of regular contractions. The second stage of labor begins when the cervix has dilated sufficiently for the infant's head to pass through; once the head is in the birth canal, the actual birth is completed in a matter of minutes. In the third stage of labor, the placenta separates from the uterine wall and is expelled; this stage is the briefest of all.

Assessing the Newborn

The physical condition of the infant is checked using the Apgar scale, which assesses heart rate, breathing, reflexes, muscle tone, and color.

Low-Birthweight and Preterm Infants

Infants who weight less than 5½ pounds (2,500 g) are considered low birthweight. Low birthweight results from two distinct causes: intrauterine growth retardation and preterm birth. The first type of infant is considered to be small for gestational age. Infants whose birth precedes the due date by more than 3 weeks are considered preterm. Because preterm infants are born before critical aspects of brain development are completed, their experiences following birth have the potential for influencing the course of subsequent brain development. The brain responds to stimulation in two related ways: the presence of stimulation facilitates the formation of connections between neurons, and the absence of stimulation results in selective cell death. The stimulation experienced by preterm infants may contribute to both types of responsiveness in ways that differ from those of full-term infants.

Key Terms

active sleep (p. 92)
actively awake (p. 93)
amniotic sac (p. 87)
Apgar scale (p. 117)
ascending infections (p. 102)
axon (p. 91)
blastocyst (p. 83)
cephalocaudal trend (p. 89)
cleavage (p. 82)
corpus luteum (p. 83)
cytomegalovirus (p. 102)
dendrites (p. 91)
ectoderm (p. 87)
endoderm (p. 87)
endometrium (p. 83)
episiotomy (p. 117)
experience-dependent mechanisms (p. 123)
experience-expectant mechanisms (p. 123)

fetal alcohol effects (FAE) (p. 107)
fetal alcohol syndrome (FAS) (p. 106)
gastrulation (p. 87)
gonorrhea (p. 103)
hedgehog genes (p. 84)
hepatitis B (p. 103)
herpes (p. 103)
human immunodeficiency syndrome (HIV) (p. 103)
inner cell mass (p. 86)
lanugo (p. 94)
low birthweight (p. 118)
mesoderm (p. 87)
morphogens (p. 84)
morula (p. 82)
neurotransmitters (p. 91)
normally distributed (p. 113)
outer cell mass (p. 86)
placenta (p. 88)
preterm (p. 119)

proximodistal trend (p. 89)
quiet sleep (p. 92)
quietly awake (p. 93)
rubella (p. 102)
sudden infant death syndrome (SIDS) (p. 105)
small for gestational age (SGA) (p. 119)
standard deviation (p. 113)
surfactant (p. 94)
syphilis (p. 103)
teratogens (p. 97)
toxoplasmosis (p. 103)
transition (p. 114)
transplacental infections (p. 102)
trophoblast (p. 86)
umbilical cord (p. 88)
vernix (p. 94)
yolk sac (p. 89)

chapterfour

Infancy and Toddlerhood
Physical Development

S oon smiles dapple the sunlight, and gurgles soften the edges of silence. The newborn emerges from its warm cocoon and balances on each new moment, unfolding a pattern of expressions and moods to the delight of all. Routines of feeding and sleeping shape the hours of parents and infant alike. Parents report that their infant's personality becomes more recognizable with each new day, few realizing the ways in which theirs are changing as well. Like partners in a dance, the steps taken by one determine the other's next movements. This chapter looks at the rhythms of growth within the first 2 years of life and at the steps, first tentative and then flowing, of the social dance.

The Newborn: The Biological Beat to Life

Birth involves neonates in the basics—breathing, keeping warm, eating, and sleeping. All of these require adjustment to life outside the uterus. Breathing is irregular, control of body temperature uneven, and swallowing unsteady. Infants startle easily and cry and sneeze at the drop of a feather. Instead of sustained behavior, they show fitful activity. Neither sleeping nor waking are well defined (Sahni, Schulze, Stefanski, Myers, & Fifer, 1995). Almost everything requires more effort than it did before or will later. As a result, neonates tire quickly.

Breathing

With the first breath, a valve inside the heart closes. The flow of blood shifts from the umbilical arteries that took it to the placenta for oxidation to the lungs. Breathing is usually irregular for the first 2 or 3 days. It is also noisy. Most neonates cough, sneeze, and wheeze, all of which helps to clear passages of mucus and fluids. Initially, infants are "belly breathers," relying on the muscles of the diaphragm to breath. When they begin to sit upright, however, additional muscles come into play, the rib cage expands, and breathing becomes more efficient (Cech & Martin, 1995).

Body Temperature

Keeping warm is another problem the newborn faces. In the uterus, regulation of body temperature, like everything else, was taken care of by the mother's body. With birth, this changes. The delivery room is 20 degrees colder than the uterine world—an especially noticeable change for the infant, who arrives naked and wet. Even when diapered and dry, neonates lack the protective layer of fat that insulates older infants from rapid changes in temperature. A light covering, even in rooms comfortable to adults, may be necessary until body temperature stabilizes.

Eating

Nourishment is no longer automatically supplied as it was prior to birth, and hunger, as such, is a new experience. Most infants lose approximately 6 to 10 ounces immediately following birth. Fluids previously supplied by the maternal system are no longer taken in, and more are lost through elimination. Once infants start to nurse or take in formula, they begin to put on weight.

States of Arousal

Patterns of sleeping and waking change dramatically in the 1st year of life. In adults, the sleep-wake cycle consists of a period of sleep lasting anywhere from 6

Active sleep accounts for about 50% of a newborn's sleep time.

to 10 hours and a longer period of wakefulness lasting from 14 to 18 hours. This cycle is sometimes referred to as a circadian cycle (from the Latin words *circa,* which means "about," and *dies,* which means "day"). Most infants will establish a stable circadian rhythm between 2 and 4 months of age. Prior to this time, they are on a 4-hour sleep-wake cycle, in which they alternate among a number of states of arousal, ranging from quiet sleep to active wakefulness (see Chapter 3). In **quiet sleep,** the body is relaxed, heart rate and breathing are slow, and brain wave activity is regular; eyelids are closed and the eyes are motionless. In **active sleep,** the infant's arms and legs occasionally twitch, facial expressions appear, and the eyes dart back and forth beneath closed eyelids. This sleep state is often referred to as REM sleep, referring to the **rapid eye movements (REM)** that characterize it. Even though the infant is clearly asleep, heart rate and breathing are irregular and the brain wave activity is similar to that of a waking state (Blumberg & Lucas, 1996). In **drowsiness,** a state in which infants are either waking up or falling asleep, the body is almost as relaxed as in quiet sleep; breathing is regular; and the eyes, though frequently open, have a glassy look to them. **Quiet wakefulness** is one of two waking states, in which the infant is relaxed, moving its body little, but keeping its eyes open and attentive. **Active wakefulness** is punctuated with brief bodily activity; breathing becomes irregular, and facial expressions appear. Crying also occurs in this state (Nijhuis, 1995).

When they are asleep, infants, just like adults, can be seen to move in and out of active, or REM, sleep. In fact, newborns spend about 50% of the time they are asleep in active sleep, in contrast to 20% for adults. This percentage steadily declines until, somewhere between the ages of 3 and 5 years, the adult level is reached. Developmental trends such as this one are intriguing and prompt developmentalists to ask why very young infants spend as much time as they do in REM sleep. In adults, dreaming most frequently occurs in REM sleep; however, it is doubtful that rapid eye movements are a sign of dreaming in very young infants. Instead, active sleep appears to plays a role in the development of the central nervous system. The spontaneous neural activity that occurs in this state may be critical in establishing neural pathways, as well as in determining which

quiet sleep A sleep state characterized by relative inactivity except for brief startles; there are no rapid eye movements (REM); also known as NREM (non-REM) sleep.

active sleep A sleep state characterized by frequent body movements; also known as REM sleep because of the presence of rapid eye movements.

rapid eye movements (REM) Rapid movements of the eyes beneath closed lids during certain sleep stages.

drowsiness A state of either falling asleep or waking up when the body is relaxed, breathing is regular, and the eyes have a dreamy stare.

quiet wakefulness A waking state in which an infant is relaxed and attentive and moves its body little.

active wakefulness A waking state characterized by frequent and vigorous movement.

Box 4.1 *Sudden Infant Death Syndrome (SIDS)*

Every year thousands of infants in the United States with no obvious health problems die in their sleep. Typically, these infants are several months old, have begun to put on weight, are happy, sociable, and well cared for. They die from sudden infant death syndrome (SIDS), the second leading cause of death among infants in the United States. They die because they simply stop breathing during the night.

Despite extensive research, the cause or, more likely, causes of SIDS remain unknown. However, a number of risk factors have been identified. One of the most important of these is the position in which an infant sleeps. A 3-year nationwide study in New Zealand identified the prone sleeping position as the leading risk factor associated with SIDS. Infants who are placed prone—that is, on their stomachs or abdomens—were more than twice as likely to die of SIDS than were infants placed on their backs (Mitchell et al., 1997). A review of other studies reports even higher odds in many of these (Henderson-Smart, Ponsonby, & Murphy, 1998; Oyen et al., 1997). Although not as dangerous as the prone position, the side sleeping position is also associated with a greater risk of SIDS (Fleming et al., 1996; Mitchell et al., 1997). Before research investigating the effects of sleeping position was done, pediatricians had actually recommended the prone and side positions over the supine position (sleeping on one's back), assuming that infants would be less likely to choke if they spit up during the night. This concern, however, has turned out to be unfounded. A large-scale study of over 8,000 infants in Britain found that infants in the supine position were not more likely to regurgitate milk or choke. In fact, sleeping in the prone position was somewhat more likely to lead to choking if infants vomited during sleep (Hunt, Fleming, & Golding, in press).

A second factor that significantly increases the risk of SIDS is parental smoking. Maternal smoking alone contributes substantially to the risk that infants will die while sleeping; and when both parents smoke, this risk is increased even further (Mitchell et al., 1997). Hillary Konoff-Cohen, an epidemiologist at the University of San Diego, found that infants exposed to cigarette smoke, either from mothers who continue to smoke during the months of breast-feeding, from caretakers, or fathers, are from 2 to 3 times more likely to die of SIDS than are those not passively exposed to cigarette smoke. In this research, a group of 200 infants who had died of SIDS was compared with a similar group of healthy infants. Care had been taken to equate the two groups for other factors associated with SIDS, such as sleeping position and whether the baby had been breast-fed

Q Why might very young infants need to spend so much time in REM sleep?

neurons will continue to exist (many more are initially produced than are needed), eliminating excessive interconnections among neurons and their targets, and in promoting the organization of neural centers (Blumberg & Lucas, 1996).

The most significant change in patterns of sleeping and waking is not so much the *amount* of time infants spend asleep or awake, but *how long* they stay in either state. Year-old infants sleep almost as much as newborns, about 13 hours in comparison to the newborn's 16 hours. However, they sleep longer when they nap, and they can stay awake for longer periods of time in between. For the 1st month, infants are awake for only short periods of time, taking as many as six or seven naps a day. By 2 months, the number of naps decreases to three or four longer ones, and by 7 months to one or two a day. Also, by this time, most infants sleep through the night. Of course, there are wide individual differences in the amount of sleep infants need and in how active they are when awake. Although parents

(Klonoff-Cohen et al., 1995). Infants with the highest risk were those who were routinely in the same room as someone who smoked, the risk of death being as much as 8 times higher than that of infants not passively exposed to cigarette smoke. As in previous research, the risk to the infant was "dose-dependent," increasing with the amount of smoke the infants were exposed to (Klonoff-Cohen et al., 1995).

Based on data collected in a Nordic epidemiological SIDS study, it is estimated that the number of SIDS deaths could have been reduced by nearly half (46.7%) had mothers not smoked during pregnancy (Oyen et al., 1997). The increased risk to the infant from smoking is dose-dependent, increasing with the number of cigarettes that the mother smokes (Henderson-Smart, Ponsonby, & Murphy, 1998). Since it is difficult to stop smoking, prospective parents should ask for help from their doctor or seek out other professional help. Smoking increases the risk not only of SIDS but also of a multitude of medical and health problems in infants.

Another condition that has been found to place infants at risk for SIDS is being too warm or, less frequently, too cold. Infants who are dressed too warmly when put to bed, who are covered with too many blankets, or who sleep in an excessively warm room are at a greater risk of SIDS. This risk is further increased if they are placed in the prone position, since the face is the primary region for heat loss when infants are covered in thick clothing or bedding. Becoming too cold is also a problem. A general rule is to clothe infants as one would dress oneself in order to be comfortable. However, if the infant has a fever, one should use fewer coverings than otherwise (Henderson-Smart, Ponsonby, & Murphy, 1998).

Finally, bed sharing is also associated with an increased risk of SIDS if either parent smokes. There does not appear to be a risk of SIDS from sleeping in the same bed with parents who do not smoke, although parents should take care that the infant does not slip beneath the covers or have its breathing blocked by pillows. In summary, parents can significantly reduce the risk of sudden infant death syndrome by

- Laying the infant on its back
- Keeping the infant in a smoke-free environment
- Preventing the infant from getting too hot while sleeping
- Not sharing a bed with the infant if the parents smoke

are always relieved to have their children sleep through the night, they also worry about SIDS; Box 4.1 discusses risk factors.

One of the landmark events, for most American parents, occurs when their infant sleeps through the night. Prior to this, new parents stumble awake several times each night to feed a hungry infant. Many attempt to forestall the inevitable by getting in one last feeding before putting the infant down for the night, hoping for an uninterrupted night's sleep. These challenges are not universally experienced in other cultures; they have more to do with the sleeping arrangements of most North American families than with the sleeping patterns of individual infants. In our culture, many infants are put to bed in a room separate from that of their parents. When infants wake in the night, parents must get out of bed and go into the other room for a feeding. By that time, everyone is completely awake. In many cultures, including industrialized ones such as Japan, infants sleep in the

Weight in pounds

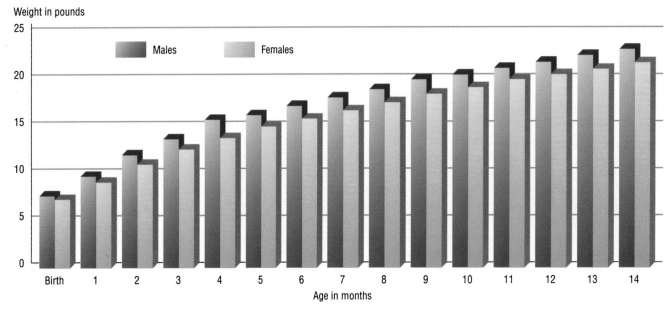

FIGURE 4.1 Mean Weight of Infants from Birth to 14 Months *Source:* S. J. Foman & S. E. Nelson. (1993). Size and growth. In S. J. Foman (Ed.), *Nutrition of normal infants.* St. Louis: Mosby.

same room as their parents, often in the same bed or in a cradle beside the bed. When the infant wakes, it is a simple matter to reach over and tend to its needs.

As basic rhythms of sleeping and waking stabilize, larger rhythms develop that include other members of the family. These rhythms are achieved largely through trial and error, learning when, for instance, to expect smiles and rapt glances with a feeding and when milk will be a sleepy punctuation to the night. Before such rhythms become established, life with a new baby has a jet set quality to it—late hours, an unfamiliar partner, and the feeling of always being on the move.

Many new parents simply have no idea of what it will be like having a new baby or of what parenting an infant will require of them. An infant's cries are particularly demanding. As Anne Lamott wrote of her infant son, "Between the tears and the cooing and his crazy drunken-old-man smiles, it's almost unbearable. There's so much joy and pain and love." Despite the complexity and maturity of her response, this mother was still not prepared for all that was involved in being a parent, at one point writing in the journal she was keeping, "I just can't get over how much babies cry. I really had no idea what I was getting into. To tell you the truth, I thought it would be more like getting a cat" (Lamott, 1993, p. 66). ◄

Physical Growth

At birth, infants weigh about 7 pounds and are about 20 inches long. Growth in the first year is rapid. Weight triples and body length increases by half again. When their first birthday comes around, most infants weigh just over 20 pounds and measure approximately 30 inches. Growth is less rapid in the 2nd year, infants adding another 5 pounds and growing 5 inches. Most children continue to add 4 to 5 pounds a year, and another 2 to 3 inches, for the next 3 years (Figures 4.1 and 4.2).

As infants grow, the proportions of their bodies also change. At birth the head accounts for one quarter of the infant's entire body, the legs contributing only one third of its length. By 2 years of age, the lower half of the body begins to catch up, and the legs account for almost half the body's length. Not all parts of the body, in other words, grow at the same rate. Growth during infancy, as well as prior to birth, reflects two growth trends, the **cephalocaudal growth trend,** in

cephalocaudal growth trend The developmental pattern in which growth begins in the regions of the head and proceeds downward.

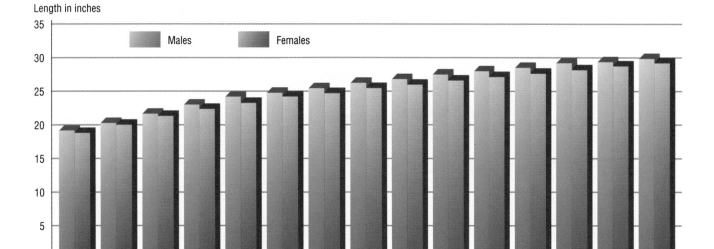

FIGURE 4.2 Mean Length of Infants from Birth to 14 Months *Source:* S. J. Foman & S. E. Nelson. (1993). Size and growth. In S. J. Foman (Ed.), *Nutrition of normal infants.* St. Louis: Mosby.

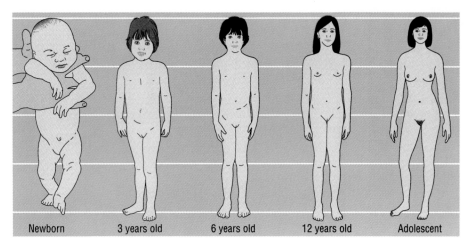

FIGURE 4.3 Changes in Body Proportions with Age *Source:* V. G. Payne & L. D. Isaacs. (1995). *Human motor development: A lifespan approach.* Mountain View, CA: Mayfield.

which growth begins in the region of the head and proceeds downward, and the **proximodistal growth trend,** in which growth progresses outward from the center of the body to the extremities (see Chapter 3). This latter growth trend can be seen in the early growth of the chest and trunk, then of the arms and legs, and finally the hands and feet (Figure 4.3).

Growth of Body Fat and Muscle

The ounces and pounds that infants add in the first weeks and months of life are due primarily to increases in body fat. Infants begin to add a layer of fat directly beneath the skin in the weeks just preceding birth and continue to do so after birth, with increases in body fat peaking by about 9 months. Body fat serves a number of useful functions, providing a protective layer of insulation that helps infants regulate their body temperature and also serving as an emergency reserve of nutrients.

Increases in muscle tissue develop more slowly. In the 2nd year, infants begin to add muscle, slimming out as they do. A spurt in the development of muscle occurs at about 2 years, followed by a relatively steady increase in muscle throughout childhood. As muscle tissue develops, the type of muscle tissue also

Q Why is it healthy for infants to have a layer of body fat directly beneath the skin?

proximodistal growth trend The developmental pattern in which growth progresses outward from the center of the body to the extremities.

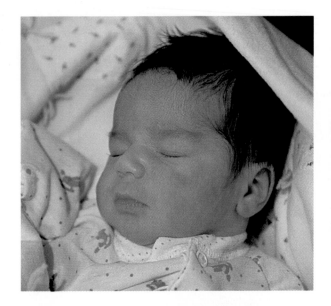

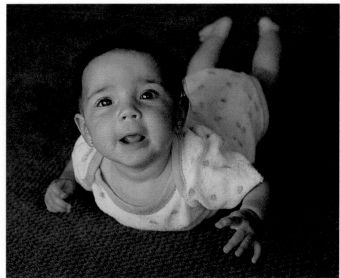

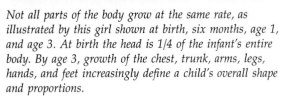

Not all parts of the body grow at the same rate, as illustrated by this girl shown at birth, six months, age 1, and age 3. At birth the head is 1/4 of the infant's entire body. By age 3, growth of the chest, trunk, arms, legs, hands, and feet increasingly define a child's overall shape and proportions.

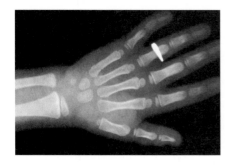 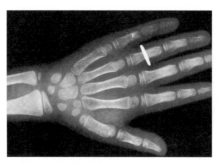 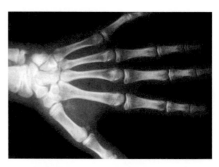

FIGURE 4.4 The Growth of Small Bones in the Wrists—at 3, 5, and 14 Years *Source:* V. G. Payne & L. D. Isaacs. (1995). *Human motor development: A lifespan approach.* Mountain View, CA: Mayfield.

changes. For the 1st year of life, muscles are predominantly fast-contracting ones. At about 1 year, slow-contracting muscles begin to develop, allowing infants greater control over their movements (Wilder, 1995).

Skeletal Growth

Bone growth occurs rapidly during both infancy and early childhood, with existing bones increasing in size and density, new bones emerging, and the overall alignment of bones changing.

The Growth of Existing Bones Prior to birth, a complete skeleton develops out of a supple substance known as cartilage, which calcifies and becomes bone. During infancy and childhood, existing bones grow both in length and in thickness. Bone growth takes place in each of two growth centers, or **epiphyseal growth plates,** near either end of the bone. These growth centers produce new cells that eventually harden into bone. As the bone reaches its adult length, the growth plates narrow and finally fuse with the ends of the bone, preventing any further bone growth (Cech & Martin, 1995).

The Emergence of New Bone Skeletal growth also occurs through the emergence of new bones. The small bones forming the wrists and ankles, for instance, develop from ossification centers, which turn into spongy bone tissue that, over time, hardens into bone (Cech & Martin, 1995). Figure 4.4 shows how new bones form in a child's wrist with age.

The bony plates forming the skull also grow in this way. At birth, the skull bones are separated by gaps, or **fontanels.** These allow the bones of the skull to overlap each other as the head squeezes through the birth canal. Following birth, in fact, an infant's head may be somewhat pointed, molded by the narrow birth canal. The fontanels also allow the skull to grow to accommodate increases in brain size. The fontanels gradually close after the 1st year (Figure 4.5).

Skeletal Alignment

As infants begin to move about, putting stresses on the skeletal system, various bones realign themselves to accommodate the forces of movement. The spine in infants, for instance, is initially much straighter than it is in adults, with the curvature in the upper region occurring as infants begin to sit upright and that in the lower region occurring as they begin to walk. Similarly, the alignment of the leg bones changes, as does that of the pelvis, once the infant begins to move about. For instance, in comparison to infants, who are bow-legged, the knees of 3-year-olds turn in, giving them a knock-kneed gait. Surprisingly, sitting upright and walking also have implications for breathing. In infants, the ribs extend out

epiphyseal growth plates In a child, areas near the ends of a bone that produce new cells.

fontanels In an infant, gaps between the bony plates of the skull.

FIGURE 4.5 The Bony Plates, or Fontanels, Forming the Skull in the Newborn *Source:* T. W. Sadler. (1990). *Langman's medical embryology* (6th ed.). Baltimore: Williams and Wilkins.

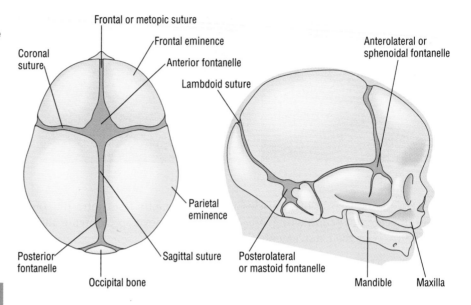

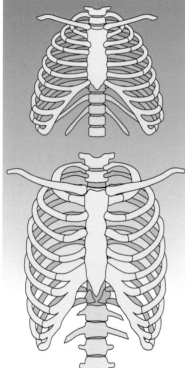

FIGURE 4.6 Changes in Skeletal Alignment with Age *The rib cage of an infant (top) and of an adult (bottom).* *Source:* D. Cech & S. Martin. (1995). *Functional movement development across the life span.* Philadelphia: W. B. Saunders.

neurons Brain cells responsible for the conduction of nerve impulses.

glial cells Cells that support and nourish neurons and produce myelin.

horizontally, rather than sloping downward as they do in adults. Gravity and the use of abdominal muscles, both involved in maintaining an upright position, pull the ribs down, increasing the space between them and, as a result, making breathing all that much easier. Figure 4.6 shows these changes (Cech & Martin, 1995).

Nutrition plays an important role in skeletal growth. Adequate amounts of protein, calcium, and vitamins C and D are essential for bone growth. Also, because bone growth is so rapid in the early years, children's bodies are especially responsive to corrective therapies of disorders such as club foot or hip dislocation.

Brain Development

The brain continues to develop following birth, doubling in weight by 6 months, at which point it weighs about half that of the adult brain. Development of the brain proceeds unevenly, with spurts of brain growth occurring between 3 and 10 months and again between 15 and 24 months. Most of the 100 billion **neurons,** or brain cells responsible for the conduction of nerve impulses, are present at birth. The increase in the size of the brain is due to the proliferation of **glial cells,** which support and nourish the neurons. Glial cells outnumber neurons 10 to 1, but since they are much smaller than neurons, they make up only about half of the brain tissue (Cech & Martin, 1995).

In addition to nourishing the neurons, the rapidly spreading glial cells serve another important function. They produce **myelin,** a fatty substance that coats the **axon** of the neuron, the long filament extending out from the cell body, by which the neuron makes contact with other nerve cells, thereby transmitting neural messages (Figure 4.7). Fibers coated with a myelin sheath conduct impulses at higher speeds than do those without a myelin covering.

Myelination of nerve fibers progresses at different rates for different parts of the brain. The **peripheral nervous system,** which connects the sensory receptors and muscles to the brain and spinal cord, as well as connecting the internal organs and glands to the brain, is first to be myelinated. These fibers are largely myelinated at birth, thus ensuring that the newborn is able to receive and act on information from the various sensory systems. The one exception are the fibers in the optic tract, those responsible for vision, which is the least mature of the senses at birth (Cech & Martin, 1995).

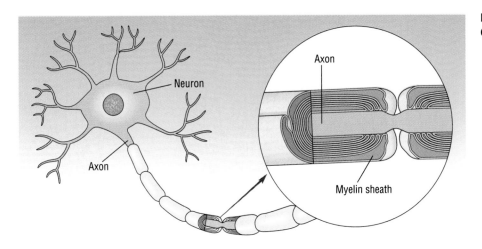

FIGURE 4.7 **Myelin Sheath Coating Axon**

Myelination of neurons within the **central nervous system,** the spinal cord and the brain itself, is completed later. Here, too, the order of myelination mirrors the order in which various areas of the brain begin to function at more mature levels. For instance, fibers in the spinal cord and the part of the brain controlling vital functions such as breathing, regulating temperature, eating, and sleeping are first to be myelinated. Myelination underlies other developments as well, which are reflected in the infant's behavior. For instance, the 24-hour cycle of sleeping and waking that develops between 2 and 4 months of age can be seen to correspond to new patterns of electrical activity in the brain. With increasing periods of alertness, there is greater opportunity for social interaction, and most parents see social smiles starting at about 2 months of age. Some of the last fibers to myelinate are those in the frontal cortex, the area most responsible for thought, conscious experience, and intentional behavior (Cech & Martin, 1995).

Even though the number of neurons does not increase following birth, the neurons themselves continue to develop with age. The length of axons increases, and tiny branchlike fibers, or dendrites, at the end of the axon increase in density over the first 2 years of life (Figure 4.8). These increases make possible many more interconnections between neurons than previously were possible.

Recall from Chapter 3 that the infant's experiences are thought to contribute in different ways to the brain's development, some types of stimulation being necessary for the *establishment* of neural connections, thereby enabling the infant to hold on to new experiences, and other types of stimulation being necessary for the *maintenance* of connections laid down by the nervous system in anticipation of usage, connections that would be lost in the absence of experience (Greenough, Black, & Wallace, 1987). The importance of early experiences is supported by research with laboratory animals which finds, for instance, that rats reared from infancy in living conditions that have been enriched with interesting things to do, such as mazes, activity wheels, and the presence of other animals, have more synaptic connections than do those reared alone in empty cages. Their brains also weigh more and produce more of an enzyme that is important in learning (Globus, Rosenzweig, Bennett, & Diamond, 1973; Rosenzweig, 1984).

The specialization of function that occurs with different types of experiences begins from birth on. With age, different areas within the cortex become specialized in their control over different types of functions. As a consequence, injuries to the brain that occur early in infancy typically have less damaging effects than do those occurring later.

Q How does an infant benefit from having toys, such as rattles and over-the-crib mobiles?

Q Why do injuries to the brain in early infancy frequently have less serious consequences than those occurring later?

myelin A fatty substance that coats axons and increases the speed of conduction of nerve impulses.

axon A long filament extending from a nerve cell, through which neural impulses are transmitted.

peripheral nervous system That part of the nervous system that connects the sensory receptors and muscles and glands and internal organs to the central nervous system.

central nervous system The brain and the spinal cord.

FIGURE 4.8 The Growth of Dendrites in the First 2 Years Following Birth *Source:* J. L. Conel. (1975). *The postnatal development of the human cerebral cortex.* Cambridge, MA: Harvard University Press.

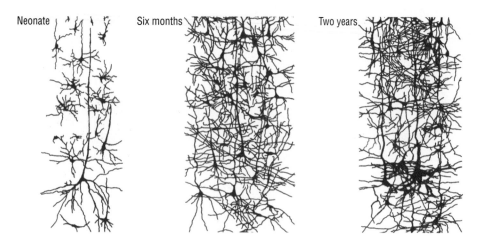

Neonate   Six months   Two years

Development of the Senses

Once thought to be passive, socially unresponsive, and possessed of senses dimmer than those of an octogenarian, our view of the newborn has changed dramatically. Only moments old, the newborn will turn toward the sound of a voice, searching for its source, or will follow a face, turning head and eyes to keep it in view. The newborn can distinguish speech from nonspeech sounds and moves in synchrony to the sounds of human voices. Newborns, in fact, appear to obtain many of the same pleasures from their senses as do individuals at any age, distinguishing not only sounds and sights, but tastes and smells as well.

Taste and Smell

Taste may provide one of the infant's first pleasures. Infants can distinguish sweet, salty, sour, and bitter tastes. They also have taste preferences right from the start, being born with a "sweet tooth," it seems, and showing an aversion to substances that taste bitter or sour.

In addition to allowing infants to savor their food, taste receptors may serve a more practical function. Research with newborn animals finds that when drops of plain water, sweetened water, or milk reach the larynx, the animals momentarily stop breathing, which prevents them from inhaling the liquid. When the water is salty, however, this protective mechanism is not triggered. A similar mechanism in neonates coordinates breathing and swallowing, taste receptors on the epiglottis triggering a reflex that stops breathing. Just like the experimental animals, neonates are less likely to inhale milk or water, both low in natural salts, than a salty solution. On a practical note, breast milk has less salt than commercial formulas (Lawrence, 1994). This is not to suggest that infants will experience difficulties when bottle-fed with a commercially prepared formula, but if an infant is choking while feeding, it might pay to check the salt content of the formula or to switch brands (Acredolo & Hake, 1982).

Much of one's sense of taste is actually provided by smell. The sense of smell, or olfaction, is triggered by molecules in the air that reach receptors inside the nose. Preterm infants as young as 28 weeks (38 weeks is full term) react to strong smells, just as do full-term infants months later (Acredolo & Hake, 1982). The sense of smell is highly developed. In fact, infants who are breast-fed can even discriminate the smell of their mother's milk from that of other nursing women, turning their head in the direction of a breast pad soaked with their mother's milk

The sense of smell in newborns is so acute that infants who are breast-fed can recognize the smell of their mother's milk.

in preference to one soaked with the milk of another mother (MacFarlane, 1975). Even infants who are not breast-fed appear to prefer the smell of breast milk to that of their formula, turning more to the breast milk when given a choice (Porter, Makin, Davis, & Christensen, 1992).

Vision

Of all the senses on which we humans rely, vision is the most important. It is also the least mature at birth. Dramatic changes occur within the 1st year in infants' ability to follow moving objects with their eyes, in visual acuity, and even in perceiving the very unity of objects at first (Johnson & Aslin, 1995).

In previous chapters, we have spoken of children as "meaning makers," continually engaged in a process of putting together, or constructing, the events to which they respond. But at what age do such constructive activities begin? Do *infants* assemble reality from the perceptual scraps offered up by their senses? And if they do, what patterns do they bring with them by which to fashion a larger whole?

Marshall Haith (1980, 1993), a psychologist at the University of Denver, has studied the way infants obtain information about their visual world. Haith recorded the eye movements of newborns, 24 to 96 hours old, as they scanned their environment. Haith discovered that, rather than passively waiting for objects to come into view, newborns actively search for things in the visual field. Comparisons of eye movements from one infant to the next revealed that all infants

Vision is the least mature of the senses at birth. As dramatic changes occur within the first year, what some research suggests are "rules for scanning" as inborn capacities emerge by which the infant actively engages the world.

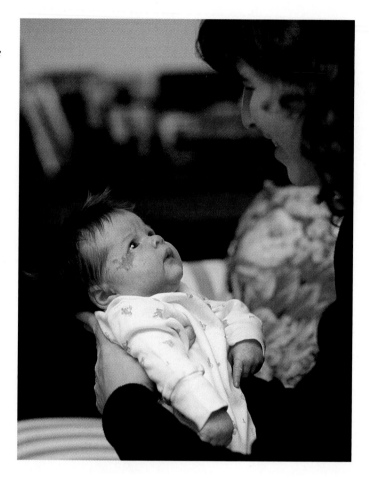

engage in the same types of searches, using what Haith refers to as **"rules" for scanning.** Since these rules are present shortly after birth, Haith assumes infants are "wired at birth" for them.

What rules do infants use? Haith (using an infrared TV camera) found that in a dark room infants open their eyes very wide and intensely scan the darkness with very small eye movements. Should even the faintest image of anything be there, such activity will improve their chances of discovering it. In contrast to the way they scan in the dark, infants scan a light-filled room with large, sweeping movements. Such scans increase the likelihood of "bumping" into an edge or a contour. When they detect a contour, infants stop scanning the field and focus on the edges of the object (Haith, 1980).

The scanning rules that infants use, whether in a darkened room or in the light, optimize their chances of discovering something if anything is there. These particular rules, however, also make it likely that infants will miss other types of information. Specifically, by focusing on the edges of objects, very young infants miss what is inside the perimeters. When shown a picture of a face, for instance, a 1-month-old will concentrate on the outer contour of the face. Not until 2 months of age will the infant scan the actual features of the face. You can see these differences in Figure 4.9. The 1-month-old, whose scanning pattern is shown on the left, seems to concentrate on the perimeter of the face, the chin and the hairline, while the 2-month-old, whose scanning pattern is on the right, spends the most time scanning the face's features, the eyes and mouth (Haith, Bergman, & Moore, 1977).

By 4 months, most infants scan objects in their visual world the way adults do, by quickly processing the global configuration, or shape, of an object and then analyzing its internal features. Janet Frick and John Columbo (1996), at the Uni-

"rules" for scanning Patterns of scanning used by infants to actively search for things in their visual field.

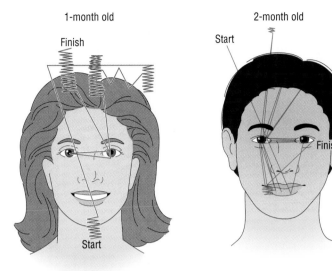

1-month old

Finish

Start

2-month old

Start

Finish

Finish

FIGURE 4.9 Differences in the Visual Scanning of a Face by 1- and 2-Month-Old Infants *Source:* P. Salapatek. (1975). Pattern perception in early infancy. In L. B. Cohen & P. Salapatec (Eds.), *Infant perception: From sensation to cognition.* New York: Academic Press.

versity of Kansas, found that by 4 months, differences among infants can be striking, with infants differing both in their speed of processing and in the strategies they use. Infants who take longer to process information also appear to use less mature strategies, being more likely to scan only the perimeter of objects as do younger infants.

Gordon Bronson (1994), at Mills College, points out that the infant's visual system undergoes rapid changes within the 2nd and 3rd months. Changes in scanning patterns parallel these developments. By 3 months, for instance, infants are able to scan a much larger visual field and do so more systematically, focusing on all of the figures that are present and comparing them by looking at first one and then the other.

Being able *not* to look at things also develops with age. The ability to inhibit automatic sweeps of the eye, or saccades, which are triggered by peripheral movement, allows infants to more systematically inspect the objects they *are* looking at (Johnson, 1995). This type of control becomes increasingly important as infants are better able to anticipate where interesting things will appear and to look in their direction. By 3 months, for instance, infants who are shown a picture first to the left of them and then to the right can detect the alternating pattern to the picture's location and will look in the expected direction. In contrast, infants younger than 3 months are unable to anticipate where an object will next appear (Haith, Hazen, & Goodman, 1988; Haith, Wentworth, & Canfield, 1993). This inability, combined with their, as yet, relatively poor motor coordination, can lead to interesting encounters with their own bodies. Anne Lamott (1993) writes of her infant son, "His arms and hands still have wills of their own. They float erratically above him, suddenly darting into his field of vision like snakes, causing him to do funny little Jack Benny double takes" (p. 101). ◄

By 6 months of age, infants not only look at the objects that interest them in more adult ways, but they also process peripheral, or contextual, visual information the way adults do, swiftly and automatically detecting features of the background without attending to it (Early, Bhatt, & Rovee-Collier, 1995).

Just as infants' ability to visually explore their world changes significantly within the first 6 months, so, too, does their **visual acuity,** or their ability to see fine detail. At birth, acuity is actually quite poor, being only one twentieth that of an adult. Acuity improves dramatically month by month until, by the end of the 1st year, it reaches that of an adult (Courage & Adams, 1990). Improvements in acuity can be traced to a number of factors, such as neurological maturation,

What information are young infants most likely to pick up when scanning a person's face, and what are they most likely to miss?

visual acuity Ability to see fine detail.

FIGURE 4.10 The Mechanism of Hearing *The outer ear funnels sound waves to the eardrum. The bones of the middle ear amplify and relay the eardrum's vibrations through the oval window into the fluid-filled cochlea.*

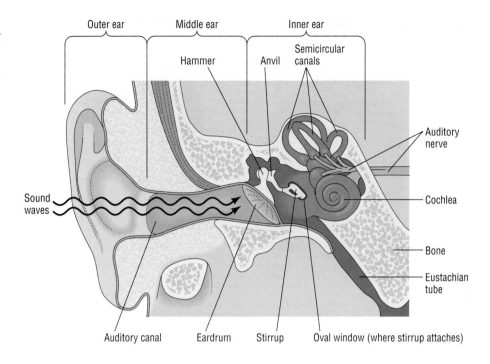

myelination of neural fibers, and changes in the eye itself. With respect to the latter, the fovea, a receptor-rich area of the retina on which images are focused, continues to develop until the 4th month. The most mature part of the visual system at birth is the "secondary visual system," cells distributed throughout the retina that are responsive to movement and gross characteristics of objects, such as changes in brightness and size (Bronson, 1982). Perhaps not surprisingly, given their relatively poor acuity, infants initially prefer to look at things that move, as well as at large patterns and bright objects, simply because it is easier for them to see these.

An object's distance from the infant is also important in determining how well it can be seen. Objects that are 8 to 12 inches away are seen most clearly. Vision blurs when the retinal image of an object does not maintain the same size, relative to the object, at all distances. In adults, the lens of the eye thickens as we focus on objects close at hand and thins out as they move further away, changing the angle at which light is refracted through the lens (and hence where the image will fall), thus accommodating for distance. Accommodation fails to occur in young infants, in part because objects are not seen well enough to prompt an attempt to bring them into focus. With foveal development, the ability to see objects either at a distance or close at hand improves to that of an adult (Maurer & Maurer, 1988).

Q Why might infants find it difficult to bring objects into focus as they look at them?

Audition

In comparison to vision, hearing is relatively well developed at birth. Sounds, whether the clatter of dishes or the rise and fall of a human voice, are transmitted as waves of pressure changes that differ in frequency (in how quickly the pattern of change repeats itself). These waves are picked up by the eardrum, which is set in motion, in turn transmitting the patterns to the cochlea of the inner ear (Figure 4.10). The cochlea contains hair cells that translate the waves to neural

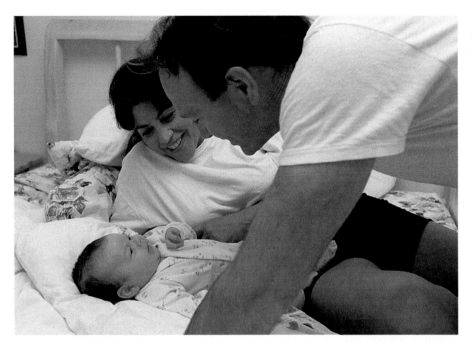

Very young infants can hear sounds that older infants and adults cannot, which suggests that they lose the ability to hear some sounds depending on their language community.

impulses. Newborns have the same number of hair cells as adults, though not all are mature at birth (Acredola & Hake, 1982).

Newborns can be seen to startle to loud sounds or to sudden changes in sound. Although their threshold for detecting sounds is not as low as that of most adults, neither are differences between them and adults that great. Electrophysiological measures, which record impulses along the auditory pathway, show that for most newborns sounds need be only twice as loud to be heard as they need to be for an adult to hear them (in comparison to vision, where objects need to be 20 times as close for a newborn to see them as well as an adult would). Considerable variation exists from one infant to the next, and some infants hear nearly as well as adults. Infants hear high-frequency sounds most easily, and, by 6 months of age, can hear these as well as adults. Their ability to hear low-frequency sounds, however, continues to improve throughout the first 18 months (Siegler, 1998).

Infants also get better with age at localizing where sounds are coming from. This improvement takes a surprising turn, in that newborns are actually better at localizing sounds than are infants several months older. Only by the age of 4 months do infants surpass the ability of newborns. This U-shaped curve reflects the operation of two separate mechanisms. Initially, in the 1st month, spatial localization is thought to be under the control of subcortical centers within the brain. As cortical activity increases in the succeeding months, subcortical centers are replaced. Even so, cortical activity is initially not fully developed, and spatial localization is not as accurate as it eventually becomes at 4 months (Siegler, 1998).

Not only can infants localize sounds, but they can also distinguish among them and show preferences right from the start. Infants only 3 days old can identify their mother's voice from those of other speakers and appear to prefer to listen to the voice of their mother. Researchers have to be ingenious when working with infants, since babies can neither answer nor understand the questions one might want to ask. To determine listening preferences, these investigators gave infants a nipple to suck. When the infants sucked, they heard either their mother's voice or that of another woman. Infants sucked more to hear their mother's voice (DeCasper & Fifer, 1980).

How do researchers use the principle of habituation to determine whether one sound can be discriminated from another?

Although infants can distinguish many types of sounds, not all are equally interesting to them. Those that are most interesting are the sounds of the human voice (Ecklund-Flores & Turkewitz, 1996). From the first days on, infants react differently to speech and nonspeech sounds, moving their faces and fingers rhythmically to the patterns of speech and turning their heads in its direction. These movements are "paced" by the rhythmic features of speech, occurring in synchrony to the rise and fall of the speaker's voice (Condon & Sander, 1974).

Speech sounds appear to be processed in a way that is qualitatively different from the way nonspeech sounds are processed. Infants, for example, are able to distinguish highly similar sounds, such as "pa" and "ba" or "s" and "z," when these are heard in the context of speech more easily than when they are not. The two hemispheres, or sides, of the brain show specialization in their processing of speech from early infancy on (Best, 1988). Sounds entering the two ears travel to the different hemispheres of the brain; but, in an interesting twist of nature, those picked up by the left ear go to the right side of the brain and those entering the right ear go to the left. Language is processed in the left hemisphere. Specialization of the hemispheres is apparent even in early infancy, in that speech sounds presented to the left ear, and processed by the right hemisphere, are not as easily distinguished as those presented to the right ear (Best, 1988).

With respect to hearing the sounds of speech, infants less than a month old can hear sounds that older infants and adults cannot, which suggests that the experience of living within a language community contributes to the development of language as much by *decreasing* the likelihood of hearing differences among sounds (those that are not meaningful in that language) as by enhancing distinctions among others. Speech sounds, you see, are actually composed of continuous signals differing along many dimensions, yet the speakers of a language hear these signals categorically—that is, as either one type of sound or another. One such dimension is voice onset time (VOT), when the vocal cords begin to vibrate in making a sound. The VOT for "ba," for instance, is short (the cords vibrate at the very beginning of the sound), whereas the VOT for "pa" is quite long. Despite very real differences along this dimension, all sounds with VOTs that are shorter than a certain value are heard as "ba" and all sounds that are longer than this VOT as "pa." As Robert Siegler (1991), a psychologist at Carnegie-Mellon University, says, "A sound is either a *ba* or a *pa*, never something in between." Except, that is, for infants less than a month old.

Perceptual Exploration

Claus von Hofsten (1982), at the University of Uppsala in Sweden, photographed arm movements from two different camera angles, giving three-dimensional information regarding the infant's actions. Von Hofsten found that although neonates were no more likely to touch an object when they were looking at it (we look at the things we reach for) than when they were not, their arm movements could be seen to come closer to the object, and the hand slowed down as it neared the object. One should not overinterpret these early reaches. Even though reaching is more likely to occur when an object is present than in the absence of an object, reaching does not necessarily mean that the infant "intends" to grab something. This type of means-end understanding develops over the course of the 1st year.

Von Hofsten suggests that the eye-hand coordination evident in neonates' reaches constitutes an "information gathering system." He views reaching as an attentional act rather than a manipulative one. According to von Hofsten (1982), looking at and reaching toward something are merely different, related ways of gaining information. From this perspective, vision becomes a way of exploring and making sense of one's surroundings. Perception, rather than a passive process triggered by external events, becomes an active process and one that is internally guided.

Ulric Neisser (1967, 1976), at Cornell, suggests that anticipatory schemata direct the pickup of information and are, themselves, refined and altered in the process. Picking up certain information creates a "readiness" for related information, preparing us to see or hear certain things and not others. The information that is received modifies the schema. The modified schema, in turn, directs the next exploration. Perception, for Neisser, is an active, constructive process. Figure 4.11 illustrates the dynamic nature of this process.

To illustrate how such schemata could account for the selective nature of perception—that is, seeing one thing and not another—Neisser devised a simple experiment in which adults watched a videotaped basketball game. Neisser assumed that the movements of the players and the ball would create anticipatory schemata based on the trajectories of each. Vision guided by these schemata should fail to pick up other, unrelated movements with different trajectories. At one point, a second videotape of a woman with an umbrella walking across the court, was superimposed over the game. People monitoring the fast action of the game failed to notice the woman. What we fail to notice, the woman with the umbrella in this case, simply is not picked up with anticipatory schemata. In a similar type of task, 4-month-old infants also failed to notice an irrelevant stimulus while attending to another (Bahrick, Walker, & Neisser, 1981). Neisser argues that, through the action of such schemata, we put together, or construct, the events to which we respond and that these constructions are fundamental to perception. Anticipatory schemata bridge perception and memory. Because the schemata are anticipations, they are the medium by which the past effects the future, information already acquired determining that which will next be experienced.

Perceptual Integration

Thus far, we have considered the senses separately. But does the activity of one sensory system ever contribute to the ability to sense something in a different modality? You have probably experienced how tasteless food becomes when your nose is stopped up with a cold or how much easier it is to hear a sound when you look in the direction of its source, even when the source is not visible. Do we taste with our noses, or hear with our eyes? Bats and dolphins can make their way unerringly in darkness, guided by echoes—forms shaped in patterns of sounds. Can we, too, use the structure of sound to see? For most of us, the answer is obscured by the very ease with which we see and hear. A look at some work with handicapped infants offers the intriguing possibility that the senses may overlap, the same information being picked up by more than one sense.

In a remarkable demonstration, a sonic guide was strapped to the forehead of a blind infant. An echoing signal indicated the presence of objects. The echo increased in pitch and loudness with size and nearness to an object. Surface texture was broadcast through the clarity of the echo, a pure tone indicating smooth surfaces and a gravelly tone rough ones. Within minutes, the infant was able to use the spatial information given by the sonic guide. At one point, as she moved her hand in front of her face, her expression changed; and, then, probing the textured darkness, she moved her hand again, this time following the movement with her head, her face sparkling in smiles (Bower, 1982). Since this initial demonstration, sonic guides have been used experimentally in programs for the blind (Humphrey & Humphrey, 1985).

The ability of infants to make almost immediate use of a sonic guide offers the promise of new aids for the visually handicapped. But how are we to understand their ability to use this information? If sensory experience is specific to each

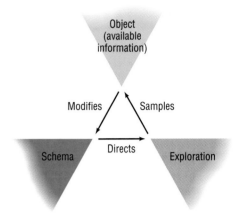

FIGURE 4.11 Neisser's Perceptual Cycle *Anticipatory schemata both direct and are modified by the pickup of information.* Source: U. Neisser. (1976). *Cognition and reality.* San Francisco: Freeman.

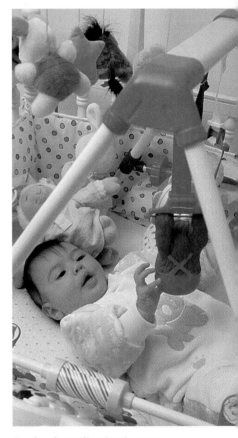

Eye-hand coordination is a way for infants to make sense of their surroundings.

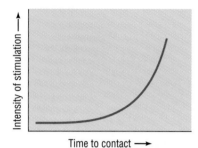

FIGURE 4.12 Changes in the Intensity of Stimulation with the Nearness of an Approaching Object *Source:* T. G. R. Bower. (1982). *Development in infancy* (2nd ed.). San Francisco: W. H. Freeman.

modality, how does the infant translate an auditory signal into a structured space that corresponds in important ways to what is seen?

T. G. R. Bower (1982), a developmentalist at Edinburgh University, explains what happens visually when an object approaches. As the object moves closer, there is a change in the pattern of retinal stimulation, the image that it projects on the retina expanding. The optical expansion that occurs with increasing proximity follows a time course. With increasing nearness, or *decreasing* time to "contact," the amount of stimulation increases (Figure 4.12). The relationship between distance and amount of stimulation is not, however, specific to vision. It can, in fact, be communicated through several senses (Bower, 1982).

To a similar approaching object, the sonic guide echoes back a change in pitch and loudness, the tone becoming both higher and louder with increasing nearness of the object. Both of these changes have the same time course—a time course that is identical to the one for optical expansion. The *information* is the same, in other words, irrespective of the sensory modality (Bower, 1982; Gibson, 1966).

Bower suggests that there may be other "amodal" variables to which infants are responsive. Consider the ability to detect radial direction. The amodal variable for straight ahead is symmetrical stimulation of both receptors, whether these be nostrils, ears, or eyes. Asymmetrical stimulation, arriving at one side before the other, signals a source that is off from the center. The order of stimulation cues direction, and the amount of difference in the time it takes the source to reach the left versus right receptors informs us as to the degree to which the object is to the side (Bower, 1982). Infants' perception of their own leg movements, also, appears to be determined, at least in part, by their detection of intermodal invariants that indicate the position of the body in its spatial surround (Rochat & Morgan, 1995). Similarly, infants respond to amodal cues, as well as specific visual and auditory ones, in listening to speech (Lewkowicz, 1996).

As already suggested, one advantage to intersensory coordination is practical; it offers therapeutic uses with handicapped infants. Bower notes a theoretical advantage, as well—that of parsimony. As pointed out in Chapter 3, the genotype does not carry sufficient information to fully specify the functioning of the nervous system. Even though the genotype can code several million proteins, this figure is still short of that necessary to explain the operation of all the senses, and the environment is believed to play an important part in modulating the process of genetic expression (see Chapter 3).

There is little doubt, however, that the genotype carries sufficient information to program amodal structures in the nervous system. For radial direction, for instance, one would only need a symmetry-asymmetry detector that would receive input from all senses. Thus one could expect a neonate to be perceptually competent despite the dramatic neural development that occurs after birth. This latter growth could be seen as fleshing out the skeletal worldview given by amodal variables (Bower, 1982). In fact, the transfer of control from subcortical to cortical centers for activities such as localizing sounds or scanning visual patterns suggests just such a development (Bronson, 1974).

Some of the simplest questions concerning perception can set the occasion for complicated answers indeed. How, for example, does an infant distinguish the sights and sounds that emanate from a single source, such as a person talking, for example, from those that merely occur together by chance? Must sensory impressions be "fused" together through the repeated association of images with sounds, smells, textures, and tastes? If the senses functioned independently of each other, as separate channels for sensory experiences, such might be necessary. If, however, perception is viewed as an *activity*, involving one or more sensory systems, by which one explores one's surroundings, what is picked up is information, and much of this can be amodal (Lewkowicz, 1996). Sensory receptors still respond to changes in stimulation, of course. However, only those changes that reflect invariant features of stimulation, those that maintain similar relationships despite differences in pitch, loudness, or size, for instance, carry the information that results in perception (Gibson, 1966).

Infants are remarkably competent at birth, having been readied for life outside the uterus in a multitude of ways. Yet there is a paradox to the richly equipped "utility kit" of biological rhythms and sensory capacities with which infants are supplied; their innate abilities place infants in a better position to explore and learn—and be influenced all the more by their experiences. This brings us to the topic of motor development and the infant's increased ability to grasp, move about, and discover more about its world and itself.

Motor Development

Perhaps nothing excites parents more than the "firsts" of motor development, seeing the first time their infant reaches out for an interesting object, for instance, or takes a first step. Physical growth and the maturation of the brain enable infants to develop new control over their bodies. Changing body proportions also contribute to increased control of movement. Were the head to remain proportionally as large, for instance, as it is in the newborn, walking would be as difficult as balancing a pumpkin on popsicle sticks. As it is, changes in body proportions, growth, and neuromuscular maturation contribute to some of the most noticeable developments of infancy—the kind that find their way into baby books—as voluntary actions begin to supplant the newborn's repertoire of involuntary reflexes.

Reflexes

Reflexes are specific responses that occur automatically to particular types of stimuli, our bodies being "prewired" to respond in distinct ways. A light tap just beneath the knee, for instance, will cause the leg to swing up in the familiar knee-jerk reflex. Tapping the tendon causes the muscle to which it is attached to stretch. Information about the muscle's movement is carried to the spinal cord along an **afferent, or sensory, pathway,** where it connects with an **efferent, or motor, pathway** leading out to the same muscle, causing it to contract, correcting for the initial movement. Simple reflexes such as this are relayed at the level of the spinal cord (Figure 4.13). More complex reflexes, such as sucking, which require the coordination of a number of related movements, involve relays within the **brain stem,** an area beneath the cortex that controls basic body functions such as breathing, eating, heart rate, body temperature, and emotional arousal.

Reflexes abound in individuals of all ages, not just newborns. Salivating to the taste of a lemon, blinking at a fast-approaching object, and swinging one's leg to a tap beneath the knee are all reflexes. Reflexes in the newborn serve highly adaptive functions, such as obtaining food, maintaining an unobstructed flow of air, and holding on to the caretaker.

Sucking and rooting are both reflexes by which the infant initially receives nourishment. The **sucking reflex** can be triggered by anything that touches the infant's mouth, whether this be a nipple, a finger, or a shirtsleeve. Simply brushing the infant's lips is sufficient to cause the lips to purse and sucking to begin. A related reflex, the **rooting reflex,** helps the infant locate the source of nourishment. Brushing the infant's cheek will prompt the infant to turn its head in that direction and to start sucking.

afferent, or sensory, pathway A series of neurons carrying impulses from the periphery (skin, muscles, joints, and internal organs) to the central nervous system.

efferent, or motor, pathway A series of neurons carrying impulses from the central nervous system to the periphery (skin, muscles, joints, and internal organs).

brain stem The area at the base of the brain that contains the midbrain, the pons, and the medulla oblongata and controls basic functions such as breathing and heart rate.

sucking reflex Sucking in response to a touch on the mouth; an adaptive reflex in infants.

rooting reflex Turning the head and starting to suck in response to a brush on the cheek; an adaptive reflex in infants.

FIGURE 4.13 A Simple Spinal Reflex

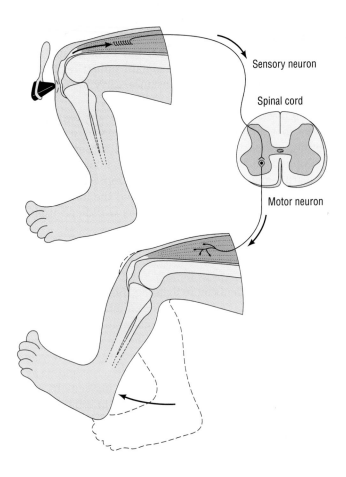

In another adaptive reflex, head turning, infants will turn their heads away from something covering their nose, thereby maintaining an adequate supply of air. As with other reflexes, this is nature's *first* defense and is not necessarily adequate in all situations. Parents need to be sure that the crib is free of objects such as pillows and soft toys that, though inviting to an adult, can be dangerous to a newborn. Breathing itself is a reflexive activity that does not require conscious monitoring. In another reflex, the swimming reflex, infants will momentarily hold their breath and kick with a swimming motion if placed face down in water. It cannot be emphasized too much that this reflex will not keep an infant from drowning if left unattended in a bath, *even if only for a moment.* An infant can drown in mere inches of water simply because it is "top heavy," and if it falls face down, its muscles are not yet sufficiently developed for it to lift its face out of the water.

A sudden loss of support or a loud noise will prompt the **Moro reflex,** in which the infant arches its back, throws its arms out, and then quickly brings them in again toward the body. The adaptive significance of this reflex is disputed. It may, in times past, have helped our ancestors cling to their caretakers, or it may have more current adaptive value in enhancing mother-infant bonding. In perhaps a related reflex, the **grasp reflex,** the infant spontaneously grasps an object that is pressed against the palms of the hands. A newborn can actually be lifted into the air as it grasps a forefinger in either hand. The Research Focus, "Science as Self-Correcting: 'The Case of The Disappearing Reflex,'" discusses the stepping reflex.

In addition to their adaptive value, reflexes are useful diagnostically, since reflexive behavior changes with age, many reflexes dropping out as the central nervous system matures. Checking an infant's reflexes is one way of assessing whether such maturation is progressing normally.

Moro reflex A reflex in infants in response to a sudden loss of support or loud noise, in which they arch their back, throw their arms out, and quickly bring them in.

grasp reflex Spontaneously grasping an object pressed against the palm of the hand.

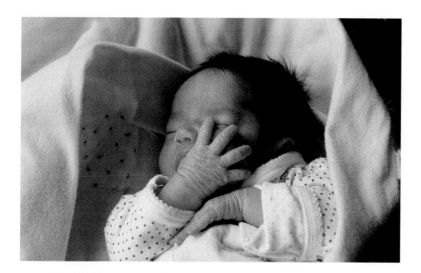

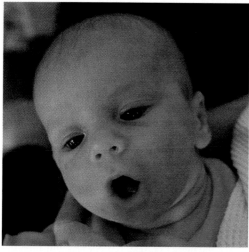

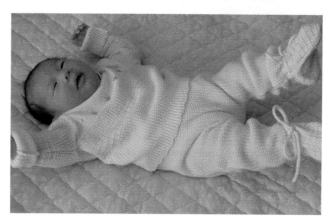

Sucking reflex (top left), rooting reflex (top right), swimming reflex (middle left), moro reflex (middle right), grasp reflex (bottom left).

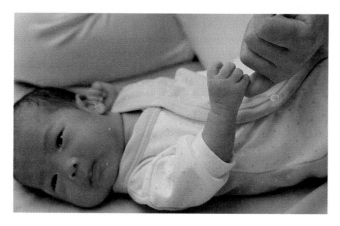

Voluntary Actions

As neurons within the cerebral cortex increase in size and complexity, and as they become myelinated, new behaviors emerge. One of the first areas to be myelinated is the **primary motor cortex,** one of two cortical areas that are important in controlling voluntary actions. This area is responsible for governing the activity of discrete muscles within the body. Figure 4.14 illustrates the way in which muscles in different parts of the body are "mapped" onto the motor cortex. As you can see, some parts of the body, such as the hands and face, are allotted more space than others. Another area that is important in the control of voluntary movement

primary motor cortex The area of the cortex responsible for governing the voluntary movement of discrete muscles.

Research Focus

Science as Self-Correcting: "The Case of the Disappearing Reflex"

Theoretical assumptions serve as lenses through which we view behavior. Frequently they lead us to look for, and enable us to see, things we otherwise would not have been able to detect. At times, however, they can blur our vision, preventing us from seeing things that are actually there. A case in point is that of the "disappearing" reflex (Thelen, 1995).

Newborn infants can be seen to make stepping movements when they are held upright with their feet touching a surface. This stepping reflex disappears after a few months, and coordinated stepping does not occur again until infants, many months later, take their first steps as they begin to walk. Presumably, the early reflexive stepping has been inhibited due to the maturation of the higher cortical centers that will eventually control the later voluntary stepping.

Esther Thelen and Donna Fisher (1982) began to question this assumption when they noticed that the movements involved in kicking, when infants are lying on their backs or stomachs, are highly similar to those of stepping. In fact, subsequent comparisons of the movement patterns involved in kicking and stepping revealed *no difference* either in the muscles that were activated or in the pattern of the movements themselves. Kicking, in other words, was essentially the same as stepping except that it involved horizontal leg movements rather than vertical ones. Yet kicking continues to occur throughout infancy and does not drop out, whereas stepping does. Surely, they reasoned, one could not expect the cortex to inhibit movements that occurred in one position and yet leave intact the very same movements when they occurred in another.

Thelen and Fisher entertained a theoretical heresy. What if movement is not simply governed by neural impulses? Isn't it just as reasonable to assume that our movements are also governed by bodily and environmental constraints, as well as by neural programming? How might these considerations explain the disappearance of stepping but not of kicking?

Thelen and Fisher noted that when posture changes from being held upright to lying down, one also has a change in the relationship between body mass and gravity. Because of this change, infants require more strength to flex their legs when in an upright position than when lying down. Also, infants are gaining weight in the months prior to the disappearance of stepping. Since most of this weight is fat and not muscle, their legs have become heavier but not correspondingly stronger. These investigators reasoned that the stepping reflex disappears not because of cortical inhibition, but because of environmental and physical constraints such as these.

When viewed from this perspective, one might expect to see the reappearance of the stepping reflex if one could counter the effects of such mechanical and environmental factors. Thelen and Fisher arranged such a test: Infants in whom the stepping reflex had dropped out were held upright in chest-high water. They found, as they had expected, that stepping once again occurred. Conversely, when weights were added to these infants' legs, they failed to kick when placed on their backs. So much for "disappearing" reflexes!

What is it about the scientific method as it was pursued by these and previous investigators that enables science to be self-correcting? First, science is *empirical;* scientists gather observations about behavior rather than basing their statements on assumptions as to what might be taking place. Second, scientists are *self-critical,* not only examining their own work for possible faults, but also publishing their work so that it can be examined by others. Third, theories, even when well established, are never considered to be proven, but instead to be *supported* or *refuted* by empirical findings.

Why do muscles of the hands and face correspond to larger areas of the motor cortex than other parts of the body do?

secondary motor cortex The area of the cortex responsible for voluntary patterned movements of groups of muscles.

cerebellum A large structure located behind the cerebral cortex that coordinates sensory input and muscle responses.

is the **secondary motor cortex.** This area, in contrast to the first, is responsible for patterned movements, in which the activity of discrete muscles is coordinated into a single action. In addition to these two regions of the cortex, the **cerebellum** also plays a critical role in movement. The cerebellum, lying beneath the cortex in the brain stem, acts as a clearing center for all of the many ingoing and outgoing signals that collectively communicate the infant's current body position. The cerebellum undergoes rapid development early in infancy, at a time when the infant is making rapid gains in the postural control and balance that are needed for walking (Malina & Bouchard, 1991).

Control over muscles in different parts of the body progresses unevenly, illustrating the cephalocaudal growth trend. Thus infants are first able to move their heads, 90% being able to lift their heads by 2 months of age. They next gain control over their shoulders, by about 3 months, raising themselves up to look around when placed on their stomachs; and, at 4 months, they can use their arms to support their weight when they do so. Similarly, the proximodistal trend is also apparent. Infants gain control over their shoulders before being able to move their

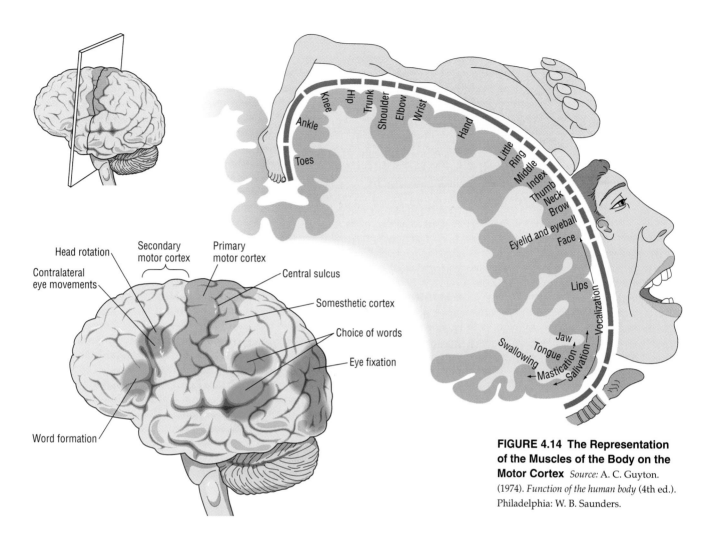

FIGURE 4.14 The Representation of the Muscles of the Body on the Motor Cortex *Source:* A. C. Guyton. (1974). *Function of the human body* (4th ed.). Philadelphia: W. B. Saunders.

arms with accuracy (their first reaches are more like swipes), only much later developing the control over their fingers that allows them, by opposing thumb and index finger, to pick up even the smallest of objects, by about 1 year of age. Box 4.2 and Figure 4.15 present the different ages at which infants accomplish the major milestones of motor development. Keep in mind, when looking at these ages, that considerable variability exists in the timing of accomplishments from one infant to the next.

Flow

Not only are parents delighted by these accomplishments, but infants appear to be as well. Anyone who has watched an infant successfully roll over after a number of abortive attempts or pick something up that has been difficult to grasp will recognize the unmistakable signs of pleasure that attend such successes. Actions that have become second nature to adults carry the heady excitement of victory for the infant.

Mihaly Csikszentmihalyi (1990), a psychologist at the University of Chicago, has analyzed what makes activities enjoyable, whether these involve perfecting one's backhand or navigating the kitchen floor in a crablike crawl. He began his study of enjoyment serendipitously, initially being interested in creativity. He noticed as he studied artists engaged in their work how absorbed they became in

What emotions are infants likely to experience as they master new motor skills?

Box 4.2 *Major Milestones in Motor Development*

1 Month

Lifts Head When Held at Shoulder
Holds Head Erect for 3 Seconds
   (Vertical)
Adjusts Posture When Held at Shoulder
Holds Head Erect and Steady for 15
   Seconds
Holds Head Steady While Being Moved
Lifts Head (Dorsal Suspension)
Adjusts Head to Ventral Suspension
Turns from Side to Back

2 Months

Holds Head Erect and Steady for 15
   Seconds
Holds Head Steady While Being Moved
Balances Head
Lifts Head (Dorsal Suspension)
Adjusts Head to Ventral Suspension
Turns from Side to Back
Maintains Head at 45° and Lowers with
   Control
Sits with Support

3 Months

Holds Head Steady While Being Moved
Balances Head
Adjusts Head to Ventral Suspension
Turns from Side to Back
Turns from Back to Side
Maintains Head at 45° and Lowers with
   Control
Maintains Head at 90° and Lowers with
   Control
Shifts Weight on Arms
Sits with Support
Sits with Slight Support for 10 Seconds
Sits Alone Momentarily
Uses Whole Hand to Grasp Rod

4 Months

Balances Head
Turns from Back to Side
Pulls to Sitting Position
Maintains Head at 45° and Lowers with
   Control
Maintains Head at 90° and Lowers with
   Control
Shifts Weight on Arms
Sits with Support
Sits with Slight Support for 10 Seconds
Sits Alone Momentarily
Sits Alone for 30 Seconds
Sits Alone While Playing with Toy
Uses Whole Hand to Grasp Rod
Uses Partial Thumb Opposition to
   Grasp Cube

5 Months

Turns from Back to Side
Turns from Back to Stomach
Shifts Weight on Arms
Grasps Foot with Hands
Pulls to Sitting Position
Sits Alone Momentarily
Sits Alone for 30 Seconds
Sits Alone Steadily
Sits Alone While Playing with Toy
Uses Whole Hand to Grasp Rod
Uses Partial Thumb Opposition to
   Grasp Cube
Uses Pads of Fingertips to Grasp Cube
Makes Early Stepping Movements

6 Months

Turns from Back to Stomach
Grasps Foot with Hands
Attempts to Raise Self to Sit
Pulls to Sitting Position
Pulls to Standing Position
Sits Alone Momentarily
Sits Alone for 30 Seconds
Sits Alone Steadily
Sits Alone While Playing with Toy
Uses Whole Hand to Grasp Rod
Uses Partial Thumb Opposition to
   Grasp Cube
Uses Pads of Fingertips to Grasp Cube
Raises Self to Sitting Position
Moves Forward, Using Prewalking
   Methods
Makes Early Stepping Movements
Supports Weight Momentarily
Shifts Weight While Standing

7 Months

Turns from Back to Stomach
Grasps Foot with Hands
Attempts to Raise Self to Sit
Pulls to Standing Position
Sits Alone While Playing with Toy
Sits Alone Steadily
Rotates Trunk While Sitting Alone
Uses Pads of Fingertips to Grasp Cube
Raises Self to Sitting Position
Moves Forward, Using Prewalking
   Methods
Moves from Sitting to Creeping
   Position
Makes Early Stepping Movements
Supports Weight Momentarily
Shifts Weight While Standing

8 Months

Attempts to Raise Self to Sit

Pulls to Standing Position
Rotates Trunk While Sitting Alone
Uses Partial Thumb Opposition to
   Grasp Rod
Grasps Pencil at Farthest End
Moves Forward, Using Prewalking
   Methods
Moves from Sitting to Creeping
   Position
Raises Self to Sitting Position
Raises Self to Standing Position
Supports Weight Momentarily
Shifts Weight While Standing
Attempts to Walk
Walks Sideways While Holding on to
   Furniture
Walks with Help

9 Months

Rotates Trunk While Sitting Alone
Uses Partial Thumb Opposition to
   Grasp Rod
Grasps Pencil at Farthest End
Moves from Sitting to Creeping
   Position
Raises Self to Standing Position
Attempts to Walk
Walks Sideways While Holding on to
   Furniture
Walks with Help
Stands Alone
Walks Alone

10 Months

Uses Partial Thumb Opposition to
   Grasp Rod
Grasps Pencil at Farthest End
Moves from Sitting to Creeping
   Position
Raises Self to Standing Position
Attempts to Walk
Walks Sideways While Holding on to
   Furniture
Walks with Help
Stands Alone
Walks Alone
Walks Alone with Good Coordination
Throws Ball

11 Months

Uses Partial Thumb Opposition to
   Grasp Rod
Grasps Pencil at Farthest End
Walks Sideways While Holding on to
   Furniture
Walks with Help
Stands Alone

Walks Alone
Walks Alone with Good Coordination
Throws Ball
Walks Backward
Walks Up Stairs with Help
Walks Down Stairs with Help

12 Months

Grasps Pencil at Farthest End
Grasps Pencil at Middle
Walks with Help
Stands Alone
Walks Alone
Walks Alone with Good Coordination
Throws Ball
Walks Backward
Walks Sideways
Stands on Right Foot with Help
Walks Up Stairs with Help
Walks Down Stairs with Help

13 Months

Grasps Pencil at Middle
Uses Pads of Fingertips to Grasp Pencil
Uses Hand to Hold Paper in Place
Stands Alone
Walks Alone
Walks Alone with Good Coordination
Throws Ball
Walks Backward
Walks Sideways
Stands on Right Foot with Help
Stands on Left Foot with Help
Walks Up Stairs with Help
Walks Down Stairs with Help

14–16 Months

Grasps Pencil at Middle
Uses Pads of Fingertips to Grasp Pencil
Uses Hand to Hold Paper in Place
Walks Alone with Good Coordination
Throws Ball
Walks Backward
Walks Sideways
Stands on Right Foot with Help
Stands on Left Foot with Help
Runs with Coordination
Jumps off Floor (Both Feet)
Walks Up Stairs with Help
Walks Up Stairs Alone, Placing Both
    Feet on Each Step
Walks Down Stairs with Help

17–19 Months

Grasps Pencil at Middle
Uses Pads of Fingertips to Grasp Pencil
Uses Hand to Hold Paper in Place
Walks Backward
Walks Sideways
Stands on Right Foot with Help
Stands Alone on Right Foot
Stands on Left Foot with Help
Runs with Coordination
Jumps off Floor (Both Feet)
Walks Up Stairs with Help
Walks Up Stairs Alone, Placing Both
    Feet on Each Step
Walks Down Stairs with Help
Walks Down Stairs Alone, Placing Both
    Feet on Each Step
Jumps from Bottom Step

20–22 Months

Grasps Pencil at Middle
Uses Pads of Fingertips to Grasp Pencil
Uses Hand to Hold Paper in Place
Walks Sideways
Stands on Right Foot with Help
Stands Alone on Right Foot
Stands on Left Foot with Help
Stands Alone on Left Foot
Runs with Coordination
Walks Forward on Line
Walks Backward Close to Line
Swings Leg to Kick Ball
Jumps off Floor (Both Feet)
Walks Up Stairs Alone, Placing Both
    Feet on Each Step
Walks Down Stairs Alone, Placing Both
    Feet on Each Step
Jumps from Bottom Step

23–25 Months

Uses Hand to Hold Paper in Place
Grasps Pencil at Nearest End
Manipulates Pencil in Hand
Laces Three Beads
Imitates Hand Movements
Tactilely Discriminates Shapes
Stands Alone on Right Foot
Stands Alone on Left Foot
Jumps off Floor (Both Feet)
Jumps Distance of 4 Inches
Runs with Coordination

Walks Forward on Line
Walks Backward Close to Line
Swings Leg to Kick Ball
Walks on Tiptoe for Four Steps
Walks Up Stairs Alone, Placing Both
    Feet on Each Step
Walks Down Stairs Alone, Placing Both
    Feet on Each Step
Jumps from Bottom Step

26–28 Months

Grasps Pencil at Nearest End
Manipulates Pencil in Hand
Copies Circle
Laces Three Beads
Imitates Hand Movements
Tactilely Discriminates Shapes
Stands Alone on Right Foot
Stands Alone on Left Foot
Jumps off Floor (Both Feet)
Jumps Distance of 4 Inches
Walks Forward on Line
Walks Backward Close to Line
Swings Leg to Kick Ball
Walks on Tiptoe for Four Steps
Walks Up Stairs Alone, Placing Both
    Feet on Each Step
Walks Up Stairs, Alternating Feet
Walks Down Stairs Alone, Placing Both
    Feet on Each Step
Jumps from Bottom Step

29–31 Months

Grasps Pencil at Nearest End
Manipulates Pencil in Hand
Copies Circle
Laces Three Beads
Imitates Hand Movements
Imitates Postures
Tactilely Discriminates Shapes
Buttons One Button
Walks Forward on Line
Walks Backward Close to Line
Swings Leg to Kick Ball
Walks on Tiptoe for Four Steps
Walks on Tiptoe for 9 Feet
Jumps Distance of 4 Inches
Walks Up Stairs, Alternating Feet
Uses Eye-Hand Coordination in Tossing
    Ring
Stops from Full Run

Source: Bayley Scales of Infant Development: Second Edition. Copyright © 1993 by The Psychological Corporation, a Harcourt Assessment Company. Reproduced by permission. All rights reserved. "Bayley" and "BSID" are trademarks of The Psychological Corporation, a Harcourt Assessment Company, registered in the United States of America and/or other jurisdictions.

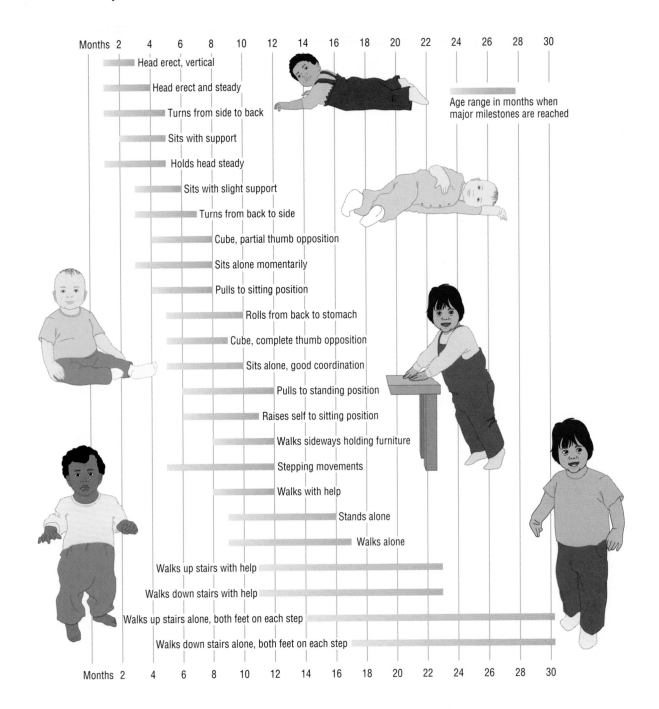

Months 2 4 6 8 10 12 14 16 18 20 22 24 26 28 30

Head erect, vertical
Head erect and steady
Turns from side to back
Sits with support
Holds head steady
Sits with slight support
Turns from back to side
Cube, partial thumb opposition
Sits alone momentarily
Pulls to sitting position
Rolls from back to stomach
Cube, complete thumb opposition
Sits alone, good coordination
Pulls to standing position
Raises self to sitting position
Walks sideways holding furniture
Stepping movements
Walks with help
Stands alone
Walks alone
Walks up stairs with help
Walks down stairs with help
Walks up stairs alone, both feet on each step
Walks down stairs alone, both feet on each step

Age range in months when
major milestones are reached

Months 2 4 6 8 10 12 14 16 18 20 22 24 26 28 30

FIGURE 4.15 Major Milestones in Motor Development

Bayley Scales of Infant Development: Second Edition. Copyright © 1993 by The Psychological Corporation, a Harcourt Assessment Company. Reproduced by permission. All rights reserved. "Bayley" and "BSID" are trademarks of The Psychological Corporation, a Harcourt Assessment Company, registered in the United States of America and/or other jurisdictions.

what they were doing. They would lose track of time, forget appointments, even forget to eat as their work began to take shape. Once the work was finished, however, their intense interest in it was gone. Their enjoyment came not so much from having a finished product as from the process by which it was created. As Csikszentmihalyi studied others who were good at what they did, he noticed that they described their experiences in much the same way, whether the activity was acting, tennis, or chess—they described the feeling of being carried away by something that took place so smoothly it occurred effortlessly. He called this experience **flow.**

T. G. R. Bower made an interesting observation of something similar in infants, one resembling Csikszentmihalyi's observation concerning *what* it is that makes something enjoyable for adults. Bower (1982) noted that early attempts to demonstrate simple forms of learning in infants frequently ran into difficulty

Infants can experience "flow" when learning to master a difficult task, such as standing up.

because the events used to reinforce the learning soon failed to hold the infants' attention. Paradoxically, the infants often learned difficult tasks, with reinforcement presented according to a complex schedule, better than simple tasks, with reinforcement presented every time the infant responded. He noticed, too, that it mattered little *what* the reinforcement was. A simple flashing light worked just as well as much more elaborate events, such as a jack-in-the-box. What appeared to be most important in holding the infants' attention was not the reinforcement at all, but the schedule by which it occurred.

"What is it about a schedule of reinforcement," Bower asked, "that can be more motivating than a reinforcement itself?" Bower's answer was that the schedule poses a problem, much like a puzzle, and *solving* the problem becomes motivating. In other words, what is enjoyable, to use Csikszentmihalyi's term, is the process of mastery. In this case, mastery involves discovering the pattern to the reinforcement. Once infants master that, they, just like Csikszentmihalyi's artists, lose interest in the task.

Under what conditions, then, might an infant, or an adult, experience flow? Paradoxically, it is not when we are relaxing, but when we are engaged in activities that are difficult enough to stretch our current level of ability—in other words, when we are involved in mastering something new. It makes sense, in that case,

flow The experience of becoming totally absorbed in a challenging activity.

to expect to see evidence of flow in infants as they master the challenges of new activities, whether in discovering the pattern to a reinforcement schedule or in mastering the movements involved in crawling.

 Louise Erdrich (1996) describes her infant daughter's initial attempts to move about on her own, attempts that, though not actually crawling, would lead to her discovery of this. Erdrich had bought herself time for writing by scattering toys about on the floor, knowing that she would have time to write only until her daughter reached the toy that was furthermost from her, a musical bird:

> This will last fifteen minutes, until she explores the last toy, a musical blue-bird with an orange beak and great black cartoon eyes. She has learned how to prop herself, how to swivel on her stomach, but she can't crawl, not yet. Instead, she lunges. She props herself on her arms and pushes with her knees, lands with a solid thump, pushes up, and throws herself again and again toward the toy. It is a paradigm of something, I think, idly, pausing to study her absolute striving concentration, but what? Turning back to this page, I know. It is what I am doing now. My face is hers. Unyielding eagerness. That is her work, just as this page is my play, just as all this is our life. It is what we do, afraid and avid, full of desire, hurling ourselves again and again toward the musical object. (p. 133) ◄

The intense concentration that Erdrich observed both in her daughter and in herself is characteristic of flow. Csikszentmihalyi refers to this aspect of flow as a *focusing of attention.* Infants, for instance, will simply become oblivious to what is going on around them as they concentrate all their efforts on what they are doing. The match between the skills the infant brings to the task and those that are required for its mastery is also critical for the experience of flow. The disparity must be just great enough to require the infant to "stretch," but not so great as to place mastery beyond the infant's reach. Finally, the nature of the activity itself is also important in determining whether flow will be experienced. Activities that provide continuous *feedback,* so that one can monitor one's performance relative to reaching a goal, are those in which one is most likely to experience flow, activities such as tennis or chess—or crawling, if one is very young (Csikszentmihalyi, 1990).

Csikszentmihalyi points out that as we focus attention on the activity, we lose awareness of ourselves, "becoming" what we are doing, losing ourselves in time. Paradoxically, the mastery that is involved in experiences in which one loses the boundaries of the self also contributes to self-definition.

Mastery and the Self

To experience the self, one must also be aware of that which is *not* part of the self. Robert Kegan (1982) speaks of the way individuals of all ages partition their experience into *subject* and *object,* into that which is "me" and that which is "not-me." I am not suggesting, by this, that young infants have a sense of self. That does not develop until about 1½ years of age. However, I am suggesting that infants begin this elemental partitioning of experience in the very first months of life and that this partitioning enables them to distinguish which of their experiences come from within and which are external to themselves. The alternative, as Kegan puts it, is to be embedded in one's senses, taking these to be what one *is* rather than what one *does,* confusing one's sensory impressions, in other words, with the self that senses.

Differentiating oneself from one's world takes a quantum leap when infants become able to coordinate their movements with the sights and sounds around them, when they can reach out to grasp an interesting toy or creep across a room

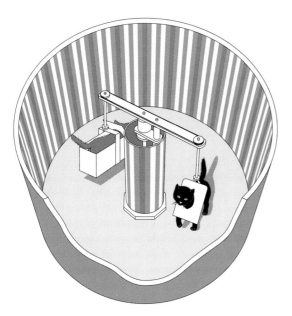

FIGURE 4.16 The Kitten Carousel Used in Held and Hein's Classic Experiment *A demonstration of the importance of active experience to development.*

they could previously only explore with their gaze. Research with laboratory animals points to the importance for understanding one's world of being able to move about in it. In a now-classic study, Richard Held and Alan Hein (1963) raised kittens in total darkness; the kittens' only chance to see anything came when they were placed, two by two, in a "kitten carousel" (Figure 4.16). One kitten was strapped into a harness attached to the end of an elevated arm that swept a circular space. The second kitten was placed in a basket hanging from the other end of the arm. As the first kitten walked, it pulled the other kitten along. Both of the kittens saw exactly the same thing, but only the first was able to coordinate what it was seeing with what it was doing. When placed in a new situation, the kitten that had been able to move about on its own was able to use visual information to position its body with respect to the things it saw. To turn an old phrase, seeing may be believing, but moving makes it real.

The development of voluntary movements, by which infants grasp, manipulate, and explore the objects around them, enables infants to discover not only the objects they are holding in their hands, but things about themselves as well. In making sense of objects "out there," in other words, the infant's sense of self in relation to these objects also changes. Infants' intense focusing on activities at this stage and their obvious enjoyment in exploring the things about them may have as much to do with the pleasures of self-discovery as with mastering the individual movements by which they explore their world. The Research Focus, "Operational Definitions: Anything You Can Do, I Can Do Too," discusses mastery motivation for those with developmental disabilities.

Nutrition and Health

It is said that an army moves on its stomach. The same can be said of development in infancy. Given that infants triple their birthweight within the 1st year and increase in length by half again, the nutritional demands of the 1st year are enormous. Because of the rate at which they grow, infants are almost always hungry, or so it seems to parents, waking every 2 to 4 hours for a feeding.

The best food for meeting infants' needs is breast milk (Hervada & Hervada-Page, 1995; Lawrence, 1994). In fact, breast milk is such a perfect food that infants

Although breast milk is the ideal food for infants, by about 6 months, additional foods can be added to the infant's diet in strained forms.

Operational Definitions:
Anything You Can Do, I Can Do Too

Carl stood quietly in the middle of the kitchen floor, looking down at his 2-year-old son, Gil, who was deliberately, and with considerable effort, putting one object after another into a large kitchen drawer that had been cleared for him to use. The 2-year-old surveyed the scattered objects on the floor about him and selected a large wooden spoon from among them. Securing his balance by gripping the drawer handle, the child painstakingly lifted the spoon over the lip of the open drawer and then, with a smile, released his grip, letting the spoon fall with a satisfying clatter to the bottom of the drawer.

The sound brought a smile to Carl's face as well. After experiencing the emotional devastation that followed Gil's diagnosis, he had thought his face might break if he ever smiled again. He had been told that Gil would never be like other kids, that he had a "developmental disability" that would prevent him from developing normally. Well, Carl thought, he might not be able to get around as well as other toddlers or hold on to things as easily, but that didn't stop him from trying just as hard. Once he set his mind to something, that little kid wouldn't give up until he'd mastered it. One thing seemed sure: Gil wasn't a quitter. Carl was proud of his son.

Was Gil unusual in this respect? Did he experience the same motive for mastery as other children his age? Mastery motivation has been assumed to serve as the basis for much of development, stimulating children to explore and rise to challenging situations. But are children with developmental disabilities as motivated to explore and master their environments as children without such disabilities?

Before one can begin to gather answers to questions such as these, an essential step has to be taken. The concepts under consideration (developmental disabilities and mastery motivation) have to be *operationally defined*. Because concepts are, by definition, abstract, there are usually a number of different ways of interpreting them. Operationally defining a concept pins it down by expressing it in terms of the methods used to measure it. Operationalizing is a fundamental process employed in all empirical science. Even a seemingly simple concept like "friendliness," in order to be studied, might be operationally defined in terms of the number of times a child smiles at others or through a questionnaire filled out by a parent. By operationalizing a concept, investigators define it in a way that others can use and follow in order to be sure they are studying the same concept.

But not all operational definitions are equally adequate. Suppose, in studying friendliness, we operationally define a "friendly" child as "any child who is smiling the first time that child is observed." Although that phase does fulfill the minimum requirement for an operational definition—that is, it specifies what operation to perform to determine if a child is friendly (observe the child and see if that child is smiling)—it is not likely to be a satisfactory definition. It is likely to be deficient with respect to the two most important criteria for any measure—*reliability* and *validity*—that is, its consistency and the degree to which it measures what we assume it is measuring.

Penny Hauser-Cram (1996) notes that previous research with children who are *developmentally delayed,* or suffer a mental disability, has found them to have lower levels of mastery motiva-

who are breast-fed need nothing else for the first 6 months, though there is debate as to whether this includes the need for some supplements, such as iron. Even though there is less iron in breast milk than in iron-fortified formulas, nearly 50% of the iron in breast milk is absorbed, compared to only 4% of the iron in fortified formulas (Lawrence, 1994). Since the composition of commercial formulas is closely patterned after that of breast milk, mothers who cannot, or simply choose not to, breast-feed need not be concerned that their infants will not be properly nourished. Infants fed with breast milk or a commercially prepared formula will receive all the nutrients they need. Parents should not feed their infant the milk they drink, however, since it contains little usable iron and almost no vitamins, has too much sodium, and can cause rectal bleeding if consumed as a steady diet (Hervada & Hervada-Page, 1995).

One of the many advantages of breast milk is that it is more easily digested than commercial formulas. As a consequence, breast-fed infants are less likely to suffer gastric discomforts; problems such as diarrhea or constipation are less likely to occur. However, they also get hungry about every 2 hours, in comparison to every 3 to 4 hours for infants who are bottle-fed.

Another advantage to breast milk is the protection that it offers infants against disease. Breast milk contains antibodies that are transferred from mother to infant,

tion. Such research, however, has examined only school-age children, leaving open the question of whether differences in mastery motivation are inherent to this type of disability or develop only with time. Furthermore, previous research has looked exclusively at children who are developmentally delayed, leaving unanswered whether the findings extend to physically disabled children. To examine the first issue, Hauser-Cram examined nondisabled infants and toddlers, comparing them to developmentally disabled children of a comparable mental age. To address the second issue, she included children who were motor-impaired (physical disability) as well as developmentally delayed.

To assess, or operationally define, children who were developmentally delayed, Hauser-Cram administered the Bayley Scales (1969) Mental Development Index (MDI). The MDI contains questions designed to distinguish children in terms of mental development. Children were considered to be developmentally delayed if they were at least one standard deviation below the mean in at least two subtests (see the Research Focus, "Descriptive Statistics," in Chapter 3). Hauser-Cram relied on determinations made by caseworkers to assess motor impairment. To assess mastery motivation, children were given problem-posing toys, such as puzzles, and were scored for such things as their persistence and focus on the task.

Were these measures reliable? One way of determining reliability is to give the measure to the same individuals on two separate occasions, assessing consistency in responding to questions from one time to the next. This method is termed *test-retest reliability*. One of the strengths of the MDI is its reliability, with children obtaining close to the same score when tested at different times. Similarly, reliability for assessments of mastery motivation was determined by having two independent observers score each child's performance. Each observer's scores were compared to yield a measure of *interobserver reliability*. Thus, rather than comparing a child's performance on two different occasions, the same performance is assessed by two different observers. Using this approach, interobserver reliability for assessments of mastery motivation was found to be high.

Of equal, if not greater, interest is whether a measure is a valid one. One way to determine a measure's validity is to see how well the measure relates to other measures of the construct. This measure of validity is known as *construct validity*. The Bayley Scales have been found to predict mental functioning in other settings, such as classrooms. Since classroom learning is assumed to reflect mental ability, this has been taken as a measure of the construct validity of this test. Similarly, the assessments of motor impairment made by caseworkers were confirmed by comparisons with children's medical records. One might question whether the measure of mastery motivation that was chosen was as valid as it was reliable. Will children focus on a task as much when being tested by an unfamiliar person with another observer present, and possibly at a time of day when they would rather be doing something else, as when they choose to sit down with a toy and play with it by themselves? Or is involvement with toys even the best measure of such a broad concept? Such questions point to the inherent difficulty in operationally defining concepts. Operational definitions, because they define concepts in terms of a set of specific procedures, are at least in principle reliable. But how well these procedures capture the underlying concept is a more difficult matter.

But back to Gil. Just how representative was this toddler of other developmentally disabled children? Hauser-Cram found that children like Gil, whether motor-impaired or developmentally delayed, did not differ from nondisabled children in measures of mastery motivation when working at tasks of comparable levels of difficulty.

protecting the infant from a number of illnesses and allergies. This advantage is particularly important in nonindustrialized nations in which death rates among infants who are not breast-fed can be up to 5 times higher than those who are (Lawrence, 1994). Even when the mothers themselves are malnourished, the nutrients contained in their breast milk do not differ significantly from those in the milk of mothers with an adequate diet. They simply produce less milk (Lawrence, 1994).

Not all mothers choose to breast-feed. For some, it is a matter of preference. Others may experience embarrassment at nursing an infant outside the home or inconvenience at having to pump their own milk into bottles for feedings when they cannot be there, such as during work hours if they are employed outside the home. For mothers who want to breast-feed but experience difficulty doing so, the La Leche League, a national organization devoted to promoting breast-feeding, provides information concerning problems such as these. Other mothers may be unable to breast-feed for medical reasons, such as a disease that could be transmitted to the infant through the milk or medication they may be taking that also would reach the infant through their milk. Although breast milk is unquestionably the best food source available to infants, the mother's comfort is also an important consideration. And mothers who choose to bottle-feed can stare with rapt delight into their infant's eyes just as well as do those who choose to breast-feed.

Supplemental Food Programs

Worldwide, approximately 190 million children below the age of 5 suffer from malnutrition (Pollitt et al., 1996). Malnutrition occurs when diets are deficient in protein, calories, or micronutrients. The first of these components, protein, provides amino acids, the body's building blocks, and is essential for growth. Calories provide energy. When diet affords too few calories, the body breaks down amino acids for energy instead of using them to build new cells. Micronutrients include essential vitamins and minerals, such as vitamin A, iodine, iron, and zinc. Deficiencies in these can result in lowered resistance to infection, goiter, anemia, and retarded growth, respectively (Brown & Pollitt, 1996). Since children who are deficient in one of these dietary components are usually deficient in others, the effects of malnutrition can be myriad. Malnourished children not only experience hunger, weight loss, and even stunted growth, but they also feel listless, are less curious, have difficulty paying attention, and get sick more often. Additionally, severe malnutrition in early childhood can impair cognitive functioning and affect later intellectual development, as well as interfere with children's emotional development and the very quality of their most intimate relationships, those they have with their parents (Brown & Pollitt, 1996; Meeks Gardner, Grantham-McGregor, Chang, Himes, & Powell, 1995; Pollitt et al., 1996).

How effective are existing intervention programs at reducing the effects of malnutrition? That depends on the degree of malnutrition, the timing of the intervention, and the presence of other conditions that frequently accompany malnutrition, such as poverty, neglect, poor medical care, and poor schools. The bottom line, however, is that when malnourished children are given supplemental food, the benefits are profound. In one such supplemental feeding program, over 2,000 pregnant women and young children living in each of several villages in Guatemala were given either of two simple nutritional supplements for a period of 8 years. One of the supplements ("atole") was a cereal that is rich in protein, an ingredient believed to be deficient in the diet of many of these children. The other supplement ("fresco") was a fruit drink containing no protein, but an equivalent supply of vitamins and minerals. Both supplements also supplied calories, though only a third as many were in the fruit drink as in the cereal.

The protein-rich cereal reduced infant mortality by 69%, and the vitamin supplement by 24%. But beyond saving lives, the supplements had long-term impact on the quality of those lives as well. Ten years later, the effects of the supplemental protein on intellectual ability were still evident, effectively counteracting differences due to income level (see left side of the figure). Dietary supplements also enabled the children to benefit from schooling in a way not possible had they remained malnourished (see right side of the figure).

These effects are not only striking in themselves but also offer the means to counter some of the most crippling effects of poverty in children's lives, even when other conditions remain unchanged. Supplemental food programs, in other words, can mitigate against the cognitive deficits that otherwise go hand in hand with poverty (Brown & Pollitt, 1996; Meeks Gardner et al., 1995; Pollitt, 1994; Pollitt et al., 1996). The importance in terms of social policy of findings such as these cannot be overstated.

In the United States some 12 million children have diets that are significantly deficient in one or more important nutrients. For instance, iron-deficiency anemia, which affects children's psychomotor development and intellectual performance, is one of the most serious of the nutritional deficiencies, affecting approximately 20% of children under 2 years of age (Yip et al., 1992). The United States currently has a number of food assistance programs, authorized under the National School Lunch and Child Nutrition Act Amendments of 1975 (Public Law 94-105). These programs provide food rich in protein, iron, calcium, and vitamins A and C to pregnant women, new mothers, infants, and children; and they provide nutritious snacks and lunches to low-income schoolchildren. Given that one in four infants and toddlers in this nation lives in poverty, such programs remain vitally important (Children's Defense Fund, 1994). Food assistance programs not only provide a better return for each tax dollar spent on education, but they also help to improve the quality of life for millions of children.

By about 6 months, additional foods can be added to the infant's diet in the form of strained cereals, fruits and vegetables, and meats; and by about 1 year of age, most infants have enough teeth to tackle whatever is served to the rest of the family, if it is cut into tiny pieces.

When speaking of feeding infants, developmentalists talk for the most part about which foods best meet the nutritional needs of infants. And rightly so. However, getting the nutritionally right foods *into* the infant, as opposed to on the walls or in your shoes is quite another thing. As Anne Lamott (1993) writes after feeding her son his newest strained vegetable, "Sam had strained carrots again tonight. Big huge mess, carrots everywhere, all over the kitty who passed by at a bad time,

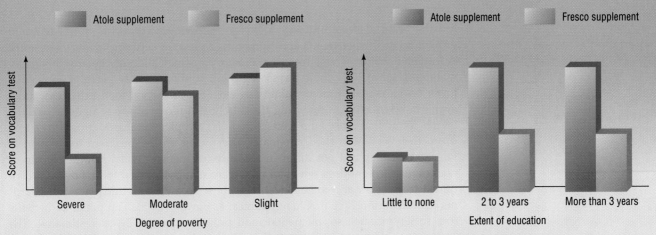

The effects of a supplemental food program on intellectual performance as a function of poverty (left). The effects of education as a function of supplemental food (right). Source: Brown & Pollitt (1996).

Guidelines for Good Nutrition

Food Category	Servings per Day	Serving Size*		
		Age 1 to 3 Years	4 to 6 Years	7 to 10 Years
Whole-grain or enriched breads, cereals, rice, pasta	6 or more	1/2 slice bread or 1/4 cup rice or noodles	1 slice bread or 1/2 cup rice or noodles	1 to 2 slices bread or 1/2 to 1 cup rice or noodles
Vegetables	3 or more	2 to 4 tbsp or 1/2 cup juice	1/4 to 1/2 cup or 1/2 cup juice	1/2 to 3/4 cup or 1/2 cup juice
Fruits	2 or more	2 to 4 tbsp or 1/2 cup juice	1/4 to 1/2 cup or 1/2 cup juice	1/2 to 3/4 cup or 1/2 cup juice
Lean meats, fish, poultry, eggs, nuts, beans	2 or more	1 to 2 oz	1 to 2 oz	2 to 3 oz
Milk and cheese	3 to 4	1/2 to 3/4 cup milk or 1/2 to 3/4 oz cheese	3/4 cup milk or 3/4 oz cheese	3/4 to 1 cup milk or 1/2 to 3/4 oz cheese

*Data from Growth and nutrient requirements of children, by P. M. Queen and R. R. Henry. In *Pediatric Nutrition*, edited by R. J. Grand et al. Butterworth, 1987. *Source:* Brown & Pollitt (1996).

on Sam's socks, in his hair, in my hair. I can see that things are going to begin deteriorating around here rather rapidly" (p. 150). ◄

Malnutrition

Maintaining adequate nutrition during infancy is vitally important, not only for physical growth, but also for intellectual development. Children who do not receive an adequate diet during infancy can suffer a number of consequences, from lethargy and loss of curiosity to physical stunting to impaired cognitive functioning. Recall that not only does the infant add inches and pounds at a rapid rate, but the brain also continues to develop following birth, with spurts of brain growth occurring between 3 and 10 months and again between 15 and 24 months. Adequate nutrition is vital for optimal development. Children who are sufficiently malnourished to have their physical growth stunted usually perform somewhat lower on measures of mental ability as well. Supplemental food programs, however, can be effective in reversing these trends. A recent study of undernourished infants found that those who were placed on a supplemental food program caught up to their well-nourished age-mates after being on the program for a year, at which point they did not differ in measures of mental ability. Another group of undernourished children who had not received supplemental food, however, continued to perform at a lower level than those receiving an adequate diet (Gardner, Grantham-McGregor, Chang, Himes, & Powell, 1995). The potential benefits to a society of such supplemental food programs cannot be overestimated. The cost of providing nutritional supplements is relatively low, certainly when compared to the misery and loss of human potential resulting from malnourishment or the costly corrective measures, such as special education classes, that may be required further down the road. See the Social Policy Focus, "Supplemental Food Programs," for a discussion of the effectiveness of these programs.

Summary

The Newborn

Birth requires adjustments in breathing, regulating temperature, eating, and sleeping. Breathing is usually irregular for the first 2 or 3 days. Most neonates cough and sneeze frequently, which helps to clear passages of mucus and fluids. Keeping warm can also be problematic in that newborns lack the protective layer of fat that insulates older infants from rapid changes in temperature. Since several days lapse before infants begin to take nourishment in the form of breast milk or formula, most also lose several ounces immediately following birth.

States of Arousal

Most infants establish a stable circadian rhythm between 2 and 4 months of age, in which they sleep for longer periods of time than they did initially. Prior to this time, they are on a 4-hour sleep-wake cycle. Both sleeping and waking are characterized by quiet and active states. In quiet sleep the body is relaxed, eyelids are closed, and the eyes are motionless. In active sleep, body movements, facial expressions, and rapid eye movements occur. Similar distinctions between states of wakefulness can be made. In drowsiness, the body is relaxed, but the eyes are open. In quiet wakefulness, the infant is relaxed and attentive, and in active wakefulness, the infant is physically and mentally active.

Physical Growth

Growth in the 1st year is rapid; weight triples and body length increases by half again. Growth is less rapid in the 2nd year, with infants adding another 5 pounds and growing 5 inches. Growth reflects two trends: the cephalocaudal trend in which growth begins in the region of the head and proceeds downward, and the proximodistal trend in which growth progresses outward from the center of the body to the extremities. Physical growth includes increases in body fat and muscle tissue as well as bone growth. The latter involves both the growth of existing bones and the emergence of new bones.

As infants move about, they put stress on the skeletal system, which causes the bones to realign. This realignment results in the familiar curvatures in the upper and lower regions of the spine and realignment of the leg bones and the pelvis as well as of the bones forming the rib cage. Nutrition plays an important role in all aspects of skeletal growth.

Brain Development

The brain continues to develop following birth. Development proceeds unevenly, with spurts of brain growth occurring between 3 and 10 months and 15 and 24 months. This growth is due largely to the proliferation of glial cells, which both nourish the neurons and produce myelin, the substance that coats the axons of neurons, thereby facilitating the conduction of neural impulses. Myelination progresses at different rates for different parts of the brain. The peripheral nervous system is first to be myelinated; among the last is the frontal cortex. Early experience also contributes to brain development, being necessary for the establishment of neural connections and for the maintenance of already-established ones.

Development of the Senses

Newborns have a well-developed sense of taste; they are able to distinguish sweet, salty, sour, and bitter substances. Their sense of smell is also highly developed. Vision, however, is the least developed of the senses at birth, maturing within the 1st year. Newborns actively scan a visual surround. These scanning patterns change markedly with age, paralleling development of the visual system. Visual acuity and distance perception also develop significantly within the first 6 months.

In comparison to vision, hearing is relatively well developed at birth. For most newborns, sounds need only be twice as loud to be heard as they need to be for an adult, whereas objects need to be 20 times as close to be seen. Infants also get better with age at localizing where sounds are coming from. Even newborns react differently to speech sounds than to nonspeech sounds, the former being processed in a qualitatively different way than the latter.

The senses can be thought of as ways of exploring and making sense of one's surround. It is suggested that anticipatory schemata guide this process, directing the pickup of information and in turn being modified by what is perceived. This information need not be tied to a particular sensory modality. Rather than functioning as separate and isolated systems, the activity of one sensory system has been shown to contribute to the ability to sense things in a different modality.

Motor Development

Both physical growth and brain development enable infants to develop new control over their bodies. Prior to the development of this control, much of their behavior is reflexive. These reflexes are highly adaptive, such as the sucking, rooting, head turning, and grasp reflexes. In addition to their adaptive value, reflexes are useful diagnostically, since reflexive behavior changes with age, and many reflexes drop out as the central nervous system matures.

Myelination of fibers within the motor cortex makes possible the emergence of new, voluntary behaviors. The primary motor cortex is responsible for governing the activity of discrete muscles within the body; the secondary motor cortex is responsible for patterned movements, in which the activity of discrete muscles is coordinated. Control over muscles in different parts of the body progresses unevenly, illustrating the cephalocaudal trend. Considerable variability also exists from one infant to the next. All infants, however, appear to experience pleasure at the mastery of new skills. The process of mastering motor skills embodies many of the same characteristics as do the activities that produce the experience of flow in adults.

The development of voluntary movements, by which infants grasp, manipulate, and explore the objects around them, enables infants to discover not only the objects they are manipulating, but things about themselves as well.

Nutrition and Health

The best food for meeting the nutritional needs of infants is breast milk. Infants who are breast-fed need nothing else for the first 6 months, with the possible exception of some supplements, such as iron. Since the composition of commercial formulas is closely patterned after that of breast milk, infants who are bottle-fed will similarly receive all the nutrients they need from the formula; however, they will not receive the antibodies contained in breast milk that protect infants from many illnesses and allergies. By about 6 months, additional foods can be added to the infant's diet in the form of strained cereals, fruits and vegetables, and meats.

Maintaining adequate nutrition during infancy is important not only for physical growth but also for intellectual development. Malnutrition can result in physical stunting and impaired cognitive functioning. Supplemental food programs, however, have been found effective in reversing both of these trends.

Key Terms

active sleep (p. 133)
active wakefulness (p. 133)
afferent, or sensory, pathway (p. 151)
axon (p. 141)
brain stem (p. 151)
central nervous system (p. 141)
cephalocaudal growth trend (p. 136)
cerebellum (p. 154)
drowsiness (p. 133)
efferent, or motor, pathway (p. 151)

epiphyseal growth plates (p. 139)
flow (p. 158)
fontanels (p. 139)
glial cells (p. 140)
grasp reflex (p. 152)
Moro reflex (p. 152)
myelin (p. 141)
neurons (p. 140)
peripheral nervous system (p. 141)
primary motor cortex (p. 153)

proximodistal growth trend (p. 137)
quiet sleep (p. 133)
quiet wakefulness (p. 133)
rapid eye movements (REM) (p. 133)
rooting reflex (p. 151)
"rules" for scanning (p. 144)
secondary motor cortex (p. 154)
sucking reflex (p. 151)
visual acuity (p. 145)

chapterfive

Infancy and Toddlerhood
Cognitive Development

L isten, Paula. I am going to tell you a story, so that when you wake up you will not feel so lost." Thus, Isabel Allende, a master at storytelling, begins a narrative for her seriously ill daughter, one intended to anchor her firmly in this world. Infants, too, are told stories, by all of us. And with each story, they are tied ever more securely to their surroundings. However, these stories are rarely in words. Instead, they take other forms—of faces moving to the rhythm of language, or mobiles spinning when touched, of shadows and light, and footsteps and fingers, and the dazzling complexity of the ordinary. For infants, you see, discover through the narrative of experience what we, as adults, no longer notice. They discover the way a door appears to change as it opens, morphing from rectangle to trapezoid, yet all the while remaining a door. Or the sameness of color as light and shadow move across surfaces. They discover the way things reappear, momentarily obscured from view, such as a hand at the end of a sleeve or a toy beneath a blanket. These daily narratives fix infants in a stable world of increasing predictability, one that invites, and yields to, their exploration.

With age, infants get better at locating and looking at things around them.

operant conditioning A simple form of learning in which the probability of a behavior is affected by its consequences.

Perceiving and Making Sense of the World

Infants are curious about their surroundings and begin to explore them from their first moments on. While still in the delivery room, infants will turn their heads in the direction of a sound, look intently at a face, and attend to the sounds of the human voice. With age, infants get increasingly better at perceiving the things around them, becoming more efficient at locating objects, following things that move with their eyes, and grasping onto what they reach for.

Getting better at the things we do is something many of us take for granted. But how is this accomplished? As you might expect, numerous explanations have been offered. Just as we saw in Chapter 1, these can be grouped as to whether they emphasize conditions that are external to the individual as primarily responsible for the changes (an environmental perspective) or whether they stress inborn processes through which individuals organize experience (an organismic or constructive perspective). Each perspective acknowledges the importance of both environmental and inner processes, but they differ in the emphasis they give to either of these in explaining developmental change.

Consider the seemingly simple activity of locating where an interesting event is likely to appear next. Marshall Haith and his associates (1993) showed 3-month-old infants pictures that sometimes appeared to the left of them and sometimes to the right. For some of the infants, the location of the pictures alternated in a predictable sequence (left, right, left, etc.), whereas for others, the sequence was unpredictable. Unlike infants for whom the pictures appeared randomly, those shown the alternating sequence quickly learned where to look for the next picture. Clearly, infants who were given a predictable sequence had gotten better at knowing where to look. But what precisely accounted for their improvement?

The Environmental Perspective: Looking Outside the Organism

Those adopting an environmental perspective would argue that the infants had learned to turn left, then right, and so on; and in each case their looking had been rewarded by actually seeing the picture when they turned their head in that direction. This type of learning, known as **operant conditioning**, accounts for changes in behavior as a result of the events that follow a behavior (see Chapter 1). An event that, when it is made contingent on behavior, increases the frequency of that behavior, is termed **reinforcement.** The behavior which is reinforced is known as an *operant.* Thus the operant in this instance would be turning to the left or right, and the reinforcement would be seeing the picture.

The Constructive Perspective: Looking Within the Organism

Ulric Neisser (1976), a psychologist at Cornell University, suggests that what is changed is not so much the behavior of looking to the left or the right as what guides the behavior. Neisser traces the infants' improvement to the development of anticipatory schemata (see Chapter 4). These are cognitive structures that prepare us to take in certain types of information and not others. Anticipatory schemata direct the way we explore things, determining the features that are sampled and guiding the pickup of information. The schemata are in turn modified and refined by the information that is picked up. This perceptual process takes the form of an ongoing activity in which what is anticipated directs the way new objects and events will be explored, with the outcome modifying and refining one's initial expectations. These tie one ever more closely to the events one is monitoring.

Neisser points out that infants come into the world with considerable "perceptual equipment." We have seen evidence of such equipment, in the last chapter, such as infants' rules for scanning in dark versus well-lit rooms. Other equipment exists in the form of their ability to visually track moving objects, reflexively reach out toward things they see, or grasp those that are placed in their hands. Even though this basic perceptual equipment does not provide infants with all they will need to know about their surroundings, it is enough to show them how to find what they need to know (Neisser, 1976). Anticipatory schemata can be thought of as plans for perceptual activity, plans that guide the constructive process by which we make sense of experience. As Haith (1993) has commented, infants don't just look at things. Instead they are analyzing what they see and creating little hypotheses as they do. But where might these hypotheses, or plans, come from?

Piaget's Developmental Constructivism

A central issue for Jean Piaget, one that gave shape to his theory of intellectual development, concerned this very question, "How do we come to know what we know?" Piaget believed that our understanding of the world begins with the development of sensorimotor schemas that are rooted in, and evolve out of, the basic reflexes that are present at birth. Piaget traced intellectual development over four stages. The first, the **sensorimotor stage,** lasts from birth to the age of 2, and is the stage that concerns us in this chapter. Like the reflexes from which they evolve, sensorimotor schemas are assumed initially to be activated only when something is actually present. With age, these become modified, spanning time to "hold" a thing in mind, whether it is there or not. For Piaget, this ability represents one of the most important cognitive achievements of infancy, the capacity to represent experience in one's mind. Before this, the infants' world is one of the here and now, a world that coincides with what they can see, hear, or touch. Only with age will they reach for things hidden from sight or be stilled by the sound of familiar footsteps. With age, also, they begin to relate to things in new and more intentional ways, at first doing so only with their hands, but eventually mentally

reinforcement An event that, when it is made contingent on behavior, increases the frequency of that behavior.

sensorimotor stage Piaget's first stage of intellectual development, during which sensory experiences are coordinated with motor behaviors.

TABLE 5.1 Stages of Sensorimotor Development in Infants and Toddlers		
Stage	**Approximate Age**	**Characteristic Behaviors**
Substage 1: Reflex modification	Birth to 1 month	Repeats reflexive behaviors, such as sucking, and becomes able to perform them efficiently
Substage 2: Primary circular reactions	1 to 4 months	Intentionally repeats actions for their own sake, such as opening and closing hands, touching them together, or making bubbles
Substage 3: Secondary circular reactions	4 to 8 months	Repeats actions directed at objects in the environment, such as kicking a crib mobile or shaking a rattle, and observes what happens
Substage 4: Coordination of secondary circular reactions	8 to 12 months	Acts for a purpose, such as crawling across room to get a desired toy, or pushing aside an obstacle, such as an adult's hand, to reach a toy
Substage 5: Tertiary circular reactions	12 to 18 months	Experiments with objects, feeling their texture, watching what happens when they are dropped or pushed; begins to use trial and error to solve problems; begins mimicking adult behaviors
Substage 6: Mental representation	18 to 24 months	Engages in make-believe play; looks at pictures in books; can point to named body part

as well, manipulating images of things that previously yielded only to their touch. Piaget distinguished six substages to this development; these are described below and summarized in Table 5.1.

Substage 1: Modification of Basic Reflexes (Birth to 1 Month)

The reflexes that infants are born with, such as rooting, sucking, and grasping, initially occur only when triggered by specific stimuli. Thus, touching the infant's cheek will trigger the rooting reflex, causing the infant to turn its head. Similarly, brushing the infant's lips will cause the infant to suck, and stroking the palm of its hand will cause it to reflexively close its fingers in a tight grasp. These reflexes soon become modified in two ways. First, they become altered, in seemingly small but nonetheless important ways, such that they provide a better fit with the conditions imposed by the immediate situation. Second, they begin to occur in the absence of the stimuli that initially had triggered them.

Consider the reflex of sucking. In the first few days of life, the infant will purse its lips and position its tongue in much the same way when it nurses, irrespective of how its head is positioned with respect to the nipple or even to differences in the shape of the nipple itself. As you might expect, the same way of sucking will not work equally well under different circumstances, and only those modifications of the reflex that produce enough suction will result in an even flow of milk. Infants soon adjust, or *accommodate,* their sucking in order to adapt to the conditions of the situations in which it is evoked.

These basic reflexes function in ways similar to Neisser's anticipatory schemata. Thus, sucking can be thought of as a biological blueprint, or plan, for drawing fluid into one's mouth. These plans are modified on an ongoing basis, involving the organism in a dynamic interaction with the environment. Thus, the infant's experience of the activity that is being guided by the schema provides information that in turn serves to modify the original schema, bringing it more closely into alignment with the requirements of the immediate situation. The way the infant initially positions its lips and places its tongue to create the pressure necessary to draw in milk is adjusted as it experiences that more or less pressure (and more or less milk) results from positioning its tongue one way or another relative to the nipple.

One soon notices a second modification. The infant can be seen to suck to the *sight* of the nipple as well as to the touch of the nipple on its lips. Similarly, other events that regularly accompany nursing, such as being held in a certain position or the sound of a bottle being prepared, will occasion sucking before the nipple touches its lips. We saw this type of modification in the discussion of classical conditioning (Chapter 1), in which reflexes were seen to occur in response to an event that predicts the arrival of the triggering stimulus. In the earlier example, dogs salivated to the sounds (CS) that preceded the arrival of food (UCS). Here, we see the infant sucking to cues, whether these are the sight of the nipple or being held in a certain position, that precede nursing. This second modification illustrates the process of *assimilation,* in which the infant incorporates new elements, such as the sight of the nipple, into an existing schema, a reflex that was originally triggered only by the touch of the nipple.

Substage 2: Primary Circular Reactions (1 to 4 Months)

In the second substage, basic reflexes are further modified, evolving into **schemas,** or action patterns, that become divorced from the stimuli that initially triggered them. This development enables the behavior to occur in new situations and to be repeated without subsequent stimulation. Infants, in other words, become able to prolong an interesting event by repeating the behavior that brought it about. The activity by which they do this takes a cyclic form, in that the completion of the behavior serves to trigger its repetition. Note, it is now the behavior itself, rather than the onset of a stimulus, that governs its occurrence. Piaget referred to these behaviors as **primary circular reactions,** primary in that they are limited to actions that involve the infant's own body and circular in that the behavior is prompted by its own completion. Thus, an infant can be seen to purse its lips as it does when sucking, but without a nipple in its mouth. When bubbles form, as they do, the infant will blow new ones as the first ones pop. Similarly, an infant may kick, enjoying the way this causes its body to wiggle, and then, once the movement stops, kick again.

Substage 3: Secondary Circular Reactions (4 to 8 Months)

In the third substage, circular reactions are extended to include objects outside the infant's body and are termed **secondary circular reactions.** Thus, an infant lying on its back with a mobile overhead might kick, and then notice the mobile moving, and kick again. Or an infant given a rattle might wave its arms, hear the sound, and then delightedly wave them again, producing the sound again. Recall that infants at this age can sit up with support and look around and are much

schemas Piaget's term for the mental structures through which the child represents experience through actions.

primary circular reactions Substage 2 of Piaget's sensorimotor stage in which infants (1–4 months) repeat a physical behavior involving their own body.

secondary circular reactions Substage 3 of Piaget's sensorimotor stage in which infants (4–8 months) repeat behaviors affecting objects outside their body.

This child is showing purposeful exploration, an indication that he has reached Piaget's fourth substage.

 During which substage of the sensorimoter period outlined by Piaget might an infant begin to delight in bathtime activities?

better at focusing on things that interest them. Their interest in the sights and sounds around them increases dramatically, and they incorporate these into their action schemas. In doing so, they become better at differentiating themselves from the things about them. For example, moving one's arms without the rattle in one's hand does not produce any interesting sounds. Piaget also believed infants first become able to imitate the actions of others at this stage, although only if this involves actions they are already capable of performing.

Substage 4: Coordination of Secondary Circular Reactions (8 to 12 Months)

Actions can be seen to become more coordinated and complex and also to reveal an intentional, goal-directed quality in the fourth substage. Piaget assumed that infants are first able to coordinate previously isolated actions into a single purposeful activity in this substage. Infants are interested in discovering all they can about the objects around them. Unlike the earlier circular reactions of the second and third substages, both of which were prompted by the accidental occurrence of an interesting event, behavior at this stage shows purposeful exploration. No longer content simply to look at something, infants pick things up, drop them, grasp them again and squeeze them, before putting them into their mouths for a final inspection. Through actions such as these, infants learn which things break, which bounce, and which quietly spill out their contents. They pursue these investigations with the determination of little scientists. As Anne Lamott (1993) writes of her son,

> He's heavily into flinging things. He dismantles everything he can get his hands on. . . . It's gratuitous looting. He almost never actually takes anything and crawls away with it, but he'll get to the coffee table and system-

atically, often without any expression, lift and then drop or fling every single magazine, book, cup, or whatever to the ground. His grim expression suggests he's got a lot to do and just really doesn't want to be bothered until he's done. (p. 219) ◄

By such activity, Piaget would observe, infants are learning what they need to know about the world they live in.

Q How would Piaget explain why infants repeatedly drop things from their high chair?

Substage 5: Tertiary Circular Reactions (12 to 18 Months)

Whereas infants in the fourth substage directed their attention to the objects around them, in the fifth substage they become fascinated with the effects of their own actions. Piaget places the beginnings of problem solving at this substage. Infants are no longer content simply to repeat a behavior that produces some interesting event; they now vary this, experimenting with all the different ways they can accomplish something. **Tertiary circular reactions** are the action schemas by which they explore new ways of acting on things. Unlike primary circular reactions in which the focus of interest is simply the activity, or secondary reactions in which focus shifts to the object, in tertiary reactions, infants focus on the relationship between their actions and the objects they are exploring, between what they are doing and the effects this has on things. The child who has noticed that a pea will bounce over the edge if she hits her high-chair tray with her hand may try to do the same by banging her cup against the tray, or her plate, looking to see with each attempt if something pops over the edge.

Substage 6: Mental Representation (18 to 24 months)

The sensorimotor period ends with the sixth substage, since Piaget believed the emerging ability to represent experiences mentally moves the child into the preoperational stage, the second of his four stages of development. Up to this point, the child's interactions with the world have been prompted by what it can see or touch, by what is actually present. But with the ability to mentally represent objects, children can think of things that are not present, thus opening up a world of imagination and fantasy. This ability is made possible by the development of *symbols*, internalized images of objects. With the ability to imagine, or anticipate, some outcome of an action, exploration is no longer a matter of trial and error, of "let's see what will happen next," but can be guided by the expected outcomes of different actions, and thought becomes symbolic and conceptual.

Object Permanence

Piaget assumed that infants only gradually become able to hold things in mind when these are not present and that it takes them 2 years to develop a full understanding of the nature of objects. Boldly put, he assumed that, initially, objects simply cease to exist for infants when they are out of sight. Piaget traced infants' understanding of objects over a series of six stages that correspond roughly to the substages of sensorimotor thought, with the last being reached only as infancy ends. Piaget developed his assumptions about infants' understanding of their world by noting their reactions to the disappearance of their toys. Many a parent has similarly observed changes in the way infants react to objects disappearing from view. For instance, Anne Lamott (1993) writes of her infant son's reactions to dropping a toy:

tertiary circular reactions Substage 5 of Piaget's sensorimotor stage in which infants (12–18 months) begin to experiment with different ways of accomplishing something; the beginning of problem solving.

During the first 2 years, children gradually acquire an understanding of object permanence (which is why peekaboo is fun for them).

Enjoying a game of peek-a-boo is a sign of what kind of development in young infants?

He's figuring out little concepts all the time these days, like that if something falls out of his hands, it is not instantly vaporized but just might be found somewhere on the floor. Even a week ago Sam was like some rich guy who drops some change and doesn't even give it a second glance, but now when he drops something, he slowly cranes his neck and peers downward, as if the thing fell to the floor of a canyon. (p. 187) ◄

Piaget observed that in the first stage of the development of object permanence (birth to 2 months), infants show no reaction when something they have been following with their eyes disappears from view. They neither look for it nor reach after it. In the second stage (2 to 4 months), infants will follow something with their eyes as it moves out of sight, but do so in peculiar ways. For instance, they will continue to track an object even after it has stopped moving. By the third stage (4 to 6 months), these tracking errors disappear. Infants also begin to reach for things, such as toys, that are only partially visible. However, they will stop in midreach if a toy is completely covered from view before they contact it. Even after grasping hold of the toy, if their hand is covered before they pull the toy out, they can be seen to look idly about, eventually pulling back an empty hand. Nor do they appear to be surprised if the hidden object is spirited away, revealing nothing there when the cover is removed. All of these reactions suggested to Piaget that objects cease to exist for infants when perceptual contact with them is lost.

In the fourth stage (6 to 12 months), infants will retrieve objects that are completely hidden from view. However, they make "place errors," looking for things where they have been found previously even when they have just seen them moved somewhere else. Unlike infants a few months younger, they show surprise when an object hidden under a cover is not there when the cover is removed, and another object has taken its place. However, they will still play with the new toy rather than looking for the first. In the fifth stage (12 to 18 months), they continue to look for the first object. They also no longer make place errors, looking for things where they last saw them. However, one last confusion remains. They have difficulty understanding that something can be moved while out of sight. If, for example, you were to show them a ball in your hand, then hide it with a fist, place your fist behind your back and transfer the ball to the other hand, and show them your empty hand, they would not think to look in the other hand. This inability to imagine movements that cannot be seen, what Piaget referred to as errors of "invisible displacement," is overcome in the sixth stage of object permanence (Piaget, 1954).

Critique of Piaget's Theory

Piaget has given us a remarkably detailed record of infants' developing abilities over the first 2 years of life, one that rings true to those familiar with infants. As a consequence, critics of his theory are less likely to take issue with the behaviors that he documented than they are to quarrel with the assumptions he based these on. For Piaget assumed, despite the significant changes that he chronicled over these years, that infants were not capable of thinking until they were approximately 2 years old. He believed not only that they lacked concepts for things, but also that, for the first half of the sensorimotor period, they did not even perceive their world as made up of three-dimensional objects. Piaget also assumed that infants had no way of bringing previously experienced events to mind or of imagining future ones. In fact, until the achievements of the sensorimotor period were completed, he believed that infants had no way of symbolically representing their world, or even had a world to represent. Why would Piaget think this?

Piaget assumed that our experience of the world is filtered through our actions on and reactions to the things around us. For the infant, these first actions take the form of reflexes, each triggered by a particular stimulus, the way a touch to the lips triggers sucking or movement in the visual field triggers tracking. Furthermore, like most of his contemporaries, Piaget believed that stimulation was specific to each sensory modality and that, as a consequence, the actions prompted by different stimuli provided information about only that one modality. Thus, one of the first things an infant had to accomplish was to integrate the different components of sensory information into a unitary percept. Only then could the infant experience a world of objects that moved and made sounds and were solid to the touch. Much of the first half of the sensorimotor period was assumed to be devoted to the construction of schemas that integrated information from the separate senses. Until this perceptual integration was achieved, objects as such could not exist for the infant nor, of course, could they be conceptualized (Piaget, 1952, 1954).

Thus, according to Piaget, an infant looking at a toy bear beating a drum would not connect the *movements* of the bear with the *sounds* of the drum. Before that connection could be made, the infant had to coordinate the various sensations arriving at the eyes, ears, and fingertips. Until then, the world was experienced as fleeting images and disconnected sounds. Piaget believed infants accomplished this integration through the development of schemas, action patterns that had become freed from the modality-specific stimuli that triggered reflexes, thus becoming available to coordinate information received from several or more senses. This integration of sensory input became one of the major accomplishments of the first year (Mandler, 1990, 1992). (The Research Focus: "Cross-Sectional Design—Slices Through Time: Visual Scanning," describes how scanning works and the way it changes from ages 6 to 13 weeks.)

Are the senses initially unconnected, and do they need to be integrated through the types of experiences Piaget has documented in the six substages of sensorimotor thought? Or do infants recognize much earlier than this that the various sights and sounds and feel of things are aspects of a single object? Can infants recognize something by sight, for instance, that they have only had a chance to feel, using information provided by one modality to recognize something they have experienced only in another? There is considerable evidence, in fact, that they

Cross-Sectional and Sequential Designs—
Slices Through Time: Visual Scanning BY MICHAEL WAPNER

Look around—at your hand, at a chair, at someone near you. As you fix your gaze on that object, you see it totally and immediately. In other words, the object does not "resolve" into view like those scenes in movies that begin out of focus and gradually become clear. Nor do you experience a bunch of isolated features assembling themselves into an object—first a patch of color, then a corner, and then an edge. Whatever object you see, you see "all at once." And yet, although you are not conscious of it, seeing an object does take time.

To be seen in its detailed entirety, an object must be *scanned*. Scanning involves movement of the eyes back and forth across the relevant portion of the visual field. The scanning movement consists of two parts—(1) brief fixations where the eye rests on some portion of the visual field and (2) intervening movements, or *saccades*, which carry the eye from one fixation point to another. Information collected by scanning must be integrated. What is seen at any given moment does not come from any single fixation, but from the integration of successive fixations— just as what is seen at any given moment on a movie screen does not correspond to any single film frame, but results from the integration of successive frames. To accomplish this integration, visual information must be circulated through various brain structures where it is collected and organized. Information from other sensory modalities (hearing, smell, touch, and the rest) and from past experience also aid in this process. What you finally see is the product of these scanning and integrative *processes*. This is what it means to say that visual perception is *constructed*.

The way we scan is not random. We do not move our eyes here and there unsystematically. Fixations must take in relevant parts of the visual field. And, especially where the environment is changing, fixations must occur in appropriate order. Depending on how well the eye is guided in its pattern of fixations and movements, it will gather more or less relevant information more or less rapidly. Because visual scanning can be more or less accurate, more or less efficient, it is a skill. And, as you might expect, this skill improves over time, with practice and maturation.

Gordon Bronson, of Mills College, undertook to assess the improvement in visual scanning by infants over different stages of development. As infants of different ages scanned simple geometric figures, their eye movements were monitored by a video camera. A computer, connected to the camera, matched location

on the figure with eye position and recorded the location, duration, and pattern of fixations. The procedure was quite complex, both because of its advanced technology and because 6- to 13-week-old infants are not much impressed with the requirements of scientific research.

Bronson chose three different age groups of infants to study—6 weeks old, 10 weeks old, and 13 weeks old. Although the 7-week age difference between the youngest and oldest groups is short, it is a time of rapid change within an infant's visual system (Bronson, 1994).

Subjects who are of the same chronological age are said to belong to the same *cohort*. Thus, in Bronson's study, 6-week-old infants constituted one cohort, 10-week-old infants another cohort, and so on. His decision to compare different cohorts made Bronson's research design *cross-sectional*. Cross-sectional research seeks to determine how a phenomenon changes over time by comparing different cohorts at a single point in time. An advantage that cross-sectional research has over longitudinal methods (see the Research Focus, "Longitudinal Designs," in Chapter 13) is that because it can be done at one time, one need not wait around while individuals grow older. However, there may also be drawbacks.

In Bronson's study, cohorts differed only by weeks, but in many studies cohorts differ by several or more years. The greater the time separating cohorts, the more likely it is that a cross-sectional approach will confront a particular difficulty. Not all differences between cohorts are attributable to age. Subjects who differ in age may also differ in other ways. Suppose, for instance, that a study is interested in whether political attitudes change with age. Suppose further that the attitudes of an adolescent cohort are compared with those of an adult cohort, a frequently used cross-sectional research strategy. We may well find that political attitudes differ between these cohorts. But we might be seriously mistaken in attributing these differences to age. They may have more to do with the social-historical context in which the members of a cohort reached a certain age than with age itself. For instance, adolescents today live in relatively plentiful times, and most grow up in urban or suburban settings. Adolescents born in 1930 grew up in the shadow of the Depression and were more likely to live in rural areas. Such *cohort differences* would likely be reflected in measures of political attitude and mistakenly attributed to age. Thus, in contrast to *longitudinal research*, which risks confounding age with times of measurement, cross-sectional research risks confusing age with cohort differences.

Is there a way around this difficulty in cross-sectional designs that also avoids the problems of longitudinal designs? A research technique called *sequential design*, which combines cross-sectional and longitudinal approaches, provides one solution. This technique tests several different cohort groups at several different times. In a way, the sequential design is a number of longitudinal studies, each starting with a different age group, as shown in the figure. By looking at the blocks that form the diagonals in the figure, we can compare 5-year-olds with 10-year-olds and 15-year-olds. The means for each of those diagonals will reflect age differences as well as cohort differences and time of measurement differences.

By taking an average of the scores for the blocks in the top row, we get a mean for the 1980 cohort. By averaging the scores for the blocks in the middle row, we get a mean for the 1985 cohort. And by averaging the scores for the blocks in the bottom row, we get a mean for the 1990 cohort. Differences among these three means provide an estimate of the amount of variability that is contributed by cohorts.

We can also estimate the effect of time of measurement. We can compare performance measured in 1990 (the blocks in the second column), for example, with performance measured in 2000 (the blocks in the fourth column). Thus, by using appro-

priate statistical techniques, we can isolate cohort and time of measurement effects and subtract these out; differences that remain reflect age changes.

To return to Bronson, when adults view figures similar to those presented to the infants, they show a characteristic pattern of scanning—long strings of brief fixations (0.3 to 0.6 seconds). On the other hand, the scanning patterns of 6-week-old infants consist of much longer fixations—some well over a second. Bronson found that the older the cohort, the greater the percentage of brief, adult-like fixations. Thus at 6 weeks the infants averaged only 27% brief fixations; at 10 weeks the average was 41%, and at 13 weeks the average was 87%. Further, even when brief fixations did occur in the younger cohorts, they tended to occur singly, between the longer, infantile fixations. The older the cohort, the more prevalent were long sequences of brief fixations. Thus, for the 6-week group only 6% of the brief fixations occurred in long strings, while by 13 weeks almost all did. Clearly then, visual scanning does change with age. And it would seem that given the small age differences between cohorts in the Bronson study and the nature of the phenomenon studied, there was little danger of cohort effects. But exercise your imagination anyway. Can you suggest some possible cohort effects that might have influenced Bronson's results? Think mobiles. Think wallpaper. Think siblings. Think HMOs.

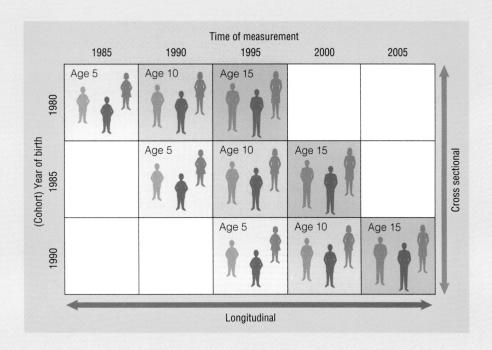

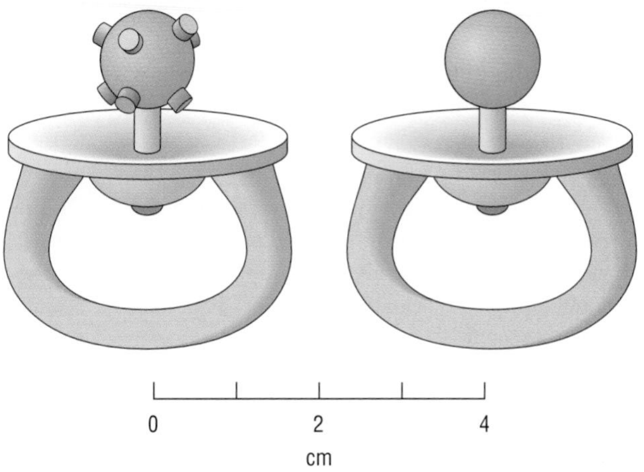

FIGURE 5.1 Pacifiers Used in Melt-zoff and Borton's Study *Infants who had been given the bumpy pacifier (on the left) spent more time looking at it than at the smooth pacifier (on the right) when both pacifiers were presented for visual inspection. The reverse was true for infants who had been given the smooth pacifier. Looking longer at the pacifier they had explored in their mouth than at the one they had not tactually explored demonstrates that infants can recognize something by sight that they have previously experienced only by touch.* Source: A. N. Meltzoff and R. W. Borton, (1979, November). Intermodel matching by human neonates. *Nature,* Vol. 282, p. 403.

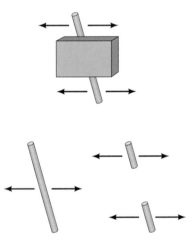

FIGURE 5.2 *Habituation display (top) and test displays from an experiment on perception of partly hidden objects.* Source: From Elizabeth S. Spelke, Perceptual development in infancy: the Minnesota symposium on child psychology, Vol. 20, p. 200.

habituation Decreased responsiveness to a stimulus with repeated exposure to it.

can. In one early demonstration of this, Andrew Meltzoff and Richard Borton (1979) gave 1-month-old infants one of two kinds of pacifiers to suck on, either a smooth one or a bumpy one. When the pacifier they had been sucking on was removed from the infants' mouths and shown to them along with the other one, infants were able to visually identify the pacifier they had only felt in their mouths but never seen (Figure 5.1).

How, you might ask, could these investigators be sure that the infants had indeed recognized the pacifier that had been in their mouths? Infants, you may recall, are curious and will spend more time looking at something that is novel, or unexpected, than at something that is familiar. Meltzoff and Borton's infants stared longer at the pacifier that had *not* been in their mouths, the one with which they were not familiar. In a comparable study, 4- and 5-month-old infants were allowed to play with two rings, one in each hand, that were connected either by a rigid bar or an elastic band. The infants' hands, as well as the rings, were hidden from their view by a cloth. Nonetheless, when the infants were presented with both pairs of rings under conditions in which they could visually, but not manually, inspect them, they recognized the ones they had explored only through touch (Streri & Spelke, 1988).

Similarly, there is large body of research indicating that infants perceive their world as made up of solid, three-dimensional objects, and that they do so well before they have mastered the action schemas Piaget believed responsible for this. Elizabeth Spelke (1988), at Cornell University, showed 3- and 5-month-old infants a moving object that was partially hidden behind another (Figure 5.2). Adults who are shown this display describe it as a stick partially blocked from view by a cube. The question is, what would infants see this as? Would they also see the two ends as belonging to a single object? Or would they see only what was visibly present, two short pieces extending from the top and bottom of a cube, without inferring the existence of a stick behind the cube?

Spelke used a **habituation** procedure to determine what the infants had perceived. In this procedure, infants were shown the figure until they lost interest and looked away. Then they were shown, on alternating trials, either a full-length stick or two short sticks as far apart as they would be if actually separated by the object that had appeared in front of them. Knowing that infants would spend more time looking at something that was unexpected, Spelke compared the time they looked at each alternative as a measure of what they expected to see when the cube was no longer there. By 4 months, infants look longer at the two separate pieces than at the single stick, indicating that they expected to see a whole stick,

Principle of Cohesion: A moving object, such as a ball, follows a single path and does not divide or move along two paths.

Illustrates cohesion

Violates cohesion

Principle of Continuity: There can be no breaks in the path followed by a moving object.

Illustrates continuity

Violates continuity

Principle of Contact: A moving object can affect the movement of another object only by coming into contact with it.

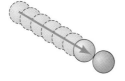

Illustrates contact

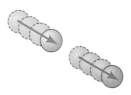

Violates contact

FIGURE 5.3 Three Types of Information Carried by a Moving Object *The arrows show the direction of movement.*

even though they could only have inferred the existence of such an object, since they had never seen it. It might be argued that two things are more interesting to look at than one, thus accounting for the longer looking time. However, Spelke controlled for this possibility by pretesting infants with each of the test displays and found no difference initially in the time they spent looking at either of these.

Important differences remain, however, in what infants and adults appear to infer about partially hidden objects. When infants are shown the same arrangement of stick and cube, but without the stick's moving, they do not, as do adults, perceive an object behind the cube (Spelke, 1988). Only when there is common motion between the several parts do they see these as belonging to a single whole (Johnson & Aslin, 1995; Johnson & Nanez, 1995).

Gretchen Van de Walle and Elizabeth Spelke (1996) suggest that infants rely on three types of information carried by movement: cohesion, continuity, and contact. *Cohesion* refers to the knowledge that a moving object follows a single path and does not divide or move along two paths. *Continuity* is the knowledge that there can be no breaks in the path followed by a moving object; that is, objects do not disappear and reappear somewhere else. *Contact* refers to the understanding that an object can have no effect at a distance, but can affect the movements of another object only if it comes into contact with the other (Figure 5.3). They found that whereas 5-month-old infants effectively use motion cues such as these to infer the existence of an object from the parts of it they can see, they are not as successful in using these cues to infer the shape of the object. In fact, cues such as shape and color, commonly relied on by adults in recognizing objects, appear not to become salient for infants until 6 to 12 months (Craton, cited in Van de Walle & Spelke, 1996).

Q How can we know when infants are paying attention to the sights and sounds around them, such as special toys and nursery rhymes?

FIGURE 5.4 *Schematic representation of the habituation and test events shown to the infants in the experimental and control conditions.* Source: L. Baillargeon, (1987), Object-permanence in 3½ and 4½-month-old infants. *Developmental Psychology,* 23, 655–664.

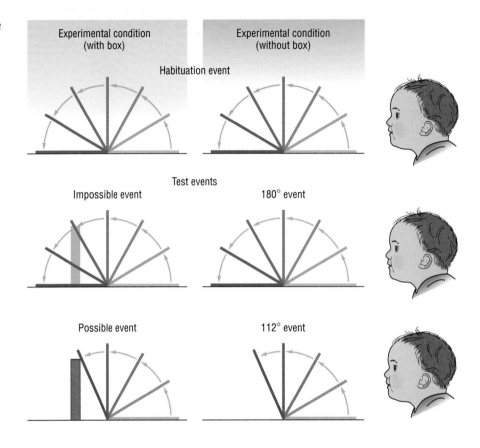

Nonetheless, a world of very real objects clearly exists for infants at an early age. By 3 months, they can determine the boundaries of objects and by 4 months they expect these objects to occupy a space of their own, to be solid and substantial, and to remain where they last saw them (Baillargeon, 1995; Spelke, 1988). Renee Baillargeon (1987) showed infants a screen, initially lying face down on a table in front of them, which swung backward through a 180 degree arc, becoming vertical at 90 degrees and proceeding back until, at 180 degrees, it again lay flat on the table. Infants watched the screen moving in this manner until they habituated, or lost interest in it. Then, with the screen again lying face down on the table, she placed an object on the table in the path of the screen's movement. The screen, as it rotated backward, soon hid the object from view. Would infants still expect the object to remain where it had been placed, even though they could no longer see it? Had they developed, in other words, a concept of object permanence?

To answer this, Baillargeon compared infants' reactions to two test conditions. In one condition, the screen stopped moving when it reached the point at which the object, now hidden by the raised screen, had been placed. In a second condition, the screen continued to rotate backward, moving through the point at which the object had been placed, until it lay flat on the table (Figure 5.4). In each case, once the screen had stopped moving, it reversed direction and rotated back until it lay on the table in front of the infant, again revealing the object behind it. Baillargeon found that infants showed surprise at the second of these tests, but not at the first, indicating that they believed the object was still behind the screen even though they could no longer see it.

How are we to reconcile findings such as these with Piaget's observations concerning object permanence? For T. G. R. Bower, the issue is not one of object per-

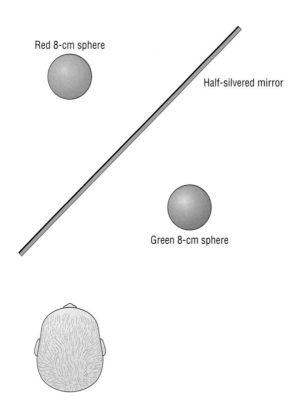

Red 8-cm sphere

Half-silvered mirror

Green 8-cm sphere

FIGURE 5.5 Object Identity Experiment *Depending on which side of the mirror is illuminated, the infant will see either the red or the green ball. By turning on the light in the side containing the green ball while turning off the light in the other side, the red ball appears to have turned into a green ball. Source: T. G. R. Bower, (1982). Development in infancy.*

manence, but one of object identity. An object's size, shape, and color, which are salient aspects of its identity for adults, appear not to be as important to young infants as other features, such as movement. Consider a 3-month-old watching a colorful toy train. The train moves down a short track, first to the right, then to the left, back and forth in front of the infant, stopping for 10 seconds each time it reaches either end. Then, instead of moving off in the other direction, the train remains in place. The infant, on schedule, removes its gaze from the motionless train and looks down the track, registering surprise when it fails to see the moving train. Surely it didn't expect to see the train after just having looked away from it? But this and other demonstrations lead one inevitably to this conclusion (Bower, 1982; Jusczyk, Johnson, Spelke, & Kennedy, 1999).

Bower (1982) suggests that the stationary train is not the same object to the infant as the train that moves. Up to 5 months of age, infants appear to rely almost exclusively on movement to determine the identity of objects. Prior to this age, a moving object that they are visually tracking can change in size, shape, and color, yet, if it reappears on the same course from behind a screen, infants will continue to follow it with their eyes, never looking back for the original object (Bower, Broughton, & Moore, 1971).

For stationary objects, place appears to enjoy a similar, privileged role in determining identity. If one object is substituted for another in the same place, by changing the illumination of different sides of a mirrored glass, thus making one or the other object disappear, the infant will continue to stare at the new object without looking around for the old one (Bower, 1982). Figure 5.5 illustrates such a procedure. Until infants reach the age of 5 months, they continue to look at the substitute object, showing no disruption in their gaze and no searching for the first object. After 5 months, movement and place lose their unique status. Infants appear to relate movement to place, realizing that movement is responsible for an object being in different places. With this, movement and place are less a part of an object's identity than of its activity or nonactivity (Bower, 1982).

How are an adult and a very young infant likely to differ in their recognition of objects?

The work of Baillargeon, in which infants as young as 3 months show evidence of object permanence, suggests that we have misinterpreted motor difficulties as conceptual difficulties. Infants who are too young to reach out and pull away a cover to expose an object hidden underneath nonetheless express surprise at events which suggest that an object hidden from view is no longer where they last saw it, such as when a screen rotates through the location in which they have seen an object placed.

Categorizing Experience

Given that infants share our understanding, more or less, of the things around them, in what other ways might their understanding of the world be similar to ours? What, for instance, do they understand about such basic dimensions as time and space? Or number? Or of ways of categorizing the things with which they come into contact, even those they cannot see or touch, such as the feelings and thoughts of others?

The Timing of Things

We take time as a given, yet it cannot be seen, heard, touched, or smelled. One might argue that time exists only as a mental construction, that we impose a grid of minutes and hours on an otherwise seamless flow of experience. If so, how is time to be experienced by infants and toddlers before they, too, weave the net of seconds, minutes, and hours through which we capture time?

Implicit in the notion of time is the experience of the succession or simultaneity of events. With respect to the first of these, infants can be shown to readily detect regularities to sequences, anticipating when as well as where something will next occur. Recall that infants who are shown photos that appear to the left or right of them in a predictable pattern anticipate when the next event will occur, turning their head in that direction before the photo appears (Haith, Wentworth, & Canfield, 1993). These investigators found that even infants as young as 3½ months can form expectations based on temporal regularities.

Many of the temporal sequences to which infants are exposed are unidirectional in nature, representing processes that naturally occur in one direction but not in another as, for example, the sequence observed when something falls or when an object breaks into pieces. William Friedman (1997, 1999), at Oberlin College, looked at infants' awareness of several temporally unfolding processes, such as liquid being poured from one container to another, blocks falling out of a hand, or a cookie being broken into pieces. Events such as these occur over an extended period of time and unfold only in a given sequence or order. At what age are infants sensitive to the temporal sequence of these events?

Friedman showed 4- to 17-month-old infants videotapes, played forward or backward, of these unidirectional events and measured how long they looked at either type of sequence. If infants can be expected to show greater attention to sequences that are discrepant with what they expect to see, they should stare longer at the backward sequences. Friedman's findings suggest that infants are aware of temporal sequence and that this awareness is related to what they have been exposed to. Thus, sequences that are readily interpretable as violating a natural direction, such as a liquid being unpoured or something falling up, show preferential staring earlier than those that are less clear violations, such as a broken cookie being reassembled. The experience of things falling down, as opposed to up, is universal; however, interpreting a unidirectional temporal sequence to

As infants' and toddlers' ability to move increases, so does their perception of things in space around them.

viewing a cookie broken into pieces is less clear, given infants' experience with blocks and puzzle pieces that can be assembled into a whole, or soft foods or clay that fuse neatly into a mass.

Space

As infants' and toddlers' activities expand, so does their perception of the space around them. At first limited to what they can follow with their eyes and then to what they can grasp within their reach, their awareness of the arrangement of things in space takes a quantum leap when they become able to crawl about. Through crawling and then walking, infants and toddlers become better able to judge distance, detour around objects in their way, and stop in time to avoid tumbling down stairs. Infants who can move about in space, either by creeping or crawling or by using a walker, are much better able to locate where things are than are infants of the same age who have not yet begun to crawl or otherwise had experience in getting about on their own (Bertenthal, Campos, & Kermoian, 1994).

How does infants' ability to get about on their own affect the way they perceive their environment?

Infants' and toddlers' perception of the form of things develops with their ability to grasp things and move them about.

Movement, either of other objects or of ourselves, informs us of space. For instance, some early work with inverted lenses by Ivo Kohler (1962), a German psychologist, suggests that our own activity is highly important in defining space. Kohler constructed a pair of glasses with lenses that inverted the images projected on the retina. When he first put these lenses on, the world flipped upside down, requiring him to cautiously feel his way about rather than rely on visual cues. With time, a most interesting thing happened. The particular things he was handling appeared right-side up, even though everything else remained upside down. However, as soon as he stopped working with these things, they too flipped upside down. Later still, the space around him appeared right-side up as long as he was moving about in it, but when he stopped moving, it turned upside down again. Only eventually did everything appear right-side up, despite the fact that the retinal images were still inverted. The research of Kohler, and of others, indicates that our perception of things, as well as of the space they occupy, is intimately related to our actions (Church, 1961; Held & Hein, 1963).

What does this research suggest about infants' experience of space? Infants' and toddlers' perception of the form of things, just like their perception of space, develops with their ability to take hold of things, to grasp them and move them about. Thus infants who can be seen to judge the size of something, by the way they adjust their grasp as they reach out to grab hold of it, can make surprising errors of judgment when simply looking at an object (Robinson, McKenzie, & Day,

1996; Sitskoorn & Smitsman, 1995). Infants will position their hands around an object similarly to the way adults do but, unlike adults, fail to anticipate the way they will have to grasp it prior to making contact with it. When a screen is placed between them and the object, with an opening through which the object can be seen, they have even more difficulty, frequently even failing to adjust the position of their hands to squeeze through the screen. Interestingly, they are better at getting their hand through when the object behind the screen is too large to pull through and can only be "petted" or touched. They appear to be better at assessing the spatial relations between themselves and an object than between one object and another (Robinson, McKenzie, & Day, 1996).

These spatial relations are important in another respect as well; they serve initially as a way of representing, or remembering, where things are located. Children's increasing ability to get about on their own and, once they get where they are going, to pick things up and move them about, contributes immensely to their understanding and memory for their surroundings. Anne Lamott (1993) captures this aspect of development as she describes her son's ability to remember the places where he previously did things that had fascinated him:

> This memory thing is really interesting. Before, every time Sam went into a room—the bathroom, for instance—he would be almost beside himself with wonder and amazement, like it was his first trip to FAO Schwartz. Now he recognizes it. It's not quite old-hat yet, but he sees the bathtub and he remembers that he loves it and he tries to thrust and squirm his way over to it. It's funny that he loves the bathtub so much. He didn't always. But mostly he loves to toss stuff into the tub when it's empty, and then he loves to gaze endlessly down into it, with wonder, like it's a garden in full bloom. (p. 218) ◄

Initially, children's understanding of space is subjective, or experienced in relation to themselves. With age, their understanding becomes more objective, and their knowledge of where things are is less dependent on their own position with respect to these. One of the earliest ways in which children represent the location of objects in space is by encoding or representing the position of the object relative to themselves. This is termed **egocentric representation.** Linda Acredola (1978), at the University of California at Davis, taught infants to crawl down a pathway and turn left to find a toy. Once they had learned this, she reversed the position from which they approached the path to the toy, such that they had to turn right, and not left. Infants continued to turn left, finding it difficult to compensate for the different location of the toy relative to their own bodies. Only by the age of 16 months were infants able to successfully turn toward the toy.

A second way of representing spatial relations, or **landmark representation,** locates objects in relation to something else in the environment. Infants can be seen to use landmarks as soon as they begin to move about on their own, by about the age of 6 months, and can even use them successfully in locating objects whose position has changed relative to their own—as in Acredola's experiment, in which they had to approach a toy from a direction opposite to the one they had previously followed. If a sufficiently distinctive landmark is available, such as Mom standing on the side nearest the toy, they are more likely to turn in the right direction (Rieser, 1979).

A third way of representing spatial relations, **allocentric representation,** does so in relation to some abstract frame of reference, such as use of a map. This form of representation comes into play when one cannot see the target destination either because it is too far away or because there is something in the way. In order to reach the target, one must envision it relative to its surround and envision these

egocentric representation Representing the location of objects in relation to oneself; typical of young children's subjective understanding of space.

landmark representation Representing the location of objects in relation to environmental landmarks.

allocentric representation Representing the location of objects in relation to an abstract frame of reference, such as a map.

Sequence of events 1+1=1 or 2

1. Object placed in case

2. Screen comes up

3. Second object added

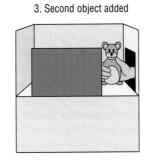

4. Hand leaves empty

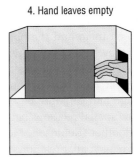

Then either: possible outcome

5. Screen drops . . .

revealing 2 objects

or: impossible outcome

5. Screen drops . . .

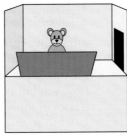

revealing 1 object

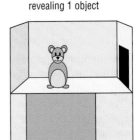

FIGURE 5.6 Sequence of Events Illustrating Infants' Understanding of Amount

in relation to oneself. Doing so requires one to organize multiple sources of information into a single system. Not only must one determine the spatial relationship between one position and another on the map, but one must also determine how that relationship corresponds to one's own position relative to where one wants to go and to the map. Despite the abstract nature of such representation, even 1-year-olds have been found to represent spatial relationships in this way (Siegler, 1998). Infants shown a toy hidden in a corner of a room have been found to use an allocentric representation of spatial relationships to locate the toy. The room in which the toy was hidden was rectangular, with identically painted white walls on all sides. It thus afforded no landmarks, but did provide allocentric information in the form of the relative lengths of the two walls forming the corner. To ensure that the infants could not use egocentric cues, they were blindfolded and then turned in a circle before being allowed to search for the toy. Only by representing the location of the toy in terms of the layout of the room—for example, the corner with the long wall on the left—could they find the toy. Since there were two corners that fit that description (remember, they had been turned in a circle), they should go to either of these corners with equal frequencies if they were relying on allocentric cues, and this is precisely what they did (Hermer & Spelke, 1994).

Q If an infant uses an allocentric method of finding a toy, what might be the most important cue?

The Number of Things

Karen Wynn (1992, 1995), at the University of Arizona, has studied infants' understanding of arithmetic operations, such as addition and subtraction. To determine their understanding of addition, for instance, she showed 5-month-old infants a hand placing a doll on a stage and then, after a screen came up hiding the stage, the hand adding a second doll to the first behind the screen (Figure 5.6). Would infants add the second doll to the first that was already behind the screen and expect to see two dolls? Since infants will look longer at things that are unexpected, Wynn measured the time they looked when the screen dropped to reveal either two dolls (possible outcome) or a single doll (impossible outcome). Infants spent more time looking at the single doll, suggesting they knew that $1 + 1 = 2$. Similarly, to access their understanding of subtraction, she placed two dolls on the stage and then, once the screen came up, removed one of these. Again, infants were tested with either one doll (possible outcome) or two (impossible outcome) and were found to look longer at the latter outcome.

These findings show that infants know that adding or subtracting a doll results in a different number of dolls. It could be argued, however, that they could do this without being able to compute the actual number of dolls that should appear. Thus, in testing for addition, a test containing three dolls might evoke as much interest as a test with two dolls, since both represent a change from what the infant has seen. Wynn tested for this possibility with 4½-month-old infants by again showing the $1 + 1$ addition procedure, and this time testing with either two or three dolls. Infants stared longer at the three dolls, indicating they were actually performing arithmetic calculations and not responding simply to a change. By the age of 5 months, infants are also able to enumerate repetitive actions, such as those of a puppet jumping up and down, distinguishing among sequences differing in the number of repetitions (Wynn, 1996).

There is, nonetheless, disagreement as to just how competent infants actually are numerically. For instance, infants who were shown displays of objects side by side, one display consisting of two objects and the other consisting of three, and who heard a drum beating out either two or three beats, looked longer at the display that matched the number of sounds they heard (Starkey, Spelke, & Gelman, 1990), prompting these investigators to assume that infants are not only capable of enumerating something that occurs in separable elements, but that they are also able to represent numerosity in different modalities in a way that allows them to relate these in a one-to-one fashion. Not all investigators, however, have been able to replicate such findings (Mix, Levine, & Huttenlocher, 1997).

Types of Things

At what age do infants begin to classify their experiences into different types of things, such as distinguishing cats from dogs or birds from bees? Research addressing this question suggests that infants begin at a very early age indeed. Once again, since young infants are limited in the ways in which they can communicate their knowledge of the world, researchers have had to be ingenious. A procedure that has been commonly used in this type of research shows infants various members of a category and then tests them with a pair of novel items, one of which is a member of the same category and the other of a different one. Knowing that infants look longer at things that are novel, and given that each of the test items is new to them, looking longer at the item from a different group would indicate they have formed some basis for categorizing, or seeing as similar, the ones they had previously seen.

"Well and good," you might say, "but *how* do they do that?" What does one do when one categorizes? There are several ways in which we might form categories. We will consider three of these: using defining features, using a probabilistic approach, and forming a theory of why things go together (Siegler, 1998).

The first of these explanations for forming categories, representing categories in terms of defining features, assumes that all instances of a category possess certain characteristics, or **defining features,** in common that identify them as a

From a very early age, infants seem to be able to categorize things and distinguish between same and different. This child is well aware that he's in an environment he's not used to.

defining features Characteristics that identify items as members of a category.

member of that category. An example of such a feature might be "wings" for the category of birds or "gills" for the category of fish. This approach assumes that when we categorize on this basis, we represent the category in terms of these defining features. Other items that possess the same defining features are also considered to be members of that category. Of course, many things with wings are not birds. Insects and airplanes come to mind. And most categories are defined by more than one feature. Birds, for instance, have feathers, lay eggs, and sing, as well as have wings and fly.

At this point, someone may say, "Wait, don't lizards and snakes lay eggs too? And ostriches have wings, but they can't fly or sing like other birds." Due to difficulties such as these in identifying which features are necessary and sufficient for category membership, Eleanor Rosch and Carolyn Mervis (1975), at Stanford University, proposed a *probabilistic* approach to defining membership in categories. Rosch and Mervis argued that we distinguish items as belonging to a category on the basis of family resemblances rather than an invariant set of features possessed by all members of a category. That is, all members of a category need not have the same set of features in common as long as they have enough in common to resemble other instances of the category.

Rosch and Mervis proposed that four factors are important in assigning items to a category: cue validity, basic-level categories, correlated features, and prototypes. *Cue validity* is the likelihood that an item is a member of a category given that a particular feature, or cue, is present. The validity of a cue refers to the extent to which a particular feature is present in members of the category and absent among members of other categories. Thus, the cue validity of wings is high for the category of birds since the likelihood of birds having wings is high relative to that of other things. Cue validity also explains how some items can be better instances of a category than others. Why are canaries better examples of birds than ostriches are? Because, even though both have wings, other cues found in canaries, such as their size, body proportions, and whether they sing and can fly, are more valid cues for birds than are those of ostriches.

Rosch and her associates note that categories are naturally arranged in a nested fashion, such that being a member of one category means that one necessarily belongs to another, more general, category as well. Thus all canaries are also birds, and all birds are animals. Most categories are arranged in such three-tiered hierarchies, with the *subordinate* level being most specific (canaries), the *superordinate* level the most general (animals), and the middle, or *basic level,* intermediate in generality (birds) and possessing the highest cue validities (Figure 5.7). Thus, "bird" is a basic-level category because the features describing birds, such as having wings, feathers, and beaks, and being able to fly and sing, have high cue validities. That is, most birds have these in common, whereas few other things do. In contrast, cue validities for "animals" are not as high as those for birds; some animals have wings, others have fins, and still others have neither. Similarly, members of subordinate categories, such as canaries, possess all the features found in basic-level categories, but are not as reliably distinguished among each other as is one basic-level category from another.

Rosch and her associates point out that the features that distinguish a category tend to be grouped, or correlated, such that the presence of one feature is highly predictive of another. Thus, things that have gills also tend to have fins and scales, whereas those with wings are likely to have feathers and beaks. This clustering of *correlated features* is characteristic of most categories. Some instances of a category are simply better examples of that category than are others. These are the ones that are the most representative, or have the highest cue validities. Such instances are termed *prototypes* in that they represent the category better than

Q How do infants use cue validity in order to classify objects?

Superordinate level: Animals

Basic level: Birds

Subordinate level: Canaries

FIGURE 5.7 Levels of Categories

any of its other instances. Canaries, for example, are prototypical birds not only because they have wings, feathers, and beaks, but also because they sing, fly, and are the right size.

Finally, we often categorize objects because of the relationships that exist among them, even when they bear little physical resemblance to each other. Robert Siegler (1998) cites the example of a category that includes children, antiques, jewelry, and family photos, an unlikely assortment unless one is asked to think of what one would remove first from a house that is on fire. Because items such as these derive their similarity from what we know about them, rather than from any physical features they might have in common, the grouping reflects a theory of why these things go together. For adults, at least, an important element in judging which things go together is the issue of whether they are the same *kind* of thing—that is, whether they are similar in nature (Mandler, Bauer, & McDonough, 1991). This basis for categorizing experience represents a theory-based approach. What makes something an animal? Is it simply that animals have legs or eyes and ears? Or is it the notion that animals are capable of self-initiated movement and this, despite large differences in how they look or in the ways they move, is what makes them animals?

By age 2½, children can distinguish basic-level categories and tell a dog from a goat, for example.

Do infants and children use any or all of these ways to categorize experience? If so, what are they most likely to base their categories on? A common assumption is that initially categories are based on perceptual similarity, and only with time do they evolve into conceptually based categories (Eimas & Quinn, 1994; Mervis, 1987). If infants and children at first categorize things based on the way they look, then basic-level categories should be the first ones that they form, since these are made up of items that are most similar in appearance to each other. Presumably when basic-level categories have been formed, children begin to group these into more inclusive, or superordinate, categories, arriving at the conceptually based hierarchical system of classifying things used by adults.

Paul Quinn and Peter Eimas (1996) found that even infants as young as 3 to 4 months of age could distinguish basic-level categories from each other. They showed infants a series of photographs of either cats or dogs and then tested them with a pair of photographs, neither of which had been seen before, one of which was a cat and the other a dog, to see which they would look at longer. Since infants look longer at things that are unexpected, their looking time was taken as a measure of whether they had formed a category based on the series they had seen. They looked longer at the photograph of the animal that differed from the series they had seen. Furthermore, when Quinn and Eimas subsequently presented only the heads or the bodies of these animals, they were able to show that infants distinguished the categories on the basis of distinctive facial features and head contours.

Jean Mandler, Patricia Bauer, and Laraine McDonough (1991) question whether basic-level categories are always the first to be formed. They suggest that children initially form rather broad categories, which they refer to as *domains* to distinguish them from superordinate categories, pointing out that the latter assume a hierarchical organization that is not necessarily present at first. They found that 18-month-olds could distinguish animals from vehicles, for instance, while still not being able to differentiate the basic-level categories, such as dogs from horses, or cars from trucks, that made these up. Only when children reached the age of 2½ did they consistently distinguish the component basic-level categories. These data suggest that, in some domains, children form broad, conceptual categories before making basic-level distinctions among the items within these.

Beliefs About Things

Given that infants and toddlers form categories for things in the world around them, what might they understand about the inner world of their own, or others', minds? Do they have a theory, that is, of the mind? Considerable data suggest that an understanding of mental states in others begins to develop relatively early. Toddlers, for instance, can be seen to establish joint attention with their mothers while engaged in an activity (Goldsmith & Rogoff, 1997), and infants can be seen to scrutinize their mother's face when in an ambiguous situation for cues as to whether the situation is threatening or safe (Hornik, Risenhoover, & Gunnar, 1987). Behaviors such as these suggest that even relatively young infants attribute inner states to others.

One of these inner states is that of desire. Betty Repacholi and Alison Gopnik (1997), at the University of California, Berkeley, explored the age at which young children, 14- and 18-month-olds, begin to understand the desires of others. These investigators used a situation that is familiar to children of any age, asking for something that tastes good. Two types of foods were used, one known to be desirable to children (goldfish crackers) and the other to be undesirable (broccoli flowerets). Children observed the experimenter take a taste of each, reacting positively to one and negatively to the other. For half of the children the experimenter expressed pleasure with the food they themselves liked (cracker) and for the other half this was reversed. What would children give the experimenter when she asked for more? The food she appeared to enjoy? Or the food they preferred? Infants who were 14 months old offered the food they preferred. However, by 18 months, infants could infer what the experimenter wanted and offered her the food she expressed delight in even when it was personally distasteful to them.

> **Q** Why may showing a toddler how much we love vegetables perhaps not be helpful in getting her to learn to enjoy them herself?

The Meaning of Things

What do infants understand of the categorical distinctions they make? Are these first categories conceptual in nature, or are they only perceptual? Asked another way, do the categorical representations infants make consist only of perceptual cues that have been abstracted from instances of the category, such as features distinguishing the faces of cats from dogs (Quinn & Eimas, 1996)? Or do they include what we would call meaningful distinctions as well? Jean Mandler (1990, 1992), at the University of California at San Diego, argues for the latter, pointing out that if language acquisition is dependent on the existence of preverbal concepts, and if infants' first words occur at about 10 months, or even earlier if they are signing (Padden & Humphries, 1989), these concepts must already be in place.

Mandler suggests that perceptual analysis results in *image-schemas* which map, or redescribe, spatial structure into conceptual structure. Such schemas represent basic forms of understanding, such as the notion of up versus down, or what it means to be supported or contained, or to follow a path. Image-schemas are thought to be based on innate perceptual processes that analyze perceptual features such as movement, border and edge, and the like. The image-schema of "path," for instance, might refer simply to an object moving along a trajectory, without necessarily identifying the object as such. Recall that infants reflexively follow a moving object with their eyes. Recall, too, that the object can appear to change in color, size, and shape, but as long as it continues along the same path, infants will not attend to differences in these dimensions. The notion of "path," Mandler argues, is a perceptual primitive, communicating information to which we are innately attentive. She suggests that image-schemas such as this make up the most fundamental level of the infant's understanding of the world.

Infants use motion cues to judge animacy.

Mandler warns that image-schemas, rather than being thought of as similar to innate concepts, should be regarded as the means by which infants derive their most basic concepts, that which equips or enables infants to conceptually order experience. Recall that Neisser (1976), too, pointed out that infants come into the world fully loaded with all the perceptual equipment they will need in order to discover *what* they will need to know.

Image-schemas, as stripped down abstractions of perceptual processes, would be capable of capturing the active interrelationships among parts. Because of their ability to capture these relational components, image-schemas could yield a syntax of sorts, one capable of specifying "truth conditions," of representing the "what's so" of experience, such as "A hits B, B moves." Possessing such a syntax would make it possible for infants to think about experience in the absence of logical, propositionally based thought, such as awaits the development of language. Mandler cautions that she is not suggesting that infants are conscious of these image-schemas. One would need at least another level of analysis in order to be aware of such processes, since consciousness, by definition, is reflective, requiring a second level from which to view the first. These image-schemas would simply provide the meaning on which concepts that are accessible to consciousness are based.

As an example of such an early image-schema, consider what it means to know that something is animate, or alive. Mandler proposes that judgments of animacy are based on three things. The first of these is *self-motion,* something that moves by itself without having to be started. *Animate motion,* or moving in a rhythmic, up-and-down fashion as we do when pushing off from a surface with every step, is thought to be a second component. In contrast to this type of motion, inanimate objects are more likely to move in a smooth trajectory, as does a missile or a ball. A third component, *contingency motion,* refers to actions that are contingent on the behavior of another, yet are prompted from a distance. We needn't be "bumped" into action, in other words; instead, we respond to the requests and behaviors of others, such as when a parent reacts to an infant's vocalizations. Infants are sensitive to such information. By 4 months, for instance, they notice the difference between an object being set in motion when another bumps into it and an object that starts to move when the first object stops just a fraction short of touching it (Leslie, 1982, 1988).

Do infants use cues such as these to form a notion of animacy? If so, things that move contingently, whether puppies, puppets, or mobiles, should initially be confused with humans. Frye, Rawling, Moore, and Myers (1983) observed 3- and 10-month-old infants' reactions to either their mothers or to toys, each of which either acted contingently or noncontingently to the infants' behavior. They found that 3-month-old infants reacted in a similar way to both their mothers and to toys when the behavior of each was contingent on their own behavior, and that in each case the infants' reactions were different than for noncontingent interactions. By 10 months, however, infants reacted differently to contingent-mothers than to contingent-toys.

Another important image-schema which Mandler discusses is that of containment. This notion, too, develops relatively early. By 5½ months, infants show surprise when containers without bottoms look like they are holding something (Kolstad, as cited in Mandler, 1992), a finding which also suggests that the notions of containment and support are closely related. George Lakoff (1987), a cognitive linguist, notes that containment connotes not only "in," but notions of "out" and "boundary" as well. He argues that containment is basic to understanding logical relations such as "A versus not-A" (that is, *in* versus *not-in*), that when we understand a set, we do so through our knowledge of containment. This notion of containment may also contribute to the meaning of the word "or," in that an object can be in *or* out, but not both. Likewise, just as containment contributes to an understanding of "in," the notion of support provides a basis for understanding the meaning of "on." Mandler points out that these two terms for indicating where something is located, "in" and "on," are among the first locative terms to develop, irrespective of the language studied and that even when children are first learning these words, they make almost no errors.

Mandler (1992) suggests that image-schemas such as these, because they represent meaningful, and not just perceptual, distinctions, can form the basis for the conceptual categories that young children will soon put into words. We turn to this achievement next.

The Development of Language

The very young think with their bodies, their intentions etched in movement. Soon thoughts slip free, loosed by words, and language branches into phrases that span place and time. Observing children as they begin to talk, however, can leave one with more questions than answers as to how they master language. How do they learn so quickly? Must they be taught? Or do they acquire language simply by listening to others? For that matter, need the voices they hear be those of people who are actually present, or could they learn just as easily by listening to a television or the radio?

It is difficult to know for certain when children actually start to acquire a language. We can note when they say their first words, but an infant's first word is only a milestone marking a journey begun much earlier. From birth on, infants are attentive to the sounds of speech, making relatively fine distinctions among these. Even newborns are able to discriminate different stress patterns in otherwise similar words (Sansavini, Bertoncini, & Giovanelli, 1997). Infants also show preferences for certain types of speech over others. They are highly attuned, for instance, to the prosodic features of speech—that is, to the rise and fall of the voice and to the rhythmic stressing of words. In fact, they prefer, when given the alternative, to listen to speech that is directed at them, in which adults characteristically exaggerate these prosodic features, than to speech directed at adults (Fernald, 1985). This is true for newborns as well as for older infants (Cooper & Aslin, 1990; Pegg, Werker, & McLeod, 1992). Infants also prefer to listen to the prosody of their own language than to that of another (Moon, Cooper, & Fifer, 1993).

First Sounds

Infants begin **babbling,** producing vowel and consonant sounds, in the 2nd to 3rd month (Menn & Stoel-Gammon, 1995). Babbling initially follows a common pattern irrespective of the language spoken at home. For the first 6 months or so all infants sound alike, from Brooklyn to Bangkok. Infants first make guttural sounds such as \g\ and \k\ combined with vowels produced mid-mouth (such as \a\). Sounds are added as other consonants (such as \b\, \p\) replace the early guttural ones. This sequence occurs in all infants, even those whose native language has many of the early guttural sounds. It thus appears that an important determinant of babbling is the child's own developing articulatory control. This control, rather than the speech sounds infants hear spoken around them, appears to determine when babbling begins and which sounds will be the first to occur. Deaf infants, for instance, begin to babble at the same age as hearing infants. The persistence of babbling, however, seems to be dependent on the ability of infants to

babbling The production of vowel and consonant sounds by infants in the 2nd to 3rd month.

Infants are highly attuned to prosodic features of speech and prefer to listen to speech directed to them.

How does babbling relate to learning more than one language?

jargon babbling Babbling that reproduces the intonation, rhythmic structure, and pitch of speech.

practice and hear the different sounds they make, as well as hear the speech of others (Menn & Stoel-Gammon, 1995). Deaf children stop babbling at about the age that babbling peaks in hearing infants, at about 9 to 12 months. Also in this later stage, differences in babbling emerge that reflect the sounds infants hear in their native language. Infants begin to reproduce the intonation, rhythmic structure, and pitch of speech. This form of babbling is sometimes called **jargon babbling** for, if one is not listening closely, it sounds very much like speech (Kent & Miolo, 1995).

Just as words themselves communicate meaning, so, too, do the prosodic features of speech. Anne Fernald (1993), at Stanford University, notes that the rise and fall of the voice, what might be thought of as the musical contours of speech, as well as the pattern of stresses, or rhythm, given to words, differ with different types of messages. Expressions of approval, such as "Good girl!" are typically drawn out, with the voice dipping and rising, whereas warnings, such as "No!" are short and staccato. Infants have been found to use cues such as these in determining how to respond in ambiguous situations. Donna Mumme, Anne Fernald, and Carla Herrera (1996) tested 12-month-old infants in a social-referencing situation in which infants, confronted with an ambiguous situation, typically look to their caregiver for cues concerning its nature. Mothers were instructed to communicate either through their voices alone, by turning their backs to the child and using words the child could not understand, or through facial expressions alone. The investigators found that infants responded more to the prosodic features of the mother's speech when communicating fear than to fearful expressions on the mother's face.

One wonders whether infants might use prosody in other ways as well. Cynthia Fisher and Hisayo Tokura (1996), at the University of Illinois, suggest that the rhythms of speech may provide cues about grammatical structure, helping children identify phrases and grammatical units. How well can one hear prosodic cues in speech directed at children? These investigators recorded mothers as they talked to their young children (13 to 14 months old) and found that these cues were easily detectable in the mothers' speech. For the most part, their sentences or phrases were separated by long pauses, with the pauses being preceded by very long vowels and an exaggerated rise and fall to the voice. Because infant-directed speech uses short, simple sentences in which there are relatively few long pauses within a sentence, the relationship between phonologically marked units and grammatical ones is high. Fisher and Tokura carried out the same procedure with native Japanese-speaking mothers and again found that the last syllable in a phrase was consistently different from preceding ones. Thus, whether in Japanese or English, the characteristic melodies of the languages were clearly present in child-directed speech. Since pauses are a reliable cue to the end of one grammatical unit and the beginning of another, they may help infants isolate, or bracket, utterances for linguistic analysis. The Research Focus, "Sampling: Baby Talk in Three Languages" describes a study that examined the way parents speak to babies in three different languages.

Infants' sensitivity to cues such as these changes with their age. Infants 7 months of age or younger, for instance, prefer to listen to speech with pauses between, rather than within, sentences. Not until they reach 9 months of age is there a similar preference at the phrase level, with infants preferring to listen to sentences in which pauses between phrases are greater than those within the phrases. These differences suggest that, with age, a more finely grained analysis of speech becomes possible (Jusczyk et al., 1992).

Infants are learning more than the sounds of words when listening to others speak. They are learning about language itself, that language is part of the way people interact with each other, a way of communicating. John Holt (1969) describes this process:

> A year or more ago, some friends and I dropped in on some people who had a six-month-old baby. She was well-rested and happy, so they brought her in to see the visitors. We all admired her before going on with our talk. She was fascinated by this talk. As each person spoke, she would turn and look intently at him. From time to time she would busy herself with a toy in her lap; then after a few minutes she would begin watching and listening again. She seemed to be learning, not just that people talk, but that they talk to each other, and respond to each other's talk with smiles, and laughter, and more talk; in short, that talk is not just a kind of noise, but messages, communication. (pp. 57–58) ◄

Why is it good for infants and toddlers to hear adults conversing?

First Words

Usually, somewhere around the first birthday infants say their first word. Considerable variability exists from one infant to the next in the timing of this event, with some doing so as early as 9 months of age and others as late as 15 months (Kent & Miolo, 1995). Also, some infants stop babbling when they start to speak, while others continue to babble as they add words to their vocabulary. On average, infants can be expected to use about 10 words by the time they reach 13 months and 45 words by 16 months. However, they understand many more words than this, comprehending over 100 words at 13 months and more than 180 at 16 months (Fenson et al., 1993).

Sampling: Baby Talk in Three Languages

After once more listening to the tape and reviewing again the last set of words, Carla hit the off button. "Enough for today," she thought. Her difficulty with this last tape had made her realize again that learning a second language wasn't that easy, and she wondered how well she'd be doing by the time she met her host family. It was exciting to think of spending a year on an exchange program, especially after hearing that her host mother had just given birth to a little boy. "Wonder how well that little guy is learning the language," she muttered to herself. "Hope he's doing better than I am." She'd never even *heard* half the sounds she was supposed to be making. "How do infants do it?" she wondered. "One thing's for sure, they don't do it by practicing with language tapes."

They definitely don't. But they appear to do something better. By simply listening to the language being spoken around them, infants' very perception of speech is modified, increasing their sensitivity to the rhythm and sounds of their native language, the sounds Carla found so difficult to hear and reproduce in a language other than her own. In other words, infants' ability to hear the sounds that distinguish their language from others is fine-tuned by the very act of listening to speech itself.

Infants are helped enormously in this task by the way people talk when they are around them. Irrespective of the particular language being spoken, speech that is addressed to infants exhibits certain characteristics. Not only do we speak in shorter and simpler sentences when talking to an infant, we also speak in a higher voice, talk more slowly, and exaggerate the cadence, or the rhythm, to our speech. Language addressed to infants has been found to exhibit these properties around the world, despite differences in the actual words that make it up. This manner of speaking is called "parentese," and, as a form of speech, it is ideal for learning one's mother tongue.

But are the individual sounds making up the words pronounced differently as well? In adult-directed speech, vowels and consonants are frequently slurred, providing a poor model of the sounds an infant needs to learn. Is this a natural handicap infants must overcome in learning their language? Or do we also articulate more distinctly the individual sounds, or phonemes, making up each word when speaking to infants? In order to answer this question, Patricia Kuhl and her associates (1997) compared the phonetic units in infant-directed and adult-directed speech by tape-recording women as they spoke either to infants or adults. Specifically, they examined the way vowels

were pronounced in either form of speech. Would these be spoken more clearly in speech directed to infants?

The speech of 10 women was recorded in each of three languages—English, Russian, and Swedish—resulting in thousands of tape-recorded words. From these tapes, individual words were selected for further analysis. But how can we be sure, you might wonder, that the acoustic properties of the words that were selected are representative of all the others? Mustn't one analyze every word in order to know with certainty whether the acoustic properties of vowels differ when speech is directed to infants?

The words that were analyzed were sampled from the larger population of all tape-recorded words. The population represents the entire set of events, or, in this case, of vowels, in which one is interested. The *sample* is a subgroup drawn from this population. If the sample is drawn at random from the population, we can be reasonably certain that it will be *representative* of that population. This is because in random sampling, each person or event has an equal chance of being chosen. How might this procedure apply to vowel sounds?

One might organize the recorded conversations into segments of a specified duration, each, for instance, lasting for 10 seconds (conversations generally lasted for 20 minutes). Such an organization would yield 6 segments per minute, or 120 segments, on average, per conversation. One could then randomly select one target word for phonetic analysis within each segment. To see how this might work, let's assume that 12 words are spoken in a given speech segment. To imagine how any given word might be sampled, think of a hat containing 12 slips of paper, one for each of the recorded words. The number written on the slip you pull would be the word that is sampled for analysis.

What did the samples of vowel sounds show? For all three languages, phonemes are spoken differently in speech addressed to infants. Specifically, vowels are stretched when speaking to infants, making them acoustically more distinct than when speaking to adults. Differences in the way in which phonemes, the building blocks of words, are articulated indicate yet one more way in which the speech to which infants are exposed provides a clear model of the language they are to acquire. This model, in turn, is thought to initiate a process by which infants' perception of speech sounds is modified, altering their ability to detect the sounds peculiar to a particular language.

Infants acquire words slowly at first, usually adding one to three new words a week. However, once their vocabulary reaches anywhere from 20 to 40 words, many infants experience a **vocabulary explosion** in which they add up to eight or more words per week, with the number of words they understand increasing even faster. Considerable variability exists from one child to the next in the timing of this event. The vocabulary explosion typically occurs late in the 2nd year, at around 19 months, but, as with other aspects of language, can vary by as much as 6 months; and in some infants it may not occur at all (Gershkoff-Stowe, Thal, Smith, & Namy, 1997). There is also a slight gender difference in how quickly children learn words, with girls doing so slightly faster than boys, although this difference is small relative to overall differences among children (Barrett, 1995).

Children's first words, just like the sounds they babble, appear to be determined as much by their ability to articulate as by their understanding of the relationship between words and what they name (Gershkoff-Stowe et al., 1997). As we have seen, children understand the meaning of many words before they can speak them. Also, research with deaf children shows that they sign their first words earlier than hearing infants speak theirs, at about 8 months rather than at 10 to 15 months. The greater ease of signing with fingers than of controlling articulatory muscles is most likely responsible for this difference.

Certainly, the regularities of articulation errors in children's first words suggest that it is quite literally a "mouthful" for them to speak. Their errors simplify pronunciation. A common error, for instance, is to reduce multisyllabic words to repetitions of the first syllable. Baby becomes "baba" or mommy is "mama." Children also simplify pronunciation by reducing words of one syllable to a single consonant and vowel. "Ba" serves for *ball* or "tu" for *shoe*. Similarly, children may delete syllables from multisyllabic words, "banana," for example, becoming "nana." Or they may reduce an initial consonant cluster to a single consonant; "stop" becomes "top" or "spoon" is pronounced as "poon." Mastery of consonant clusters continues to develop over the next several years. Some children may have difficulty with these until 4 or 5.

Children also simplify pronunciation by using the same place of articulation for all consonants in a word. "Kitty" becomes "titty" or "doggy," "doddy." Another common form of pronunciation is to replace unvoiced initial consonants, such as \t\, \p\, or \k\, with voiced ones, such as \d\, \b\, or \g\, at the beginning of words. Words such as "toe" and "pie" become "doe" and "bie" (Menn & Stoel-Gammon, 1995). Some errors arise as well from hearing adult speech incorrectly. Perception of speech sounds continues to improve through the 2nd and 3rd years. Even so, children initially are better at perceiving words than at producing them.

Children's use of single words has intrigued parents and psycholinguists alike. How much do they intend to communicate with that one word? Do children use single words to function as phrases or even whole sentences, commenting on their experiences in addition to simply labeling them? Some have suggested they do (McNeill, 1970). Used in this way, single words are termed **holophrases.** "Milk," for instance, might be an observation that the milk is all gone, a request for more milk, or a comment that the cup has milk in it and not juice. While such interpretations of early words are intriguing, they are challenged by others who caution that interpreting single words as holophrastic speech is not warranted by the data. The evidence from single words is simply not sufficient to convict an infant of having a sentence in mind.

Patricia Greenfield and Joshua Smith (1976) suggest, instead, that single words are one component of a communicative expression that, along with gesture, expresses a thought. Thus, "up," combined with raising both arms over the head,

> Which do you think comes first, the ability to understand language or the ability to use speech to express language?

vocabulary explosion The rapid addition of new words to a toddler's vocabulary; usually occurs late in the 2nd year.

holophrase A single word used to represent a phrase or sentence; typical of the first stage of language acquisition.

In the early stages of speaking, single words are often combined with gestures to communicate a thought.

communicates one thought ("Pick me up"), whereas the same word combined with pointing to a balloon that has floated free communicates a different thought ("The balloon is going up"). Thus, although the word itself is not the equivalent of a sentence, the combination of word with gesture functions as one.

Whether used as holophrases or simply to name, many of the child's first words may refer only to some, but not all, of the instances for which they are used by adults. Examples of such **underextensions** would be using "bottle" to refer only to plastic nursing bottles or "cut" only to cutting with a knife (Barrett, 1995). Conversely, in **overextensions,** children use a word to refer not only to all members of the group that it labels for adults, but to other referents as well. Thus, "doggie" might be used for all dogs, but also for cats and lambs, or "bath" might be used for the tub, water, or the toys that float in the bath. Some of these overextensions last for months; others will be used only briefly until the correct name for another object is learned. Children typically have no trouble distinguishing the objects they group this way. When asked to bring the rubber ducky, for instance, a child will correctly bring that and not another toy, even though both may be called "bath." Recall, children's comprehension of words far exceeds their ability to spontaneously produce them at first (just as does ours when learning a second language). In a pinch, they will use whatever word comes closest to what they have in mind. They may even deliberately overextend a word as a way of finding an object's name, knowing that parents will supply the right word when correcting them (Barrett, 1995). All children display these regularities of speech, irrespective of their gender, ethnicity, or social class. Despite such regularities, tremendous differences can exist in richness of the experience their environments provide. The Social Policy Focus, "Early-Intervention Programs: Money Well Spent?" describes the success of early intervention programs in countering the effects of impoverished environments.

Naming Things

What is the "right" word to use when naming things for children? One could supply any of several possible names, from the specific to the general. One could refer to the family car, for instance, as a Mustang, a Ford, or simply a car. Similarly, one could refer to a banana or an apple by name or as a piece of fruit. Naming things is something that most of us do without thinking. Yet, despite the many ways we might refer to things, we are amazingly consistent in the way we name things for children. Roger Brown (1958, 1965), at Harvard University, has noted that the names we supply correspond to the distinctions we anticipate children will need to make in using what we are naming. Thus, children are told to get into the "car" and not the "Mustang" unless, of course, there happens to be more than one car in the family. Similarly, cats remain undistinguished as to ancestry or Persian pedigree—all are "kitty." It is enough for toddlers to distinguish a car from a truck, or a cat from a cow, without knowing which type of car or cat it is. Which type of fruit they want for breakfast, however, is a meaningful distinction. As a consequence, most fruits are identified specifically by name. With a few exceptions, we tend to call things by base-level names—children live in a world of cars and cats, not Mustangs and Persians and not vehicles and animals (Lakoff, 1987).

These names, furthermore, tend to be associated with distinctive actions. We name things in meaningful contexts, as part of an ongoing and natural dialogue, in which we might bounce a ball that rolls underfoot, calling it "ball" in the process; peel a piece of banana, offering some "banana" to a child; or smell a

underextension A child's use of a word to refer to only some but not all of the instances for which it is used by adults.

overextension A child's use of a word to refer not only to all members of the group that the word labels for adults but also to other referents.

Early-Intervention Programs: Money Well Spent?

BY ANDREA HAYES

How important are the years from birth to age 3? Do infants' and toddlers' earliest experiences affect their ability to profit from later ones, contributing to their cognitive and social skills in middle childhood and adolescence? Conversely, do impoverished environments contribute to later problems, such as academic failure or youth violence? What might a toddler's environment, for instance, have to do with social problems such as school dropout rate, teen pregnancy, or joblessness? Given the possibility of such influences, might intervention programs that provide rich, stimulating environments for at-risk infants affect the general well-being of all, disadvantaged and advantaged alike?

For the past 25 years, a program at the University of North Carolina has been laying the groundwork for answers to questions such as these. The program is known as the Abecedarian Project, named for the first four letters of the alphabet (Campbell, Helms, Sparling, & Ramey, 1998). Starting at the age of 6 months, 111 at-risk infants from low-income families were placed in an intensive child care program with one supervisory adult for every three infants and were given year-round child care 8 hours a day until they were ready to enter school. Once they reached school age, children received additional intervention until they entered the 2nd grade. The program also offered assistance to their families, providing such things as training in parenting and encouraging parents to become involved in their children's schooling (Burchinal, Campbell, Bryant, Wasik, & Ramey, 1997).

Children who were enrolled as infants in the Abecedarian Project were followed until they reached the age of 21. A comparison of the Abecedarian children with a comparable group of children not enrolled in the program shows that intensive early intervention can significantly improve the odds for at-risk children. Specifically, children who had been enrolled in the project had higher reading and math scores when they reached school age, lower school dropout rates and delayed pregnancy as adolescents, and higher rates of college attendance and higher rates of employment as young adults.

In contrast to the success of the extended intervention provided by the Abecedarian Project, research has repeatedly discovered that 1- or 2-year early-intervention programs fail to protect children against poor academic outcomes (Reynolds & Temple, 1998). Similar research finds that children enrolled in intervention programs that do not cover the transition period from preschool to 2nd grade are less likely to maintain the gains they initially make in reading, math, and grade progression (Reynolds & Temple, 1998). Such findings, together with those demonstrating the effectiveness of intensive long-term intervention that covers the transitional period, call for a renewed examination of existing social policy with respect to early intervention programs. Although the funding of intensive programs such as the Abecedarian Project may seem expensive when compared to conventional preschool programs (roughly $10,000 covers one child for 1 year), such programs are likely to offer society a savings in the long run. It has been estimated that for every $1.00 spent on such programs, society saves $7.00 in reduced costs for crime, premature births, and increased unemployment (Maugh, 1999). In addition to more effectively utilizing public and private funds on social programs, the savings in human potential are incalculable, in the form of reclaiming purposeful and productive lives for at-risk youth. Results from the Abecedarian Project, and others similar to it, focus our attention on *what works*, not what *might* work.

flower we have just named (Brown, 1965; Iverson & Goldin-Meadow, 1997). Most verbs in child-directed speech, for instance, name actions that the child or others are currently engaging in. Such actions distinguish these objects as neatly as do their names, the proof of which is seen in games such as charades. Thus our first names for things are names that correspond to distinctive ways of interacting with, or acting on, those things (Brown, 1965). However, the very actions so helpful in distinguishing flowers from, say, bananas or balls are of no help in distinguishing one type of flower from another. Brown (1965) notes that categorizing experience "begins at the level of distinctive action" and only proceeds upward to superordinate categories by "achievements of the imagination" (as quoted in Lakoff, 1987).

Even when illuminated by gesture, when spoken by others, a new word can refer to any of a myriad of different things that may be present. Which of these does it name? Despite the daunting demands that naming places on young children, children are often able to learn the meaning of new words after hearing

If this girl is like most children her age, many of the names she learns for things will be associated with distinctive actions.

them used a single time. **Fast mapping** refers to children's ability to map the meaning of a new word onto a referent after hearing the word used in context just once. This first mapping does not capture all of the word's meaning. The full meaning of a word can develop over years, but fast mapping enables children to establish a lexicon with many entries, which in itself contributes to language development by making it easier for children to talk to others, putting them in a position to learn even more (Clark, 1995). In one study, children were asked by an adult to bring "the chromium tray, not the blue one, the chromium one." Even though they had never heard the word "chromium" before, they brought the right tray and a week later remembered that the new word referred to a color (Carey, 1978).

Children apparently assume that a new word refers to something for which they presently have no name. Names, in other words, are assumed to be *mutually exclusive*; if a thing has one name, it is not likely to be called by another. Hence children look for unnamed, or novel, items or actions on hearing a new word (Merriam, Evey-Burkey, Marazita, & Jarvis, 1996; Merriam & Stevenson, 1997). Children, for instance, who were shown *Sesame Street* characters performing familiar or unfamiliar actions and were asked "Which one is glorping?" picked the unfamiliar action as a referent for the novel verb. They also extended the meaning of this novel verb to a later picture of another character performing the same action (Golinkoff, Jacquet, Hirsh-Pasek, & Nandakumar, 1996).

fast mapping Children's ability to map the meaning of a new word onto a referent after hearing the word used in context just once.

More than assumptions of mutual exclusivity are important in learning names for things. Young children also appear to rely on social criteria in establishing whether unfamiliar words are actually being used as names for things. One of the most powerful social cues is that of joint attention with another person to something that is present or going on. In one study, 18- to 20-month-olds heard a new word ("peri") spoken by someone while they were looking at a new toy. In one case, the new word was spoken by someone who was also looking at the new toy. In the other case, it was spoken by someone out of view of the infant and the toy. When infants were shown the new toy, together with another one, and asked "Where is the peri?" they correctly identified the new toy only when they had heard it named by someone who was also looking at the toy, even though in both instances, the toy was the only new object around to be named. In order for a new word to be taken as a name for something, then, it cannot simply be uttered in the presence of the object. It must be clear that the speaker is referring to that object—that is, naming it (Baldwin et al., 1996).

Children use other strategies, as well, in learning names for things. In **bootstrapping**, children appear to use their knowledge of word class, of whether a word is a verb or a noun, for instance, to learn the meaning of new words (Clark, 1995). To those of us who didn't get the parts of speech right until we reached the 7th grade, this may sound implausible. Yet Roger Brown offers convincing support for this idea. Brown (1957) showed children a picture of hands working on a spaghetti-like substance in a bowl. To some he said the picture showed "how *to sib*"; to others he said it showed "*a sib*"; and to some others he referred to it as "*some sib*." Different aspects of the picture, in other words, were isolated by the syntactic cues of "to (+ verb)," "a," and "some." The verb "to sib" cues children to look for movement. Similarly, the cue "a" denotes a noun whose referent should have a well-defined shape. In contrast, "some" is used to refer to something with ill-defined borders, such as milk, sand, or spaghetti.

After describing the picture in one of these three ways, Brown showed separate pictures of the hands, the bowl, and the spaghetti, and asked which one "sib" referred to. Those who had been told that the picture showed "how to sib" picked the hands, those who had heard "a sib" picked the bowl, and those who had heard "some sib" picked the spaghetti. Each had learned the meaning of a strange word by relying on syntactic cues, cues that told them to look for movement, something with a well-defined shape, or an amorphous substance. By assuming that a word is one type or another, children know what to look for when hearing a new word.

How can parents help their child to learn words more quickly?

First Sentences

At about 18 months to 2 years, children begin putting words together. Their sentences are simple at first, never more than two words. The number of these two-word combinations initially develops slowly, and then takes off, increasing rapidly. Over a period of 7 months, for example, one child put together 14, 24, 54, 89, 350, 1,400, and then over 2,500 different combinations (Braine, 1963). Children can express most of the same relationships expressed in adult speech in these early constructions. They can identify agents and objects of actions, who did what (Doggie run) and what happened to whom (Bump head), as well as indicate possession (Jenny shoe), location (Kitty chair), recurrence (More cookie), and disappearance (Allgone milk). Word order, important in communicating meaning in adult speech, is similarly important in children's first sentences; the meaning of sentences such as "Davey hit" (Davey hit me) is clearly different from that of "Hit Davey" (I hit Davey).

bootstrapping A strategy children use to learn names for things through their knowledge of word classes and syntactic cues.

What children talk about reflects their understanding of their world. Children are beginning to understand what causes things to happen, and distinctions between agent and object sprinkle their observations of events. Similarly, frequent mention of possession, as in "Mommy cup" or "Billy sock," reflects their awareness of which things they are allowed to touch or play with and which are forbidden. And always, as they explore, they are ever mindful of where others are in relation to them.

Another milestone in language development is reached when children begin putting three or more words together. The age at which this occurs varies considerably, from 2 years in one child to 3 years in the next. These sentences, just like earlier ones, have their own organization. Children frequently begin with a short, two-word sentence and expand it, inserting another phrase similar to the first, "Fix it . . . Joshua fix it." The presence of units in these sentences is revealed by the child's intonation, by hesitations in the pattern of speaking, as well as by the choice of words. Pauses occur at the borders of a unit, as in "Put . . . big boots . . . on." The length of these utterances increases with their developing language skills. In fact, the **mean length of utterance,** determined by counting the number of different units, or **morphemes,** that communicate meaning, is a more reliable measure of language development than is age. Using this measure, "Kick boots" would have a MLU of 3, since it contains three morphemes ("kick," "boot," "s"), even though the sentence contains only two words.

The length of children's utterances has been found to correspond to their use of ever-more-complex rules for communicating meaning (Brown, 1973). Brown has identified five such stages of language development. In the first stage, corresponding to an MLU of 1.0 to 2.0, children speak in two-word sentences, adopting the rule of word order in communicating meaning. Examples would be "Davey hit" or "Billy sock," the order of the words in each communicating agency or possession, respectively. In the second stage, with an MLU of 2.0 to 2.5, children can use rules to inflect words, adding "s" to form plurals and "ed" to indicate past tense, as in "Two kitties" or "Ellie jumped." In the third stage, with an MLU of 2.5 to 3.0, children use rules to get from one form of a sentence to another, known as transformation rules ("Kristina hugged Ginger" or "Ginger was hugged by Kristina"). Some of the first transition rules children use are for questions—the who, what, where, and why ones. Children follow an interesting progression in their mastery of these.

One of the first rules children use in this third stage is the rule of preposing, or putting first, the "wh-" word ("*What* does she want? Or *Where* does he sit?"). Unlike adults, however, children do not invert the subject and auxiliary verb, as in "What *does she* want?" or "Where *does he* sit?" Instead, they say "What she want?" or "Where he sit?" At about the same time that they ask questions using the preposing rule, they also begin to use another rule, the rule of inverting, or transposing, the subject and predicate—"*Can I* go out?" as opposed to "I can go out." Though both preposing and inverting rules are available to them in this stage, children do not use both in the same question. It seems that early sentences are limited by performance factors such as memory span or just how much can be programmed and thought out at once.

Children appear to be able to employ only a limited number of rules in producing a sentence. Initially, they are limited to one rule ("What she can ride?" or "Can she ride?"). Then they can use two rules within a single sentence, preposing and transposing ("What can she ride?"). But at this point, they cannot produce sentences requiring the use of three rules: preposing, negating, and inverting, as in "Why can't she ride?" Instead, they ask "Why she can't ride?"

In the fourth and fifth stages, with MLUs of 3.0 to 3.75 and 3.75 to 4.5, respec-

mean length of utterance (MLU)
The average number of morphemes in a child's sentences.

morphemes Units of language that communicate meaning.

In the third stage of language development, children learn to ask questions using who, what, where, why.

tively, children's sentences become increasingly complex. They begin to use clauses and compound and complex sentences. Language continues to develop through early childhood, and continues to develop even through the school years. Table 5.2 charts milestones in language development.

Theories of Language Development

How are we to explain the development of language? What role, for instance, does the language that children hear spoken around them play in language learning? Or are environmental influences, such as spoken language, relatively unimportant? Noam Chomsky (1965), at MIT, devalued the importance of the speech children hear, assuming it was not an adequate model of grammatical speech. Chomsky assumed instead that children are born with a language-acquisition device, neural centers that are prewired for detecting the phonological, semantic, and syntactic categories that constitute a spoken language. The evidence that language is indeed biologically based is abundant and convincing. Such evidence in itself, however, does not rule out the importance of other factors.

Research examining the way individuals speak to young children reveals important differences between that and speech directed toward adults, differences that make child-directed speech ideal for someone new to a language. Sentences are short, simple, and grammatical. Speakers use familiar words, refer to things in the here-and-now, and talk about whatever the child is paying attention to. All of these aspects of child-directed speech make it an excellent model of language. Thus, it seems that adults *fine-tune* the way they speak to infants and young children, adjusting their speech to correspond to what the child can understand and to capture the child's attention (Snow, 1995).

Q Why is reading to a child so important to language development?

TABLE 5.2 Milestones in Language Acquisition

By Age 1	
Milestones	**Activities to Encourage a Child's Language**
• Recognizes names • Says 2 to 3 words besides "mama" and "dada" • Imitates familiar words • Understands simple instructions • Recognizes words as symbols for objects	• Responding to coos, gurgles, and babbling • Talking to the child throughout the day • Reading colorful books to the child every day • Telling nursery rhymes and singing songs • Teaching the child the names of everyday items and familiar people • Taking the child to new places and situations • Playing simple games, such as peek-a-boo and pat-a-cake

Between Ages 1 and 2	
Milestones	**Activities to Encourage a Child's Language**
• Understands "no" • Uses 10 to 20 words, including names • Combines two words, such as "daddy bye-bye" • Waves good-bye and plays pat-a-cake • Makes the "sounds" of familiar animals • Gives a toy when asked • Uses words such as "more" to make wants known • Points to his or her toes, eyes, and nose • Brings object from another room when asked	• Reading children's stories to the child • Talking to the child about what you're doing as you do it • Talking simply and clearly • Talking about new situations before you go, while you're there, and after you return • Looking at the child when he or she talks to you • Describing what the child is doing, feeling, hearing • Playing children's records and tapes • Praising the child's efforts to communicate

Fine-tuning takes its cues from the child. This sensitive interplay between speaker and child can first be seen in the way we talk to infants. "Baby talk" is characterized by a high-pitched voice and exaggerated prosodic features, or the rise and fall of the voice and the stress given to words (Garnica, 1977). These same characteristics are true of speech to infants in languages other than English as well. It is noteworthy that these speech characteristics are precisely the ones that are most likely to capture an infant's attention (see Chapter 4).

When young children begin to say their first words, we again fine-tune our speech, but this time by enunciating our words more clearly. Sounds, such as final consonants, that would ordinarily be "swallowed" in speech that is directed toward another adult are now carefully articulated. We usually stop doing this by the time children reach the age of the vocabulary spurt. Even in terms of syntax, there is evidence of fine-tuning. Thus, we see a close correspondence between the degree to which parents will add words, elaborating on the speech of the child, and the degree to which children drop them. That is, the more telegraphic the child's speech, the more likely the parent will elaborate. Elaboration decreases as children spontaneously add the parts of speech they originally had omitted in telegraphic speech. Fine-tuning is most evident in the speech of mothers, and less so in that of fathers and siblings (Snow, 1995).

So far, our discussion of the factors that contribute to language development has stressed input from adults. How active a role do children assume in these dialogues? Lois Bloom and colleagues (1996) propose that children, and not adults,

TABLE 5.2 Milestones in Language Acquisition

Between Ages 2 and 3 Milestones	Activities to Encourage a Child's Language
• Identifies body parts • Carries on "conversation" with self and dolls • Asks "What's that?" and "Where's my . . . ?" • Uses two-word negative phrases, such as "no want" • Forms some plurals by adding *s* • Has a 450-word vocabulary • Gives first name; holds up fingers to tell age • Combines nouns and verbs, such as "mommy go" • Understands simple time concepts, such as "last night" and "tomorrow" • Refers to self as "me" rather than by name • Tries to get adult attention: "Watch me" • Likes to hear same story repeated • May say "no" when meaning "yes" • Talks to other children as well as adults • Solves problems by talking instead of hitting or crying • Answers "where" questions • Names common pictures and things • Uses short sentences like "me want more" or "me want cookie" • Matches 3 to 4 colors, knows big and little	• Repeating new words • Helping the child listen and follow instructions by playing games: "pick up the ball," "touch my nose" • Taking the child on trips and talking about what you see before, during, and after the trip • Letting the child tell you answers to simple questions • Reading books every day, perhaps as part of the bedtime routine • Listening attentively as the child talks to you • Describing what you are doing, planning, thinking • Having the child deliver simple messages for you • Carrying on conversations with the child • Asking questions to get the child to think and talk • Showing that you understand what the child is saying by answering, smiling, and nodding your head • Expanding what the child says. If the child says, "more juice," you say, "You want more juice?"

Source: Adapted from Learning Disabilities Association of America. (1997, July 9). *Speech & language milestone chart.* KidSource OnLine. Retrieved from the World Wide Web: http://www.kidsource.com/LDA/speech_language.html.

take the lead in these early conversations. In her **intentionality model** of language development, Bloom assumes that the impetus for language development comes from the child, fueled by the growth of the child's mind rather than by the conversational skills of the adult. Consequently, the rate at which language is acquired reflects children's growing understanding of their world and their desire to communicate this. It is primarily the abilities of the child, rather than structure provided by the adult, that determine the course of language learning in general and the nature of conversational discourse in particular.

In contrast to Bloom's intentionality model is the **scaffolding model** (Bruner, 1983). This model assumes that adults are the ones to take charge of these early conversations, both by initiating them and by providing a structure, or scaffold, which supports the emergence of new language forms. The concept of a scaffold is similar to Vygotsky's zone of proximal development, in which the adult models forms of speech that are just beyond the capacity of the child to perform independently, yet still within the child's reach when assisted. Different predictions follow from the two models about the form that early conversations between children and their caregivers will take. The intentionality model assumes that

intentionality model Lois Bloom's model of language development, which assumes that the impetus for language development is the growth of the child's mind rather than the conversational skills of the adult.

scaffolding model A model of language development that assumes that the impetus for language development is adults' initiation of conversation and providing of a scaffold, or structure, to support the emergence of new language forms.

children will be the ones to initiate a conversation and that when mothers do initiate a conversation, they will be more likely to state what is on their mind than ask questions to foster speech in the child. Conversely, the scaffolding model predicts that mothers will initiate most conversations and that they will use questions rather than statements in order to prompt turn-taking and help the child build on what they have just said.

At least some evidence seems to favor the intentionality model. Bloom, Margulis, Tinker, and Fujita (1996) followed children from the ages of 9 months to 2 years, recording their conversations with their mothers. They found that most conversations were initiated by children and that when mothers responded, they were more likely to do so with a statement than a question. Thus these early conversations appear to reflect children's desire to communicate and do not appear to require elaborate scaffolding from their conversational partners.

What might children want to talk about? Children talk about what they see ("Ball go"), what they are doing ("Shoe on"), and what they are feeling ("Billy sleepy"). Jean Mandler (1992), recall, has suggested that children's ongoing analysis of activities such as looking at moving objects, understanding agency, and animacy results in image-schemas which represent basic forms of understanding. She further suggests that such image-schemas provide the foundation for the conceptual vocabulary that children later put into words.

What forms of understanding would such a vocabulary include? The narrative of experience suggests some answers. Consider an event such as a cat tapping a ball with its paw. As we have seen earlier in the chapter, even very young infants can abstract information about agency (the cat), action (tapping), object (the ball), location (a room in the house), and path (of the ball). Such preverbal conceptualizations translate into the more familiar questions of what happened, who did it, to what or to whom, and where it took place.

Mandler suggests that these image-schemas function at an intermediate level between perception and language, with preverbal concepts being based on a perceptual analysis of actual ongoing events taking place in space and time. This earliest of grammars, rather than being an abstract formal system, becomes spatial in nature and thus continuous with the way we process other information about our physical world (Armstrong, Stokoe, & Wilcox, 1995; Lakoff, 1987).

How might image-schemas serve as a primitive grammar? These schemas, recall, are assumed to have an internal structure, to consist, in other words, of parts. For instance, the image-schema for "path," as in the path a moving ball follows, would join the beginning, the trajectory, and the destination of the ball. This structure, then, would allow the child's gaze to anticipate and more easily follow points along the path and be surprised should the ball deviate. The analogue nature of such schemas makes it possible for them to embed information about regularities of relationships among the parts. A child following the path of the ball, for instance, can shift her attention from where it starts to where it will be the next moment. The relationship among these elements is rule-governed, just as it is among the words of a spoken language. We know that infants are aware of these rules from the work of investigators such as Van de Walle and Spelke, Baillargeon, and others. Infants are aware, for instance, that objects do not simply disappear and then reappear as they move along a path (principle of continuity) and that for something to start to move, it must be set in motion by something else or itself be animate.

In attending first to one element and then to another within such schemas, children are guided by their knowledge of such rules. In this grammar of experience, they can distinguish such things as agent (the animate cat) from action (the tap which sets the ball in motion) or object (that which moves when it is hit) or

What is this toddler likely to notice? In addition to sharp teeth or furry ears, children can distinguish agent from action, object, or location, and this "grammar of experience" is reflected in the grammar of their speech.

location (the path followed by the moving ball) (Fillmore, 1982). This grammar, since it is based on the same analysis of experience as other perceptual and cognitive processes, provides a foundation for talking about what infants are experiencing.

A perceptually based approach to language such as the one proposed by Mandler assumes that language is processed the way we process other information about our physical world, in terms of basic schemas that capture fundamental distinctions such as part-whole, agent-object, container, support, and the like. Approached this way, grammar, just like other forms of thought, can be traced to the way we perceive and interact with our physical world. Language, rather than beginning as an abstract, formal system that must later be connected to other aspects of experience, becomes continuous with such basic cognitive processes as object recognition or perceptually guided movements such as walking or reaching (Armstrong, Stokoe, & Wilcox, 1995).

Summary

Making Sense of the World

Infants begin to explore their surroundings from the moment of birth. With age, they become increasingly better at perceiving the things around them. These improvements can be interpreted as reflecting the operation of both reinforcing contingencies present in infants' surroundings and internal anticipatory schemata. Reinforcers are events that increase the frequency of the behaviors on which they are contingent. Anticipatory schemata are cognitive structures that direct perceptual exploration, preparing individuals to take in certain types of information and not others. The

schemata are in turn modified by the information that is sampled.

Piaget's Developmental Constructivism

Piaget believed that infants' understanding of the world begins with the development of sensorimotor schemas that evolve out of reflexes present at birth. Piaget believed that sensorimotor thought, characteristic of infancy, develops over six substages. In the first substage (modification of basic reflexes) inborn reflexes become modified, providing a better fit with the conditions under which they have occurred and occurring in the absence of the stimuli that initially triggered them. In the second substage (primary circular reactions) infants develop circular reactions in which they are able to repeat behaviors that lead to interesting outcomes. In a third substage (secondary circular reactions) circular actions are extended to include objects outside infants' own bodies. In a fourth substage (coordination of secondary circular reactions) intentional, goal-directed behavior can be seen; and in a fifth stage (tertiary circular reactions) the use of trial and error in problem solving is believed to first occur. In a final substage (mental representation) Piaget believed infants become able to represent their experiences mentally with the emergence of symbolic thought.

A central concept in Piaget's theory of infant intelligence is that of object permanence. Piaget assumed that it takes infants several years to develop a full understanding of the nature of objects; and in the first substages of this development, objects cease to exist for infants when they are out of sight.

Critique of Piaget's Theory

Piaget assumed that each of the sense modalities functioned independently of the other and that only through experience did infants come to integrate these. More recent evidence shows that infants can use information provided by one modality to recognize something they have experienced in another modality. Similarly, research strongly suggests that infants are aware of objects' existence, even when these can't be seen, well before Piaget believed they are able to do so.

Categorizing Experience

Infants' awareness of time, like that of adults, appears to be based on their sensitivity to the temporal sequencing of events. Infants' perception of space and of the form of things develops with their ability to move about and with their ability to take hold of things and grasp them. Initially, infants represent the location of objects in relation to themselves (egocentric representation). Infants come to locate objects in relation to other things in their environments (landmark representation) when they begin to move about on their own. Finally, infants become able to represent spatial relations according to some abstract frame of reference (allocentric representation). Infants also show a rudimentary understanding of simple arithmetic operations that result in an object being added to or taken away from a set.

Even young infants have been shown to be able to classify objects into different categories. Three explanations for forming categories were considered: using defining features, using a probabilistic approach, and forming a theory of why things go together. Categories could be represented in terms of defining features, or features that all members of a category possess in common. A probabilistic approach assumes that we distinguish items as belonging to a category on the basis of family resemblance rather than an invariant set of features. This approach assumes that four factors are important in assigning items to a category: cue validity, basic-level categories, correlated features, and prototypes. Finally, objects can be categorized on the basis of the relationships that exist among them, reflecting a theory of why things go together. The first categories are most likely conceptual in nature, reflecting image-schemas, which map spatial structure into conceptual structure.

The Development of Language

From birth on, infants are attentive to the sounds of speech and prefer to listen to the sounds of their native language. Infants begin to babble in the 2nd to 3rd month. Later, their babbling reflects the sounds they hear in their native language. Infants also attend to the prosodic features of speech, using these as cues in ambiguous situations. Infants typically utter their first word at about the age of 12 months. Word acquisition occurs slowly at first, but late in the 2nd year a vocabulary explosion often occurs. Difficulties in articulation underlie regularities in children's pronunciation errors.

Children may use single words not only to name things but also, in combination with gestures, to communicate more complex thoughts; this usage is referred to as a *holophrase*. When naming things for children, adults use names that correspond to the distinctions they anticipate children will need to make in using the objects named. Children are often able to learn the meaning of new words after hearing them used a single time. *Fast mapping* refers to their ability to map the meaning of a new word onto a referent on hearing the word used in context just once. In learning the names for things, names are assumed to be mutually exclusive: If a thing has one name, it is not likely to be called by another. Children also use a bootstrapping strategy in learning names for things, in which they use their knowledge of word class to learn the meaning of new words.

Children begin putting two words together at about 18 months, and three or more words together anywhere from 2 to 3 years of age. The length of children's utterances (mean length of utterance) has been found to correspond to their use of ever-more-complex rules for communicating. Using this index, five stages of language development have been identified. In the first, children speak in two-word sentences. In the second, children use rules to inflect words, indicating plurality and tense. In the third, children can use rules to transpose meaning from one form of a sentence to another. In the fourth and fifth stages, their sentences become increasingly complex.

Theories of Language Development

There is abundant evidence indicating that language is biologically based; this does not, however, rule out the importance of other factors. Child-directed speech, using sentences that are short, simple, and grammatical, provides an excellent medium through which children can learn aspects of language. Adults fine-tune the way they speak to children, adjusting their speech to correspond to what the child can understand. Children also play an active role in these dialogues, often taking the lead in directing early conversations. In contrast, the scaffolding model of language acquisition assumes that adults are the ones to take charge of conversations, providing a scaffold that supports the emergence of new language forms.

Key Terms

allocentric representation (p. 187)
babbling (p. 195)
bootstrapping (p. 203)
defining features (p. 189)
egocentric representation (p. 187)
fast mapping (p. 201)
habituation (p. 180)
holophrase (p. 199)
intentionality model (p. 206)

jargon babbling (p. 196)
landmark representation (p. 187)
mean length of utterance (MLU) (p. 204)
morphemes (p. 204)
operant conditioning (p. 170)
overextension (p. 200)
primary circular reactions (p. 173)
reinforcement (p. 171)

scaffolding model (p. 207)
schemas (p. 173)
secondary circular reactions (p. 173)
sensorimotor stage (p. 171)
tertiary circular reactions (p. 175)
underextensions (p. 200)
vocabulary explosion (p. 199)

chaptersix

Infancy and Toddlerhood
Psychosocial Development

A toddler stands, legs planted in the doorway, casting a brief shadow, and then with a squeal steps into the outside. Horizons widen in infancy, and beginning steps quicken to a run as mastery brings surer footing and a firmer sense of self. Parents who kept pace initially may find it hard to keep up, as the emotional security of deepening relationships enables infants and then toddlers to move beyond the familiar. The infant's exploration of the world without enables the toddler to discover a world within, one which reveals a realm of emotions and the startling discovery of the self. Households and schedules are rearranged to avoid the wreckage that comes with life in the fast lane, as first the infant and then the toddler fine-tunes shifting emotions and masters corners on the run. It is a fast, wild, joyous, and tumultous ride into childhood.

This chapter marks the developmental route taken. We will stop first to look at the bonds of attachment that form between infants and their caregivers. Much of the exuberance of these first years can be traced to the emotional foundation provided by secure and trusting relationships in infancy. Infants contribute to the building of this foundation just as do their caregivers. In a second stop, we will look at differences in temperament among infants that are apparent even at birth and that give shape to these first relationships. In a final stop along the route into childhood, we will look at the emotional developments that accompany an emerging sense of self. Emotions such as guilt and shame emerge as infants move from reactivity to self-regulation and as toddlers move from stormy demands for autonomy to a more relaxed exploration of their limits. Not all of the moves are smooth, however. There's many a "glitch" as those youngest on the road of life shift gears, find their own pace, and learn to coordinate their needs with those who care for them.

Infants are biologically prepared to become attached to those who care for them.

Attachment: The Bonds of Love

In the first days and weeks of life, infants react in the same way to everyone, showing little preference for one person over another. In a sense, any shoulder or lap will do. This sweet indiscretion becomes less true with time, until by the end of the first 6 months, infants clearly prefer those closest to them, such as parents or siblings, to others. **Attachment** refers to the affectional bonds that infants form with those who care for them and to the ways in which infants organize their behavior around these people, using them as a base from which to explore and to which to return for safety when stressed (Seifer & Schiller, 1995; Waters, Vaughn, Posada, & Kondo-Ikemura, 1995).

Are infants biologically prepared to become attached to those who care for them? It would appear that they are. Not only are they equipped perceptually to discover what they will need to know about their world, as we noted in the last chapter, but they are also equipped socially in much the same manner. This is not to say that infants have social skills, but simply that their initial behaviors are sufficient to ensure that, under most circumstances, their needs will be met. Among the most important behaviors equipping infants for social encounters are their reflexive cries to changes in their body states. Infants need not wait for others to wonder whether they might be hungry or cold. Their cries clearly signal their needs (Seifer & Schiller, 1995). Similarly, a second factor equipping them socially is their soothability. They *stop* crying when fed, are soothed when picked up, grasp fingers that are offered, stare quietly at faces, and still to voices. Each of these responses to those who care for them knits infants and their caregivers ever more closely into a social unit.

Why do infants become attached to their caregivers? Is it because these are the ones who feed them when they are hungry, keep them warm when cold, and amuse them with whispers and kisses? Is love won by sweet talk and warm milk? Initial assumptions about the basis for affectional bonds in infants focused on the satisfaction of physical needs, such as the reduction of hunger, cold, or discomfort.

How does attachment differ form affection?

attachment The affectional bonds that infants form with those who care for them; the ways in which infants organize their behavior around these caregivers, using them as a base from which to explore and to which to return for safety when stressed.

In Harlow's experiments with attachment in monkeys, infants preferred the cloth surrogate mother to the one that gave milk.

Sigmund Freud (1933/1961) assumed that the behavior of humans as well as of other organisms is motivated by biological drives. These drives are experienced as states of arousal, such as hunger and thirst, which individuals seek to reduce. Satisfying biological drives such as these is not only necessary for our survival, but is also pleasurable. The reduction of drives is so pleasurable, in fact, that Freud believed it to serve as one of the basic motivating principles throughout life. Freud assumed that infants associate the pleasure derived from reducing the drive of hunger with the very person who is most closely associated with this activity, the mother. Thus, for Freud, drive reduction became the basis for attachment.

Harry Harlow, a psychologist at the University of Wisconsin, was one of the first to actually put these assumptions to the test. Harlow raised rhesus monkeys with inanimate surrogate mothers, wire forms with plastic faces. These surrogates provided either milk, in the form of a bottle that protruded below the neck, or contact comfort, a soft terry cloth covering the wire form. When allowed to spend time with these surrogates, infants would bound over to the surrogate with the milk. But after satisfying their hunger, they left her for the terry-cloth surrogate. In an even more dramatic test of surrogate preferences, the infants were scared with a raucous toy to see which surrogate they would seek for comfort. Once again, the infants preferred the surrogate they could cling to and cuddle against over the one that gave milk (Harlow & Zimmerman, 1959). This research argues strongly against any simple explanation of attachment in terms of hunger reduction.

The Development of Attachment

John Bowlby, a British psychiatrist, approached attachment in terms of its adaptiveness. Infants are completely helpless at first and must rely on others to meet all of their needs. Survival depends on staying close to those who will care for them. However, infants also experience a growing curiosity about their world, one which increases with age and which can lure them from the safety of their mother's side. The attachment bond balances these competing needs, the need for

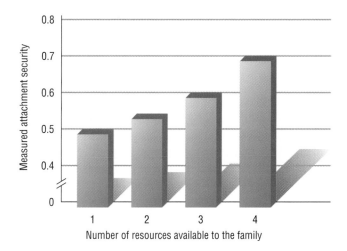

FIGURE 6.1 Security of Attachment Between Fathers and Their Sons As a Function of the Personal and Collective Assets Within the Family *Source:* J. Belsky, (1996). Parent, infant, and social-contextual antecedents of the father-son attachment security. *Developmental Psychology*, 32, 905–913.

marriage, job satisfaction, the family's financial situation, and the presence of social supports that together predict attachment security. For instance, it has been found that mothers who experience satisfaction with their maternal role are more likely to have securely attached infants. The degree to which mothers experience role satisfaction, however, is affected by the amount of social support they receive (Isabella, 1994). The Social Policy Focus, "The Importance of Fathers: Child Support Versus Emotional Support" examines two contextual factors: the absence of the father and the absence of financial support from the father.

Most of the research on attachment has focused on infants' relationships with their mothers. Still, we know that by the end of the 1st year, the affectional bonds infants establish with their fathers are very similar to those with their mothers (Lamb, 1977, 1981). But are similar processes at work in each case? That is, are contextual factors similarly important in determining the quality of infants' attachment to their fathers? Belsky (1996) examined father-son attachment at 1 year of age using the strange-situation procedure. He also assessed the presence of factors that could serve as stressors or supports, such as personality types, quality of the marriage, and work-family relations. He found, just as with mothers, that as the number of resources available to the family increased, so did the security of attachment between fathers and their sons. We can see this relationship in Figure 6.1, in which attachment security is shown to increase with the number of resources that fall above the median.

One of the most obvious factors contributing to the quality of the relationship that develops between parents and their children is the sheer amount of time they have to spend together. For a majority of mothers, this translates into the length of their maternity leave. By the late 1990s, 60% of women with children under the age of 6 were employed, and a majority of mothers returned to work within the 1st year of their child's life (U.S. Bureau of Labor Statistics, 1999).

Is length of the maternity leave related to the quality of mother-child interactions? Roseanne Clark, Janet Shibley Hyde, Marilyn Essex, and Marjorie Klein (1997), at the University of Wisconsin, examined this relationship in the context of what the infant and the mother each bring to it. These investigators were not as interested in determining whether employment in itself affected the relationship as in determining the conditions under which it might and the processes responsible for this.

The Importance of Fathers: Child Support Versus Emotional Support BY ANDREA HAYES

An American father recently spent 11 years searching for his two children, who had been abducted by their mother. The mother had a severe drug addiction and yet effectively kept their whereabouts unknown. This father repeatedly attempted to gain some sort of support or assistance from police and other agencies to help find his children, but to no avail. Predictably, the children ended up in foster care. At the time, the foster care agency claimed the father could not be located for dependency proceedings. Interestingly, this same public entity eventually tracked him down as a "deadbeat dad" in order to garnish his wages to pay for the benefits his children received while they were on welfare. Is it fair to say that this agency was more interested in tracking down a "deadbeat dad" than in helping him to function as a real one?

As a result of welfare reform, Congress has addressed the growing concern for children's health and welfare by passing legislation that strengthens child-support enforcement. Child support is defined as "payments to children from nonresident parents." One third of American families were headed by a single parent in 1996 (Rockefeller, 1998), yet only 60% of this nation's eligible children have a legal agreement for child support. Of those, 25% receive no payment at all. When we consider that the number of eligible children grew from 10% in 1960 to 33% in 1990, it leaves many children at risk for poverty-related problems such as poor nutrition, inadequate health care, and unsafe housing (Garfinkel, Miller, McLanahan, & Hanson, 1998).

Through the 1998 Child Support Performance and Incentive Act, the federal government rewards individual states for better performance and enforcement of child-support laws. The actual implementation of this policy began in the year 2000. While the development of this policy seems logical and necessary, is it an example of the tail wagging the dog?

Some researchers believe that the money spent on incentives for states that enforce child support could be better spent on intervention programs. Certain studies seem to point to fathers' involvement being interdependent on their developmental life stage, economic situation, ability to pay, and relations with other family members. Without attending to these underlying issues, forced payment may actually cause further estrangement (Coley & Chase-Lansdale, 1999). One intervention program called the Parent's Fair Share Demonstration seeks to increase child-support payments and paternal involvement through education, job training, social support groups, and mediation services. Time and further research will tell which approach is most effective: broad legislation or community intervention.

The development and implementation of social policy always has pros and cons. Due to the tax burden on most working Americans, the drain of welfare made reform imperative, and part of this reform requires fathers to take personal responsibility for their children. However, one can't help but wonder if future research will find more children *monetarily* cared for, but *emotionally* bereft due to the absence of their father.

When mothers were depressed or when they perceived their infants as difficult, shorter leaves of absence (6 weeks) were associated with less sensitivity and responsiveness and less pleasure in being with their infants. However, these effects disappeared with longer leaves of absence (12 weeks). It may be that longer maternity leaves provide the opportunity for working mothers to resolve the competing demands of family roles and work. Longer leaves may be especially helpful with difficult infants, by increasing the mother's sense of effectiveness and competence. By 3 months, infants are more responsive and their habits are more regular. Each of these can increase a mother's feelings of competence, which in turn can affect the way she interacts with her infant, enabling her to be more sensitive and simply to enjoy her infant more.

These findings have implications for public policy. The Federal Family and Medical Leave legislation of 1993 guarantees the mother's job and her benefits for a minimum of 12 weeks' leave; but the leave is unpaid, and many working mothers cannot afford to take this length of leave without pay. A shorter 6-week disability leave is currently mandated and often includes pay. While this may be adequate for many mothers, these findings indicate that individual differences in mothers and infants make a longer leave desirable for some. Following the birth of an infant, parents need time not only to care for the infant, but also to develop relationships with the infant and to adjust to new roles within the family.

High-quality day care has no negative developmental effects and may benefit children's social and intellectual development.

Day Care

The number of mothers with young children who work outside the home has increased substantially over the past three decades, with just over 60% of mothers whose children are 6 years of age or less being employed outside the home (U.S. Bureau of Labor Statistics, 1995). As a result, many more young children today experience day care for some number of hours each week than did so in the past.

What effect does early day care have on children's development? Is attachment security likely to be affected? Are other aspects of development, such as intelligence and social behavior, affected? And will the family still continue to exert as strong an influence on a child's development as it might were the child not being cared for by others? Questions such as these have arisen for parents who face the need to find alternate sources of care when they return to work.

Initial research on the effects of day care did not offer comfortable assurances to concerned parents. In fact, based on a review of the existing research to that point, Jay Belsky (1986) suggested that placing infants in day care for 20 hours or more a week during the 1st year of life could pose a risk to the development of secure attachment. Additionally, the effects of extended early day care were thought to carry over into childhood, resulting in poorer social adjustment once children reached school age. Subsequent research has not supported these early generalizations. Research focusing only on the number of hours a child is in day care each week, without considering the many contextual conditions that are present, can lead to more confusion than clarity. See the Research Focus, "The 'File Drawer Problem': Day Care and Attachment."

What contextual conditions need to be considered? The two contexts that are most important, as one might expect, are the day care facility itself and the context of the family. We will consider each of these in turn.

With respect to the day care facility, research has found that when the quality of child care is high, day care has no negative developmental effects and may even beneficially affect aspects of social and intellectual development (Burchinal,

The "File Drawer Problem": Day Care and Attachment BY MICHAEL WAPNER

1. Every year over a thousand tickets pay off more than $500 in the lottery.

2. At least 500 cases of cancer have improved after treatment with medicines made of apricot pits.

3. I personally know of four people who have had bad luck after breaking a chain letter.

What's wrong with these claims as guides to behavior? What's wrong is that they don't tell the whole story. They trumpet the number of *positive outcomes*—that is, the number of times some event or behavior was followed by a particular effect. But they omit the *negative results*—the number of times that the particular effect did not follow. Consequently the claims are misleading. Consider:

1. It may be true that every year more than 1,000 lottery tickets pay over $500. Does that make it a good idea to buy lottery tickets? What if you knew that every year over 10 billion lottery tickets pay nothing? That would make the probability of getting a winning lottery ticket 1 in 10 million.

2. Perhaps 500 cases of cancer did improve after being treated with medicines made of apricot pits. But in how many cases did no change or even deterioration follow the same treatment? Maybe the improvement had nothing to do with apricots.

3. Perhaps I do know four people to whom bad things happened after they failed to respond to a chain letter. But how many people experienced nothing unusual after doing the same thing? (Not to mention the number of people to whom bad things occurred even though they did respond or never received a chain letter.)

We have come to expect that people who are trying to sell something may "forget" to report the negative cases. But that the same problem may occur in science is a bit more surprising. And yet it may occur, not out of an intentional desire to mislead, but as the unintended consequence of the way the results of research are disseminated.

The failure to report negative outcomes in science is called the "File Drawer Problem." The phrase refers to the effect of two related tendencies: First, scientists tend not to submit negative results to journals (but to "file" them); and, second, journals tend not to publish research with negative results. In the extreme, the consequence of the file drawer problem would be that in some cases only the handful of positive results that occur by chance would be published, while the much larger proportion of negative results would remain unknown.

One antidote for the file drawer problem is for researchers to replicate studies that had positive outcomes and to publish the results even (or particularly) if they are negative. Lori Roggman and her colleagues did precisely that in an area of particular social and psychological importance—the relationship between infant day care and mother-infant attachment. The authors chose for replication four published studies which had found that infant day care was significantly related to insecure attachment to the mother. Appropriate to the point in question, the replication (Roggman, Langlois, Hubbs-Tait, and Reiser-Danner, 1994) used data from research which had not been published because it had produced no significant results. However, because the procedures and the subjects in the research by Roggman and her associates were comparable to the studies being replicated, it made sense to reanalyze the unpublished data. In contrast to the earlier published studies, Roggman and her associates did not find a consistent relation between day care and attachment. This is not to say that no significant effects were found. It did appear that anxiety in the mother-infant relationship was greater for infants in part-time day care than for infants in no day care or full-time day care. However, part-time day care also tended to be more irregularly scheduled, with a greater variety of caregivers, reflecting the parents' partial and irregular employment. Thus, the greater insecurity in mother-infant attachment might well have come from factors more complex than day care itself. But in any case, no simple statement about the relation between day care and attachment could be made.

The authors discuss a number of factors which might account for the conflicting results between these studies, including different ways of selecting subjects and different definitions of day care. And certainly there must be reasons for the differences. But the bottom line is that unless negative results, when they occur, are published, there will be no differences to explain.

Ramey, Reid, & Jaccard, 1995; Pungello & Kurtz-Costes, 1999). Determining what constitutes high-quality care, however, is not always that easy for parents.

What does one look for in determining whether a facility offers high-quality care? To get answers, parents need to be able to walk into a facility and look for various conditions. The first thing to notice is the number of children in the facility and the ratio of children to caregivers. For infants and toddlers especially, these ratios should be low. A ratio of one caregiver for every three infants or every six toddlers is desirable, whereas a higher ratio of one to eight is possible with preschoolers (Berezin, 1990; McCartney, Scarr, Phillips, & Grajek, 1985). Another thing to look for is whether children have ample opportunity to interact with the adults who are caring for them. Are they able, that is, to be held, to climb into a lap, or to be listened to or read to? Keep in mind that day care centers with larger numbers of children are likely to have more rules in place and be less flexible in accommodating the interests and needs of individual children than are smaller facilities. Irrespective of the size of the facility, parents should be able to stop by at any time, unannounced and with no appointment necessary.

In addition to the number of staff, both their training and their commitment to caregiving are also important. Day care facilities have been found to differ widely in these respects. For instance, sensitivity and responsiveness, the two dimensions of interaction that Ainsworth found to be important in the formation of attachment, have been found to differ markedly among caregivers. In this respect, parents could follow Ainsworth's lead and notice how responsive adult caregivers are to children's overtures as they show them through the facility, just as Ainsworth noticed how responsive mothers were to their infants while being interviewed. Do caregivers respond promptly? Are they attentive to expressions of delight and pleasure as well as those of distress (Pungello & Kurtz-Costes, 1999)? Additionally, the consistency of staff over time is important for children's emotional comfort. A high turnover of staff can be problematic not only with respect to children's comfort in relating to their caregivers, but also in terms of signifying underlying administrative problems.

Day care facilities also need ample space, both inside and out, for a variety of activities to be going on at any one time. Finally, it is important to be sure that health and safety standards are met. A personal tour of a facility can reveal some things, such as whether dirty diapers are disposed of in a sanitary way or adequate protections exist around stairs and the sharp edges of furniture. It is also important to make sure that the facility has met state licensing requirements.

Even so, parents may not always be able to see what they need to see in order to judge the quality of a facility. They simply can't be there throughout the day to observe, and often find it difficult to interpret the meaning of the things they do see. For instance, how is one to interpret signs of distress in a child? Does a child's tearful clinging simply indicate separation anxiety or a real problem in the type of care the child is experiencing? Perhaps the best measure of a facility's quality is the overall attitude and behavior of the children themselves. Is their behavior spontaneous? Are they busily engaged in play with each other? Do they appear to be happy?

> **Q** What should parents look for in a day care center to determine whether it offers high-quality care?

A disturbing finding to emerge from studies assessing the quality of child care is that most facilities, whether child care centers or family day care homes, do not offer high-quality care. Among child care centers offering care for infants and toddlers, only 8% were found to provide good care and as many as 40% were found to have health or safety problems (Helburn et al., 1995). Similarly, irrespective of age, for children cared for in homes, either by relatives or in family day care homes, just under 10% were found to receive good-quality care whereas 35% received care that was potentially harmful to development (Kontos, Howes, Shinn, & Galinsky, 1995). Box 6.1 is a checklist for day care quality.

The quality of care has been found to vary with the income level of the children attending the facility. Children from upper-income homes generally receive the highest quality of care. Interestingly, children from low-income homes receive higher quality care than do those from middle-income homes, with the exception that care providers in these centers have been found to be less sensitive and more emotionally detached than are those in centers attended by children from middle- or high-income homes (Pungello & Kurtz-Costes, 1999).

Box 6.1 *Checklist for Day Care Quality*

How can parents determine the quality of care provided by a facility? Child Care Aware, a joint venture of the National Association of Child Care Resource & Referral Agencies (NACCRRA), suggests asking the following questions.

Caregivers/Teachers

- Do the caregivers/teachers seem to really like children?
- Do the caregivers/teachers get down on each child's level to speak to the child?
- Are children greeted when they arrive?
- Are children's needs quickly met even when things get busy?
- Are the caregivers/teachers trained in CPR, first aid, and early childhood education?
- Are the caregivers/teachers involved in continuing education programs?
- Does the program keep up with children's changing interests?
- Will the caregivers/teachers always be ready to answer your questions?
- Will the caregivers/teachers tell you what your child is doing every day? Are parents' ideas welcomed? Are there ways for you to get involved?
- Do the caregivers/teachers and children enjoy being together?
- Is there enough staff to serve the children? (Ask local experts about the best staff/child ratio for different age groups.)
- Are caregivers/teachers trained and experienced?
- Have they participated in early childhood development classes?

Setting

- Is the atmosphere bright and pleasant?
- Is there a fenced-in outdoor play area with a variety of safe equipment? Can the caregivers/teachers see the entire playground at all times?
- Are there different areas for resting, quiet play, and active play? Is there enough space for the children in all of these areas?

Activities

- Is there a daily balance of play time, story time, activity time, and nap time?
- Are the activities right for each age group?
- Are there enough toys and learning materials for the number of children?
- Are toys clean, safe, and within reach of the children?

In General

- Do you agree with the discipline practices?
- Do you hear the sounds of happy children?
- Are children comforted when needed?
- Is the program licensed or regulated?
- Are surprise visits by parents encouraged?
- Will your child be happy there?

Source: Child Care Aware. (1999). A project of the National Association of Child Care Resource and Referral Agencies (NACCRRA), Washington, D. C.

How can we promote the selection of high-quality care facilities by parents? Educating parents is a first step. Providing information about the potential impact of low-quality care as well as guidelines on what to look for in high-quality care is important. Also important are public policy changes that would institute better regulation of such facilities as well as the training of increased numbers of qualified providers. Training, however, will accomplish little unless there are sufficient incentives for individuals to pursue this line of work. Thus, the suggestions just made need to go hand in hand with legislation guaranteeing adequate compensation for child care providers. Finally, we need public policies aimed at helping parents pay for high-quality care, making such care accessible, in other words, to all income groups.

What can we say with respect to the second context, that of the family? Will parents continue to exert as strong an influence on their children's development as they might were their children not being cared for by others? Comparisons of children in day care with those cared for at home by their mothers have found that dimensions of family life are no less closely related to children's development when they attend day care than when they are cared for at home. Rather, exposure to developmentally sound experiences, such as less authoritarian attitudes toward child rearing and more sensitive mothering, is related to more positive development in children whether they are cared for at home or in day care (NICHD, 1998).

Finally, how might the effect of day care vary as a function of differences in family contexts? Although research has found that high-quality day care can have beneficial effects, it is nonetheless true that not all children are equally likely to benefit by such care. Rather, day care appears to have a buffering effect with respect to family variables. In other words, day care appears to serve as a protective factor, mitigating the negative effects of family variables that have been found to be associated with poorer cognitive, social, or emotional functioning. Conversely, however, the very same buffering effects may work in the opposite direction as well, in that beneficial family variables may also have less impact on children's development (Burchinal et al., 1995; NICHD, 1998).

Temperament

Perhaps because infants are small enough to fit in the crook of an arm and are dependent on others for their every need, it is all too easy to think that they would be "putty" in the hands of adults. But are infants so many lumps of biological clay, to be shaped by their caretakers? Observations of a single infant, no matter how carefully they are conducted, would do little to resolve this question. However, even a casual comparison of two newborns reveals noticeable differences between them, and a glance at a roomful of babies, such as in a hospital nursery, would leave no doubt as to the individual nature of each. Infants differ from one another from the moment of birth. They differ not only in their weight, the length of their fingers, and the shape of their ears, but also in what one might refer to more generally as their disposition, or their characteristic mode of responding. Infants begin life very much as individuals.

Differences in infants' characteristic ways of responding are referred to as temperament. More specifically, **temperament** consists of the underlying predispositions contributing to infants' activity level, emotionality, and sociability (Goldsmith et al., 1987). Since differences in temperament are evident even in very young infants, they are assumed to be biologically based, genetically predisposing an infant to

temperament Underlying predispositions contributing to an infant's activity level, emotionality, and sociability.

From birth, infants differ from one another in their temperament.

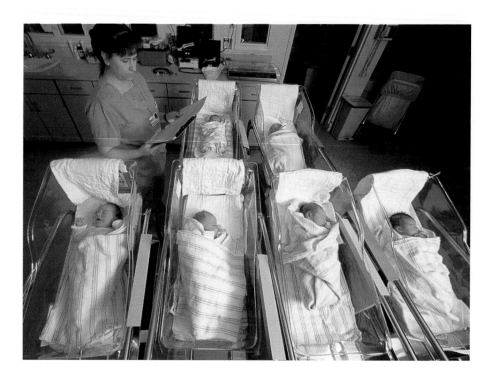

react in certain ways rather than in others (Emde et al., 1992; Kagan, 1997). This is not to say that the resulting behaviors are fixed at birth, but simply that, for any infant, certain ways of behaving are more likely than are others. In the final analysis, the characteristics that infants eventually develop are as much a function of the ways in which their caretakers *respond* to what infants initially do as they are to any behavioral predispositions themselves. Thus, not only would an infant who shies away from new situations be likely to develop in different ways from one who excitedly approaches them, but the first infant would also be likely to develop in different ways from one who, though initially just as shy, is gently encouraged to explore new things (Kagan & Snidman, 1991).

Genetic and Cultural Contributions to Temperament

The influence of heredity on temperament has been studied in a number of ways. One approach is to compare the correspondence in traits among individuals with different degrees of genetic similarity to each other, such as is done in twin and adoptive studies. A second approach is to identify certain index behaviors that, because they are presumably related to temperament types through underlying processes that are partially inherited, predict later differences in temperament among children.

Comparisons of identical (monozygotic) with fraternal (dizygotic) twins illustrate the first of these approaches. Because monozygotic twins (see Chapter 2) develop from the same fertilized ovum, they are genetically identical. Dizygotic twins, on the other hand, develop from two separate fertilized ova and are no more similar genetically than any other two siblings with the same set of parents, sharing 50% genetic relatedness. Greater similarity in a given trait among monozygotic twins than dizygotic twins can be taken as an index of the contribution of heredity to that trait.

Shyness and emotionality appear to be genetically influenced.

There are presently several large-scale longitudinal studies examining genetic contributions to temperament, one comparing identical with fraternal twins and another comparing adopted and matched nonadopted children with their biological and adoptive parents. These are the Louisville Twin Study (Wilson & Matheny, 1986) and the Colorado Adoption Project (Plomin, DeFries, & Fulker, 1988), respectively. Although it is somewhat difficult to generalize across the various situations and measures used in various studies, two temperament traits emerge as showing some genetic influence. These are emotionality and shyness (Goldsmith, Buss, & Lemery, 1997; Plomin et al., 1988; Wilson & Matheny, 1986). Together, these traits describe a more general characteristic that might be described as behavioral inhibition, which other research has also identified as having an hereditary component (Kagan, 1997). Of equal interest, however, is the broad range of genetic influence for different aspects of temperament, ranging from virtually no influence for some traits to moderate levels of influence for others (Emde et al., 1992).

Jerome Kagan and his associates (1981, 1997), at Harvard University, have explored the contributions of heredity to temperament through the second of these two approaches. These investigators assumed that the biological processes that predispose a child to some, although not necessarily all, temperament traits are genetically influenced and that these processes are indexed by the presence of certain behaviors. These investigators found, for instance, that infants who become agitated when exposed to unfamiliar events, reacting by arching their backs and sticking out their tongues, are likely to later be shy as children, whereas those who do not exhibit these behaviors are more likely to be sociable. Thus, the behaviors of arching the back and sticking out the tongue can be used as *index behaviors* for later shyness.

Kagan (1997) began by classifying 4-month-olds according to behavioral differences in the way they reacted to unfamiliar events. Differences were assumed to be indicative of different thresholds of excitability in neural centers that are involved in organizing responses to novelty. Would these differences predict later temperament differences? Specifically, would they predict which infants would be inhibited and which would be uninhibited as toddlers?

Using crying and physical agitation as index behaviors, they identified 4-month-old infants as either *high reactive* or *low reactive*. Approximately 20% and 40% of the 462 infants they studied fell into these two categories, respectively. The index behaviors for these categories were assumed to reflect genetically influenced differences in the processing of information. When these infants were tested with unfamiliar situations at 14 and 21 months of age, a third of the high-reactive infants proved to be extremely fearful, with very few (3%) showing little fear. Just the opposite pattern of responding was observed in the other group. A third of these infants showed very little fear, with very few (4%) being highly fearful.

Thus, the constellation of behavioral reactions that were associated with a lower threshold of excitability was in fact predictive of which infants would become most fearful as toddlers in new situations. These findings strongly suggest that these traits, those of being either inhibited or uninhibited, are influenced by heredity. Furthermore, differences between these groups persisted into childhood. When these two groups of children were tested again when they were 4–5 years old, those who had originally been identified as inhibited smiled less and talked less than did those who had been identified as uninhibited.

To what extent are differences in temperament apparent across cultures? A number of studies have found reliable differences. A comparison of Japanese and Caucasian infants found the former to be less likely to show distress during well-baby examinations (Lewis, Ramsay, & Kawakami, 1993). Comparisons of Chinese and Caucasian infants have found the former to be calmer and more easily soothed when distressed. They were less likely, for instance, to pull off a cloth that had been placed over their face and, when placed in a crib, tended to stay in that position, whereas Caucasian infants were more likely to reposition themselves, lifting their heads or turning them to one side (Freedman & Freedman, 1969). A more recent comparison of 4-month-old Chinese and Caucasian infants found Caucasian infants to have higher levels of arousal and to differ more among themselves than did Chinese infants. They moved more, fretted more, vocalized more, and cried more (Kagan et al., 1994).

Temperament Types

Some differences can clearly be seen to persist into childhood, such as differences in fearfulness or reactions to the unfamiliar (Kagan & Snidman, 1991). And some have been found to persist into early adulthood (Newman, Caspi, Miffitt, & Silva, 1997). However, for most differences in temperament, the link with behavior becomes increasingly complex with age (Goldsmith et al., 1987). How well one can predict temperament qualities in children from assessments made in infancy depends in part on the age of the infant when temperament is first assessed (Rothbart, 1986). By 4 months of age, individual differences in infants' temperament clearly exist, although multiple observations over several sessions may be necessary for these to be reliably assessed (Seifer, Sameroff, Barrett, & Krafchuk, 1994).

Using procedures involving such multiple measurements, Alexander Thomas, Stella Chess, and Herbert Birch (1963) conducted the New York Longitudinal Study, a pioneering study of newborns in which they interviewed parents over several years. These investigators identified nine aspects to temperament.

1. *Activity*. Some infants are more active than others. They move more when held or even when simply lying awake in their cribs. They also move about more in their sleep. Differences in activity are also apparent before birth, in

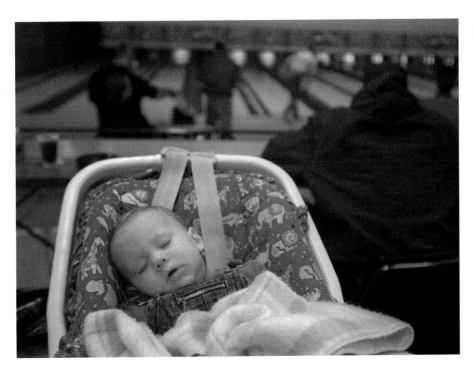

Infants differ in the intensity of stimulation required to elicit a reaction.

movements of the fetus. Parents of these children seem always to be chasing after them. In contrast, less active children can sit quietly in one spot, amusing themselves for long times at a stretch.

2. *Regularity.* Infants and toddlers differ in the regularity of their biological functioning. Some children become hungry at the same time each day and have predictable nap and bed times, enabling parents to plan day and evening activities around them. Other children never seem to be hungry at the same time, are wide awake at nap time, and wired by bedtime.

3. *Approach versus withdrawal to new situations.* Infants and toddlers also differ in the way in which they respond to new situations. Some welcome new experiences and change, whether these involve people, foods, toys, or routines, whereas others are cautious and uncomfortable.

4. *Adaptability.* Infants differ in how quickly they modify their responses to new situations, irrespective of whether they tend to welcome change or withdraw from anything new.

5. *Sensory responsiveness.* There are differences as well in the intensity of stimulation that is required to bring about a reaction. Some infants and toddlers can sleep through a loud party, while others startle awake when the lights to their room softly click on.

6. *Quality of mood.* One can characterize children in terms of their overall mood, by whether they are predominantly happy or unhappy. Some children fuss when they wake up, cry when they go to bed, and mumble over their food and toys in between. Others smile or hum to themselves.

7. *Intensity of response.* Infants and toddlers differ in the energy with which they react to things, irrespective of whether their reactions are positive or negative. Whereas some will smile or whine, others will laugh out loud and howl.

8. *Distractibility.* Infants differ in their ability to concentrate, some, for example, taking a bottle no matter what is happening around them and others being distracted at the slightest sound or movement. Distractibility, however, is not always a disadvantage; distractible children can also be diverted when crying or hurt.

9. *Attention span and persistence.* Infants as well as older children and adults differ in their persistence. For instance, one infant can be seen to persevere in trying to reach something just beyond its fingertips while another will give it only a passing swipe. Children also differ in the length of time they can focus on a task, some jumping from one toy to the next and others playing for a long time at a single activity.

Thomas and Chess (1977) distinguished three temperament types based on clusters of the characteristics listed above. These types identified some infants as easy, others as difficult, and still others as slow-to-warm. These researchers caution that temperament types simply reflect *how* children do what they do and not *why* they do these things. Temperament, in other words, describes the style that characterizes a child's behavior and does not explain the motives that may underlie this.

Easy infants tend to be cheerful and playful, regular in their biological functioning, such as in patterns of sleeping and waking and becoming hungry, and easily adaptable to changes. Approximately 40% of the infants originally studied by Thomas and Chess fell into this category. **Difficult infants** tend to be negative in mood, have irregular body functions, and be slow to adapt to changes. They cry a lot as infants, have irregular sleep patterns, do not take new foods well, and react intensely when frustrated. About 10% of the original sample could be classified as belonging to this temperament type. **Slow-to-warm infants** have low activity levels, give mild reactions, are slow to adapt to changes, tend to withdraw from new situations, are slightly negative in mood, and react to situations in a mild way. Fifteen percent of infants studied could be placed in this category.

Not all infants "fit" into one of these categories, of course. Thirty-five percent of the original sample studied by Thomas and his co-workers could not be categorized according to any of these temperament types. In fact, some researchers, such as Mary Rothbart, at the University of Oregon, prefer not to include a "difficult" category, pointing out that behavior that might be considered difficult in one situation is not necessarily difficult in another. For example, persistence in play, such as when a child is called away by a parent or teacher to do something else, might be labeled as "difficult," yet the same persistence when fitting pieces of a puzzle together would be seen as laudatory. Similarly, what might be perceived as problematic at one age can be an advantage at another. A preschooler who is easily distracted may have trouble getting dressed in time in the morning, but a similar distractibility becomes an advantage for an infant who, by being distracted from sources of discomfort, can be more easily soothed. Instead of labeling a particular constellation of traits as being of one type or another, Rothbart reminds us that each trait has its "social costs" as well as its benefits.

An alternative to classifying infants into temperament types is to identify higher-order factors, or more general temperamental differences, that can be derived from the nine or so traits originally identified. When this is done, five factors emerge (Rothbart & Ahadi, 1994). Two factors, fearfulness and irritability, describe a general negativity, and a third describes a positive mood, as seen in a general tendency to approach things. A fourth factor is related to activity level and the fifth to persistence. These factors roughly correspond to similar dimensions of the adult personality (Eysenck & Eysenck, 1985; Rothbart & Ahadi, 1994; Watson,

easy infants Infants who tend to be cheerful and playful, regular in their biological functioning (such as in patterns of sleeping and waking and becoming hungry), and able to adapt easily to changes; a temperament type identified by Thomas and Chess.

difficult infants Infants who tend to be negative in mood, irregular in their biological functioning (such as in patterns of sleeping and waking and becoming hungry), and slow to adapt to changes; a temperament type identified by Thomas and Chess.

slow-to-warm infants Infants who have low activity levels, give mild reactions, are slow to adapt to changes, tend to withdraw from new situations, and react to situations in a mild way; a temperament type identified by Thomas and Chess.

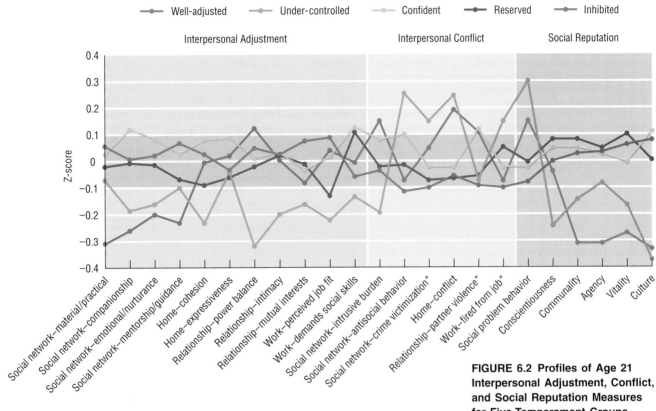

FIGURE 6.2 Profiles of Age 21 Interpersonal Adjustment, Conflict, and Social Reputation Measures for Five Temperament Groups
Measures with asterisks are interpolated z-scaled percentages of cases in groups. Source: D. L. Newman, A. Caspi, T. E. Moffitt, and P. A. Silva (1997). Antecedents of adult interpersonal functioning: Effects of individual differences in age 3 temperament. *Developmental Psychology*, 33, p. 213.

Clark, & Harkness, 1994). Thus, fearfulness and irritability correspond to a tendency in some adults toward negative affect or mood. Similarly, the factor of positive mood, as well as that of activity, corresponds to differences in adults in positive emotion or extroversion, in which individuals seek out and approach situations. Finally, the factor of persistence corresponds to differences among adults in control or constraint, presumably resulting from attentional factors involved in regulating behavior.

But do differences in temperament in childhood predict different styles of behavior in adulthood? A longitudinal study that followed 3-year-olds into adulthood suggests that they do (Newman et al., 1997). Over 900 3-year-olds were classified into one of five behavioral styles on the basis of three temperament differences: sociability, activity level, and behavioral control. Eighteen years later, when these children reached adulthood, they were again assessed for the way they functioned in a variety of settings, such as at home, at work, and in romantic and social relationships. Young adults who as children were classified as either well-adjusted, reserved, or confident differed little among themselves. However, those who had been inhibited or undercontrolled differed as adults from the others in ways that could be anticipated based on their temperament. For instance, young adults who had been undercontrolled as children reported more conflictual relationships, more difficulty at work, and scored higher on measures of antisocial behavior. Conversely, young adults who had been inhibited as children were described as less outgoing, confident, and popular. These trends can be seen in Figure 6.2: Both undercontrolled and inhibited 3-year-olds scored lower as adults on measures of interpersonal adjustment and social reputation. With respect to measures of interpersonal conflict, only the former were higher (Newman et al., 1997).

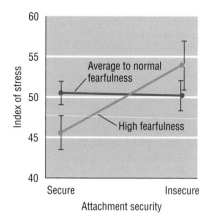

FIGURE 6.3 Attachment Security Moderates the Relationship Between Temperament and Stress
The number of infants in each condition were: secure, high fearful = 9; insecure, high fearful = 8; secure, average-to-low fearful = 32; insecure, average-to-low fearful = 14.

Temperament and Attachment

Differences in temperament not only thread their way into adult personalities but can also affect the ways in which parents interact with their infants. Researchers are still untangling the complex ways in which children and parents influence each other and how this relationship affects the child's development. Does temperament, for instance, affect the quality of attachment? Or does attachment affect the manner in which temperamental traits are expressed? For instance, might children who are predisposed to fearfulness evidence this trait only when they do not have a secure attachment relationship or when their caregiver is not present? Megan Gunnar, at the University of Minnesota, has explored the intricate relationships between temperament and attachment within the context of children's reactions to stressful situations.

Gunnar and her associates (1996) assumed that patterns of attachment actually moderate the way children of different temperaments would cope with stress. Thus, the attachment relationship should serve to buffer or protect children when stressed, and this buffering should be particularly evident in those who are temperamentally most in need of it. Put another way, one should not be able to predict how successful children are at coping simply by observing differences in their temperament. One would also need to know something about their attachment relationships. Gunnar and her associates observed toddlers who were either high or average in fearfulness in a mildly stressful situation. Would children who were temperamentally fearful, or inhibited, but securely attached cope better than those who were equally fearful yet insecurely attached? As expected, fearful toddlers showed greater evidence of stress than those who were less fearful. However, this was true only for those who were insecurely attached. Among toddlers who were securely attached, those who were high in fearfulness actually coped better than the less fearful (Figure 6.3).

Can temperament similarly be shown to affect attachment? For instance, might infants who are temperamentally irritable be more at risk for developing insecure attachment relationships, perhaps because of the difficulty mothers may have in sensitively responding to their demands?

Dymphna van den Boom (1989), at the University of Leiden, wondered whether one could predict the quality of attachment in older infants from assessments of their irritability, or proneness to distress, shortly after birth. Following the same group of infants and their mothers over a year's time, she found that irritability was a better predictor of attachment than the mother's sensitivity and responsiveness. Intrigued by this, van den Boom looked more closely at the way these infants and their mothers interacted. She found that irritable infants were not only more easily distressed, but also less fun in general to be with. They cooed and smiled less and fussed and cried more than other infants, with the result that mothers devoted a disproportionate amount of time to "fixing" things rather than to having fun and playing with their infants. Also, when the infants stopped fussing, their mothers appeared loath to initiate any new activities for fear they might provide more fussing. Thus, an unhealthy pattern of interaction had become established.

In a follow-up study, van den Boom (1994) was interested in whether mothers of irritable infants such as these could be taught to interact in more positive ways with their babies. As before, all of the infants were assessed for irritability shortly after birth; however, only those who were prone to distress were selected this time. When the infants were 6 months old, they and their mothers were randomly assigned to either an intervention or a control condition lasting for several months. Mothers who were given the intervention training were shown how to be more attentive to their infant's signals and how to respond more appropriately.

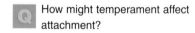

How might parents help a fearful child cope with new situations?

How might temperament affect attachment?

They were also instructed to play more with their infants. At 1 year of age, 78% of the infants in the intervention condition were securely attached, whereas only 26% of those in the control condition were. Infants in the intervention condition also were more sociable, better able to soothe themselves, cried less, and explored their surroundings more. In subsequent research, van den Boom (1995) found the effects of the intervention to persist into early childhood. Furthermore, there was a spillover from the mothers who participated in the intervention group to their husbands, with the latter also becoming more responsive with their children.

Temperament Types and Parenting

Most parents are unsure of themselves at first, and infants can do much to either make them feel competent or reinforce their initial fears. Parent-child relationships, in other words, show *bidirectional effects* in which infants influence their parents as well as being influenced by them. Easy infants, for instance, more often than not make parents feel effective. They stop crying when they are picked up, relish a bottle when it is offered, and snuggle into the fold of one's arms. These simple reactions of being soothed, comforted, and quieted allow parents to feel competent. They also make it likely that parents will respond to their infants' needs in similar ways in the future. By way of contrast, few experiences are more frustrating to a parent than not being able to soothe a crying infant. Parents of irritable or difficult infants face such frustrations on a daily basis. When infants cannot be soothed, refuse a bottle, or stiffen when held, parents feel helpless, and can even feel resentful or hurt. They are also likely to become inconsistent in the approaches they adopt when such infants fuss, since what they have done in the past has only occasionally been successful. The way infants respond to their parents, in other words, can influence the consistency of the care that they receive.

Children, as well as parents, try to maintain the other's behavior within a range acceptable to them.

Until relatively recently, attempts to understand the course of development have focused on factors outside the child, such as the home environment or parenting practices. Only occasionally have trained eyes been turned toward children themselves to see what they contribute to their own development (Bell, 1968; Scarr, 1993). When one does look at development from this perspective, one sees that children, as well as parents, exert an influence. This influence frequently takes the form of *upper and lower limits* for the other's behavior. These limits reflect how much or how little activity each one expects, or can tolerate, from the other, such as how intense a reaction can be or the extent of physical contact needed by one or the other. Both parents and children will try to maintain the other's behavior within a range that is acceptable to them. When an upper limit to a behavior has been exceeded, the other will act to reduce the behavior in some way. This reaction is termed an *upper-limit control.* Similarly, when a lower limit has been surpassed, attempts will be made to increase the behavior, by exercising a *lower-limit control.*

We should expect the control behaviors that parents use to be stepped, with each successive action depending on what has been tried before. Thus, with toddlers, first an explanation may be offered in a soft voice, then a request for a change, then crisp demands, and finally physical restraints. We might also expect to see more upper-limit controls with difficult children or with those who are extremely active or impulsive. These parents have a long history in which they have learned that other approaches, such as verbal reasoning or subtle changes in their emotional expression, frequently have little or no effect.

The behaviors of children will also be stepped, as they attempt to maintain their interaction with parents within limits that are most comfortable to them.

Consider a toddler who attempts to engage her busy mother's attention with a soft "Mommy." If the mother fails to respond, the toddler is likely to raise her voice a bit the next time, calling out more loudly until, if the mother is still unresponsive, her initial verbal request may become physical, as she tugs at the mother while loudly demanding her attention. It is all too easy for parents to respond only when children's stepped requests reach an upper limit such as this.

The way children cope, their eventual feelings of self-esteem and their willingness to step out on their own, evolve out of their early relationships with parents. Children, as well as parents, give shape to the form these relationships take. Whether children are easy, slow-to-warm, or difficult will influence the ways their parents approach them. Each of these temperament types can bring about, and react differently to, differences in the approaches parents bring to the situation. These early relationships shape the course of future development for parents and children alike.

Emotional Development

Many a new mother or father has watched smiles play across a sleeping infant's face. But do the smiles of newborns signal pleasure? Do infants' cries mean they are unhappy? When do babies first laugh? And when are they first angry? For that matter, what does it *mean* to experience emotions such as pleasure, happiness, anger, or joy? Can emotional states such as these be reduced simply to feelings, or do they play some larger role in our lives? And what do we know of the emotional life of infants and toddlers?

The feelings that emotions occasion in us are certainly one of their most immediate aspects. However, emotions are also highly adaptive behavioral states, organizing the way we react to events. A large, noisy dog occasions not only the experience of fear in a toddler, for instance, but also prompts a characteristic pattern of behavior that includes a physical drawing back or turning away and a general mobilization of the body. Thus, emotions have not only a felt, or experiential, component but also a behavioral component, so that they play a role in motivating behavior (Barrett, 1995; Mascolo & Fisher, 1995). Most emotions also have a cognitive component as well. Whether a child experiences one emotion or another results from that child's evaluation, or appreciation, of the particular significance of a situation. Thus, children may experience anger or amusement at such actions as having ice dropped down their shirts or a hand thrown over their eyes, depending on whether they interpret these actions to be hostile or friendly.

Not all emotions depend on such an appraisal for their instigation, leading some researchers to classify emotions as either basic or complex (Lewis, 1995; Lewis & Michaelson, 1983). According to this distinction, basic emotions are present from early infancy and, since they are not assumed to involve an appraisal of the event occasioning the emotional reaction, their expression is thought to be universal, occurring in all members of the species and taking much the same form from one culture to the next (Ekman, 1984, 1994; Izard & Maletesta, 1987). Complex emotions are assumed to be derived from, or differentiate out of, these more fundamental emotions and to reflect a cognitive appraisal of events.

By what age do infants express emotions such as happiness, surprise, and sadness?

The Growth of Emotions in Infancy

There is less than perfect agreement on which emotions are present in very young infants. Carroll Izard (1983, 1994), who developed a system for reliably coding infants' facial expressions, believes that newborns are likely to experience only

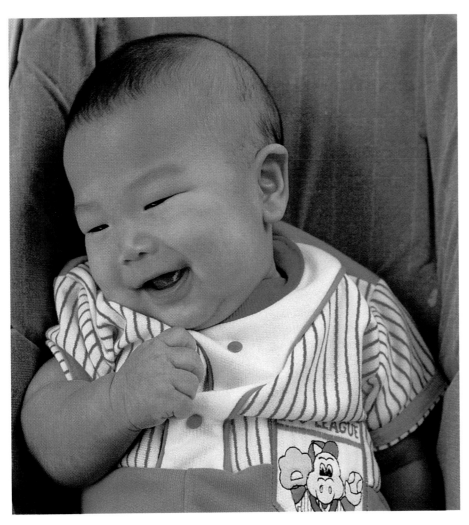

By 3 to 4 months, infants begin to laugh at things that tickle their fancy.

interest, distress, and disgust. Other investigators distinguish only calm or distress in the newborn (Rothbart & Ahadi, 1994). By the age of 1 month, however, mothers report they can detect a number of distinct emotions, such as interest, happiness, fear, anger, surprise, and sadness, based on their infants' facial expressions and their vocalizations (Johnson, Emde, Pannebecker, Stenberg, & Davis, 1982).

Also at about this age, between 4 and 6 weeks, infants begin to smile in response to what is taking place around them, or to engage in **social smiling** (Emde & Harmon, 1972; Izard, 1983). Infants smile much earlier than this, even when they are only days old, but they do so at first only when they are sleeping. Robert Emde and Jean Robinson (1979) traced the development of smiling in infants over the first several months of life. They noted that these earliest smiles appear to be prompted by changes in brain-wave activity in the brain stem, rather than to reflect emotions such as pleasure or happiness, and referred to them as **REM smiles.** By the 2nd week, infants begin to smile when they are awake. These smiles, however, are accompanied by the same brain-wave pattern as those that occurred in their sleep and are unrelated to what is taking place around them. REM smiles decrease in frequency over the next several weeks and are gradually replaced by smiles that occur in response to events that are taking place around the infant. Not until the age of 2 to 3 months, however, do infants appear to

social smiling Smiling in response to what is taking place around one; expression of emotion that begins between 4 and 6 weeks.

REM smiles Early smiles in infants prompted by changes in brain-wave activity in the brain stem.

discriminate between people and other interesting things, smiling back at others who are smiling at them. And by 3 to 4 months, infants begin to laugh at things that tickle their fancy (Maletesta, Culver, Tesman, & Shepard, 1989). Many of the things infants find fanciful are the commonplace events that we take for granted. Anne Lamott (1993) describes her 6-month-old son's reactions to the family cat:

> We were in the kitchen and Sam was lying on his back on a blanket on the floor, and suddenly the cat came in and started rolling around on the floor near him. . . . Sam laughed for ten straight minutes. He wounded like a brook. The kitty would stop rolling for a moment, and Sam would kind of get a grip, catch his breath, and all but wipe his eyes like an old man, and then the kitty would fling herself into the rolling motion again and Sam would just go nuts. (p. 156) ◄

At the opposite end of the emotional spectrum is another behavior familiar to parents—that of crying. This, too, shows a developmental progression. At birth, infants have two distinct types of cries: cries of pain and cries of hunger. Just as with infants' first smiles, these initial cries are involuntary, or reflexive, being coordinated at the level of the brain stem, rather than involving the cerebral cortex. The pattern of sound for each type of cry differs. Pain cries are loud and have a sudden onset, without any preliminary fussing, whereas hunger cries are more likely to build in intensity over a period of time. Most adults, even those who are not parents, can distinguish between these two cries (Gustafson & Harris, 1990; Zeskind, Klein, & Marshall, 1992).

Just as with smiling, after several months, crying comes under voluntary control as centers within the cortex become involved in its coordination. Not only does the crying of an older infant sound different, becoming somewhat lower in pitch, but it can now also be prompted by different circumstances. Voluntary, or *instrumental crying*, can be in response to things such as boredom as well as to hunger or pain (Lester, Boukydis, & Zachariah, 1992). This change introduces a new problem for parents. In addition to wondering whether their infant is hungry or in pain, now they may also wonder whether they will make crying more likely in the future by picking their infant up if the occasion for crying is simply restlessness or boredom.

Q Do parents need to worry they will spoil their infant by picking it up when it cries?

With respect to such fears, parents can feel reassured that picking up a crying infant will not "spoil" their child. Instead, doing so has just the opposite effect. Despite one or two discrepant findings (Gewirtz, 1976), research in this area strongly supports the notion that being responsive to an infant's cries—that is, picking the infant up and soothing it—promotes the development of trust and security in the infant. These emotions translate into a healthy independence, just the opposite of the excessive crying seen in insecure or emotionally dependent children. Recall, Ainsworth and Bell (1969) found that mothers who were responsive to their infants' cries when they were 3 months old, had infants who cried less at the age of 12 months than did less responsive mothers who were less likely to comfort their infants when they cried.

At about 6 months, infants develop a wariness of unfamiliar people and new situations, pulling back or looking away when someone unknown to them tries to talk to them or pick them up, even though a familiar caregiver such as the mother may be present. Shortly afterward, at about 8 months, they can also be seen to look to the mother or caregiver for cues as to how to respond when confronted with someone new. "Is this person okay?" they seem to ask both with their eyes and with their general body language, "or is this someone to be afraid of?" This behavior, known as **social referencing,** signals a significant conceptual development as well as an emotional one, because it suggests that infants at this age

social referencing Checking with a caregiver or other familiar figure for cues about how to respond to a new or ambiguous event.

become aware of mental states in others. For instance, they will look at what is being pointed at rather than at the hand that is pointing, or they will follow another's gaze, establishing joint attention with respect to some object or event, suggesting that they understand that the emotion or interest of the other is in response to the object or event. This referencing is an attempt to "read" others, either through their facial expressions or the intonation of their voices, for emotional messages concerning their world.

By 6 to 8 months, then, infants are capable of expressing a range of emotions, such as interest, disgust, joy, fear, anger, sadness, surprise, and wariness (Lewis, 1993, 1995). These emotions continue to develop throughout infancy and toddlerhood, both in the ways in which they are expressed and in the situations that occasion them.

Emotional Development in Toddlerhood

As infants enter the 2nd year of life, new emotions appear. Toddlers are capable of feeling pride, guilt, shame, and jealousy in addition to basic emotions such as happiness, anger, and fear. These new emotions differ from earlier ones in having an evaluative and self-conscious quality to them. They reflect toddlers' increasing concerns with "measuring up." The yardstick toddlers hold up to themselves reflects their emerging sense of standards and an increasing self-awareness. Because of the self-reflective component to these new emotions, we might expect them to follow a developmental course, one that mirrors toddlers' developing capacity to evaluate their own actions and also their growing awareness of the self (Lewis, 1995).

A Sense of Standards Jerome Kagan (1996) argues that a singularly human characteristic is our tendency to symbolically evaluate things. Whether these are our own actions, those of others, or naturally occurring events such as rainstorms and traffic jams, we habitually appraise things along a dimension of "good versus bad." He further argues that this evaluative aspect of our nature emerges early in life, at about the age of a year and a half. Thus, 14-month-olds who are given toys to play with that are dented or marred in some way will happily play with them. But by the age of 19 months, toddlers notice and even comment on these imperfections, telling the experimenter the toys need to be "fixed" and preferring to play instead with toys that are not marred (Kagan, 1981). Similarly, Grazyna Kochanska, Rita Casey, and Atsuko Fukomoto (1995), at the University of Iowa, found that toddlers preferred to play with whole, and not flawed, toys even though they expressed more interest in the flawed toys. This interest underscores their developing sensitivity to violations of standards concerning the "way things should be."

Furthermore, toddlers' tendency to evaluate the things around them extends to themselves. Deborah Stipek and her associates (1992, 1995), at the University of California at Los Angeles, looked for toddlers' first signs of pride in accomplishing something. One of the difficulties in determining when self-conscious emotions such as pride are first experienced is in knowing what toddlers are actually feeling from simply observing their behavior. Can a smile after accomplishing something be taken as a sign of pride? Or is it simply an indication of pleasure?

Stipek observed the way 13- to 39-month-old children reacted when a pin was knocked down by a ball, either by themselves or an adult. When the pin fell, they noticed that the children frequently smiled or looked up at the adult. They found, however, that children were no more likely to smile when they themselves had

Why do emotions such as pride, guilt, and shame not appear until children become toddlers?

TABLE 6.1 Percentage of Children Engaging in Social Referencing (Looking at the Experimenter) Following Another's or Their Own Success

Age (in months)	Other	Self
13–21	22	30
22–29	15	45*
30–39	10	65*

*statistically significant

Source: D. Stipek, S. Recchia, & S. McClintic. (1992). Self-evaluation in young children. *Monographs of the Society for Research in Child Development, 57* (1, Serial No. 226).

knocked the pin over than when the adult had. Smiles, apparently, are as much a reflection of simple pleasure as they are of pride. Looking up at the adult, however, was a different matter. Starting at about the age of 22 months, toddlers looked up at the adult more frequently when they had been the ones to successfully knock the pin over than when the adult had (Table 6.1). This behavior suggests that as children near the age of 2, they develop an interest in others' reactions to what they do—in social recognition for their accomplishments. For children 2½–3½ years old, this difference was even more pronounced, with only 10% looking over at an adult who had knocked the pin down, but 65% doing so when they had accomplished the same thing.

We've seen that even very young children react to success with pride. Do their reactions change as they get older? And are there similar self-conscious reactions to failure? These same investigators compared reactions to success and failure in 2- to 5-year-olds by giving them tasks that were possible to complete in a matter of minutes, such as fitting pieces of a puzzle together or arranging a set of nested cups, or that were impossible to complete because of missing or wrong pieces. Irrespective of age, when children were successful, they acted the same way— smiling, saying things like "I did it," looking at what they had done or calling attention to it, and looking up at the experimenter. Even their posture communicated pride, with head up, shoulders back, and arms wide. Thus, despite the large difference in their ages, toddlers and kindergartners alike reacted to success in highly similar ways.

Similarly, their reactions to failure did not noticeably differ with age. Even 2-year-olds would sigh, attempt to divert the adult's attention from their efforts, avoid eye contact, and sit with hunched shoulders and their arms crossed over their bodies. However, with children younger than 2, these investigators found it impossible to create a situation that they would experience as failure. When 18-month-olds, for instance, couldn't do something the experimenter had shown them how to do, they just changed the task, happily playing with the pieces according to their own whims. Thus, below the age of 2, children appear not to take an adult's behavior as a standard for their own or to feel self-conscious for not matching it.

Standards can be defined in a number of ways. They can be set by the requirements of the task itself or established by the accomplishments of others. Completing a puzzle in which the pieces obviously fit together is an example of the first, whereas racing to see who is the fastest is an example of the second. When standards are defined competitively, as in the second example, failure is then experienced as losing and success as winning. At what age, wondered Stipek and her associates, would young children begin to judge their accomplishments in terms of competitive standards such as this? These investigators found that 2-year-olds were oblivious to the competitive standards set by having another child work

Between 2 and 3 years of age, children start to show pride in their accomplishments.

alongside them at the same task, expressing just as much pleasure when they finished after the other had as when they finished first. But by 33 months of age, things changed. Those who finished first were obviously more pleased with themselves than were those finishing second. Furthermore, although the youngest children continued to work at their task even after the other child had "won," by the age of 3½, a fourth of those who did not finish first stopped working when the other child "won"; and by the age of 4 to 5, approximately half stopped working. What makes for success? For the very young, it is the sheer pleasure of completing what they have set out to do. Only with age is one's success at something also measured against the accomplishments of others.

A Sense of Self Emotions such as pride, guilt, or shame have a self-conscious quality to them as well as an evaluative component. Toddlers are aware of themselves in a way that infants are not. One might think that something as abstract as self-consciousness would be hard to observe and measure. Yet, an ingenious procedure has made this development relatively easy to study. A spot of rouge is surreptitiously dabbed on the child's nose, and the child is then placed in front of a mirror. Before the age of 15 months, infants do not touch their noses when they see the reflection in the mirror. They act instead as if they were seeing another

Toddlers begin to have a consciousness of self, as can be seen by their delight in finding themselves in a mirror.

child in the mirror and attempt to look behind the mirror, or they reach out to touch the image. Starting at about 18 months, however, one can see them reach up and touch their own noses when they see the rouge on their nose in the reflection. Three quarters of the 18-month-olds who were tested in this way and all of the 24-month-olds touched their noses, indicating that they recognized the image in the mirror as themselves (Lewis & Brooks-Gunn, 1979).

There is more than one way in which we are aware of ourselves, however. Over a hundred years ago, William James (1890) distinguished between the "I" and the "Me." The I is that part of the self that is the agent; it is the "do-er" and "knower." The Me is the part of the self that is known; it is what we know *about* ourselves. Sandra Pipp-Siegel and Carol Foltz (1997), at the University of Colorado, studied the development of these aspects of self-knowledge in 12-, 18-, and 24-month-olds, along with their growing ability to distinguish themselves from others. They found that the sense of self as an agent, or the I, increased as one would expect with age. Two-year-olds, although not those who were younger, clearly distinguished themselves from others. Furthermore, as expected, there was a corresponding increase with age in toddlers' knowledge about the self, although even 12-month-olds had more knowledge about themselves than about others.

Perhaps it should not be surprising that toddlers readily distinguish themselves from others, since one of the issues they face at this age is that of autonomy, of separating self from other. Toddlers, in short, are full of themselves. They are, in fact, one of their biggest discoveries. New bodily control informs them that they can do things or not do things. Physical maturation makes many new skills

A toddler's claiming something as "mine" may be an expression of a developing sense of self rather than selfishness.

and types of control possible. They can pick up, hold on to, or throw away, and in doing so they experience themselves as separate from the things around them. However, even while their maturing bodies place new skills within their reach, they also inform them of their limited grasp on what they hold.

Although toddlers are quick to master activities such as running, grabbing hold, and throwing, inner restraints are slower to develop. Parents often find themselves several steps behind, cautioning *not* to run, touch, drop, or throw. With the development of control over events outside themselves, toddlers learn to control their inner worlds as well. Toddlers almost burst with an awareness of themselves as they claim new territories with flags of "me" and "mine." They prize having things their way. Yet they are dependent on others too. It is a time of contradictions. At one moment, a toddler will snuggle into a parent's lap, only in the next to squirm free.

The toddler's developing sense of self divides the world into two opposing encampments—mine and yours. The presence of others may only increase toddlers' need to define their boundaries by claiming things. For instance, toddlers high in self-definition were found to claim toys more and comment on a peer more than those low in self-definition. The latter were more likely to hold toys up and show them or exchange them, but were not as likely to claim them. Once the issues of "me" versus "you" and "mine" versus "yours" were settled, however, toddlers high in self-definition showed an interest in the other child (Levine, 1983). Claiming toys, in other words, is not always simply selfish. Toddlers do this even when there are plenty of toys to play with. Parents who expect their toddlers to share before boundaries have been established may be expecting too much.

By being allowed to do some things on their own, toddlers develop feelings of accomplishment and self-worth. Children's emotional needs are similar to their parents' in this respect. They value their independence, which, because it is newly won, is all the more precious, and they want the respect of others. Their desire to do things themselves can take the form of being demanding and stubborn, however; and Erikson (1963) suggests that parents be firm, so that toddlers' desires to do things on their own do not lead to premature efforts and a sense of failure and shame.

Research Focus

Ethnographic Field Research: Who's Telling This Story, Anyway? BY MICHAEL WAPNER

Life is continuous from fertilization to death. But the self is defined by episodes—salient events in which we participate as the star or victim or hero or supporting player or simply as onlooker. Whatever role we play in the episode itself, its self-defining significance is not fully realized there. What the episode means to and about us is more deeply defined, is reinforced or modified, in its subsequent telling and retelling. It is in these narrative acts that we present ourselves and our experiences to our group—family, friends, colleagues, tribe. For one's stories to be listened to is itself to be affirmed as a participant in the life of the group and thus to have one's selfhood acknowledged. Wiley, Rose, Burger, and Miller (1998) observe that

> selves are constructed in interaction with others, . . . they develop through participation in sociocultural practices. . . . children come to enact certain kinds of selves by virtue of their everyday participation with other people in characteristic self-relevant practices—what Markus, Mullally, and Kitayama (1997) called "selfways."

The way our narratives are listened to communicates how autonomous a participant we are considered. May we initiate a story or must we wait to be asked? Is there silence once we begin to speak or do others continue to talk? Are we interrupted? And most important, are we truly the authors of our own stories (with *narrative autonomy*) and hence of our own experience, or does our narrative become a *co-narrative* in which our story is "corrected" and modified by the perspective of oth-

ers? (When two or more people participate in the telling of a story it is termed a co-narrative.)

The way a group structures storytelling is termed its *narrative practice*. And at no other time in life does narrative practice have more importance for the development of an individual's social self than in his or her third year, for it is then that issues of personal autonomy are likely to appear. Not every culture grants such young children "speakers' rights," for all cultures do not value individual autonomy equally. In Western Samoa, "young children are not considered appropriate conversational partners for parents" (Ochs, 1988, cited in Wiley et al., 1998), and when the children are allowed to speak, "their speech is directed by a higher status person . . . and therefore not 'authored' by the child." In Taiwanese families, parents frequently co-narrate stories with their young children and insist that the child accept their version of the story. Thus, children are granted the right to speak but are denied authorship of the story. These observations suggest that these cultures value deference to authority over individual autonomy. European American families, on the other hand, do place a high value on individual autonomy, and their narrative practices reflect this. However, even within this group there may be differences.

Hypothesizing that family narrative practices will differ across socioeconomic levels, Wiley and associates (1998) compared middle-class with working-class families in the way they allowed their 2-year-old children to tell their stories. The methodology the researchers employed was an **ethnographic**

Shame is the feeling of being exposed, of being visible before being ready to be seen. Feelings of shame increase a child's sense of smallness. Rather than causing toddlers to try harder, shame prompts them to try to get way with things, to not be caught or seen. *Guilt,* on the other hand, is the result of some wrongdoing that one has committed and involves a sense of responsibility for it. Karen Barrett, Carolyn Zahn-Waxler, and Pamela Cole (1993) reasoned that children who experience shame should try to hide, whereas those who experience guilt should try to repair what they have done. These investigators gave toddlers a toy clown to play with, one which they identified as a "favorite doll," and then left the child alone in a room with the mother, who was busily filling out forms. The doll was constructed so that when the toddler picked it up, its leg fell off. Children could be expected to experience either shame or guilt at this occurrence, shame at having violated some standard of care for someone's favorite doll or guilt at having broken something.

They found that some toddlers were prone to shame ("avoiders"), whereas others were prone to guilt ("amenders"). Those who experienced shame averted their eyes when the experimenter returned, were more likely to hide what had happened (only one of them "confessed" about the doll), and were less likely to try to remedy the situation, with less than half trying to fix the doll before the experimenter mentioned the leg. Of those who reacted with guilt, all tried to fix the doll, and three quarters of them promptly told the experimenter what had happened as soon as she came into the room.

244

field study. That is, the investigators went into the homes of their subjects and observed the interactions of interest as they occurred in their natural settings. The investigators did not establish the conditions under which the behavior would take place and did not control it as it occurred. The authors describe their presence in the following way:

> During the taping sessions the researchers tried to behave in a way that was least disruptive to the communicative norms of the family. . . . They aimed not to be invisible or silent nor to "lead" the conversation but to observe and participate in a relaxed, low-key way, joining in the conversation when appropriate, following up on narrative topics when appropriate. This stance on the part of the observer was intended to maximize the ecological and cultural validity of the samples of narrative talk.

The researchers selected 12 children (half male, half female) and their families, six from each socioeconomic level. The neighborhoods from which the families were selected were heavily Catholic, and so were all of the families selected. All 12 were two-parent families, and in all families the mothers were not currently employed outside the home. In the working-class families, the parents were high-school graduates; the fathers were employed in blue-collar jobs such as truck driver, grave digger, and construction worker. The parents in the middle-class families were college educated, and the fathers held white-collar jobs such as businessman, lawyer, salesman.

Data were collected on two occasions, when the child was 2 years, 6 months and when the child was 3 years old. But because no age differences were found, the data form the two occasions were combined. On each occasion the researchers videotaped the family for 2 hours on each of 2 successive days. In almost all cases the father had already left for work and thus interactions were between the child and her or his mother.

The researchers found patterns of both similarities and differences in the narrative practices of the two groups. In both groups, it was common for children at 2½ and 3 years of age to participate as speakers. There were no differences in the extent to which children began the narratives—in both groups children initiated stories as frequently as half of the time. In both groups the mothers participated in the telling of almost all stories, either by asking questions, coaching, or correcting. Thus at this age, children's narratives are really co-narratives.

The differences between the two groups were primarily in the frequency of occurrence of co-narratives and the way disagreement was handled. Both the frequency and duration of co-narratives was far greater in working-class than in middle-class homes. In both groups, when conflict occurred as to the details of the child's story, it was usually the mother who initiated the conflict by disagreeing or correcting. However, the way disagreements were handled differed significantly between the two communities. Children were allowed more latitude to express their stories in the middle-class homes. When a conflict arose, middle-class mothers were more willing to allow an obviously incorrect telling rather than infringe on the child's authorship. In contrast, working-class mothers were more likely to insist on a correct rendition, and thus their children were forced to defend their version of the story if they wished to retain authorship. Apparently, narrative practice in working-class homes is also a lesson in standing up for one's views.

Guilt and shame are social emotions. They derive their significance, in other words, from involvement with other people. As a result, we would expect socialization to play an important role in the development of these emotions. Socialization not only provides information about the standards that toddlers are increasingly expected to live up to, but it also imbues these standards with significance because they are valued by people whom toddlers look up to. As a consequence, we might expect that parenting practices, because they communicate social values, would be related to the development of these emotions. And they are. Toddlers are most likely to attempt to remedy a wrongdoing, for instance, when parents give explanations as to why it is important. These explanations are most effective when they are accompanied by appropriate feelings. Recall that, by late infancy, children engage in social referencing, reading the emotions of others from their facial expressions and tones of voice. The emotional overtones of parents' explanations most likely help children understand the personal relevance of what parents are saying (Barrett, 1995). See the Research Focus, "Ethnographic Field Research: Who's Telling This Story Anyway?" for a discussion of one form of parent-child communication about events.

Toddlers' emerging ability to regulate their behavior coincides with the onset of parental demands that they control their behavior. In fact, a high proportion of the expectations for toddlers relates to the development of inhibitory control. Grazyna Kochanska, Kathleen Murray, and Katherine Coy (1997) suggest that aspects of temperament that are related to inhibitory control in toddlers have

ethnographic field study Observational research conducted in natural settings that facilitates the study of the unique contributions of the social groups to which individuals belong.

conscience That part of the personality that is concerned with issues of right and wrong.

implications for the later development of **conscience.** These investigators followed toddlers into the early school years in a longitudinal study. Measures of inhibitory control included such things as the ability to slow down an ongoing activity, such as walking a line on the floor or drawing a circle, or suppressing or initiating a behavior when instructed, such as in the game of "Simon says." Conscience was assessed by such things as compliance with mothers' requests, even when the mother was not present, resistance to temptation to violate a rule, or internalizing another person's rules concerning the way to play a game.

These investigators found inhibitory control to increase with age and to be a remarkably stable characteristic of children; that is, a child's position relative to others in the group changed little from toddlerhood to early school age. Such stability is what one would expect in a traitlike characteristic and suggests this to be a genuine individual difference.

Summary

Attachment: The Bonds of Love

Attachment refers to the affectional bonds that infants form with those who care for them and to the ways in which infants use caregivers as a secure base from which to explore and to which to return for safety when stressed. Freud assumed that drive reduction was the basis for attachment, due to infants' association of the mother with hunger reduction. However, research with infant monkeys reared with cloth or wire surrogate mothers showed that infants preferred the cloth surrogate they could cling to over the wire one that gave milk.

Bowlby distinguished four phases in the establishment of attachment. In the preattachment phase, infants experience no distress when cared for by someone other than their primary caregiver. In the attachment-in-the-making phase, infants become wary in the presence of unfamiliar persons. In the phase of clear-cut attachment, infants attempt to stay close to the mother (proximity seeking), show distress when they cannot (separation anxiety), and use the mother as a secure base from which to explore their surroundings (secure base). In the phase of reciprocal relationships, the toddler is able to comfortably spend longer periods of time away from the mother. Bowlby assumed that children develop an internal working model for subsequent relationships based on their initial attachment to the mother.

Types of Attachment Relationships

Ainsworth's research on attachment focused on the security infants derive from their relationship with the mother. Three types of attachment relationships were identified: infants who are securely attached, anxious-avoidant infants, and anxious-resistant infants. Ainsworth attributed differences in attachment security to the accuracy with which the mother interpreted the infant's signals (sensitivity) and the promptness with which she responded (responsiveness), with both sensitivity and responsiveness being positively related to security of attachment and to less frequent crying in infants. Similar processes contribute to attachment with fathers. The quality of attachment of the infant with either parent is affected as well by contextual factors that can both support and strengthen the relational bond between infant and parent and create stress in the relationship. Attachment security increases with the number of supportive factors present in a family.

Day Care

An increase in the number of mothers with young children who work outside the home has resulted in many more young children experiencing day care today than in the past. When the quality of child care is high, day care has no negative developmental effects and may even beneficially affect aspects of social and intellectual development. Furthermore, comparisons of children in day care with those cared for at home by their mothers have found that dimensions of family life are no less closely related to children's development when they attend day care than when they are cared for at home. Rather, exposure to developmentally sound experiences, such as less authoritarian attitudes toward child rearing and more sensitive mothering, is related to more positive development in children whether they are cared for at home or in day care.

Temperament

Temperament consists of underlying predispositions contributing to infants' activity level, emotionality, and sociability. Nine aspects of temperament have been identified: activity, regularity, approach versus withdrawal to new situations, adaptability, sensory responsiveness, quality of mood, intensity of response, distractibility, and attention span and persistence. Based on clusters of these characteristics, three temperament types have been distinguished: infants who are easy, difficult, and slow to warm. An alternative to classifying infants into temperament types is to identify higher-order factors that can be derived from these traits. The nature of infants' attachment relationship has been found to moderate the way children of different temperaments react. Similarly, temperament has been found to affect attachment.

Temperament Types and Parenting

Parent-child relationships show bidirectional effects in which infants influence their parents and are, in turn, influenced by them. This influence often takes the form of upper and lower limits for the other's behavior, with both parents and children attempting to maintain the other's behavior within a range that is acceptable to them.

Emotional Development

Basic emotions, which are not assumed to involve an appraisal of the event occasioning the emotional reaction, take the same form from one culture to the next. Complex emotions are assumed to reflect a cognitive appraisal of events and occur later in development. By 1 month, distinct emotions such as interest, happiness, fear, anger, surprise, and sadness can be detected. Both smiling and crying initially occur involuntarily but come under voluntary control by 6 to 8 weeks following birth. By 6 months, infants develop a wariness of unfamiliar people and situations and by 8 months engage in social referencing as a means of appraising unfamiliar situations. By this age as well, infants are capable of expressing a range of emotions, which continue to develop throughout infancy and toddlerhood, both in the ways they are expressed and in the situations occasioning them. New emotions of pride, guilt, shame, and jealousy appear in toddlerhood. These emotions differ from earlier ones in that they reflect toddlers' increasing self-awareness.

 Key Terms

attachment (p. 215)
conscience (p. 244)
difficult infants (p. 232)
easy infants (p. 232)
ethnographic field study (p. 245)
proximity seeking (p. 217)

REM smiles (p. 237)
responsiveness (p. 219)
secure base (p. 217)
sensitivity (p. 219)
separation anxiety (p. 217)
slow-to-warm infants (p. 232)

social referencing (p. 238)
social smiling (p. 237)
strange situation (p. 218)
temperament (p. 227)

chapterseven

Early Childhood
Physical Development

Young children know what we have forgotten. They know the pure joy of simple actions, of running wild into the wind, or splashing light in puddles like sparks, and spinning under the moon to the heaving breath of the night. They know these things as they know the taste of sweat and dew in their mouths. They have no need to be told. Other things, those we would try to tell them, await their understanding. They know just as surely, despite our protests, that dolls and stuffed animals have feelings too and that, though they themselves sort their world into "big" and "small," they will never be big like us.

Ursula Hegi (1995) captures this perception in describing a young child and her mother in *Salt Dancers:*

> My mother woke me up, whispered for me to get dressed, and brought me along on her moon-walk which she usually took alone when the moon was at its brightest . . . and when my legs grew tired, my mother swirled me into the air and propped me on her shoulders in one fluid motion; her hands spanned my ankles—light, yet secure—and as she took steps longer than any I could have managed, I was rocked by the motion of her body.
>
> "Someday," she said, "you'll be tall too."
>
> My hands in her hair, I smiled to myself, knowing better than to believe that old story which most adults seemed compelled to tell children. I'd figured out a long time ago that children didn't grow up—they stayed children, just as adults stayed adults. (pp. 17–18) ◄

Children make their own sense of the stories we tell them, just as they figure out so many other things, by understanding these in terms of what they already know. And they know that at times they still need to be carried, just as they know

Walking with a grandparent can make a child feel big and small all at once.

that their steps are not as sure as ours. Their experiences of what they can do, or not do, influence their perceptions of themselves and others—of the reality they take as a given.

This take on reality illustrates the constructive approach adopted in this text. Events are rarely perceived in the same way by those who experience them. The reality to which each person responds will differ depending on that person's experiences, for reality is constructed, or assembled, from what we bring with us to each moment. The reality of children's knowledge, such as the idea that they will never be big, comes from the immediacy of their experiences—of having to take two steps to every one of ours or looking down from the dizzying heights of our shoulders. Our reality comes from the same experiences, seen from the other side.

Children not only grow in size during these years, but they also become increasingly adept at the things they do, whether simply running without falling or managing the complexities of silverware or dressing themselves. These developments, in turn, change their relationship to their world. Growth is never simply a matter of inches and pounds. Instead, each new skill necessitates in some way a readjustment on the part of the child to the world as it has been known. The environment that the child experiences is not arbitrarily given by circumstances but, as Erikson (1968) puts it, is an "expectable environment" that itself is differentiated out of many potential ones by the child's own maturation, which makes possible new ways of reacting and, as a consequence, the possibility of new experiences. Thus, a child who can walk enters an environment where interesting things can be approached or where one can get lost. Similarly, a preschooler who is toilet-trained becomes part of an environment where she can be a "big girl" by not soiling her pants versus one where, as a baby, she needed "changing."

This chapter examines the physical growth that takes place during the preschool years and the implications this growth holds for broader aspects of development. Before considering growth itself, we will look at three developmental snapshots to give us an overview of the preschool years. Physical development has both behavioral and psychological consequences for young children, making possible not only a host of new skills but also a new sense of self. These receive attention in separate sections of the chapter. Concluding sections of the chapter examine issues of health and well-being: children's nutritional needs, injuries resulting either from accidents or maltreatment, and the reserves of social capital on which children and their families can rely.

Developmental Profiles

Three-year-olds can be just as animated as toddlers, but can also sit quietly and play, inhibiting movements that a year ago were a nervous jitter throughout the house. Crayons and puzzles suit their improved motor coordination. They have better control of larger movements as well. They can stop and turn when running and take corners in stride. Perhaps because of their improved coordination, they are tidier. There is a "sense of order" in the 3-year-old (Gesell et al., 1940). Despite their new control, modulating behavior can still be a challenge, whether it involves lowering their voices or slowing down at the curb. It will be another year before they develop this flexibility. By that time they will be more responsive to instructions as well, waiting their turn or putting down a noisy toy when asked.

Four-year-olds enjoy showing off, even practicing in order to accomplish something new. Increased skills reflect individuation, a developmental process in which structures and functions become increasingly separate with growth. For

New skills make four-year-olds
self-reliant and independent.

example, by 4, children begin to throw a ball with their arms instead of their whole bodies. Children now dress themselves easily, buttons and zippers yielding to their fingers. New skills, whether buttoning a shirt or wielding scissors, make 4-year-olds more self-reliant and independent. Yet a 4-year-old who has just told you "I can do it myself" may be afraid to hang a jacket in the closet, for fear there could be something lurking in one of its corners.

By 5, children have good balance and are more agile than before. Increased control can be seen in fine motor movements as well, which are more precise than they were a year earlier, enabling children to pick up small things quickly and easily. In mental games as well, they are nimbler than 4-year-olds, adopting a more flexible approach when they encounter problems. Independent, self-sufficient, assured, and confident, they can dress themselves, go off to kindergarten, make their own friends, and help out around the house. Despite their maturity, they are still very much children. Fantasy and fact are easily confused (perhaps explaining a deadpan response to an adult's humor). Emotionally, too, they are just gaining the controls that will allow them to be less impulsive and more in control of themselves. They may be entering a new world, but fairies and giants can still be found there. For 5-year-olds, the tooth fairy is as real as their kindergarten teacher.

Physical Growth

Three-year-olds stand just over 3 feet tall and weigh a little over 30 pounds. Growth in early childhood occurs at a more even pace than during infancy and toddlerhood, and preschoolers gain 2 to 3 inches in height and add 3 to 5 pounds a year (Figure 7.1). By the time they are ready to go to school, most will weigh 38 to 45 pounds and be 42 to 46 inches tall (Allen & Marotz, 1989).

One can still clearly see evidence of the cephalocaudal trend in patterns of growth. Some of the first visible changes, in 3-year-olds, involve a lengthening of the neck and torso. Recall that in infants and toddlers, the head is much larger in proportion to the rest of the body than it is in adults. With the lengthening of the torso and then the legs, body proportions come closer to those of older children and adults. Also, the longer torso means that internal organs fit more easily within the body cavity, eliminating the "potbellied" look of the toddler.

Q Why do preschoolers lose the "potbellied" look of toddlers?

Bone growth occurs rapidly in early childhood. The long bones of the arms and legs grow noticeably, giving the 3-year-old a more lithe and streamlined appearance than the toddler has. The normal pressures of movement placed on the skeleton through activities such as walking and running contribute to a realigning of the bones in early childhood, causing the legs to rotate from the bow-legged gait of the toddler to the knock-kneed gait of the 3-year-old. In infancy, recall, we saw a similar effect on the curvature of the spine from the pressures of sitting upright and then walking. By 4, most children walk with a mature gait, swinging their arms in synchrony with their legs; and by the age of 5, body proportions have become adultlike.

Bodily strength also increases throughout the preschool years. The muscles develop more rapidly in early childhood than do other aspects of the body. This is especially true for muscles in the legs, since children are continually using them. In fact, approximately 75% of the increase in body mass during the 5th year can be attributed to the development of muscles throughout the body. Along with increases in strength, there are also increases in stamina, or endurance, due to changes in the respiratory and cardiovascular systems. Breathing becomes deeper and slower as lung volume increases and as the chest muscles, as well as the diaphragm, contribute to breathing. With respect to the cardiovascular system, the

Weight-for-age percentiles (girls)

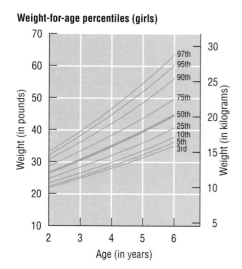

Weight-for-age percentiles (boys)

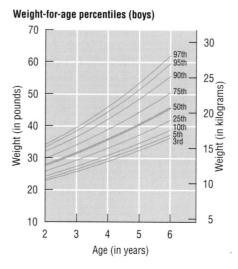

FIGURE 7.1 Growth Charts for Ages 2–6 *Source:* Centers for Disease Control (CDC) (2000), Washington, D. C.

Body mass index-for-age percentiles (girls)

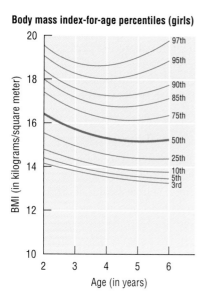

Body mass index-for-age percentiles (boys)

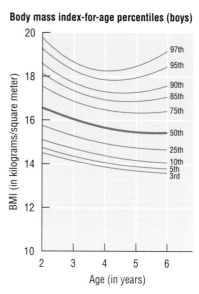

Stature-for-age percentiles (girls)

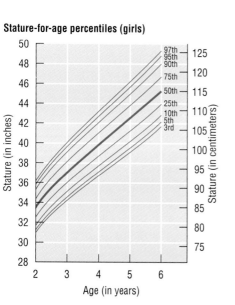

Stature-for-age percentiles (boys)

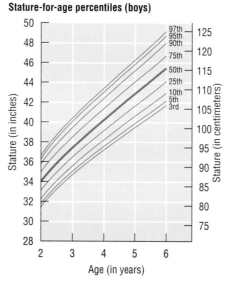

By preschool age, most children lose the toddler's potbelly and their arms and legs are more elongated. This girl is more streamlined than her little sister.

heart beats more slowly and steadily, and blood pressure gradually increases. These changes make it possible for children to be more active, as well as faster and more coordinated (Cech & Martin, 1995; Mitchell, 1990; Wilder, 1995).

Physical differences between boys and girls remain insignificant. Although boys have a slight edge in height and weight, children of both sexes are about the same in muscle strength. Also, there are few differences in physical skills, such as speed, balance, endurance, or agility. Differences in their behavior, however, are apparent. Boys are more active and "rowdy" in their play; and, when disagreements arise, they are more likely to resolve these physically. Chances are, the bully on the playground is a boy, even though a girl is physically just as able to push someone else around. This is not to say that girls don't do their share of pushing. But, as Charlie Brown would tell you, they are more likely to do so, as Lucy does, with words.

Differences in height and, to a lesser degree, weight tend to remain fairly stable from early childhood on. Three-year-olds who are tall for their age, for instance, are likely to be tall at 5 as well, and one can even predict adult height with some accuracy from about the age of 3 (Tanner, 1978). This stability does not mean, of course, that factors such as diet, exercise, or neglect cannot affect a child's weight and even a child's height. However, height and weight are more highly correlated among monozygotic, or identical, twins who share the same genotype than among dizygotic, or fraternal, ones, whose genotypes are no more similar than those of ordinary siblings, suggesting that heredity contributes substantially to stature, or body build (Bouchard, Malina, & Perusse, 1997; Cratty, 1986).

Behavioral Consequences of Physical Development

Preschoolers, especially the youngest among them, have an abundance of energy, coupled with less-than-perfect control over their motor activities. As a consequence, one of the tasks they face is developing self-restraint, learning, for instance, that they cannot simply reach over to grab hold of something that looks interesting or run through a crowded room. They are learning to regulate their movements, to sit still and not fidget, and to put things down or stop when asked. "Simon says" is fun for preschoolers precisely because it's a challenge for them: It is hard for them to restrain actions that have been mentioned without first asking "May I?"

The implications of this challenge became all too clear to me, many years ago now, when I took our 3-year-old son, Joshua, shopping with me at the local mall. We had been to a number of stores, looking at such things as bed linens, mice, and shoes and had accumulated a number of packages. Standing by the escalator to the second level, I released his hand briefly to get a better grip on the packages, only to discover, when I reached for his hand again, that he was no longer by my side. I frantically scanned the area, knee-high to the floor, where we had been standing, but he was nowhere to be seen. As moments passed, anxiety turned to panic. Then, my eyes were caught by a man coming *down* the escalator, holding Joshua in his arms. He explained that Joshua had placed his hands on the outer handrail of the escalator and, as the railing moved up with the rising steps, had been lifted off the ground, hanging outside the escalator as it climbed to the second floor. Only because this stranger had dashed up the steps and grabbed hold of my son was Joshua saved from a terrible fall. One of the developmental challenges facing young families is that parents and children often learn from many of the same experiences, especially with their oldest child.

Compounding problems of restraint is the fact that preschoolers have more aerodynamic bodies than toddlers, making them faster and more agile, a surprise to parents who still expect a trail of carnage as their children move through a

By age 5, children have mastered the use of utensils.

room. Because stopping and turning corners is difficult for toddlers, 2-year-olds frequently find themselves in unexpected situations—two steps from the stairs and at a full run or riding the tray of the highchair on its way to the floor. Three-year-olds, however, can turn corners while running and stop at will. Their agility, however, does not extend to such things as balancing or moving backwards. And, because they run with their heads tilted back for better balance, they often trip and bump into things. Only by about the age of 5 can preschoolers routinely navigate obstacles at a full run.

Especially during the early years, most preschoolers are still mastering the basic routines of daily life, such as dressing, eating, making it to the bathroom in time, falling asleep at night, and navigating a body that is changing almost weekly. At meals, for instance, 3-year-olds can observe such niceties as chewing with their mouths closed and using utensils, feeding themselves with a spoon, or spearing their food with a fork. Knives, however, have yet to be mastered and remain of interest primarily for entertainment purposes, serving as catapults or seesaws, rather than implements for cutting. Five-year-olds, by contrast, can not only manage tableware but can also fix themselves simple meals, such as a bowl of cereal for breakfast or a peanut-butter-and-jelly sandwich for lunch.

By 3, most preschoolers can stay dry through the day, with periodic reminders to use the bathroom. However, even 5-year-olds can have occasional accidents, for the most part due to poor timing. Most 3-year-olds also begin to sleep dry through the night, though this is a transitional time and children who have been successful for nights or even weeks in a row can then wet the bed again for a while. Bladder control continues to develop over the next year and a half. Mature bladder control becomes possible when the bladder can hold nearly double the amount of urine that has been voided during the day, usually before the age of 4½ (Cech & Martin, 1995).

Even the nature of sleep changes in early childhood. Normally, individuals move into and out of two types of sleep states throughout the night: NREM sleep and REM sleep. NREM sleep is associated with a slowing down of bodily functions such as blood pressure, rate of breathing, and basal metabolic rate, as well as the development of characteristic slow-wave brain activity, with decreases in

Children's fears of monsters are the downside of the same active imagination evident in their fantasy play.

How might improved coordination and new skills contribute to tension and outbursts in preschoolers?

brain-stem activity. In REM sleep, the state in which dreaming occurs, brain-wave activity does not become slower, the heartbeat becomes irregular, and rate of breathing actually increases. REM sleep in adults lasts anywhere from 5 to 40 minutes, punctuating NREM sleep every hour and a half or so (Cech & Martin, 1995).

The development of mature sleep patterns involves a fundamental change in the alternation of these two states. In infancy, sleep begins with REM sleep and moves to NREM sleep, whereas in adulthood, sleep begins in the NREM state and is punctuated with episodes of REM sleep. After about the age of 5, children experience the same amount of REM sleep as do adults (Short-DeGraff, 1988), perhaps reflecting the ability of an increasingly mature central nervous system to inhibit REM sleep. The increase in NREM sleep during early childhood is important because it is associated with the release of growth hormone and increased protein synthesis (Cech & Martin, 1995).

More obvious differences to many parents are the fears that children can develop in early childhood that affect both how well they sleep and how easily they fall asleep. Some children wake with nightmares; others have difficulty falling asleep in the first place, imagining monsters in the closet or under the bed or simply being afraid of the surrounding darkness. Each of these fears is the downside of the same active imagination evident in their fantasy play during the day, either alone or with others, talking to themselves, to others, or their toys.

Throughout the preschool years, children continue to become more coordinated and skillful in what they do, whether their activities are as simple as carrying things without dropping them or more complex, such as getting themselves dressed or using a knife to cut their food. Continuing improvements in ordinary activities such as these lead to increased self-confidence and independence. The somewhat uneven progress that young children experience, however, often results in frustration. Perhaps as a result, they still find it easiest to do things when adults are around, a condition that can lead to a test of wills. Having once done something on their own, even young children are not as compliant or cooperative when help is offered as they had been earlier. On the positive side, their testiness over seeming challenges to their independence is offset by their genuine desire to help.

As preschoolers increase in size and become better coordinated, more is also expected of them in both physical coordination and impulse control. Physical development, in other words, has its psychological costs. Parents who might still see the toddler in a 3-year-old and overlook accidents or errors in judgment, for instance, are willing to hold 4-year-olds accountable for their actions in ways they would not have earlier. Perhaps as a result, 4-year-olds live with more tensions and are more likely to have emotional outbursts and tantrums or engage in other nervous outlets, such as biting nails, than are 3-year-olds. They also tire easily. Muscles are not yet attached firmly to the skeleton, with the result that children at this age experience muscle fatigue and need opportunities to rest during the day (Mitchell, 1990). By 5, preschoolers are calmer, have more emotional control, and are more self-confident. Box 7.1 summarizes the self-care and daily routines that 3-, 4-, and 5-year-olds are usually able to manage.

With respect to the routines of daily life, preschoolers have well-formed daily schemas, ordering their day in terms of predictable sequences of activities. They know, for instance, to dress before coming to breakfast or that it is time to get up when they hear a parent switch on the morning news or that bedtime comes after a bath and a story or favorite TV show. Changing the order of activities as familiar as these can be as disorienting as entering a different time zone, or jet lag, is to adults. I recall one futile attempt to rush our two young children as they dawdled through a late dinner one night after arriving home from visiting relatives. I flew around the kitchen throwing together something for us all to eat. We were

Box 7.1 *What Preschoolers Can Do: Self-Care and Daily Routines*

A 3-Year-Old

Dressing and Caring for Self

- Can dress and undress self, with help.
- Has very few toilet accidents, but needs to be reminded to go to the bathroom (boys may still have occasional bladder accidents).
- Can wash and dry face and hands, take a bath, and brush teeth with help.

Eating

- Can feed self at table without help.
- Can use spoon, but spears food with fork.
- Pretty good appetite, but "dawdles" when not hungry.

Sleeping

- Can get ready for bed with some help, likes stories.
- Needs 10–12 hours of sleep a night and a nap or quiet time in afternoon.
- Beginning to sleep dry through the night, with periods of success followed by short periods of bed-wetting.
- Begins to have nightmares.

A 4-Year Old

Dressing and Caring for Self

- Can dress self, managing buttons as well as zippers, but may need to pass "inspection" to make sure shirts and blouses are on right-side out. Tying shoes remains problematic, but can fasten buckles on sandals.
- Can manage most toileting needs, such as brushing teeth, washing faces and hands, and bathing self, but needs help shampooing hair (to keep shampoo out of eyes).
- Can go to the bathroom without help, but may need to be reminded to flush.
- Frequently expect privacy when in bathroom.

Eating

- Can eat with fork and spoon; can spread jelly on bread, cut soft things with knife.
- Develops food dislikes.
- Frequently prefers talking to eating when at the table.
- Enjoys helping out, setting the table, putting things on plates.

Sleeping

- Goes off to bed without much trouble, especially if bedtime is part of a regular routine.
- May be afraid of the dark; a small light helps.
- Needs 10–12 hours of sleep each night; may need a nap in the afternoon or a quiet time.
- Can wake during the night to go to the bathroom, but may need help getting settled down again.

A 5-year Old

Dressing and Caring for Self

- Can dress self, notices if clothes are inside-out.
- Learning to tie shoes.
- Has full bladder and bowel control, but occasional accidents due to putting things off.

Eating

- Can make self breakfast (cereal) or lunch (sandwich).

Sleeping

- Can get ready for bed by self, even helping a younger sibling.
- Sleeps 10–12 hours a night; few need an afternoon nap.
- May have difficulty falling asleep if excited about the next day.
- Dreams and nightmares are common.

Source: Allen & Marotz (1989).

hungry, and it was well past their bedtime. Tomorrow would be another full day, and we still had the evening ritual of a bath, pajamas, and a story ahead of us before the lights went out. My comments about how late it was, pointing out that it was already past their bedtime, went unnoticed as they walked peas, stuck to the tines of their forks, across their plates and made snowbanks with the mashed potatoes. Only much later, after the shouting was over, did I realize why they hadn't paid any attention to me. It simply wasn't bedtime to them. It was dinner time. Why? Because bedtime comes after a bath, when they are in their pajamas, and have been read a story. When one is fully dressed and sitting at the table, it's obviously dinner time. Had I wanted them to hurry, I should have gotten them into their pajamas before sitting down to eat. Then they would have realized that it was time for bed.

Brain Maturation

The brain develops faster during early childhood than does any other part of the body, reaching 90% of its adult size before the age of 6 (Lecours, 1982; Reiss, Abrams, Singer, Ross, & Denckla, 1996). This development makes possible the many motor skills that emerge in early childhood. The maturation of different regions of the brain parallels their anticipated functions. For instance, one of the earliest regions to develop is the cerebellum, a region involved in coordinating movement and maintaining balance; it matures in time for the postural control that is necessary as infants begin to walk. In general, during early childhood all brain regions undergo rapid maturation (Hudspeth & Pribram, 1992).

Brain maturation takes a number of forms. In addition to significant growth in volume, there is the progressive myelination of neural fibers, or the formation of an insulating sheath of myelin around the axons of neurons. This sheath facilitates the conduction of neural impulses, enabling neurons to communicate more effectively with neighboring ones (see Chapter 4). Neural communication, in turn, contributes to what Reiss and his associates (1996) refer to as a remodeling of the brain through the selective elimination of neuronal connections that are not frequently stimulated (Thatcher, 1997). The Research Focus, "Inferential Statistics: Children as Witnesses," on pages 260–261 examines issues related to children's memory.

Robert Thatcher (1997) has found two nearly identical cycles of change in cortical activity with age, the first occurring in early childhood and the second in middle childhood. These cycles involve the establishment of neural interconnections between the frontal lobes and other cortical areas, making possible the creation of new psychological units or ways of functioning. Robbie Case (1992) has suggested that these units underlie not only the motor developments that are so evident in early childhood but also developmental changes in self-awareness. The frontal lobes are involved in monitoring cognitive activity and, as a consequence, in the awareness of oneself engaged in various activities. Interconnections involving the frontal lobes also contribute to children's developing ability to restrain, or inhibit, responses, as is involved in the regulation of activity.

How does brain maturation affect preschoolers' behavior?

Motor Development

Gross motor skills involve large-muscle movements, such as those used in activities that require moving the whole body—running, skipping, or riding a bike, for example. In contrast, fine motor skills involve precise movements controlled by small muscles and usually entail the hands and fingers; examples are the skills involved in using crayons and scissors or fastening buttons. Of course, many activities, such as throwing a ball, require both types of motor skills. Although most basic motor skills develop by the end of the preschool years, there is considerable variability in motor coordination from one child to the next, and significant percentages of even 6- and 7-year-olds are not adept at all basic skills. There is considerable variability even from one day to the next in early childhood. Thus a child who can repeatedly catch a ball on one day may just as consistently fail to do so on the next (Malina & Bouchard, 1991). Box 7.2 summarizes typical skill development in preschoolers.

Gross Motor Skills

One can predict with fair accuracy what a preschooler can do by knowing the child's age. Individual differences, even when extreme, are unlikely to place a child in the next age or skill category. Thus, even well-coordinated 3-year-olds are

Box 7.2 *Skill Development in Preschoolers*

A 3-Year-Old

- Can go up stairs alternating feet, but not down
- Can jump and hop on one foot
- Can kick a ball, if it's a large one
- Can throw a ball overhand
- Can pedal a tricycle or "big wheeler"
- Can draw a circle or a square, and make some letters

A 4-Year-Old

- Better control in drawing, can copy shapes of letters
- Is able to cut with scissors
- Can go up and down stairs alternating feet
- Can pedal a tricycle, turn and stop and not bump into things
- Can skip and stop and turn corners when running
- Good at climbing, whether jungle gyms, stairs, or trees

A 5-Year-Old

- Has good control using pencils and crayons; can color within the lines
- Can cut following a line with scissors
- Walks down stairs as easily as up
- Can walk backwards
- Has good balance; can stand on one foot or walk a balance beam
- Can catch a ball that is thrown a short distance

Source: Allen & Marotz (1989).

unlikely to run as well as an average 4-year-old (Mitchell, 1990). Most 3-year-olds, for instance, run with a flat-footed gait, never completely leaving the ground when they run, and have difficulty with sudden turns. However, by 4, children have a longer stride, actually getting airborne at one point, with both feet off the ground. They are also better at stopping and starting. By 5, coordination has improved even more, enabling them to maneuver sharp turns without falling.

One sees a similar progression with respect to hopping. Three-year-olds can hop with both feet, but have difficulty doing so on one, moving their arms a lot as if they were flying. Even 4-year-olds still hop stiffly, but by 5 most hop by springing from their ankles, knees, and hips. One sees similar progressions with skipping, jumping, and climbing. There are few sex differences in motor skills in the preschool years. One exception is in throwing; boys can throw farther and faster than girls. Since this difference is not reduced when girls later join athletic teams, it may be biologically based (Mitchell, 1990; Thomas & French, 1985).

Fine Motor Skills

Fine motor skills also improve rapidly. Children get better not only in picking things up, but also in manipulating what is already in their hands; this is referred to as **in-hand manipulation.** Thus, they become more adroit at moving an object around in one hand without the help of the other hand—in getting a crayon from the palm of their hand to their fingertips, for example. Three-year-olds can hold

in-hand manipulation The ability to move an object around in one hand without the help of the other hand, such as moving a crayon from the palm of the hand to the fingertips.

Inferential Statistics: Children as Witnesses

BY MICHAEL WAPNER

Imagine you have been falsely accused of a crime. Imagine also that the main witness against you is a 4-year-old child who says she recognizes you as the one in the store who took the watch from the counter and put it in your pocket. True, you were in the store. And when you passed the child, your eyes met, you smiled, and she smiled back, so you know she saw you. But you are innocent of shoplifting. However, unless the child remembers that it was not you she saw at the counter or unless the child's testimony changes or is not believed, you are in danger of being convicted anyway. To add to your danger your lawyer tells you that children of that age are very suggestible and the more you are mentioned to the child in relation to the crime, the more likely the child will "remember" that you committed it.

Of course, this scenario is fictitious. But the problem that it depicts is real. Unfortunately, it is not unheard of for preschool children to be called to give testimony as a witness to a crime. And when they are, it is natural for there to be concern. "Can children adequately process, retain, recall, and report events?" ask James Lampinen and Vicki Smith, of Northwestern University. These authors point to two competing views of children as witnesses. "On the one hand, children are perceived as innocent and truthful; on the other hand, they are viewed as suggestible and prone to fantasy." Actually, both views are correct. When simply asked to tell what they witnessed (called "free recall"), young children are quite accurate (Cole and Loftus, 1987; Marin, Holmes, Guth, & Kovac, 1979, both cited in Lampinen and Smith, 1995). But their accounts tend not to include much detail. If, to fill in the details, they are asked suggestive and misleading questions, their memory may well be distorted.

The reason that such questioning may distort memory is that while a question is presumably a way of *eliciting* information, it is really, to one degree or another, also a way of transmitting information. Of course, how much information is transmitted by the question depends on how the question is phrased. Sometimes the question establishes a context or has an embedded assumption, restricting the range of appropriate answers. "Did you see this defendant put the object in his pocket?" is such a question, since it assumes the defendant put something in his pocket and asks only whether the witness saw it. Other times the questioner may simply add or change details of the event and ask the witness to affirm or deny that it happened that way. However the questioning takes place, the interrogated witness receives information about the event from two sources—the event itself and the questioner. Moreover, misleading interrogation is only one of several possible ways that misinformation can influence what people recall of an earlier event. Another way is simply for the witness to hear a different, false version of the event told by another (alleged) witness.

Lampinen and Smith (1995) raise an interesting question about the suggestibility of children. Does the effect of misinformation on children's memory depend on the credibility of the source of that misinformation? Earlier research had shown that adults' memory is more influenced by misleading suggestions from people with acknowledged authority than from people with less or no authority. The effect on children, however, was not as clear. Lampinen and Smith designed research to clarify this issue.

The experimental design was fairly simple. There were three stages. First, children were given information to be remembered. Second, some of them were exposed to misleading information (while the rest received correct information) about what they had just heard and seen. The (mis)information in this second stage came from sources of varying degrees of credibility. Finally, the children were tested to see whether their memory for the original information had been influenced by the misinformation and whether the credibility of the source made a difference.

One hundred and twenty preschool children from 3 to 5 years old participated in the study. Each child was read a story, which he or she would later be asked to recall, about a girl named Lauren. The story was accompanied by illustrations, including two drawings, one of Lauren eating eggs, the other of Lauren with a stomachache. The information about the eggs and the stomachache was available only in these two drawings and not in the spoken narrative. Ten minutes later the child viewed a videotape of another person, "Anthony," who had also heard the story of Lauren and was now being questioned about it. Depending on the condition, Anthony was either an adult or a child of the same age as the subject. For some subjects the adult was simply introduced as a 24-year-old who had heard the story. For others the adult was introduced as a *silly* 24-year-old who had heard the story. Thus, for each subject, Anthony in the videotape was one of the following: a child, an adult, or a "silly" adult. Thus, the researchers established three levels of credibility. For the 3- to 5-year-old subjects a 24-year-old adult is presumably a credible authority. However, when he is described as "silly," we would expect this credibility to be undermined. And finally, a child who is the same age as the subject would be expected to have less credibility than an adult, although where he would stand with respect to a "silly adult" remained to be seen.

All the videotapes showed Anthony being questioned about what Lauren had for breakfast and in what way she got sick. In half of the videos Anthony answered correctly. In the other half he answered incorrectly, saying Lauren had cereal for breakfast and got a headache. This latter condition, of course, constituted the misleading suggestive information.

Ten minutes later all children were shown two pairs of pictures. One of each pair illustrated the actual event in the story (the ones they had originally seen of Lauren eating eggs and Lauren with a stomachache). The other picture in each pair, which they had never previously seen, illustrated the misleading information of Lauren eating cereal and Lauren with a

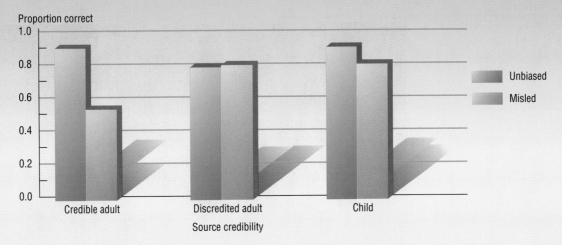

Proportion correct

Source credibility

headache. Each child was asked to choose the picture that had been in the original story.

The figure shows the results. The red bars show the number of questions answered correctly by the children who had seen the misleading videotape. Children who were misled by the credible adult made more errors (got fewer correct) than those who were misled by the discredited (silly) adult or the child. So it does seem, as Laminen and Smith supposed, that children's memory is more vulnerable to misinformation from credible sources than from sources that are discredited or nonauthoritative.

One general but very basic question remains to be asked. To what extent can we rely on these results? To answer this question we must turn to *statistical inference*, a method that allows one to generalize from a sample to the larger population from which that sample was drawn. After all, we are interested not just in the subjects of this study but in children in general. But how can we conclude anything about children in general without having tested all children? It is because, although we actually compare only a *sample* of children, we *infer* that whatever differences we find hold for more than our sample. For such an inference to be justified a number of requirements must be satisfied. First, we must assume that the members of our sample are not systematically different from the members of the population to which we wish to generalize. (See the Research Focus, "Sampling," in Chapter 5.) Second, we must assume that our findings were not the result of chance differences. You will notice from the figure that although *on the average* the children were more misled by the credible adult, not all were misled. (Over 50% answered correctly despite hearing wrong answers from the credible adult.) And although fewer children were misled by incorrect information from the silly adult or the child, about 20% were misled. Finally, even some of the children hearing the correct information answered incorrectly. What these results indicate is that whether a child remembered the actual details or got them wrong did not totally depend on the variables of the study. Each group had variability, and its sources aren't clear. Unexplained variability not due to the variables being studied is termed *random error*. Maybe *all* the differences observed in this study (or any study), including the ones attrib-

uted to the different treatments, were due to random error. It is the probability of differences occurring due to different treatments versus random error that *inferential statistics* is designed to estimate. Given the existence of random error, what is the probability that the differences found in a given study occurred just by chance?

The basic concept of inferential statistics is the *sampling distribution*. The sampling distribution is derived in the following way: First, assume that there is no difference between the populations being compared (in our case between the effects of credible and discredited sources on children's memory). This is called the *null hypothesis*. Second, assume that we repeat our experiment an indefinitely large number of times using the same size sample every time. Because of random error (that is, simply by chance) the difference between the groups will not be the same each time. If the variables that we are studying really make no difference (by the null hypothesis), then most of the chance differences between our groups will be very small and in no particular direction. But if we do the experiment over and over enough times, sometimes large differences will occur just by chance. The sampling distribution tells us the probability of differences of various sizes occurring by chance. Thus, if we compare the results of the current study with the sampling distribution, we can determine the probability of getting a difference this size just by chance. This comparison is called a *test of significance* (which is really not a very good name for it since it does not indicate the "significance" or importance of the result, but only how likely we would be to get one this large simply by chance).

Frequently used inferential statistics (that is, tests of significance) are chi-square, t-tests, and F-tests (or analysis of variance). Limpinen and Smith used an F-test to assess the significance of the differences due to the source of misinformation. Their results were significant at the .01 level. This means that a difference between groups as large as the one they found could be expected to occur by chance about one time in a hundred. Whether this is enough security depends on how important the results are and how the conclusions will be used. For instance, if the results of an experiment could send someone to prison, we might demand that the test of significance be set at one in a thousand.

Fine motor skills improve with age and by age 5, most children can cut with scissors.

a crayon between the first two fingers and their thumb, rather than encircling it in their fist as they did earlier (see Figure 10.5). Four-year-olds have even better control in using crayons and pencils and can begin to copy the shapes of letters; some can print their names. Five-year-olds have good control when using pencils and crayons and can cut along a line with scissors (Allen & Marotz, 1989).

Children also improve in **bimanual coordination,** or using both hands simultaneously, one for doing one thing and the other for doing another, as in holding a paper with one hand while using the other hand to cut with scissors or in opening a jar by turning the top in one direction and the jar in the other. As a result, activities such as grasping hold of and using things of different shapes and sizes, such as buttoning a shirt while dressing oneself or holding a doll to brush her hair, improve greatly. Children who may have difficulty with these when attempting them alone are frequently successful when they can watch someone else. Thus a 4-year-old attempting to use scissors is often able to do so better when an older, already-adept child is present (see Chapter 1 for a discussion of Vygotsky's zone of proximal development).

Hand preference also develops during the preschool years, becoming well established by 4 to 6 years. Hand preference refers to the tendency to use one hand over the other for such things as throwing a ball, writing, or using a fork, even when marked superiority is not apparent with the preferred hand. When brain lateralization occurs, however, by the age of 6 or 7, **hand dominance** occurs; and with this, the use of one hand becomes superior to that of the other (Vansant, 1995).

bimanual coordination The ability to use both hands simultaneously but to do different things, such as holding a paper with one hand and cutting with scissors with the other.

hand preference The tendency to use one hand instead of the other to do such things as throw a ball, write, or use a fork, even when marked superiority is not apparent with the preferred hand.

hand dominance The superiority of one hand to the other for doing such things as throwing a ball, writing, or using a fork; occurs at the time of brain lateralization.

Being allowed to do some things on their own contributes to children's feelings of accomplishment and self-worth.

Psychological Implications of Physical Development

Children develop a sense of themselves in early childhood. The issue for them is no longer *whether* they are autonomous and separate beings, as it was in toddlerhood, but rather of discovering what *kind* of person they are, a task characterized by Erikson as involving **initiative.** Physical development plays an important role in this discovery. New skills, whether simply walking without bumping into things, climbing a jungle gym, or sitting quietly with crayons and scissors or a picture book, make it possible for them to attempt new things, gaining a sense of mastery and success.

New skills also equip preschoolers to play a more active role in the daily routines of their lives. Young children are ready to have a say in things and can profit from being given choices. Being allowed to do some things on their own contributes to their feelings of accomplishment and self-worth. In this sense, their emotional needs are similar to those of their parents. They value their independence, which, newly won, is all the more precious. Although their need to do things for themselves can at times lead to stubborn demands, discernment on the part of parents as to what they can reasonably attempt is usually sufficient to protect them from failure (Erikson, 1959).

Q In what ways might physical development contribute to a child's sense of self?

initiative The term used by Erik Erikson for a child's sense of purposefulness and effectiveness.

Physical development, by its very nature, seems to prompt comparisons with others. Such comparisons fuel preschoolers' seemingly endless curiosity about who is biggest, strongest, and so on. Their new skills also prompt them to imagine themselves in the roles of others, envisioning possibilities that only the future holds. The most significant comparisons they make, of course, are with those who are closest to them, the very people whom they most want to be like—their parents. Erikson suggests that children's perceptions of their parents are not as simple as we might imagine, that though they see them as "powerful and beautiful," they also perceive them as "often quite unreasonable, disagreeable, and even dangerous" (Erikson, 1968, p. 115).

Q Why do giants and monsters seem so real to young children?

Children can also regard their own thoughts and feelings as dangerous, confusing these, as they do at times, with real events. With age, they come to separate feelings from actions, knowing that they cannot kill with a wish or a word. Until this time, fantasy and feeling receive little balance from reality testing (Elkind, 1978a). Just as new freedom of movement expands children's outer world, imagination expands their inner one. This, together with increasingly sophisticated language skills, allows children to conjure up the unknown and to question everything. The giants and monsters that rule the dark places in children's minds are a reminder of how small they still feel in comparison to their rapidly expanding world. Rational explanations by parents that monsters don't exist have little impact on this netherworld.

When are children ready to abandon one explanation for their feelings and experiences and accept another? An explanation, at 5 or 50, is a way of relating something new to what we already know. Children have to be ready for a new idea for it to make sense. Piaget, for instance, described children's reactions to his explanation for the origin of Lake Geneva. He had first asked them to explain how the lake had come into being. One of the common explanations they gave was that a giant threw a rock and rain had filled in the hole that it made. Piaget listened and then offered an alternative, scientific explanation, talking about the movement of glaciers that carved out the basin of the lake and then melted, filling it with water. Although the children could accurately repeat what Piaget had told them, when later asked how the lake had been formed, they earnestly explained that a giant had done it. There is a time for giants and myths and another for science. For something to be an explanation, it must fit what one knows; and at 5, one knows there are giants.

Impulse Control

It is not at all simple for young children to stop doing something when they have been told to or to wait to do something until told it is okay.

Inhibition and Verbal Control Toddlers can do something that is asked of them, but they cannot as easily stop what they are doing when they are asked. By 3, children can inhibit an activity when asked but they have difficulty not acting if they see someone else doing what they want to do—a difficulty shared by 4-year-olds as well. When verbal instructions are inconsistent with visual cues, in other words, the latter are likely to win out (Saltz, Campbell, & Skotko, 1983).

The difficulty young children have in inhibiting an ongoing activity can create problems with parents who may interpret noncompliance with their requests as a power struggle. Toddlers and young children cannot easily bring their behavior under verbal control, either theirs or anyone else's, including an angry parent's. If another toy or activity is substituted for the prohibited one, however, compliance is easier. A harried mother, tired from a day at work and driving home

Scenes like these become less frequent with age as children develop better control over their behavior.

from day care, may find herself dangerously close to the edge after repeatedly telling her 3-year-old *not* to blow the whistle on her spare set of keys. However, if she offers her sunglasses or the photo foldout in her wallet as a substitute, the child is likely to accept the trade happily.

Verbal control over behavior develops gradually. The process is usually not complete until about age 5. Certainly before this age, children have difficulty inhibiting a behavior, especially if tempers flare and parents shout. We know this from research in which children were given a game to play requiring that they follow instructions either to do, or not do, simple things. The instructions were given in a loud, medium, or soft voice. Younger children found it more difficult to inhibit an action when instructions were shouted. However, children older than 5 were more likely to comply under these conditions. Just a note of warning, however. Children who are shouted at will learn to shout like their parents (Saltz et al., 1983).

Children develop better control over their behavior with age. Not only can they stop what they are doing when asked, but they are also better at modulating the pace of their activities. However, even this is difficult for young children. For a preschooler, it is easier to run than walk, to shout instead of talk, to throw rather than hand something, or do anything fast instead of slow. Cautions to slow down, stop running, or wait at the curb go unheard. In addition to this high activity level, preschoolers may be easily distracted from the task at hand. When these behaviors continue into childhood, they may be a sign of attention-deficit disorder, the topic of the Research Focus, "Within-Subjects Designs: Attention-Deficit Hyperactivity Disorder."

Parents can help by anticipating the difficulty young children have in bringing their behavior under control. Instead of telling children what to do, or not do, it is more effective to build habits through consistent routines and consequences for behavior that children can anticipate. David Elkind (1978b) reminds us that young children do not learn through rules. Admonitions such as "Don't hit," "Say please," or "It's not nice to hurt someone" go in one ear and out the other.

Young children learn best by experiencing the consequences of their actions. The liberal and consistent use of positive consequences, such as praise and hugs, and the consistent use of negative ones, such as time out or benching, is effective with young children. Even young children can anticipate the consequences of their

Q Why do young children not always stop an activity when they are told to stop?

Within-Subjects Designs:
Attention-Deficit Hyperactivity Disorder

Although most preschoolers are not likely to be characterized in terms of their capacity for self-restraint or sustained attention, these qualities are considerably less evident in some than in others. For a small percentage of children, the inability to sit still and pay attention to anything for very long reaches clinical proportions. Attention-deficit hyperactivity disorder (ADHD) is thought to affect upwards of 5% of children (American Psychiatric Association, 1994). Children with this disorder are distractible and impulsive; most are also in seemingly constant motion (those who are not hyperactive are said to have attention-deficit disorder, or ADD).

Paradoxically, despite the difficulty these children have in attending to things, they appear to have no trouble watching television. In this, they are like most children their age. Even so, one might wonder whether they are as likely to remember what they have watched as are other children. Most children, in fact, have no difficulty remembering a program they have watched even though playing with toys while doing so. Presumably they are able to successfully divide their attention by monitoring auditory cues accompanying the program; these cues direct their attention back when something is about to happen.

Steven Landau, Elizabeth Lorch, and Richard Milich (1992) wondered whether ADHD children would be able to control their attention in similar ways. They videotaped both ADHD boys and control boys as they watched a television program, either with appealing toys present or without toys in the room, and, once the program was over, asked both groups of boys what they recalled of the program they had seen.

These investigators used a *within-subjects design*. In this type of design, each boy experienced both of the experimental conditions; that is, each boy watched television once with appealing toys present and once with no toys present. This design can be compared with a between-subjects design in which each subject experiences only one condition (see the Research Focus, "Between-Subjects Design," in Chapter 11). Within-subjects designs are *economical*, requiring fewer subjects because the same subjects react to all conditions. They are also *sensitive*. A design is sensitive to the extent that it can pick up, or detect,

differences resulting from the experimental treatment. Within-subjects designs are sensitive because they use the same subjects in all conditions, thus reducing variability due to individual differences.

Despite these important advantages, this type of design has several serious disadvantages. One runs the risk of *carryover effects*, in which the effect of one treatment is still present when the next is given. In this example, boys might confuse the contents of the first program with that of the second, resulting in poorer memory for the second program. Carryover effects are not necessarily symmetrical for each of the orders in which different subjects watch programs. Watching the first program with distracting toys present may result in less carryover, if the toys actually do distract subjects from the program, than watching without toys present. In addition to carryover effects, there can be *order effects* with this design. These reflect systematic changes in performance over time due to factors such as practice, fatigue, boredom, and so on.

Both carryover and order effects introduce the potential for *confounding*. Confounding exists when the difference between treatments can be explained in more than one way—that is, when an experiment lacks internal validity (see the Research Focus, "Internal and External Validity," in Chapter 14). Landau, Lorch, and Milich *counterbalanced* the order in which boys watched programs under the two toy conditions. Counterbalancing presents each condition an equal number of times in each order, thus balancing any effects due to order equally across conditions.

What did these researchers find? When no toys were present, ADHD boys spent as much time watching television as did the control boys. When toys were present, however, they spent only half the time watching that the control boys spent. Nonetheless, ADHD boys recalled just as much of the program's content as did control boys. These findings suggest that although ADHD children are more distractible, under some circumstances, at least, they can utilize the same cues to guide their attention as used by other children.

actions when these are consistent and predictable. Soon, even the thought of a misdeed is enough to cause anxiety—and restraint. This is not to say that parents should not accompany a hug with a remark such as "That was so kind," or to comment, as a child is benched, that one can play with others when one does not hurt them. But words alone are not sufficient for the very young.

Finally, parents should know when to use external restraints. Childproof doors handles, locked cabinets, a gate to the yard, hand-holding when crossing the street, and seat-belt use are all simple precautions that help children who are at an age when external constraints are more reliable than internal ones.

Waiting: Delay of Gratification   Perhaps even harder for young children than total restraint is waiting for something they have been told they can have. Children's ability to delay gratification has been studied using a number of procedures. In one of these, they are shown two snacks, one more desirable than the other, and told they must wait in order to get the more desirable one, but can have the less desirable whenever they want—but taking the less desirable snack means forfeiting their chances of ever getting the better one. Thus, they might be shown a marshmallow and a pretzel; the adult leaves, taking both, explaining that they can have the marshmallow if they are willing to wait but if they call the adult back beforehand, they get the pretzel. The first thing social scientists found, something any parent could have told them, is that ability to delay gratification, to wait for the better reward, increases with age (Mischel & Rodriguez, 1993).

Even 3-year-olds will consider how long they must wait if they are told in familiar terms how long it will be, such as "until bedtime" or "when Sesame Street ends." However, it seems that while younger children can make choices that are just as adaptive as those of older children, they cannot carry them out as well. That is, they may choose to wait for something better, but they do not have the strategies that help them wait for what they have chosen (Schwartz, Schrager, & Lyons, 1983).

Older children have learned that it is easier to wait if they do not look at what they want. It is also easier to wait if they do not think about what they are waiting for, if they distract themselves with other thoughts or with other things to do. They have learned that "hot thoughts," about how sweet, chewy, or yummy a promised treat will be, make it harder to wait. "Cool thoughts" that focus on abstract qualities of the goal, such as its shape or color, make it easier. Also, when children focus on what they are doing, such as "I am waiting for _____," they can wait longer than when they focus on the reward itself, as in "The _____ is yummy" (Cole & Newcombe, 1983, Miller, Weinstein, & Karniol, 1978).

But how much do young children know about these strategies? Mischel and Mischel (1983) asked preschoolers and third- and sixth-graders what makes it easier to wait. Preschoolers did not seem to know any of the strategies for waiting. Third-graders, however, were more knowledgeable, and sixth-graders were downright sophisticated. Preschoolers, for example, could not spontaneously think of any delay strategies when asked. Third-graders knew that it helped to think about the relationship between waiting and the reward, as in "If I wait, I will get more." Sixth-graders used sophisticated techniques to reduce the temptation to opt for a smaller or less desirable reward that could be had right away. For example, one child repeated over and over, "It would taste soapy." Another said, "I don't want this now, but I will when the experimenter comes back."

These investigators found an interesting trend among the preschoolers. The youngest children, those under 4, showed no preference either for covering up or looking at what they were waiting for, but 4-year-olds thought it would actually help them wait if they could look at what they were waiting for. This seems to be a genuine strategy rather than simple wish fulfillment, since they also suggested it for others (Mischel & Mischel, 1983; Mischel, Shoda, & Rodriguez, 1992).

These same 4-year-olds also knew they would have to distract themselves while waiting, but they did not realize the difficulty they would have in doing so. Thus, they set up self-defeating situations by putting the tempting object in full view, not realizing how difficult it would be to overcome temptation. By 4½, children realize it will not help to look at what they are waiting for, but they also do not think to cover the source of temptation from view. Only by the end of the 5th year do they think to remove the tempting object from view (Mischel & Mischel, 1983; Mischel et al., 1992).

Finally, children find it easier to wait for things when they trust adults to keep promises. Parents who want their children to be able to wait must be prepared to follow through with what they have said. In this case, it is better to promise something that is within one's reach, even if it is small, than something bigger that may not be. Children can wait more easily when they experience a sense of control over the situation and over themselves, when they can trust themselves as well as others to "deliver the goods" (Maccoby, 1984).

Erikson believed children's experience of their parents' trustworthiness to be the foundation on which all later development builds. Keeping promises to children, both the spoken ones and the unspoken ones implicit in the orderly nurturing care they give, is central to this trust. Sam Keen (1970) describes the power of promises kept in an essay about his relationship with his father. He begins

> Once upon a time when there were still Indians, Gypsies, bears, and bad men in the woods of Tennessee where I played and, more important still, there was no death, a promise was made to me. One endless summer afternoon my father sat in the eternal shade of a peach tree, carving on a seed he had picked up. With increasing excitement and covetousness I watched while, using a skill common to all omnipotent creators, he fashioned a small monkey out of the seed. All of my vagrant wishes and desires disciplined themselves and came to focus on that peach-seed monkey. Finally, I marshaled my nerve and asked if I might have the monkey when it was finished (on the sixth day of creation). My father replied, "This one is for your mother, but I will carve you one someday." ◄

His father didn't carve that peach-seed monkey for him that summer, and Keen soon forgot his fascination with it. Years later, as an adult listening to his father taking stock of his life just before dying, Keen told his father how trustworthy he had always been with him, "In all that is important you have never failed me. With one exception, you kept the promises you made to me—you never carved me that peach-seed monkey."

Shortly after this conversation—two weeks before he died—his father gave him a peach-seed monkey that he had carved. For Keen, that carving became a symbol of "all the promises which were made to me and the energy and care which nourished and created me as a human being."

Developing Restraints: How Parents Can Help

Children differ in the amount of control they have over their activity, as well as in their ability to wait for what they want. But initially, all are impulsive compared to later, and parents need to provide many of the controls children need until they develop their own. Parents can help in a number of ways. Especially important for developing restraints as structuring situations, regulating the child's activities, and being controlled themselves (Maccoby, 1984).

Q How can parents help children develop necessary restraints in their behavior?

Structuring Situations   Regular predictable routines and settings help children to cope with new experiences. It is not by chance that preschoolers are likely to be at their crankiest when Grandma and Grandpa come to visit. Schedules are disrupted; naps are missed; meals, baths, play time, and quiet time are all likely to differ. Young children have difficulty integrating their activities into those of others. It is even difficult for them to integrate one activity of their own with another. Their actions are prompted more by immediate, external conditions than by a planned ordering of events. A predictable schedule, familiar routines of eating, sleeping, and such, give a structure to their experience that is not easily provided from within.

Because preschoolers have trouble anticipating future needs, parents need to plan for them by bringing things for them to do.

Parents frequently need to structure play activities. Young children find it difficult to sustain play over any amount of time. It is not unusual for a parent to hear "I have nothing to do" from a child standing in the middle of a room filled with toys. Children may have the toys to play with, but they lack the plans that will transform them into play. Parents can help by supplying plans. Although one might think first to shoot back a testy remark, it is just as easy to suggest a way to play. "Why don't you build a house with those, make a bridge, give your dolly a meal?" Each of these suggestions is a blueprint for play (Maccoby, 1984).

Parents can help young children manage their impulses by not making them wait. Children lack strategies for filling time and can get out of control when asked to wait. Running, squirming, teasing, fighting, and shouting soon follow.

Regulating Children's Activities   Young children have difficulty anticipating future needs. Five minutes out the door they can announce, "I have to go potty." "Why didn't you think of this before?" an exasperated parent retorts. "I didn't have to go then," is the answer. Children who are told to bring along crayons, skates, paper dolls, or airplanes are likely to answer that they won't be bored, and then drive an adult crazy every 10 minutes with "I'm bored," "Can't we go yet?" and "I want to go home NOW." They weren't bored when told to bring something along and couldn't imagine feeling any way other than how they felt then. Some of these problems can be avoided by building in routines. Trips in the car, whether to the market or the next state, mean going to the bathroom first and bringing along something to do—books, puzzles, crayons, dolls, or action figures.

Because young children find it difficult to anticipate the consequences of their decisions, parents need to make some decisions for them. "Can I have a pet mouse, bird, puppy, kitten, water buffalo? Please, Mom, please? I'll take care of it. Please, pretty please, P-L-E-A-S-E?" Many a tender-hearted parent has fallen prey to such pleadings only to regret it while cleaning out the mouse cage, chasing the bird, or picking up buffalo chips. Preschoolers fail to anticipate that a pet must be fed, bathed, and cared for. Parents who are unwilling to share the burden of these consequences by building in new routines of pet care may find it easier to make their children wait until they are ready to assume the responsibilities themselves. One may feel like a heel when denying a small child, yet the alternative of giving in may be setting the child up for failure ("You promised you would feed it, walk it . . .") and feelings of guilt or inadequacy (Maccoby, 1984).

Many decisions can be shared by parent and child. Parents can simplify choices to several alternatives, any of which would be manageable and acceptable for the child. The child decides between these. When the number of alternatives is small, children can consider each and reach a decision that they and their parents can live with.

Parental Self-Control   Parents can also help their children develop control through their own self-control. Children can manage their emotional outbursts more easily when parents control their tempers. A child's angry outbursts can lead to anger in the parent, making it all too easy to shout back or spank, leading to more tears and precluding further communication. But when parents are calm and firm, children can take in information even while being disciplined.

Parents can help children develop habits that provide structure when they themselves are predictable and regular. Even though a parent may be dying to skip the nightly routine of chores, homework, bath, and bedtime stories, routines that are set aside too frequently fail to be routine and do not provide structure to the child's daily experiences.

Similarly, children will think of strategies to help them wait or to remember things if parents teach such strategies through example. If children see parents bringing something along to occupy themselves while they wait at the car wash or the dentist's office, it becomes natural for them to do the same. Similarly, strategies for remembering can be built in by teaching children to routinely put the item to be remembered where it will be seen, such as homework by the front door or milk money on the kitchen counter (Maccoby, 1984).

Helping children develop controls requires an investment of time. It takes time, in other words, to teach the skills children need to do things on their own, and it takes time to follow through to see that they carry out what they have been given to do in a responsible way. When children have skills, they have options. Teaching children how to do things on their own, gradually introducing them to difficult tasks and letting them experience success with each new level of difficulty, builds tolerance for frustration and fosters the development of inner controls (Maccoby, 1984).

Health and Well-Being

The dramatic changes in height and weight that take place during the preschool years depend on adequate nutrition. These very same changes also make it possible for preschoolers to increasingly get about on their own, getting into just about anything, and increasing their risk of accidental injuries as a consequence. We will look at the dietary needs of preschoolers and the risk of injury in the following sections.

Nutrition

Rapid skeletal and muscular development, as well as continuing brain growth, all require adequate nutrition. As a consequence, preschoolers need more energy per ounce than do adults. However, because the rate of growth slows in early child-

CALVIN AND HOBBES © 1988 Watterson.
Reprinted with permission of Universal
Press Syndicate. All rights reserved.

hood, they need less than they did as toddlers. As a result, their appetites are likely to decrease, often causing some alarm in parents. Preschoolers can even become "finicky," picking through their plates for just the right things to eat. Food not only has to taste good, it also has to look "right," and so foods that are the wrong color or texture are frequently rejected, with little consistency from one day to the next. However, unless parents notice a marked change in weight or persistent fatigue, a diminished appetite is not a problem (Mitchell, 1990).

It is not how much children eat but what they eat that contributes to their health during these years. A healthy diet should include an adequate supply of fruits and vegetables, whole grains, and foods rich in calcium and protein, such as dairy products and meats. Colorful foods, such as oranges, apples, tomatoes, and green vegetables are not only appealing to preschoolers, but also highly nutritious.

Q Why do preschoolers have less of an appetite than they did as toddlers?

TABLE 7.1 Sources of Essential Vitamins and Minerals

Young children are most likely to be deficient in vitamins A, C, and B$_6$, folic acid, calcium, iron, and zinc. The following foods adequately supply these nutrients.

Whole grains, fortified cereals, and breads	6 servings	Iron, zinc, vitamin B$_6$, folic acid
Fruits	2 servings	Vitamins A, B$_6$, C, folic acid
Milk, cheese, yogurt group	3 servings	Calcium, zinc, vitamins A, B$_6$
Meat, fish, poultry group	2 servings	Iron, zinc, vitamin B$_6$
Vegetables (dark yellow; leafy greens; potatoes)	2 servings	Vitamins A, B$_6$, C, folic acid

Source: W. H. Dietz and L. Stern (eds.). (1999). *American Academy of Pediatrics: Guide to your child's nutrition.* New York: Villard.

TABLE 7.2 Substituting Foods for a Balanced Diet

Vitamins

For children who don't like vegetables	Vitamin A: apricots, cantaloupe, mango, peaches, plums, prunes; milk; eggs
	Vitamin C: grapefruit, oranges, cantaloupe and other melons, strawberries

Calcium

For children who don't drink milk	Part-skim and low-fat cheeses, yogurt; broccoli, dark-green leafy vegetables; chickpeas, lentils; canned sardines, salmon, and other fish with bones; calcium-fortified orange juice. Some pediatricians recommend an over-the-counter antacid containing calcium carbonate

Protein

For children who don't eat meat	Lentils, tofu; beans, and other legumes in combination with grains; peanut butter; eggs; fish; nuts; dairy foods

Source: W. H. Dietz and L. Stern (eds.). (1999). *American Academy of Pediatrics: Guide to your child's nutrition.* New York: Villard.

A number of deficiencies, however, are sufficiently common to bear mention. One common form of malnutrition during these years, and one not limited to poor or developing countries, is protein deficiency. Adequate supplies of protein are necessary to support rapidly developing muscles and body tissues. Malnutrition, when chronic, can stunt physical growth and affect brain development. Even mild forms of malnutrition, however, can result in fatigue, poor concentration, apathy, and a generally decreased ability to cope with the demands of one's environment (Pollitt et al., 1996).

Most children's eating habits in the United States fail to meet established nutritional guidelines. Only about a third of children in a recent national survey met the daily recommendations for the five food groups of fruits, vegetables, grains, meat, and dairy products. In general, fats and sugars were found to provide about 35% to 40% of the energy children consumed daily from food, much more than is considered healthy. Objectives for healthier eating include eating more complex carbohydrates and high-fiber foods by having at least five servings a day of fruits and vegetables and at least six of grains (that is, breads and cereals), increasing daily calcium intake, and reducing the intake of fat to about 30% of the caloric intake (Munoz, Drebs-Smith, Ballard-Barbach, & Cleveland, 1997). Table 7.1 summarizes a healthy daily diet for young children, and Table 7.2 suggests alternatives for finicky eaters.

Public school lunch programs help to combat inadequate nutrition among children from low-income families.

The total energy consumed daily by children is related to their income level (Munoz et al., 1997). Not surprisingly, children who live in poverty are not as well nourished as those who do not. What may be surprising, however, is that inadequate nutrition poses a serious health problem not only to children living in poor countries, but to significant numbers of low-income children in the United States as well. Paradoxically, we have come to downplay the importance of biological risk factors such as poor nutrition for development because of the very success of our nation's public health system during the first part of this century, which improved children's nutritional status and dramatically reduced communicable childhood diseases (Pollitt, 1994).

What are the nutritional consequences of poverty, and how can these be corrected? The most serious nutritional deficiency among low-income children in the United States is iron-deficiency anemia (Pollitt, 1994). Overall, about 17% of children from low-income families are estimated to have iron-deficiency anemia, whereas only 3% to 5% of middle-income children are estimated to suffer this nutritional deficiency. Iron deficiency can result in retarded growth, greater susceptibility to infectious diseases, and diminished physical and cognitive functioning (Filer, 1995).

Many of these effects are reversible with daily supplements of iron. Research in which iron-deficient infants and toddlers were randomly assigned to either a supplemental iron or a placebo condition found a reversal of such developmental delays in the children treated with iron but not in those given the placebo. Since these studies included double-blind controls, in which neither those receiving the supplements nor those evaluating their effects knew which of these conditions the children were in, the initial symptoms as well as their reversal could clearly be attributed to the deficiency itself and not to social or environmental conditions typically associated with poor nutrition (Idjradinata & Pollitt, 1993).

Just as programs giving supplemental iron have been found to be effective in combating iron deficiency, those giving supplemental food to low-income children have been found effective in combating malnutrition. Support for the effectiveness of supplemental food programs comes primarily from research conducted in other countries (Engle, Gorman, Martorell, & Pollitt, 1992; Joos, Pollitt, & Mueller, 1982; Super, Herrera, & Mora, 1990). In this research, children have been assigned at random either to control conditions in which they did not receive nutritional supplements or to those in which they received supplemental food. Research of this nature has found that supplemental feeding results in improved motor and mental development in children. Furthermore, this improvement carries over into the preschool years, even after the supplemental program has terminated. In one long-term follow-up, in which children were again tested 11 years later, benefits of such programs extended even into adolescence (Engle et al., 1992). In this study, nutritional supplementation was so effective that differences in performance ordinarily associated with socioeconomic status disappeared for the low-income adolescents who had received supplemental food as young children (Engle et al., 1992; Joos et al., 1982; Super et al., 1990).

Overweight

Quite a different problem is faced by other children. The percentage of children in the United States who are overweight has increased substantially in recent years, paralleling a similar trend among adults (Troiano & Flegal, 1998). Given that wide differences in weight are common among children at any age, how is one to determine what constitutes overweight? Body mass index, or BMI, offers a convenient formula for calculating both overweight and underweight. BMI expresses one's weight relative to one's height, by dividing one's weight by the square of one's height (see Table 7.3 for the formula). Is a 3-year-old who weighs 33 pounds overweight? It depends. For a boy who is 37 inches tall, this weight yields a BMI of 16.9, which places him at the 50th percentile. However, a boy weighing 33 pounds who is only 35 inches tall has a BMI of 18.9, placing him at the 95th percentile in weight for that age. Children who are **overweight** are at or above the 85th percentile of weight for their height. Since body fat varies not only with age but also with sex, separate growth charts are necessary for girls and for boys.

Children slim down in the preschool years due both to rapid bone growth, which adds inches to their height, and to muscle development. These developmental changes are reflected in growth charts that use BMI as an index-for-age (see Figure 7.1). One can see a decline in BMI from the age of 2 to approximately 6. After age 6, BMI increases, and approximately 10% to 15% of 6- to 17-year-olds are overweight, which is twice the number who were overweight 30 years ago (CDC, 2000). A number of factors are most likely responsible for this trend in weight gain among children, some of the more important being changes in patterns of physical activity and in eating habits (CDC, 2000; Hill & Trowbridge, 1998).

Both children and adults are less physically active today than in the past. This change is important since being overweight is negatively correlated with physical activity. That is, the *less* active one is, the *more* likely one is to be overweight (Harsha, 1995). What might account for today's more sedentary lifestyle? Both work and leisure pursuits are likely culprits. The work habits of parents, for instance, can affect the entire family's activities. Working parents do not always have time to spend tying on roller skates, balancing a child on a bicycle, or playing catch. And more children today are being raised in families where both parents work or in families with a single working mother. Many days of the week parents may arrive home from work at the same time as their children, having picked them up from day care on the way, only to face the need to fix dinner before beginning the evening's activities. Depending on the quality of the day care, children may or may not have had ample opportunity to run and play outside.

With respect to leisure activities, children today spend more time in sedentary recreational activities than in the past. For some children this decision is

overweight A condition in which children are at or above the 85th percentile of weight for their height.

TABLE 7.5 Foods That Are Unsafe for Toddlers

Because children don't begin to chew with a grinding motion until approximately 4 years of age, toddlers can easily choke on the following foods.

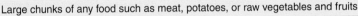

Hot dogs (unless cut in quarters lengthwise before being sliced)

Hard candies, including jelly beans

Nuts

Chunks of peanut butter—spread peanut butter thinly on bread or cracker—never give chunks of peanut butter to a toddler

Popcorn

Raw carrots, celery, green beans

Seeds (such as processed pumpkin or sunflower seeds)

Whole grapes, cherry tomatoes (cut them in quarters)

Large chunks of any food such as meat, potatoes, or raw vegetables and fruits

Source: Adapted from W. H. Dietz and L. Stern (eds.). (1999). *American Academy of Pediatrics: Guide to your child's nutrition.* New York: Villard.

1993). Even when children eat vegetables, these are not always the ones a dietitian would choose. Among children who said they ate five or more servings of fruits and vegetables a day, 25% of the vegetables they listed were french fries (Krebs-Smith et al., 1996).

Establishing Healthy Patterns

A number of factors affect children's food choices and eating patterns. Perhaps the most obvious of these is the accessibility of various foods. Children eat what is available. Those who attend day care centers and schools, for instance, where more fruits and vegetables are served, eat more fruits and vegetables (Birch & Fisher, 1998). The same holds for preschoolers at home. Parents can establish healthy eating patterns by offering cut-up vegetables or fruits as snacks instead of sweets or crackers; by replacing fast-food meals with microwavable meals that contain less fat; by using low-fat milk instead of whole milk; and by limiting high-calorie drinks, including juices, offering fruit or water to drink instead (Christoffel & Ariza, 1998). Table 7.4 lists some other healthful snacks and Table 7.5 lists foods that are unsafe for children under 4.

Children do what they see others doing. Preschoolers who see other children eating vegetables, even those that they do not especially like, will nonetheless increase the frequency with which they select and eat those vegetables (Birch, 1980). Modeling is a pervasive and powerful influence, even when it comes to establishing food preferences. Very young children are more likely to put different foods in their mouths, for instance, when they see these being eaten by their mother than by a stranger (Harper & Sanders, 1975). Similarly, when weight is a salient issue in families, due to obesity or dieting, children's eating patterns are likely to be influenced by those of their parents (Fisher & Birch, 1996).

Controlling the availability of different foods can sometimes backfire. Parents run the risk of inadvertently increasing children's preferences for certain foods by making them forbidden. The old adage, "Forbidden fruit tastes sweeter," holds true at all ages. Restricting children's access to certain types of foods can increase their value to children (Birch & Fisher, 1998; Smith & Epstein, 1991). We frequently send mixed messages to children about such foods, saying they are bad for them on the one hand, but on the other hand offering them as the food to be eaten on festive occasions, such as birthday parties and other celebrations. It might be better to include these foods in children's daily fare, teaching them to enjoy them in moderation.

How sensitive are children to their energy needs, such that they could be expected to regulate what and when they eat? Research in which children are given food over a series of two courses suggests that they are sensitive. Two groups of children were given the same amount to eat in the first course, but the energy content of the food differed for the two groups, by varying the amount of carbohydrates and fat. After the first course, all were given a second course in which they were allowed to self-select their food. Those who ate the energy-dense food in the first course ate less in the second course (Birch & Deysher, 1986; Birch, McPhee, Shoba, Steinberg, & Krehbiel, 1987). Children's responsiveness to the energy content of food, furthermore, is evident in the foods they select over an extended period of time. Thus, if more energy-dense foods are consumed in one meal, fewer will be consumed even in a much later meal (Birch, Johnson, Andersen, Peters, & Schulte, 1991).

Children's responsiveness to internal cues such as these is reduced when they are encouraged to rely on external cues, such as how much is left on their plate. There appears to be a natural tension between parental attempts to regulate what children eat, which must for the most part rely on external cues, and children's own self-regulatory patterns, which are based primarily on internal cues. Thus, research in which children are fed over two courses has found that children whose parents exercise a high degree of control over what they eat do not adjust their food selections in the second course to compensate for the energy they have taken in as much as do children whose parents exercise less control (Johnson & Birch, 1994). For most children, the tension between parental control and self-regulation introduces few problems. But for those where there are issues related to eating within the family, this tension may be problematic. Parents are more likely to attempt to regulate what their children eat when they have problems themselves in terms of eating, the very conditions under which external cues are likely to be least reliable.

Illnesses, Injuries, and Accidents

The health status of children differs significantly with ethnicity, presumably due to associated differences in socioeconomic status. Thus, African American children are nearly twice as likely to be in fair or poor health as White children, and children from low-income families 3 times more likely to be in poor health than those from middle-income families. Statistics such as these strongly suggest that low-income minority children are more likely to be affected by common illnesses and less likely to receive the medical care they need (Pollitt, 1994).

Comparisons of children from a nationally representative sample give support to this concern. When children at risk due to low income, minority status, or lack of health insurance were compared with a control group of middle-income, White children who were covered by insurance, substantial differences were found in the availability and type of care they received. In addition to being less likely to be cared for by a particular doctor familiar with their health history, at-risk children also had to spend more time traveling to the doctor and more time waiting once they got there. They were also less likely to have access to after-hours medical care in case of emergencies. Perhaps as a result of their difficulty in seeing a doctor, children in the at-risk groups were less likely to be taken for treatment when they were ill than were control children and were less likely to have received all their vaccinations (Newacheck, Hughes, & Stoddard, 1996).

Immunization Programs

Due to widescale immunization programs in developed nations, many infectious diseases that were once life-threatening to children, such as smallpox, diphtheria, polio, and measles have been effectively controlled. In the United States, for instance, rubella (German measles) was a common childhood disease and a common cause of birth defects. Due to a national immunization program, the Centers for Disease Control (1995d) reported only five cases of congenital rubella in 1994. In underdeveloped nations, measles continues to be a common childhood disease and kills upwards of a million children a year (CDC, 1993). Given the success of immunization programs and the potential dangers to children in their absence, one might expect parents, to the extent they are able, to make sure their children are current in all their vaccinations. Such is not the case for many children, however. Paradoxically, the very achievements of these programs threaten to undermine their continued success, as parents and the public in general have become less aware of the potential danger of the diseases that immunization programs control.

Although 90% of children in the United States are immunized by the time they enter elementary school, immunization rates for 2-year-olds frequently fall well below this figure. This discrepancy is especially true for children living in major urban areas. For example, a 1993 survey of families in the Houston area revealed that only 36% of 2-year-olds had received all their immunizations by their 2nd birthday. This figure, though alarmingly low, is not unrepresentative for children living in major U.S. cities. The percentage of 2-year-olds living in Los Angeles and Dallas who were fully immunized, for instance, was 27%; the percentage was 48% for those living in San Diego (Hanson et al., 1996, as reported in McCormick et al., 1997).

Given the low rate of immunizations of young children, it is important to understand why parents are not keeping their children's immunization status up-to-date. It is one thing to be able to say that parents of children living in major urban areas are less likely to have their children immunized. But it is another thing to be able to say *why* they are less likely to do so. Some of the research aimed at understanding the causes behind parents' behavior has started with the assumption that to have their children immunized, parents must *plan* for it and that their plans are affected by their beliefs (Prislin, Dyer, Blakely, & Johnson, 1998). When parents of young children were interviewed, a clear link emerged between parents' beliefs and their likelihood of maintaining up-to-date immunizations.

Such links can improve educational programs aimed at increasing immunization. Well-educated parents, for instance, were somewhat more likely than parents with less education to incorrectly believe that a child with a cold should not get immunized. *All* parents, not only less-educated ones, need accurate information concerning contraindications for immunization.

Other beliefs, however, were found to differ as a function of sociodemographic groups. For instance, low immunization rates among African Americans were related to beliefs in natural immunity. Thus, educational programs targeting this particular group, to be effective, should emphasize the effectiveness of vaccines over natural immunity. Similarly, parents with little formal education were found to be concerned about the safety of vaccines, an issue needing to be addressed in educational programs directed to this segment of the population. An encouraging finding to emerge from this research was the effectiveness of the WIC program (see Chapter 4) in promoting immunization. Those participating in this program were more likely to believe that immunizations protected their children from disease and to perceive fewer barriers to immunization.

Thus, there are nonfinancial as well as financial barriers to health care for many children. Some of these are being addressed through increased federal funding for community health centers and training for health care providers who are willing to practice in low-income neighborhoods. Additional steps will need to focus on improving the availability of transportation and child care, arranging office hours that meet the needs of working single parents, reducing waiting times, and providing more trained providers who are "culturally competent" with respect to those for whom they are caring (Newacheck, Hughes, & Stoddard, 1996). The Social Policy Focus, "Immunization Programs," looks at the effectiveness of parent education programs in improving the immunization rate.

Because they are so active, running across yards or playgrounds at full tilt, climbing anything that's higher than they are, and exploring whatever presents itself as new, preschoolers experience their share of accidental injuries. Most of these do not require medical attention. However, girls have a 25% chance of sustaining an injury that does; and for boys, this figure rises to 33% (Fried, Makuc, & Rooks, 1998).

The increased use of child-restraint devices is primarily responsible for the prevention of automobile fatalities among preschoolers.

Injuries are, in fact, the leading cause of death for children between the ages of 1 and 4. Death from an accidental injury is 4 times more common than the next most common cause (Scholer, Mitchel, & Ray, 1997). The percentage of injury-related deaths among children, however, has decreased substantially. Over a 14-year period from 1978 to 1991, the death rate due to unintentional injuries decreased by 39%. The largest decreases involved motor vehicle deaths and deaths due to drowning (Rivara & Grossman, 1996).

The increased use of child-restraint devices, such as seat belts, is primarily responsible for the prevention of automobile fatalities among children under the age of 5. In 1991, for instance, 63% of the children who died in automobile accidents were not using seat belts or, if younger, were not belted into infant car seats. Belts securing a child across the lap alone are not as effective as lap-shoulder restraints and, though they decrease the risk of fatal injuries, may be a source of serious nonfatal injuries in themselves (Viano, 1995).

Drowning is the second most frequent cause of accidental fatalities among children and adolescents, most of which involve preschoolers. Drowning in swimming pools is largely preventable by making sure that these are fenced in on all sides and secured with a self-latching gate and by having an adult present at all times whenever children are in the pool. Drowning in bathtubs, accounting for approximately 10% of all drownings, is similarly preventable (Rivara & Grossman, 1996). Most of these deaths involve toddlers or children who suffer seizures, such as those with epilepsy. Toddlers should never be left in a bath by themselves, and it is best for children who suffer seizure disorders to take showers rather than baths, even beyond the preschool years.

The risk to a child of dying from an accidental injury increases under certain conditions. Seth Scholer, Edward Mitchel, and Wayne Ray (1997), who studied the population of children born in Tennessee between 1985 and 1994, found a substantial association between injury death rates and certain maternal and child characteristics. Injuries were more than 50% more likely when the mother had less than 12 years of education, had more than two other children in the family, and was less than 20 years old. Race and income level were not related to injury mor-

Box 7.3 *Types of Maltreatment*

Abuse

- *Physical abuse:* Involves substantial injuries that last for at least 48 hours and often, as in the case of burns, broken bones, or internal injuries, longer. Examples might include bruises or fractures from being hit or punched, burns from cigarettes, or cerebral hemorrhages from being shaken. Fifty-one percent of children who are abused are physically abused.
- *Sexual abuse:* Involves exposure, molesting or fondling, or actual penetration. Examples might include a father fondling his 4-year-old son during visitations, or a daughter being molested by her mother's live-in boyfriend. Twenty-nine percent of children who are abused are sexually abused.
- *Emotional abuse:* Involves behavior that undermines a child's sense of well-being and self-esteem. Examples could include denigrating or derisive remarks ("You stupid little brat!"), locking a child in a closet as a form of punishment, or threatening physical or sexual abuse, such as a father taking his children to a gun store to buy a gun which he said he would use to kill their mother. Twenty-eight percent of children who are abused are emotionally abused.

Neglect

- *Physical neglect:* Involves a failure to provide for a child's physical or medical needs or to provide adequate supervision. Examples might include failure to provide treatment for a medical condition, driving while intoxicated, leaving a child unattended in a car, or not attending to obvious hazards around the home. This type of neglect has more than tripled over the past two decades.
- *Educational neglect:* Involves permitting truancy (approximately 5 days/month), not enrolling a child in school, or keeping a child home to care for other siblings. This is the most common form of neglect.
- *Emotional neglect:* This differs from emotional abuse in that this is a passive emotional rejection of the child, taking the form of giving little or no emotional support, attention, or affection. Although the least common form of neglect, it has also risen substantially in the past two decades.

Source: Sedlak & Broadhurst (1996).

---

tality when other variables were controlled for. When children were classified according to these three variables, those identified as high-risk had an injury mortality rate more than 15 times greater than that of low-risk children. If all children had the same risk of injury as the low-risk children, more than 75% of deaths from injury would not have occurred (Scholer, Mitchel, & Ray, 1997).

Most serious accidents are preventable. Thus, using smoke detectors and child car seats, lowering the thermostat on the water heater, not putting infants in walkers, and instituting home visitation programs for young or poorly educated mothers can all substantially reduce injuries to young children.

Maltreatment

Not all injuries to children are accidental. **Maltreatment** refers to instances of harm to children that are nonaccidental and avoidable, whether from abuse or neglect. Abuse can be physical, sexual, or emotional in nature and often involves some combination of these. Similarly, neglect is categorized as a failure to provide for

maltreatment Nonaccidental and avoidable harm done to children, whether from abuse or neglect.

the child's physical, educational, or emotional needs. Box 7.3 distinguishes among these types of maltreatment.

Well over a million children are maltreated in the United States each year, somewhat over half of these through neglect and just under half through abuse. When one also includes children who are *endangered,* for whom there is no proof of harm but reason to believe they are in danger, the number of children affected by maltreatment is closer to 3 million (Sedlak & Broadhurst, 1996; U.S. Dept. of Health and Human Services, 1998). How do we turn statistics such as these into meaningful figures? An estimate of approximately 3 million children translates, when counting by hundreds, into 4 children out of every 100, or 1 child in 25, an easier figure to put a face to and a figure where 1 becomes a very large number indeed.

How believable are figures such as these? Is maltreatment this common a problem? A national sample of over 3,000 families surveyed by phone suggests that it is. Parents were asked how they resolved family conflicts when these arose and were asked specifically whether acts such as hitting a child with an object, kicking, biting, burning, or using a gun or a knife had occurred during the course of the conflict. By parents' own reports, 110 children per 1,000 had experienced one or more of these forms of violence (Straus & Gelles, 1986). Given that this survey was conducted over a decade ago and that the frequency of maltreatment has increased over the past two decades (U.S. Dept. of Health and Human Services, 1998), these figures are not likely to overestimate the problem.

The toll of abuse extends beyond the immediate effects of the violence, permeating children's lives with a quiet dread. Scott Peck (1995) describes this dread, as a young boy, living with an abusive stepfather in *All American Boy:*

> Somewhere in this night, it is all still happening.
>
> We sit together on the grass, we three. My mother, her dancer's legs drawn up tightly against her chest, her face looking old in the glow of our block's lonely street lamp.
>
> Quiet. She is quietly afraid, quietly listening for sounds from the porch where he sits—her husband, my stepfather. I can see the red tip of his cigarette, flaring on cue every two minutes as he inhales, flaring and sending illuminated little butterflies twitching to the floor. He sits in darkness, still and silent in his rocking chair, like some Mayan king, while his wife and children huddle closely together on the grass of the front lawn. Floridian night breezes, soaked in the smell of gardenias, lap around our heads and necks, chilling.
>
> He will dictate this night to us; we wait for his decree.
>
> When he stands, we scatter like frightened sparrows, Mother grabbing each of us by a wrist and moving out toward the sidewalk.
>
> "Get ready," she hisses. (p. 9) ◄

Most children who experience maltreatment (74%) are maltreated by their parents. Another 13.6% are maltreated by another adult in the home, such as a stepparent or a foster parent. The type of maltreatment children are likely to experience differs as a function of the perpetrator. Mothers, or some other female caretaker, are responsible for 87% of neglect. In contrast, all forms of abuse are more likely to be committed by a male: 89% for sexual abuse, 63% for emotional abuse, and 58% for physical abuse (Sedlak & Broadhurst, 1996).

Rather than assuming that a single factor, such as family income level or characteristics of the child or the parent, is responsible for maltreatment, taking an approach that views contributing factors at many levels is more reasonable (Bronfenbrenner, 1979). These factors could either predispose toward or protect a child from maltreatment. Predisposing factors at the level of the microsystem might take the form of a parent's loss of a job, whereas at the level of the macrosystem, predisposing factors may be the acceptance of violence in society or media portrayal of conflict resolution. Conversely, protective factors at the level of the microsystem might consist of a family income sufficient to buffer stresses, and at the level of the macrosystem they might take the form of cultural beliefs about the innocence of children and legal protections against abuse.

Both risk and protective factors can be either enduring or transient. *Enduring risk factors* represent relatively permanent conditions, such as a parent's inability to tolerate stress. In contrast, *transient risk factors* are short-term challenges, such as the loss of a job, an illness, or a child's entering a difficult developmental period. Similarly, *enduring protective factors* might be the parent's own history of good parenting as a child or the existence of other supportive relationships within the family. *Transient protective factors* buffering a child from maltreatment might be improvement in conditions at work or a new neighbor with a child the same age to play with (Cicchetti & Lynch, 1995).

What can lead parents to maltreat their children? Is it lack of love? Can one look to mental illness as an explanation? Or to catastrophic life circumstance? No simple answers are to be found. Most of these parents love their children and experience genuine remorse for what they do. Similarly, relatively few would be diagnosed as suffering from a mental illness. Nor could one predict maltreatment simply by knowing their life circumstances. In fact, research on maltreatment has failed to identify any single factor that necessarily leads to maltreatment (Cicchetti & Lynch, 1995). Most maltreating parents in many ways are not that different from average parents.

Even so, some differences have been found. One important difference concerns the way they respond under stress. Parents who maltreat their children appear to experience more difficulty coping with stress than do other parents. Not only are they likely to find the normal stresses of life more aversive than are other individuals, but they also tend to overreact when they are stressed, experiencing more difficulty controlling their impulses. In addition, parents who maltreat their children are more likely to interpret events as being outside their control and to react angrily and defensively than are other parents (Brunquell, Crichton, & Egeland, 1981). Thus, although parents who maltreat their children may behave in ways that are similar to the ways other parents behave under most circumstances, they are likely to respond differently when stressed.

Maltreating parents also appear to differ in what might be termed their worldview. They are less likely to have a positive outlook on life, seeing the world instead as a hostile place and life as a struggle, with them on the defensive. This defensive attitude can extend to their interactions with their children, in which they are more likely than are other parents to interpret their children's behavior as intentionally disobedient or otherwise "aimed" at them. A tired toddler's tearful outburst, for instance, is apt to be seen as an expression of anger directed at them rather than as distress experienced by the child. With their own feelings so much in the foreground, it also becomes easy for parent-child relationships to undergo a reversal in which the child is expected to be responsive to their feelings and meet their needs. This reversal, in which the child is *parentified,* places the burden for caring for the parents' needs on the children. In fact, maltreated children frequently are more nurturing than are their parents (Cicchetti & Lynch, 1995; Macfie et al., 1999).

Maltreating parents also tend to hold inappropriate expectations concerning what children of different ages are capable of. These unrealistic expectations can fuel their tendency to perceive their children's behavior as willfully disobedient rather than as normal behaviors for children of that age. Thus, a preschooler who continues to toot on a toy horn after being told to be quiet is likely to be seen as defiant rather than as having difficulty inhibiting an ongoing behavior to a verbal command. Similarly, unrealistic expectations that very young children be able to stay dry through the night, avoid accidents during the day, understand complicated instructions, or keep even younger siblings out of trouble can lead to children being seen as irresponsible or careless and deserving of punishment.

Maltreating parents differ as well from average parents in the types of discipline they are likely to use, being less likely to use effective parenting styles. They are more likely instead to punish, threaten, and otherwise use coercive measures with their children, and they are less likely to use reasoning. They are also less consistent in their discipline and less warm and affectionate in general in their relationships (Cicchetti & Lynch, 1995).

Maltreating parents are not only able to bring fewer personal resources to bear when facing stressful life events, but they also have fewer interpersonal resources on which they can rely. Perhaps the most important of these for most parents is their relationship with their spouse. These relationships are less satisfying for maltreating parents. Partners of maltreating parents have been found to be less supportive and warm than those of comparison parents, as well as more aggressive (Cicchetti & Lynch, 1995; Howes & Cicchetti, 1993). In general, relationships within the home, whether these be with spouse or children, are less positive and warm than in other homes.

None of these characteristics, in themselves, can be regarded as responsible for maltreatment. Maltreatment typically results from a combination of conditions rather than a single factor. Thus, a parent who has difficulty coping with stress may still be able to function adequately unless something untoward happens. The loss of a job, however, or a child entering a "difficult" developmental stage may be enough to precipitate maltreatment. One such condition that places families under significant stress is poverty. Although maltreatment is by no means limited to low-income families, it is unusually high among such families. Life below the poverty line can involve cascading stress on an almost daily basis. A case in point might involve something as simple as an appliance, such as a refrigerator, breaking down and needing repair. But when money is short, food that has spoiled may be difficult to replace. To repair the appliance would leave nothing for groceries; however, without a refrigerator, frequent trips to the market become necessary, taxing the reserves of an already overtaxed parent. Coupled with inadequate transportation and perhaps the need to take along cranky, hungry children, an event that might have been an ordinary stressor in another family can precipitate maltreatment in an impoverished one.

We have talked so far about characteristics of parents that are associated with maltreatment, but are there characteristics of children as well that affect the likelihood of maltreatment? That is, are some children more likely to be maltreated than others? We need to be very clear that in asking such a question we are not suggesting that children who are maltreated are in any way responsible for the treatment they receive. Rather, to ask about characteristics of children who are maltreated is to look for factors that are associated with an increased risk of abuse when coupled with other risk factors. When we do so, we find a number of such characteristics. Plainly put, children who present special difficulties to parents are more likely to be maltreated than are those who do not. These difficulties can take a number of forms.

Children who are in poor health are more likely to be maltreated. Thus children who because of discomfort or developmental lags are fussy, cry a lot, are difficult to soothe, or require special attention are more likely to be maltreated. Not

Q How might poverty increase the likelihood of a child being maltreated?

only are maltreating parents more easily stressed under such conditions, but these parents are also more attuned to their own needs than they are to those of their children, and they expect their children as well to be responsive to these parental needs. When children continue to fuss, maltreating parents can react angrily and defensively. Consider, as an example, a mother who attempts to soothe her crying infant, first by offering a bottle that is spurned with a wail and then by placing the infant on her shoulder, only to have the baby stiffen and cry even harder. Even though very little is expected of infants by way of "appropriate" behavior, most parents expect their infants to be soothed when they are held, their bodies relaxing as they tuck their heads into the crook of one's shoulder. Infants who continue to cry can be perceived as rejecting by maltreating parents. It is all too easy for such parents to lash out in anger. But a parental education program might give this mother permission to let her child cry after she has checked on its well-being and attempted to soothe the infant, enabling her to close the door on a potentially abusive situation and have a much needed cup of tea or a supportive chat with a neighbor.

Children are also at greater risk for abuse when their temperaments or personalities are a poor match with those of their parents. That is, it's not so much the energy level of the child per se that can become problematic, but the degree to which this complements the needs and expectations of the parent (see Chapter 6 for a discussion of upper-limit and lower-limit controls). An active child might ideally match the temperament of one parent but be perceived as unduly demanding by another. Additionally, children whose temperaments fall outside the range of most children, being either hyperactive or, at the other extreme, lethargic, are also at greater risk for some forms of maltreatment.

All forms of maltreatment are more likely among children from lower-income families. Comparing just two income levels, families earning $30,000 or more a year and those earning less than $15,000, children from the latter are more than 22 times as likely to be maltreated. They are also nearly 14 times as likely to be harmed by some form of abuse and more than 44 times as likely to be neglected (Sedlak & Broadhurst, 1996).

One might ask whether these differences in maltreatment are actual or are merely due to differences in reporting. It could be argued, for instance, that maltreatment is simply more visible when families must interface with social workers and public health agencies. This argument is unlikely, however, since agencies such as these are responsible for relatively few (12%) of the reported cases of maltreatment, whereas schools are responsible for most instances of detection (59%), with the consequence that most maltreated children are identified by persons who come into contact with children from all income levels. Furthermore, to assume that differences are due to a failure to report maltreatment among families with incomes of greater than $15,000 a year is to assume that there are vast numbers of children as yet unidentified who are being maltreated (Sedlak & Broadhurst, 1996). Rather, the myriad factors that are associated with poverty, such as fewer social support systems, poorer neighborhoods, fewer educational and occupational opportunities, higher incidence of crime and of substance abuse, are likely contributors to maltreatment (Sedlak & Broadhurst, 1996).

Each of the factors listed can pose either an enduring or a transient risk, raising the level of stress within a family or in other ways reducing the ability to cope. We see, for instance, that maltreatment is also more likely in single-parent households. This is not to say that the custodial parent is necessarily the abusive one, but it does suggest there are additional responsibilities and stresses in single-parent families and a greater likelihood that these will tax or exceed the personal resources of the parent. Similarly, maltreatment is also more likely in larger families, with four or more children, than in those with two to three children or with a single child, again suggesting the importance of stress and reduced family resources in contributing to maltreatment (Sedlak & Broadhurst, 1996).

The overall incidence of maltreatment has risen steadily over the last two decades. The risk of a child suffering some form of maltreatment was more than 2⅓ times greater in 1993 than it was in 1980, and it continues to increase (U.S. Dept. of Health and Human Services, 1998). Furthermore, the increase is greatest for those seriously injured and those suffering emotional abuse (Sedlak & Broadhurst, 1996).

How are we to interpret this increase? Does it reflect an increase in the actual numbers of children who are maltreated or, once again, does it simply mean that professionals in the community are better able to recognize maltreatment when they see it? The answer this time is, most likely, both. The very fact that there has been an increase in the number of children seriously injured argues strongly for the former. Injuries such as these would be difficult *not* to notice. These cases do not, in other words, require a heightened awareness of maltreatment in order to receive attention, and the number of them has quadrupled since 1986 (Sedlak & Broadhurst, 1996). It also seems likely that professionals are better able to recognize abuse than previously. Support for this can be found in the increase in the number of children perceived as endangered—that is, children *without* any visible signs of maltreatment but recognized as potential victims nonetheless. Box 7.4 describes cues to possible abuse.

Just as no single factor can predict the occurrence of maltreatment, no single factor can predict its effects on a child. In attempting to assess these effects, one must consider not only the type of maltreatment but also its severity and how frequently it occurred, as well as the relationship of the perpetrator to the child and the point in development at which the maltreatment occurred (Cicchetti & Lynch, 1995). Protective factors, such as the personal strengths and coping strategies of the child or the general healthiness of relationships within the family must also be entered into the equation (Finkelhor, 1990).

What are the effects of maltreatment on children? Its effects are more far-reaching than any visible injuries a child may have suffered, serious as these frequently are. Physically, these effects can take the form of specific injuries or a general failure to thrive. Behaviorally, maltreatment can result in fearfulness, nightmares, poor peer relations, and aggressive play with other children. Most children, however, do not become delinquent as youths or violent as adults. Similarly, with respect specifically to children who have been physically abused, most do not perpetuate the cycle of abuse when they become parents themselves, although figures are somewhat higher than for those who have not been abused (Cicchetti & Lynch, 1995).

Children who are maltreated also often have difficulty in school, with problems paying attention and concentrating. However, perhaps no single effect of maltreatment is more significant than its potential for affecting a child's trust. Erikson (1968) believed trust to include not only the child's awareness of living in a stable world in which one's needs will be met, but also the awareness that one is worthy of having one's needs met. The myriad effects of maltreatment, influencing as it does everything from the way children play with their peers and their performance in school to the development of language, suggest that maltreatment touches the very core of a child's sense of self (Cicchetti & Lynch, 1995).

The effects of sexual abuse, both the immediate and long-term, are especially marked. Among the more common immediate effects are fearfulness, problems in sleeping, distractedness, depression, anger, and sexually inappropriate behavior.

Box 7.4 *Cues to Possible Abuse*

When is an injury likely to have resulted from abuse, rather than accidental causes? Angelo Giardino, Cindy Christian, and Eileen Giardino offer the following as cues:

- *Nonplausible injuries:* These are injuries that are not likely given the events that are mentioned as happening. Examples might be "minor" accidents that result in extensive injuries, such as internal injuries from falling off a bike. Conversely, other types of accidents, such as falling down stairs or out of bed, do not typically result in extensive harm even though they appear to be major. For instance, one study of 363 children treated in a pediatric emergency department after falling down a stairway found that most needed to be treated only for scrapes and bruises and that none required extensive treatment. Such falls are unlikely to result in fractured bones or abdominal injuries (Joffe & Ludwig, 1988).

- *Peculiar injuries:* This class of injuries includes such things as pattern burns, as would come from a cigarette lighter, "stocking" burns resulting from holding a child's feet in hot water, or patterned welts suggesting the use of a stick or switch for beating.

- *"Magical" injuries:* These are injuries for which the parent has no knowledge of cause; that is, the parent was not present, did not see/hear anything, etc. Of course, many times children do hurt themselves when a caregiver is not present as a witness. However, abuse becomes increasingly suspect as the age of the child decreases. For the first 6 months, infants simply are not capable of inflicting serious injury on themselves. With toddlers and preschoolers, who can run into another room or outside by themselves, this is more likely.

- *Self-inflicted injuries:* The child is reported to have been responsible for its own injuries, but because of the nature of the injuries, this explanation doesn't make sense given the developmental level of the child. Most injuries that children bring about by themselves are minor, although serious ones are certainly possible, such as a toddler pulling a pot from the stove over on itself. Similarly, although fights between siblings and peers are common, few result in serious or multiple injuries.

- *Delay in getting treatment:* Abuse is more likely when caregivers do not immediately bring the child in for treatment. Frequently, following abuse, they will wait until the injuries are partially healed or will try to treat these themselves; for example, treatment may be sought only when burns that have failed to heal have become infected. Other reasons for delay can reflect real obstacles in the parent's life, such as low income, lack of transportation, no one to care for other siblings, or an inability to get off work.

Source: Giardino, Christian, & Giardino (1997).

Long-term effects frequently persist into adulthood and include anxiety, anger, depression, lowered self-esteem, self-destructive behaviors, substance abuse, and sexual problems (Finkelhor, 1990). Children of either sex respond to sexual abuse in similar ways, with the exception that girls are somewhat more likely to be depressed and boys to be more aggressive (Finkelhor, 1990; Swanston, Tebbutt, O'Toole, & Oates, 1997).

Children draw strength from their communities, such as these children attending church.

Once the sexual abuse terminates, children typically begin a process of recovery in which symptoms can be seen to lessen. The most obvious improvements, usually occurring within the first year to a year and a half, involve a lessening of fearfulness and fewer sleeping problems, although a sizable number of children show a worsening of symptoms (Gomes-Schwartz, Horowitz, & Cardarelli, 1990). A recent follow-up of sexually abused children found the effects of abuse to be strikingly present 5 years later. Children who had been sexually abused showed more disturbed behavior, had lower self-esteem, and were more depressed and anxious than were a nonabused comparison group of children (Swanston et al., 1997). Findings such as these underscore the importance of state and federal commitments to the prevention of abuse and care of children who have been abused.

Wellness and Resiliency: With a Little Help from Their Friends

Children do not grow up by themselves. Development unfolds in the multiple contexts of their lives, in families and neighborhoods, day care settings and schools, and churches and synagogues. Children draw their strength from these surroundings, just as they do from the food they eat and the medical attention they receive. **Social capital** refers to the personal relationships that contribute to resiliency in children, both within the family and in the community. These relationships promote children's development not only through the love they provide them but also through the expectations and obligations to which others hold them (Coleman, 1988).

How effective are these reserves of strength in the face of various risk factors? Desmond Runyon and his associates (1998) followed a large group of preschoolers over time, all of them sharing certain factors that placed them at risk for abuse or neglect. Some of these children were eventually reported for maltreatment; however, others were not. These investigators compared the two groups of children, those who fared well with those who did not, first matching them in terms of their sex, socioeconomic status, and ethnicity, so that they differed simply in terms of their social capital. The measures of social capital used were (1) two parents, or parent figures, in the home, (2) the mother's sense of personal support, such as having someone to talk with, (3) no more than two children in the home, (4) a supportive neighborhood, such as neighbors who could be counted on to look out for each other, and (5) a mother who attended church at least several times a month.

Children who fared well were found to have greater reserves of social capital on which they could rely. "Doing well," in other words, was not a function of demographic variables such as ethnicity, gender, or maternal education. Instead, variables indicative of social capital, or relationship variables, predicted how well children were likely to fare. In fact, the greater the number of social capital indicators that were present in a child's life, the greater the odds of that child doing well. The three indicators that were found to be of greatest importance were church affiliation, mothers' perceptions of personal support, and support from the neighborhood. Thus, just as the accumulation of risk factors increases the likelihood of developmental problems, so does the accumulation of social capital indicators increase the likelihood of doing well (Runyon et al., 1998).

Do some children have personal attributes that enable them to "bankroll" more social capital than others, establishing the relationships and receiving the affirmation from others that contribute to their personal reserves of strength? Children who fare well, even in the face of adversity, have been found to have a number of characteristics in common (Cohler, Stott, & Musick, 1995). These children

social capital The relationships, both within the family and the community, that contribute to resiliency in children.

One of the most important things contributing to a child's resiliency is the presence of an adult who cares about that child.

tend, as a group, to be good with people. As a consequence, people enjoy being around them. These children tend to be intelligent, personable, and positive in their approach to life, an attitude that includes both good self-esteem and a sense of humor. They also tend to be self-reliant. Rather than sitting around feeling blue, for instance, they will find something to do. Other people usually feel good about themselves just by being around these children. Perhaps this is because these children are sensitive to those they are with and responsive to them, listening to what they say, being attentive to their feelings, and caring for them. These dimensions of personal interaction are the very same ones that have been found to be important in parents as well (Ainsworth & Bell, 1969).

Attributes of children's families also contribute to resiliency and faring well in the face of adversity. Perhaps the most important of these is the presence of a single adult who cares about that child and, in Bronfenbrenner's (1990) words, finds the child "somehow special, especially wonderful, and especially precious" (p. 31). This adult need not be the child's parent. A grandparent, aunt or uncle, or sibling can also provide this caring presence in a child's life. What *is* important is the continuity of the child's relationship with this person (Cohler, Stott, & Musick, 1995; Kaufman, Grunebaum, Cohler, & Gamer, 1979; Musick, Stott, Spencer, Goldman, & Cohler, 1987).

Characteristics of children's neighborhoods also contribute to their reserves of personal strength. Attending schools with supportive classroom environments and, once again, the concern of even just one teacher for the child's welfare; living in a neighborhood where the streets are safe; and the absence (or minimal presence) of conditions related to poverty, such as gangs and substance abuse, are all important (Cohler et al., 1995).

These findings are consistent with those of other research that finds that the type of neighborhood children live in can exert a strong influence, especially on children from high-risk families (Garbarino & Sherman, 1980). What distinguishes one type of neighborhood from another? The most important differences do not necessarily go hand in hand with income level. For instance, neighborhoods that might otherwise be classified as "poor" nonetheless differ among themselves in

Q What personal attributes of children are likely to affect how well they fare when risk factors are present in their lives?

important ways. Perhaps the most important of these differences is in terms of the network of supporting relationships which they provide to those who make them up. Neighborhoods with a higher percentage of families that could be said to be functioning well are characterized by what one might call "a sense of community." Individuals living in these neighborhoods have an investment in where they live and who they live with. They keep up their property, talk to their neighbors, watch out for each other, and belong to various community groups and organizations. This investment is only loosely tied to income level (Coulton, Korbin & Su, 1999; Korbin & Coulton, 1995).

Income becomes increasingly important, however, as families function closer to the poverty level. And roughly 20% of children in the United States live in poverty, a figure that is twice as high as that for most other industrialized nations. Additionally, the percentage of children living in poverty is disproportionately high for African American and Hispanic children. The experience of poverty itself is also likely to differ for White than for many ethnic minority children, for whom it is more likely to be chronically present and who are more likely to live in neighborhoods with fewer supports and greater risks (Huston, McLoyd, & Coll, 1994).

Although official definitions of poverty are based on income, poverty should not be confused with low income or low socioeconomic status. Poverty, in fact, does not result from a single condition, such as how much money a parent makes, but varies along a number of dimensions (Huston, McLoyd, & Coll, 1994). Thus, a mother and child could live for several years on a poverty-level income in a low-income neighborhood while the mother finishes her education, making ends meet by buying clothes, furniture, and toys at thrift stores, yet not be considered poor by other socioeconomic status indicators, such as the parent's educational level or occupational objective. Furthermore, such a child may even experience an enriched environment, in terms of indices such as the number of books in the home, conversational patterns, exposure to various cultural events (music, museums), and attendance at a university-sponsored day care. Home environments that are supportive and stable, irrespective of income level, contribute to healthy development (Bradley et al., 1994).

Two important dimensions defining the experience of poverty are the duration of the poverty and the surrounding context (Huston, McLoyd, & Coll, 1994). The longer children live below the poverty level, for instance, the more the quality of their home life decreases (Garrett, Ng'andu, & Ferron, 1994). The neighborhoods in which children live also contribute significantly to their experience of poverty or well-being. Neighborhoods differ not only in immediately obvious ways, such as the exteriors of their homes or buildings, but also in the quality and safety of recreational areas, access to and quality of health care facilities, the availability of libraries, the safety of being on the street, and the sense of order to life given by living in a neighborhood that is well tended and cared for, irrespective of the size of the homes, versus one that is not. These are not simply physical properties of neighborhoods, but affect the ways in which people interact with each other. Thus, having a safe and inviting park near one's home means that neighbors are likely to use it and, in the process, get to know each other, establish friendships, perhaps work out cooperative day care arrangements, arrange to shop for each other, organize a car pool, and so on.

Even when one is looking for differences in neighborhoods, they are not always obvious. Thus, day care facilities attended by high-income children have been found to provide better quality care than those attended by low-income children. The difference, however, is subtle, and not likely to be caught by a simple count of the better known indices of quality, such as the ratio of caregivers to children. Comparisons of day care centers have found this ratio to be similar across income levels. Only when the interactions between the caregivers and the children were observed did differences emerge, showing that caregivers in low-income neighborhoods were less sensitive and harsher with the children (Phillips, Voran, Kisker, Howes, & Whitebook, 1994).

Further, children's sense of well-being depends on how parents communicate their own concerns about the family's welfare. Edgar Bledsoe (1996) writes of his experiences as a youth when his family was going through hard times. After he was laid off from his job, his mother, the only other person bringing in any money, became ill and could not work. When bills could not be paid, first one utility and then the next was cut off until finally the family was reduced to eating vegetables from their garden cooked over a fire in the backyard. Then, as he describes it,

> One day my younger sister came skipping home from school saying, "We're supposed to bring something to school tomorrow to give to the poor."
>
> Mother started to blurt out, "I don't know of anyone who is any poorer than we are," when her mother, who was living with us at the time, shushed her with a hand on her arm and a frown.
>
> "Eva," she said, "if you give that child the idea that she is 'poor folks' at her age, she will be 'poor folks' for the rest of her life. There is one jar of that home-made jelly left. She can take that."
>
> Grandmother found some tissue paper and a little bit of pink ribbon with which she wrapped our last jar of jelly, and Sis tripped off to school the next day proudly carrying her "gift to the poor." After that, if there ever was a problem in the community, she just naturally assumed that she was supposed to be part of the solution. ◄

Summary

Developmental Profiles

Control over both small- and large-muscle movements continues to develop through the preschool years, enabling children to work at tasks requiring fine motor coordination, such as puzzles and coloring, and those involving larger movements, such as running, skipping, or riding a bike. However, preschoolers continue to be impulsive and to have difficulty inhibiting their behavior in response to instructions.

Physical Growth

Preschoolers gain 2 to 3 inches in height a year and add 3 to 5 pounds. Growth reflects the cephalocaudal trend, with the neck and torso first lengthening, followed by the legs. Bone growth is rapid in early childhood, as is muscular development, contributing to increases in body size and strength. Physical differences between boys and girls remain insignificant.

Behavioral Consequences of Physical Development

Preschoolers are learning to regulate their movements, in terms of both physical coordination and impulse control. They also become increasingly better with age at self-help routines such as dressing and feeding themselves. By 3, most can stay dry through the day and are beginning to sleep dry through the night. Mature bladder control becomes possible at about 4½, though many children have occasional accidents for the next several years. Sleep patterns also change during the preschool years, from a pattern that starts with REM sleep and moves to NREM sleep to sleep beginning in the NREM state and being punctuated with episodes of REM sleep. As preschoolers increase in size and become better coordinated, more is expected of them, both in terms of physical coordination and impulse control.

Brain Maturation

The brain develops faster during early childhood than does any other part of the body, reaching 90% of its adult size before the age of 6. The brain increases both in volume and in the progressive myelination of neural fibers. Resulting increases in interneural communication contribute to a remodeling of the brain through the selective elimination of neuronal connections that are not frequently stimulated. Cortical activity undergoes cycles of change, involving the establishment of connections between the frontal lobes and other cortical areas, contributing to a greater ability to monitor and regulate activity.

Motor Development

Both gross motor skills, which involve large-muscle movements, and fine motor skills, which involve precise movements controlled by small muscles, improve with age. With respect to fine motor skills, improvements can be seen in in-hand manipulation and bimanual coordination. Few sex differences in motor skills are evident during the preschool years.

Psychological Implications of Physical Development

Children develop a sense of themselves in the preschool years. New skills contribute to a sense of mastery and equip them to assume a more active role in the daily routines of their lives. Being allowed to do some things on their own contributes to feelings of accomplishment and self-worth. Just as new physical skills expand children's outer world, imagination expands their inner one, often leading them to confuse feelings with fantasy.

Impulse Control

Verbal control over behavior develops gradually. Before the age of 5, children have difficulty inhibiting an ongoing behavior when instructed to. Parents can help children through the use of consistent routines, providing consequences for behavior, in addition to stating rules, and using external restraints. The ability to delay gratification increases with age, facilitated by the development of strategies.

Developing Restraints: How Parents Can Help

Parents can help children develop restraint by structuring situations, regulating children's activities and by being controlled themselves. Structuring situations means using predictable routines to provide a structure to children's experience that is not provided from within. Regulating activities means limiting alternatives to manageable choices and then letting children decide among these. Being controlled means being calm, firm, and self-controlled.

Health and Well-Being

Rapid skeletal and muscular development and continuing brain maturation all require adequate nutrition. However, because rate of growth slows in early childhood, preschoolers need to eat proportionately less and may have a diminished appetite. Both protein deficiency and iron-deficiency anemia are relatively common. Supplemental food programs have been found to be effective in counteracting the effects of specific deficiencies as well as of malnutrition more generally. In the United States, most children's diets fail to meet established national guidelines. Recommended dietary objectives include eating more complex carbohydrates, foods high in fiber, and fruits and vegetables, as well as increasing intake of calcium and reducing intake of fat.

Overweight

The percentage of children in the United States who are overweight has substantially increased. Children are less active physically, spending more time in sedentary recreational activities than in the past. Overweight children also are more likely to have diets that are high in fat and low in complex carbohydrates.

Establishing Healthy Patterns

One of the most important factors affecting children's food choices is the accessibility of various foods. Healthier eating patterns can be established by offering vegetables and fruits as snacks instead of sweets or crackers, replacing fast-food meals with those containing less fat, using low-fat milk instead of whole milk, and limiting high-calorie drinks. Modeling is also an important influence in determining food preferences, and children's eating patterns are likely to be influenced by those of their parents. Children are also responsive to internal cues such as the energy content of foods.

Illnesses, Injuries, and Accidents

Low-income and minority children are more likely to be affected by common illnesses and less likely to receive the medical care they need than are middle-income children. Recommended steps for reducing barriers to health care among these children include increasing the number of community health centers, training health care providers willing to practice in low-income neighborhoods, improving the availability of transportation, and extending office hours to meet the needs of working single parents.

Death due to accidental injury is 4 times more common than the next most common cause among preschoolers. The use of child-restraint devices such as seat belts and car seats has significantly reduced fatal injuries. Accidental injuries could be further reduced by instituting home visitation programs for young or poorly educated mothers.

Maltreatment

Maltreatment refers to instances of harm to children that are nonaccidental and avoidable; it includes both abuse and neglect. Abuse can be physical, sexual, or emotional and often involves some combination of these. Neglect refers to a failure to provide for a child's physical, educational, or emotional needs. Over a million children in the United States are maltreated each year, most of these by their parents. Maltreating parents are more likely than other parents to experience difficulty coping with stress, to have difficulty controlling their impulses, to interpret their children's behavior as intentionally disobedient, to hold inappropriate expectations for their children's behavior, to use less effective modes of discipline, and to have fewer personal resources. The likelihood of maltreatment increases with children who require special attention or are exceedingly active or lethargic. Maltreatment has cognitive and emotional effects as well as physical ones, leading to difficulties in school and in relationships with peers.

Wellness and Resiliency

A number of factors contribute to resiliency in children. The presence of stable, caring relationships within the family and in the community are important. Characteristics of the children themselves, such as good social skills, intelligence, self-reliance, and having a positive outlook on life, also contribute. Attributes of the community, such as supportive classroom environments, safe streets, and the minimal presence of conditions related to poverty, are also important. Two important dimensions defining the experience of poverty are the length of time a child's family income is below the poverty level and the stability and orderliness of the neighborhood in which the child lives.

Key Terms

bimanual coordination (p. 262)
hand dominance (p. 262)
hand preference (p. 262)

in-hand manipulation (p. 259)
initiative (p. 263)
maltreatment (p. 281)

overweight (p. 274)
social capital (p. 288)

chaptereight

Early Childhood
Cognitive Development

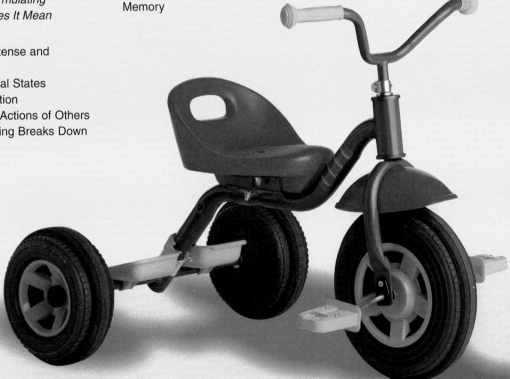

Margery, age 3, dimpled and adorable, carefully poured tea into a cup, giving a satisfied sigh after doing so, for she had spilled not a drop, and handed it to the bear on her right. Less successful with the second cup, she murmured a soft "Ohhh," as she had so often heard her mother do, and wiped the imaginary spill with her fingers—for there was no tea in the pot—before handing the cup to the one-eyed doll on her left. Passing the cookies, she opened the conversation by remarking that Grandma was coming to visit today.

A voice from the other room, that of her mother, called out that it was time for a bath. Margery protested that her favorite television show hadn't come on yet, so it couldn't be time for a bath. Appearing at the door with a towel and clean clothes, her mother said they had to hurry in order to meet Grandma at the train station. Margery, still busy with tea, replied that it would be dark by then—and Grandma wouldn't see if she were dirty or not.

Frequently, we are so caught by the imaginary creatures that populate the world of preschoolers that we fail to notice the neatness of their logic. Margery's logic is impeccable. She reasons that it can't be time for a bath since she has not yet seen her favorite show, the one that always precedes taking a bath. Or, in the words of a logician, "If A, then B; and if not A, then not B." Since she has not seen her show, in other words, it can't be time for her bath. Further, she notes that by the time she has taken a bath and they have driven to the station, it will be too dark for her grandmother to see anything clearly.

This mix of fantasy and logic is one of the most striking characteristics of preschoolers' thought, an aspect of their development that we will explore more closely in this chapter. We will look at what young children understand, as well as what they don't, and at how this understanding develops. Along the way, we will consider some of the practical implications of cognitive development, such as how to answer their questions, how much they can be expected to remember, and just what they will understand.

Piaget's Stage of Preoperational Thought

Cognitive development, for Piaget, is a gradual freeing of thought from experience, enabling children to imagine the fanciful as well as consider the actual. Preschoolers' thought illustrates this new freedom. Their understanding of their world is imaginative and playful, as well as serious and sensible, a construction of fantasy and fact pieced together from everyday experiences. Like artisans who have been given a mix of traditional and unusual materials to work with, the resulting product at times gives a curious twist to an otherwise familiar model of the world we live in.

Piaget believed these characteristics to result from the emergence of **preoperational** thought, a way of thinking that is qualitatively different from the sensorimotor thought of infancy. The underlying competence that develops and is presumed responsible for the emergence of preoperational thought is the ability to use symbols to represent experience. As infants become able to hold objects in mind, representing them symbolically, they can differentiate the "existence" of the object from their "experience" of it. With symbolic representation, the external world of objects emerges from the inner world of experience, and the sensorimotor stage of infancy comes to an end (Piaget, 1952).

Thus, the most significant aspect of preschoolers' thought for Piaget was their use of symbols, something that is evident both in their play and in their approach

preoperational thought Piaget's second stage of intellectual development, thought to characterize toddlerhood and early childhood, during which experience is represented symbolically.

to everyday problems. Piaget believed their use of symbols, however, not only freed but also constrained their vision of the world. At this point, we will look more closely at this aspect of preschoolers' thought.

Symbolic and Imaginative Play

Preschoolers chatter to themselves when alone, talk to their stuffed animals, tell their troubles to their pets, assume the identities of their action figures, and spend hours in make-believe play, enacting fantastic adventures as well as the more familiar routines of their lives. In all of this, they are representing their world symbolically, through language, imagination, fantasy, and playful pretense.

Vivian Paley (1997), a teacher at a nursery school maintained by the University of Chicago, tape-recorded children's conversations for a year, enabling her to capture their dialogue as they engaged in imaginative play. Typical of these conversations is that of Mollie, a 3-year-old. Paley describes Mollie's conversation as follows:

> Today, for example, she puts "Mushroom in the Rain," "The Three Pigs," and "Hansel and Gretel" into a Wonderwoman story. In the original "Mushroom in the Rain," a butterfly, a mouse, and a sparrow are drenched in a heavy downpour, then sheltered under a mushroom by a kindly ant. A frightened rabbit and a hungry fox also enter the story, but Mollie gives star billing to the wet butterfly.
>
> "I want to be the wet butterfly and Wonderwoman. First he goes under the mushroom. Now we got to do the big, bad wolf and the three pigs and the fox is going to catch the butterfly and put it in the cage, that one from Hansel. Then Wonderwoman comes. Then I open the cage and the wet butterfly goes under the mushroom because the ant says to come in."
>
> How has Mollie learned to integrate these bits and pieces into a sensible whole? No one else offers Christopher [another child at the nursery school] blackberries and milk if he is good or unites the big, bad wolf with a fox to make trouble for a butterfly. However, it is the sort of storytelling that is heard every day during play: Cinderella and Darth Vader put the baby to bed while Superman serves tea and saves the baby from the witch just as Daddy comes home from work and sits down to eat a birthday cake. (pp. 139–140) ◄

Children, of course, engage in symbolic play well before they reach the preschool years (Bornstein, Haynes, O'Reilly, & Painter, 1996). But their earlier play differs in at least three important respects from the symbolic play of preschoolers. It involves simpler sequences of activities, is dependent more on the characteristics of the objects with which they are playing, and is not well coordinated with the play of other children (Singer & Singer, 1990).

With respect to the first of these differences, for instance, toddlers may "quack" as they push a floating duck around the bath, pretending that the toy is alive or that they themselves are a duck. In contrast, bath time for preschoolers can involve extended battles with bobbing toys, with armaments lined up along the rim of the tub for future battles, or elaborate psychodramas enacting the roles of various family members in familiar daily routines. Second, the objects preschoolers incorporate into their play need not bear as close a resemblance to what they are imagining as these must for toddlers. Thus, a stone can serve as a turtle, a mountain, or a rocket ship for a preschooler, depending on the imaginative script being enacted. In contrast, for a 2-year-old to call a stone a turtle, the

These 4-year-olds aren't bothered by their messy playroom as they enact a script for familiar daily routines—one of the advantages to fantasy play.

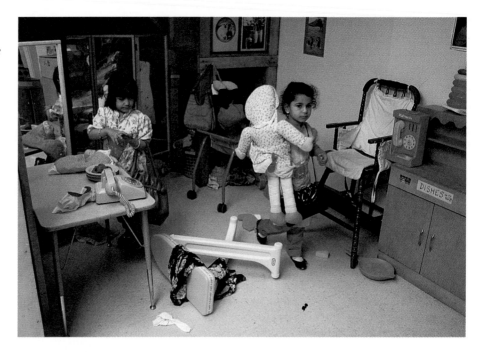

stone must bear some resemblance to a turtle; and, once seen that way, it cannot easily be transformed into a rocket ship. Finally, preschoolers are able to coordinate their fantasy play with that of other children, all sharing in the same imaginary world. Toddlers, however, even when playing near another child their age, do not share in one another's fantasy worlds and simply play alongside one another.

By the age of 4, children engage in pretend play both by themselves and with others for extended periods of time, assuming different roles as they act out various **scripts,** or schematic representations of familiar routines. Examples of scripts familiar to preschoolers might be going to the market, eating in a restaurant, or visiting the doctor. Of course, there are wide individual differences among children in the extent to which they engage in fantasy play, just as there are among adults in so many aspects of their behavior (Taylor & Carlson, 1997).

Fantasy play with others involves considerable social skill as well as imagination, in that children must first enlist the interest of another child, assign each other various roles, and develop a shared reality. How do they go about accomplishing all of this? Children in our culture do this primarily by explaining what they are doing and negotiating with their play partner—for example, "I'll be the teacher this time and you can be teacher next time." But do children from other cultural backgrounds establish a shared reality in this way as well?

Jo Ann Farver and Yoolim Shin (1997) reasoned that the strategies children use to communicate with each other when playing should reflect the broader social conventions of their culture. North Americans, for instance, value individualism and "saying what you think." In contrast, Asian cultures value group harmony and sensitivity to the needs of others, such that the others need not even voice them. Would these differences be reflected in the strategies preschoolers use to organize and maintain their play with each other?

The investigators compared the social pretend play of children in a predominantly Anglo-American preschool with that of children in two all-Korean preschools. As expected, communication strategies were found to differ as a function of the children's cultural backgrounds. The Anglo-American children's strate-

scripts Schematic representations of familiar routines used by young children to organize and recall everyday events.

gies reflected both individualism and self-expression, these preschoolers being more likely to describe their own actions ("*I'm* going into the forest"), use directives when speaking to the other ("*Put the king over there*"), and reject suggestions made by their partner (A: "You can be the princess. B: "*No, I'm the queen!*"). Similarly, Korean American children communicated in ways that both minimized conflict and promoted harmony and also reflected their sensitivity to their partner's intentions. Thus, they were more likely to agree with suggestions made by their partner (A: "Let's put these bad guys in the dungeon." B: "*Yes, let's lock them up*"), make polite requests ("*Could I be the . . . ?*"), use tag questions as a way of eliciting agreement ("We're playing prince and princess, *right*?"), and describe what their partner was doing ("*You're* going into the forest").

Pretend play also involved different themes for children from the two cultures. Korean American children were more likely to act out everyday activities, such as putting a child to bed, and to portray family roles. The pretend play of Anglo-American children, on the other hand, was more likely to be about fantastic or dangerous situations. These differences held for girls and boys alike. In fact, the pretend play of children of either sex differed little in the strategies they used to communicate their fantasies or the themes they played out together.

Knowing What Is "Real"

How real *is* pretend play for preschoolers? Adults, at least, have little difficulty distinguishing reality from fantasy. We know better than to squeeze life into a teddy bear or offer seconds to a doll. Clear lines have been drawn. For children, sorting fantasy from reality is an ongoing task. So too is discovering who shares their inner world—who knows what they know, which of their experiences are held in common with others, and which are private and known only to them. When one is 3 or 4, fairies and giants are no more fantastic than ballerinas and firefighters and more may be fuzzy than the stuffed bear in one's arms.

In a classic children's story, *The Velveteen Rabbit*, Margery Williams (1983) gives voice to this earliest of realities for children, an inner world where desires can take precedence over beliefs. In this story, a toy horse, much loved by the little boy who plays with him, explains to a recent arrival to the toy closet what it means to be real:

"What is REAL?" asked the Rabbit one day. . . .
"Real isn't how you are made," said the Skin Horse. "It's a thing that happens to you. When a child loves you for a long, long time, not just to play with, but REALLY loves you, then you become Real." ◄

Children understand the Skin Horse's description of what makes things real. It is an explanation that makes sense to them, given their own need to be loved and the way they feel toward their favorite toys. But does this understanding mean that they *actually* think toys talk and have feelings? Would they unblinkingly accept it if one of their stuffed animals audibly answered them back? Or would they run out of the room in wide-eyed amazement to tell anyone within earshot what had just happened? How firmly are their feet planted in the same sod as ours?

Piaget, for one, believed their tread to be considerably lighter than ours. Despite their capacity to symbolically represent their experiences, his observations of young children suggested that they often accepted as fact what others easily recognized as fiction. He attributed this confusion to the absence of **mental operations,** a concept that is reflected in his use of the term *preoperational* thought to refer to this stage. Piaget defined a mental operation as any action that could be

Like most preschoolers, this young boy most likely believes he's really talking to Mickey, even though his brother may have told him it's just a person wearing a costume.

Q Do we as adults ever think in ways that are characteristic of preoperational thought?

mental operations Piaget's term for actions that can be carried out in one's head and then reversed or undone.

carried out in one's head and then reversed, the mental equivalent of taking a step forward and then back. What possible advantage could come from taking a step such as this, considering that one ends up in the same spot as before? The advantage, argues Piaget, is one of perspective. Being able to envision an action that one can undo gives individuals two perspectives from which to view a situation, rather than a single one. Piaget believed that—in the absence of mental operations—preschoolers' thought suffered from a number of characteristic limitations.

Piaget noticed that when thinking through a problem, preschoolers tended to focus on one aspect of, or approach to, the problem to the exclusion of others. Piaget referred to this characteristic of thought as **centration.** Typically, when a second approach was pointed out, they lost sight of the first, illustrating their difficulty in considering several aspects of a situation at once. Piaget's measures of **conservation** illustrate this quality of thought. Tests of conservation assess a child's ability to see that something actually remains the same despite changes in its appearance. Since many of these tests are quite simple to do, you may want to carry out one or two, with a child, for yourself.

In one of these, Piaget showed children two identical balls of clay and asked if there were the same amount of clay in each. When they agreed that there was, Piaget rolled one of the balls into a sausage shape and again asked if there were still the same amount of clay in each. Preschoolers frequently said "no," usually indicating that the sausage now had more because it was longer. However, when Piaget pointed out that the sausage was also thinner, they would agree that the ball had more, since it was fatter. Thus, they either focused on the sausage's length, in which case it was judged as having more, or on its thickness, and believed it to have less. Piaget believed centration to result from preschoolers' inability to undo, or reverse, the action he had performed by mentally rolling the sausage into a ball again and thereby see that the two were still equivalent.

This inability to move something around in one's mind and catch it from another angle gives thought a static, or "stuck," quality. How something looks to the preschooler is how it is, and there is no moving beyond this by inference to how it must be. Piaget identified this second limitation by referring to preschooler's thought as *intuitive,* noting that their thought was dominated by the appearance of things. In one of his measures of this, Piaget showed a child two sheets of green cardboard, each the same size, and placed a plastic cow on each "field," asking, "Do the two cows have the same amount to eat?" The child assures him that they do. Piaget then places a block on one of the fields, calling it a barn, and again asks if each cow has the same amount of grass. The child answers "no" this time, indicating that some of the grass is covered by the barn. However, when Piaget adds a barn to the second field, the child again agrees that the two cows have the same amount of grass to eat.

Barns are added, one field at a time. With each addition, the child points out that the amount of grass is unequal, until a barn is added to the other field. In adding barns, Piaget was careful to arrange them neatly along the edge of one field while scattering them randomly across the other. At some point in the process of adding barns, a critical mass of "barn-ness" is reached, and the child's reasoning that the amount of grass must remain the same breaks down in the face of the overwhelming perceptual evidence to the contrary. Simply put, anything that looks that different can't be the same.

Piaget believed that preschoolers' thought was characterized by yet another limitation, which he referred to as **egocentrism,** also reflecting a failure in perspective. Piaget did not mean by this term that children are selfish, but rather that they are self-centered, simply failing to realize that the way they see something is not the way it may look to others. Because young children are unaware of their

Q Will preschoolers agree that glasses of different shapes filled from identical cans of soda will contain the same amount of soda?

Q Why might a preschooler be distressed if her mother dyes her hair a different color?

centration Piaget's term for the tendency to focus on one aspect of an object to the exclusion of others; characterizes preoperational thinking.

conservation The realization that something remains the same despite changes in its appearance.

egocentrism The failure to realize that one's perspective is not shared by others.

When asked to describe what the train engineer sees, preschoolers will describe what they see from their own vantage point, an example of Piaget's concept of egocentrism.

view as a perspective, they assume that others see things the same way. Piaget used a model of three mountains, one covered with snow, one with a house at the top, and one with a red cross at the peak, to demonstrate egocentrism. Children were first asked what they saw and then what a doll saw as it was placed at different positions around the mountains. Each time the doll was moved to a new position, children were asked what the doll saw. Could children literally take another's point of view and recognize that the same set of mountains seen from a different position would not look the same? Children younger than 6 or 7 typically described how the mountains appeared from where they were sitting rather than from where the doll was positioned, demonstrating egocentrism.

Piaget noted that preschoolers have difficulty distinguishing other aspects of their own and others' knowledge as well. In particular, they are unsure which aspects of what they know are private, and known only to them, and which are public, and hence knowable by others too. Thus, preschoolers fail to realize that what they know is not automatically known by others. As a consequence, they frequently give themselves away by denying something for which they otherwise would not be caught. A preschooler who tips over an ink bottle might never be picked out of a "line-up" of siblings and household pets were it not for crying out in alarm, "I didn't spill the ink!" Such denials are only necessary if you assume that others know what you know.

Margaret Donaldson (1978) has questioned whether tasks such as those used by Piaget to identify egocentrism actually make sense to young children. She points out that when children are tested with tasks that do make sense, they can be shown to adopt the other person's perspective. Martin Hughes (as cited in Donaldson, 1978) presented children with two dolls, one a policeman and the other a little boy. These were separated from each other by two walls that intersected in a cross, forming four open areas, each hidden from the others (Figure 8.1). When the policeman stood at the end of one wall, he could see into only the two sectors

FIGURE 8.1 A Measure of Perspective-Taking in Preschoolers

on either side of the wall he faced; the remaining two were hidden from him. The little boy was placed in each of the four sectors and children were asked each time if the policeman could see him. Preschoolers made virtually no mistakes on this task.

Even when a second policeman was added and they were told to hide the boy so that he could not be seen by either of them, they still performed well, even though doing so required them to coordinate two separate perspectives. When children 3½ to 5 years old were given this task, 90% of their answers were correct. Donaldson points out that hiding makes sense to young children. They can understand the motives of the little boy, who does not want to be seen by the policemen. Piaget's task, on the other hand, had no interpersonal motives to give it intelligibility. As Donaldson (1978) remarks, "It is totally cold-blooded. In the veins of three-year-olds, the blood still runs warm" (p. 17).

Donaldson also suggests that preschoolers' failure to do well on other of Piaget's measures reflects the way his questions were worded. Based on their answers to his questions about classification, for instance, Piaget assumed that preschoolers could not classify a group of related objects into subclasses while still realizing they retained their membership in the larger class. Piaget believed that in order to group objects into subclasses, children had to be able to view the objects from several perspectives. Thus, the class of animals can be divided into cats and all other animals. One knows that all cats are animals, that some animals are not cats, and so on. A central inference is that the number of items in the class (animals) is greater than the items in any of the subclasses (such as cats).

When Piaget gave tasks such as this to young children, they consistently made mistakes. In one of these tasks, Piaget showed children ten flowers, seven of them red and the remaining three white, and asked, "Are there more red flowers or more flowers?" Most preschoolers answer that there are more red flowers. Piaget assumed from their answer that they are not able to think of the class (flowers) at the same time as the parts (red or white ones) and so cannot compare the parts with the class. In other words, centration limits their performance here as it did with the sausages. Donaldson suggests, instead, that they misunderstand Piaget's question. She points out that there are natural and unnatural, or strange, ways of saying things. For instance, it is natural to say that the flowers are on the television. It is strange, however, to say that the television is under the flowers. It is also strange to ask, "Are there more red flowers or more flowers?" She argues that children do their best to make sense of questions such as this. Surely, this person must mean something by asking that, they think, and so they give a "reasonable" answer. Donaldson calls it "acquiescing in the bizarre." When children were asked, for instance, "Is milk bigger than water?" they all tried to give serious answers. "Yes," said one, "cuz it's got color." Only a 4-year-old didn't try to answer the question. According to Donaldson (1978), he just "grinned his head off."

Despite these criticisms, Piaget has contributed more to our understanding of children's thinking than perhaps any other single person. For some he has helped by providing a theoretical framework for explaining the course of development. For others, he has helped primarily by stimulating research aimed at disproving his theory. In either case, we know considerably more about the course of intellectual development because of Piaget than we would otherwise have known.

Making Wishes and Living with Superheroes

Preschoolers live in a world in which magic, making wishes, and superheroes are served up to them with their morning cereal, yet they show considerable skill in distinguishing fantasy from reality. Jacqueline Woolley (1997), at the University of Texas at Austin, argues that even 3-year-olds can distinguish their thoughts from those of others and know the difference between "pretend" and what is really so. Nonetheless, fantasy and reality still mix somewhat more freely in the world of young children than of adults.

Perhaps one of the most common areas in which fantasy and reality mix in children's minds concerns what it means to make a wish and what to expect after one does. Most preschoolers, when asked, believe that wishing is more than simply thinking about something and probably involves some magic. They also believe that some people are better at making wishes than others. For wishing to be effective, one must know how to do it. As we might expect, children's beliefs in the effectiveness of wishing decrease with age and vary, as well, from one child to the next, with some children being much more credulous than others (Vikan & Clausen, 1993; Woolley, 1997).

Even young children know the difference between events that are possible and those that are not, but when faced with explaining occurrences of the latter, most preschoolers are open to the possibility that magic may be involved (Phelps & Woolley, 1994). The youngest among them believe magic to entail the exercise of special powers. By 5, however, preschoolers are more likely to believe magic to be a trick that anyone can learn to do (Woolley, 1997). Whether children offer magical explanations appears to be more a function of their knowledge about the physical causes of the event they are trying to explain than of their age (Taylor & Carlson, 1997). When children are aware of more naturalistic explanations, even young preschoolers prefer these. Nonetheless, when something happens for which they have no explanation, especially when this runs counter to everything they would normally expect to see, preschoolers resort to magic as an explanation. These conditions, by the way, are pretty much the same as those in which adults become superstitious.

Children also know that fantasy figures, such as Batman, Barney, and Cookie Monster, are not real in the way that other rarely encountered things, such as parrots, bullfrogs, and porpoises are, but the distinctions they make are not as clear as they will later become (Woolley, 1997). In part, these distinctions may blur because children are continually invited by adults to believe in such fantasy figures. Books, movies, logos on T-shirts, and references in everyday speech underscore their existence. With some fantasy figures, such as Santa Claus, there is even what one might call a cultural conspiracy to promote their acceptance. Children are taken to shopping malls to sit on his lap, are encouraged to write him letters, and wake on Christmas morning to find that their stockings have been filled, as

Most preschoolers believe that wishing probably involves some kind of magic.

Q Under what circumstances are preschoolers most likely to rely on magic to explain things?

promised, and that the cookies they left the night before have been eaten, all of this orchestrated by conspiring adults (Taylor & Carlson, 1997). In the absence of information to the contrary, there are many situations in which children do not know what is most reasonable to believe. As one young child explained to a researcher, "I didn't know; I'm still little" (Subbotsky, 1993, as quoted in Taylor & Carlson, 1997).

Consider a 3-year-old, standing at the top of a short flight of stairs in his Superman shirt and a pillowcase cape. The child raises his hands over his head and utters what he believes to be the "important words." "Up, up to the way [sic]," he says. After waiting several moments, poised for flight, he walks down to level ground, muttering to himself, "I guess I wasn't going fast enough," and gathering himself in his cape, prepares to try again with a running start. What part of this sequence represents fantastical thought and what part the use of an adultlike logic? Only by experimenting with such things as capes and "important words" do preschoolers discover what is likely to happen and what is not.

Similarly, I remember mailing out bills, many years ago, licking stamps and pressing them on each envelope in turn as our daughter Jenny, then 3, looked on. When I next looked up, I saw her pull off a stamp, turn to the wall next to her, and press the stamp onto the wall. Since she had missed the part about licking the stamp first, it slid to the floor. Perplexed, she took another stamp and tried again, pressing even harder. No cape and incantation were involved here, but getting a stamp to stick to the wall must have seemed to involve as much magic as flying.

Woolley (1997) points out that the fantasy figures associated with holidays and actual events, such as Santa is with Christmas or the tooth fairy is with losing a tooth, are more likely to be taken as real than those, such as monsters and dragons, that are not. Perhaps this difference reflects the very real evidences of their appearances that are left behind, such as toys, colored eggs, and money under one's pillow, as well as the degree of cultural endorsement they receive. With respect to the latter, it is important to keep in mind the cultural context for children's beliefs. Our culture, like so many others, invites children to believe in the fantastical. As a consequence, figures such as Santa Claus and Cookie Monster, not to mention Disney creations such as Pluto and Mickey, can have more recognizable personalities than the neighbor next door (Woolley, 1997).

Not all developmentalists accept Woolley's arguments. Michael Chandler (1997), at the University of British Columbia, takes issue with her suggestion that differences between children's and adults' willingness to accept the fantastic are due primarily to children lacking the knowledge by which they could realize the fantastical nature of their beliefs or to their living in a subculture in which they are both invited by others to participate in fantastical beliefs and less likely to have their view of the world challenged. Chandler retorts that children, unlike isolated primitive peoples who are rarely exposed to alternative perspectives, are continually exposed to other perspectives. Their failure to attempt to reconcile these perspectives with their own assumptions he takes as evidence, in fact, of a very different way of approaching discrepant beliefs than one finds in adults.

Given that children can distinguish fantasy from reality as well as they so often do, why, then, do they become afraid of things that are obviously fantastic, such as monsters under their beds at night? Woolley suggests that in considering the possibility of such things, negative emotions such as fear are aroused and that these emotions *are* very real. Children, also, may not be as good as adults at dismissing their thoughts by saying such things as "monsters aren't real" and deriving comfort from such assurances. One of the cognitive abilities that appears to develop with age is the ability to recruit related information to either confirm or

Some beliefs are harder to give up than others. Preschoolers like this girl may wonder who brings the presents each year if there isn't a Santa—and what will become of what she has just whispered in this Santa's ear.

disconfirm ideas and events. This ability is probably related to increases in domain-specific knowledge with age, and to information-processing capabilities, which we will consider later in the chapter (Woolley, 1997).

Paul Harris (1997), at Oxford University, argues that it is incorrect to think of logical thought as necessarily displacing magical thinking, pointing out that magical and scientific thinking cannot always be separated as neatly as we might believe, even among scientists. Harris notes, for instance, that Newton developed his theory of gravity, which has become a fundamental scientific law, from his belief in alchemy, which was regarded as magical. The alchemists believed in hidden forces of attraction and repulsion. And gravity is, after all, an "invisible pull." At the time, many considered direct impact (one object hitting another) as the only "scientifically valid" cause of movement. Some even criticized Newton for "magical thinking." We see a similar blending of different forms of thought when anyone looks beneath the surface to explain some action. Thus, we don't mechanistically talk only about bodies in motion when explaining goal-directed behavior, but infer beliefs and desires which, like gravity, exist as unseen forces. The fact that preschoolers sometimes attribute motives to inanimate things, such as trees or clouds, does not mean they have abandoned reason for magic.

Distinguishing Appearances from Reality

Even though preschoolers are relatively successful in distinguishing fantasy from reality, they nonetheless improve with age. John Flavell, Eleanor Flavell, and Frances Green (1983) showed 3-, 4-, and 5-year-olds objects that looked like one thing but were actually another, such as a sponge that had been painted to look like a rock and a stone that had the same shape and color as an egg. After letting the children touch and play with these, so that they could discover the objects' true properties, they asked them what the objects looked like and what they "really, really" were. Five-year-olds nearly always answered each of these questions correctly, easily distinguishing what things looked like from what they actually were. Four-year-olds also answered correctly most of the time, demonstrating that they, too, knew that things are not always as they appear to be. Three-year-olds, however, had difficulty distinguishing appearances from reality, saying, for instance, that the sponge not only looked like a rock but actually was a rock.

Most 3-year-olds encounter few sponges painted to look like rocks or rocks that look like eggs. However, other equally deceptive experiences are a common part of their everyday world. Among these are the images they see on their television screens. Do young children understand that these are in fact images, or do they believe them to be real objects inside the television? Flavell and his associates first showed 3- and 4-year-olds a real bowl of popcorn, tipping it over to show that the popcorn spilled out, and then a photograph of a bowl of popcorn, showing that the popcorn did not spill when the photo was turned upside down. Following this, they played a videotape showing popcorn in a bowl and asked whether the popcorn would spill if the television were turned upside down. Once again, 4-year-olds are relatively good at distinguishing what they see on television from real objects. Nearly 90% of the 4-year-olds in this study answered the question correctly, indicating, when asked what they were really seeing, that they were looking at pictures and not real objects ("No, the popcorn wouldn't spill"). Three-year-olds, predictably, were more likely to interpret the television images as real objects, agreeing that the popcorn could spill if the television were tipped (Flavell, Flavell, Green, & Korfmacher, 1990).

Are there conditions under which 3-year-olds understand that things actually can be different from the way they appear? Catherine Rice and her associates (1997) suggested that children "fail" tests such as the above because of the way they are presented. If the questions are embedded within a meaningful, real-life type of experience with which children are familiar, even 3-year-olds should be able to make the appropriate distinctions. For instance, 3-year-olds are familiar with the experience of playing tricks on people. These investigators first showed children the rock-sponge and asked them what it looked like. When children responded that it looked like a rock, they answered, "That's right, it looks like a rock." Then they allowed the children to touch it and asked them what it felt like, indicating, "That's right, it's really and truly a sponge." At this point, they said, "I played a trick on you with this tricky sponge. Let's play a trick on someone else who's never seen this before and hasn't touched it." When asked under these conditions what the object really was, and whether the other person would think it looked like a rock or a sponge, nearly 80% of 3-year-olds answered correctly, saying that it was really a sponge but that the other would think it a rock.

Children who are given training in understanding the beliefs of others also do better on standard tasks measuring their understanding of the mental states of others (Slaughter & Gopnik, 1996). However, when the tasks themselves are made intuitively understandable, such as when they are related to children's own experiences of tricking others, even 3-year-olds need no training to do well. Thus, providing children with a familiar context, such as tricking someone, in which questions such as these become meaningful makes the task intelligible to them.

A corollary to this observation is that preschoolers will function in a more adultlike manner in their everyday world than they do in a social scientist's laboratory. In the former, they are the ones to set goals, plan, and make decisions, all of which imbue the activities they are engaged in with intrinsic meaning. In the latter situation, they can only guess as to the exotic interests of the adults who have invited them to play, making the best sense they can of the strange situa-

Q Why might preschoolers be better at understanding another person's false belief when they have intentionally tried to deceive that person?

tions to which they are introduced, before returning to their own world of purposeful action. This is not to say that there are not important differences in the ways in which preschoolers and older children think. There are. But the differences are not as consistently evident as preschoolers' lapses in the labs of social scientists might lead one to expect.

In general, preschoolers, just like adults, think best when the situations they are asked to think about are familiar to them. When they are asked to think through problems that can be related to immediate, real-life situations, where goals and intentions are evident, they perform well. Reason breaks down, however, when they are asked to think about problems that are removed from daily experience. Thus, one of the things that appears to develop with age is the ability to think about things that are increasingly abstract. Perhaps one of the most important differences between the thought of younger and older children is not so much the particular form it takes, but whether it can move beyond familiar experience. The Research Focus, "Formulating Hypotheses: What Does It Mean to Be Rich?" examines the ways children's surroundings can affect their development, including their intelligence.

What Children Know About the Mind

"Come on, Jenny, move over. I can't see," says Joshua with a tug, peering over the pages of the book his mother is holding.

"Here, you hold one page of the book, Joshua, and you hold the other, Jenny. Now, let's see what happens next," says Mom, continuing with the story.

> "Who is it?" called the grandmother in a weak voice.
>
> "It's Red Riding Hood, Grannie, bringing you fresh bread and cakes," answered the wolf, making his voice small.
>
> "Just press the latch, child," the grandmother cried.
>
> The wolf pressed the latch and pushed open the door. He walked in and before the poor grandmother knew what was happening he opened his mouth and with one gulp swallowed her up. Then he put on a nightgown and cap and got into bed and drew the curtains. . . ." (Tudor, 1980)

"See, the wolf is pretending to be Grannie," says the mother, pointing at a picture of the wolf in Grannie's clothes. "Will the wolf try to trick Red Riding Hood and eat her too?"

Jenny, age 3, staring at a picture of the wolf innocently dressed as a grandmother, answers that the wolf will be nice to Red Riding Hood. But Joshua, age 5, knows better and says that the wolf is only pretending to be innocent so that he can eat her as well.

How much do preschoolers actually understand of the stories we read them? The wolf in this story is pretending to be other than he is in order to deceive someone. Are young children able to distinguish the intentions of the characters from the way the characters present themselves to others? Children's everyday activities suggest that they should be able to, since these activities so frequently involve a world of make-believe. Preschoolers spend endless hours in pretend play, and even the very youngest can understand deception when it is they who are planning to play a trick on others. Since both pretense and deceit involve a form of make-believe, in that each involves making up a separate version of reality, one would expect children to be able to follow bedtime stories such as this with ease, participating as well in the fabricated reality.

Formulating Hypotheses: What Does It Mean to Be Rich?

Dorrie's family was poor, but her life was rich. Although she was only 3, she knew everyone who lived on her floor of the building. Two doors down there was old Miss Casterline. Dorrie and her Mom would pick things up for her at the market. And next to her were the Garcias. Sometimes Dorrie had supper at their house when her mother went to night school. Across the hall from Miss Casterline were the Ramsey twins; they went to Head Start every day with Dorrie. Yes, Dorrie knew everyone, and they all knew her.

How much do Miss Casterline, the Garcias, and the Ramseys contribute to the quality of Dorrie's development? And how can their contributions be distinguished from those of Dorrie's home life? One might expect that how well children fare in life will reflect the quality of the environments to which they are exposed, but it is another matter to disentangle the effects of the many environments that are present in any child's life. Such environments surround children at a number of levels, like the concentric layers of an onion, and include, as in Dorrie's case, not only their families but also their neighbors and their neighborhoods. Do each of these environments exert the same effect on a child's development irrespective of the child's age, or does the impact of a particular environment, such as the family or the neighborhood, change with the child's age? And how does one go about separating the immediate effects of children's families from those of the neighborhoods in which they and their families live? Questions such as these are interesting, but difficult to answer. What does one look for first?

What one looks for, or expects to see, takes the form of a research hypothesis. Hypotheses are guesses as to why something might happen. When these guesses are formulated concretely enough to be empirically tested, they take the form of research hypotheses. A *research hypothesis* is a statement specifying the particular conditions under which one expects to observe certain events (Ray & Ravizza, 1985). Hypotheses are based on prior research findings either alone or in conjunction with existing theory (see the Research Focus, "The Role of Theory in Research," later in this chapter). Research by Pamela Kle-

banov, Jeanne Brooks-Gunn, Cecelia McCarton, and Marie McCormick (1998) illustrates how, building on the findings of other investigators, these researchers were able to arrive at a conceptual framework for characterizing the quality of both neighborhoods and families and for separately examining the influence of each on development.

Much research on neighborhood effects has categorized neighborhoods simply in terms of their economic level. But how do neighborhoods affect the families living within them? Is it through the positive effects of having affluent neighbors or the negative effects of living among those who are poor? With respect to problem behavior in adolescents, for instance, research has found the presence of affluent neighbors, not poverty per se, to be more important (Crane, 1991). Similarly, among school-age children, having affluent neighbors has been found to be associated with verbal ability (Chase-Lansdale, Gordon, Brooks-Gunn, & Klebanov, 1997). Klebanov and her associates suspected that for preschoolers, as well, the most important determinant of a neighborhood's quality would be the presence of affluent neighbors, not simply the presence of poverty. In order to translate this expectation into a testable research hypothesis, they had to specify what they meant by affluence versus poverty as well as specify the particular way in which preschoolers' development would be affected.

With respect to the first of these tasks, they defined neighborhood affluence and poverty in terms of the percentage of neighbors who earned over $30,000 a year. Affluent neighborhoods were thus defined as those in which 30% or more of the neighbors earned over $30,000 a year. Conversely, poor neighborhoods were defined as those in which fewer than 10% of neighbors earned over $30,000. To determine whether it was affluence or poverty that affected development, children from each of these types of neighborhoods were compared with those living in middle-income neighborhoods, defined as those in which 10%–29% of neighbors earned over $30,000.

With respect to the second task, these investigators chose to look at the way intelligence in preschoolers might be affected,

Understanding Pretense and Deception

Joan Peskin (1996), at the University of Toronto, read illustrated stories to 3-, 4-, and 5-year-olds about a villain who disguises himself in order to deceive the main character, Susan, in a fashion directly analogous to what the wolf does in Red Riding Hood. After listening to the story, children are asked who the villain really is, who he is pretending to be, who Susan thinks he is, and whether he will still be mean even though he is disguised to look nice. Almost all of the children, irrespective of their age, understood that the villain was pretending and had not actu-

again concretely defining this in terms of scores on standard scales of intelligence. Thus, their research hypothesis was that intelligence scores in preschoolers would be higher for children living among affluent neighbors than for those living among poor neighbors. To test this hypothesis, they compared the intelligence of preschoolers from families *of the same income level* who lived either in affluent neighborhoods or poor neighborhoods, in each case making their comparisons with those living in middle-income neighborhoods.

To assess the quality of the home environment, they used the Home Observation and Measurement of the Environment (HOME), a scale that evaluates such things as parental warmth, types of discipline, and the availability of stimulating experiences. Based on previous research findings, these investigators hypothesized that the effects of neighborhood and family poverty on children, specifically on measures of their intelligence, are likely to be mediated by the quality of children's home environment. For home environment to act as a mediator, however, three conditions must be present: (1) both neighborhood and family poverty should be correlated with the home environment, (2) the home environment should be correlated with measures of intelligence, and (3) the relationships between neighborhood poverty and intelligence, and between family poverty and intelligence, should be significantly reduced when the influ-

ence of the child's home environment is removed (see figure).

Because these investigators had defined the quality of children's neighborhoods and of their home environments in the precise way that they did, they were able to determine whether the data they collected supported their research hypotheses. As they had expected, these investigators found that by the time children reached the age of 3, it was the proportion of neighbors who were relatively affluent, such as the Garcias, rather than the proportion of those who were poor, that was associated with higher intelligence in children. They also found, as they had hypothesized, that the relationship between neighborhood affluence and children's intelligence was mediated by the quality of home environment. Finally, these investigators found that environmental effects are ordered in terms of their proximity to children's lives. At 1 year of age, lower intelligence scores reflect only conditions present in a child's immediate environment, such as having a mother who is very young, has little education, or is depressed. By the age of 2, more general family variables, such as family income, can be seen to be related to children's intelligence, perhaps through such things as the ability to buy interesting toys or books or go on family outings. And by the age of 3, when children such as Dorrie begin stepping out into their neighborhoods, we see the effects of even larger, and more distal, surrounds.

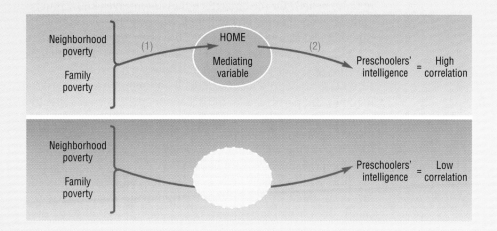

ally changed character, confirming that children as young as 3 actually do understand the difference between make-believe and real. The 4- and 5-year-olds also understood that the villain was attempting to deceive Susan by changing his appearance and knew as well that since Susan had agreed to play with the villain, she must have been deceived, falsely believing the villain to be other than he was. Three-year-olds, however, failed to understand the implications of the deception, fully half of them believing that the villain would act in a way consistent with his new appearance and not try to trick Susan. Nor did they understand that Susan must have been deceived.

Does all of this mean that we should pick simpler stories, ones that do not involve deception, or even forget about stories altogether until we are sure children can understand what the story is about? Not in the least! Stories can be appreciated at many levels. The sense of excitement, danger, and adventure are certainly there for even the youngest children, even if they miss the intrigue of deception. Mention of hungry wolves, dangerous forests, or houses made of candy guarantees their interest. Moreover, of far greater importance than understanding the story is the time children spend together with parents and those who love them.

In fact, most classic children's stories involve an element of deception, whether this is the wolf in Red Riding Hood, the witch in Hansel and Gretel, or the queen in Snow White dressed as a kindly old lady with an apple. How is it that young children fail to understand deception in stories such as these when we know from other research (Rice, Koinis, Sullivan, & Tager-Flusbergf, 1997) that 3-year-olds understand very well what it means to play tricks on others? One possibility is that in order for children to understand the deception, they must be the ones trying to deceive the other and that simply hearing about the actions of someone else may not be enough. Recall that Rice had to involve children in the actual trick for them to understand that someone would be deceived.

Most measures of children's understanding of deception involve creating false beliefs in others, typically by telling the children a story. In a typical task, children are told about a boy who puts candy in a box for safekeeping, only to have it removed to another box by some other child. Children are then asked which box the boy will look in to find his candy when he returns. The box he initially put it in (false belief)? Or the box which they themselves know it to be in (correct belief)? Only answers that the boy will look where he falsely believes the candy to be indicate that children understand that the other has been deceived.

Suzanne Hala and Michael Chandler (1996) argue that because 3-year-olds have no personal stake in understanding what another person might believe in such tasks, they do not perform well on them. When the tasks are structured such that they can participate in the deception, their answers should demonstrate a better understanding of the other's perspective. Thus, when children are allowed to move the candy themselves, they should correctly predict that the person whom they are tricking will believe the candy to be where it had been left and not where they themselves know it to be.

But what, precisely, is responsible for children's improved performance? Is it involving them in the procedure, by having them choose a place to move the candy, or is it making the procedure itself meaningful, by involving them in the goal of deception? Hala and Chandler (1996) argue that it is the latter. They compared two conditions for establishing false belief, each of which required 3-year-olds to remove cookies placed in a container by someone else and put them in a second container without that person's knowledge. In one condition, the cookies were removed because the first container was found to be wet. However, in the second condition the cookies were removed specifically to deceive the person. When asked where the person would look for the cookies, only children who had attempted to deceive the other were more likely to answer that the person would look for the cookies in the first container.

These findings suggest that it is the planning to deceive that is important, by making salient what others know and think. In order for children to plan how they will deceive someone, in other words, they must take into consideration what that person is thinking, or knows to be true, as well as their own goal, which is to make that belief false and so "trick" the other. Older preschoolers, on the other hand, have already developed an appreciation for this on their own.

One of the ways in which children develop an appreciation of what others know and think is by constructing a shared reality in pretend play.

Awareness of Mental States

One of the ways in which children develop such an appreciation is by talking about their own and others' mental states in their play together. Jane Brown, Nancy Donelan-McCall, and Judy Dunn (1996) analyzed 4-year-olds' conversations with each other for their references to mental states. They reasoned that children should refer to mental states frequently when playing together, since much of their play involves pretense and, with this, the need to construct a shared reality. As anticipated, children made frequent reference to mental states when playing, clearly revealing their awareness of such states in others as well as themselves. In this respect, the conversations of these 4-year-olds differed little from those of younger children. However, it was also evident from what they said that, unlike younger children, 4-year-olds were aware that they could mentally construct one reality or another in any given play situation and hence needed to communicate which direction they wanted their play to take. Thus, their view of mental states reflected a more active, "agentic" role to the mind. One 4-year-old, for instance, was heard to direct a friend as to how they would find a pile of gold when pretending to be pirates:

CHILD: All the silver things hafta go in here, and then you can use the swords when they find the gold.

FRIEND: You mean it's gonna be under the bed like that?

CHILD: No, it's gonna be on top of the bed so that we can find it.

FRIEND: But we'll still know where it is.

CHILD: I know, that's okay. That's okay, cause we're gonna walk from that way.
(Brown et al., 1996, p. 847)

As Brown and her associates remark, "the activity of creating fantasy worlds and sustaining interactive games with other children must surely provide multiple opportunities for the fledgling theorists to appreciate the workings of the mind" (p. 847).

Not only play, of course, but also other types of interactions, such as garden-variety household routines, contribute to preschoolers' understanding of the mind. These interactions can be especially helpful if they involve children with those who are older than they are. In a sense, children become social apprentices, being tutored by those who are older in reading the mental states of others. Support for the importance of children's social environments in contributing to this understanding comes from research showing that preschoolers who have older siblings or friends to play with, and who interact more with adults, have a better understanding of mental states in others (Lewis, Freeman, Kyriakidou, Maridaki-Kassotaki, & Berridge, 1996).

Mental Representation

Research investigating children's understanding of pretense and deception is interesting in its own right. However, it is also interesting for the insights it provides into the ways children understand what the mind does. Consider, for a moment, what it means to pretend. Typically, when one pretends, one *does* something, as when a child pretends to be a kangaroo and hops. What distinguishes something as pretense, however, is not the way one acts but the way one represents oneself mentally, which may or may not be evident in one's behavior. No matter how well one hops, in other words, if one does not see oneself as a kangaroo, one is not pretending to be a kangaroo (Lillard, 1996).

Do preschoolers understand this distinction? The research of Angeline Lillard (1993), at Stanford University, suggests they do not. Lillard found that even 4- and 5-year-olds, when told of a troll who had never heard of kangaroos and didn't know they could hop, still believed the troll was pretending to be a kangaroo when it hopped like a kangaroo, thus judging pretense on the basis of action rather than mental representation. Similarly, when preschoolers were shown pictures of children either pretending to be something, thinking about something, or performing some action and were asked whether each of these was something one could do "just inside your head," without using your body, or using only your body and not your mind, she found that fewer than half of the 3-, 4-, and 5-year-olds believed that pretending involved the mind. Thus, only 42% thought you needed your mind to pretend to be a kangaroo, but 96% thought that you needed your mind to think about things, in contrast to only 5% who thought you needed your mind to perform an action such as falling over if pushed (Lillard, 1996).

Similarly, Craig Rosen, David Schwebel, and Jerome Singer (1997) found that preschoolers who were shown episodes from a children's television show could distinguish those that involved pretense from those portraying realistic activities well before they could infer what the characters were thinking about when they were pretending. Thus, after viewing an episode in which characters were pretending to be in an airplane while sitting on a bench, children were asked, "Are they really in an airplane or just pretending to be in an airplane?" and then "Are they thinking about being on an airplane or sitting on a bench?" As can be seen in Figure 8.2, close to half of all 3-, 4-, and 5-year-olds could identify pretense but not infer the pretenders' thoughts. One can also see from this figure that the ability to do the latter systematically increases with age, with 9% of 3-year-olds, 24% of 4-year-olds, and 56% of 5-year-olds being successful in this.

Understanding the Actions of Others

Findings like those illustrated in Figure 8.2 should not be taken to mean that preschoolers cannot understand why people do what they do. Beginning with the preschool years, children's language reveals that they are aware of mental states,

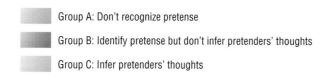

Group A: Don't recognize pretense

Group B: Identify pretense but don't infer pretenders' thoughts

Group C: Infer pretenders' thoughts

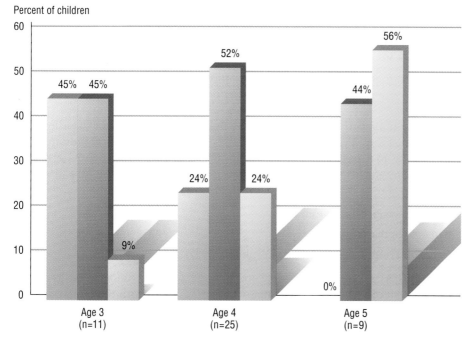

FIGURE 8.2 Age Differences in Children's Ability to Identify Pretense and Infer the Pretender's Thoughts *Source*: C. S. Rosen, D. C. Schwebel and J. L. Singer (1997). Preschoolers' attributions of mental states in pretense. *Child Development*, 68, 1133–1142.

both in themselves and others. How does their understanding compare with that of adults? Adults know, for instance, that others' actions are motivated by thoughts and feelings. But do children also attempt to understand the actions of others in terms of underlying beliefs and desires? In order for children to understand behavior as adults do, they must be able to understand that individuals' actions are prompted by what they believe to be so, rather than by what may actually be, by their beliefs *about* reality versus reality itself. They must be able to think of the mind, in other words, as *representing* reality. Do they do this?

Karen Bartsch, at the University of Wyoming, and Henry Wellman (1995), at the University of Michigan, studied children's everyday language as a way of discovering how they conceive of the mind. These investigators found that preschoolers routinely refer to both their own and others' thoughts and feelings in their conversations. Looking for evidence, first, of children's awareness of thinking, they found that children start to use words such as *thinking* and *knowing* in their everyday speech just before they turn 3. Furthermore, it was clear from the way children were using these terms that they were doing so to refer to mental states. Listen to one 3-year-old as he explains a remark he has just made in terms of what he had been thinking:

ABE (3 years, 4 months): Hey, don't eat it.

ADULT: I'm not.

ABE: I thought you were. (Bartsch & Wellman, 1995)

Or consider the exasperated remark of one 4-year-old, "He (Mark) thinks finished is not finished. Marky, not finished is not finished." This child is clearly making reference to what Mark is thinking and distinguishing that from what he knows to be so. Similarly, another 3-year-old explains an adult's behavior in terms of what he knows the adult must have been thinking:

ADAM (3 years, 11 months): No, dat not de right wheels.

ADULT: Oh, why isn't that the right one?

ADAM: Dis de right wheel to de bus.

ADULT: Oh.

ADAM: You thought that was the wheel to that. (Bartsch & Wellman, 1995, p. 45)

How can we know that pre-schoolers are aware of mental states in others?

What can be seen in each of these examples is that even very young children are aware of thinking and that they distinguish their own thoughts from those of others.

Children refer to feelings even earlier than they do to thoughts, starting anywhere from 1½ to 2 years of age. Again, the way they do so clearly indicates they are referring to a psychological state and are not simply using these words as a way of asking for something, such as saying "I want the ball" for "Hand me the ball." Thus, Ross (2 years, 6 months) says to his father

ROSS: You want it (a button) off?

FATHER: No, thank you.

ROSS: You want it on? (Bartsch & Wellman, 1995)

If all Ross asked were the first question, he could be understood as saying "Can I take it off?" But Ross does not try to do anything with the button. Instead he tries to find out what his father wants, as we see in the second question. He is clearly trying to figure out what his father's goal is, not expressing his own. Even at an early age, then, children's use of desire terms indicates that they understand that desires are feelings within a person that motivate a person's behavior, yet are themselves different from the actual behavior.

Thus, very young children appear to share many similarities with adults in the way they understand the actions of others. There are, however, important differences. Children, as you may recall, talk about desires before they begin to talk about beliefs, suggesting the possibility that, at least initially, they may not take people's beliefs into consideration as a way of understanding their behavior. Bartsch and Wellman suggest, in fact, that children progress through several phases in understanding why people do and say what they do. In the first of these, the *desire phase*, children are not yet aware of their own or others' thoughts and understand people's behavior only in terms of their feelings. At about the age of 3, children enter a second phase, the *desire-belief phase*. At this point, they are aware of others' thoughts and beliefs, but fail to realize that these are important in explaining what people do. Thus, children still explain behavior the way they did earlier, by referring only to people's desires.

How reasonable is it to assume that children, even though they recognize beliefs in themselves and others, still do not take these into account in explaining their behavior? Bartsch and Wellman draw an analogy to adults' understanding of imagination. Adults know that people imagine things—that is, that they frequently think about things that do no exist. Yet we rarely take what they imagine into consideration when explaining their behavior. We simply know that people do not act on the basis of the fictional accounts they make up, real as these may be. Similarly, children in this transitional phase may recognize the existence of beliefs but do not have to regard them as important in explaining what people do. Three-year-olds' predictions of where a story character would look for a desired object in a false-belief task were found to support such a transitional phase (Bartsch, 1996).

At about the age of 4, children enter the third and final phase, the *belief-desire phase*. At this point, they realize not only that people have beliefs and thoughts but also that these are central to explaining their actions. They understand, in other words, that what people do is largely determined by their beliefs—specifically, that what they do is what they *believe* will be effective in getting what they want.

Part of the problem may be that preschoolers fail to realize at first that their thoughts can affect their feelings. When asked, for instance, what strategies they might use to regulate their emotional states, preschoolers do not usually suggest mental strategies, such as changing their thoughts. Instead, they suggest changing the situation, which suggests they believe that feelings follow directly from events.

At what age do children understand the relationship between thinking and feeling? Kristin Lagattuta, Henry Wellman, and John Flavell (1997) asked specifically whether children understood that remembering something that had happened to them could cause them to feel happy or sad. Children were read a story in which the character, Mary, felt sad because of some event, such as a dog chasing her pet rabbit away. Later in the story, the character was said to feel sad when a friend asked her to play with a puppy that looked similar to the one that chased her rabbit. The children were then asked why the character felt sad.

Although preschoolers were aware that the character's thoughts could affect her feelings, their knowledge of the relationship between thought and emotions clearly develops in these years. Thus, although a majority of 4-year-olds and even some 3-year-olds understood why the character felt sad, only the older children could put this into words, explaining that Mary felt sad because she was reminded of a sad event. Once again, it's important to emphasize that children's ability to articulate their understanding of a situation will vary from child to child and from one situation to the next, depending on how closely it relates to their own experiences.

All in all, preschoolers understand quite a bit about thinking. They know that thinking is something people do. More generally, they know that something must be alive to think. They also know that thinking is a mental event, as opposed to a physical event, and that thinking is something you do in your head. That is, they know that one thinks with one's brain and that the brain is in one's head. They are also beginning to realize that thoughts are internal, not external—that is, public or tangible—and that a person who is not seen to be doing anything could still be thinking (Flavell, Green, & Flavell, 1995).

Preschoolers gradually realize that thoughts are internal mental events and not necessarily reflected by physical action.

Where Understanding Breaks Down

From here on, however, things start to get murky. One of the big differences between preschoolers and older children is the former's failure to realize how *much* people think. They, unlike older children, do not appear to understand that people are constantly experiencing one mental state or another, whether thinking, noticing something, or simply being aware of feelings; that is, they don't understand that there is a continuous stream of consciousness. Older children, for instance, will attribute consistent mental activity to a person who outwardly appears to be doing nothing, whereas preschoolers do not. Thus, when shown a picture of a person sitting quietly on a bench, fewer than 40% of 4-year-olds agreed with the statement "something is always going on in people's minds, so there *must* be something going on" in this person's mind (Flavell, Green, & Flavell, 1993). Because preschoolers lack this awareness, they are more likely to rely on observable cues, such as a person's actions or aspects of the situation that would prompt

Q Why might a preschooler interrupt his father when he is reading, even though his father has already told him that he is busy?

thought. However, even when they see people engaged in activities that are known to require thought, such as seeing someone reading a book, listening to or looking at something, or even talking to someone, preschoolers do not necessarily assume that the other is thinking.

Even when preschoolers do recognize that a person is thinking, they still have difficulty guessing what that person is thinking about. Flavell, Green, and Flavell (1995) describe a procedure used to study preschoolers' awareness of thinking in which one person asks another a question about one of two objects. The second person responds, "That's a hard question. Give me a minute. Hmmm," and turns to look at the object. When preschoolers are asked which of the two objects the person is thinking about, they do not, as one might expect, automatically choose the correct object. Even with additional cues, such as the person actually touching the object while looking at it, some of the youngest preschoolers fail to guess correctly.

Part of the problem may be that preschoolers do not understand that attention is focused—that is, that when one is thinking about one thing, one is not simultaneously thinking about something else. Flavell likens focused attention to a flashlight, something one can point in one direction or another, but not in several directions at the same time. Preschoolers appear to think of attention, or focused thinking, more like turning on a light in a room, allowing one to simultaneously take in any number of things. Given this understanding, it makes sense that they would not necessarily know which of two objects a person is attending to even though that person has every appearance of being deep in thought.

We can see similar limitations to preschoolers' understanding when they talk about their own thoughts. One of their more noticeable difficulties is in recalling the content of their thoughts. Thus, when 5-year-olds are given questions to answer—such as "What room do you keep your toothbrush in?"—many fail to recognize that they had been thinking when coming up with an answer. Even when they do realize this and are asked what they had been thinking about, they do not necessarily mention either their toothbrush or the bathroom (Flavell, Green, & Flavell, 1995).

Adults, on the other hand, understand that individuals are continually involved in some mental activity and that this activity can be prompted either internally, such as by another thought, or externally, by events outside ourselves, but that in either case, what is set in motion is a train of related thoughts. This understanding illustrates a central assumption we make about thoughts—namely, that they are part of a causal network of mental events.

Young children are not as aware of their thoughts as are adults and are not likely to spontaneously think about them. As a consequence, when they are asked to do so, they tend to regard their thoughts as isolated mental events, rather than as a chain of interrelated events that can arise as a result of either some other thought or something that has happened. Thus, preschoolers have no explanation for what causes their thoughts, nor do they see thoughts as causes of anything else. As a consequence, thoughts remain outside the flow of explainable behavior. For this reason, preschoolers underestimate the extent to which others engage in mental activity in going about their ordinary activities. And because they conceive of thoughts as isolated events, rather than as part of a stream of consciousness, they find it difficult to understand how one might go beyond the information immediately given to arrive at an interpretation of an event that might differ from that given by another person. Simply put, preschoolers are literalists (Flavell, Green, & Flavell, 1995).

If preschoolers are in fact not aware of the pervasiveness of thought in themselves or in others, we should expect to see evidence of this in their behavior. They should, for instance, have more difficulty than older children in saying how they arrived at an answer or a decision, since they would not be as aware of the mental steps leading up to it. And because they are less aware of the process of attending to something, they should be less aware of having their attention or thoughts distracted from what they were doing. By the same token, they should have difficulty realizing when they are distracting others, not being likely to assume that others are engaged in any mental process from which they could be distracted. They should also be less likely to know when something is beyond their understanding, since they are less aware of the processes contributing to various aspects of problem solving (Flavell, Green, & Flavell, 1995).

Thus a 4-year-old, enthusiastically driving his "big wheels" through the house, would be surprised to hear his father, who is sitting nearby quietly thinking about a problem, tell him that the noise he is making is distracting his thoughts. Similarly, a preschooler would be amazed that his mother could know he was the one who had stained the carpet when he unwittingly answers "grape juice" when she muses as to what might have been spilled. So, too, preschoolers fail to realize that they will not necessarily be able to later remember a list of things simply because they can readily identify them all at the moment.

What Children Know About the Body

"Why aren't there any more dinosaurs?" "Is it the same time of day all around the world?" "What's a nymphomaniac?" Only the last of these is likely to cause a parent to blush, stammer out an answer, or develop sweaty palms. Very few parents think their children will become paleontologists when answering questions about dinosaurs, yet many harbor fears that questions about sex reveal childhood obsessions.

Preschoolers have questions about nearly everything, including questions about their bodies and sex. They want to know how mosquitoes find you in the dark, why ice is cold, how come animals don't talk, and, yes, where babies come from. When questions are answered in ways they can understand, their curiosity is satisfied and they move on to something else.

Birth

Children typically ask questions about their bodies by the age of 3 or 4. These first questions are usually about such things as the function of different parts of their bodies or pregnancy and birth. Many of the questions that preschoolers have are prompted by the birth of a younger sibling. Most parents who are expecting another child have carefully prepared answers to questions about how people get babies. However, most are not prepared for the way their children will interpret their answers. Hours spent thinking of ways to translate the action of ova and sperm into familiar examples involving birds and bees can be reduced in a micromoment to misunderstandings of gigantic proportions. "It's where? . . . You swallowed a baby?"

Children understand the answers we give them in terms of what they already know. A child who has been told, for instance, that babies grow within the mother's womb, may nonetheless confide to a friend that babies come from the mommy's tummy. What most children know about how things get inside you is that you swallow them; this knowledge is garnered from the alarmed reactions of their parents to things the children have put in their mouths. It sometimes helps

The first questions a 3 or 4-year-old asks are typically about the function of different body parts and about pregnancy and birth.

to ask children what they think the answer to a question might be before giving them one of your own. At least this way you can know what you are dealing with.

Many parents, and educators as well, assume that if they can translate the facts into terms that are simple enough, children will automatically understand. The weight of the evidence is against this. Children translate the facts, whether simple or not, into their own way of understanding. And initially they do not understand that things must come into being, rather than having always existed. Anne Bernstein and Philip Cowan (1975), at the University of California, Berkeley, found that part of preschoolers' difficulty in understanding birth is their limited grasp of biological causation, of understanding that a baby is *created* rather than having arrived from some other place. The question of how people get babies is understood, instead, in terms of knowing where to look. The 3- and 4-year-olds they interviewed assumed that the newest addition to a family had always existed. They simply didn't know where the child had been before. Questions about the origin of babies were interpreted spatially, in other words, and not in terms of causation. As one child responded when asked about a younger sibling prior to the child's own birth:

ADULT: You said the baby wasn't in there when you were there.

CHILD: Yeah, then he was in the other place. In . . . in America.

ADULT: In America?

CHILD: Yeah, in somebody else's tummy. (Bernstein & Cowan, 1975, p. 86)

Adoption

Similar misunderstandings can exist concerning what it means to be adopted, specifically as this concerns preschoolers' understanding of the ways in which children can be expected to resemble their birth parents or their adoptive parents. Gregg Solomon, Susan Johnson, Deborah Zaitchik, and Susan Carey (1996) read 4-year-olds an illustrated story in which a woman who gives birth to a daughter dies without ever seeing the baby, and the infant is adopted by a second woman who "brought her home to live with her." Children were then asked which woman the girl would resemble in terms of both physical and nonphysical traits when she was older. Children had difficulty understanding that the child would be likely to resemble the birth parent in terms of her appearance, but would resemble the adoptive parent in her beliefs. Instead, young preschoolers appear to expect that members of a family will simply resemble each other, and that's that. The mechanisms that might underlie biological inheritance await their understanding (Johnson & Solomon, 1997). By the age of 5, they are better at differentiating which traits are inheritable when judging family resemblances, but continue to improve with age (Springer, 1996).

Many adoptive parents want to know the best time to tell their children they are adopted. Most agencies tell parents to begin early and to add more facts as the child gets older. However, there are few guidelines on what to say and when. The guidelines that exist mostly concern how to tell the child initially and not how to handle later questions. As a result, many parents remain unsure about how to answer their children's questions. This issue has become increasingly salient as adoption policies have changed from requiring that the identities of each set of parents be withheld from the other to allowing varying degrees of contact between them. The issue is no longer simply whether to inform children of their adoption but how much information about, and contact with, their birth parents is best.

Gretchen Wrobel, Susan Ayers-Lopez, Harold Grotevant, Ruth McRoy, and Meredith Friedrick (1996) interviewed adopted children to determine whether the amount of information they had been given was related to various outcome variables. Measures of self-esteem were high for all adopted children, as were measures of global self-worth, irrespective of how much they had been told. These investigators also found that children's satisfaction with how much they knew was unrelated to how much their parents had told them. However, they caution that one cannot conclude from this that children would remain that satisfied if they understood all that they might know. Most children, irrespective of how much they had been told, indicated being curious about their birth parents. In general, these findings suggest that giving adopted children information about their birth parents has little affect on their feelings about themselves or their satisfaction with their present state.

Perhaps a more fundamental problem than one of giving children information is the issue of how children will understand the information they are given. David Brodinsky, Leslie Singer, and Anne Braff (1984) interviewed several hundred adopted and nonadopted children ranging in age from 4 to 13 to determine their knowledge of adoption. They found that most preschoolers are not likely to understand adoption even though they may have discussed it with parents. Even

Preschoolers may have difficulty understanding the concept of adoption and distinguishing adoptive parents from birth parents.

children who spontaneously refer to themselves as adopted may fail to distinguish adoption from birth, assuming the same biological process explains both. The fact that adopted children overall knew no more about adoption than nonadopted children suggests that what children know is not just what they have been told, since adopted children are much more likely to have been told about adoption, but what they are able to understand.

By 6, most children distinguish adoption from birth as different ways of becoming a parent. They also know that adoption is a permanent relationship, but not necessarily how it takes place or why. They simply know that children cannot be taken away from their adoptive parents. Most likely, they have been told this by parents and have accepted the information on faith. By middle childhood, uncertainties about the permanence of adoption can arise. Fears that the biological parents can reclaim an adopted child may bother some children. Others may see the relationship with the adopted parents as less secure than before. Not until adolescence are children likely to understand that adoption is a legal procedure that transfers rights and responsibilities from biological to adoptive parents and, because of this, is permanent (Brodinsky, Singer, & Braff, 1984).

Most adoptive parents are encouraged to tell their children early of their adoptive status. One advantage to doing so is that children learn they can trust their parents to tell them about important issues. Early telling is also recommended so children are first likely to hear of their adoption at home in a loving context rather than as a taunt or a casual remark disclosed unintentionally by someone else. The findings from Brodinsky and his associates suggest, however, that children may not understand the meaning of adoption, just as they don't understand birth, even when they are told. This can come as a surprise to parents who may think their children know more than they do. After having told them of their adoptive status and hearing their children spontaneously refer to themselves as adopted, parents may not be prepared for children's concerns later on, when they do distinguish adoption from birth. Being told that one is adopted can have the same impact on young children as being told that one has brown hair or red hair—perhaps less, since they cannot see differences between adopted children and those living with their biological parents the way they can see differences in hair color. And what small child can imagine having any parents other than Mom and Dad?

Perhaps the best course is to tell children early, so that the term is familiar and not threatening. Parents should anticipate, however, that very young children will not fully understand what adoption means. By telling their children, they have merely neutralized a word that could hurt if used thoughtlessly by others. Parents and concerned adults need to know that children's ability to understand concepts such as adoption and birth develops with age and that children who comfortably refer to themselves as adopted may nonetheless at some later point experience fears about their adoptive status that need to be discussed.

Information Processing: Acquiring Basic Skills

Some things are so second nature to us that we hardly pay them any mind, such as making inferences from our experiences, knowing that "three" is more than "two," or that we are likely to forget unless we do something to remember. What do preschoolers grasp of the knowledge we have come to take for granted? And how does this develop? Those who adopt an information-processing approach to cognition focus on the specific processes involved in developmental change, rather than on the characteristics of any stage of thought. Such processes include the way information is coded, the ways in which it is stored, and how it is retrieved from memory. A central assumption of this approach is that individuals face real constraints on their ability to process information at any age. In studying the ways individuals approach different types of problems, the strategies they use to overcome these constraints, and the particular demands of the tasks, investigators guided by this approach attempt to explain the mechanisms underlying developmental change.

Reasoning

Reasoning allows one to know something without checking it out. It is a way of extending one's knowledge, in other words, without having to experience things directly. How easily do preschoolers discover new things in this way? In deduction, for instance, one reasons from a premise, concluding that if one thing is true, something else must be. If Princess is a dog, for example, one knows she cannot also be a cat, or if Alisa is older than Anthony, and Anthony is older than Eddie, then one knows that Alisa must also be older than Eddie.

Laboratory tests of preschoolers' ability to reason through simple problems such as these often find they have difficulty doing so. Margaret Donaldson (1978) argues that their failure is due more to the nature of the tasks preschoolers are given than to their ability to reason. Simply put, some laboratory tasks are sufficiently removed from the routines of daily life that preschoolers are not sure what is being asked of them. However, in observing preschoolers as they go about their normal activities, one finds that examples of spontaneous reasoning are common. For instance, Donaldson tells of one 4-year-old's confusion when shown a picture of a wedding in which the groom had shoulder-length hair, giving him the appearance of a woman. When told this was a wedding picture, the child retorted, "But how can it be? . . . You have to have a man too" (p. 52). Rephrasing what the child said in a way that shows reasoning from premises to conclusions, the remark takes the form

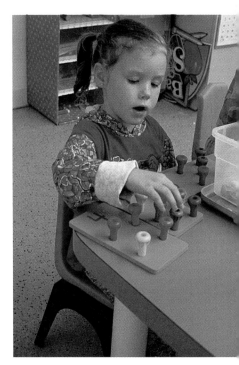

Premise: If there is a wedding, there is a man in it (If P, then Q).

Premise: There is no man (Not P).

Conclusion: Therefore, this is not a wedding (∴ Not Q).

When children's reasoning falters, it is usually because they do not argue from the premises, either bringing in their own instead or ignoring the given ones. A young mother, for instance, who wistfully says, "If this were Saturday, we could go to the beach," is likely to be corrected by her preschooler that this is a weekday. Young children, more so than older ones, have difficulty isolating a problem from the rest of experience, from what they know to be true. However, even adults can find this difficult at times, especially when the premises are at all controversial or touch them personally. The Social Policy Focus, "Schooling Children Not Proficient in English" looks at issues of bilingualism and cognitive abilities.

Counting and Numbers

Preschoolers are also developing an understanding of numbers and what it means to count. By age 3 most preschoolers are beginning to count, know more from less, and can add and "take away." For instance, one 3-year-old, on being passed a plate of cookies a second time around, was heard to mutter, "Someone musta' took one cuz there's only two now. There were three."

Touching each object as it is counted helps the preschooler count each one only once.

Schooling Children Not Proficient in English

Over 6 million schoolchildren in the United States speak a language other than English at home (U.S. Bureau of the Census, 1996). Being able to speak more than one language carries a number of advantages. Beyond the obvious advantage of expanding the number of people in their lives with whom children can communicate, knowledge of another language gives children an understanding of another culture as well and, with that, a better awareness of their own. Bilingualism has also been found to promote children's conceptual understanding and to increase their cognitive flexibility (Diaz, 1983). One might wonder whether these advantages occur at any cost. Are children who are bilingual, for instance, less fluent in either or both of their languages than those who grow up speaking only one? Research suggests that when both languages are spoken in the home while children are growing up, children become as proficient in each of these as do children who grow up speaking only one language (Oller, 1999).

Yet approximately half, or 3.3 million, of all children who speak another language at home are *not* proficient in English at school (Hakuta, 1999). These children come from homes in which English is only infrequently used. In a historic 1974 decision (*Lau v. Nichols*), the Supreme Court ruled that these children are denied equality of treatment even if taught by the same teachers, using the same materials they use for native English-speaking students, unless their schooling also fosters the acquisition of English—since only with the latter is a meaningful edu-

cation accessible to them. Ever since this decision, schools have been faced with the dual task of making sure students who are not native English speakers learn English in addition to the academic content of their courses. It is left to local schools to determine, however, how best to accomplish these dual goals. As a consequence, educating children who are not proficient in English has taken a number of forms.

In one type of program, known as *English as a second language* (ESL), students with limited proficiency in English are taught their academic subjects in the same classrooms as other students, but are given special times of instruction in which they learn English. Thus they are taught English as a subject, just as native English-speaking students might be taught a foreign language, with instruction in vocabulary and grammar. Although this approach addresses the dual concerns of *Lau v. Nichols*, it can be argued that students who are not proficient in English will have difficulty grasping basic concepts through English-based instruction in science or social studies, for example, even though they are also being taught to speak and write in English. A further disadvantage to this approach is that these children may find it more difficult to discuss their schoolwork with their parents than if this work were being taught in a language they share with their parents.

In an alternative to ESL, students are also taught English as a subject, but receive instruction in all their other coursework in their native language. As a consequence, they spend much of

In order to count, children must follow certain rules. They must know, for instance, that you can use each number only once, that numbers must be used in the right order, and that the number of items is indicated by the last number counted. They know, too, that it doesn't matter which item you count first, as long as you count each one only once, using a different number for each ("You're not supposed to count something twice . . . it doesn't make it more") and that it doesn't matter what type of things one is counting because the rules work the same way with any set of objects, from buttons to toes. Once they have these rules down, preschoolers can use counting to do simple arithmetic by about the age of 4 or 5.

Memory

Preschoolers are known for their poor memories. When asked what they did at day care, for instance, they are likely to respond with one-liners such as "We played on the jungle bars" or "I ate some ice cream." Even with prompts such as "Didn't you go on a field trip?" they rarely recall the sequence of activities that filled the day. Similarly, one can send them to the closet for a pair of boots only to find them, much later, playing with an old toy they discovered there. And forget about using them as couriers or message-bearers. Dad has no more than an

their school day in classes that are separate from those being taught in English. This approach is called *bilingual education,* or bilingual-bicultural education. It can be argued that children are in a better position to master basic concepts when these are taught in the language in which they think. It is also argued that it takes a certain amount of time for children to learn a language and that, until they do so, they will fall behind in their basic coursework. This approach also has the advantage of making it easier for the parents of these children to help them with their schoolwork. Those critical of this approach argue that continued instruction in their native language only further delays the acquisition of English, which can be learned more rapidly the younger children are. An additional disadvantage to this approach is that it segregates children who are not proficient in English in separate classrooms, effectively creating two school cultures.

A third approach offers instruction to all students in English, adjusting this instruction to make it easier for those who are not English-proficient to understand. Thus all students are instructed together in the same classrooms. This approach is termed *immersion,* or sheltered instruction. Immersion has the advantage of not isolating students from different cultural backgrounds from each other, thus promoting socializing among children from each language group. Since children learn language best when using it to communicate in real-life settings, this approach should speed the acquisition of English among those not proficient in it.

Are there data to indicate which of these approaches is more effective? Considerable research exists; however, comparisons among the various approaches are difficult to interpret due to the presence of other variables that are frequently confounded with instructional approaches, such as socioeconomic differences. Thus, ESL and immersion are more frequently offered in schools with somewhat higher socioeconomic status (Hakuta, 1999). Notwithstanding, a review of existing research supports a number of conclusions: (1) there is no intrinsic disadvantage to bilingualism and often very real advantages, (2) it takes children a relatively long time to learn a second language, often as long as 3 to 5 years, and (3) how successful children are in becoming literate in a second language depends strongly on the support they receive at home. Most important, however, the research we have to date suggests that bilingual education is more successful than the other two approaches in achieving the dual objectives laid out in *Lau v. Nichols* (Hakuta, 1999). Children master basic concepts more easily *and* become proficient in English more quickly using this approach.

Kenji Hakuta, a researcher and educator in this field, warns that by focusing on comparative evaluations of approaches such as these we may blind ourselves to a more fundamental problem—the fact that students with limited proficiency in English are more likely to experience poverty than are others. Also, even though research supports bilingual education, students being educated in this manner still perform significantly below national norms, by about 1 standard deviation (see the Research Focus, "Descriptive Statistics," in Chapter 3). For these children to get all they should be getting from their education, we need to address the presence of poverty in their lives.

even chance, for instance, of getting a cup of coffee if a preschooler is sent to ask if he would like one.

One of the best-established truths to development, however, is that memory improves with age. But what, precisely, is responsible for the improvement? Robert Siegler (1998), at Carnegie Mellon University, suggests four possibilities: children's basic memory capacities improve; they are better at using strategies to remember; children develop an awareness, or metacognition, of their memory; and their knowledge base increases, making it easier for them to relate new material to what they already know.

Siegler compares *basic capacities* to the hardware of a computer, likening them to the size of a computer's memory, for instance, or its speed. As Figures 8.3 and 8.4 show, research has found that both speed of processing and the number of items children can hold in short-term memory increase with age (Dempster, 1981; Kail, 1991). However, the observed differences in capacity are most likely due to the greater speed with which older children recognize items, thereby functionally increasing the number of items they can work with in a given amount of time. Memory capacity, on the other hand, is more likely to remain constant with age (Siegler, 1998).

The same cannot be said regarding the use of memory strategies. A **strategy** is any activity that is consciously used to improve one's memory, from verbally

strategy Any activity that is consciously used to improve one's performance or attain a goal.

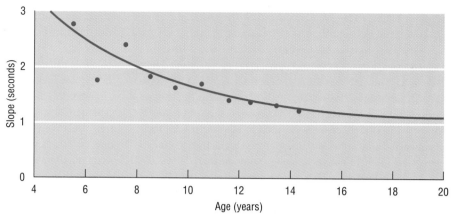

FIGURE 8.3 Age Changes in Speed of Processing Items in Short-Term Memory
Source: R. Kai (1991). Developmental changes in speed of processing during childhood and adolescence. *Psychological Bulletin*, 109, 490–501.

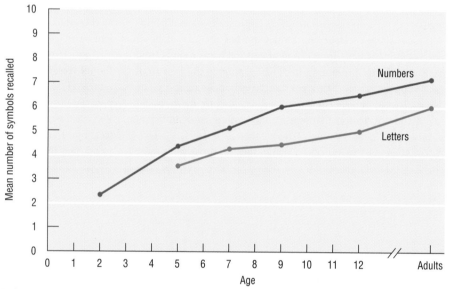

FIGURE 8.4 Age Changes in Number of Items Children Can Hold in Short-Term Memory *Source*: F. N. Dempster (1981). Memory span: Sources of individual and developmental differences. *Psychological Bulletin*, 89, 63–100.

rehearsing the items to be remembered to tying a string on one's finger. In contrast to basic capacities, which are akin to the hardware of a computer, strategies are similar to the particular programs, or software, on a computer. The use of strategies dramatically improves with age, in at least three ways. Older children are more consistent in their use of strategies, use more effective strategies, and are better at generalizing the strategies they use to new situations.

Age differences in the use of rehearsal illustrate the first of these points. **Rehearsal** is a common strategy for holding on to items for a relatively short time, simply by repeating them over and over to oneself. In a classic study, John Flavell, David Beach, and Jack Chinsky (1966) showed children pictures of objects, pointed to several of these, and told the children they would be asked later to remember which ones had been pointed to. Very few of the preschoolers could be heard rehearsing the names of the objects or seen moving their lips. By contrast, most of the 10-year-olds did so. One sees a similar difference in the use of *clustering*, a

rehearsal Repeating items to be memorized; a common strategy for retaining items in short-term memory

recurrent events such as these is thought to be organized in terms of scripts, which help children anticipate, understand, and later reconstruct these daily routines (Schank & Abelson, 1977; Nelson, Fivush, Hudson, & Lucariello, 1983). We saw such scripts at work earlier in the chapter, guiding the pretend play of preschoolers. The scripts themselves are assumed to be organized representations of the events, in that they reflect the relationships among the actions that make them up and are organized in terms of clusters of related components surrounding central events.

Evidence for children's use of scripts can be seen in various aspects of their memory. For instance, if children are told stories about familiar routines, but with the events mentioned out of order, they remember these events in the correct order when recalling the story, just as do adults. Children also mention the various components making up each particular event together, clustering them, in other words. Thus, a script for going to the park might include bringing the dog along as one of the events of the script. When recalling such trips, the activities related to this event are clustered, preschoolers mentioning together such things as getting the dog's leash, fastening it to the collar, and bringing a toy for it to fetch before moving to the activities making up the next event (Price & Goodman, 1990).

 ## Summary

Piaget's Stage of Preoperational Thought

Each stage of thought differs qualitatively from the preceding stage. Preoperational thought is distinguished by the ability to use symbols to represent experience. The use of symbols is characteristic of children's play as well. Symbolic play differs in preschoolers from the form it took in toddlers: It involves more complex sequences of actions, is less dependent on the characteristics of the objects with which they are playing, and is coordinated with the play of other children. Fantasy play among preschoolers is guided by *scripts,* which take the form of schematic representations of familiar routines. In addition to imagination, children's play involves the use of social skills and strategies that reflect the social conventions of their culture.

Preoperational thought derives its name from the lack of *mental operations,* actions older children can carry out in their heads and then reverse. Because of the absence of operations, preschoolers' thought was assumed to suffer from characteristic limitations: (1) *Centration* is the tendency to focus on one aspect of a problem to the exclusion of others. Tests of *conservation* assess a child's ability to see that something actually remains the same despite changes in its appearance. (2) *Intuition* refers to thought that is dominated by the appearance of things. (3) *Egocentrism* reflects a failure to realize that the way something appears to the child is not the way it may look to others. Other investigators have argued that it is the way Piaget's measures are presented to children that causes them to do poorly

rather than the particular way children of this age think. When children are tested in ways that make sense to them, they are able to assume the perspective of another and to group objects into subclasses.

Making Wishes and Living with Superheroes

Preschoolers experience more difficulty distinguishing fantasy from reality than older children. With respect to making wishes, young children consider these to involve the use of magic and special powers. The extent to which children offer magical explanations is more a function of their knowledge of the physical causes of events than of age. Similarly, preschoolers also know that fantasy figures are not real, but the distinctions they make are not as clear as they are to older children. Cultural endorsement of such figures most likely contributes to their difficulties in making distinctions.

Distinguishing Appearances from Reality

Even young children can distinguish appearances from reality when questions are embedded within meaningful and familiar contexts. Similarly, children appear to have little difficulty understanding the mental states of others when the measures used to assess their understanding provide them with a familiar context in which questions about others' beliefs become meaningful. In general, preschoolers think best when the situations they are asked to think about are familiar to them. When problems can be related to real-life situations in which goals and intentions are evident, they perform well. One of the most important differences between the thought of younger and older children is not so much the actual form thought takes, but whether it can move beyond familiar experience.

Understanding Pretense and Deception

Most measures of children's understanding of deception involve creating false beliefs in others by moving an object a person believes to have been left in a certain location and assessing whether children will distinguish their knowledge of the object's new location from the false beliefs held by the other person. Three-year-olds fail to distinguish what they know from the beliefs of others unless the task is made meaningful by involving them in plans to deceive the other. Four- and five-year-olds are able on their own to distinguish what they know from what the other person knows.

Awareness of Mental States

Children's symbolic play, in which they talk about their own and others' mental states, helps them distinguish their own thoughts from those of others. Everyday interactions with older siblings and friends also help children understand the mental states of others.

Understanding the Actions of Others

Children first use words referring to their own and others' mental states just before the age of 3. They progress through several stages in understanding others' behavior. Initially, children appear to understand behavior only in terms of feelings (desire phase). Subsequently, they become aware of thoughts as well, but fail to recognize their importance in explaining behavior (desire-belief phase). By the age of 4, they realize that others' beliefs are central to explaining their behavior (belief-desire phase).

Preschoolers have a relatively well developed understanding of thinking: They know that something must be alive to think, that thinking is a mental event that is carried out in one's head, and that thoughts are internal and not available for public inspection.

Failures of Understanding

Preschoolers do not understand that people constantly experience one mental state or another and so do not assume that a person is thinking unless there are observable cues as to this. Preschoolers also have difficulty recognizing what another person is likely to be thinking about, based on contextual cues, perhaps due to their failure to realize that attention is focused. Preschoolers also tend to regard their thoughts as isolated mental events rather than as part of a stream of consciousness.

Questions About Birth and Adoption

Many of children's questions about birth are prompted by the birth of a younger sibling. Because children understand the answers they are given in terms of what they already know, it is helpful to ask what they think before supplying an answer. Many children fail to understand that babies are created rather than having arrived from some other place. Thus answers concerning how people have babies are understand in terms of knowing where to look. Confusion concerning adoption also arises. Preschoolers have difficulty understanding that an adopted child is likely to resemble birth parents in appearance but resemble adoptive parents in beliefs. In general, most preschoolers are not likely to understand adoption even though they may have discussed it with parents.

Information Processing: Acquiring Basic Skills

An information-processing approach focuses on the processes involved in developmental change rather than on the characteristics of stages of thought. These processes include the way information is coded, stored, and retrieved from memory. Even young children use strategies when given problems to solve. Furthermore, children use a number of strategies, and changing from one to the next does not necessarily mean moving from less efficient to more efficient ones.

Both deductive and inductive reasoning are commonly employed by preschoolers. When reasoning breaks down, it is usually because children fail to argue from the premises. By 3, most preschoolers are beginning to count and are aware of the need to follow rules when doing so.

The improvement of memory with age is likely to be due to children's better use of strategies, to improvements in their metamemory, and to an increasingly expanded knowledge base. With age, strategies are used more consistently and effectively and can be generalized more easily to new situations. Metamemory, or knowledge about memory, also improves with age. Finally, the more children know about any area, the easier it is to remember new facts about it. In general, older children have more information, or content knowledge, than younger ones.

Key Terms

centration (p. 300)

conservation (p. 300)

egocentrism (p. 300)

mental operations (p. 299)

metamemory (p. 325)

preoperational thought (p. 296)

rehearsal (p. 324)

scripts (p. 298)

strategy (p. 323)

chapternine

Early Childhood
Psychosocial Development

I've got a lot of problems," whispers a 4-year-old to his grandmother at bedtime. "It's hard to fall asleep . . . my shoes come off when I run . . . sometimes kids don't want to play with me . . . and I can't catch a ball very well. Don't I have a lot of problems, Grandma? Goodnight."

It's popular to think of early childhood as carefree, when one's biggest problems are learning the alphabet or how to skip rope and when the only things to fear are monsters in dark places. Mothers hurrying children into clothes or through meals often fail to give skipping rope and closet creatures their proper due. And questions such as "Where does el-em-en-o-pee go, Dad?" can receive an impatient answer from fathers who forget they too started with the alphabet. Thank goodness for grandparents, who know the shadows on the wall are real.

The years of early childhood fairly burst with energy and activity. Preschoolers are into everything, inspecting the contents of desk drawers and pants pockets, scrutinizing dead insects, and racing around corners, leaving the rest of the world behind them. Viewed from the outside, their activity looks like random bursts of energy. Looked at from within, the glimmer of a purpose can be seen. Running, climbing, poking, and peering all confirm their awareness of themselves. Like striking a light in the dark, their actions are a means of discovering what they can do and what kind of person they are becoming.

Recognizing the Self

Most children can recognize themselves in photos and mirrors, saying "That's me" or calling out their name by about 18 to 24 months of age. Developmentalists have studied the emergence of *self-recognition* in the laboratory by placing a dot of rouge on an infant's nose and determining the age at which the infant touches its own face when it sees the dot in its reflection in the mirror. Touching one's nose has been taken to mean that children recognize that what is true of one's image must be true of the self. Such behavior has been taken to signify the existence of an objective self-concept (Bertenthal & Fischer, 1978; Lewis & Brooks-Gunn, 1979).

But how similar is this early self-concept to that of adults? Central to adults' understanding of themselves, for instance, is their recognition that despite changes in how they might feel or look from one time to the next, they remain the same person. Do preschoolers have a similar sense of themselves as continuous over time?

Ulric Neisser (1992) argues that they do not, suggesting that initially children experience the self only with respect to the activities in which they are currently engaged. The **ecological self** is the self that is directly perceived through one's actions. This awareness of the self is direct and immediate, based, as it is, on feedback from ongoing activity in an actual surround. It is the awareness of holding something, for instance, as well as of what one is holding, or of kicking one's feet in addition to the ball one is kicking. In addition to this awareness of their present selves, children increasingly remember their past experiences and imagine future possibilities. Neisser refers to this awareness as the **extended self.** Through imagining what they will do and recalling what they have done, children extend the self over time, beyond the immediate moment.

Daniel Povinelli, Keli Landau, and Helen Perilloux (1996) examined the temporal dimensions to preschoolers' self-concept through the use of delayed images. They videotaped 2-, 3-, and 4-year-olds as they played a game and then invited the children to watch on television what they had done just moments before. While they had been playing, a sticker had been covertly placed on the child's

How can you test whether a child recognizes itself in a mirror?

ecological self The self that is directly perceived in terms of one's ongoing actions.

extended self The self that includes not only what one is doing at the present moment but also memories of one's past experiences and imaginings about one's future.

Initially children are aware of the self only in terms of what they are doing at the time.

head. Would children appreciate the causal connections between past and present instances of the self and reach up to touch their heads?

Such an appreciation develops only with age. None of the 2-year-olds, 25% of the 3-year-olds, and 75% of the 4-year-olds reached up for the sticker, even though children of all ages could identify themselves by name as the child in the video-tape. These investigators suggest that the emergence of a concept of self that extends over time occurs considerably later than the "on-line" self-concept, or eco-logical self, that is revealed through live feedback, such as in mirrors. Even though young children realize that the image they are looking at is of themselves, they appear not to understand that the way they experience themselves currently is related to previous states. Only the 4-year-olds in this study were likely to under-stand that the sticker that had been on their heads several minutes ago must be there now.

Interestingly, even though the younger children labeled the delayed image as themselves, they spoke about it as if it were someone else, saying things such as "it's on *his* head" rather than "*my* head." In fact, the likelihood that children would reach up for the sticker was associated with the pronouns they used to refer to

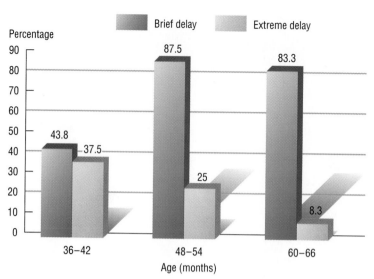

FIGURE 9.1 Percentage of Preschoolers Reaching to Touch a Sticker on Their Heads as a Function of Age and Delay Conditions

themselves in the videotape. Of those who reached up, 83% used the first person to refer to their image, whereas only 3% of those referring to their image in the third person reached for the sticker.

Findings such as these support the distinction between an ecological self and an extended self, suggesting that young children initially think of themselves in terms of their ongoing actions. Information about this aspect of the self is communicated by cues such as contingent movement, like what would be reflected back in a mirror. Delaying the image eliminates this cue, making it difficult for young preschoolers to relate to this image of themselves. As awareness of the extended self develops over time, children should get better at understanding how the self that they presently experience is related to their past experiences. For instance, they should know that the more delayed the image of themselves is, the less reflective that image is likely to be of their present state.

Povinelli and Simon (1998) videotaped preschoolers on two separate occasions, 1 week apart, as they played a game. The videotapings took place in recognizably different rooms. As in the earlier experiment, a sticker had been surreptitiously placed on the child's head during play. Children watched either the video taken just moments ago or the one that had been taken a week ago. In each case, when the video was shown, they were asked, "Can you get that sticker for me?" If awareness of the extended self improves with age, older preschoolers should be less likely to reach up for the sticker when viewing the video from a week ago than when viewing the one taken moments before. Conversely, when watching the recent video, they should be more likely to reach for the sticker than younger children. Both of these expected age differences were found. Thus, the older preschoolers understood that something that had happened just a few minutes ago could still be causally relevant to their present self, but that something that had happened a week ago could not be. The youngest preschoolers, however, did not make this distinction. Figure 9.1 shows the results of this experiment. These trends give support to the development of an extended self, or the awareness, as William James (1890) put it, that "I am the same self I was yesterday" (p. 332).

The conversations children have with their parents contribute to the development of autobiographical memory.

Self-Concept

What might underlie the growth of such a sense of self? Katherine Nelson (1992), at City University of New York, suggests that a new type of memory, which she terms an **autobiographical memory,** emerges at about the age of 4. Autobiographical memories make up an individual's life history. They form the personal narrative that tells the story of oneself. Prior to this age, children may recall particular events, but these do not become part of their life story. Nelson considers language in general, and conversations in particular, to be important for the development of such memory. By the age of 4, children are better able to understand language as a representational system; they are able to step back from the pragmatics of communication and understand language as a way of representing their experiences and communicating these to others. Thus, children begin to use language not simply to communicate their needs or label things around them, but also as a way of representing what they know and what others must know as well. Autobiographical memory represents the same sort of change with respect to memory that one sees in their use of language, the development of an awareness, that is, that these memories are *about* something, namely themselves.

The conversations children have with their parents are assumed to contribute to the development of this memory. Just as Vygotsky (1978) stressed the social context of development, in which children acquire the skills of their culture by working alongside those who are more skilled, children's conversations with parents support the development of an autobiographical memory, both in terms of what is remembered and how it is fit into a personal narrative. Parents provide the narrative structure for this memory by showing children how to make sense of past events.

At what age do childhood memories start for most people?

autobiographical memories
Memories that constitute the personal narrative that tells the story of oneself; emerges at about age 4.

Melissa Welch-Ross (1997), at Georgia State University, assumed that children's ability to participate in these conversations should reflect their developing cognitive capacities (see Chapter 8). Preschoolers were tested for their ability to mentally represent what others know and to coordinate this with their own understanding. Their conversations with their mothers were also recorded. As anticipated, children who had a better understanding of the way in which they and their mothers mentally represented shared experiences participated more actively in conversations about events they had experienced, offering information on their own about these rather than simply responding to what their mothers said. Their participation suggests that they understood that such conversations represented a "meeting of the minds," in which it was necessary for both parties to share information for each to know what the other remembered.

Several distinct conversational styles have been identified in these conversations between parents and children (Reese & Fivush, 1993). Typically, parents either weave past events into a narrative that describes not only the event but also how it relates to the child's other experiences, or they analyze events in terms of general semantic categories rather than the child's experiences. Nelson has noted that children's memories tend to reflect the style in which their personal experiences have been discussed. Parents, in other words, teach their children how to remember things, telling them what is important and which things are related to what other things.

Not only can differences between one parent and the next be expected to influence the nature of parent-child conversations, but so can differences between one culture and the next. One such difference concerns the emphasis cultures give to the individual versus the group. Western cultures have been characterized as emphasizing the personal characteristics that make individuals unique, reflecting a high valuation of personal independence, and Asian cultures as emphasizing the self in relation to others, reflecting the value given to the interdependence that exists among members of a group (Markus & Kitayama, 1991).

Given that parents from different cultural backgrounds might be expected to emphasize somewhat different past experiences in these conversations, what implications might this have? Are differences such as these associated with cultural differences in the way children think of themselves—that is, in the way they construe the self? Do American parents, in other words, foster a construction of the self that is more independent, by encouraging self-expression and telling stories in which the child stands out from others in some way? And do Asian parents foster one that is more interdependent, by discouraging emotional displays or focusing on the self?

Jessica Jungsook Han, Michelle Leichtman, and Qi Wang (1998), at Harvard University, interviewed North American, Korean, and Chinese children, from 4 to 6 years old, asking them about their recent experiences. As expected, American children spoke less about others relative to themselves, talked more about their feelings and thoughts, and gave more details than did the Korean or Chinese children. Consider the responses of two children, one Chinese and one American, when asked to describe what they did at bedtime the evening before:

CHINESE CHILD: "After I washed my face, I asked Dad to tell me a story. Then my mom covered me with the blanket. Then my mom went over there and read magazines. And finally I fell asleep."

INTERVIEWER: What else did you do?

CHINESE CHILD: "Watched TV before going to bed. After watching TV, I went to wash. After washing, I watched again. Just after I finished dinner, my dad asked me to practice writing. After practicing writing, he asked me to play the piano. Just after playing the piano, the TV program began. Then my dad watched TV together with me. After watching TV, I went to sleep."

Personal storytelling about happy occasions is a means of socializing children to their culture.

U.S. CHILD: "I read, did I read last night? No, I played computer, instead of reading, but I liked the book better than the computer."

INTERVIEWER: What else did you do?

U.S. CHILD: "I played with my toys, I think, and then I'll tell you what game I played on the computer. There's a dictionary thing, and there's a word finder, and there's hangman, and other games, and three games, and then there's all different things, and to find a word, you just click on the word finder, and after two or three letters it just finds the word." (p. 708)

These findings show that children acquire the values of their cultures at an early age and that these values shape the way they talk, and presumably think, about themselves.

Peggy Miller, Angela Wiley, Heidi Fung, and Chung-Hue Liang (1997) examined personal storytelling as a means of socializing children into the values of their culture by comparing the narratives told to European American and Chinese children. In particular, they examined mention of past wrongdoings as a way of teaching children and communicating social standards. Although they found the similarities to be greater than the differences, they also found Chinese families to be more likely to mention transgressions as a way of teaching children what was expected of them than were European American families, 35% versus 7% of the stories reflecting transgressions, respectively. Further, when European American parents did mention transgressions, these were typically peripheral to the story line or otherwise marked as nonserious, suggesting these parents did not use past transgressions as a teaching tool. These findings should not be taken to mean that

Box 9.1 *The Use of Personal Storytelling as a Means of Socializing Values*

As the co-narration begins, the grandmother is holding the child in her arms. After the first few words, he gets up and stands by his grandmother.

GRANDMA: Oh, right. This morning when Mom was spanking you, what did you say? You said, "Don't hit me!" Right?

CHILD: Hmn. (nods)

GRANDMA: Then, what did I tell you to say?

CHILD: "I won't push the screen down."

GRANDMA: Oh right. So, what would you say to Mom?

CHILD: I would say to Mom, "Don't have the screen pushed down." (Child moves closer and speaks in a very low tone into Grandma's ear)

GRANDMA: Oh, you would talk to Mom, saying, "Mama, I won't push the screen down."

CHILD: Hmn.

GRANDMA: So, Mom wouldn't hit you.

CHILD: Hmn.

GRANDMA: Right? Hmn. If you asked Mom, "You don't hit me," Mom would have hit you, right?

CHILD: Hmn. (Nods)

GRANDMA: So you would directly say to Mom in this way, "Mom, I won't push the screen down." Then how would Mom have reacted?

CHILD: [Unintelligible]

GRANDMA: What?

CHILD: [Unintelligible]

GRANDMA: Then she wouldn't hit you, right?

CHILD: Hmn. (Nods)

GRANDMA: Oh. So, next time when Mom is going to spank you, which sentence is better for you to say to her?

CHILD: Hmn. Hmn. (Moving close to Grandma's ear) "I won't have [unintelligible] won't have the screen pushed down."

GRANDMA: Oh, right. Now you have choices. You say, "Mom, I won't push the screen down." In that way, Mom won't spank you. So next time when Mom is spanking you, you shouldn't say, "You don't hit me. (High pitch) You don't hit me." (High pitch) You shouldn't say that way.

CHILD: (Laughs)

GRANDMA: You say, "Don't hit me." (Raises her voice) Mom will hit more. Right? Instead, you say to Mom, "I won't push the screen down." What will Mom do to you?

CHILD: Will give me [unintelligible] a tender touch (in Taiwanese).

GRANDMA: What?

CHILD: A tender touch (in Taiwanese).

GRANDMA: A tender touch (in Taiwanese), oh, give you a tender touch (in Taiwanese). OK. (Laughs loudly and holds child in her arms.)

This co-narration ends as it began with the grandmother holding the child in her arms.

Source: Miller, Wiley, Fung, & Liang (1997).

European American parents did not take misbehavior seriously, but rather that they dealt with it in a different way. Similarly, it would be wrong to interpret Chinese families' use of transgressions as being overly critical. The parents found ways to end these stories on a positive note, often giving the child the opportunity to suggest a more appropriate behavior and then praising the child (Box 9.1).

Even with these differences, it should be emphasized that the similarities in the use of personal stories were greater than the differences. In both cultures, most of the stories were about things such as holidays, family outings, or other happy occasions, not about something the child had done wrong.

Age Differences in Self-Concept

The way children think about themselves also changes with their age. Research finds a consistent developmental progression in the way children conceptualize the self. Preschoolers tend to describe themselves in terms of their physical characteristics, such as how tall they are, whether they wear glasses or have freckles; they also mention objective information, such as their age or where they live. As they get older, children increasingly mention aspects of their personality, such as being kind or brave or having a good sense of humor. They are more likely to characterize themselves, in other words, in terms of their psychological makeup. They are also more likely to describe themselves in terms of their relationships and in terms of membership in social groups (Brinthaupt & Lipka, 1985; Livesley & Bromley, 1973).

Richard Ely, Gigliana Melzi, and Luke Hadge, at Boston University, and Allyssa McCabe (1998), at the University of Massachusetts, Lowell, looked at the way children, 4 through 9, conceptualize the self by listening to the way they described themselves in their conversations. These investigators focused on two aspects of personal functioning. Conversations were coded for **agency** when they were about mastery or achievement, such as stories involving some dynamic action, and for **communion** when they were about sharing feelings, friendship, and being together (Bakan, 1966). These two modes of functioning capture both the physical and the psychological dimensions of the self-concept and are more or less balanced in adults (McAdams, Hoffman, Mansfield, & Day, 1996). But we know very little about how children perceive themselves in terms of each of these modes.

These investigators found that children regularly described themselves with respect to both of these modes of functioning, but that activities, rather than feelings and relationships, dominated their descriptions. Although this was true at every age, the frequency with which they mentioned others when talking about themselves increased with age, a finding that is consistent with other research showing that children are more likely to characterize themselves in terms of their social world as they get older. Girls, also, were more likely than boys to mention others and, in general, to mention themes of communion.

Gender and the Self

One of the most important ways in which children come to think of themselves is in terms of their gender. By the time they are 2, most children can identify themselves as a boy or a girl, a process known as **gender labeling.** How much they understand of what this means, however, is another matter. Misunderstandings arise from confusing sex with gender. Sex refers to whether one is biologically female or male and is determined at the moment of conception. **Sex differences** are biologically based. Examples include differences in the reproductive systems

Q How would a preschooler be likely to describe her older sister? And how would that description most likely differ from the sister's description of herself?

agency An aspect of mature functioning characterized by achievement and mastery; the complement of communion.

communion An aspect of mature functioning characterized by empathy and friendship; the complement of agency.

gender labeling The ability to label oneself as a boy or girl; develops by about age 2.

sex differences Biological and physiological differences distinguishing the sexes.

Between the ages of 3 and 5, children develop notions of which behaviors are appropriate for their sex.

and genitals of females and males or differences in the average height and body proportions of each sex. Gender refers to the distinctions a culture makes in what it considers masculine or feminine. **Gender differences** are socially determined. For example, our culture expects boys to be assertive and noisy and girls to be helpful and understanding. One is *born* female or male, but one is *socialized* to be feminine or masculine.

Initially, most children do not distinguish sex from gender. They do not realize, for instance, that changes in one's appearance will not result in changes in one's sex. Thus, a 3-year-old boy may be afraid to put on a dress, fearing he will become a girl, or a girl may not want to get her hair cut short, thinking that she will turn into a boy. **Sex constancy,** also referred to as gender constancy, is the understanding that one's sex is permanent and will not change as a function of how one looks or dresses. This understanding develops between the ages of 3 and 5. So, too, does **gender stereotyping,** or preschoolers' notions of which behaviors are appropriate for either sex. These stereotypes encompass such things as types of dress, which toys are appropriate to play with, and the occupations children envision for themselves as adults, and they contribute to children's **gender identity,** or experience of themselves as male or female (Lips, 1997).

Children develop gender stereotypes in various ways. Perhaps the simplest is by observing which people do what things. Thus, children can easily sort through pictures of hammers, baby rattles, cooking utensils, and power tools, labeling these as masculine or feminine. Adults' understanding of gender, however, extends beyond objective and concrete examples such as these to what might be called a metaphorical knowledge, or one based on characteristics drawn from other domains of experience and only extended to gender. Examples of this understanding would be to think of girls as "sweet," or of boys as "rough," characteristics borrowed from the domains of taste and touch, respectively. Does this understanding of gender extend to preschoolers as well?

Mary Leinbach, Barbara Hort, and Beverly Fagot (1997) showed children pictures of objects, such as hammers and ironing boards, that were easily stereotyped as masculine or feminine in terms of their usage by males or females, and also pictures of objects embodying characteristics that could only be extended to either

Why might clothing such as a Wonder Woman belt or a Superman cape be significant to very young preschoolers?

gender differences Culturally determined differences in masculinity and femininity.

sex constancy The understanding that one's sex remains the same and will not change as a function of how one looks or dresses; also termed *gender constancy.*

gender stereotyping Culturally based expectations of behaviors that are appropriate for each sex.

gender identity Experience of oneself as male or female.

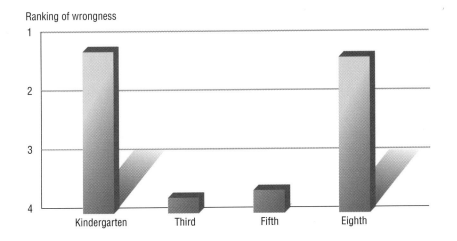

Ranking of wrongness

FIGURE 9.2 Evaluations of Sex-Role Transgressions as a Function of Age

Source: T. Stoddart and E. Turiel (1985). Children's concepts of cross-gender activities. *Child Development*, 56, 1241–1252.

sex metaphorically, such as burlap (rough) and butterflies (soft). Children demonstrated an awareness of gender stereotyping not only for the objects typically used by one sex or the other, but also for those that were only metaphorically associated with either sex. The latter basis for stereotyping was evident even in 4-year-olds, as well as in older children. Thus, burlap, bears, and fir trees were sorted as "mostly a boy kind of thing" whereas cotton, butterflies, and flowers were thought of as "mostly a girl kind of thing."

Even with a metaphoric understanding, preschoolers' gender stereotypes are considerably more rigid than those of older children or adults. Adults understand, for instance, that sex roles are culturally determined and, as such, represent relative rather than absolute standards for behavior. Do young children share this understanding of gender stereotypes? Trish Stoddart and Elliot Turiel (1985) asked children of different ages to evaluate whether sex-role transgressions, such as a boy wearing a barrette or a girl wearing a boy's suit, were wrong and to state why. Preschoolers evaluated transgressions such as these as very wrong and cited concern over maintaining sex constancy as the most frequent reason. In contrast, third- and fifth-graders evaluated sex-role transgressions as only minimally wrong. Eighth-graders, for whom puberty again raises issues of gender, also considered sex-role transgressions to be wrong, but for different reasons, viewing them in terms of their psychological implications rather than possible physical ones (Figure 9.2). Preschoolers' understanding of sex roles as absolute and inflexible makes sense, given their confusion over what might happen were they to violate them. After all, who knows what they might wake up to be were they to wear the wrong clothes to bed at night!

How do children know which behaviors are appropriate for either sex? How do they come to know, in other words, what it means to be a boy or a girl? Once again, different answers have been offered by different schools of thought. We will consider three of these: a social-learning-theory perspective, a psychodynamic perspective, and a developmental constructive perspective.

The Social Learning Approach   Social learning theory derives from the environmental model (see Chapter 1). As such, it emphasizes the role of external forces in shaping gender-appropriate behavior. Social learning theorists assume that one's gender role and one's gender identity are learned, just as they assume most other behaviors are (Bandura, 1977). Specifically, children learn gender-appropriate behaviors by *observing* people around them, who serve as *models*, and *imitating* what they do. Not all of the behaviors they imitate, of course, are appropriate for

Hammering like daddy: By imitating their same-sex parent, children acquire both gender-appropriate roles and the skills necessary to fill them.

their sex. Little boys not only do the things they see their fathers, big brothers, and uncles do, but they also may, on occasion, do some of the things Mom and their big sisters do as well, such as put on lipstick or dress up in high heels. Differential reinforcement of behaviors that are appropriate for their gender role makes these more likely to occur, whereas ignoring or even punishing inappropriate behaviors makes these progressively less likely.

Parents play an important part in this learning process, both as the models whom children imitate and as those actively involved in shaping their children's behavior. This does not mean that parents always act intentionally. Parents, in fact, may not know just how differently they actually treat children of either sex. One study, for instance, observed mothers as they interacted with an infant who was dressed up either to look like a boy, in blue pants, or a girl, wearing a pink dress (the infant was actually a boy). These mothers offered the infant different toys when they believed it to be a boy than when they thought it a girl, and smiled more and held the infant more closely when they believed it to be a girl. Yet all of these mothers told the researchers that they would not act differently toward their own sons and daughters (Will, Self, & Datan, 1976).

How do parents influence children's sex-role behavior?

Eric Lindsey, Jacquelyn Mize, and Gregory Pettit (1997), at Auburn University, observed parents as they played with their children, to see whether parents model different types of play for children of either sex. Eleanor Maccoby (1988, 1990), for instance, has noted that boys and girls engage in noticeably different play styles, boys in more rough-and-tumble play and girls more in pretense play. Children of either sex also use different strategies in attempting to influence their peers. Boys are more likely to use direct commands when attempting to get others to do what they want, whereas girls more frequently use polite suggestions (Cramer & Skidd, 1992). What part do parents play in shaping these differences? Lindsey, Mize, and Pettit (1997) found, first, that the play styles of boys and girls differed in the expected ways. They also found that the play patterns of parents differed as well. Fathers engaged in more physical play than did mothers, thus modeling this form of behavior, and mothers similarly modeled, or engaged in, more pretense play than fathers. Children appeared to be sensitive to these differences, as evidenced by the type of play they attempted to engage the parent in. Children of both sexes, for instance, were more likely to engage in pretense play when with mothers than with fathers.

How differently do parents treat daughters and sons? In terms of general socialization, such as in matters of discipline, time spent with their children, and how warm their relationships are, the differences are slight. It is primarily with respect to gender-related behaviors that the differences are more apparent. Thus, parents dress children differently, give them different toys, and frequently ask them to do different chores around the house. Finally, with respect to gender socialization, differences due to both socioeconomic status and ethnicity are evident. Gender stereotyping is more pronounced in lower-income than in middle-income families. Also, African American families are more likely to socialize females to be more androgynous, to be not only caring, but also economically independent, by fostering responsible attitudes toward work (Lips, 1997).

The Psychoanalytic Approach   The psychoanalytic approach derives from the organismic model, and so gives greater importance than does social learning theory to biological forces within the individual. Rather than explaining gender differences through the imitation of external models, psychoanalytic theory focuses on the internalization of standards for behavior through a process of **identification**. In identification with the same-sex parent, children internalize, or take on for themselves, all of the behaviors and attitudes of that parent, making it possible for them, in a sense, to carry that parent about with them wherever they go. Identification thus lays the foundation for gender differences and for adult sexuality. The process of identification also resolves one of the central dramas in the young child's life. Freud termed this drama the **Oedipal complex** after the Greek myth of a young man who unknowingly murdered his father and married his mother. Freud believed that every boy falls in love with his mother, and every girl with her father. The resolution to this love triangle, according to Freud, lays the foundation for fundamental differences between the sexes. We shall look at the Oedipal complex in boys first, since Freud framed his theory around the male experience.

During the phallic stage of personality development (see Chapter 1), the libido seeks expression through the genitals. The young boy derives sexual pleasure from masturbating, an activity that imbues his penis with such significance that when he notices a girl without one, he is horrified and assumes she has been mutilated. He also thinks that the same could happen to him if he is not careful. Before you think he is overreacting, consider the reason for his fears. His sexual feelings for his mother have transformed his father into a rival. Castration, he fears, would be a fitting punishment for these emotions. Freud believed the boy's fear, termed *castration anxiety,* to be so great that he represses his sexual desire for his mother. In yielding to his father, he identifies with him, and, in so doing, he takes on the father's values. Thus the boy's fear of castration motivates him to move beyond his incestuous desires, repressing these and identifying with the father. The superego that emerges from this process is strong, since it reflects the power that the boy sees in his father.

The girl falls in love with her father and views her mother as a sexual rival. For her the **Electra complex** revolves around a different set of motives. Instead of anxiety, she experiences longing and inferiority. She sees that she has "come off badly" in comparison with boys and feels inferior because she does not have a penis. She wants her father to give her one, too. Of course, these longings, termed

identification The child's internalization of parental behaviors and attitudes.

Oedipal complex A Freudian concept in which the young boy is sexually attracted to his mother.

Electra complex A Freudian concept in which the young girl is sexually attracted to her father.

Freud believed that every boy falls in love with his mother, and every girl with her father.

penis envy, cannot be satisfied and are finally replaced by a compensatory wish: that her father give her a baby. Freud writes, "Her Oedipus complex culminates in a desire, which is long retained, to receive a baby from her father as a gift—to bear him a child" (Freud, 1925a/1961, p. 124). Freud believed that the girl's longings for a penis and a child intermingle in the unconscious and prepare her for her future roles of wife and mother.

Notice that the girl never cleanly resolves the Oedipal complex; she retains a lingering longing in the unconscious that imbues her personality with its essential feminine features, one of which is a feeling of inferiority. Freud believed that the female moves from feelings of personal inferiority to contempt for all women. Once she realizes that her lack of a penis is not a personal form of punishment for something she has done, but is shared by all women, "she begins to share the contempt felt by men for a sex which is the lesser in so important a respect" (Freud, 1925b/1961, p. 253).

Freud was ahead of his time in many ways in his acceptance of women. He freely admitted women into his analytic circle and frequently referred patients to women analysts (Tavris & Wade, 1984). However, his theory of the feminine personality is uniquely uncomplimentary. Freud believed females to be masochistic, vain, and jealous. The masochism (deriving pleasure from pain) stems from the frustrated longing for their fathers. The vanity and jealousy he attributed to penis envy. "If she cannot have a penis, she will turn her whole body into an erotic substitute; her feminine identity comes to depend on being sexy, attractive, and adored. Female jealousy is a displaced version of penis envy" (Travis & Wade, 1984, p. 182).

Freud also believed that the female superego is not as strong as that of men; the implication is that females are less moral. Two things account for their weaker superegos. Females are never as highly motivated as males to resolve Oedipal issues, since they literally do not have as much to lose. Also, they identify with a weaker figure than do males; the mother is more nurturant and less threatening and powerful than the father.

Karen Horney, a contemporary of Sigmund Freud, objected to Freud's interpretation of the feminine personality. She countered that he had not properly taken into consideration the male-dominated society in which his patients lived. While women might want the power and privileges that men have, this is a very different matter from Freud's penis envy. Further, women's economic dependence on men creates a psychological dependence and a need to have men validate their self-worth (Horney, 1967).

Horney contended that it is impossible to test Freud's concept of penis envy as long as women do not have the same status in society as men. Though from wealthy families, Freud's female patients lived in a male-dominated society. They were economically dependent first on their fathers and later on their husbands, enjoying few outlets for creativity or productivity. Did they envy a man for his penis? Or did they envy him for his privileged position in society?

Horney also questioned Feud's assertion that masochism is a central feature of the female personality. Freud maintained that since the Oedipal complex is never fully resolved in the girl, she retains a frustrated desire for her father, which becomes associated with later sexual pleasure. Horney pointed out that, although some women may obtain pleasure by sacrificing themselves to the needs of others, so do some men (Tavris & Wade, 1984).

Horney observed that numbers of her male patients expressed envy and fear concerning pregnancy and childbirth. She suggested that men cope with these feelings by reacting with compensatory emotions: Rather than feeling inferior because they are not able to become pregnant, they feel contempt for women for

penis envy A Freudian concept in which the young girl longs for a penis.

not having a penis. Rather than fearing women's power to give birth, they feel contempt for their weakness.

The Constructive Approach   The constructive approach derives from the organismic model, just as does the psychoanalytic, and similarly stresses forces within the individual in giving shape to behavior. However, important differences exist between these two approaches when it comes to explaining gender differences. The constructive approach assumes that children construct their sexual identities by selectively attending to gender-appropriate behaviors in others, whether these behaviors are evidenced by a parent or another person. Thus, selective perception, and not identification, is the process assumed to be responsible for the development of gender-appropriate behavior. Also, the behavior of any individual, not simply that of a parent, is assumed to be important in the formation of children's gender identities (Martin & Halverson, 1981; Bem, 1981, 1985).

This process of selective perception is guided by **gender schemas;** these are cognitive structures that direct the pickup of information about the self as it relates to one's gender (Bem, 1981). Gender schemas operate as anticipatory schemata (see Chapter 5), creating a readiness to perceive certain types of information, cues that are consistent with one's gender schema and not others. Thus, a young boy whose gender schema for the way boys play includes information about how active and "physical" the play is would be more likely to notice these as elements in climbing on jungle bars, a form of play engaged in more by boys than girls, than as elements in skipping rope, which few boys engage in, even though the latter involves just as much physical activity as the former.

The ability of gender schemas to influence both perception and memory has been dramatically illustrated. Carol Martin and Charles Halverson (1983) showed 5- and 6-year-olds drawings of children performing various activities. The activities were either consistent with their sex role (a girl cooking, a boy boxing) or inconsistent (a boy cooking, a girl boxing). When asked about the pictures a week later, children's memory was more likely to be faulty for those pictures in which the activity was inconsistent with their gender schema. Moreover, the errors they made frequently "corrected" what they had seen; for instance, they remembered a picture of a boy cooking as being that of a girl. Similarly, Bruce Carter and Gary Levy (1988) assessed preschoolers' awareness of gender stereotypes prior to showing them pictures of males and females engaged in activities either consistent or inconsistent with their sex role. As they had expected, they found that children with more firmly established gender schema had more difficulty remembering pictures of activities inconsistent with sex roles and were more likely to make errors in which they "corrected" the sex of the character to fit the activity in the picture they were recalling.

Why might children organize their experiences in terms of gender as opposed to other, equally visible, characteristics? Sandra Bem (1981, 1985) argues that gender has "cognitive primacy" over other social categories because of the importance given it by our society. This is not to say, of course, that children do not organize their experiences according to other categories as well, for they do. However, the extent to which children use gender schemas to process information about themselves or other children most likely depends on the extent to which gender has been emphasized in their socialization.

Bem recommends that parents mention anatomical differences, rather than behavioral ones, when first teaching children about sex differences, since these have the double advantage of being both concrete and precise. She and her husband did so with their preschooler, who, even at a tender age, could identify himself as a boy because he had a penis. Such distinctions, however, do not cover the

gender schemas Cognitive structures that direct the pickup of information about the self as it relates to one's gender.

difficulties children will encounter with friends whose parents have been less objective. Bem (1985), for instance, recounts a conversation their son had with another preschooler when he wore barrettes to nursery school one day:

> Several times that day, another little boy told Jeremy that he, Jeremy, must be a girl because "only girls wear barrettes." After trying to explain to this child that "wearing barrettes doesn't matter" and that "being a boy means having a penis and testicles," Jeremy finally pulled down his pants as a way of making his point more convincingly. The other child was not impressed. He simply said, "Everybody has a penis; only girls wear barrettes." (p. 216)

Ethnicity and the Self

Children's conceptions of themselves also include their ethnicity. The term *ethnicity* has been used to include individuals who differ racially as well as culturally, for several reasons. Both genetic and behavioral variation among individuals of European, African, and Asian descent are greater *within* any racial classification than *between* classifications (Lewontin, 1982; Rowe, Vazsonyi, & Flannery, 1994; Zuckerman, 1990). The *significance* of ethnicity/race can best be understood from a contextual perspective. The community and cultural contexts in which people live and the responses of others to physical features such as skin pigmentation and facial characteristics are what contribute to one's sense of identity (Phinney, 1996).

Ethnicity can influence children's self-concepts in ways not limited to skin color, one's hair, or facial features. Language is one example, as shown in the way Maxine Hong Kingston (1976), who grew up in a Chinese immigrant community in Stockton, California, describes having to talk in school: "It was when I found out I had to talk that school became a misery, that the silence became a misery. I did not speak and felt bad each time that I did not speak. I read aloud in first grade, though, and heard the barest whisper with little squeaks come out of my throat. 'Louder,' said the teacher, who scared the voice away again. The other Chinese girls did not talk either, so I know the silence had to do with being a Chinese girl." ◄

Children who belong to a minority become aware sooner of the racial or ethnic differences that distinguish them than do those who belong to the majority. Majority children may even be unaware that they are also members of a so-called racial group. Thomas Kochman (1987) found that Whites distinguished each other in terms of ethnicity, but not race. They would, for example, refer to themselves as Irish or Polish, never as "White." The terms *minority* and *majority* are relative, of course. Whites are actually in the minority throughout the world, though in the majority in the United States. Similarly, within this country, White children can experience minority status if they live in a community or attend a preschool in which some other group predominates (Phinney, 1996).

But what does it mean to belong to an ethnic group? Jean Phinney (1996), a psychologist at California State University, Los Angeles, points out that ethnicity cannot be thought of simply in terms of labels for groups of people who are neatly distinguished from one another. People using the same label often differ widely from one another, including the ways in which they interpret and use the very terms by which they identify themselves. Rather than sorting people into categories, it is necessary to examine ethnicity with respect to at least three *dimensions* along which individuals vary: their cultural values and attitudes, their sense of

"Hey, Laf, let's play," James urged his friend. James loved basketball. . . . James, who was short for his age, dreamed of playing professional basketball.

"I don't wanna play ball with them," Lafeyette said, referring to the children by the jungle gym. "They might try to make me join a gang."

About a week earlier, members of one of the local gangs had asked Lafeyette to stand security, and it had made him skittish. His mother told the teenage members she would call the police if they kept after Lafeyette. "I'd die first before I let them take one of my sons," she said.

. . . Lafeyette and James constantly worried that they might be pulled into gangs. Lafeyette knew what might happen: "When you first join you think it's good. They'll buy you what you want. You have to do anything they tell you to do. If they tell you to kill somebody, you have to do that." James figured the only way to make it out of Horner was "to try to make as little friends as possible."

So while a group of young boys shrieked in delight as the basketball ricocheted through the jungle gym's opening, Lafeyette, James, and a few other boys perched idly on the metal benches in front of their building. (pp. 30–31) ◄

Some children have difficulty reading a social situation and knowing when and how to join a group.

Social Competence   What children usually do is play. Simple as this may appear to be, some children are better at playing than others. Play, in other words, requires a certain amount of skill. Research has isolated several important components of social competence (Dodge, Pettit, McClaskey, & Brown, 1986). The first component, *assessing the situation,* is simply to see what's going on, to accurately "read" the social situation, so that one can adapt one's behavior accordingly. In a sense, joining others in play may involve some of the same skills adults use in entering fast-moving traffic. One has to judge the speed of the ongoing activity, get up to that speed oneself, and then move into the thick of things. Pulling onto a freeway at 30 miles an hour requires everyone else to slow down to your speed: It doesn't work.

When preschoolers "pull into the fast lane" with a remark such as "What are you doing?" they're asking others to stop for them, an unwelcome request if they are enjoying themselves. Entry remarks that call attention away from the ongoing activity are likely to be rebuffed. Similarly, remarks about oneself are usually unsuccessful ways of getting a group's attention. Instead, fitting into a group appears to be a matter of figuring out what the group is doing Children who are better at this are more popular. Simply put, one needs to be able to know what the group is doing in order to join in.

Figuring out what is going on, however, is not a matter of simply seeing what others are doing. Recall that the constructive approach taken in this text assumes that individuals read meaning into situations, interpreting them in terms of their own expectations. As a consequence, factors related to one's personality enter into the equation as well. Mary Lynne Courtney and Robert Cohen (1996), at the University of Memphis, showed a videotape to school-age boys who had been rated by their classmates for aggressiveness (see the Research Focus, "An Experiment," in Chapter 1). The tape of two boys playing tag showed one boy falling down after being tagged by the other. Some of the boys had been told the two were good friends (benign prior information); others had been told they did not like each other (hostile prior information); and still others had been told nothing (neutral condition). Boys who were more aggressive perceived the videotaped sequence differently than did those who were less aggressive. The difference was most noticeable when they had the least information about the situation (neutral condition), suggesting that aggressive boys are more vigilant in ambiguous situations.

Q How do socially competent children enter a group of children playing?

In general, more aggressive children are likely to attribute hostile intentions to others more frequently than less aggressive ones (Crick & Dodge, 1996; Waldman, 1996).

Children's perceptions of others' intentions are related to their early experiences within the family, experiences that appear to affect the way they process social information. Specifically, their perceptions are related to the way their own intentions are perceived by their parents. Gregory Pettit, Kenneth Dodge, and Melissa Brown (1988) found that preschoolers whose mothers were likely to perceive their children's actions as motivated by hostility when provoked by them were not as socially competent as those whose mothers attributed benign intentions to them. The former children could not think of as many solutions to problems, such as making new friends or getting someone to give them what they wanted, as did the latter. Research such as this points to the importance of parents' values and expectations in shaping children's expectations about their social worlds and, in turn, affecting their social competence.

How accurately preschoolers can predict and understand the emotional reactions of others is directly related to how well liked they are. Susanne Denham, Marcia McKinley, Elizabeth Couchoud, and Robert Holt (1990), at George Mason University, found that children who couldn't say how someone would feel in a given situation were more likely to be disliked by their peers. As with most skills, there are noticeable and relatively stable individual differences from one child to the next. Likability, in other words, is fairly well differentiated among 3- to 5-year-olds.

The second dimension of social competence is *responding appropriately* to others' behavior. Children who are popular are distinguished not as much by their own initiation of encounters as by their positive response to the initiations of others. In fact, popular children approach others infrequently; but they *are* better at keeping things going, and other children appear to have a better time with them (Dodge, 1983). Mothers have been found to contribute to children's social competence by serving as "social coaches," both making suggestions for future behavior and giving feedback on what children have already done. For instance, children who are popular have been found to have mothers who give better advice on how to join a group of children playing together and who are more likely to use feedback as a way of fostering more appropriate behavior than are mothers of unpopular children (Russell & Finnie, 1990).

Jacquelyn Mize and Gregory Pettit (1997) showed videotapes of conflict situations to mothers and their children and observed the ways in which mothers "coached" their children concerning the sources and possible solutions to the conflicts they were viewing. Children whose mothers interpreted the source of the conflicts as unintentional rather than hostile and who suggested positive solutions, such as "I don't think he meant to do that. You can build it again, right?" were more socially skilled and were liked better by their peers. The relationship between maternal practices and children's reactions appears to hold across cultures (Zahn-Waxler, Friedman, Cole, Mizuta, & Hiruma, 1996).

Children's play differs not only as a function of their social competence, but also as a function of their gender. Peer interactions become segregated by sex by the age of 3. A frequently noted gender difference is that boys are more likely to play in groups and girls to play in dyads, or pairs. Joyce Benenson, Nicholas Apostoleris, and Jodi Parnass (1997), at McGill University, examined the development of dyadic and group play by forming play groups of five to six children and observing them as they interacted. Rather than coding play as *either* dyadic or group play, they coded instances of both types of play as these occurred. Thus a child could be interacting with one other child (coded as a dyad) while participating in an ongoing group activity (coded as group play) and coded for each type of play.

When play behavior was coded in this way, the percentage of time spent in dyadic interactions did not differ as a function of sex. Dyadic interactions, however, when they did occur, were maintained for a longer period of time by girls than they were by boys. Whether this difference reflects greater social skills among girls, as has been found to be true for popular children, or whether it reflects gender preferences for one type of play versus another remains unclear. Although the amount of time spent in group play among 4-year-olds did not differ for boys and girls, by the age of 6, boys were more likely than girls to play in groups.

Whether playing with one or several children, preschoolers are more open and relaxed when they are with their friends than with others. They smile, laugh, and talk more; are more likely to say what they want and why; and affirm each other more, answering one another and picking up on each other's play. They are also better at resolving conflicts when these arise (Hartup, 1996). Richard Fabes, Nancy Eisenberg, Melanie Smith, and Bridget Murphy (1996), at Arizona State University, found that preschoolers get just as angry when playing with friends as when playing with peers whom they don't like as well, but that what causes them to get angry differs. With friends, they are most likely to get angry at what might be called relationship issues, such as being rejected or violating the conditions of play—when a child doesn't play by the rules, for instance. In contrast, physical acts, such as being pushed or having a toy knocked over, were the most common causes of anger with less-liked peers.

Children are also more generous in interpreting the motives of those they like, being less likely to see their behavior as intentionally provocative (Fabes et al., 1996). This "generosity" again illustrates the constructive nature of perception. Fabes and his associates found, for instance, that just as with the aggressive boys studied by Courtney and Cohen (1996), the assumptions children made concerning the intentions of others affected the way they perceived the others' behavior. A child who has just been pushed, for example, would be more likely to perceive this behavior as hostile when pushed by someone who is not well liked than when pushed by a friend. The very same behavior by a friend would more likely be interpreted as an invitation to rough-house or as simply clumsy.

Parenting

Most parents are not prepared for the sheer number of things to be done at once, all at once, all the time. Conversations, for example, are rarely held with just one other person—not, at least, when there's more than one child in the family. As soon as one child starts talking, another joins in. Reminders not to interrupt or requests that something be repeated frequently don't help, since it's not always clear who has interrupted whom or what one has missed. All of this typically takes place while the parent is doing something else, such as making lunches before having breakfast or telling a child where to find a misplaced shoe. Parenting, most would say? This had better not be one more thing to think about.

In fact, it usually isn't. Parenting, like life, is what one does while waiting for something else to happen. It's helping a child find the pet mouse before the cat does or listening to a joke your son has just told. People learn how to parent not from reading books or taking a course, although both of these can be helpful, but from the way they were parented. In this sense, parenting is more a matter of who one is than what one does, passed on from one generation to the next much like eye color or body build.

TABLE 9.1 Parenting Style and Social Competence

Parenting Style	Characteristics	Resulting Social Behavior in Child
Authoritative	Demanding, encourages independence; responsive, warm, and nurturing; disciplines with explanation; maintains open dialogue	Social competence and responsibility
Authoritarian	Demanding; consistent in enforcing standards; restrictive, controlling	Ineffective social interaction; inactive
Indulgent	Responsive, warm, and nurturing; undemanding; uses punishment inconsistently and infrequently; exercises little control	Social competence, well-adjusted; peer oriented; misconduct
Neglectful	Unresponsive, little warmth or nurturance; undemanding, sets few limits and provides little supervision	Poor orientation to work and school; behavior problems

Source: D. Baumrind. (1989). Rearing competent children. In W. Damon (Ed.), *New directions for child development: Adolescent health and human behavior* (pp. 349–378). San Francisco: Jossey-Bass.

Diana Baumrind (1967, 1971, 1996), at the University of California, Berkeley, has distinguished four styles of parenting in terms of differences in parental responsiveness and demandingness (shown in Table 9.1). *Responsiveness* refers to how sensitive, supportive, and involved parents are, and *demandingness* to the degree to which parents hold high expectations for their children's behavior and supervise their activities.

Authoritative parents are both responsive and demanding. They are warm and nurturant, listen openly to their children's ideas and plans, yet are willing to assert their own authority and do so in a way that consistently enforces their standards. These parents stress self-reliance and independence, maintain an open dialogue with their children, and give reasons when they discipline. **Authoritarian parents** are equally demanding but less responsive than authoritative ones. They, too, are consistent in enforcing their standards but, perhaps because they value obedience over self-reliance, are less open and responsive to the other's perspective. Instead, they expect their children to do as they are told and not to question. Rather than backing up their discipline with reasons, they are more likely to use force. **Indulgent parents** are responsive to their children, as are authoritative parents; however, they are not demanding. These parents are warm and nurturant, but make few demands for responsible behavior, punish infrequently and inconsistently, and exercise little control or power over their children's activities. **Neglectful parents** are neither responsive nor demanding. These parents provide little nurturance or supervision, are cold and uninvolved, and set few limits, letting their children do whatever they choose. Several studies have found that the quality of parenting is strongly influenced by the kind of social support the parents have (see the Research Focus, "Questionnaires: Social Support and the Quality of Parenting" on page 362).

Both authoritarian and authoritative parents provide strong models, but in different ways. Authoritarian parents attempt to control their children; authoritative ones to guide them. In line with this difference, the latter place greater value on autonomy and self-discipline and the former on obedience and respect for

Q How is an authoritative parent likely to differ from an authoritarian parent when confronting a child who has done something wrong?

authoritative parenting A style of parenting that stresses self-reliance and independence; parents are consistent, maintain an open dialogue, and give reasons when disciplining.

authoritarian parenting A style of parenting that stresses obedience, respect for authority, and traditional values.

indulgent parenting A style of parenting characterized by warmth and nurturance but little supervision.

neglectful parenting A style of parenting characterized by little warmth, nurturing, or supervision.

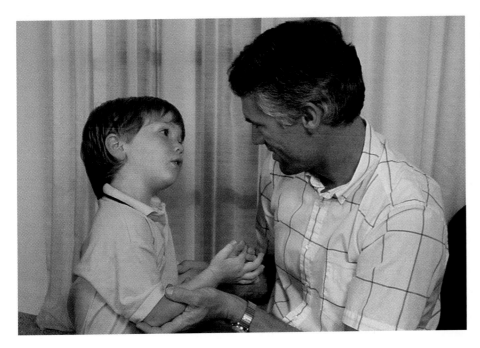

Authoritative parents are warm and nurturant and listen openly to their children's ideas and plans but are also willing to assert their own authority in a way consistent with their standards.

authority. Both types of parents define limits and set standards. Authoritative parents, however, are more willing to listen to reasons and arguments, tending to draw the line around issues rather than set absolute standards.

Authoritarian parents are more likely to use physical punishment than are authoritative ones. The use of harsher forms of discipline has been associated with increased hostility and aggression in children (Hart, Nelson, Robinson, Olsen, & McNeilly-Choque, 1998; Rothbaum & Weisz, 1994). Research finding such a relationship, however, has been based almost exclusively on the study of European American families. Little is known concerning the use of physical discipline in other ethnic groups. Kirby Deater-Deckard, Kenneth Dodge, John Bates, and Gregory Pettit (1996) compared the use of physical discipline by African American and European American mothers in a longitudinal study that followed children from kindergarten through the third grade. Disciplinary practices were assessed through interviews with both mothers and children, and levels of aggression were established through teacher and peer ratings.

These investigators found the relationship between physical discipline and children's aggression to be different in African American than in European American families. Only in the latter was the use of harsher discipline related to children's aggression. Findings such as these suggest that children's perceptions of punishment may differ across ethnic groups. Similar differences have been found for parental attitudes. Among European American parents, for instance, the use of physical punishment is associated with parent-centered child-rearing attitudes rather than child-centered ones. The latter, in contrast, are associated with the use of reasoning and nonphysical discipline. Research with African American mothers, however, finds no such relationship between child-rearing attitudes and the use of physical punishment (Kelley, Power, & Wimbush, 1992).

Similar cultural differences have been found among Chinese and North American mothers. Chinese mothers have been found to be not only more protective and more concerned, but also more punishment-oriented than the latter. These differences in child-rearing attitudes and practices were found to be associated with different behavioral outcomes in children (Chen et al., 1998). With North American

Questionnaires: Social Support and the Quality of Parenting BY MICHAEL WAPNER

Teenage mothers who live with their parents have been found to punish their children less (King & Fullard, 1982). It's also the case that mothers who have more friends parent more competently (Corse, Schmid, & Trickett, 1990), that mothers who have supportive friends are more emotionally responsive to their children (Crnic, Greenberg, Ragozin, Robinson, & Basham, 1983), and that parents who live in friendly communities mistreat their children less (Garbarino & Sherman, 1980).

What are we to make of findings such as these? In general, it appears that the quality of parenting that children receive depends a lot on the kind of social support their parents receive. In the worst case, parents who are isolated, lonely, alienated from family, and distant from friends tend to suffer from psychological distress, low self-esteem, and poor parenting skills. And their children pay for it. Frequently this worst-case scenario is the result of poverty (Golding & Baezconde-Garbanati, 1990). However, not all differences in social networks among families can be attributed to socioeconomic factors. The traditions of different cultures also give rise to different kinds of interpersonal structures. For instance, some cultures value the maintenance of close ties and cooperation among members of the extended family. Other cultures value autonomy and independence more. Thus, loose or abbreviated social networks may result for different reasons. We might ask, then, whether parents from different ethnic backgrounds find support in different kinds of social networks? And is the relationship between social support and child rearing the same from one ethnic group to the next?

David MacPhee, Janet Fritz, and Jan Miller-Heyle (1996) investigated this question. They looked at three ethnic groups: Native American, Hispanic, and Euro-American. All participants were residents of Colorado. All were low-income parents

with children between 2 and 5 years old who were referred to an early prevention project by a community agency. Thus, all participants lived in poverty or near-poverty and had children below the age of 5 who were considered at risk by some social or mental health agency.

To assess the relationship between the parents' social support and their child-rearing practices, MacPhee and his associates administered a series of questionnaires. Because the degree of literacy among these parents varied considerably, the questionnaires were read to them; however, respondents were still required to respond in writing. Each questionnaire elicited a great deal of information, including (1) the type of relationship, closeness, and function served by up to 20 people with whom the parent had contact; (2) the parent's satisfaction with available social support; (3) child-rearing practices; and (4) the parent's self-esteem.

Questionnaires, along with interviews, are a type of *survey research*. Both elicit a *self-report*. That is, both ask the respondents to give information about themselves. A major strength of questionnaires is the chance they offer to study behavior that could not otherwise be observed. For instance, patterns of parenting and interactions with friends and relatives, the behaviors under consideration here, extend over innumerable times and places. Having parents report on these in a questionnaire offers a convenient alternative to what otherwise would require many hours of direct observation. Obtaining self-report data through questionnaires is also useful when the behavior of interest is potentially embarrassing or perhaps even illegal. In the MacPhee study, parents might have felt easier about acknowledging that they occasionally abused or neglected their children given the relative *anonymity* of the questionnaire, in contrast to the per-

mothers, for instance, behavioral inhibition was positively related to the use of punishment and lack of acceptance. That is, the more punishment mothers used, the more inhibited were their children. With Chinese mothers, however, inhibition was positively related to acceptance and encouragement of achievement, and *negatively* related to punishment and expression of anger. Thus, mothers who used more punishment had children who were *less* inhibited.

Differences such as these in the relation between child-rearing practices and behavioral outcomes can be better understood in the context of each culture's values. In China, behavioral inhibition in children is considered to be socially appropriate and is fostered within the context of an accepting mother-child relationship. In North America, behavioral inhibition is viewed as a sign of immaturity and inferior social skills and is fostered by the same parenting practices that are associated with other less favorable developmental outcomes. Even so, differences such as these should not overshadow the similarities in child-rearing attitudes that were observed in these two cultures. Although mothers differed in the ways men-

sonal exposure of an interview. However, even information from questionnaires is often subject to distortion because the respondents prefer to give the *socially desirable* rather than the true or accurate answer.

Another advantage to questionnaires is that most rely on *closed-ended* questions that supply alternative answers from which to choose. Data from these *multiple* or *forced choice* questions are easy to score, in contrast to the data obtained from interviews, which require elaborate preprocessing or coding before being analyzed. Because of this ease of scoring, questionnaires, as we have already seen, can be administered to large numbers of people at relatively little expense.

There are also disadvantages to the use of questionnaires. In general they can be given only to people who can read, thus eliminating their use with very young children or others with limited reading skills. Even when the questions are read to groups of respondents, as they were in the study under discussion, subjects must be able to respond in writing (orally posed questions responded to orally convert a questionnaire to an interview and change the nature of the data considerably). Individuals also often find responding to questionnaires tedious and even boring, especially when, as in the MacPhee study, they are presented with many questions that require considerable thought. Even for subjects who agree to complete a questionnaire, attention and motivation may change appreciably between early and late items. An even more serious disadvantage, however, is that, unlike an interview, the investigator cannot explain or elaborate on questions for subjects who do not understand or who misinterpret them.

What, then, did this study discover about ethnic differences in types of support networks and about the way these related to patterns of parenting? Support networks for Native American parents most frequently included extended family, with very few members of the network being nonfamily. The most supportive networks were likely to involve intense and frequent contact among all members. For Hispanic parents also, networks most frequently included family, but also included friends. However, for emotional support, Hispanic parents depended most on members of their immediate families. As with Native Americans, networks involved frequent contact among the members. Support networks for Euro-American parents had the greatest number of nonfamily members. These networks were also more diffuse, with less frequent contact among the members. Euro-American parents were likely to rely on family and friends alike for emotional support. It is always possible, of course, that these differences may reflect differences in mobility, community acceptance, and patterns of housing as much as they do tradition and preference.

What about the relationship between social support networks and parenting? To begin with, the investigators had hypothesized that social networks exercise much of their influence on parenting by providing parents with emotional support and thereby raising their feelings of self-esteem and competence, which, in turn, presumably facilitate parenting. The hypothesis was supported to the extent that for all groups, healthy, effective child-rearing practices were more frequently found among parents who reported feeling competent as parents. Of course, with correlational data, no causal direction can be inferred. To the authors' surprise, the data showed only a very weak overall correlation between social support and feelings of self-esteem. When looked at group by group, the data showed a significant correlation between emotional support and self-esteem only for the Native American and Hispanic groups. There was no such relationship for the Euro-American group. Thus, while it can be said that both the presence of appropriate social support and parental self-esteem are correlated with effective parenting, the ways in which they are related may well be different for different ethnic groups. Perhaps the greater emphasis on individual autonomy made the self-esteem of the Euro-American group less dependent on emotional support.

tioned, their rankings of what they considered to be most important in child rearing were highly similar.

Ruth Chao (1994), at the University of California, Los Angeles, argues that parenting styles cannot be separated in any simple way from their cultural contexts. She points out that Chinese American parenting, often referred to by developmentalists as "authoritarian," "controlling," or "strict," nonetheless is very different from the authoritarian style of parenting identified by Baumrind. "Strictness" and "control" simply do not exist as ways of interacting for most Asian parents. For instance, control, instead of taking the form of a unidirectional exercise of power by parents over the child, in Asian cultures is bidirectional, carrying with it an obligation to nurture and support the child. Thus, parents are as much governed by the child's needs as the child is expected to comply with parental expectations.

Compliance with parental directives is particularly important in Asian cultures, not only as a means of getting children to follow the directives of those who

Research into attitudes and practices among parents from different cultures finds much similarity in parenting styles.

are older but, more generally, as a means of teaching them to consider others when making decisions—that is, as a means of fostering interdependence. Hiroko Kobayashi-Winata and Thomas Power (1989) compared the relationship of compliance to child-rearing practices among Japanese and North American parents. They found that providing children with opportunities for engaging in desired behavior was positively related to compliance in both cultures. Similarly, the use of punishment and physical interventions, such as forcibly taking forbidden objects from the child, resulted in poor compliance. Although Japanese parents were somewhat more likely to rely on verbal reprimands and explanations and American parents to supplement these with opportunities for desired behavior and the use of praise and punishment, children's compliance in each culture was related to parenting that could be characterized as authoritative. Generally, research examining attitudes and practices among parents from different cultures finds considerable overlap (Stevenson-Hinde, 1998).

Baumrind sees authoritative parenting as clearly superior to the other styles and considerable research supports her position, at least for European American families (Baumrind, 1996; Pratt, Kerig, Cowan, & Cowan, 1988; Steinberg, Lamborn, Darling, Mounts, & Dornbusch, 1994). She stresses, however, that it is not a simple way to parent, nor is it stress-free. In fact, parenting authoritatively seems to be distinguished by the presence of tensions produced by the need to balance opposing forces: tradition with individualistic innovation, cooperation with autonomous behavior, and tolerance with principled firmness. The benefits are worth the hassles. Authoritative parents, more so than authoritarian, indulgent, or neglectful ones, are likely to have children who are independent, competent, and responsible. These parents have stressed self-reliance and have paved the way for independence by involving their children in decision making from early childhood on. Similarly, setting high standards and following through to see that these are

Meta-Analysis: Noncustodial Fathers

BY MICHAEL WAPNER

It's rough enough when your parents get divorced. But it's rougher when your dad stops coming around. Or is it? Fathers who don't live with their children are called "nonresident" or "noncustodial" fathers. But that doesn't mean they stop being fathers. A father can maintain contact in many ways with the children he no longer lives with. But how much does it matter to the well-being of his children that he does? This is an important question given that about 50% of marriages end in divorce. So what do we know about this matter? Both a lot, and not that much.

There are some socially important questions that we know too little about because there just hasn't been much research on them. And then there are questions that have received a lot of research attention but still do not have a definitive answer. Sometimes when we have the results of many studies, the question under investigation starts to look more complex than it did at the start. The problem then is not that there is too little information, but that we need some method of bringing order to the results of the many studies that we do have. That is the case with research about the relationship between the involvement of nonresident fathers and the well-being of their children. For instance, of 32 studies on the question, 15 found that contact between a child and a nonresident father was positively related to the child's well-being, 7 found a significant negative relationship, and 10 found no relationship at all (Amato, 1993).

In a more extensive examination of the findings on this question, Paul Amato and Joan Gilbreth (1999) compared the results of 63 studies dealing with nonresident fathers and their children's well-being. The technique they used is called *meta-analysis*. It consists of a set of statistical procedures that compare the *size* and the *significance level* (see the Research Focus, "Inferential Statistics," in Chapter 7) of a given relationship across many studies. In their selection of studies for meta-analysis, Amato and Gilbreth chose studies that contained data relevant to four independent variables indicating the father's involvement and three dependent variables indicating the children's well-being. The indicators of the father's involvement were (1) payment of child support, (2) frequency of contact, (3) feelings of closeness, and (4) authoritative parenting. The indicators of child well-being were (1) academic achievement (test scores, grades, teacher's ratings), (2) externalizing problems (delinquency,

misbehavior, aggression), and (3) internalizing problems (depression, anxiety, low self-esteem). However, not every study contained every variable. Nor did every study use the same terms to characterize the variables. And even when the variables were referred to in the same terms, they were not always measured in the same way. Thus the authors had to use considerable judgment about whether the variables were sufficiently similar to pool and compare. For instance, with regard to payment of child support, some studies reported the amount of child support a mother received during some particular period, while other studies simply distinguished fathers who paid from those who didn't.

More complicated was the variable of "authoritative parenting." Different studies reported on different behaviors engaged in by the fathers toward the children, and Amato and Gilbreth had to decide which behaviors constituted authoritative parenting. They ultimately selected listening to children's problems, giving advice, monitoring school performance, helping with homework, and using noncoercive discipline to deal with misbehavior. But they did not include taking children to dinner or to the movies.

So what did the meta-analysis of 63 studies find? Interestingly, Amato and Gilbreth found that although fathers' payment of child support was positively associated with their children's well-being, frequency of contact was not. However, feelings of closeness and authoritative parenting were positively related to academic success and negatively related to children's externalizing and internalizing problems. In fact, authoritative parenting was the most consistent predictor of child outcomes. So what conclusions can we draw? First, the payment of child support is important. Clearly, children living in homes suffering from financial problems are subject to many kinds of pressures, not the least of which come from mothers coping with economic distress. Second, the father's simply maintaining contact with the child is not enough. How often the father sees the child is less important than what happens when they are together. It matters more that the father engage in actual parenting—guidance, discipline, modeling.

Thus, the message from a meta-analysis of many studies is that divorce cannot relieve fathers of the responsibilities of parenting. It only makes it harder.

met are associated with competence and responsibility in children. The Research Focus, "Meta-Analysis: Noncustodial Fathers," looks at the importance of authoritative parenting for noncustodial fathers.

Interestingly, it is not high standards or rigorous demands that lead to rebelliousness in children, but arbitrary ones. Parental strictness, per se, does not appear to be the issue. Parents encounter rebelliousness, it seems, when they are inconsistent, when they break their own rules, and when punishment is meted out arbitrarily. Baumrind stresses the importance of modeling responsible behavior, of practicing what you preach, in other words. Children do what they see others doing, not what they hear others say. Children are also more responsible when parents are warm and not rejecting. Baumrind is careful to point out that she is not advocating unconditional acceptance of whatever the child does. Parents often need to express displeasure and to punish. In doing so, however, it is important to distinguish the *absence* of emotional warmth from the *presence* of emotional rejection. Rejection is harmful; absence of warmth is at times necessary. Similarly, anger is often a reasonable reaction to some behaviors and can be useful in communicating the unacceptability of those behaviors. Again, however, it is important to distinguish between angry remarks and derogatory ones. The latter belittle and disparage children and can undermine their sense of self (Eisenberg, 1996).

Parents are more effective when they are fair. Being consistent, encouraging children to listen, and taking the time to listen to them are all important. When parents do punish, it is important to avoid forms of punishment that raise children's anxiety to such a level that they cannot appreciate the connection between the punishment and what they have done. For children to be able to generalize the consequences of their actions to other situations, they need to know which particular behavior was unacceptable.

Simple enough to say, you might be thinking. But how much does a 3-year-old understand concerning the logic behind parental rules? When a parent gives a child permission to do something, as "In order to do X, you must meet condition Y," does the child actually know which conditions make the behavior permissible? That is, can the child distinguish which actions would be in keeping with the permission rule and which would violate it? Paul Harris and Maria Nunez (1996) studied 3- and 4-year-olds' understanding of such conditional rules. Children heard a story in which a child was given permission to play outside *if* the child put on a coat. Three-year-olds, for most part, as well as four-year-olds recognized the conditional nature of this rule, distinguishing as "naughty" a picture of a child playing outside without a coat from that of a child also not wearing a coat, but playing inside.

Discipline

Mentioned in the right circles, the word *discipline* can create as much confusion as yelling "fire" in a theater. Many parents equate discipline with punishment. Others protest that discipline can break a child's will. Discipline, however, is not the same as punishment; and, instead of breaking a child's will, it can give children a sense of mastery and accomplishment.

What *is* discipline then? According to most dictionaries, discipline can be defined in a number of ways: as a branch of knowledge or learning, as training that develops self-control, as the acceptance of authority, and as treatment that corrects or punishes. Broadly defined, from the child's perspective, discipline involves learning and self-control; and, from the parent's perspective, it involves teaching and correction. When parents discipline, they teach children what is acceptable and what is not acceptable. They set limits, in other words. These limits can create freedoms both for parents and for their children. Setting limits can mean, for one thing, that within those limits children are free to do as they please. Furthermore, disciplined children, who know the rules and are self-controlled, can be trusted to do things without continual supervision. Their parents, in turn, are freed from nagging. Preschoolers, of course, are still learning the self-control that makes these freedoms possible; and until they do, parental supervision and monitoring are vitally important.

The same principles that apply to learning in any situation apply to effective discipline. Four in particular are important. First, it is important for parents to keep directions clear. Rules need to be stated clearly and maintained consistently. Consistency adds to clarity. It is not always clear what a rule is, if it is broken as much as it is kept. This does not mean that parents must be rigid and inflexible in order to communicate a set of standards. There will always be times when rules need to be modified or relaxed. Second, it is important for parents to keep the number of rules to a minimum. Doing so makes it easier to enforce them, while at the same time making it easier for children to learn what is important. Third, parents need to remember that encouragement and rewards are more effective than criticism and punishment. Letting children know, for instance, how pleased one is that they did a chore without being nagged is more effective than criticizing them for not having done it. Fourth, children do best when they earn their responsibilities. For example, they might be allowed to use scissors only when they learn to carry them point down or to have a pet when they show they can manage simple chores without continual reminders.

Why might it be important for parents to keep the number of rules in the home to a minimum?

Parenting and Poverty

The same dimensions of parenting that foster healthy development in all children also serve as protective factors for children who are at risk for developmental problems. Poverty is associated with a number of risks for young children, such as greater family stress, more medical problems, poorer medical care, and, not surprisingly, poorer developmental outcomes. However, not all children who grow up in poverty are equally affected. There are individual differences here as there are in other areas of development. Children who have one or more risk factors present in their lives, but who develop into healthy individuals, are termed **resilient** (Boyce & Jemerin, 1990; Werner, 1989). Protective factors, however, just like risk factors, can be assumed to have a cumulative effect; the more factors that are present, the greater the chances of resiliency.

Robert Bradley and his associates (1994), at the University of Arkansas, looked at factors present in children's home environments that are related to resiliency. These researchers were especially interested in the way in which such contextual factors interacted with the presence of a biological risk factor. Specifically, they looked at resilience among low-income, premature infants (37 weeks or less gestational age), following them into the preschool years. Prematurity in itself is not associated with developmental problems. However, when coupled with an inadequate environment, such as poor caregiving, it is frequently associated with multiple problems.

As expected, resilient children were found to have more protective factors in their home environments than nonresilient children, with at least three such factors being critical for healthy development. Sixty-nine percent of the 3-year-olds who were identified as resilient, for instance, had three or more protective factors present, whereas 64% of nonresilient children had two or less. In all, children with three or more protective factors in their home environments were nearly 9 times more likely to be resilient at 1 year of age and approximately 3 times more likely at 3 years of age.

These findings strongly suggest that it is the cumulative effect of protective factors, rather than the presence or absence of any one critical factor, that is impor-

resilient Able to recover readily from illness, change, or misfortune.

Building Social Capital

The term *capital* is commonly used to refer to a person's wealth, as measured in terms of such things as money or property. Capital provides a developmental "edge" for children, since it is associated with numerous advantages, such as better schools and safer neighborhoods. Wealth comes in a number of forms, however, and a significant one for children is the presence of supportive relationships within the family and in the community. This type of wealth is referred to as social capital. Children who are developmentally "at risk" due to factors such as poverty or parental substance abuse but who have reserves of social capital on which they and their families can draw are more resilient than those who lack such reserves (Klebanov, Brooks-Gunn, McCarton, & McCormick, 1998; Runyan et al., 1998). This type of capital is to be found not only in children's homes, but also in their neighborhoods, and is associated with differences in developmental test scores and cognitive functioning, both in children who are school-age and even in the preschool years (Klebanov et al., 1998).

How can we as a nation increase the social capital available to children and their parents? One approach is to build the potential for such capital into the neighborhoods in which children live. Presently, many of the children most in need of social capital live in neighborhoods that themselves are bereft of the conditions that could foster their personal growth, conditions such as safe streets, parks and libraries, and neighborhood businesses. Ironically, this circumstance has resulted in part from some of the very policies designed to help families in need. Policies governing public housing are a case in point. Such policies typically cluster public housing in large projects, rather than scattering it throughout the community, at the same time establishing income limits that preclude middle-income families from living in the same area (Garbarino, 1999).

When the proportion of middle-income families making up a neighborhood falls below a certain point, known as a "tipping point," neighborhoods have been found to undergo a relatively rapid decline (Wilson, 1993). Public policies that limit public housing to families whose incomes fall below a certain level virtually ensure the eventual decline of these housing projects through the inclusion of a built-in tipping point. In *There Are No Children Here* (1991), Alex Kotlowitz describes such a process in the Henry Horner neighborhood, a public housing development that sprawled across 34 urban acres in Chicago:

> The neighborhood slowly decayed, as had many urban communities like Horner over the past two decades. First, the middle-class whites fled to the suburbs. Then the middle-class blacks left for safer neighborhoods. Then businesses moved, some to the suburbs, others to the South. Over the past ten years, the city had lost a third of its manufacturing jobs and there were few jobs left for those who lived in Henry Horner. Unemployment was officially estimated at 19%; unofficially, it was probably much higher. (pp. 10–11)

In order to maintain communities that are rich in social capital, we need a healthy mix of families from a range of income levels. Opening public housing to families of varying income levels is one way of increasing a community's social capital and of creating supportive community environments. In fact, Chicago is not only tearing down its decayed high-rise public housing units but is also replacing them with "low-rise housing buffered by playgrounds and lawns"—housing that will include units for working- and middle-class families (Downey & McCormick, 2000, p. 37).

tant for healthy development. The caregiving conditions that were found to serve as protective factors were parental responsiveness; parental acceptance; and having adequate living space, safe play conditions, and a variety of stimulating things to play with. Such factors are related to social capital, the topic of the Social Policy Focus, "Building Social Capital." These conditions, by the way, are the same as those that promote healthy development in all children, presumably because they promote feelings of efficacy and self-esteem. In other words, children feel competent and good about themselves when they are able to discover what they can do and to have their achievements shared and celebrated by those who matter most to them. Being able to play in safety, having interesting things to play with, and having their explorations affirmed by a responsive and accepting parent not only help children develop necessary skills but also contribute positively to a sense of themselves. The presence of caregiving conditions such as these assumes a certain level of organization and stability within the home, in terms of both the actual living space and the quality of children's relationships.

Summary

Recognizing the Self

Self-recognition, as measured by an infant's touching its own face when it sees a dot of rouge in its reflection, emerges between 18 to 24 months of age. This behavior has been taken to signify the existence of an objective self-concept. Unlike adults, however, preschoolers lack a sense of themselves as continuous over time. Initially, children's sense of self is limited to the ecological self, the self that is directly perceived in terms of their ongoing activities. The self becomes extended over time, in the extended self, as children remember past experiences and imagine future possibilities.

Self-Concept

The emergence of an autobiographical memory at about the age of 4 appears to underlie the growth of the extended self. Autobiographical memories are those that make up an individual's life history. Prior to this age, children are apt to recall particular events, but these do not become part of their life story. Developments in language in early childhood are assumed to contribute to the development of this memory. Parents also teach children how to remember things, telling them what is important and which things are related to what other things. Children's self-concepts reflect cultural differences in the way the self is construed.

Age Differences in Self-Concept

A child's self-concept changes systematically with age. Preschoolers tend to describe themselves in terms of their physical characteristics. Beginning by abut age 5 or 6 children are more likely to characterize themselves in terms of their psychological makeup and their relationships.

Gender and the Self

Children are able to correctly label themselves as to gender by the age of 2 but fail to distinguish sex differences, which are biologically based, from gender differences, which are socially determined. An understanding of sex constancy, the understanding that one's sex is permanent and will not change as a function of how one looks or dresses, develops between the ages of 3 and 5. Gender stereotyping, beliefs concerning which behaviors are appropriate for either sex, also develops between the ages of 3 and 5 and contributes to gender identity, or the experience of oneself as male or female.

Three theoretical explanations for the development of sex roles were considered. Social learning theory assumes that one's gender role and gender identity are learned by observing and imitating the behavior of others, such as parents and brothers and sisters, who serve as models. Differential reinforcement of behaviors that are appropriate for one's gender role makes these more likely to occur. Parents are assumed to be important, both as models and as those who shape, through differential reinforcement, their children's behavior.

Freud's psychoanalytic theory focuses on the internalization of standards for behavior through the process of identification, in which children internalize the behaviors and attitudes of the same-sex parent. Identification is involved in the resolution of the Oedipal complex in boys and the Electra complex in girls. Freud assumed that females never completely resolve this complex, but develop feelings of inferiority; he also thought that females have weaker superegos.

The constructive approach assumes that children construct their sexual identities by selectively attending to gender-appropriate behaviors in others. The process of selective perception is guided by gender schemas, cognitive structures that direct the pickup of information about the self as it relates to gender. Gender schemas operate as anticipatory schemata, creating a readiness to perceive certain types of information, cues that are consistent with one's gender schema.

Ethnicity and the Self

Children are aware of ethnicity at a relatively early age and refer to themselves and others according to their ethnicity. These references include an awareness of differences not only in physical appearance, but in cultural behaviors as well. The concept of racial constancy, that one's ethnicity does not change with age or circumstances, develops later. Children's awareness of differences among themselves contributes to the way they evaluate others only when differences are used as a basis for forming social categories.

Liking the Self: Self-Esteem

Bowlby assumed that children form an internal working model of the self based on their relationships with attachment figures. The quality of these early attachment relationships appears to contribute to children's self-esteem. Children with high self-esteem are better adjusted and have better peer relationships. They also are more confident and curious, show more initiative, and are more independent.

Emotional Development

With age, preschoolers become better able to talk about their feelings, incorporate them into their pretend play, and understand the emotions of others. However, they easily confuse overt expressions of emotion with what a person is likely to be feeling; older children are better at inferring the conditions under which others are likely to experience different emotions. There is some evidence suggesting that children's ability to explore their own emotions is related to the quality of their relationships with attachment figures. Despite increases in emotional understanding, preschoolers are still learning ways of managing their emotions; parents help by communicating social standards.

Friendships and Peer Relations

Friends give children a feeling of belonging and contribute to their sense of themselves. There are developmental progressions in the way children think of their friends; they move from an emphasis on physical characteristics to an emphasis on psychological ones. Children's views of the nature of friendship change with age from seeing it as an activity to seeing it as an enduring relationship that transcends the way they may feel at the moment. What children value in their friendships also changes with age, with affection and support becoming more important with age.

Several skills contribute to social competence. Children must be able to assess a social situation in order to determine what is taking place so they can adapt their behavior

accordingly, and they must be able to respond appropriately to others' behavior. Mothers contribute to children's social competence by serving as social coaches, suggesting future behavior and giving feedback on what children have done.

Peer interactions become segregated by sex by the age of 3. Although the percentage of time spent in dyadic interactions as opposed to group play does not differ as a function of sex among preschoolers, dyadic interactions are maintained for a longer period of time by girls than they are by boys. By the age of 6, boys are more likely than girls to play in groups. Children are more open and relaxed when they are with their friends than with others, are better at resolving conflicts when they arise, and are more generous in interpreting the motives of those they like, being less likely to see their behavior as intentionally provocative.

Parenting

Four styles of parenting can be distinguished in terms of differences in parental responsiveness and demandingness. *Responsiveness* refers to how sensitive, supportive, and involved parents are, and *demandingness* to the degree to which parents hold high expectations for their children's behavior and supervise their activities. Authoritative parents are both responsive and demanding. Authoritarian parents are also demanding but less responsive than authoritative ones. Indulgent parents are responsive to their children, as are authoritative parents; however, they are not demanding. Neglectful parents are neither responsive nor demanding. Although parenting practices have been found to differ with ethnicity, attitudes and practices among parents from different cultures show considerable overlap.

Discipline can give children a sense of mastery and accomplishment. Discipline involves learning and self-control for children and involves teaching and correction for parents. For discipline to be effective, it is important that rules be clearly stated and consistently maintained and that the number of rules be kept to a minimum. It is also important that encouragement and rewards rather than criticism and punishment be used, and that children earn the responsibilities they request.

Poverty is associated with increased numbers of risks for children. Children who have risk factors present in their lives but develop into healthy individuals are termed resilient. The greater the number of protective factors in a child's life, such as a supportive family, church, or school, the greater the likelihood of resiliency.

Key Terms

agency (p. 341)
authoritarian parents (p. 360)
authoritative parents (p. 360)
autobiographical memory (p. 337)
communion (p. 341)
ecological self (p. 334)
Electra complex (p. 345)

extended self (p. 334)
gender differences (p. 342)
gender identity (p. 342)
gender labeling (p. 341)
gender schemas (p. 347)
gender stereotyping (p. 342)
identification (p. 345)

indulgent parents (p. 360)
neglectful parents (p. 360)
Oedipal complex (p. 345)
penis envy (p. 346)
resilient (p. 367)
sex constancy (p. 342)
sex differences (p. 341)

chapterten

Middle Childhood
Physical Development

was running down the Penn Avenue sidewalk, revving up for an act of faith." So Annie Dillard describes the time one afternoon when she tried to fly, simply for the joy of attempting something that would challenge everything she brought to it, despite knowing it to be impossible. "I ran the sidewalk full tilt. I waved my arms ever higher and faster; blood balled in my fingertips. I knew I was foolish. I knew I was too old really to believe in this. . . .

"I crossed Homewood and ran up the block. The joy multiplied even as I ran—I ran never actually quite leaving the ground—and multiplied still as I felt my stride begin to fumble and my knees begin to quiver and stall . . . even as I slowed bumping to a walk. I was all but splitting, all but shooting sparks. Blood coursed free inside my lungs and bones, a light-shot stream like air. I couldn't feel the pavement at all" (Dillard, 1987, pp. 107–109). ◄

The middle years of childhood are filled with exuberant activity—skateboarding and roller blading, bicycling and skipping rope, soccer games and sandlot baseball, shooting baskets, and, of course, running with the hope of flying. Mixed in with these unearthly glories is the more pedestrian jumble of schoolwork, chores, and down-to-earth matters such as looking after one's kid sister and remembering one's lunch money for school.

Physical growth and continuing brain maturation contribute to these developments, as do the press of changing expectations and the pleasures to be found in their accomplishment. We will look at changes in height, weight, and body proportions during the school years and at the developing skills that characterize middle childhood before considering the underlying maturation that supports their development. Finally, we will look at the contexts for growth that are provided by families, schools, and communities. The emerging skills of middle childhood depend not only on physical growth and maturation but also on the presence of a supportive environment for their development.

Developmental Profiles

By the age of 6, children are relatively self-sufficient. They can get themselves dressed in the morning, fix a snack when hungry, help with chores around the house, find their way around the neighborhood, look after a younger sibling, and walk to school or the bus stop by themselves. At school they can work alone on projects that challenge their developing skills as well as participate with others in organized activities.

Life is not without its problems, however. And many of the problems 6-year-olds experience can be traced to what some would call "growing pains." Molars start to come in; ear infections are more common than at any time since they were toddlers; those who will need glasses may first experience difficulty at this time; and arm and leg muscles frequently ache as muscles stretch to fit growing limbs. Six-year-olds are also adjusting to school. Still somewhat impulsive, they approach their world in a hands-on fashion, touching and feeling things, rather than appraising them at a distance. Sitting quietly can be difficult. Children in a first-grade classroom are constantly in motion, walking about, fidgeting in their seats, and whispering and talking (Mitchell, 1990).

By 7, children are quieter and more settled. Their actions are controlled and purposeful, and there is a tidy air about them as they move about. This new sense of control may reflect their increasing ability to order their lives in time and space, according to the constraints of clocks and calendars, enabling them not only to find their way about but also to know where they should be at different points in the day and to get there reasonably on time. At school, they move around less,

Seven-year-olds have a new sense of control, which may reflect their growing ability to order their lives in time and space.

and when they do, it is with some clear purpose. They are able to sit quietly for longer periods of time, but can still jump out of their seats at odd moments.

Older children, 8 through 10, move easily in their worlds, with an air of competence, self-possession, and independence. They have not yet begun to experience the stresses of pubertal growth and are over any earlier growing pains. There is an air of practical realism about them. They know they are capable and enjoy being trusted with freedoms and responsibilities. They can manage things around the house when necessary, such as getting younger siblings ready for school or fixing meals when a parent is sick, as well as the more familiar routines that fall within their own domains. They are bigger than many of the other children they find themselves with, such as at school or around the neighborhood, and enjoy being looked up to. Although as yet untouched by puberty, their gatherings are usually segregated by sex, with those of either sex showing a certain interest, albeit motivated more by curiosity than desire, in each other. At school, they are relatively composed and restrained, show more concentration when working, and are generally more businesslike in their approach to what they are doing (Mitchell, 1990).

Discretionary Time: Being on Their Own

The years from 8 through 10 are the ones best remembered from childhood, when children grow up, so to speak. Children spend increasing amounts of time on their own in these years, whether by themselves or with friends, away from the watchful eyes of adults. Even when an adult is present, the presence is more nominal than literal. It is not unusual for an adult to be in the house and for children to be off somewhere in the neighborhood, at a friend's house, a playground, or someplace in between. Supervision takes the form, on the one hand, of *having access* to an adult should one be needed, and on the other, of *being accessible* to an adult, such that someone responsible knows where children are and who they are with (Belle, 1994).

What kind of adult supervision is appropriate for grade school children?

Even then, there's a certain amount of slippage between where they might be at any time and where they are thought to be, mainly for older children, and mostly on weekends and vacations. Summer days, especially, can stretch on endlessly, punctuated only by hunger and boredom or the random occurrence of a truly exciting find. Gerald Haslam (1988) describes such days in his short story "The Horned Toad," in which he has just brought home such a find:

> "Expectoran su sangre!" exclaimed Great-grandma when I showed her the small horned toad I had removed from my breast pocket. I turned toward my mother who translated: "They spit blood."
> "De los ojos," Grandma added. "From their eyes," mother explained, herself uncomfortable in the presence of the small beast.

Haslam describes how he and other neighborhood kids would spend their free time playing on a vacant lot across the street, at the edge of the California desert, the lot on which he had found the horned toad:

> Despite the abundance of open land, plus the constant lure of the river where desolation and verdancy met, most kids relied on the vacant lot as their primary playground. Even with its bullheads and stinging insects, we played everything from football to kick-the-can on it. The lot actually resembled my father's head, bare in the middle but full of growth around the edges: weeds, stickers, cactuses, and a few bushes. We played our games on its sandy center, and conducted such sports as ant fights and lizard hunts on its brushy perimeter. (pp. 139–140) ◄

Such unstructured activities are common in middle childhood and play an important role in development. Giving children time in which they are responsible for themselves, doing such things as getting across streets safely, not getting lost, organizing a game with friends, knowing which things are relatively safe to play at and which are not, and finding their way back home at the expected hour, is important in building independence and responsibility. In other words, continual and close supervision in middle childhood is not necessarily the best form of care.

Finding the right balance between adult supervision and expectations for responsible autonomy, however, is the trick for most parents. Children need time to be on their own. But they also need the structured support and emotional warmth that parents and other caregivers provide. How are these to be balanced, and what form does such a balance take? Brenda Bryant (1994) notes that this balance combines two forms of support. The first of these is having a caring adult either present or immediately accessible, not only as an emotional base but also to offer practical help in coping with immediate problems, such as minor accidents or emergencies. The second form of support comes from the way parents socialize children to be competent and autonomous when they are on their own. (The Research Focus, "Basic Versus Applied Research: After-School Activities," looks at issues of supervision and autonomy in various forms of after-school care.)

Baumrind's (1971, 1996) authoritative parenting (see Chapter 9), in which children are empowered through choices that are coupled with parental measures to ensure responsible decision making, illustrates the second form of support. The two defining dimensions running through authoritative parenting are warmth and demandingness, with the latter reflecting expectations for competent autonomy. Paradoxically, it is autonomy, and not dependence, that is fostered by parental warmth and acceptance. Parents who can accept their children's feelings, emotionally supporting their children, for instance, as they experience and talk about feelings, enable children to think through their feelings in more complex ways. This, in turn, enables children to solve their own problems more effectively.

Q How do children benefit from spending time in unstructured activities by themselves or with friends?

Parental warmth and acceptance during childhood fosters confidence and autonomy in children.

After-School Hours: Latchkey and Supervised Care

Not only summer vacation, but also after-school hours can include long stretches of unsupervised time for many children. Approximately 2½ million children spend a substantial amount of time after school without adult supervision (Cain & Hofferth, 1989). Most of these children get out of school at 3:00, with parents returning from work several hours later. In the absence of grandparents, older siblings, or other family members, these children spend the time alone or with friends. Children who have no adult to supervise them after school have been referred to as "latchkey" children.

Deborah Belle (1994), in reviewing research on latchkey children, notes that the single point that most clearly emerges from this research is the variability in children's responses to self-care. No single statement can be made, in other words, about the effects of self-care on children. It should be kept in mind that children experience unsupervised time in a variety of ways. Furthermore, children who spend part of the day looking after themselves are not necessarily left to fend for themselves. Many of these families appear to make good use of the community resources available to them while parents are at work. Thus, it has been found that children looking after themselves are almost twice as likely as those who are supervised to attend clubs after school, participate in sports, or have after-school lessons. Many also regularly spend time at friends' houses after school (Steinberg & Riley, 1991, as cited in Belle, 1994).

A number of the findings from such research are surprising. For instance, Vandell and Corasaniti (1988) compared the effects of self-care, home care with a mother present, home care with a sitter present, and care in after-school programs for third-graders. Using reports from the children, their parents, teachers, and friends, they found no differences on a variety of measures between self-care children and those supervised by their mothers. Unexpectedly, though, children who attended after-school centers or who were at home with a sitter were perceived more negatively by peers than were self-care children or those at home with their mothers. Those who attended centers also did more poorly academically. It is possible that the children who attended centers or were watched by a sitter differed

Basic Versus Applied Research: After-School Activities

Tanesha had heard people talking about time stopping, always when they referred to something momentous in their lives. For her, time stopped 5 days a week, Monday through Friday, at the same time each day—40 minutes before school let out. That was when they started their last subject for the day, geography. "How could Mrs. Pfannen make this stuff so dull?" she wondered. She would have loved to go to most of the places they had studied. Just thinking about some of them made her happy. "Those islands, what were they called?" she wondered, as her eyes slid over the dirty snow caked outside her classroom window. The book had said the sand was as soft as silk. Imagine how it would feel, in between your toes, and the water as blue as flowers. She'd paint a beach today, she decided, and put herself in it, soon as she got to her after-school program. Tanesha, like most of her classmates, attended an after-school program at her elementary school.

How do most children spend their time each day once they leave school? Relatively little research exists in this area. That which does finds that boys and girls have somewhat different experiences. Boys are supervised less closely than girls their age and get about the neighborhood more. They also spend more of their time in sports and watching television. Girls spend somewhat more time doing homework than do boys and more time doing chores around the house (Posner & Vandell, 1999; Timmer, Eccles, & O'Brien, 1985).

The question of where and with whom children spend this time is of more than academic interest, in that increasing numbers of schoolchildren have parents whose work prevents them from being at home at the end of the school day. Jill Posner and

Deborah Vandell (1999) were interested in identifying which child and family factors were associated with the types of after-school activities children experience and in determining the developmental implications of these experiences. These investigators followed a group of urban third-graders growing up in Milwaukee for 2½ years, through the fourth and fifth grades, using telephone interviews to determine the types of activities in which they were engaged in their after-school hours.

These investigators had designed a program of applied research, aimed at answering pressing questions concerning after-school experiences. Research can be classified as either basic research or applied research. Those doing basic research are interested in getting answers to key questions concerning basic developmental processes. Frequently, these questions are generated by developmental theories and address general issues in development. Those doing applied research are interested in obtaining answers to specific, practical problems. Both types of research are important, and together they advance our understanding of development. The findings of basic research, for instance, frequently serve to direct and stimulate applied research questions. Applied research on the effects of day care, for example, has been guided by Mary Ainsworth's basic research on attachment (see Chapter 6). Similarly, findings from applied research often stimulate a closer examination of basic research findings. Most recently, legislators overseeing research-granting agencies have questioned the value of basic research and pressed for more socially relevant research. However, it is difficult to anticipate when findings about basic processes can be put to practical use. Skinner, for instance, devoted years to

initially in some way from the others, perhaps by being less mature. This difference may have been the reason parents felt they needed supervised care.

Fourth- and sixth-graders who looked after themselves also were found to feel just as good about themselves, in terms of self-worth and self-esteem, as other children (Berman, Winkleby, Chesterman, & Boyce, 1992). However, those who were looked after by older siblings suffered in this respect, feeling less competent than children who looked after themselves or those who were supervised by an adult. Once again, findings such as these may be unexpected, but make a certain sense, after the fact. Children, for instance, are frequently more severe with each other than are adults, both in their judgments of the acceptability of various behaviors and in the way they communicate these. Thus the care children receive from older siblings may be harsher than that from an adult. Children may also internalize reprimands differently, depending on whom these come from. Being told they have done something wrong by an older sibling, with whom they expect to share a similar outlook on many things, may cause children to doubt themselves more than would the very same words from an adult. Since children are less likely to expect to share the views of an adult than someone closer their age, they may be less apt to doubt their competence when reprimanded by an adult, even though told in much the same way.

programmatic research on operant conditioning with rats and pigeons for which there were no immediately practical uses. However, as we have seen in this chapter, a very real problem faced by a number of schoolchildren, bed-wetting, has been helped by the principles Skinner discovered in his basic research with laboratory animals (Cozby, 1997).

The research of Posner and Vandell identified four types of after-school arrangements. The first of these involved *formal programs,* such as an extended-school program (3 P.M. to 5 P.M.), sponsored by the school district, in which children could participate in two of three activities each day: academic ones such as computers or creative writing, recreational ones such as basketball or art, and tutorial ones such as help with homework. The other three arrangements were *informal neighbor or relative care, self-care,* and *parental care.* Children were contacted periodically during the course of the study to determine where they had spent their time after school, who else was present, and the kinds of activities in which they had engaged. Their answers were coded based on categories arrived at from previous research (see the Research Focus, "Coding," in Chapter 12). Since these investigators were interested in the developmental implications of after-school activities, they obtained measures of academic, social, and emotional adjustment as well.

With respect to the question "How do children spend their time after school?" they found gender differences in the types of activities children experienced. Girls spent more time in academic activities and socializing, and boys spent more time participating in coached sports. Boys also spent more time playing video games and watching television. Few family variables were found to be related to the types of activities in which children engaged, with the exception that White children from single-parent households had somewhat less supervision, spending more time outside in unstructured activities than

did those from two-parent households. Age was also related to the types of activities children experienced. Between the third and fifth grades, the time spent in unstructured outside activities decreased by half, and the time spent socializing, such as just talking, doubled. In general, children who were in formal after-school programs spent more of their time doing academic and extracurricular types of things. Children who experienced informal care spent more time watching television and socializing.

These investigators also found an association between enrichment activities and adjustment in schoolchildren. Children who experienced more enrichment activities, whether participating in extracurricular activities or socializing with friends, benefited emotionally from these experiences. Among the African American children in this study, these activities were also found to be positively related to grades in school and work habits. White children's grades in school were also related to their after-school activities, with those spending more time in unstructured outside activities getting poorer grades. Unfortunately, perhaps, it looks as if the days in which children could freely wander about their neighborhoods, meeting friends and spending time by themselves without adult supervision, may be behind us—at least in many urban settings.

Findings such as these offer practical suggestions concerning after-school care, as one would expect from an applied research project. However, they also raise questions that can stimulate basic research, such as why seemingly similar after-school experiences were associated with different outcomes in African American children than in White children. In research, coming up with a good answer often means coming up with another question as well.

Once again, it is important to keep in mind that it is not simply what one person says to another, but the way one *hears* what the other has said that matters. The very same words that make for good-natured banter among friends could be heard as a stinging rebuke if spoken by someone else. In ordinary conversation, as in so many other aspects of our lives, we construct the events to which we respond, hearing what we expect to hear, given the context in which something has been said. In the short story "The Body," Stephen King (1998) illustrates the way the remarks of others can be given a meaning quite apart from any literal interpretation of the words that have been said. Listen to the rough banter of four friends, hanging out in a tree house and playing cards. Their tough talk serves to solidify their friendship, affirming that the tough image each projects is accepted by the others:

"So what are you pissing and moaning about, Vern-O?" Teddy asked.

"I knock," Chris said.

"What?" Teddy screamed, immediately forgetting all about Vern. "You friggin liar! You ain't got no pat hand. I didn't deal you no pat hand."

Chris smirked. "Make your draw, shitheap."

Teddy reached for the top card on the pile of Bikes. Chris reached for the Winstons on the ledge behind him. I bent over to pick up my detective magazine.

Vern Tessio said: "You guys want to go see a dead body?"

Everybody stopped. (p. 299) ◄

These same epithets, said by anyone other than a close friend, would be heard as a challenge to their identity rather than an affirmation of the way they wanted to be seen by each other.

The time children spend with each other in unstructured play, whether in supervised or unsupervised settings contributes to their development in untold ways. Yet one of the findings to come out of research assessing the effects of different types of care was that children had relatively little time to spend with their friends after school (Belle, 1994). This was true for all children, irrespective of the type of after-school arrangements they had. Those who had activities after school, for instance, said their friends were likely to be in different activities. Similarly, those in self-care often said their friends' parents wouldn't let them visit other children unless one of the parents was at home.

Belle and her associates (1994) also found considerable variability in the amount of time children spent by themselves, without an adult present. Many of the children typically never experienced unsupervised care whereas others were left to care for themselves for several hours each day. Most of the children who were allowed to look after themselves were allowed to go out of the house and also to have friends over. These investigators also found a range of reactions among children experiencing self-care, from tremendously enjoying their independence to very much wanting a parent around. However, none of these measures showed differences in children's experience of social support, such as having someone to talk to when needed or simply receiving emotional support, among the various after-school arrangements. Thus, self-care children were just as likely to feel supported as were those in various forms of supervised care. Also, children's *dis*satisfaction with the types of support they experienced was not found to be a function of any of the various types of after-school care.

The satisfaction elementary school children experience in supervised programs should reflect many of the same variables found to be important in preschool programs. Robert Rosenthal and Deborah Vandell (1996) found this indeed to be so, with smaller student-staff ratios, smaller overall programs, and more highly trained staff improving the quality of after-school child care programs for elementary school children just as they do for preschool programs. These variables appear to contribute to the success of such programs by increasing their flexibility, something that becomes particularly important with elementary school children for whom most of the hours during the day have been tightly structured. The things children mentioned as most important for them in supervised after-school care were the sense of emotional support they received from staff; their experience of autonomy and privacy, such as in being able to do what they wanted when they were there, including being by themselves at times; and the chance to be with others their age. These three aspects of programs accounted for more than 55% of the variance in children's satisfaction with them.

Belle (1994) warns, however, that one cannot assume that what is experienced as supportive by one child will necessarily be experienced that way by another. As we saw earlier with respect to the dialogue among Stephen King's friends in the tree house, the meaning that one takes from what another says or does cannot be separated from the context in which this occurs. Thus, some children might feel supported by being placed in a small, friendly after-school child care program, whereas other children could feel undermined by having to be in such a pro-

Q What qualities should an after-school program have to make it attractive to grade school children?

Many school-age children participate in team sports after school where they learn the importance of fair play and teamwork as well as develop physical skills.

gram, taking it as a sign that they were not considered old enough or sufficiently responsible to look after themselves. Similarly, some children will feel affirmed by after-school self-care arrangements, taking this as a sign that their parents consider them to be trustworthy, and others might take the same arrangement as a sign that their parents are not involved in their lives or would rather be anywhere but with them.

Mentoring

An effective alternative to supervised after-school child care programs is to be found in mentoring programs. These programs involve children in one-on-one interactions with someone who is both older and wiser and, equally as important, who develops a caring relationship with them. Such programs have been found to be highly effective in promoting healthy development in at-risk children and adolescents (see the Research Focus, "Randomized Versus Quasi-Experimental Designs: What's in a Name? Communication Across the Ages"). Children with mentors not only develop healthier personal habits, but their schoolwork also improves, and they develop more positive attitudes toward life in general and their own futures in particular.

Getting Around the Neighborhood: Children as Pedestrians

Children increasingly move in a world of their own in middle childhood. Their lives are organized around school, not only the time they actually spend at school but also the time it takes getting there and back, the time they spend on homework, and, increasingly with age, the activities that take place there, such as pageants and plays, practices and recitals, and team sports. They spend these hours in their own society, away from home and parents, in the company of each other and of adults their parents know only by name. Many walk to and from school, further increasing the reach of their independence.

Research Focus

Randomized Versus Quasi-Experimental Designs: What's in a Name? Communication Across the Ages

Joey was beginning to like his name. He liked the soft way it sounded when Mrs. Thomas spoke to him, even though this was usually when they were talking about his homework. Funny, a year ago he would never have thought of doing homework. Or going to a museum with his class, or even to school basketball games. But he did now, and his mom did too, every now and then, when Mrs. Thomas called her. For that matter, a year ago he would never have thought he'd even know anyone as old as Mrs. Thomas. She must be at least 60, he thought, as he watched her coming into the room with a pencil and another piece of pie.

Joey lives in a low-income, high-crime neighborhood in Philadelphia. His sixth-grade class is part of an intergenerational mentoring program in which older members of the community, such as Mrs. Thomas, volunteer time with students, doing things such as helping with homework or school projects, going to games or cultural events, and taking part in community service activities. The purpose of the program is to increase the protective factors in the lives of high-risk children. By working with these students, mentors serve as friends and role models, as well as advocates and challengers, helping to build the self-esteem, confidence, and skills they need to stay drug-free.

In addition to mentoring, this unique program includes three additional components. It also involves students in community service, offers classroom-based instruction in life skills, and includes a workshop for parents. The community service aspect of the program enables these students to see how they can help others, giving them a sense of personal and social responsibility and contributing to their self-esteem. In contrast, instruction in real-life skills takes place in the classroom, teaching skills applicable to students' real-life problems within their families, with friends, and with peer pressure. Finally, the workshop for parents helps them develop more effective parenting skills and more positive ways of interacting within the family. Essential to the success of the program are the teachers and school personnel who have been trained in its implementation and evaluation.

Programs like this are expensive—not only in money, but also in a community's investment of its limited reserves of passion and hope. How might one determine whether an intergenerational mentoring program such as this is effective? Leonard LoSciuto, Amy Rajala, Tara Townsend, and Andrea Taylor (1996), at Temple University, employed a *randomized pretest-posttest control group design*. Three sixth-grade classes per school were randomly selected from all of the sixth-grade classes in schools that were willing to participate in the study (almost all of them). Within each school, each class was randomly assigned to one of three conditions:

1. Students received the complete program of mentoring, community service, instruction in life skills, and parent workshops.
2. Students received everything but mentoring.
3. Students received no intervention at all. They were the control condition.

At the beginning of the academic year, prior to beginning the intervention program, students were pretested on a variety of measures assessing their knowledge, attitudes, and behavior related to the program goals. All students were tested again, with a series of posttests, at the end of the academic year. This type of design, because it employs random assignment of subjects to conditions and the use of a separate control comparison (see the Research Focus, "An Experiment," in Chapter 1), in addition to comparing pretest with posttest performance, has high internal validity (see the Research Focus, "Internal and External Validity," in Chapter 14), enabling the investigators to conclude that the changes they observe are actually due to the program and not to some other factor.

Because the students are randomly assigned to conditions, and each student has the same chance as any other of being assigned to each group, one can be reasonably certain that individuals in the three groups do not differ in any systematic way at the outset of the program. Additionally, pretesting students before they begin the intervention program makes it possible to determine whether equivalence has, in fact, been achieved.

This independence, for the most part, is rightfully earned. Children become increasingly knowledgeable concerning their surroundings and rapidly improve in their judgment concerning what is likely to be safe or unsafe in these years. Their very improvement, however, means that the youngest among them are likely to make more than their share of poor decisions. Some of these decisions carry a fair degree of risk. Children are 4 times more likely than adults, for instance, to be injured as pedestrians. Given that they are less likely than adults to be near traffic, this difference has developmental significance. Children younger than 9,

382

Pretesting offers other advantages as well. Pretests allow investigators to assess the extent to which individuals *change* over time. Thus, if some students are responsive to the treatment, whereas others are not, pretesting may suggest clues that can be followed up in subsequent research as to why some are more responsive than others. Pretesting is also useful when subjects drop out of the program, as is likely with lengthy programs. Loss of subjects in this manner is known as *subject mortality* and is a potential source of bias if it is systematically related to the experimental conditions. For instance, poorer students might be least responsive to the demands of mentoring and community service and most likely to drop out, leaving proportionately more of the better students in the intervention group. In this way, even interventions that have no effect might appear to result in improved performance. By inspecting the pretests of students who drop out, however, one can determine whether these subjects differed from the ones who remained in the program. Pretesting has its disadvantages as well. One potential disadvantage is that it can *sensitize* subjects to the purpose of the investigation, making it possible for them to figure out what is expected of them and potentially affecting the way they respond to the experimental treatment.

Many intervention programs are not able to randomly assign subjects to experimental and control conditions. Research that relies only on comparisons of pretest and posttest performance is termed *quasi-experimental*. A number of problems exist with quasi-experimental designs. Because there is no control condition, we don't know how to interpret the findings. Suppose, for instance, one finds that posttest scores are no better than pretest scores. Can we conclude that the program is ineffective? Not necessarily. It's always possible that performance could have declined during that time, and that only because of the program did scores remain the same. Similarly, increases in performance on the posttest do not lend themselves to a simple interpretation. Several potential *confounds* exist. These can be due to maturation, testing, history, instrument decay, or statistical regression.

Maturation reflects any systematic changes that occur over time. These can be long-term, such as the developmental changes in intelligence discussed in Chapters 4 and 10, or short-term, such as changes due to fatigue, boredom, or practice. *Testing* reflects any changes that might occur due to familiarity with the tests. Since pretests usually involve the same type of question as posttests and frequently measure knowledge about the same subject matter, testing effects are likely. *History* refers to events that occur during the time between testings that can affect the behavior being measured. Television might run a series of public service spots featuring famous athletes who warn kids against the use of drugs at the same time as the intervention program. *Instrument decay* reflects changes in the instruments being used to make measurements. Such changes are especially likely when the instruments are people themselves, whose judgments of various behaviors provide the measures that are being recorded; we might expect people to become more practiced over time or in other ways to have their standards change.

Statistical regression can occur when students are selected for a program because they are atypical, because their scores are either especially low or high. When they are retested, as they are on the posttest, most scores will change somewhat simply because the two tests are not perfectly correlated (no two tests ever are). Students who are selected because of especially low scores will look like they have improved due to the program. In actuality, because they were at the bottom of the distribution, their scores could *only* go up. Of course, by the same token, students with especially high scores on a pretest would show a drop in performance on the posttest. In each case, scores "drift" or regress toward the mean of the distribution, since that is where most scores are to be found.

None of these confounds, however, threaten the validity of LoSciuto's research. What, then, can we say about the effectiveness of this intervention program? These investigators found that students who received all four components of the program were likely to do best. They were more likely to react appropriately when they were offered drugs; were absent from school less; and had more positive attitudes toward school, community service, and their own futures. There is also some indication that mentoring resulted in increased feelings of self-worth and well-being and reduced sadness and loneliness.

for instance, are not good at identifying which places are safe when crossing the road. As long as there isn't a car in sight, they assume that one place is as safe as another, irrespective of whether they are standing at the brow of a hill or at a bend in the road (Ampofo-Boateng et al., 1993).

When grade school children were taken to a number of intersections and asked to point to the route they would follow in crossing them, most of the 5-year-olds indicated ways to cross that were either very dangerous or moderately so. Seven-year-olds were better, but were still likely to choose an unsafe route

At what age can children usually be trusted to cross streets safely?

FIGURE 10.1 Percentage of Routes Falling into Safe and Unsafe Categories by Age *Source:* K. Ampofo-Boteng, J. A. Thompson, R. Grieve, T. Pit-cairns, D. N. Lee, and J. D. Demetre. "A developmental and training study of children's ability to find safe routes to cross the road," *British Journal of Developmental Psychology,* March 1993, Vol. II, Part I, pp. 31–46.

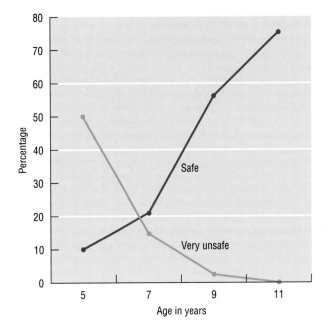

FIGURE 10.2 Sample Routes from Very Unsafe (1) to Safe (4)

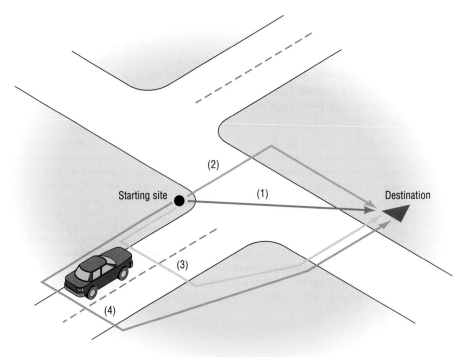

across a complicated intersection. Only 9- and 10-year-olds were likely to choose a safe route across (Ampofo-Boateng et al., 1993). Figure 10.1 shows the results of this experiment.

It should be pointed out that these were familiar crossings to all of the children, since the intersections were within walking distance from their schools. Even so, the younger children were not aware of the dangers present in these situations, such as trying to cross an intersection where traffic comes from several different directions, as shown in Figure 10.2. In fact, many of the 5-year-olds indicated the

Walking home from school with friends can give children a sense of independence. However, younger children have difficulty knowing when or where it's safe to cross the road.

best way to cross such an intersection would be to walk directly to the other side, which would require walking *diagonally* across the intersection. Selection of a safer route would have meant adopting a strategy that would take them away from where they wanted to go, a difficult solution for the youngest children to envision. Although 7-year-olds realized the dangers of such a solution, they were still unaware of other dangers, such as crossing between parked cars. Even when they did realize the dangers and suggested moving to a new place to cross, they frequently chose one equally as dangerous (Ampofo-Boateng et al., 1993).

New Responsibilities

Barbara Rogoff (1996) notes that in most cultures children between the ages of 5 and 7 are entrusted with increasing responsibilities. Not only are they expected to do such things as care for younger children, tend animals, or do chores around the house, they are also expected to act in more adultlike ways, to be well-mannered, for instance, or to remember to do the things they have been told to do. We expect this of them not simply because we believe they have better social skills or better memories than younger children, but because we assume they share with adults an understanding for *why* certain things are important.

Rogoff argues that the behaviors one sees developing in children at this age are not solely, or even primarily, a function of developments occurring within the children themselves, but result as much from the expectations of their communities for different types of behavior. She points out that in the United States, for instance, we expect that children cannot handle sharp knives until at least the age

The skilled behaviors that young children develop depend as much on the expectations of their community as on their own physical and cognitive development.

of 5 without seriously endangering themselves. However, Efe toddlers living in Zaire are able to use a machete by themselves to cut fruit, without injuring themselves, and Fore infants in New Guinea are trusted to handle knives by the time they can walk and do so carefully (Rogoff, 1996). Similarly, Asian children (Miller, Wiley, Fung, & Liang, 1997) are expected to act with sufficient restraint for the family to keep fragile objects around without fear of their being broken or damaged.

Rogoff points out that the adults in these communities are not being irresponsible, as some might assume, by allowing young children to handle sharp implements or by leaving precious but delicate objects about the house. Rather, they are providing children with the skills they will need in their culture. Such provisions, however, cannot be imported in any simple way from one culture to the next. Fragile objects can be left in their places, for instance, because Asian children are socialized in ways that make them at least as attuned, if not more so, to the needs and desires of others (seeing a delicate vase on a table) than to their own needs (picking it up). Rogoff notes that these very same parents would view many of the things North American children are allowed to do as equally dangerous for their age, such as sleeping by themselves or growing up in isolated nuclear families, removed from grandparents, aunts, and uncles.

Rogoff suggests that rather than attempting to chart development in terms of which behaviors can first be seen to occur at any age, researchers look at the activities in which children already participate, focusing on how their roles in these activities change with age. These activities include not just the child, but also those with whom the child is interacting, the materials they are working with, and the traditions that guide what they are doing. Rogoff speaks of this participation as either *guided participation,* when focusing on the interpersonal aspect of the activity, or as *participatory appropriation,* when focusing on the individual. The concept of participation makes explicit the notion that the activity involves others and that children do not develop in isolation from those around them or apart from the cultural traditions that give their roles meaning.

One such role, which shows clear developmental changes during middle childhood, is that of doing chores. Six- or seven-year-olds, for instance, are expected to help with things when they are asked to. By the age of 7, for instance, 63% of a large urban sample of low-socioeconomic-status children reported that they regularly performed several household chores, such as dusting or vacuuming, running errands, and babysitting (Entwisle, Alexander, Olson, & Ross, 1999). These investigators found that the number of chores increased substantially with age. Furthermore, older children are expected to carry out tasks on their own, without having to be asked.

By about the age of 9, clear gender patterns exist in children's chores, with girls' chores more frequently involving work inside the house and those of boys involving work outside the house. Thus, over 80% of boys versus 50% of girls report having to take the trash out (Entwisle et al., 1999). And by 9 or 10, they are expected to carry out tasks on their own, without having to be asked. In *Gryphon* (1999), Charles Baxter gives us a picture of a young boy at the first of these stages, as he arrives home from school after another day with a substitute teacher:

> I kissed my mother. She was standing in front of the stove. "How was your day?" she asked.
> "Fine."
> "Did you have Miss Ferenczi again?"
> "Yeah."
> "Well?"
> "She was fine, Mom." I asked, "Can I go to my room?"
> "No," she said, "not until you've gone out to the vegetable garden and picked me a few tomatoes." She glanced at the sky. "I think it's going to rain. Skedaddle and do it now. Then you come back inside and watch your brother." . . .
> "Do you feel all right?"
> "I'm fine," I said, and went out to pick the tomatoes. (p. 918) ◄

Attitudes toward work and leisure show surprising continuity through large segments of the life span. Many of the attitudes adults hold toward work, for instance, can first be seen by the time children enter adolescence. Adults who are asked to report how they feel about what they are doing while they are working are likely to indicate they would rather be doing something else. Yet these same individuals acknowledge that work, more than leisure, contributes significantly to their sense of self and frequently is more deeply satisfying (Csikszentmihalyi, 1997).

In a similar fashion, 10- and 11-year-olds report activities they label as work as being less pleasurable than those they label as play, even though they acknowledge that the former more frequently contribute to feelings of high self-esteem. Adolescents as well, when asked to indicate how they feel while they are working, report they are less happy than if doing something else even though their feelings of self-esteem are higher when they are working than at other times, and they are likely to regard what they are doing as important (Csikszentmihalyi, 1997).

Physical Growth

By the age of 6, children stand about 3½ feet tall and weigh about 45 to 50 pounds. Growth is steady in middle childhood, though slower than in early childhood, with children adding between 2 to 3 inches in height each year and gaining

The pattern of growth changes in middle childhood. The school-age child on the left has longer legs relative to the rest of her body and a slimmer look than does the preschooler.

Q The lower part of the body grows faster during middle childhood than it did in early childhood. How might this change in physical growth affect children's activities?

secular trends The differences in size, both in height and in weight, that occur from one generation to the next.

approximately 5 pounds in weight. Even though the numbers of inches and pounds they add are about the same as those gained by preschoolers, the increases in height and weight are *proportionately* less given the relative difference in their sizes. Thus, the rate of growth slows in middle childhood (Hagerman, 1999).

The pattern of growth also changes. The lower part of the body grows faster during middle childhood, whereas in early childhood, the upper body grew at a faster rate. As a consequence, school-age children have longer legs relative to the rest of their bodies and a slimmer look than do preschoolers. This pattern of growth is a continuation of the cephalocaudal trend evidenced earlier in development, in which skeletal growth proceeds downward from the region of the head.

Smooth growth curves such as those appearing in Figure 10.3 can be deceptive, because they suggest that growth occurs evenly over time. When frequent measurements are taken at regular intervals, however, growth is found to occur in spurts, each spurt separated by longer periods in which growth is much slower. On average, these spurts in growth occur at the ages of 6½, 8½, and 10 years in girls, and approximately half a year later, at 7, 9, and 10½ in boys (Butler, McKie, & Ratcliffe, 1990; Johnson, Veldhuis, & Lampl, 1996). Similar research in which measurements of an adolescent's height were taken on a nearly daily basis over a year's time also found evidence of growth spurts rather than gradual increases (Lampl & Johnson, 1993).

Considerable variability in growth exists not only from one time to the next in any given child, but also from one child to the next. Differences in height and weight between any two classmates, in fact, can be as great as those between children separated in age by as much as 4 years. Individual differences such as these tend to increase with age throughout middle childhood, especially with respect to weight (Hagerman, 1999).

Gender differences in height and weight remain insignificant in middle childhood. In fact, it is frequently difficult to distinguish one sex from the other at a distance, given similar forms of dress and the length of their hair. Girls' shoulders are just as wide as boys', and boys' hips are no slimmer than girls'. Nor does size differ appreciably, although boys have a slight edge in height. However, even this changes midway through the school years. After the age of 9, girls are slightly taller than boys, as the early hormonal changes accompanying puberty affect their rate of growth. On average, girls will begin puberty 2 years earlier than boys (Mitchell, 1990).

Because the lower portion of the body is growing faster, children's center of gravity changes as well, moving downward. This change enables them to maintain their balance better when actively moving about, and having longer legs means they can run faster. They also have increased strength and endurance. Lung capacity increases in middle childhood, and muscles are stronger. In all, children are longer-limbed, better coordinated, faster, and stronger than they were before.

As a group, children today are somewhat taller than they were generations ago. Differences in size from one generation to the next are referred to as **secular trends** in growth. Recently, there have also been secular increases in weight. The number of children who are overweight, or are in the 85th percentile of weight for their height, has approximately doubled in the last 25 years (Freedman, Srinivasan, Valdez, Williamson, & Berenson, 1997). This increase is most noticeable among older children, those approaching or already in adolescence; however, a similar trend has been observed among 4- and 5-year-olds. Although there are no gender differences in obesity among older children, among 4- and 5-year-olds, obesity is more prevalent among girls (Freedman et al., 1997). Because this trend has occurred over such a relatively short period of time, it most likely is the result of environmental factors, such as diet or physical activity, rather than genetic ones.

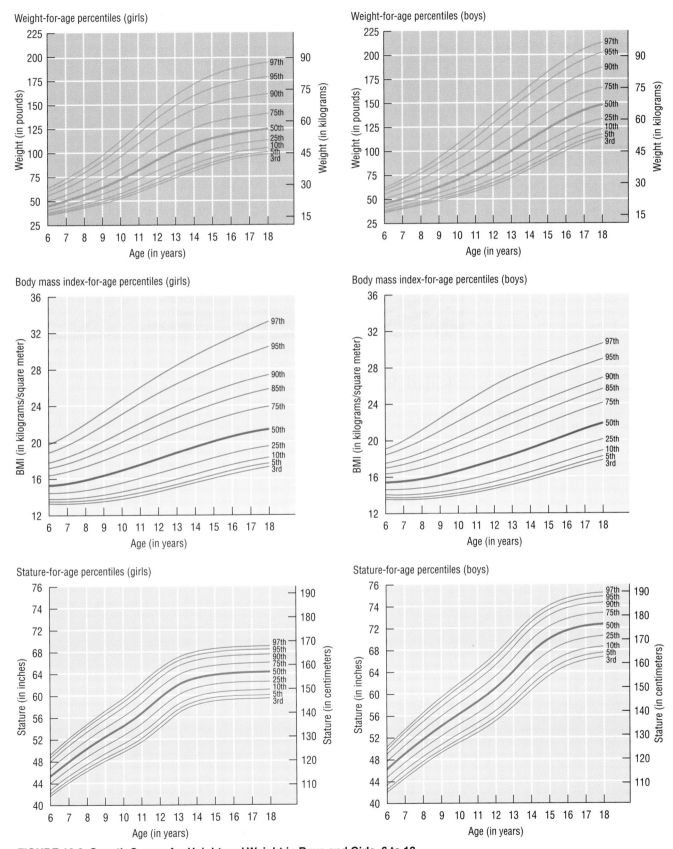

FIGURE 10.3 Growth Curves for Height and Weight in Boys and Girls, 6 to 18

One of the most obvious aspects of physical development in middle childhood is increased coordination.

Skilled Behavior

With each year, children become more accomplished at various activities that require motor skills—such as running, jumping, and maintaining their balance while moving. Stamina and strength also increase year by year, enabling school-children to play actively for longer periods of time without tiring. One of the more obvious aspects of physical development is the increased coordination one sees, both in tasks involving fine motor skills, such as handwriting or drawing, and in those involving larger muscle groups, such as running, biking, skipping rope, and playing ball.

Fine Motor Skills

Children's control over small body movements, such as those involving the fingers and hands, increases steadily in middle childhood. One sees this control not only in the way they hold a pencil or cut with scissors (Figure 10.4) but also in other activities requiring manual dexterity, such as fitting together the pieces of model airplanes and ships, outfitting Barbie, and mastering the fingering on a musical instrument (Pehoski, Henderson, & Tickle-Degnen, 1996, 1997). Most children can print all the letters of the alphabet by the first grade, but find uppercase letters easier than lowercase ones, since the former involve more straight lines and fewer curves. Cursive writing, for the same reason, is more difficult than printing, and children usually do not master this until the third grade. Also, as their motor skills improve, their lettering becomes smaller and more regular.

Gross Motor Skills

Our house is at the end of the road at the top of a slight hill, and children in the neighborhood congregate in the turnaround to play. One day there were several groups, one kicking a soccer ball around and another, older group on skateboards.

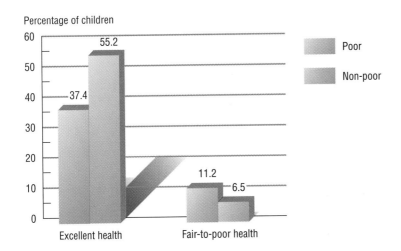

FIGURE 10.8 The Percentage of Poor and Nonpoor Children in Excellent Health and Fair-to-Poor Health

Poverty is unequally distributed among children. Those who are most likely to be poor are those who live in single-parent or large families, those who are members of racial or ethnic minorities, and those whose parents have little education. Children living with single-parent mothers, for instance, are over 5 times as likely to be living below the poverty line as are those in two-parent families. Similarly, African American and Latino children are over 2½ times as likely as are Euro-American children to be poor (Corcoran & Chaudry, 1997).

The effects of poverty permeate the lives of these children, from how much food they have to eat and where they will live, to the safety of their neighborhoods and how good their schools will be, to what kind of health care they receive. However, even more important than *whether* children experience poverty is the *duration* over which they experience it. The effects of poverty are approximately twice as great when the poverty is long-term, lasting for 10 years or more, than when it is experienced for a single year or two. This difference has been found to be independent of factors such as family structure, mother's education or age, or the health of the children (Korenman, Miller, & Sjaastad, 1995). Fifteen percent of children who have ever been poor have experienced long-term poverty (Corcoran & Chaudry, 1997).

The effects of poverty can follow children from birth through adulthood. With respect to physical development, poverty can affect both growth itself and general health. Poor children are likely to weigh less at birth and are more likely to have their growth stunted during childhood. Even though relatively few poor children do not actually have enough to eat, poverty is nonetheless associated with significant nutritional deficits, resulting in a greater likelihood of poor children being short for their age, or evidencing *growth stunting*. Their health, as well, can be affected. Children who are poor are significantly less likely, by two thirds, to be in excellent health than other children and nearly twice as likely to be in fair or poor health (Brooks-Gunn & Duncan, 1997; Figure 10.8).

Since children who live in poverty often have less food to eat, how are they likely to be affected?

Preventive and Interventive Programs

A number of federal programs have been found to be effective in reducing the harmful effects of poverty as these relate to physical growth and health. These programs are directed toward improving nutrition, health care, and housing. Included under the former are the Food Stamp Program, a special supplemental program for women with infants and small children (WIC), and school nutrition programs. Medicaid is directed toward health care, and a federal housing program makes up the latter.

School-based nutrition programs supply a significant portion of some children's food.

Nutrition Even though most children consume nutritious diets, the same cannot be said for the poor. Children living in poverty receive on average less than 70% of the recommended daily allowance for many, if not most, nutrients. Research suggests that participation in the Food Stamp Program has improved the dietary status for these children, especially with respect to calcium, iron, and vitamin C (Devaney, Ellwood, & Love, 1997). Similarly, WIC, which not only provides vouchers for supplemental food, but also educates women about nutrition and health care, has been found to be especially effective in combating iron-deficiency anemia and in promoting immunizations.

A school-based nutrition program, the National School Lunch Program and the School Breakfast Program, is available to low-income children on a daily basis. These meals are frequently a significant portion of what some children get to eat on any day and thus are an important supply of nutrients. The School Lunch Program, for instance, is designed to supply one third of the required daily allowance (RDA) for a number of nutrients, and the School Breakfast Program to supply one fourth of the RDA. Among other foods provided, each meal must include milk and a fruit or a vegetable. As of 1996, this program has also been required to reduce the fat content in school meals (Devaney et al., 1997).

How effective are school-based nutritional programs? Nearly all public schools participate in the school lunch program, making it available to over 90% of schoolchildren. Over half of those for whom it is available participate on any day. Participation varies with family income, with nearly 80% of children who can receive free meals participating, 75% of those eligible for reduced-price meals doing so, and just under half of all others participating choosing to buy their lunches at school rather than bringing them from home. The school breakfast program is available to considerably fewer students, just over half of those who are school age. It is more likely to be in place in those schools whose students are predominantly from lower-income homes. Children are sensitive to the stigma associated with poverty and may choose not to participate to avoid this. Others simply don't like the food. Even so, children who participate in these programs get more of the nutrients they need (Devaney et al., 1997). Box 10.1 lists nutritious

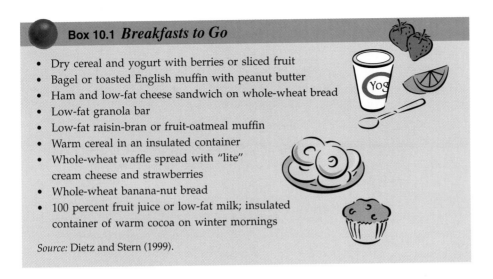

Box 10.1 *Breakfasts to Go*

- Dry cereal and yogurt with berries or sliced fruit
- Bagel or toasted English muffin with peanut butter
- Ham and low-fat cheese sandwich on whole-wheat bread
- Low-fat granola bar
- Low-fat raisin-bran or fruit-oatmeal muffin
- Warm cereal in an insulated container
- Whole-wheat waffle spread with "lite" cream cheese and strawberries
- Whole-wheat banana-nut bread
- 100 percent fruit juice or low-fat milk; insulated container of warm cocoa on winter mornings

Source: Dietz and Stern (1999).

breakfasts that children can carry with them—for those who don't have time to eat at home.

Receiving help, even when it is needed, can be a cause for shame among some children. Dick Gregory (1964) writes of such an experience at school when a collection was taken in class one day for the families of children in need. His family was one of them. He lived in a single-parent home with his mother, sisters, and brothers. He had money in his pocket that he had earned on his own and wanted to impress one of his classmates, a girl on whom he had a crush:

> The teacher opened her book and started calling out names alphabetically.
> "Helene Tucker?"
> "My Daddy said he'd give two dollars and fifty cents."
> "That's very nice, Helene. Very, very nice indeed."
> That made me feel pretty good. It wouldn't take too much to top that. I had almost three dollars in dimes and quarters in my pocket. I stuck my hand in my pocket and held onto the money, waiting for her to call my name. But the teacher closed her book after she called everybody else in the class.
> I stood up and raised my hand.
> "What is it now?"
> "You forgot me."
> She turned toward the blackboard. "I don't have time to be playing with you, Richard."
> "My Daddy said he'd . . ."
> "Sit down, Richard, you're disturbing the class."
> "My Daddy said he'd give . . . fifteen dollars."
> She turned around and looked mad. "We are collecting this money for you and your kind, Richard Gregory. If your Daddy can give fifteen dollars you have no business being on relief."
> "I got it right now, I got it right now, my Daddy gave it to me to turn in today, my Daddy, said . . ." (pp. 184–185)

But he had no father, and the teacher knew that, and soon everyone else did as well. Still standing, he started to cry, further adding to his humiliation. He later reflected, "It seemed like the whole world had been inside that classroom, everyone had heard what the teacher had said, everyone had turned around and felt sorry for me" (p. 185). ◄

About 9 to 11 million children have no health insurance, meaning they are less likely to get medical care when they need it or regular check-ups and immunizations.

Even with programs such as the School Breakfast Program, some 12% of schoolchildren do not eat breakfast before going to school. The number of students failing to do so, however, does not appear to differ as a function of the availability of such programs. In a natural experiment, test scores before children began to participate in the school breakfast program were compared with their scores after being in the program for several months; the comparison showed that test performance had improved. Students in the program were also absent from school less and tardy less (Meyers, Simpson, & Weitzman, 1989). Even so, more research is needed on the effectiveness of these programs in meeting the dietary needs of school-age children and on ways of increasing participation in such programs by those most in need of them.

Health Care Medicaid extends health care coverage to low-income children by providing them with health insurance. This program provides children with preventive care, such as periodic visits to a health care provider and immunizations, as well as treatment of injuries and illnesses. Although not all low-income children are eligible and standards of eligibility vary from one state to the next, new federal mandates concerning eligibility have increased the number of children whose health needs can be met under this program. Even so, anywhere from 9 million to 11 million children remain uninsured. Of these, 25% most likely are eligible but are simply not enrolled (Devaney et al., 1997).

How effective is Medicaid? Children enrolled in this program have more access to health care services than do children with no insurance. However, they still do not receive the same benefits as those who are privately insured. Additionally, they appear to be less likely to make use of the services available to them. For instance, children insured through Medicaid see a physician less frequently during the year than do those who are privately insured. Given that the health of poor children in general is not as good as that of those who aren't poor, this difference means they are less likely to get medical care when they need it. Children under Medicaid are also less likely to receive all their immunizations than those who are privately insured and are less likely to see a dentist.

Underutilization of programs such as Medicaid reflects a variety of factors. Low-income parents may experience difficulty, for instance, in getting children to health care facilities, given work constraints, poor transportation, and the need for child care for siblings. Part of the problem, too, may be that clinics are not available in low-income and rural areas (Delaney et al., 1997).

Housing   In addition to nutritional programs and health care, assistance with housing is also available to low-income families. This federal program is designed to reduce the cost of housing to 30% of a family's net income. Although providing a place to live meets a fundamental need, federally subsidized housing is not an entitlement program, in which anyone who meets the eligibility requirements will receive benefits. Thus, when funds run out, families must wait. The wait can be long, up to 19 months for public housing and 31 months for subsidized rent, in the form of vouchers, for existing units. A large percentage of those waiting is made up of very low income families with children. By providing vouchers for existing housing, housing programs attempt to avoid isolating poor families from the mainstream of society by concentrating them in public housing projects, which tend to be characterized by higher rates of crime, joblessness, substance abuse, and poorer neighborhood schools. Vouchers, together with counseling on how to search for housing and programs that screen potential tenants, can be used to help low-income families move out of poor neighborhoods.

It is important to keep in mind that the very government measures that were so successful in reducing the rate of poverty among the elderly, from 35% to 11%, offer hope for our children as well. Similar measures can reduce poverty among them.

Summary

Developmental Profiles

In middle childhood, children become increasingly self-sufficient; they are able to find their way around the neighborhood, look after younger siblings, help out with chores, and get themselves to and from school.

Discretionary Time: Being on Their Own

In middle childhood, children begin to spend more time on their own. Unstructured activities can play an important role in development, giving children time in which they are responsible for themselves. Structured support from parents, in the form of providing an emotional base and socializing children to be autonomous, contributes to children's growing competence. These two forms of support parallel the two defining characteristics of authoritative parenting, warmth and demandingness.

After-School Hours: Latchkey and Supervised Care

Approximately 2½ million children are latchkey children, with no adult supervision after school until parents return from work. Children respond to self-care in a variety of ways; in general, few differences are found between self-care children and those supervised by a parent on a variety of measures, including children's experience of social support. With respect to supervised care, most important to children are the sense of being emotionally supported by staff, having a choice in how they will spend their time, and being able to be with others their age. An effective alternative to supervised after-school programs are mentoring programs that involve children in one-on-one interactions with someone with whom they can develop a caring relationship.

Getting Around the Neighborhood

Many children walk to and from school and around their neighborhoods after school. Children are 4 times more likely than adults to be injured as pedestrians; they have difficulty identifying safe routes for crossing intersections and roads even when these routes are familiar to them. Children make increasingly better decisions with respect to pedestrian safety with age.

New Responsibilities

Children are entrusted with increasing responsibilities in most cultures between the ages of 5 and 7. The new behaviors children develop reflect the expectations of their communities as much as they do developments within the children themselves. Children's roles change from being expected to help when asked to being expected to carry out tasks on their own without being asked.

Physical Growth

Growth slows in early childhood; children gain between 2 and 3 inches in height and approximately 5 pounds each year. The lower part of the body grows at a faster rate than the upper body, as a continuation of the cephalocaudal trend. Growth occurs in spurts rather than gradually; these occur at the ages of 6½, 8½, and 10 years in girls and approximately half a year later, at 7, 9, and 10½ in boys. Strength, endurance, and coordination increase as well. Secular trends in growth are evident in that children are somewhat taller and heavier today than in previous generations. The number of children who are overweight has doubled in the last 25 years.

Skilled Behavior

Coordination improves with age both in tasks involving fine motor skills and in those involving large-muscle groups. Most children can print all the letters of the alphabet by the first grade and master cursive writing by the third grade. With respect to gross motor skills, hand-eye coordination improves steadily, as does agility and balance.

Brain Maturation

By the age of 9, the brain has reached 95% of its adult size. Brain growth is characterized by two interrelated processes. Cell proliferation, which takes place through the first several years of life, consists of the overproduction of neurons and interconnections; and cell pruning, which continues throughout childhood, consists of the selective elimination of excess cells and the cutting back of connections. These two processes enable neural development to be fine-tuned by experience, with interconnections that are frequently used being retained and those infrequently used being pruned. Brain metabolism changes throughout childhood, presumably reflecting the differing energy demands of these growth processes.

Plasticity, or the degree to which one area of the brain can assume the functions governed by another following an injury, decreases with age. Paralleling a decrease in plasticity is a progressive lateralization of the brain, in which the two halves of the cortex become specialized for different functions. The frontal lobes also develop, contributing to increases in attention, planning, and self-awareness.

Developmental Asynchronies

Many school-age children experience sleep-related problems, which can take the form of difficulty falling asleep, fear of the dark, waking in the night, and enuresis. Enuresis, or bed-wetting, is a relatively common problem in middle childhood, affecting as many as 10% of 7-year-olds and even higher percentages of younger children. Enuresis has a strong genetic component; 75% of children who are enuretic have a close relative who was also enuretic. Children who are enuretic produce less of the hormone that is responsible for decreased production of urine during sleep, and they may also find it harder to wake to the sensation of a full bladder. Even though most families do not seek treatment, enuresis is a highly treatable disorder.

Physical Development and Poverty

Approximately 15 million children, or 1 out of every 5, live in poverty. Those who are most likely to be poor are those who live in single-parent or large families, who are members of racial or ethnic minorities, and whose parents have little education. Poverty can affect both physical growth and general health. Poor children are more likely to weigh less at birth, to suffer significant nutritional deficits, and to have their growth stunted during childhood; they are nearly twice as likely to be in fair or poor health as other children.

Preventive and Interventive Programs

A number of federal programs are effective in reducing the harmful effects of poverty. With respect to nutrition, these include the Food Stamp Program, a supplemental program for women and infants and small children (WIC), and school nutrition programs. The Food Stamp Program has improved the dietary status of children primarily with respect to calcium, iron, and vitamin C. WIC has been found to be effective in combating iron-deficiency anemia and in promoting immunizations. Nearly 80% of children eligible for school-based nutrition programs participate in these. These programs provide a significant portion of what many children eat on any day and are an important source of nutrients. Medicaid, by extending health insurance to low-income children, provides for preventive care, such as immunizations, as well as treatment of injuries and illnesses. In addition to nutritional programs and health care, assistance with housing is also available to low-income families.

Key Terms

cell proliferation (p. 391)
cell pruning (p. 391)

enuresis (p. 396)
lateralization (p. 393)

plasticity (p. 392)
secular trends (p. 388)

chaptereleven

Middle Childhood
Cognitive Development

A foot in two worlds: that's what it's like to be on the short side of 10. Kids this age are sure that with a bit more time, say a year or two, they could have everything figured out. Like school and sex and what life is really all about. After all, multiplication tables weren't that bad; they discovered where babies really came from; and they finally got it straight about Wonder Woman, Spiderman, and Santa Claus. Too bad in a way. Sometimes it's hard knowing everything. Can't even get anyone to tickle them anymore, except when others forget how grown up they really are.

Quite grown up, in many ways. In the middle years children hone skills they will keep a lifetime. They master the Internet, make legitimate double plays in Little League, win spelling bees, and do homework that can make their parents scratch their brows. Yet with it all, Band-Aids still work better with a hug, and tickling is too good just for the little kids.

Part of what makes children so grown up in these years is the way they think. They appreciate the complexities of time, of tomorrows that turn into today and todays that become yesterday. They are beginning to use strategies to remember things from one day to the next, they can order experience by classes and categories, and their reasoning becomes more logical and less intuitive. Even their sense of humor changes. We will examine several explanations for these developments, before moving to a consideration of the practical side of intellectual development, that of schooling.

Perhaps the single most important factor contributing to the changing world of middle childhood is school. School represents an abrupt change from the life children have been used to, even for those who attended preschool. With time no longer their own, children must follow new rules, form new relationships, and be away from home for a significant portion of the day. Some children adapt to these changes more easily than others. We will look at factors that affect adjustment to school, as well as at the skills children develop there.

The success children have in navigating changes such as these depends in large measure on the support they receive from others—from families, teachers, and friends—and the communities in which they live. We will examine these sources of support at the conclusion of the chapter.

Piaget's Stage of Concrete Operational Thought

Perhaps because of his background as a biologist, Piaget's theory of intellectual development shows the influence of Darwin's theory of evolution. Piaget approached human intelligence, in other words, with questions a biologist might ask if discovering a new organism. How does this creature adapt to its surroundings? What does it do that allows it to survive? How is it changed by the processes that maintain it? Piaget viewed intelligence as a means of adapting to one's environment, in which only those forms of thought that promoted adaptation survived with increasing age. He assumed adaptation to take place through the complementary processes of assimilation and accommodation (see Chapter 1). These processes actively shape the individual's exchanges with the world at every age and are responsible for the growth of thought.

Piaget traced the intellectual developments of middle childhood to the emergence of **mental operations,** internalized actions that children could perform in their heads and that were presumed to develop with the maturation of centers and pathways within the brain (see Chapter 10). Piaget believed that mental operations evolved out of the action schemes of infancy and early childhood. Once these became internalized, they enabled children to carry out in their heads what

mental operations Piaget's term for actions that can be carried out in one's head and then reversed or undone.

Mass
(continuous
substance)

Two identical balls of playdough are presented. The child agrees that they have equal amounts of dough.

One ball is rolled into the shape of a snake.

Conserving child recognizes that each object contains the same amount of dough (average age, 6–7).

FIGURE 11.1 A Demonstration of Conservation, Using Two Balls of Clay *Source:* From Life-Span Human Development, 1st edition by C. Sigelman and D. Schaffer.

previously they could do only with their hands (Piaget & Inhelder, 1969). You can see what infants are thinking, in other words, by watching what they are doing. But you have to ask school-age children what they are thinking and then wonder if they have really told you. The Research Focus "Between-Subjects Design: Tolerance" looks at how children distinguish among thought, speech, and action.

Piaget considered reversibility to be an important quality to mental operations. By this he meant that children could not only imagine performing some action but could also think of reversing, or undoing, that action to get back to the point from which thought had started. This mental "two-step," one step forward and one back again, enables children to consider the same problem from several perspectives, greatly increasing the flexibility of their thought. Such flexibility can be seen in perhaps the best known of Piaget's many measures of intellectual functioning. Children are shown two identical glasses, each filled with the same amount of liquid, and watch as the liquid from one of these is poured into a tall, narrow glass, where it rises to a higher level. Piaget then asks whether the amount of liquid in the narrow glass is the same as that remaining in the other, wider glass. School-age children, who can mentally reverse what they have just watched and imagine pouring the liquid back into the wider glass, understand that the liquid would again come to the same level as before. Preschoolers, who lack this flexibility, can only answer on the basis of how the liquid appears in each of the containers.

Operations have a second quality that, like reversibility, makes thought more flexible. Each operation belongs to a set of operations, making it possible to see how the effects of one are related to those of another. Think, for a moment, what it means for children to understand the concept of "six." They know, for example, that six pencils, six erasers, and six pennies are alike in that all are "six things." They can also imagine moving the pencils, erasers, and pennies into groups of 3s, or 2s. A mental operation such as this allows children to appreciate relationships between the class of "six things" and other classes, such as classes of "two things" and "three things." They realize not only that 6 is larger than 3, but also that 6 is the same as two 3s, and so on. Being able to relate one operation to another, to see how one thing relates to another, enables children to impose a new order on experience instead of taking it as a given. Thinking, as a result, becomes more logical.

This logic takes a number of forms. Unlike preschoolers, school-age children understand that if a ball of clay is rolled into the shape of a snake the amount of clay is unchanged, an understanding that Piaget referred to as conservation. (Figure 11.1). Children's achievement of conservation rests on several principles. The first of these, already mentioned, is the principle of *reversibility*. This is the understanding that one could roll the snake back into a ball, thereby reversing or nullifying the effects of the first operation. This understanding, that the amount of clay in the two must be the same because one can reverse, or undo, the effects of the first action, is related to a second principle, the *identity* principle. Children also realize that the clay making up the snake is the same clay that was in the ball, that the substance of each, in other words, is unchanged despite changes in the

How might mental operations enable a child to understand that a tall, narrow glass contains the same amount of liquid as a low, wide one?

Children who have entered the stage of mental operations can follow a recipe and understand how to transform raw ingredients into cookies.

Between-Subjects Design: Tolerance

BY MICHAEL WAPNER

The scene was repeated every few days for several weeks. But each time it was worse. First came the voices, raised in anger and argument. Then came pickets with their signs of protest. Then the store windows were broken. Then there were fistfights and the police came. People were arrested. The broken windows were boarded up and the store was closed.

The owner of the store was a Vietnamese immigrant. So were the protesters. All had come to this small community in Southern California to escape the oppression, violence, and death of the war in Vietnam and its aftermath. What precipitated the confrontation was that the store owner had displayed a picture of Ho Chi Minh in the window—a picture of the same "Uncle Ho" whose victorious forces had 25 years before overrun South Vietnam and driven out so many South Vietnamese, along with all their American allies.

One letter to the newspaper criticized the protesters harshly and observed that immigrants to the United States must learn that in a democracy "we are tolerant of the views of others, even when we strongly disagree." Another letter argued that it was a provocative affront to display the picture of the very man who was responsible for the death or imprisonment of family members of the residents of this community and that the store owner should have expected just what he got. A third letter pointed out that many who rejected the demonstrators' intolerance as un-American would have sung another tune had the picture been of Adolf Hitler.

Without tolerance we would always be at each other's throats. Every difference would be a provocation. On the other hand, indiscriminate tolerance invites chaos. Surely we must speak up and even act when we observe behavior of which we disapprove. But these examples are extremes. Tolerance need not be an all-or-nothing matter. One is not simply tolerant or intolerant. Distinctions must be made. Is the display of an "objectionable" picture free speech or the creation of a hostile environment? Do hateful thoughts lead to hateful words and then hateful deeds? And if so, where does one draw the line? Shall we allow words but suppress deeds? Or if words incite deeds, perhaps we should control speech also? And what about thought . . . ? And what about motives? For example, suppose you believe, as most of us do, that doctors cure illness and that it's a good thing they do. Is your tolerance for parents who refuse their sick child medical attention because they believe it is of no benefit (a factual disagreement) different than it is for parents who accept that medicine might help but reject it for religious reasons (a values disagreement)?

When viewed in these more complex terms, "tolerance" becomes a social-cognitive phenomenon. It depends both on the value system one has developed and on one's cognitive capacity to distinguish among thought, belief, and action, among error, evil, and disagreement. Consequently, it should not be surprising, as we shall see below, that the boundaries of tolerance follow a developmental course (Enright and Lapsley, 1981).

Wainryb, Shaw, and Maianu (1998) designed a study to examine the way tolerance for disagreement differs with age. Two of the questions they asked were (1) Does age affect the way subjects distinguish among objectionable beliefs, speech, and actions? and (2) Does tolerance at different ages depend on whether the disagreement is over facts or values? To investigate

appearance of either. A third principle, that of *compensation*, is the realization that changes along one dimension, such as length, are compensated for by changes along a second dimension, that of width. Although the snake is longer than the ball, it is not as wide, and the differences in width make up for those in length.

The dawning of operations burns through the mists of childhood thought like the morning sun. Ideas emerge from shadow, etched crisply in logic. New skills follow as the day follows night. At school, mathematical concepts such as place value emerge from addition of single-digit numbers. In social studies, it's possible to understand that one's state is larger than a city and smaller than the nation. At home, stamp albums, baseball cards, and doll collections reflect a new ability to mentally order one's world.

Piaget assumed that because these intellectual changes are biologically based, younger children lack the capacity to think the way school-age children do. Other developmentalists (Donaldson, 1978; Siegler, 1996a) point out that younger children frequently show these forms of thought, although more often they do not. Why, then, might they not? We turn to an information-processing approach for an analysis of factors influencing children's approaches to problems.

these issues they compared students at four grade levels: first grade (mean age 7.3), fourth grade (mean age 10.4), seventh grade (mean age 13.6), and college undergraduates (mean age 20.1). All participants were presented with short stories describing a person engaged in a practice which was harmful or unfair and of which all participants disapproved. One of the stories, for instance, was about a teacher who criticizes and insults her students when they make mistakes. The investigators made sure that all subjects disapproved of the behavior described in the story. For half the participants the behavior of the character in the story was based on deviant values (that is, "It is okay to be mean to children"). For the other half the character's behavior issued from deviant factual beliefs (that is, criticism and insult are the best way to educate children).

Randomly assigning half the subjects a value disagreement and the other half a factual disagreement constitutes a *between-subjects design*. In this type of design, each subject experiences only one condition of the independent variable. This is in contrast to a *within-subjects design* where each subject receives all conditions of the independent variable. A major advantage of the between-subjects design is that investigators need not worry that subjects' responses will reflect the effects of a previous condition that may still be present. In other words, what if subjects responding to the factual disagreement condition had just been exposed to the value disagreement condition? Could we safely assume that these subjects would be able to separate their reactions to each situation? In a between-subjects design, one need not worry about such matters. Also, because subjects can be assigned at random to conditions, investigators can be reasonably confident that groups do not initially differ until they impose different treatments. Both assumptions involve the issue of internal validity (see the Research Focus, "Internal and External Validity," in Chapter 14). To the extent that guarantees exist in experimental research, between-subject designs offer high guarantees of internal validity.

After reading the stories, subjects were questioned regarding their tolerance for the story character's *belief* (Is it all right for the character to believe X?), *speech* (Should the character be prevented from expressing X?), and *action* (Should the character be allowed to do X?).

One of the most salient, but not very surprising, findings is that the distinction between thought, speech, and action becomes more important with increasing age. A majority of all ages tolerated differences of belief (although 40% of first-graders were intolerant even of that). When it came to contrary speech, a large majority of first-graders and half of fourth-graders expressed intolerance. All age groups refused to tolerate actions with which they disagreed, if the actions were harmful. Interestingly, it was only with respect to speech that it mattered whether the disagreement was factual or over values, and then only slightly. The relative intolerance of the younger subjects for both belief and speech becomes more understandable when we look at the reasons they gave. The older the child, the clearer he or she was about the distinctions between thought, speech, and action. First-graders think that to think something leads necessarily to doing it. Older subjects were not so likely to make that equation. Of course, because younger children are not as able as older ones to inhibit behavior, an idea, once thought, is more likely to be manifest in action. So for them thought, speech, and action are indeed closely related.

These results raise an interesting possibility. Could it be the case that adults who have trouble with impulse control will tend to be intolerant of the ideas of others with which they disagree? Not being able to separate thought, speech, and action in oneself may cause one to distrust the thoughts of others. It would make an interesting experiment.

An Information-Processing Approach to Cognitive Development

Information-processing theorists view thinking as the processing of information and approach its study by looking at how information is encoded or represented in children's minds, and at the processes involved in its transformation and use. Robert Siegler (1998), summarizing two fundamental characteristics of cognition, points out that thinking is both limited and flexible. Simply put, we are limited in just how much we can attend to at any point in time, and we are very good at adapting the way we think to the demands of the task or the moment. With age, children develop increasingly efficient processes for overcoming these cognitive limitations.

Three of these processes are automatization, encoding, and the use of strategies. **Automatization** refers to increases, with continued experience, in the efficiency with which children can engage in various mental activities, such that these require less of their attention, thereby placing fewer demands on attention and memory (Siegler, 1998). For instance, school-age children can recognize words at

automatization Increases, with continued experience, in the efficiency with which children can engage in various mental activities.

The ability to categorize underlies the collecting enthusiasm typical of middle childhood, making it possible for these boys to organize players according to their teams, positions, and scoring/assist records.

a glance that younger children have to sound out letter by letter. Differences in the ease of pronouncing words also reflect automatization.

Encoding refers to the formation of mental representations for one's experience. The specific features of a situation that children notice, or encode, change with age. Older children are better at recognizing which features are most important as well as at processing these more efficiently. They are also able to focus on more features of a problem at once, whereas preschoolers typically limit their attention to a single feature. Siegler (1996a) points out that it is not simply what children of either age think to notice on their own, but also how much they can profit from instructions to solve problems in new ways. And this is related to what they have encoded.

Siegler (1976) has studied differences in the way children encode features of a problem through the use of a simple balance. Pegs are positioned at equal distances along each of the two arms so that weights can be added without slipping off. Children are asked to predict whether the arms will be balanced, or whether one will tip down, when various combinations of weights are placed at different distances along each arm (Figure 11.2). The amount of weight on either arm is a joint product of both the number of the weights that have been added and the distance of each from the center. Thus, to solve such a problem children must attend to both the number and the distance of the weights.

A common initial solution is to look only at the number of weights, without taking into consideration their distance from the center of the balance. When 8-year-olds were given feedback that distance was also important, they were able to adjust the way they approached the problem, whereas the same feedback didn't help the 5-year-olds. Siegler (1996a) reasoned that perhaps this was because the 5-year-olds were not looking at, or encoding, the relevant aspects of the problem as they were given feedback. He could see, for instance, that the 8-year-olds not only looked up and down at the number of weights added to any arm, but also back and forth at their distance from the balance point. Five-year-olds, by

encoding The formation of mental representations for one's experience.

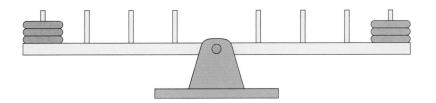

FIGURE 11.2 Siegler's Balance Problem *Source:* R. S. Siegler (1976). Three aspects of cognitive development. Cognitive Psychology, 8, 481–520.

contrast, only looked up and down. When 5-year-olds were taught to encode distance as well as weight, they were then able to profit from feedback and solve problems that required attending to two dimensions for their solution. The difference between the younger and older subjects was that the younger ones needed to be shown to look for a second dimension, whereas older ones did this spontaneously.

Why might older children be likely to encode more information in problems such as this? Siegler (1996a) cites three possible factors. The first relates to increases in the ease with which they can process new information, due to processes such as automatization, even when faced with an unfamiliar task. Younger children, by way of contrast, need to narrow their focus when faced with problems that tax their processing ability, such as those that are unfamiliar. In doing so, they are likely to focus on whatever stands out as the most perceptually salient dimension. By attending to less, younger children thereby reduce the amount of information they must process and remember.

> Why might older children be better at solving Siegler's balance problem than younger ones?

Siegler also suggests that children's beliefs, or worldviews, can contribute to the solutions they adopt. Older children are less likely than younger ones to believe that simple comparisons, such as which arm of a balance will tip down, or in which glass liquid will rise to a higher level, are explained by equally simple differences. Thus, they are prompted to look for more than the first difference that catches their attention. They also encode information differently, scanning the features of objects more systematically than younger children, with the result that they are less likely to be influenced by a particularly noticeable, but misleading, dimension, such as the height of the weights on any peg or the water level in a glass.

Finally, school-age children enjoy not only greater automaticity and are more likely to spontaneously notice, or encode, multiple aspects to a problem, but they are also likely to use more efficient strategies when solving problems. A strategy is simply any activity that is deliberately used to improve one's performance at a task. Even simple strategies, such as using one's fingers when counting (see later section on arithmetic), can be effective when an answer does not immediately come to mind. Children of any age have available a number of strategies, or differing approaches, to a problem (Alibali, 1999; Canobi, Reeve, & Pattison, 1998). Siegler (1996b) points out that these strategies coexist over an extended period of time in each child's life. It is this diversity, in fact, that creates the necessity of selecting among various approaches, with the result that the more adaptive ones eventually come to characterize more mature forms of thought. Development for Siegler, then, takes the form of changes in the frequency with which *existing* strategies are used, as well as of the appearance of new ones (Figure 11.3). Thus, just as Darwin identified competition among the various species as resulting in evolutionary change, Siegler sees the same process accounting for cognitive change.

One of the areas in which the use of strategies shows obvious improvement in middle childhood is that of memory. We turn to a consideration of this topic next.

FIGURE 11.3 Cognitive Development as the Use of More Efficient Strategies

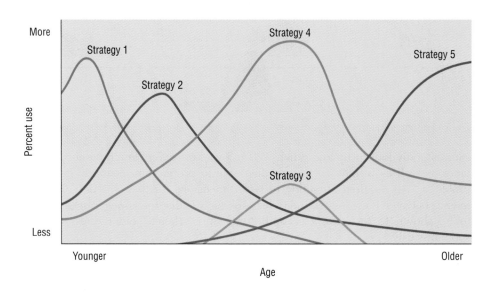

Memory

Have you ever asked a person to repeat something, only to find you know what that person said before hearing it again? How many times have you found yourself repeating a phone number you have just looked up until you can reach the phone and dial it? And have you ever noticed that you know what you *don't* know in addition to what you *do* know?

Rather than existing as a single system, memory exists as a number of interrelated systems, each with different characteristics. **Sensory memory** is very brief, lasting for half a second or less. This is the memory that allows you to reconstruct that lost snippet of conversation you asked someone to repeat, before hearing it again. There are no real age differences in sensory memory, 8-year-olds, for instance, doing as well as adults on tasks measuring this.

A second memory system is that of **short-term memory,** also known as working memory. This is the memory we rely on when dealing with information immediately surrounding us, such as holding a phone number in mind before dialing it. Short-term memory is limited in what it can hold, or work on, at any time to about seven items, give or take a few. This limitation is relatively constant over a wide range of items, being as true for small items such as numbers and letters, as larger ones such as words or even sentences. As long as the item exists as a single unit, or "chunk," it matters little whether it is made up of one letter or five. "Zebra" is as easy to remember as "z."

Short-term memory is also limited in duration, holding information for only 15 to 20 seconds. For information to be kept alive longer than this, it must be rehearsed, or repeated over and over, as one does with a phone number before dialing (see Chapter 8). Older children can hold on to more information in their working memories than can younger ones. It is not clear precisely why they can. Perhaps this difference reflects age changes in the actual capacity of memory, or perhaps it reflects processing differences. With respect to the latter, older children are able to rehearse items more rapidly than younger children, as pronunciation improves with age, thereby enabling them to keep a larger number of items alive in memory.

Long-term memory lasts from a minute to a lifetime. Because of the vastness of this memory, differences in capacity are essentially irrelevant. Information is semantically encoded, or stored according to meaning, in long-term memory. To

Q When a child who is trying to memorize a phone number repeats it over continuously, which memory system is likely to be involved?

sensory memory A very brief form of memory, lasting for less than a second, that is used during the processing of information.

short-term memory The form of memory used for immediate tasks; its capacity is about seven items at one time; also known as *working memory.*

long-term memory The form of memory in which information is semantically encoded, or stored according to meaning, for later retrieval.

As children grow older, they can retain more information in their short-term and long-term memories than preschoolers can and therefore are capable of memorizing lines for a play.

hold on to long-term information, one must relate it to things one already knows. Even though long-term memory has no time or capacity limitations, there is no guarantee that one will always be able to use the information that is encoded in it. Retrieving information is the biggest problem. Imagine misplacing a book in a large city's public library. How likely are you to recover the book if you can't remember which part of the library you were in when you put it down? The book is likely still there, but you can't retrieve it without using the system by which it was coded.

We also find age differences in long-term memory, a number of which reflect speed of processing—in this case, how quickly children can reach and retrieve information as it is needed. Age differences also include knowledge about one's memory. School-age children know more than do preschoolers about their memories, and they use their knowledge to monitor what they do. This knowledge is called *metamemory*. Older children know, for instance, that they are likely to forget things. They also know that they will be more likely to forget the more time has passed. Thus, when 6- and 8-year-olds were asked how much of something they would remember either 1 day or 1 week later, most 8-year-olds knew they were likely to remember less after a week than after a day. However, none of the 6-year-olds predicted this (Howe, O'Sullivan, & Marche, as cited in O'Sullivan, Howe, & Marche, 1996).

Julia O'Sullivan, Mark L. Howe, and Tammy Marche (1996) studied the development of metamemory by telling children (preschoolers, first- and third-graders) a story in which the characters tried to remember what had happened at a party

Q Why might young children be likely to believe that their memories are faithful representations of their experiences?

the day before. Children were asked how successful the characters would be and whether their memories would be affected by what others might tell them or by what they experienced subsequently. The researchers found systematic increases in metamemory with age. Preschoolers, for instance, believed that their memories faithfully represented reality and would not be affected by such things as suggestibility and interference. By the first grade, however, children become aware that memory can be influenced by having experienced something similar to what they are trying to remember. But not until the third grade do children become aware of the way their own memories can be influenced by the failings of someone else's memory—that is, their suggestibility to false memories.

Metamemory should develop hand in hand with children's more general awareness of their minds (see Chapter 8). Adults, for instance, are able to monitor their thoughts and describe these to others. The years of middle childhood appear to be particularly important in the development of such an awareness. John Flavell, Frances Green, and Eleanor Flavell (1995) looked at changes with age in children's ability to introspect, or look in on their own mental activity. They showed children "impossible" events, such as a scarf changing color as it was pulled through someone's hand and, after a few moments, asked them whether they had just been thinking about anything. If the children said they had, they asked them to describe their thoughts.

Nearly 70% of the time, 5-year-olds said they had not been thinking of anything. When they did mention something, it was twice as likely to be about something other than what they had just seen. Sixty-three percent of the 7- and 8-year-olds, on the other hand, said they had been thinking about what they had just seen. Note, however, that even at these ages, over a third of the times they were asked, they reported not having thought of anything. Thus even second- and third-graders seemed relatively unaware of their thoughts, not being that good at reporting the contents of the thoughts they had had even moments before. However, even 5-year-olds can accurately report other types of mental activity, such as mentally rotating a figure to determine whether it is the same as an upright one, suggesting that metamemory, just like other aspects of cognition, does not develop at the same pace across all domains (Estes, 1998).

Children also appear to be aware at an earlier age of those aspects of their mental activity over which they have control than they are of those aspects over which they do not have control (Kipp & Pope, 1997). Adults, for instance, realize that people often find it difficult to prevent themselves from thinking about things they don't want to consider. But at what age do children begin to realize that they are not the masters of their own minds? Flavell, Green, and Flavell (1998) traced the development of children's understanding of what they termed "mental uncontrollability" by telling children, adolescents, and adults a story about a person who sees something that is likely to trigger an unwelcome thought (getting a shot in a doctor's office) and asking them how successful the person would be in *not* thinking about that.

Adolescents and adults agreed that it would be very difficult not to think of getting the shot. Five-year-olds, on the other hand, indicated that people could keep themselves from thinking about such things if they wanted to. By the age of 9, children admitted the existence of unwelcome thoughts. They were also aware by this age of other aspects of mental life over which they had no control, such as not being able to stop for any appreciable amount of time the stream of consciousness that characterizes thought. These investigators conclude that most of our understanding of the uncontrollability of our own minds develops in middle childhood. Children's understanding of the limitations to their minds is important

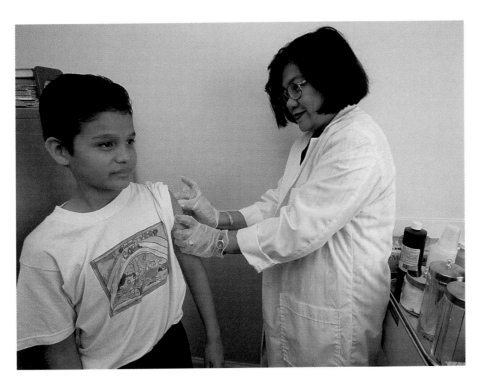

By the age of 9, children realize that they cannot always control unwelcome thoughts, such as fear of getting a shot at the doctor's office.

because it leads to a more careful monitoring of what they are thinking about and consequently leads to checking up on, or monitoring, themselves.

Limitations of Thought in Middle Childhood

Although children's thought is flexible in middle childhood, it is limited as well. Children do not think easily about things they cannot see. Their thought is not abstract. Children think of things that are absent only through simple extensions of their thoughts about what is present. Thought, in other words, is still prompted by the here and now.

Because school-age children tend to focus on aspects to a problem that can be seen, they tend to miss alternatives they could reach only by turning something around in their minds. Failure to speculate about other possible solutions frequently means they fasten on thoughts with finality. David Elkind (1978b) points out that school-age children frequently mistake their assumptions for facts, erroneously assuming that their first answer is the only answer and not looking for alternatives. Adults and adolescents check their assumptions out, rejecting them if they are not supported by facts.

Elkind says children operate according to **assumptive realities,** assumptions that they make on the basis of limited information. One assumptive reality, common during the school years, is what Elkind calls "cognitive conceit," or children's belief that they are clever, whereas adults are not. In contrast to preschoolers who believe that their parents know everything they know (see Chapter 8 for a discussion of egocentrism), school-age children realize they know things their parents don't know. On the basis of this, they jump to the conclusion that their parents must be ignorant and know nothing. Elkind wonders, in fact, whether cognitive conceit contributes to children's frequent reluctance to grow up. He points to numerous stories in which children outwit adults—Tom Sawyer

assumptive realities Assumptions made on the basis of limited information.

What children find funny changes with age.

outfoxing Aunt Polly, Nancy Drew solving mysteries for which her father hadn't a clue, and Peter Pan fooling Mr. And Mrs. Darling (even the *dog* knew what was going on).

Sometimes logic like this can only be taken with a grain of salt or a pinch of humor. Children develop a sense of the ludicrous in these years. Their appreciation of humor, just like their intellectual functioning in general, shows a developmental trend, which we will consider next.

Why are stories such as Peter Pan, Tom Sawyer, and Nancy Drew so appealing to school-age children?

Humor: A Sense of the Ridiculous

What makes a situation funny? Jokes that can turn an 8-year-old into jelly with giggling may only get a yawn from an adolescent. Paul McGhee (1979) identifies at least three ingredients to any humorous situation, each of which can be expected to change with age.

The first element in humor is what might be called the incongruous. We laugh, or smile, at things that violate our expectations. School-age children are able to appreciate incongruities that go over the heads of younger children. Many of these incongruities are provided by the multiple meanings some words have, which form the basis for many of the jokes and riddles children enjoy at this age. School-age children find this type of joke particularly funny, appreciating the ambiguity arising from the several possible meanings of a word, whereas preschoolers, failing to catch more than one meaning to the word, miss the joke. Consider the joke, "Order! Order in the court!" "I'll have a ham and cheese on rye, your honor."

A second ingredient to humor is the emotional release it affords. Humor provides a way of coping with situations and feelings that cause us to feel anxious by poking fun at them (Freud, 1961). Because different situations are problematic for children of different ages, the things that children find funny should also change with age. Preschoolers, for instance, are concerned with issues of bodily control, especially as these reflect elimination. Consequently, much of their humor could be characterized as "bathroom" humor. School-age children, on the other hand, are concerned with issues of mastery, as reflected in the riddles that characterize so much of humor in middle childhood. In a sense, riddles can be viewed as a microcosm of the schoolchild's experiences of being questioned and needing to have the right answers, but not always being sure what makes these right. However, the one who asks the riddle is the one who knows the answer, putting that person in control of the situation. This makes for a pleasant reversal of who is in control of knowledge.

A final component to humor is intellectual (see the Research Focus, "Generative Interview: An Astronomical Joke"). Concepts that are recently mastered are sufficiently challenging to be humorous. A joke about a man who orders a whole pizza for dinner and, when asked whether he wants it cut into six or eight pieces, responds "You'd better make it six, I could never eat eight!" is particularly funny to school-age children. Children who have just mastered conservation enjoy a joke where the same quantity cut into eight pieces could be thought to be more than it would be as six pieces (McGhee, 1979).

The content of much of children's humor during these years reflects their growing concerns over mastery and the development of new skills. An important component of intellectual development in middle childhood is the acquisition of the skills that will equip them for life in the larger culture. We turn next to a consideration of school and the mastery of basic skills such as arithmetic and reading.

The World of School

Perhaps no single transition is greater in children's lives, other than the birth of a sibling or the breakup of a family, than going off to school. School-age children spend most of their hours each day away from home, surrounded by other children, sitting still for longer periods of time than they are initially comfortable with, and bending their minds to tasks they have not chosen for themselves. And yet most children eagerly rise to all of this.

For some children, this transition can be harder than for others. In school, children not only learn to master basic skills such as reading and writing, but also take their first steps toward becoming members of a larger society, one that awaits them outside the intimate confines of their homes. To the extent that this society, as mirrored in their schooling, does not reflect the comfort and safety they have known within the privacy of their families, the step is a difficult one to take. In *Hunger of Memory,* Richard Rodriguez (1982) writes of his reluctance to take this step, by adopting English, the public language used in school:

> Without question, it would have pleased me to hear my teachers address me in Spanish when I entered the classroom. I would have felt much less afraid. I would have trusted them and responded with ease. But I would have delayed—for how long postponed?—having to learn the language of public society. I would have evaded—and for how long could I have afforded to delay?—learning the great lesson of school, that I had a public identity.
>
> Fortunately, my teachers were unsentimental about their responsibility. What they understood was that I needed to speak a public language. So their voices would search me out, asking me questions. Each time I'd hear them, I'd look up in surprise to see a nun's face frowning at me. I'd mumble, not really meaning to answer. The nun would persist, "Richard, stand up. Don't look at the floor. Speak up. Speak to the entire class, not just to

Generative Interview: An Astronomical Joke

BY MICHAEL WAPNER

Here's a joke.

A famous astronomer is giving a public lecture. When he is finished regaling his very impressed audience with the latest findings on black holes, white dwarfs, and quarks, he asks for questions. Immediately a small, gray-haired man jumps up and furiously waves his hand for recognition. The astronomer calls on him.

"I want a straight answer and no evasions," challenges the little man.

"I'll do my best," replies the famous scientist, just a touch patronizingly.

"O.K. then. What holds up the earth?"

Obviously pleased with himself for asking so fundamental a question, the man from the audience smiles knowingly at the people around him as he awaits his answer.

The scientist, having in his years of public lectures encountered flat-earthers, UFO abductees, and telepaths in direct thought contact with Mars, is not much surprised by the question. He attempts to get around it without offending.

"Well, you see, there is a problem with the way the question is put. Strictly speaking nothing holds up . . ."

"Enough!" breaks in the little man, triumph in his voice and on his face. "I knew you would try to wiggle out. All you academic smarties dodge the hard ones. As a matter of fact, I know the answer to my own question. It's a turtle. A turtle holds up the earth."

The scientist, condescension growing with impatience, responds, "And what holds up the turtle?"

The little man, gracious on the edge of victory: "Another turtle, of course."

The scientist, now in full sarcasm, "And what, pray tell, holds up that . . . ?"

The little man, not waiting for the end of the challenge, pounces for the *coup de grâce*. "I got you now. It's another turtle. And then another turtle under that one. In fact, it's turtles all the way down!"

However funny we find this story (and I hope you find it as funny as I did the first few times I heard it), there is more than humor here. Overlooking for the moment his turtle explanation, the little man's conceptual problem is quite understandable and not at all unusual. All of us, even small children, know that the earth is round and moves in empty space around the sun. We have heard and read about it over and over. We have even seen pictures, taken from space, of the round earth. But it is one thing to know this as a isolated fact. It is a deeper and more difficult thing to internalize the astronomical frame of reference into which this fact fits and still more difficult to reason on the basis of this broader frame of reference. The man in the audience is having just this difficulty. He knows, as an isolated fact, that the earth is an object in space. But his frame of reference has not caught up with that fact. He wants to know how the earth remains in space without falling. It is his, as it is everyone else's, common experience that heavy, unsupported objects fall. And the direction in which they fall is down. But everyone's common experience is from an earthbound perspective, in which earth is not itself an object but the "floor of the world." When we take an astronomical perspective, then we no longer speak of "falling" and there is no meaning to the term *down*. The man in the audience has confused these two perspectives.

Stella Vosniadou (1994; Vosniadou & Brewer, 1992) was particularly interested in how children and adolescents deal with this same problem, with how they reconcile what they have heard about the roundness of earth with their more deeply internalized earthbound perspective. To investigate this question she used what she terms a *generative* interview. A generative interview is one in which the interviewer does not stop with the

me!" But I couldn't believe that the English language was mine to use. (In part, I did not want to believe it.) I continued to mumble. I resisted the teacher's demands. (Did I somehow suspect that once I learned public language my pleasing family life would be changed?) Silent, waiting for the bell to sound, I remained dazed, diffident, afraid. ◄

Arithmetic

The expression "It's as simple as two plus two" is a common way of saying that something couldn't be easier. Yet learning basic arithmetic, such as addition and subtraction, is not necessarily easy at first. In fact, children frequently resort to the use of one or more strategies to help them arrive at the right answer. Robert Siegler

answers to factual questions, but gives the subject problems that probe the reasoning behind the factual answers. Consider the following interview with Jamie, a third-grader:

E: What is the shape of the earth?

J: Round.

E: Can you draw a picture of the earth?

J: (Child draws a circle to depict the earth.)

E: If you walked for many days in a straight line, where would you end up?

J: Probably in another planet.

E: Could you ever reach the end or the edge of the earth?

J: Yes, if you walked long enough.

E: Could you fall off that end?

J: Yes, probably.

Clearly, had the interviewer stopped when Jamie said the earth was round, she would have left with a seriously mistaken understanding of Jamie's view of the earth. If one can "reach the end of the earth by walking long enough" and then "probably" fall off, one is not walking on the surface of an earth that is "round" as astronomers understand that term.

By posing astutely chosen questions, (which are more like problems to be solved than questions to be answered), Vosniadou and Brewer are able to infer the cognitive model of earth the child must have constructed.

You may have noticed that the *generative interview* owes a great deal to the *clinical interview* of Jean Piaget. Piaget also posed "diagnostic" questions that allowed him to infer the way children think. The generative, or clinical, interview is to be contrasted with the *survey interview*. This latter form is designed to elicit *facts* or *opinions* of which the respondent is consciously aware. The generative interview, on the other hand, focuses more deeply, on the cognitive structures that lie beneath conscious facts and opinions. To conduct a generative interview, the interviewer must be much more skilled, since each question must build on the child's last response and thus cannot be totally scripted beforehand. The standardized protocol of a survey interview is much too rigid to serve a generative function. On the other hand, the necessity to ask somewhat different questions of different subjects in the generative interview makes standardization, and hence data interpretation, more complicated. There is also a greater danger, in a generative interview, of the questions suggesting and hence contaminating the responses, since the material elicited is more complex and hence more vulnerable to suggestive influence.

In spite of these dangers, the generative interview is wonderfully productive of insights on children's cognitive models. Here is Matthew, a first-grader:

E: If you walked and walked for many days, where would you end up?

M: If we walk for a very long time we might end up at the end of the earth.

E: Would you ever reach the edge of the earth?

M: I don't think so.

E: Say we kept on walking and walking and we had plenty of food with us?

M: Probably.

E: Could you fall off the edge of the earth?

M: No, because if we were outside the earth we could probably fall off, but if we were inside the earth we couldn't fall off.

Matthew has done pretty well in imagining the earth to be round. Where his cognitive model seems to disagree with conventional science is that he has us living *inside* the sphere. That's why we don't fall off.

and Mitchell Robinson (1982) studied the strategies children used by giving them problems in which they were asked to add two numbers, neither of which exceeded the number of fingers on each hand. One of the first things they noticed was that children typically had available to them a number of different strategies. Sometimes children would raise the number of fingers that corresponded to each number of items to be counted, counting the fingers that were raised (counting fingers strategy). Or they might raise that number of fingers but without any appearance of counting them (fingers strategy). At other times, children would count, without using any fingers (counting strategy). And sometimes they appeared to do nothing, simply retrieving the answer directly (retrieval strategy).

These strategies were clearly different, both in their accuracy and in the time it took to use them. The use of retrieval, for instance, was much faster than the

TABLE 11.1 Speed, Accuracy, and Frequency of Use of Strategies for Counting by Preschoolers

Strategy	Seconds	Accuracy	% Trials Used
Counting fingers	14.0	87	15
Fingers	6.6	89	13
Counting	9.0	54	8
Retrieval	4.0	66	64

Source: R. S. Siegler & M. Robinson. (1982). The development of numerical understandings. In H. W. Reese & L. P. Lipsitt (Eds.), *Advances in child development and behavior* (Vol. 16). New York: Academic Press.

One of the first strategies children use when doing math is counting with their fingers—and it works.

other strategies, but not nearly as accurate (Table 11.1). Also, children did not necessarily use the same strategy each time they solved the same problem. When given the same problem on different weeks, children used a different strategy 34% of the time. And the change was not necessarily because they moved to a more sophisticated strategy.

In addition to differences within any individual child such as these, there are large cultural differences both in the efficiency of the strategies that children use and in their general mathematical skills (Geary, Bow-Thomas, Fan, & Siegler, 1993, 1996). American children tend to place near the bottom of rankings comparing students from different countries (Youth Indicators, 1996; Figure 11.4). Such disparities have been explained in the past in terms of cultural expectations for achievement and differences in instruction. However, the language children speak also contributes to their relative ease in acquiring certain mathematical skills. A comparison of schoolchildren from China and the United States, for instance, found marked differences in the strategies they used when doing addition problems. When not immediately able to think of an answer, Chinese students preferred to verbally count, whereas American students were more likely to count on their fingers. The reliance on verbal counting as a strategy by Chinese children reflects the more rapid rate at which numbers can be pronounced in Chinese (Geary et al., 1996).

Many Asian languages confer a second, and more important, advantage when doing simple math problems. The names for numbers communicate information about the place value of the numbers. Children in the United States have difficulty understanding the concept of place value well into the second and even the third grades. Asian children find this concept considerably easier to grasp (Kamii, 1991). When one looks at the names given to numbers in Chinese and English, for instance, one sees the relative advantages of the former. Thus, the word for "11" in Chinese is translated as "ten one," and for "12" as "ten two."

Children must understand the concept of *place value,* that the value of a number changes depending on its place within a double-digit number, to know what they are doing when they add two-digit numbers. Adults have come, through long usage, to take this understanding as a given. This concept remains a mystery, however, to many schoolchildren even though they come up with reasonably good scores on tests of addition or subtraction of double-digit numbers.

Mieko Kamii (1991) demonstrated the types of misunderstandings American schoolchildren have by asking them to count out the number of items in a pile of 25 poker chips and to write down their answer. Then children were asked about the values of the "2" and the "5" in their answer. Kamii describes one second-grader who, when asked about the 5, answered that it stood for five chips, which

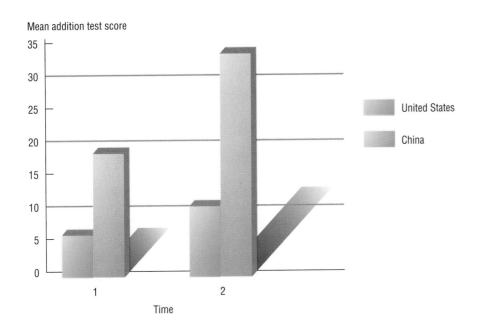

FIGURE 11.4 Performance in Addition by Chinese and U.S. Kindergarten Children near the Beginning (time 1) and End (time 2) of the School Year. *Source:* D. C. Geary, C. C. Bow-Thomas, L. Fan, and R. S. Siegler. (1996). Development of arithmetical competencies in Chinese and American children: Influence of age, language, and schooling. *Child Development, 67,* 2022–2044.

he then counted out, but when asked about the 2, responded that it stood for the two piles he had just created. Another second-grader answered that the "5" stood for five chips and the "2" for two chips, and the two-digit number for all 25 of them. Even though third graders did better in mentioning such things as "tens" and "ones," their failure to understand the meaning of what they were saying became evident when they were given two numbers to add, such as 18 and 13, in which they had to "carry" the "1." When asked to show the number of chips the "1" stood for, they were likely to indicate 1 chip, not 10.

Over and above such things as the advantages communicated by language are differences in how mathematics is taught. This latter difference is perhaps of paramount importance in contributing to cultural differences in mathematics achievement (Stigler & Stevenson, 1991). James Stigler and Harold Stevenson have compared the way mathematics is taught to American and Asian students and summarize a number of differences. In Asian classrooms, students spend more time interacting with each other and the teacher than they do working alone at their desks. Lessons also typically begin with a concrete problem, enabling children to become active participants in a process of discovery, rather than passive recipients of information. Finally, up to 8 times as much time is devoted to reviewing and summarizing what they have learned than in American classrooms. Let's take a look at one of the examples Stigler and Stevenson give; this is a fifth-grade class in Japan, a typical lesson:

> The teacher walks in carrying a large paper bag full of clinking glass. Entering the classroom with a large paper bag is highly unusual, and by the time she has placed the bag on her desk the students are regarding her with rapt attention. What's in the bag? She begins to pull items out of the bag, placing them, one-by-one, on her desk. She removes a pitcher and a vase. A beer bottle evokes laughter and surprise. She soon has six containers lined up on her desk. The children continue to watch intently, glancing back and forth at each other as they seek to understand the purpose of this display.
>
> The teacher, looking thoughtfully at the containers, poses a question: "I wonder which one would hold the most water?" (p. 14)

Active lessons with concrete items and problems to work on with classmates have been shown to be more successful in students' comprehension of math concepts than are lessons where students work out problems alone on paper.

Q Why is it effective to teach mathematics in elementary school using real-life problems?

After getting a number of different answers, she asks how they can discover which answer is correct. The class agrees on a way of measuring each and is divided into familiar working groups, each assigned to measure one of the containers. Students move about the classroom, each group carrying out the procedures agreed on by the class and recording their observations in a notebook. When they are finished, the teacher stands at the blackboard and asks a child from each group to report what that group has found:

> She has written the names of the containers in a column on the left and a scale from 1 to 6 along the bottom. Pitcher, 4.5 cups; vase, 3 cups; beer bottle, 1.5 cups; and so on. As each group makes its report, the teacher draws a bar representing the amount, in cups, the container holds.
>
> Finally, the teacher returns to the question she posed at the beginning of the lesson: Which container holds the most water? She reviews how they were able to solve the problem and points out that the answer is now contained in the bar graph on the board. She then arranges the containers on the table in order according to how much they hold and writes a rank order on each container, from 1 to 6. She ends the class with a brief review of what they have done. No definitions of ordinate and abscissa, no discussion of how to make a graph preceded the example—these all became obvious in the course of the lesson, and only at the end did the teacher mention the terms that describe the horizontal and vertical axes of the graph they had made. (pp. 14–15)

Stigler and Stevenson liken such lessons to a good story. They are organized around a central drama and capture students' interest. Like a story, they have a beginning in which a problem is introduced, a middle that is characterized by a search for a solution, and an end in which the problem is mastered. They also, like good stories, maintain children's interest and capture their imaginations. Fur-

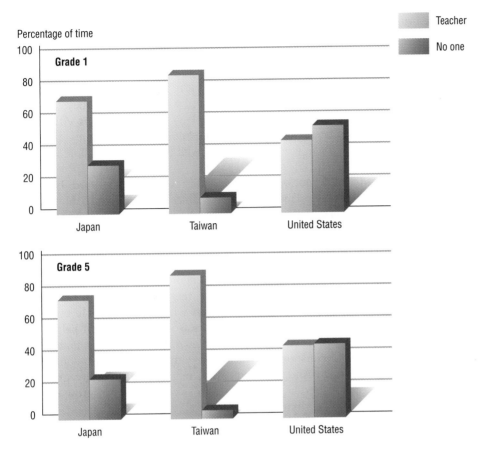

Percentage of time

Grade 1

Grade 5

FIGURE 11.5 Percentage of Time Students in Japan, Taiwan, and the United States Spend in Teacher-Led Instruction Versus Instruction Led by No One *Source:* J. W. Stigler and H. W. Stevenson. (1991). How Asian teachers polish each lesson to perfection. *American Educator,* (Spring) 12–20, 43–47.

thermore, lessons are not interrupted by extraneous activities that would break students' interest or lessen the experience of discovery and mastery at their conclusion. Nearly 50% of American fifth-grade math lessons, for instance, experienced some interruption, whereas fewer than 10% of classes were interrupted in Asian classrooms.

Finally, the amount of time devoted to actual instruction is greater in Asian classrooms. American lessons are more likely to have students working on problems at their seats, with the teacher walking around answering questions. Teacher-led instruction accounts for only 46% of class time in U.S. classrooms, in contrast to 90% of class time in Taiwan and 74% in Japan (Figure 11.5). Put another way, there was no one guiding the instructional period for only 9% of the time in Taiwan and 26% in Japan, but this was true for 51% of the time in American classrooms, leaving U.S. children to work by themselves for relatively long periods of time during which they may have had difficulty focusing on their work or understanding how it was relevant (Stigler & Stevenson, 1991).

Reading

In addition to learning mathematical mysteries, such as the place value of numbers and how to add or subtract, schoolchildren learn the mysteries of reading, of breathing sound into letters on a page, and of discovering the meaning behind these. Most are prepared to begin this adventure by the time they reach school. Before ever beginning school, most children can already recognize many letters if they are printed in uppercase, and they engage in pretend reading, telling a story while holding and looking at a book (Worden & Boettcher, 1990).

Learning to read involves a number of skills. At the most elementary level, children must be able to visually scan a word to identify individual letters. Laboratory research in which children are asked to search for a target letter among nontarget letters has found that the speed and accuracy with which they are able to detect the letter they are looking for is also related to their reading efficiency. Those who perform well at such a search task are better readers, reading at a rate that is 1½ times that of those who perform less well (Casco, Tressoldi, & Dellantonio, 1998).

Children need to know not only the names of the letters in a word, but also the sounds these letters make. This knowledge enables them to decode the sounds that make up a word. One of the difficulties children face, however, is that each letter can have more than one sound. There are only 26 letters in the alphabet, but over 50 different sounds, or **phonemes,** for which these can stand. The word "hot," for instance, has three phonemes, "huh," "ah," and "teh," one for each letter. However, the word "hope" also has three phonemes, "huh," "oh," and "peh," even though it contains four letters. Furthermore, the "o" in "hope" makes a different sound than does the "o" in "hot." Hidden within the scramble of letters and phonemes to be found even among these two words is a key that helps children unlock some of the mysteries of the sounds letters make. The key, that words ending in "e" give a different sound to the vowel within them, is itself something additional they must learn. And, just like Alice, many have difficulty grasping hold of this key as they experience the vagaries of vowels that can grow shorter or longer with seemingly no rhyme or reason.

Children use their knowledge of the name of the letter when learning the sound it will make, "mapping" the sound in the name onto the corresponding phoneme (Treiman, Tincoff, Rodriguez, Mouzaki, & Francis, 1998). For some letters, this approach works well. For others it can lead to errors, such as mistaking the letter "y" ("wai") as standing for the sound of a "w." An important difference among letters is whether the sound they make occurs in the name of the letter. Also important is whether this sound occurs at the beginning of the letter's name (b, c, d, g, j, k, p, t, v, and z) or at the end (f, l, m, n, r, s, and x). For a few letters, such as "h," "q," "w," and "y," the sound is absent altogether. Even though children can name one type of letter as accurately as another, they find it considerably easier to identify the sound a letter will make when it occurs at the beginning of the letter's name than at the end, and both types of letters make it easier to "map" the corresponding phoneme than when the sound is absent from the letter's name altogether.

Phonological skills, or the ability to sound out words, are fundamental to learning how to read (Ball, 1997). However, children also rely on context when faced with unfamiliar and phonologically ambiguous words, such as "beige," "diesel," or "canoe." In general, children who have better reading skills are better both at phonologically decoding new words (Booth, Perfetti, & MacWhinney, 1999) and at using context more effectively in recognizing new words (Nation & Snowling, 1998).

These differences among readers increase with age, with better readers becoming even better with time and poorer readers becoming relatively worse. In reading, as in other aspects of life, those who have get even more, and those who have not, fall even further behind. A 3-year longitudinal study of schoolchildren in the Netherlands suggests that the increasing differences between skilled and nonskilled readers largely reflect differences in their word-recognition skills, which

phonemes The smallest distinguishable units of sound in a language.

One Saturday morning I entered the kitchen where my parents were talking, but I did not realize that they were talking in Spanish until, the moment they saw me, their voices changed and they began speaking English. The gringo sounds they uttered startled me. Pushed me away. In that moment of trivial misunderstanding and profound insight, I felt my throat twisted by unsounded grief. I simply turned and left the room. But I had no place to escape to where I could grieve in Spanish. My brother and sisters were speaking English in another part of the house.

Again and again in the days following, as I grew increasingly angry, I was obliged to hear my mother and father encouraging me: "Speak to us *en inglés.*" Only then did I determine to learn classroom English. Thus, sometime afterward it happened: One day in school, I raised my hand to volunteer an answer to a question. I spoke out in a loud voice and I did not think it remarkable when the entire class understood. That day I moved very far from being the disadvantaged child I had been only days earlier. Taken hold at last was the belief, the calming assurance, that I *belonged* in public. ◄

Even written schoolwork becomes problematic for students who have difficulty translating the ideas they frame easily in the intimate language of their home into Standard English. Additional complications arise when corresponding terms are not available in the two languages (Feldman, Stone, & Renderer, 1990).

Overcoming the Differences The increasing ethnic diversity of our society makes it progressively difficult to characterize students in terms of simple behavioral and motivational profiles. Recognizing the distinctive approaches that characterize different ethnic groups can be a start and can be used to advantage in the classroom. Research on ethnic groups reveals distinct differences along four dimensions of personal interaction: group versus individual orientations, active versus passive coping styles, attitudes toward authority, and expressive versus restrained mannerisms.

Group Versus Individual Orientations Some cultures, such as Asian and Hispanic cultures, stress affiliation, interdependence, and cooperation. Other cultures, such as northern European, stress individual achievement, independence, and competition. Within the United States ethnic differences emerge along this dimension. Chinese, Hispanic, and African American children, for instance, are more group-oriented than those from the dominant culture (Rotheram & Phinney, 1987). These children are more attentive to the feelings and expectations of others than their White counterparts are. A Hispanic or an African American child may pay as much attention to the feelings of others as to the demands of the task at hand, an orientation many teachers may not understand or appreciate. However, in learning situations that require students to work together, this orientation will serve these students as well inside the classroom as outside it (Rotheram & Phinney, 1987).

Active Versus Passive Coping Styles Cultures characterized by active coping styles stress the importance of controlling one's environment and being productive. Those with passive styles place more emphasis on being than on doing. The sense of the present is greater in the latter and of the future in the former. These differences—like those of group versus individual orientation—can translate into either strengths or weaknesses in the classroom. Children with a take-charge attitude may find it difficult to wait for others, or to take enough time to explore all the issues. The strength of this approach is the way that it fosters achievement.

The strengths of the passive approach are the freedom it gives students to turn themselves over to the moment and learn what it can teach them. The disadvantages to this coping style are most apparent in classrooms structured according to active coping strategies. Children from cultures with a passive coping style are not as likely to ask for help or materials, and, if teachers and classmates assume that no help is needed unless asked for, these students will not receive the help they need to keep up (Rotheram & Phinney, 1983).

Attitudes Toward Authority   Clear ethnic differences exist for this dimension as well. Hispanic and Asian American children, for instance, are likely to have been raised in authoritarian homes (see Chapter 9) and taught to be respectful and not to question those in authority. Certain Native American and many White children have been socialized to make decisions for themselves and are less accepting of authority (Rotheram & Phinney, 1987). It should not be surprising that some students want to be told what to do and do their best work under those conditions, whereas others want to make decisions for themselves and do not fare well with authoritarian teachers.

Expressive Versus Restrained Mannerisms   Interactions in some cultures are informal and open and in others are ritualized and private. The former is more characteristic of Black and White children, the latter of Asian American children. Black children express their feelings even more openly than Whites; theirs is a high-intensity culture, in which feelings are given more open expression. An Asian American student might easily misread a Black student's expressions of anger as aggression or a White student might regard an Asian American's reaction to an incident as timid simply because each is not familiar with the other's culture.

Children are not very accurate in predicting how those from another culture will react. Differences along each of these dimensions underscore the importance of developing cross-ethnic awareness among students as well as teachers.

Many minority children have difficulty predicting their own experiences as they move from home, to school, to community. Urie Bronfenbrenner (1979) describes the experiences that make up one's reality in terms of overlapping spheres of influence. At the most immediate level, the *microsystem,* are one's first-hand experiences—interactions at home, in the classroom, and with friends. The *mesosystem* arises from interactions among one's different microsystems. Minority children frequently experience problems with interactions involving the mesosystem. They may see their parents distrust the system or teachers communicate less respect for their parents than for those of other students.

Children experience the *exosystem* at the level of their communities. Available housing and the types of schools they attend reflect decisions made at the community level but influence their lives directly. The *macrosystem,* which consists of the underlying social and political climate, is even further removed from children's daily experiences, yet it impinges on their realities in very real ways. Laws concerning compulsory education, the mainstreaming of students with special needs, and the separation of grades into elementary, junior high, and high schools all illustrate the direct ways the macrosystem can affect the lives of schoolchildren. A less observable, but no less real, effect of the macrosystem is experienced in the form of beliefs, biases, and stereotypes. The values of the macrosystem can be at odds with those of the home microsystem for children from some minority groups (Spencer, 1985).

John Ogbu (1981, 1992) offers a disturbing analysis of the plight of many minority students. He notes that educational programs have assumed that the problems many minorities experience at school (poor attendance, high dropout rates, low achievement) should be addressed at the level of the microsystem—by improving the home environment or enriching educational experiences. Ogbu suggests that the problem is generated at the macrosystem level and can only be solved by changes introduced at that level. He attributes poor academic performance and high dropout rates among minorities to a "job ceiling," or discrimination in job opportunities, and to their perception that members of their own families have not been rewarded for their achievements.

If all children progressed through the same *social mobility system,* one in which mobility, or social class, reflects their abilities, then the most effective method of intervention for minorities who are failing would be at the microsystem level, reaching into the home or classroom to bring their abilities and skills up to the level of the others. But *do* all members of our society move through the same mobility system? Is there more than one system, similar to that of academic tracking, once students reach high school, but with respect to economic rather than educational opportunities?

If there is more than one mobility system, what factors other than ability and skill determine the system in which individuals participate? Notice that if we have more than one social mobility system, social class is an *effect* rather than a cause, and minority problems must be addressed at another level. Social status among minorities, argues Ogbu, reflects the realities of a job ceiling: a consistent set of social and economic obstacles preventing equal selection based on ability imposed on certain minorities at birth—that is, a society stratified by ethnic and racial castes as well as by class. The problems of minority groups can be resolved only at the macrosystem level, by addressing social ills such as prejudice and discrimination.

Children at the Edge

Two other groups of students have special needs and frequently find themselves out of step with the rest of the class. These children come from all backgrounds. They are the gifted and those with learning disabilities.

Gifted Children   In 1925, Lewis Terman of Stanford University defined the gifted as those who place among the top 2% on a test of intelligence. Seventy years later, the most common criterion for placing students in special educational programs is still a score on an intelligence test: 130 or higher (Horowitz & O'Brien, 1986). The following descriptions come close to what the average person is likely to think of as gifted: the super-smart, the ones who ace school, the kids behind the books.

In 1981 Congress passed the Education Consolidation and Improvement Act, which defines giftedness more broadly. The gifted and talented are those "who give evidence of high performance capability in areas such as intellectual, creative, artistic, leadership capacity, or specific academic fields, and who require services or activities not ordinarily provided by the school in order to fully develop such capabilities" (Sec. 582).

Howard Gardner (1983) also includes more than traditional measures of intelligence in defining giftedness. Gardner considers seven domains of intelligence: musical, bodily-kinesthetic, logical-mathematical, linguistic, spatial, interpersonal, and intrapersonal. Children can be creative in any of these different domains, and, for Gardner, creativity is the highest form of functioning. Creativity and giftedness, however, are not neatly related. Many gifted individuals are also highly creative, but many are not. Also, many creative people are not intellectually gifted.

Some characteristics of giftedness, such as being bored or restless, are often not seen as signs of intelligence.

Q Why might it be difficult to identify gifted children by their performance in the classroom?

Identifying the Gifted Perhaps because intelligence reflects our personalities, gifted students fail to fit any stereotype. It is easy to identify those who have large vocabularies or who top out on standard tests of achievement. But what about the ones who never see things the way others do, have zany senses of humor or vivid imaginations, those who get bored easily or who, when they can't do things perfectly, fail to do them at all? Gifted children are likely to fit any of these descriptions as well.

Barbara Clark (1988), an educator at California State University, Los Angeles, offers the characteristics listed in Box 11.1 as indices of cognitive giftedness. Many of these characteristics would not be taken as signs of unusual talent or intelligence by most of us. Some, in fact, seem to signal just the opposite.

Do gifted children apply their intelligence to advantage in areas of their lives other than academic ones? Research offers a tentative yes. Various studies have found the gifted to be more mature, to have better social skills, and to be more self-confident, responsible, and self-controlled than age-mates of average intelligence (Hogan & Weiss, 1974; Hogan, 1980). Terman (1925) even noted that his gifted children were slightly more likely to be physically superior to average children, to be heavier at birth, to walk earlier as infants, grow taller, and generally have fewer physical defects. So much for the negative stereotypes of the gifted as bookworms and wimps.

Being gifted does not offer immunity to social and emotional setbacks. In fact, it may make them harder to take. Social injustices can be especially difficult for those concerned with social or political problems, and slights can easily be exaggerated by those who react to life intensely and with passion.

Educating the Gifted Educational programs follow one of two alternatives: enrichment or acceleration. The goal of *enrichment* is to provide gifted students with more opportunities and experiences than they would normally get, without moving them to a higher grade. An example would be offering special courses in literature, math, science, or the arts, along with the normal course of studies.

Box 11.1 *Some Characteristics of a Gifted Student*

Asks many questions
Has much information on many topics
Adopts a questioning attitude
Becomes unusually upset at injustices
Is interested in social or political problems
Has better reasons than you do for not doing what you want done
Refuses to drill on repetitive tasks
Becomes impatient when can't do an assignment perfectly
Is a loner
Is bored and frequently has nothing to do
Completes part of an assignment and leaves it unfinished for something else
Continues to work on an assignment when the rest of the class moves on
to something else
Is restless
Daydreams
Understands easily
Likes to solve problems
Has own ideas as to how things should be done
Talks a lot
Enjoys debate
Enjoys abstract ideas

Source: Clark (1988).

Acceleration allows gifted students to advance beyond their grade level at a faster than normal rate—that is, to skip grades (Horowitz & O'Brien, 1986). Advocates of enrichment point to the social and emotional needs of gifted students, arguing that these are best met by keeping them with others their age. Although many gifted children are socially and emotionally more advanced than their peers, this argument is especially compelling for late maturers, especially boys.

On the other hand, failure to advance the highly gifted can present as many problems as acceleration. Students who experience little or no intellectual challenge in their classes and feel they are simply "marking time" can face intellectual stagnation, loneliness, and apathy—difficulties as serious as any introduced by moving ahead of their age-mages (Horowitz & O'Brien, 1986).

Children with Learning Disabilities For some students, marking time takes a very different form. They, too, have difficulty maintaining interest in their classes but for reasons very different from those of gifted students. These students have experienced difficulty in school almost from the beginning. Many live with the bewildering sense that something is wrong, though they can't say what. Most feel stupid, though they are not. These children have a learning disability.

Having a learning disability is not to be confused with intelligence. Learning-disabled children are just as intelligent as other children and perform as well as their classmates on tasks that do not require them to process information in particular ways. Thus one type of learning disability might take the form of a child having difficulty understanding instructions when these are stated orally to the class as a whole, but not when they appear in writing at the top of her worksheet.

Conversely, another learning-disabled child might be unable to distinguish b's from p's and d's on a printed page, making reading difficult, but be able to comprehend a story that is read to him as well as any of his classmates.

 John Dixon (1997), research director for the American Shakespeare Theater, describes his experiences as a gifted child who also had a learning disability:

> It was a combination of mystification and depression that set in when Mrs. Wilson struggled at introducing me to reading in the first grade. As I looked around at my classmates, their ease at turning written words into the correct spoken words seemed to make them coconspirators. They possessed a secret wisdom to which I was not privy. Mrs. Wilson looked upon them with eyes of pleasure. They were her teacher's delight, her measure of success. She looked upon me with eyes of forlorn patience. I was the stumbling block in her attempt to deliver a class full of readers to the second grade teachers. I remember sitting bent low at my school desk, eyes downward, hoping not to be noticed as I bumbled over Dick and Jane. . . .
>
> Throughout these eight years there was an interesting discrepancy. Although my reading never changed from a slow to halting pace, I nevertheless loved reading. Sometimes I would spend every minute possible devouring whole sets of books from the library bookcase in the back of the classroom; slowly, ruminatingly, but devouring. There was no way my reading could be rushed. Deep twinges of anguish accompanied speed reading drills. I would pretend to be reading faster than I could because I didn't want to be the last student to raise his hand to indicate being finished. Most of all I hated reading tests. If I didn't rush through tests much faster than I could possibly comprehend the material, I would find myself far from the end of the test when the time was called. Yet there were times when I spent all the time I could reading. Books were the entry way to the larger world. The ideas in books were marvelous even if my reading mechanics were tortuous. The ideas in books came to be an important focus of my life, and I would learn to put up with the difficulty for the sake of learning. (pp. 174–175) ◄

Estimates of the number of school-age students with learning disabilities range from 2% to over 30%, depending on how learning disabilities are defined (Lovitt, 1989). Of those with learning disabilities, approximately 33% will eventually graduate with a diploma. Another 5% will graduate through certification, but 19% of all learning-disabled students will drop out of school (U.S. Department of Education, 1988).

Defining Learning Disabilities   Who are these students, and what special problems do they face? Only recently have experts achieved some consensus in answering these questions. Their answers focus on three defining features of learning disabilities: (1) a discrepancy between expected and actual performance, (2) difficulty with academic tasks that cannot be traced to emotional problems or sensory impairment, and (3) presumed neurological dysfunction.

First, learning-disabled students show a *discrepancy between expected and actual performance.* Students with a learning disability are of average or above-average intelligence but don't perform at the level one would expect based on their intelligence, frequently falling behind their peers in academic skills. Second, their *difficulty with academic tasks* cannot be traced to emotional or sensory dysfunction. They may experience difficulty in one or more specific areas (for example, reading or math) or in the general skills needed for many areas, such as being able to pay attention or to monitor their performance (such as remembering which subroutines they have completed in a math problem in order to begin the next). They do not have a learning disability if the source of the difficulty is an emotional problem, problems at home, or a sensory impairment, such as a hearing loss. Finally, students with a learning disability are presumed to have some *neurological dysfunction,* because they are of at least average intelligence and their difficulties are not primarily the result of sensory, emotional, or cultural causes (Lovitt, 1989).

Addressing Problems   Learning-disabled children face problems both inside and outside the classroom. In the classroom, programs can range from difficulty paying attention or following class discussions to failure to turn in written assignments. Learning-disabled students have difficulty keeping up with classmates. In addition, most learning-disabled students have poorer study habits, are less likely to do their homework, and, when it comes to demonstrating what they *have* learned, have poorer test-taking skills. Frequently, nonattendance, incomplete assignments, and failure to turn in homework contribute to their failure in a course as much as their scores on tests do (Lovitt, 1989).

The problems of learning-disabled children don't end when they leave the classroom. As a group, they have poorer social skills than other students. They are less likely to pick up on another's mood and respond appropriately and are less aware of the effect their behavior has on others. Subtle cues can go right by them. The same problems that make it difficult for them to understand what their teachers are saying in class can affect their interactions with friends. They may miss nuances of conversation and respond inappropriately or miss rule changes in a game and feel they've been taken advantage of when the old rules no longer apply. Frequently they prefer the company of those who are younger, just because they are more compliant.

The learning-disabled are less likely to be involved in extracurricular activities than other students (Spreen, 1988). Perhaps this fact reflects their general disenchantment with school. Or it may reflect a poorer self-image and expectations of failure in these activities as well. Increasing learning-disabled students' involvement in extracurricular activities such as teams, clubs, and music and drama productions might be one of the most important ways of increasing their participation and their motivation to stay in school (Lovitt, 1989).

Schooling the Learning Disabled   *Mainstreaming* places learning-disabled children in regular classes in which teachers attempt to accommodate their special needs. Perhaps because so little can be done to meet the special needs of the learning-disabled in most classrooms, mainstreaming can introduce special problems of attendance. A growing number of schools that mainstream learning-disabled students provide a *special education consultant* who meets with regular teachers to discuss ways of managing the needs of these students. This procedure allows students to attend classes with their peers while receiving materials designed by someone who has specialized in learning disorders.

The other extreme from mainstreaming places learning-disabled students in *special education classes*. The obvious advantages of such an approach are small classes in which materials can be personalized to the needs of students and a teacher who is experienced in the special needs of the learning-disabled. Disadvantages are that association with nondisabled students who might serve as positive role models is limited, and teachers may not hold the learning-disabled to the same standards that are required of other students (Lovitt, 1989).

Children who are mastery oriented enjoy situations that challenge them.

Success, Failure, and Patterns of Achievement   The attitude children take toward their successes and failures is an important determinant of future success. It's not so much whether they fail or succeed—all children experience their share of both; the important thing is what they attribute their failure or success to that determines whether they will persist and eventually achieve. Research distinguishes two quite different patterns of achievement behavior: one defined by a focus on the task and what it takes to master it (a *task-mastery orientation*) and the other by a focus on one's performance or ability (a *performance-ability orientation*). The first approach is adaptive; the second is not (Dweck, 1989).

Children who are task, or mastery, oriented enjoy situations that challenge them, and they work at them even when they are difficult. They even take pride in how much effort they have to put into mastering something new. Children who are performance, or ability, oriented avoid challenging situations and show little persistence in the face of difficulty. They view any effort they must expend negatively, because having to try hard puts their ability in question. If at first they don't succeed, they find something else to do (Burhans & Dweck, 1995; Dweck, 1989).

Performance-oriented students tend not to pursue challenging material unless they're sure they will succeed. They choose situations that will not reveal what they regard as their lack of ability. These students are likely to prefer tasks that are either very easy or very difficult; failure at the first is unlikely, and failure at the second cannot be taken as a measure of their ability. Even above-average students who are performance-oriented will avoid situations that involve risk in preference to those they can perform effortlessly, thereby making them feel smart. In doing so, however, they miss situations that promote further understanding (Dweck, 1986).

The difference between students who stick it out and those who give up is basically one of attitude, which researchers term *attribution of outcome*. Children who persist when they experience failure tend to attribute the outcome of their actions to their efforts. Believing they haven't tried hard enough, they increase their efforts. They are task-oriented (Dweck & Reppucci, 1973; Heyman & Dweck, 1998).

Those who are disrupted by failure, frequently to the point of giving up, are performance-oriented. Because they interpret failure to mean that they lack the ability for what they have attempted, they defensively withdraw in the face of it. To believe that failure means that one lacks ability is also to believe that trying harder isn't going to help. Rather than trying harder, these students explain their failure as bad luck or the task's being too difficult. For them, having to try too hard is dangerous; it's just another way of calling their ability into question.

Claudia Mueller and Carol Dweck (1998) point out that praising children's intelligence when they do well by telling them they are smart may cause them to focus more on their performance than on what they are working on. These investigators gave fifth-graders problems to complete, after which they were told they had done very well. Some were praised for their intelligence ("You must be smart at these problems"), some for their effort ("You must have worked hard at these problems"), and those in a control condition were given no additional feedback. All were then given a choice as to whether they wanted to continue with problems they could "learn a lot from" even though they might not "look so smart" (learning goal) or with those that were "pretty easy" in which they could expect to "do well" (performance goal).

They found that children's choice of what type of problem to continue with was definitely affected by the type of praise they received. Two-thirds of those who had been praised for their intelligence chose to work on problems on which they could expect to do similarly well. In contrast, over 90% of those who had been praised for working hard at the first set of problems chose to work with ones

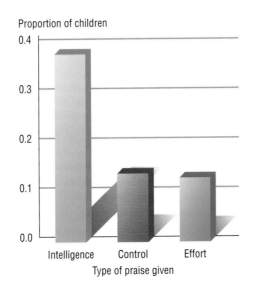

Proportion of children

Type of praise given

FIGURE 11.6 Proportion of Children Misrepresenting Their Success on Problems After Being Praised for Their Intelligence or Their Effort or Receiving No Feedback. *Source:* C. S. Mueller and C. S. Dweck. (1998). Praise for intelligence can undermine children's motivation and performance. *Journal of Personality and Social Psychology, 75,* 33–52.

from which they could learn something. Approximately equal numbers of children in the control condition chose either of the two types of problems.

In order to discover whether praise also affects how children interpret failure experiences, all children were told they had done worse on the second set of problems. It was found that those who initially had been praised for being smart were more likely to attribute their subsequent failure to lack of ability, whereas those who had been praised for working hard were more likely to attribute this to lack of effort. Finally, when children were asked to describe for another child how well they had done on these problems, those who received praise for their ability were more likely to misrepresent how well they had done, nearly 40% lying about the number of problems they had actually solved (Figure 11.6). In contrast, only 13% of those praised for how hard they had worked misrepresented their performance, a number close to that for children who received no feedback (14%).

The Contexts of Development: Supportive and Responsive Environments

Children's pleasure in learning, understanding what their successes and failures communicate about themselves, and their persistence at challenging tasks are as much a product of their experiences at home as they are of those in the classroom. Supportive parenting has been found to be positively related to children's intellectual development as well as to their social and emotional well-being. Supportive parents are characterized by their warmth and firmness in their interactions with children, their use of reasoning when disciplining, and their involvement in the various aspects of their children's lives (Baumrind, 1967, 1989).

Supportive parenting, additionally, is related to children's overall adjustment to school. Gregory Pettit, John Bates, and Kenneth Dodge (1997) found academic performance among kindergarten children to be related to parental warmth and involvement and, among the same children when they reached the sixth grade, to parental involvement and the use of reasoning. In addition, supportive parenting acted as a protective factor for children who might otherwise be at risk for school adjustment, such that the relation between supportive parenting and adjustment in the sixth grade was strongest for children from low-income and single-parent families.

Cognitively stimulating home environments motivate children academically.

Adele Gottfried, James Fleming, and Allen Gottfried (1998) followed a group of largely middle-class, European American children from 8 to 13, examining the relation between home environments and students' intrinsic academic motivation. They found, as might be expected, that children who grow up in homes that are cognitively stimulating are more likely to find academic pursuits intrinsically interesting. Furthermore, growing up in a cognitively stimulating home environment had an impact on academic intrinsic motivation in ways that could not be explained simply in terms of differences in family income level. This is not to say that family income level is not important, but that its effects are filtered through the more immediate environment of interactions within the family and the transmission of family values. This environment not only fosters curiosity and exploration, but also promotes the development of competencies.

Parents who otherwise might not offer sufficiently optimal environments can be shown ways of making these more stimulating. Terry Cronan, Sonia Cruz, Rosa Arriago, and Andrew Sarlom (1996) tutored parents of Head Start children in effective ways of reading to their children. Children were randomly assigned to either a high- or low-intervention program or to a no-intervention control. Parents of children in the first group attended 18 sessions in which a tutor met individually with them and their child and showed them effective ways of reading to their children. Parents were also shown how to teach basic concepts, such as naming colors and shapes, and told the importance of asking their children questions and of talking to them. Tutors met with families on an average of once a week. Parents of children in the low-intervention group received similar instruction, but only for three sessions.

These investigators found that parents in the high-intervention group not only read to their children more often, but also were more likely to build this into a ritual, such as having a regular time or place for reading. These parents were also more likely to use the library, checking out books to read together with their children and by themselves, and were more likely as well to bring their children to the library than were those in the control condition. Children whose parents were given the intensive training showed improved language skills and improved conceptual development. Intervention programs such as this one are important, because they help to create a more responsive environment for children by building in patterns of interaction, such as reading together, sharing more activities, and, in general, talking more with each other.

Other attempts at intervention have focused on day care programs. Participation in day care during the first 3 years of life has been found to serve as a protective factor for at-risk children whose home environments are otherwise impoverished. Children who are enrolled in early day care programs do better once they reach school than those not enrolled, showing improvement in both mathematics and reading skills. Reading skills, especially, are affected by early intervention, with children who are enrolled by the age of 2 showing the strongest effects. Day care has not been found to affect all children the same way. Children from impoverished environments have been found to especially benefit from day care if enrolled early in such programs, before reaching the age of 1, perhaps because their responsiveness to their environment is increased (Burchinal, Campbell, Bryant, Wasik, & Ramey, 1997). Enrollment this early has an opposite effect on children from more optimal home environments (Caughy, DiPietro, & Strobino, 1994).

Although participation in preschool programs such as Head Start has been found to contribute to children's cognitive development and to their success in school (Barnett, 1992, 1995; Neisser et al., 1996), exposure to such programs cannot protect children from the effects of poverty indefinitely. One of the recommendations to come out of research on early childhood intervention programs is

Parental involvement in children's education has a strong positive effect on children's school performance.

that intervention be extended into the school years, such that its effects can better take root in children's and families' lives (National Head Start Association, 1990). Being able to continue in a program for the first several years of schooling, as opposed to ending with kindergarten, may be an important source of stability, by providing continuity not only in a learning environment, but also in a social environment, preserving supportive relationships with peers and teachers. Such programs may also be effective in involving parents in their children's schooling.

Arthur Reynolds and Judy Temple (1998) compared school achievement between children who participated in an extended intervention program, lasting from preschool to the second or third grade, and children whose participation ended when they were in kindergarten. They found that extended intervention significantly improves the effectiveness of early-intervention programs. This is not to say that preschool and kindergarten programs are not effective, because they are. However, enrollment in an extended intervention program through the second and third grades for children who had previously been enrolled in preschool and kindergarten programs significantly increased the benefits of the earlier intervention. Furthermore, these benefits persisted through the seventh grade and held up even when other important factors, such as family background variables, parents' attitudes toward education, and level of achievement among children at the completion of kindergarten, were controlled.

The parents of children in extended intervention also become more involved in their children's schooling, participating more in the activities of the school, volunteering in the classroom and interacting more with other parents (Reynolds & Temple, 1998). In general, parental attitudes of children enrolled in early intervention programs are quite positive; they express optimism about their children's education and affirm their belief in the importance of doing well in school (Galper, Wigfield, & Seefeldt, 1997).

The importance of parents' involvement in their children's education cannot be stressed too much. James Comer (1985, 1988), at Yale University, has created a program in which parents, along with teachers, administrators, and staff, are responsible for administering the activities of the school. This program addresses

Educational Equality and School Choice

BY MICHAEL WAPNER

One unhappy reality of American public education is that not every school provides quality instruction. As measured by achievement test scores, likelihood of finishing high school, and the proportion of graduates entering and completing college, there are wide gulfs between the best and poorest public schools (Godwin, Kemerer, Martinez, & Ruderman, 1998).

A second unhappy reality is that despite legislation against intentional segregation and the widespread busing of students to achieve desegregation, schools still show great disparities in racial and ethnic populations. Approximately two thirds of African American students and nearly three fourths of Hispanic students who attend public schools go to schools in which the student body is predominately minority. For over a third of these students, 90% of the students in the schools they attend are members of an ethnic minority group (Godwin et al., 1998; Orfield, 1993).

At the intersection of these two unhappy realities lies a third. Schools with the highest concentration of minority students are among those that provide education of the lowest quality. High among the variables that influence the quality of learning in a school are the social class and ethnic composition of its student body (Bryk, Lee, & Holland, 1993). These two variables are tightly linked. A student in an intensely segregated minority school is 14 times as likely to be in a high-poverty school as is a student in a school where black or Latino students make up less than 10% of the student body (Orfield, 1993). Thus, race is linked to poverty, both are linked to segregation, and segregation is linked to poor schools and educational failure (Orfield, 1993).

One strategy for breaking the pattern of separation and underachievement would be to broaden the selection of schools that minority students can attend—to dilute the concentration of poor minority students in particular schools, to place students at risk for low achievement among higher-achieving students in better schools, and, as a very desirable bonus, to increase the cultural diversity of the student body. There are a number of ways this might be achieved but, in addition to questions regarding educational effectiveness, every one of them raises knotty economic, political, social, and ethical issues.

Busing

Since the Supreme Court struck down the "separate but equal" formula that had rationalized school segregation and educational inequality, one of the most frequently employed mechanisms for achieving school integration has been transporting groups of students by bus. However, busing often generates hard feelings in the community. It often requires enforcement by the courts and even police, it does not allow for student or parental choice, and it is expensive.

Changing Residence

The greatest determinant of school choice is housing. Everything else being equal, children go to the schools that are closest to where they live. Unfortunately, where people live depends overwhelmingly on what they can afford. Poor people are forced to "choose" low-cost housing, frequently in ethnically segregated neighborhoods where the schools are poor.

Magnet Schools

Specializing in some particular academic area (science, arts, and the like), magnet schools accept qualified students from throughout a school district or, sometimes, from neighboring school districts. In large urban districts, about 20% of high

the social and developmental, as well as the educational, needs of students. Comer believes, for instance, that social skills and ties to the community are as important as academic subjects, especially for lower-income students, who often lack these assets. In two inner-city schools using Comer's model, student performance so improved that the schools tied for third and fourth place in the district, with the students testing up to a year above the average for their grade. Attendance also improved dramatically, and behavior problems practically disappeared.

It is easy to understand why such a program could work: teaching becomes more relevant when academic subjects are translated into the daily concerns of students and their families. In turn, what is learned in the classroom receives the support of parents who are committed to educational programs they help plan. The Social Policy Focus, "Educational Equality and School Choice," examines various attempts to provide inner-city students with better educational opportunities.

school students are likely to attend magnet schools. Outcome studies have shown that magnet schools have a positive effect on student performance (Godwin et al., 1998). However, these schools frequently skim the best students from the local schools, thus leaving the latter even worse off than before.

Open Enrollment

Another mechanism for achieving desegregation and greater equality of education is to give students and their parents the freedom to enroll in any school they choose rather than to restrict them to single school districts. While this principle seems good in theory, its effect is frequently to *increase* rather than decrease ethnic and economic segregation (Wells, 1996). The more affluent and knowledgeable families in a school district are more likely to be able to afford transportation costs and to know the relative qualities of the various schools. Thus, as with magnet schools, open enrollment tends to skim the least at-risk students, leaving local schools even more economically and educationally disadvantaged.

School Vouchers

A voucher system gives families a certain amount of money (usually some percentage of the cost to educate a child in the local public schools) to send their children to private schools. The basic idea behind this system, clearly, is to open education to the forces of the marketplace. Presumably, parents will patronize those schools that provide the best education for their children. This competition will force schools to improve—or lose enrollment, which will ultimately force them to close. Studies of the use of vouchers in Great Britain, France, the Netherlands, and Chile suggest that when vouchers are made available to families at all socioeconomic levels, more affluent families are more likely to use the vouchers to send their children to private schools. The result is even greater economic and ethnic segregation in the schools (Ambler, 1994; Pary, 1996).

In the United States, the Milwaukee Parental Choice Program has systematic outcome data available. This program provided vouchers only to low-income families; 95% of the participating students were either African American or Latino. The results are mixed but promising. Witte and colleagues (1994) found no difference in test scores between students using their vouchers to go to private schools and a random sample of students in the public schools. But other studies found that voucher students who remain in private schools show significantly greater improvement than students who applied to but could not enroll in private schools because of space limitations (Godwin et al., 1998).

The private schools involved in the Milwaukee study were all nonreligious. Current interpretations of constitutional restrictions preclude the use of publicly funded vouchers in religious schools. Interestingly, among private institutions, it is Catholic schools that appear to bring out the greatest educational achievement with poor, minority students—better test scores and higher percentages graduating from high school and from college (Witte, 1996; Bryk et al., 1993).

So, what can we conclude? The bottom line is that schools do not exist in a vacuum. They reflect the social, cultural, economic, and political conditions under which the students, their families, teachers, and friends live. Thus, well-intentioned programs for improving the educational opportunities for low-income children cannot succeed without breaking the vicious cycles which these conditions converge to create. Poor people get poor educations. Poorly educated people live in poverty. Whom you go to school with influences how much you learn. But how much you know determines whom you go to school with. A democracy must provide its citizens with equal opportunity for education. But without education one cannot take advantage of educational opportunities. The one good thing about circles, however, is that there are many places to enter and many from which to exit.

Summary

Piaget's Stage of Concrete Operational Thought

Piaget traced the intellectual developments of middle childhood to the emergence of mental operations, internalized actions that children can perform in their heads. Mental operations are reversible, enabling children to imagine both performing an action and reversing that action to get back to the point from which they had started. Each operation belongs to a set of operations, making it

possible to see how the effects of one are related to those of another. Being able to reverse an operation carried out in one's head and to relate one operation to another causes thinking to become more logical.

School-age children, when given tests of conservation, are capable of understanding that an object can remain the same despite having changed in appearance. Conservation reflects three processes: (1) reversibility, or the understanding that one could nullify the effects of the operation

443

that resulted in the changed appearance, (2) identity, or the realization that the substance in each of the two states has not changed, and (3) compensation, the realization that changes along one dimension are compensated for by changes along a second dimension.

An Information-Processing Approach to Cognitive Development

Information-processing theorists view thinking as the processing of information and approach its study by looking at how information is encoded, or mentally represented, and at the processes involved in its transformation and use. With age, children develop more efficient ways of processing information. Automatization refers to increases with age in the efficiency with which children engage in various mental activities such that these require less of their attention. Encoding also changes with age such that older children are better able to recognize which features are important. Encoding appears to become more efficient with age due to increases in the ease of processing new information, to more systematic searches for relevant information, and to the use of more efficient strategies when solving problems.

Memory

Memory exists as several interrelated systems, each with different characteristics. Sensory memory, which lasts for no more than half a second, does not reveal age differences. Short-term memory is limited in both capacity, to approximately seven items, and duration, to no more than 15 to 20 seconds. For information to be held longer than this, it must be rehearsed, or continuously repeated. Age differences exist in the number of items children can hold in short-term memory. Long-term memory is unlimited both in capacity and duration. Age differences in long-term memory are evident primarily in information retrieval. With age, children can retrieve information more rapidly and develop greater awareness of their memory known as metamemory, which enables them to monitor what they are doing and increases the likelihood of using strategies for remembering.

Limitations of Thought in Middle Childhood

Thought in middle childhood is not abstract; thus, it is difficult for children to think of things they cannot see. Because children focus on visible aspects of a problem, they fail to speculate about other, less immediately evident solutions. Consequently, they frequently operate according to assumptions that they make on the basis of limited information.

Humor: A Sense of the Ridiculous

Three ingredients to humorous situations have been identified; each of these changes with age. The perception of incongruity, or violations of one's expectancies, increases in middle childhood due to children's ability to appreciate multiple meanings of words. This component of humor forms the basis for many of their jokes and riddles. Emotional release is a second component of humor; because different situations are problematic for children of different ages, the things that children find funny will also change with age. The third component of humor is intellectual. Concepts that are recently mastered are sufficiently challenging to be humorous.

The World of School

The intellectual developments that occur in middle childhood ready children for school. Even so, many of the basic tasks they must master are difficult and require the use of strategies. Children typically have available for their use a number of strategies that differ in their efficiency. Changes in strategies do not necessarily reflect movement to more sophisticated approaches. In arithmetic, children from different cultures differ in the efficiency of the strategies they use and in their general mathematical skills. Language has been found to contribute to both their choice of strategies and their understanding of basic mathematical concepts such as place value. Differences in how mathematics is taught also contribute to achievement.

Learning to read involves a number of skills. Children must be able to identify individual letters and must know the sounds these letters make. This knowledge enables them to decode the sounds that make up a word. Children use their knowledge of the name of the letter when learning the sound it will make, mapping the sound in the name onto the corresponding phoneme. Children also rely on context when sounding out unfamiliar or phonologically ambiguous words. Reading has been taught through either of two basic methods. The basic-skills approach starts with letters and sounds before moving to words, whereas the whole-word approach teaches by exposing children to contexts that facilitate the discovery of principles.

Culture and Gender in the Classroom

Some gender-role stereotyping still exists in teaching materials. In textbooks, males are still pictured more frequently than females, appear in more diverse occupations, and need rescuing less frequently. But these differences represent tremendous improvements over the materials in use a generation ago.

The use of male generic language represents another form of bias. Using the masculine pronoun generically predisposes students and their teachers to think of males, not of individuals in general. Their evaluations of the competence of students of either sex for different types of work are thereby skewed.

Jigsaw classrooms, where students work in small groups, each contributing a different part of the lesson, foster cooperation and promote better relations among students from different ethnic backgrounds. Presenting material from several cultural perspectives is helpful to minority students who may not always share the perspective assumed in the textbook or other materials used.

Communication problems arise for some minority students when language is used differently at school and at home. Four distinctive approaches characterize different ethnic and racial groups: group versus individual orientations, active versus passive coping styles, attitudes toward authority, and expressive versus restrained mannerisms. Intervention programs that heighten teacher and student awareness of these differences improve the quality of multicultural education.

Most intervention programs have focused on problems minority students may experience at the level of the microsystem—that is, in the home and the classroom. Problems of poorer achievement may have to be addressed at the level of the macrosystem.

Children at the Edge

Children who score 130 or above on an intelligence test or who have creative, artistic, leadership, or other special talents are defined as gifted. Gifted children fail to fit any stereotype. Educational programs for the gifted can offer enrichment, providing them with more experiences than they would ordinarily get, or acceleration, allowing them to advance beyond their grade level.

Children with learning disabilities are of average or above-average intelligence and show a discrepancy between expected and actual performance. They have difficulty in academic tasks that presumably can be traced to a neurological dysfunction. Learning-disabled students fall at least two grade levels behind classmates and their difficulties cannot be traced to emotional or sensory dysfunction. Social skills are also affected for many.

Mainstreaming places learning-disabled students in regular classes. A consulting special education teacher may advise regular teachers on the special needs of these students. At the other extreme, learning-disabled students may be placed in special classes with specially trained teachers. Each of these educational options has different advantages.

Success, Failure, and Patterns of Achievement

Achievement motivation patterns distinguish schoolchildren. Task-oriented children focus on the task and work to increase their mastery. Performance-oriented children focus on their performance and use it as a measure of their ability. Task-oriented children are less likely to be disrupted by initial failure, believing it to result from a lack of sufficient effort rather than inability. Performance-oriented children are likely to withdraw in the face of failure and attribute it to an external cause rather than their own lack of effort. Praising children's intelligence when they do well may cause them to focus more on their performance than on what they are working on. Conversely, praising children for working hard appears to cause them to focus on the effort they must put into a task in order to succeed.

The Contexts of Development: Supportive and Responsive Environments

Supportive parenting, which takes the form of parental warmth, involvement, firmness, and use of reasoning when disciplining, is positively related to children's intellectual development, adjustment to school, and intrinsic academic motivation. Parents who otherwise might not offer optimal environments can be shown ways of making these more stimulating. Participation in extended day care programs, lasting from preschool to the second or third grade, offers another effective form of intervention. One of the benefits of such programs is the increased involvement of parents in their children's education.

Key Terms

assumptive realities (p. 417)	jigsaw classroom (p. 429)	phonemes (p. 426)
automatization (p. 411)	long-term memory (p. 414)	sensory memory (p. 414)
basic-skills approach (p. 427)	male generic language (p. 428)	short-term memory (p. 414)
encoding (p. 412)	mental operations (p. 408)	whole-language approach (p. 427)

chaptertwelve

Middle Childhood
Psychosocial Development

B ye, Dad! Charlie's mom is here to take us to practice. See you at the talent show tonight—get a seat where I can see you this time, okay?"

"Sure thing," he muses, reviewing the evening—pick Jessie up from basketball tryouts, bring home some take-out for diner, and work up that report for tomorrow. "Front row center," he calls back.

Perhaps never faster than in middle childhood does time rush by. As one wise uncle said, "The years go faster than the days." They do in fact, compressed by school and homework, soccer games and basketball practice, and, of course, household chores and talent shows.

These are rich years, filled with growth and change. Children are not only physically stronger and intellectually more adultlike than they were just a few years ago, but they are also beginning to master activities they could only dream about earlier. They will spend hours for instance, practicing rim shots, doing scales on a clarinet, and completing complex projects for school, such as constructing an igloo from sugar cubes, complete with an explanation of how one can stay warm inside a house made from ice. In mastering these accomplishments children learn not only the particular skills involved but also, in each case, something about themselves. They discover what they can do when they really try. They also discover that their earlier fantasies of extraordinary feats are no longer as satisfying as their actual, if less than perfect, accomplishments.

The Self

Erikson (1968) spoke of this new satisfaction as a sense of **industry.** By *industry* he meant the sense of accomplishment that comes from being able to make things and that comes with doing things well. Children come to know themselves

In middle childhood, children are especially ready to apprentice themselves as learners.

industry (versus inferiority)
Erikson's term for the sense of accomplishment that comes from being able to make things and that comes with doing things well.

through the things they can do, through their skills. Erikson believed that children are especially ready to apprentice themselves as learners when they reach middle childhood. They want to be big by sharing in the activities of those whom they regard as big. They willingly work alongside parents and teachers, watching what they do and attempting the same themselves. Accomplishment comes only with perseverance and discipline, however, and Erikson points out that a sense of inferiority can develop in children who are not willing, or able, to persist at the things they attempt until mastery is achieved.

Children become more reflective during the school years as well. In combination with their newly developing skills, this reflection lays a foundation for changes in the ways in which they think of themselves, of their self-concept.

Self-Concept

How do children think of themselves? What are they most likely to say, for instance, if asked to describe themselves? Listen to what two children have to say. We will first hear from Lisa, who is 8, and then from her 4-year-old brother Jason. Lisa says this of herself:

> I'm in third grade this year, and pretty popular, at least with the girls.
> That's because I'm nice and helpful and can keep secrets. Most of the boys
> at school are pretty yukky. I don't feel that way about my little brother
> Jason, although he does get on my nerves. I love him but at the same time,
> he also does things that make me mad. But I control my temper, I'd be
> ashamed of myself if I didn't. At school, I'm feeling pretty smart in certain
> subjects, Language Arts and Social Studies. I got A's in these subjects on
> my last report card and was really proud of myself. But I'm feeling pretty
> dumb in Arithmetic and Science, particularly when I see how well the other
> kids are doing. Even though I'm not doing well in those subjects, I still like
> myself as a person, because Arithmetic and Science just aren't that impor-
> tant to me. How I look and how popular I am are more important. (Harter,
> 1996, p. 208)

Jason, who is still a preschooler, also has quite a bit to say about himself:

> My name is Jason and I live in a big house with my mother and father and
> sister, Lisa. I have a kitty that's orange and a television in my own room. I
> know all of my A, B, C's. listen: A, B, C, D, E, F, G, H, J, L, K, O, M, P, Q,
> X, Z. I can run faster than anyone! I like pizza and I have a nice teacher. I
> can count up to 100, want to hear me? I love my dog, Skipper. I can climb
> to the top of the jungle gym, I'm not scared! Just happy. You can't be happy
> and scared, no way! I have brown hair and I go to pre-school. I'm really
> strong. I can lift this chair, watch me! (p. 208)

These self-descriptions illustrate several characteristic differences between the way older and younger children think of the self. Older children, for instance, describe themselves in terms of general traits. Thus, Lisa says of herself that she is smart and gives examples of school subjects in which she has done well, mentioning that she got A's on her report card. Younger children, in contrast, describe themselves in terms of specific behaviors. Jason, for instance, talks about how well he can climb a jungle gym, not how good he is at sports in general.

Older children are likely to describe themselves interpersonally, in terms of their relationships with others, whereas younger children are more likely to describe themselves in terms of their preferences and possessions. Lisa, for instance, talks about how she is with others and how she feels toward them,

As children grow older, self-perceptions of both strengths and weaknesses become more realistic.

School-age children are able to describe themselves in terms of contradictions and inconsistencies, whereas younger children cannot. What explanation might Piaget offer to explain this difference?

Older children have been found to compare their present performance at a task with how well they have done before, whereas younger children do not. How might we expect children's perceptions of themselves to change based on this difference?

describing herself as popular, telling us what she thinks of boys, and using such relational terms as "helpful" and being able to "keep secrets." Jason, on the other hand, tells us that he likes pizza and that he has a cat, a dog, and his own television.

Self-characterizations also become more complex with age, tolerating contradictions and inconsistencies, whereas those of younger children remain relatively simple, describing themselves and others as either all good or all bad in any particular domain. Jason argues, for instance, that one cannot be both "happy *and* scared," whereas Lisa recognizes that she can be smart in one subject and "pretty dumb" in another. As a consequence, preschoolers tend to have a positive bias when describing themselves, whereas older children tend to be more self-critical. Jason describes himself in glowing positive terms, saying he knows all of his ABCs, can run faster than anyone, and is really strong. Older children admit to weaknesses as well as strengths. Lisa feels "pretty smart" in some subjects but not that smart in others. Similarly, she considers herself popular, but only with other girls.

With respect to this latter point, children's self-perceptions tend to become more realistic with age, their initial optimism declining as their appraisal of their strengths and weaknesses becomes more realistic (Marsh, Craven, & Debus, 1998). But on what basis do children make these evaluations? Do they compare their performance with what they have done in the past, or do they evaluate themselves in comparison with others?

Ruth Butler (1998) gave children the task of tracing a path from one point to another and told them either that they had done better or worse than another child or better or worse than they had done on a previous attempt. Irrespective of age, she found that children appraised themselves more positively when they were told they had done better than another child as opposed to having done worse. However, only older children used information from their previous performance in appraising themselves. This latter finding is to be expected given young children's difficulty in recognizing the continuity of the self over time (Povinelli et al., 1996; Povinelli & Simon, 1998), suggesting that comparisons with previous attempts would not provide a meaningful basis for self-appraisal for younger children (see Chapter 9).

Self-appraisal can also be seen in the expression of socially derived emotions, such as pride and shame (see Chapter 9). Harter notes that children's experience of these is dependent on the existence of an internalized standard, such as that provided by parental values, against which children evaluate the self. One might expect that prior to the internalization of such a standard, parents would actually have to be present for children to experience such feelings about themselves, whereas once parental values are internalized, children should experience such emotions even when others are not present.

Harter (1996) examined this possibility by telling children a story in which a child took something after being told not to and then was either discovered or not. When children were asked how the child and the parent would feel in either case, preschoolers talked only about the child being scared or worried if discovered and not about being ashamed. Although 6- and 7-year-olds mentioned being ashamed, this was only if the child had been caught. Only 7- and 8-year-olds said the child would feel shame even though no one might have seen what had been done.

The way children think of the self reflects their culture as well as their age. Maxine Hong Kingston (1976), a novelist and poet, illustrates this point when writing of the difficulty she experienced as a schoolgirl, growing up with Cantonese as her first language, when she tried to understand the way the words for "I" and "you," words used to describe the self versus others, were written in English:

> It was when I found out I had to talk that school became a misery, that the silence became a misery. I did not speak and felt bad each time that I did not speak. I read aloud in first grade, though, and heard the barest whisper with little squeaks come out of my throat. . . .
>
> Reading out loud was easier than speaking because we did not have to make up what to say, but I stopped often, and the teacher would think I'd gone quiet again. I could not understand "I." The Chinese "I" has seven strokes, intricacies. How could the American "I," assuredly wearing a hat like the Chinese, have only three strokes, the middle so straight? Was it out of politeness that this writer left off the strokes the way a Chinese has to write her own name small and crooked? No, it was not politeness; "I" is a capital and "you" is lower-case. I stared at that middle line and waited so long for its black center to resolve into tight strokes and dots that I forgot to pronounce it. ◄

The problem she experienced in reading English had very little to do with the mechanics of reading itself, of knowing which symbols stood for which sounds. Rather, it had to do with the sense to give to these symbols. And this sense was intimately tied to the sense of self she had acquired as a Chinese American, one that reflected her culture's value of modesty, as well as civility and respect for others.

Self-Esteem

If the self-concept is what one takes to be true about the self, then self-esteem is how good one feels about this. A boy who might describe himself as smart, witty, a leader, loyal to his friends, and not very athletic does not stop there. He evaluates each of these qualities. "So I'm a wit, but is that as good as being athletic? Is

Children's friendships affect not only the way they think of themselves but also what they expect from relationships in general.

it really okay to be as social as I am, or should I be more concerned with my studies? Am I loyal enough with my friends? And what about the times they do things I can't support?" The way he answers questions such as these contributes to how he feels about himself, to his feelings of self-worth. Self-esteem refers to children's overall positive or negative evaluation of themselves.

Q Why are children's relationships with their parents so important for their self-esteem?

Relationships with parents provide the foundation for self-esteem. When parents are loving, children feel lovable and develop feelings of self-worth. These feelings become established early in life. Infants quickly learn whether the world in which they live will meet their needs; when those around them are responsive, they develop a sense of trust. The establishment of trust in these first, basic relationships permeates all later ones. Self-esteem in children then, as well as their more general self-perceptions, will reflect their interactions with parents (Bowlby, 1969, Erikson, 1968).

When do most children first begin to evaluate themselves in terms of their overall worth? Harter (1996) first finds evidence of an overall evaluation of the self in terms of self-worth at about the age of 8. She is quick to point out, however, that the absence of such evaluative remarks in younger children cannot be taken to mean that they do not differ with respect to how good they feel about themselves; rather, they simply do not articulate these feelings in relation to a self. Instead, one sees differences reflected in such things as their confidence in being able to do things versus their reluctance to show what they can do.

Constructing the Self with Others

Q What quality primarily distinguishes children's friendships from their relationships with their parents?

Children's friendships affect not only the way they think of themselves, but also what they come to expect from relationships in general. Because of the egalitarian nature of their relationships with friends, as opposed to those they have with parents, children come to appreciate the importance of taking others' ideas into consideration. The reciprocity that characterizes friendships fosters an awareness in children of the obligations that one person has toward the other. This interdependence, in fact, is what distinguishes their relationships with friends from those they have with others (Youniss, 1994).

James Youniss (1994), at Catholic University, extends the constructivist position elaborated at earlier points throughout this text to include the social construction of reality through interaction with others. Thus, for Youniss, the basic unit in which knowledge is constructed is the interaction that takes place between children. Youniss notes that when children are together, they respond to each other's ideas, creating a shared meaning, each child putting forth his or her own understanding and reacting in turn to the way others receive it. In other words, children do not simply want to understand what is going on or how something makes sense, they want to share that understanding with someone else. In this way, the reality to which each responds is co-constructed, in that each child works toward the end of creating an understanding that is shared by the other. We see an example of such an interactive exchange between several boys in grade school as they attempt to give meaning to the somewhat unusual behavior of a substitute teacher who has just appeared in their classroom. Charles Baxter (1999), a novelist and short-story writer, describes the scene as follows:

> Therefore it was a surprise when a woman we had never seen came into the class the next day carrying a purple purse, a checkerboard lunchbox, and a few books. She put the books on one side of Mr. Hibler's desk and the lunchbox on the other, next to the Voice of Music phonograph. Three of us in the back of the room were playing with Heever, the chameleon that lived in a terrarium and on one of the plastic drapes, when she walked in.
>
> She clapped her hands at us. "Little boys," she said, "why are you bent over together like that?" She didn't wait for us to answer. "Are you tormenting an animal? Put it back. Please sit down at your desks. I want no cabals this time of the day." We just stared at her. "Boys," she repeated, "I asked you to sit down."
>
> I put the chameleon in his terrarium and felt my way to my desk, never taking my eyes off the woman. . . . Her fine light hair had been done up in what I would learn years later was called a chignon, and she wore gold-rimmed glasses whose lenses seemed to have the faintest blue tint. Harold Knardahl, who sat across from me, whispered, "Mars," and I nodded slowly, savoring the imminent weirdness of the day. (p. 909) ◄

This example illustrates, as well, the cooperative nature of children's interactions. Youniss regards cooperation as an essential feature of the social construction of reality. Friends implicitly agree, in other words, to be guided by the perceptions and promptings of each other. The alternative is to take one another's remarks as an occasion to offer a countering remark of one's own, resulting in a "stalemate" as both defend their own positions. Instead, friends agree to jointly order reality, understanding that in doing so they can rely on each other to validate their perceptions. "Yes," these boys were agreeing, "this is going to be a weird day."

Friendships are important as well in constructing the self, contributing to the way children come to see themselves. Friends provide feedback not only about the activities that they co-construct, but also about themselves as they engage in these. The shared meanings that friends arrive at, in other words, involve the ways in which they come to see themselves as well as the way they see their world. Children whose opinions are not listened to at home, for instance, may discover they have something to say when their friends come to them for help with problems. Similarly, children who are used to being protected by an older sister or brother may see themselves as able to stand up for others when their friends look to them for support. Friends also help each other sort through feelings, letting each other know that the way they feel is normal and shared by others. As one young girl put it, a friend is "someone who helps you understand how you feel" (Youniss, 1994).

Such feelings are not always positive, nor do friends always contribute to children's understanding of themselves through the experiences they share. Sometimes the awareness children gain of themselves is even more powerful when they have been left out or left behind. Nora Ephron (1972), an essayist and screenwriter, describes such an experience:

> I am eleven years old, about to enter the seventh grade, and Diana and I have not seen each other all summer.... We are meeting, as we often do, on the street midway between our two houses and we will walk back to Diana's and eat junk and talk about what has happened to each of us that summer. I am walking down Walden Drive in my jeans and my father's shirt hanging out and my old red loafers with the socks falling into them and coming toward me is...I take a deep breath...a young woman. Diana. Her hair is curled and she has a waist and hips and a bust and she is wearing a straight skirt, an article of clothing I have been repeatedly told I will be unable to wear until I have the hips to hold it up. My jaw drops, and suddenly I am crying, crying hysterically, can't catch my breath sobbing. My best friend has betrayed me. She has gone ahead without me and done it. She has shaped up. ◄

Because friends contribute in such important ways to children's sense of themselves, having even a single good friend should be especially important for children whose sense of self-esteem cannot be derived from their relationships with their parents. We know, for instance, that maltreated children have less positive self-concepts than do other children (Okun, Parker, & Levendosky, 1994) and, when maltreated in early childhood, have lower self-esteem (Bolger, Patterson, & Kupersmidt, 1998). Is it reasonable to expect, then, that self-esteem would be higher among maltreated children who have a close friendship with at least one other child than among those who do not?

Kerry Bolger, Charlotte Patterson, and Janis Kupersmidt (1998) reasoned that it would be. Friendships can provide the emotional security children need in order to explore their worlds, just as healthy relationships with parents have been found to provide a secure base for children who have not been maltreated (see Chapter 6). Also, children learn appropriate social skills through interactions with friends, skills that maltreated children are less likely to acquire in their interactions at home. These investigators conducted a longitudinal study in which they followed a group of maltreated children and a matched control group of nonmaltreated children over a 3-year period. They found that having a good friend was particularly important for chronically maltreated children, such friendships being associated with greater increases in self-esteem over time than for their nonmaltreated peers.

Friendships

Who are children most likely to have as friends? By the time they reach middle childhood, friends are almost exclusively of the same sex (Kovacs, Parker, & Hoffman, 1996; Oswald, Krappmann, Uhlendorff, & Weiss, 1994). In fact, school-age children rarely interact with peers of the opposite sex and, on the occasions when they do, follow a strict code of unspoken rules. Such rules maintain that these contacts must be accidental or, if intentional, must appear to be unfriendly and dismissive; and under no circumstances must they occur unless accompanied by someone of one's own sex (Sroufe, Bennett, Englund, Urban, & Shulman, 1993).

In addition to being of the same sex, friends are likely to be similar in race, socioeconomic background, and grade in school, and to have the same social status with peers. None of these similarities, however, is as important as that of being of the same sex (George & Hartmann, 1996; Hartup, 1992). Finally, friends are likely to share similar perceptions of others (Haselager, Hartup, van Lieshout, & Riksen-Walraven, 1998).

What contributes to the quality of children's relationships? When interviewed about their friends, children are most likely to talk about the assistance they receive from each other, whether through offers of encouragement, helping each other out, or sharing confidences. Of course, fooling around together and having fun are also important (Oswald et al., 1994). Hans Oswald and his associates (1994) found that children described upwards of eight or nine important relationships when asked to describe their friends. These friendships were remarkably individual, with very different patterns of qualities characterizing the relationships children had with their different friends. Important to all, however, was the assistance they could count on from each other. It is all too easy to overlook the very real difficulties children experience on a day-to-day basis and the importance to them of being able to rely on each other for support. It is no less difficult for an 8-year-old to stand up to a playground bully or to work problems at the blackboard than it is for parents to resolve a dispute with a neighbor or to fill out their tax returns. In each case, having the support of a friend can make all the difference.

In middle childhood, children's friends are almost always of the same sex.

Peer Relations

Children's social status, or their relative popularity with peers, is fairly stable, showing little change throughout the grade school years (Downey, Lebolt, Rincon, & Freitas, 1998; George & Hartmann, 1996). By using measures in which children are asked to name those they most and least like to play with, researchers have been able to identify a number of such statuses. What behaviors, especially, distinguish children of one status from those of another?

Popular children behave very much like average ones in many ways. Both are cooperative, good at taking turns, and play well with others. Both, in other words, engage in many prosocial behaviors and relatively few antisocial ones. In addition, popular children tend to set the norms for their group, reminding others of the rules and giving suggestions. Perhaps because they have better social skills, they are able to maintain their play with other children for longer periods of time, and others appear to have more fun when they are with them (Dodge, 1983; Coie & Kupersmidt, 1983). The children, in other words, engage in the types of supportive behaviors that Oswald and his associates found children to value in their relationships with others.

This happy picture does not hold for all children. Children whom others indicate they least like to play with are classified as rejected. Also, some children are not mentioned by any of their classmates, either as being liked or disliked. These children are classified as neglected. Since most of this research has been conducted with boys, we will specifically refer to the children in these studies as boys.

Rejected boys tend to be very active and often aggressive when they play with others, taunting and teasing as well as being physically aggressive. They are more likely than other children to exclude others when playing, and they engage in more inappropriate behavior, such as grabbing something away from someone or standing on a table. Unlike popular boys, they have difficulty sustaining an activity, even when it involves play. They are also at greater risk for adjustment

Popular children seem to instinctively know how to enter an ongoing group; other children may need help building social skills.

problems as adolescents and adults. Neglected boys spend most of their time in solitary play. This, however, does not appear to be out of preference, since they initially make numerous social overtures to others. Their behavior, just like that of rejected boys, is at times inappropriate; however, it does not take an aggressive form. Unlike rejected boys, they are not at risk for later adjustment problems. They hold down jobs and live comfortably with themselves as adults despite the stringent criteria defining this status in childhood; that is, these boys have no friends (Dodge, 1983).

John Coie and Janis Kupersmidt (1983) formed play groups of boys who did not know each other, in order to study the emergence of social status among their peers. These investigators initially determined boys' social status among their classmates and, based on this, formed play groups consisting of rejected, popular, neglected, and average boys. The play groups met for 1 hour a week. These investigators found that social status became established quickly. By the 3rd week, after only 3 hours of playing together, a boy's status in his group corresponded to his status at school. Findings such as these indicate that the successes or the failures children experience with their peers are not simply accidental, but reflect very genuine social skills. Coie and Kupersmidt also found, however, that neglected boys frequently benefited from being among a new group of peers, suggesting that children's reputations as well as their skills affect their social status.

The studies of Dodge and Coie and Kupersmidt have implications for intervention programs. It isn't enough simply to encourage children who are having problems in making friends to interact with others more. These children have already tried to do so and failed. Instead, intervention needs to focus on building social skills. Reputation may also be more important than previously thought, in that the same behaviors in popular and rejected children are responded to differ-

How helpful is it to encourage a child who is always off by him- or herself, watching others play, to simply go over and start to play with others?

Conflict Resolution in the School System

BY ANDREA HAYES

It is clear that national concerns over school safety have risen to a high level. Traditionally, our approach to solving the problems of interpersonal conflicts and school violence has been crime-focused; such problems are seen as resulting from the behavior of chronically disruptive, or "bad," kids. These students are suspended, transferred to alternative schools (filled with other youths on probation), and effectively isolated from nonproblematic, "successful" students (Dupper, 1995). This approach, though effective with respect to the immediate, or precipitating, problem, can result in the early marginalization of youth, as well as foster the assumption that crime-focused legislation (such as tougher laws, stricter sentencing, and trying children as adults) is the only response. With our juvenile and adult prison systems currently overcrowded, we are in a position to reevaluate this approach and to ask whether isolating these youths has solved the problem of violent conflicts at school (Irwin & Austin, 1997).

Have our beliefs about the cause of violence been too narrow? Some social scientists believe that they have. In spite of well-intentioned interventions and tougher laws, the juvenile arrest rate for aggravated assault and murder rose more than 50% from 1987 to 1996. Furthermore, homicide rates among youth in small towns and rural communities increased by 38% in 1997 (Garbarino, 1999). We can no longer hide behind the assumption that violence happens only among ethnic groups in the inner city. In the school environment alone, a national survey of high school students found that 8% were threatened or injured with a weapon, 16% participated in a physical fight, and 34% had their personal property stolen or deliberately damaged (Centers for Disease Control, 1996c).

Comprehensive, multifaceted, environmental approaches to resolving conflicts in the school environment are receiving attention. These approaches change a school's *culture* by teaching students, parents, teachers, and the community skills for building personal responsibility and resolving conflict in a nonviolent way. One such program, called the Bullying Prevention Program (Olweus, Limber, & Mihalic, 1999), attempts to reduce the opportunities and rewards for bullying behavior by involving the students themselves through anonymous questionnaires, discussion groups, and peer-based supervisory roles. The classrooms are a place for regular conflict-resolution discussions, empathy development, and teacher enforcement of prosocial behavior. Parents are considered an invaluable resource and involved in all levels of the program. The Bullying Prevention Program has reduced the frequency of bully/victim student and teacher reports by 50%. Students also report significant reductions in vandalism, theft, and truancy.

A second program, Building the Peace: The Resolving Conflict Creatively Program (RCCP), offers a national model for conflict resolution (DeJong, 1999). RCCP focuses on creating *school* change through public policy at the school administration level. It requires administration buy-in and philosophical alignment. Teachers can then promote an appreciation of diversity and shared decision making among students and can facilitate the recognition of common purposes. Students *daily* practice skills in communication, cooperation, bias awareness, mediation, and conflict resolution. Parents are taught to help implement new skills at home to resolve family conflict as well. Studies among different school sites around the country have indicated that students experience less violence in the classroom, the student dropout rate decreases significantly, and teachers report more positive classroom climates and observe students using conflict resolution skills spontaneously around campus (DeJong, 1999). Why rely on metal detectors that cost $100,000 annually to create safe school environments? A program like RCCP costs $33.00 per student per year while teaching lifetime interpersonal skills *and* creating a safer school environment. Punishment or prevention? Which seems the wiser choice?

ently, children reacting more positively to popular boys, even when they are aggressive, than to others. Although it is certainly possible that children's reactions may be due to subtle differences in the behaviors themselves, it is also possible that children are reacting not just to the momentary exchange, but also to a history of interactions. The Social Policy Focus, "Conflict Resolution in the School System," looks at some comprehensive conflict resolution programs aimed at changing a school's culture.

Research on entry behaviors finds that popular children are better at entering ongoing groups. They seem to try to determine the frame of reference of the groups, what the others are doing, and then share in this. Unpopular children appear to divert attention to themselves. Rather than fit themselves into the group, they ask the group to shift gears to include them. They are more likely to ask what others are doing, to disagree as a way of inserting themselves into an activity, to talk about themselves, or to state their feelings. Each of these only draws other children's attention away from the activity that interests them and is likely to be ignored or rebuffed (see Chapter 9) (Putallaz, 1983; Putallaz & Gottman, 1981).

Although it is relatively easy to imagine friendships among children who are cooperative, take turns, and play well with others, it is less easy to imagine the types of friendships that children have who are aggressive. Before considering these, however, we need to distinguish two forms of aggression. **Overt aggression** involves physical acts such as hitting, punching, and kicking. **Relational aggression,** on the other hand, involves acts aimed at manipulating the relationship, such as divulging secrets or spreading lies. The former is more characteristic of boys and the latter of girls, although children of either sex can be seen to engage in both forms of aggression (Grotpeter & Crick, 1996 as cited in Crick & Grotpeter, 1995).

To determine how the friends of aggressive children fare, Jennifer Grotpeter and Nicki Crick (1996) identified children as either relationally aggressive, overtly aggressive, or nonaggressive, and asked children in each group and their friends to describe the qualities of their friendships. Are children who are aggressive with peers aggressive in their friendships as well? The answer, it seems, is both a yes and a no. These investigators found that although relationally aggressive children enjoyed many of the qualities to friendships that characterize those of nonaggressive children, such as intimacy, caring, and companionship, they nonetheless engaged in the same forms of relational aggression with friends that distinguished their interactions with their peers. Thus, for example, they rarely disclosed much about themselves even though their friends reported relatively high amounts of self-disclosure, putting the former in a position to control the friendship through threatening to tell the other's secrets. So, yes, children who show this form of aggression with peers are likely to do the same thing in their friendships.

In contrast to the friendships of relationally aggressive children, those of overtly aggressive children are characterized by an *absence* of aggression. Instead, these children were found to direct their aggression toward those outside the relationship, enlisting the support of their friends in the aggression as well. This was true whether their friends were initially aggressive or not. Thus, children who form friendships with either type of aggressive child run certain risks, either of being the object of relational aggression themselves or of being drawn into aggressive interactions with others. On a final note, Grotpeter and Crick observe that children's friendships, just like those of adults, are a complex mix of positive and negative qualities, a point that is especially true for aggressive children and those who befriend them.

A significant number of children, approximately 10%, are bullied at school. Furthermore, pretty much the same children get picked on from one time to the next. Victimization, just like aggression, is a relatively stable characteristic of children. Children identified by their classmates as victims are the same ones to be identified a year later as most likely to be bullied. Those who are likely to be victimized are children who cry easily, have poor social skills, and are submissive when attacked, thereby rewarding their aggressors. However, having a friend decreases the likelihood of being victimized, as well as buffering the effects of this when it does occur (Hodges, Boivin, Vitaro, & Bukowski, 1999).

Not all bullied children are submissive. Some victims are actually aggressive, being easily provoked by others and reacting angrily, their outbursts apparently targeting them for retaliation. Their aggression differs from that of bullies, however, taking the form of unwitting emotional outbursts rather than being used intentionally to dominate others. These victims, who more typically are boys, are more likely to have been physically abused and treated harshly when growing up. In fact, David Schwartz, Kenneth Dodge, Gregory Pettit and John Bates (1997) found that 29% of boys who had been physically harmed became aggressive vic-

overt aggression Hostility expressed in physical acts such as hitting, punching, and kicking.

relational aggression Hostility expressed in acts manipulating the relationship, such as divulging secrets or spreading lies.

A parent's remarriage is usually more difficult for adolescents than for younger children, who are better able to form a genuine attachment to a stepparent.

& Booth, 1989). Economic hardship can contribute to children's distress in intact families as well. In this case, however, it does so primarily by undermining the marital relationship that then affects the way each partner relates to the children (Ge et al., 1992).

Remarriage and Stepparents   Parents who divorce are likely to remarry and to introduce a stepparent into their children's lives. Close to 20% of children under the age of 18 live with a stepparent, who in most cases is a stepfather. Remarriage usually occurs soon on the heels of the divorce, typically within 3 years. Many stepparents bring a stepsibling or two (residential or weekend) in the process. For many children, this series of events comes on top of the changes introduced by moving to a new residence, changing schools, and making new friends. Fewer changes would still be enough to disrupt anyone's equilibrium. Yet many families weather the stresses of these new relationships, and some even thrive (Giles-Sims & Crosbie-Burnett, 1989; Glick, 1989).

One sees differences in adjustments to divorce and remarriage as a function both of children's gender and their age. Following divorce, boys exhibit more problems than girls. However, following remarriage, girls exhibit more problems. Boys' relationships with their mothers following divorce tend to be somewhat negative and coercive, whereas those of girls tend to be closer and more positive. The introduction of a stepfather may be more of a threat to girls' relationships with their mothers than to boys', because boys have less to lose in the first place and may have something to gain by the appearance of a warm and supportive older male.

Marital transitions, whether divorce or remarriage, are difficult for children of all ages. However, remarriage appears to be most difficult for early adolescents, for a number of reasons. Younger children appear to be better able to form genuine emotional attachments to stepparents. Also, early adolescents may have had to shoulder adult responsibilities while living with a single parent and, while welcoming more discretionary time, may resent any threats to their autonomy by the introduction of a stepparent. Finally, early adolescents' concerns with their own sexual feelings may compound their reactions to a parent's new sexual relationship.

We don't have much information about the conditions that facilitate or hinder healthy stepfamily relations (Giles-Sims & Crosbie-Burnett, 1989; Hetherington & Clingempeel, 1992). Yet some general statements can be made. Perhaps the first is to underscore the importance of **role clarity**, the understanding among family members regarding each person's role and how it affects the others (Giles-Sims & Crosbie-Burnett, 1989; Visher & Visher, 1989). The most successful families establish clear guidelines for interactions. Families with the most ambiguity in roles are those with a stepmother and at least one child in common (Pasley & Ihenger-Tallman, 1989). The difficulties facing stepmothers are especially acute, because they are likely to oversee the management of the household, a role that can bring them into direct conflict with stepchildren who may resent their presence. For families experiencing problems, support groups and counseling can help establish guidelines for daily living, such as who supervises homework, who disciplines, buys clothes, cleans up, and so on. Mundane matters can easily become explosive unless defused with professional help (Visher & Visher, 1989).

In research comparing children in nondivorced families, divorced single-mother families, and remarried families, Mavis Hetherington and Glenn Clingempeel (1992) found that when differences among the three types of families emerged, they favored children in nondivorced families. Significant numbers of children living in divorced single-mother families evidenced problems in adjustment both at home and at school for up to 4 or even 6 years following the divorce. Children also had difficulty adjusting to their parent's remarriage, showing more problem behavior than children from nondivorced families. Two years after remarrying, however, mothers' relationships with their children differed little from those of never-divorced mothers. However, relationships between stepparents and stepchildren frequently, though not always, remained problematic.

Children and Their Families

Even when the family structure remains stable, children's relationships with parents change in middle childhood. At the most immediate level, children and parents simply spend less time together. As we have seen (Chapter 10), children have more discretionary time in middle childhood to spend on their own or with friends. They also spend more hours a day in school than do younger children, and many spend additional hours after school in activities such as clubs or sports, band practice or play rehearsals—or they simply spend time at a friend's house.

In order to study changes such as these, Reed Larson, Maryse Richards, Giovanni Moneta, Grayson Holmbeck, and Elena Duckett (1996) had children and adolescents wear pagers for a week, asking them to record what they were doing and how they were feeling when beeped at random intervals during the day and evening. Larson and his associates noted dramatic changes with age, as well as important continuities, in the ways children interacted with their families. Fifth-graders, for instance, spend about 35% of their waking hours with their families. By the time children are in the twelfth grade, however, this figure is down to about 14%. Despite the dramatic reduction with age in the amount of time children and parents spend together, children still spend the same amount of time alone with each of their parents when they become adolescents as they did in middle childhood and just as much time as before talking with them.

Not only the time parents and children spend together, but also the way they interact changes. Parents spend less time in hands-on caretaking activities and more in monitoring activities at a distance, keeping track of where children are when they're not at home and whom they are with. Irrespective of distance, how-

role clarity An understanding among family members about each one's role.

ever, communication within the family becomes increasingly important as children and parents begin to redefine their roles relative to each other when children become more independent with age.

Central to any effective communication is one's acceptance of the other person. Frequently, there isn't any need to offer help or give advice; all that's needed is simply to listen. Parents' comments are usually motivated by good intentions: They only want to help their children learn new skills ("Here's how you should do that") or to prevent them from making unnecessary mistakes. ("Watch out, that could spill.") However, such comments communicate nonacceptance, letting the child know that the parent's way is better. Active listening offers an alternative.

Listening to Children: Active Listening   **Active listening** is a way of drawing children out and helping them explore their feelings by feeding their message back to them. In the process, you find out if you have understood what they said. Consider the following example:

ALLEN: Do I have to get up? [He has just been told it's nearly time to leave for a baseball game.]

FATHER: You don't feel like playing baseball today?

ALLEN: I'll miss messing around with my friends.

FATHER: You'd rather mess around with your friends than play baseball?

ALLEN: Yes. We have fun together.

FATHER: It's not fun to play baseball?

ALLEN: No. Sometimes the other guys razz me when I don't get a hit.

FATHER: You don't like being teased?

ALLEN: It makes me feel like I'm not a very good player.

FATHER: You'd like to be good at baseball?

ALLEN: Yes, I felt terrific that day I got that base hit.

FATHER: Would you like to practice before the game?

ALLEN: Hey, Dad, that'd be great. I'll get dressed.

Notice how Allen is able to discover how he really feels when his father actively listens. Notice, too, that his father does not offer a solution, give advice, or do anything other than feed back what his son is saying.

An essential ingredient to active listening is communicating acceptance to the other person. The paradox in accepting people as they are is that as they feel accepted, they are free to change. Many parents, and children for that matter, communicate nonacceptance, believing that if you want someone to change, you must let the other person know what needs improvement. Telling children, or parents, that they need to improve communicates that they are not all right the way they are. This communication puts the person on the defensive—and closes off the conversation.

Active listening takes time. Each must be willing to let the other feel his or her way through a problem. If you don't have the time, it is important to say so and arrange some other time to talk. Parents must also genuinely want to let the child find a solution to the problem and not use active listening merely as a way to get her or him to do what they think should be done. They must accept the problem as the child presents it and accept the child's feelings about it. Parroting words without reflecting feelings is not active listening. You need to feed back all of the message, and feelings are an important part of it.

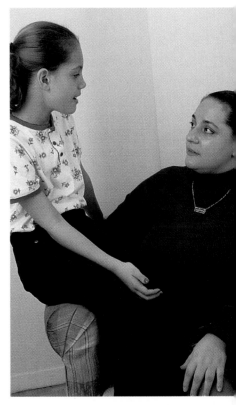

As parents and children begin to redefine their roles toward each other, "active listening" keeps conversations open, and helps them discover how they feel about these changes.

Q Why does active listening usually make children more willing to talk with their parents?

active listening A way of listening that reflects the message and feelings back to the speaker.

Talking to Children: You-Messages and I-Messages Let's turn the situation around and look at how parents can talk so that children will listen to them. The simplest approach would be to let children know how they feel, but parents rarely do that. Instead, they are likely to tell children what to do ("Pick up your clothes"), warn them what will happen if they don't ("If I have to tell you one more time, you've lost your clothes allowance"), moralize ("You should contribute your share of the work around the house"), or make a suggestion ("Why don't you put your clothes in the hamper when you take them off?"). Each of these approaches is usually met with resistance. After all, who likes being told what to do, warned, or made to feel wrong?

The parental comments in the preceding paragraph are examples of **you-messages.** They communicate that parents do not expect children to be helpful unless they are told to be. And by offering a solution without letting children help in defining the problem, such remarks subtly communicate that parents don't think children can help or are willing to find a solution.

An **I-message** tells children how their actions make others feel. Children can hear such messages as a fact about the parent, not as an evaluation of themselves, and thus they have little need to be defensive. A parent who says "I can't hear what she's saying to me when you interrupt" communicates a different message than one who says "It's rude of you to interrupt." I-messages let children know how their behavior affects others. These messages also communicate to children that parents trust them to find a solution and put the responsibility for change with the recipient. Because I-messages do not accuse, suggest, or warn, they are easier for children to hear.

Family Conflict and Changing Domains of Authority Perhaps at no time are their changing roles more evident than when parents and children discuss their perceptions of family conflicts. Judith Smetana and Rusti Berent (1993), at the University of Rochester, asked seventh-, ninth-, and eleventh-graders and their mothers to respond to vignettes describing typical conflicts that occur at home, such as those involving household chores, keeping one's room clean, or personal appearance. Each conflict was presented both from the parent's perspective and the child's, by giving justifications each might use in appealing to the other. (Table 12.1 shows the different perspectives.)

Perhaps not surprisingly, given their responsibility for maintaining family ways, mothers considered conventional justifications to be more adequate in resolving conflict than did children. Children, on the other hand, saw this type of reasoning as a source of conflict. This was especially true of mid-adolescent ninth-graders, for whom family conflict is likely to have reached a peak as gains in autonomy are won by questioning parental authority.

Mothers also considered appeals to authority and threats of punishment to be more effective in getting their children to comply with their wishes than did the children, a difference that increased with the children's age. Children and adolescents, on the other hand, appealed to practical considerations, perhaps because such arguments are less likely to be challenged by parents. Smetana has found that, although children may believe their position can be justified by appeals to personal jurisdiction ("It's my room and I can keep it as I like"), they will use pragmatic reasons ("It doesn't matter if it's messy; I can find whatever I need") when arguing with a parent. Parents are not as likely as children to view the behaviors in question as rightfully within the child's purview (Smetana, Braeges, & Yau, 1991).

Children's appeals to social convention in resolving family conflict are likely to generate more conflict than they settle, usually because the conventions referred to are those of their peers, perhaps already a sore point for many parents.

you-message A message communicating what you think of another person.

I-message A message that tells the listener how his or her actions make one feel.

TABLE 12.1 Differences in the Parent's and the Child's Attempts to Resolve Conflict

The examples below are responses to a typical conflict: Mother wants Anne to wear something else, but Anne doesn't want to.

	Type of Justification	Example
Parent	Conventional	Reference to behavior standards, arbitrarily arrived at by family members; e.g., "I'd be embarrassed if any of my friends saw you looking like that."
	Pragmatic	Consideration of practical needs or consequences; e.g., "You'll catch a cold."
	Authoritarian	Reference to authority and punishment; e.g., "I'm your parent, and I say you can't dress like that."
Child	Conventional	Reference to standards of behavior shared with peers; e.g., "My friends would think I'm weird."
	Pragmatic	Consideration of practical needs or consequences; e.g., "I'm comfortable in these clothes."
	Personal	Portraying the issue as one of maintaining personal jurisdiction in an area; e.g., "The way I dress is an expression of me and my personality."

Source: J. G. Smetana & R. Berent. (1993). Adolescents' and mothers' evaluations of justifications for disputes. *Journal of Adolescent Research, 8,* 252–273.

The complexity derives from the fact that different domains of authority exist within the family. Only in some domains is there a shift in parental authority as children grow older. In others, parents continue to be perceived as having a legitimate say, both by themselves and by their children. Conflict arises over which issues lie within which domains: Children and parents, in other words, don't always see things eye to eye (Smetana & Asquith, 1994).

Judith Smetana and Pamela Asquith (1994) asked sixth- through tenth-graders and their parents to indicate the legitimacy of parental authority concerning various hypothetical issues, shown in Box 12.1. Almost all children and parents agreed that parents have the authority, even the obligation, to set rules concerning *moral issues,* in which a person's actions can affect the well-being of another. Similarly, most children and parents considered *conventional issues* to be the legitimate province of parental decision making, although parents saw themselves as having more authority here than did children. These perceptions, by the way, did not change with age, suggesting that parents are seen as rightfully the ones to establish and maintain the social as well as the moral order and children as the ones seeking greater autonomy within this.

There was similar agreement between children and parents about *personal issues,* both believing that children should have the say concerning these. When disagreements arose, they were most likely to concern *friendship issues, multifaceted issues* (involving both personal and conventional concerns), and *prudential issues,* which involved children's well-being or possible harm. Children, for instance, believed their friendships to be matters of personal choice, whereas parents considered these to more legitimately fall within their domain, feeling obligated to step in when they disapproved of certain friends. Similarly, even though parents and children agreed that parents had the authority and were even obligated to set down rules concerning prudential issues, disagreements arose over which specific issues fell within this domain, with parents seeing themselves as having more authority to govern children's behavior than children did. The large differences in parents' and children's perceptions of these issues indicate where the struggle for increasing independence is fought—not on moral or even conventional grounds, but on what constitutes children's personal prerogatives.

> ### Box 12.1 *Issues Concerning Parental Authority*
>
> **Moral Issues**
>
> Hitting brothers and sisters
> Lying to parents
> Breaking promises to parents
>
> **Conventional Issues**
>
> Not doing assigned chores
> Eating with elbows on table
> Cursing
>
> **Multifaceted Issues**
>
> A boy wearing an earring
> A girl wearing makeup
> Not cleaning one's room
> Not putting clothes away
>
> **Friendship Issues**
>
> Going to a friend's house without telling parents
> Seeing a friend whom parents do not like
> Inviting a friend over when parents are away
>
> **Personal Issues**
>
> Watching cartoons on TV
> Choosing own clothes
> Spending allowance money on games
>
> **Prudential Issues**
>
> Trying cigarettes
> Eating junk food
> Driving with older sibling's friends who are new drivers
>
> *Source:* Adapted from Smetana and Asquith (1994).

In general, for both children and parents, the realm of issues considered to be properly the domain of children increased with age, with more items being considered personal as children got older, thus expanding the sphere of their independence (Bosma et al., 1996; Smetana & Asquith, 1994). Smetana and Asquith point out, however, that this sphere remains narrower for parents than for their children, the former continuing to see themselves as legitimately setting rules governing children's bodies, physical appearance, and choice of friends. Issues of parental authority and children's rights are considered in the Research Focus, "Coding: 'Hey, I'm 10, and I Got a Right to See My Friends!'"

Samuel Vuchinich, Joseph Angelelli, and Antone Gatherum (1996), at Oregon State University, followed 63 families in a 2-year longitudinal study of family problem solving, making their first observations when the children were in the fourth grade. These investigators found that the struggle for increasing independence, or autonomy, begins in preadolescence, even before the ages observed by Smetana and Asquith. Families were videotaped as they discussed an issue that had been a problem in the family during the past month. As preadolescents got older, from 9½ to 11½ years, problem solving became less effective, with family members finding it more difficult to reach a solution or even take the other's perspective. With age, preadolescents became more negative. Fathers, especially, appear to react negatively to this, mothers being more the "peacemaker." Consistent with the findings of Smetana and Asquith, difficulties in communicating were not so much a matter of *what* was being discussed, mundane issues generating as much difficulty as significant ones, as was the age of the child.

In general, however, it is not children, but their parents who are responsible for changes in the emotional climate within the family. Reed Larson and David Almeida (1999) point out that this climate changes as emotions are transmitted from one person to another through daily interactions. In fact, one can actually follow the path of an emotion as it moves through a family. A parent, for instance,

Coding: "Hey, I'm 10, and I Got a Right to See My Friends!"

"What do you mean I can't have friends over after school? I've got rights around here too, you know!" Terry shouted as he slammed his bedroom door inches from his mother's face.

"You come out here this minute and we'll talk about those rights, mister!" his mother fumed.

"You have the right to be taken care of," she continued as Terry appeared in the doorway, "and that means I need to know something about the company you keep. And while we're on the issue of rights, I have the right to be addressed with respect by you, no matter how you feel about what I've just said."

"If you were here when I got home, you'd know who my friends were," Terry answered his mother sullenly. "You know how I hate being alone after school."

"Some days that can't be helped. If a meeting runs late, I can't just get up and walk out. And with Nana only a phone call away, you always have someone to call on if you need help."

Terry and his mother had both mentioned his rights, but were they talking about the same thing? What *are* the rights of children? And how do children think of these rights? For that matter, what do we as adults understand these rights to be?

Until relatively recently, considerations of children's rights focused almost exclusively on their right to be cared for and protected. More recently, those working with children, such as social service providers, legislators, and the courts, have also taken into consideration children's right to exercise some control over decisions affecting their lives (Hart, 1991). Terry was talking about the latter, what some call *self-determination rights;* his mother was talking about the former, or *nurturance rights.* But how do children understand each of these types of rights?

Martin Ruck, Rona Abramovitch, and Daniel Keating (1998) presented children (8 to 16) with hypothetical vignettes describing situations in which a child's right to either nurturance or self-determination conflicted with the desires of a parent or a teacher, and they asked the children to describe in their own words what the story character should do and why. This approach involves the use of *free-response data* or *descriptive data.* When researchers begin to investigate an area in which relatively little is known they will frequently simply observe what people do in natural settings, or, when this is impossible given the sensitive nature of the behavior, they will listen to what people have to tell them. Open-ended questions such as those used by Ruck, Abramovitch, and Keating are useful when one wants to know what people are thinking (Cozby, 1997). Another

advantage to descriptive responses is that they generate a rich source of data, useful in formulating future research questions. An additional advantage is the increased *external validity* of the research or the likelihood that the answers one gets are representative of the way people actually think.

There are disadvantages to the use of descriptive free responses as well. Perhaps the most formidable of these is the need to *code*, or classify, the specific answers that people give into broader classes of answers. Instead of attempting to work with everything people say, for instance, one looks at categories of answers. This approach makes it easier to detect relationships. Patterns emerge showing the frequency of different types of answers for different people, such as those given by older versus younger children. How does one arrive at the codes to be used in analyzing descriptive responses? One might simply decide in advance to look for certain types of answers, given what other investigators have found. One might also look at the actual answers that are given by a sample of the respondents, grouping specific answers into larger categories based on similarities in their meaning. These investigators had two independent raters code each of the response protocols; each rater was ignorant of the age of the respondent whose answers he or she was reading. The use of more than one coder makes it possible to determine the *reliability* with which answers are coded, or the degree to which the two raters working independently of each other agree in their coding.

The use of free-response or descriptive data is a time-intensive procedure. Raters must be trained to identify responses accurately, and this takes time. The actual scoring of the data also takes more time. In a sense, one enters a stream of behavior with a net—ready to catch (code) certain specimens of interest—but there is little way of speeding up the rate at which the behaviors flow by.

These investigators found that for younger children self-determination rights were not nearly as salient as were nurturance rights, as one might expect given the frequency with which young children need to be cared for and helped and the relative infrequency with which they get to participate in decisions about themselves. By the age of 14, however, adolescents were just as aware of their rights of self-determination as they were of nurturance rights. The salience of self-determination rights for adolescents most probably reflects their perception of themselves as able to fend for themselves in a variety of situations as well as their increasing need for autonomy.

might come home after work tense and irritable and yell at a child, who then fights with a sibling.

Research on such **emotional transmission** reveals a number of characteristic patterns. First, negative emotions are more easily transmitted than are others. It is easier to pass on anger, anxiety, or depression, for instance, than joy or peacefulness; or as Larson and Almeida put it, "negative emotions may trump positive ones." In general, however, families with greater psychological resources are less likely to experience the transmission of negative emotions than those with fewer resources.

Second, some members of the family are more likely than others to transmit emotions. The flow of emotions from one person to another is often unidirectional rather than reciprocal. Specifically, the emotions of men are more likely to affect their wives and children than vice versa. It is unclear whether this pattern reflects individuals' relative power within the family or, with respect to women, a greater sensitivity to the emotional states of others and also greater responsiveness to these. Emotions are also more likely to flow from parents to children than vice versa (Larson & Gillman, 1999). However, when they do, these are more likely to be the father's emotions than the mother's. This is not to say that mothers do not pass on their emotional states at the moment to their children, but that they are just less likely to do so.

Many of the negative emotions fathers pass on can be traced to stresses they experience at work. Mothers seem to be better at keeping these from spilling over into the emotional life of the family and may even become more responsive to their children when stressed at work. Marital tensions, on the other hand, are likely to be transmitted by mothers and fathers alike (Almeida, Wethington, & Chandler, 1999; Repetti, 1993).

Finally, it is common for an emotion that is passed from one person to assume a different form in the next person. Thus, the transmission of anger on the part of a parent may result not in anger in the child, but in anxiety. In this way, the effects of "secondhand" emotions on children can include physiological symptoms and patterns of behavior as well as emotional states. Thus, children can experience nervous stomachs or headaches, form "defensive alliances" within the family, or simply experience anxiety.

The way children react to the emotions of others depends in large measure on the way in which they interpret these emotions. Children actively construct, or make sense of, the emotional states of others just as they do other aspects of their world. Simply because an emotion is expressed does not mean that it will be experienced in the same way by different individuals. Geraldine Downey, Valerie Purdie, and Rebecca Shaffer-Neitz (1999) compared anger transmission from mother to child in mothers who experienced chronic pain and those who did not. They found that anger in the latter was likely to result in consequent anger in the child, but not in children in families in which the mother experienced chronic pain. Children of mothers with chronic pain simply did not interpret the anger the same way as they would were it not for the pain—that is, as a statement about themselves.

Families and Ethnicity

Over the past two decades, the number of ethnic families in the United States has increased dramatically. Twenty percent of all children under the age of 17 belong to an ethnic minority. By the year 2010 one third of all those in school will be Asian American, African American, Hispanic, Native American, or a member of some other minority. Ethnicity is an important factor contributing to the impact

Q Why are emotions more likely to be transmitted from men to their wives and children than vice versa?

emotional transmission Transference of emotions from one person to another, especially in a family, through daily interactions.

Family roles and relationships in minority-culture families are likely to differ from those typical in the dominant culture.

of the family on development. The organization of the family system often takes typically different forms in families with differing cultural backgrounds.

Asian American Families   Less than 4% of children in the United States are Asian and Pacific Islander American (Federal Interagency Forum, 1997), and most of them are of Chinese and Japanese backgrounds, although Vietnamese, Korean, and Filipino groups are growing in number. Asian traditions emphasize the importance of the group rather than the individual, and Asian American children feel strong loyalties to their families. Chinese Americans, as adults, continue to see their parents frequently, 2 to 3 times a week (Ying, 1994). Roles in Asian American families are more rigidly defined than in Western families, and relationships are vertically, or hierarchically, arranged, with the father in a position of authority at the top. Family relationships reflect the roles of members more than in individualistic, Western cultures. An aspect of the children's role is to care for their parents. This sense of responsibility to the family characterizes Asian American children (Huang & Yin, 1989; Nagata, 1989). Socialization practices emphasize duty, maintaining control over one's emotions and thoughts, and obedience to authority figures within the family (Nagata, 1989). Even with proportionately higher educational achievements, more Asian and Pacific Islander two-parent families (12.4%) experience poverty than do European American families (4.7%); however, the reverse is true for female-headed families. This difference might be attributable to the fact that the earnings of Asian and Pacific Islander males are 87% of those of European American males, whereas the earnings of Asian and Pacific Islander females are generally comparable to those of European American females (Day, 1996).

African American Families   Approximately 15% of children in the United States are African American (Federal Interagency Forum, 1997). Family roles are more flexible and are less gender-specific than in the dominant culture; parents assume responsibilities within the household according to work hours and type of task rather than according to gender-based roles. Parents also show less differentiation in the roles and tasks they assign to children of either sex (Gibbs, 1989). Support from extended family members is also more common than in majority families (Levitt, Guacci-Franco, & Levitt, 1993). The median income of African American families with children is approximately 67% that of European American families, and usually both parents must be employed for families to have middle-class status (Baugher & Lamison-White, 1996).

Hispanic Families   Nearly 14% of U.S. children are Hispanic. Most of these are Mexican American, although large numbers come from Puerto Rican, Cuban, and South and Central American backgrounds (Federal Interagency Forum, 1997). For children from Spanish-speaking homes, the sense of being between two cultures is especially strong. Traditionally, Hispanic families are patriarchal, with fathers making the decisions and supporting the family (Webster, 1994), and mothers caring for children and the home. These roles have changed as more Hispanic women find work outside the home. Employment is associated with higher status for the wife and greater decision making in the family (Herrera & DelCampo, 1995). Children are socialized into well-differentiated gender roles (Casas, Wagenheim, Banchero, & Mendoza-Romero, 1994; Ramirez, 1989). As do African American families, Hispanic families enjoy greater extended family support than do majority families (Levitt, Guacci-Franco, & Levitt, 1993). And, as with Asian and Pacific Islander and with African American families, more Hispanic families (27%) experience poverty than do non-Hispanic families (11%) (Baugher & Lamison-White, 1996).

Native American Families   Native Americans include Indians, Eskimos, Aleuts, Alaska Natives, and Metis, or people of mixed ancestry (LaFromboise & Low, 1989). One percent of children are Native Americans. Over 500 different native entities are recognized by the federal government. Each has its own customs and traditions, and over 200 Native American languages are spoken today (LaFromboise & Low, 1989).

Native American children frequently experience a cultural shock when they begin school. Many speak another language and have been raised with cultural values that run counter to those of the dominant culture. Often parents can be of little assistance, because they have not successfully assimilated themselves (LaFromboise & Low, 1989).

Siblings

Another aspect of the family system that affects children's development is its size. Children growing up with sisters and brothers experience a different family life, and are affected differently by it, than do those without siblings. Most children find that, despite the conflicts that inevitably arise, they develop close bonds of affection with siblings. Gene Brody, Zolinda Stoneman, and Kelly McCoy (1994), at the University of Georgia, followed 70 families over a 4-year period, assessing the quality of sibling relationships. In general, siblings reported that their relationships with each other improved over time. However, as siblings reached early adolescence, they reported relationships with other children in the family as being more negative, a finding that corroborates that of Larson and associates (1996),

Older siblings are models for younger ones. This young boy wants to be just like his older brother.

who also found adolescents' emotional experiences, when they were with their families, to become more negative by junior high.

The quality of the relationships siblings enjoy with each other is moderated, in part, by the relationships their parents have with other children in the family. This is especially true for their parents' relationships with the older child (Brody, Stoneman, & McCoy, 1994). Gene Brody, Zolinda Stoneman, and Kenneth Gauger (1996) found this "spillover" effect to be especially noticeable when the temperament of the older sibling was "difficult." The quality of each parent's relationship with the older child is only marginally associated with sibling relationships when the older sibling's temperament is "easy," but dramatically so when it is "difficult." Good parental relationships with difficult children appear to buffer those children's relationships with their siblings, perhaps through building better interpersonal skills, or by affecting self-regulatory skills, or simply by creating the expectation that relationships can be rewarding. Considering only relationships among the siblings themselves, the temperament of the older child rather than that of the younger is most important in determining the quality of the relationship, because older children are better able to dominate a relationship, influencing the form their interactions will take.

Older siblings are models for younger ones. Through their interactions with parents and others, they illustrate expected forms of behavior and family standards.

Their achievements influence younger siblings' aspirations and interests. A girl's interest in sports, for example, will be influenced by having an older sister on the varsity field hockey team. She sees the interest her parents take in her sister's activities and the pride her sister has in her team role. The girl takes it for granted that girls participate in sports and intends to try out for the swimming team herself when she reaches junior high.

Siblings provide friendship and company for each other. Because they are closer in age to each other than to a parent, they are often more in touch with the problems each faces and can frequently offer better advice than a parent. An older brother can advise a boy that the problems he is having at a new school will soon end. He knows, because that was his experience a year ago when he was the new boy at school. A parent would be less likely to have this information.

Siblings often describe their relationship as a mixture of rivalry and love. Here is how two girls talked about their relationships with their older brothers. Nilmarie, age 9, says, "My brother is sixteen and he treats me like a baby. He calls me shrimp and I hate that. And he's always torturing me . . . like there's this huge sofa and everybody in the house loves sitting on the sofa. So when my brother sits on the sofa, I say, 'Mom wants you in the kitchen.' So he goes to the kitchen and I stretch out on the sofa. Then he comes back and throws me on the floor." Anna, who is 10, responds by saying that her 18-year-old brother is even worse, holding her upside down until her face turns blue, and sums it up by saying, "I'm telling you, big brothers are trouble." But then, after a reflective moment, Anna adds, "last month we took him to college, and I just had to go back into the car because I was crying. Because he was going to stay there for five months." When asked if she were going to miss him, Anna nodded, surprised at her own reaction, "I was sobbing. I couldn't believe it. I mean, that's the brother that I fight with the most, that I kick, who beats me up. And there I am crying" (Samalin, 2000, pp. 73–74).◄

A Developing Morality

The development of moral reasoning undergoes a number of significant changes in middle childhood. Children internalize the standards of their communities and begin to use these in evaluating their own and others' behavior. They also begin to take intentions into consideration rather than judging actions simply in terms of their consequences, such as whether they were punished or praised. Finally, they begin to examine values that they once unthinkingly accepted and to formulate their own principles for evaluating the acceptability of various behaviors. What is responsible for these developmental changes? The answers will differ depending on who we turn to. We will consider four explanations of moral development in the section that follows: social-cognitive theory, which derives from the environmental model, and the theories of Kohlberg, Gilligan, and Freud, all of which reflect the assumptions of the organismic model.

Social-Cognitive Theory and Moral Development

Why do children internalize the standards of their communities? Why do they take intentions into consideration and examine their values? Social-cognitive theorists look to principles of learning for explanations.

Internalizing Standards   Those who adopt the social-cognitive approach assume that rewards and punishments regulate behavior. These incentives are initially effective in young children only when other people, such as parents and teachers, are around to administer them. As children imitate adult models, they also tell themselves when they have been good or bad, administering their own rewards and punishments (Mischel & Mischel, 1976).

Community standards determine which behaviors are to be rewarded and which ones punished. In learning the consequences of their behavior, children also acquire the standards of the group. These internalized controls tend to be concrete at first. Children learn specific actions and their consequences; they learn to say thank you, for example, or not to interrupt. In time they also acquire the principles behind these actions. Being polite, for instance, can take the form of a thank you or considering others' feelings by not interrupting. Thus, social-cognitive theory offers an explanation for internalizing the standards of one's community.

Considering Intentions How does social-cognitive theory explain age-related changes in moral thought? Children at first do not take the intentions of others into consideration; they judge actions in terms of their consequences. This literal focus is one of the facts that any theory of moral development must address. Social-cognitive theorists point out that the experiences of children make this type of reasoning likely. Adults rarely use reasoning with young children, often simply relying on physical restraints. Because physical rewards and punishments are common with young children, they are more likely to attend to the rewards or punishments that follow what they do than to the reasons that directed their actions (Mischel & Mischel, 1976).

Parental reactions to damage and messes probably contribute to children's literal focus. Most parents become more upset over big messes than small ones, even though both can be equally unintentional. Consider a child who, keeping out of his mother's way as she fixes dinner, attempts to pour himself a glass of milk. His grip slips as he positions the milk carton, and he watches, transfixed, as a stream of milk sends the cup scudding, flooding the countertop with milk. Is this mother likely to comment on his thoughtfulness at not disturbing her? Probably not. This child, like most, will be scolded for making a mess. It makes sense that children fail to understand that intentions can enter into one's evaluation of a situation when their intentions are so imperfectly considered.

Questioning Values Social-cognitive theory also explains the questioning of values that occurs as children get older. Parents and teachers expect older children and adolescents to start thinking for themselves, to evaluate ideas on their merit instead of accepting the endorsement of authorities. Social-cognitive theorists argue that we subtly reward older children and adolescents for questioning the very ideas we taught them to uncritically accept as younger children. Similarly, learning experiences explain the relativistic form of thought that emerges in many adolescents as they near their 20s. Exposure to new values challenges them to consider their own set of values as only one of a number of possible belief systems.

How does social-cognitive theory explain the questioning of values that occurs in older children and adolescents?

Acting Morally How likely are children to act in ways that reflect their moral understanding? In part, it depends on the incentives. *Incentives* are the rewards and punishments for acting in particular ways. For instance, if children believed they would be rewarded for doing certain things, or if they could be sure nothing bad would happen to them if they acted irresponsibly, they might be more likely to act in either of these ways.

Factors other than incentives also effect the likelihood of action. Children are more likely to imitate the actions of prestigious people than of those whom they don't regard as important. Models who are nurturant are also more likely to be imitated, perhaps because we like them more than less-nurturant people and want to be like them. Models who are similar to us in one or more ways are also likely to be imitated, again perhaps because we can imagine being like them (Mischel & Mischel, 1976).

Critique of Social-Cognitive Theory   How well does this approach explain particular forms of moral behavior? We can look at how well it explains a very practical form of behavior: cheating at school.

Cheating   Cheating in most students is motivated by the fear of failing or the need for approval. However, whether students with those motives will actually cheat is influenced by situational variables such as the normative behavior of classmates, incentives either for being honest or for cheating, the amount of risk involved, and characteristics of models for honesty and dishonesty.

Both personality and situational variables are related to cheating. In one experiment, schoolchildren worked at unsolvable problems that could be finished only if they cheated. Some worked for a tangible prize and others just for recognition. The likelihood of cheating was related both to the students' personalities and to the incentives they were working for. Both self-esteem and need for approval predicted cheating. Students with high self-esteem and low approval needs were least likely to cheat. Those with equally high self-esteem but high need for approval were as likely to cheat as those with low self-esteem. Regardless of personal motives, students working for a tangible prize were more likely to cheat (Lobel & Levanon, 1988). Cultural differences have also been found in what students consider to be cheating. Even so, similarities seem to be greater than differences, with all students, irrespective of their nationality, understanding that cheating involves, in one way or another, a shirking of their responsibilities to their studies (Evans, Craig, & Mietzel, 1993; Waugh, Godfrey, Evans, & Craig, 1995).

Little mention has been made about conscience in this discussion. Social-cognitive theory suggests that many internalized controls are not necessarily related to moral values or to conscience; they simply reflect conditioning. Children become helpful or law-abiding in order to avoid the anxiety they associate with doing otherwise. Conscience, when it does apply to behavior, is merely the set of standards one internalizes with the learning process (Seiber, 1980). For social-cognitive theorists, there is no inner voice other than the echo of the voices around them.

Kohlberg and Moral Development: Morality as Justice

What makes one moral? Is it simply that one internalizes the standards of one's community? Is it ever possible for individuals to function at a higher level than the society in which they live? Where does a sense of justice come from if it is not present in the social order? Lawrence Kohlberg's theory of moral reasoning addresses these questions.

Kohlberg's (1976, 1984) theory bases its assumptions about moral development on the organismic model, stressing the importance of the inner forces that organize development. The most important of these forces is a sense of justice, which underlies the highest forms of moral thought.

Kohlberg's theory traces moral reasoning over a number of discrete stages. Movement from one stage to the next is prompted by the need to resolve conflict. This conflict arises when one realizes that others view things differently. Children gain insight into the perspectives of others through increases in role-taking skills. As they become able to put themselves in the place of another, they can see things as that person does. Cognitive maturity—the ability to think about and balance the competing demands produced by examining several perspectives—also contributes to moral development. Kohlberg (1976, 1984) assumes that children's level of cognitive development places limits on the sophistication of moral thinking.

Kohlberg traces moral development over three levels of moral reasoning, with two stages at each level. The levels reflect the stance individuals take in relation to the standards of their community. Not all standards reflect moral issues. Some standards exist as laws, others simply as conventions or customary ways of behaving. It is the law, for example, that one not take another person's life; it is customary that one not giggle when hearing of another's death. Both of these reflect a common value—the sacredness of life. But only when individuals reach the postconventional level of moral reasoning do they distinguish social convention, whether codified as laws or customs, from the values these conventions reflect. And only then, according to Kohlberg, can they distinguish conventional concerns from moral ones.

Preconventional Moral Reasoning   Children at the level of **preconventional moral reasoning** want only to satisfy their needs and not get punished while doing so. They have not as yet internalized the standards of their community, even though they know what these standards are. They abide by the rules only when someone else is around. The rule enforcers, and not the rules, constrain their actions. In the absence of the former, anything goes as long as you don't get caught (Kohlberg, 1984).

Stage 1: Obedience   Children at this stage assume that everyone else sees things as they do, not realizing that their view of a situation is just one of several possible perspectives. Consequently, they experience little or no conflict in their interactions with others. Their actions reflect only a need to satisfy their own desires, without getting punished for doing so. Stage 1 morality is not reflective; children do not take motives and intentions into consideration (they do not understand others' feelings and points of view easily). They judge behavior simply in terms of its consequences. Actions that are rewarded must have been good; those that were punished, bad.

Stage 2: Instrumental, or Considering Intentions   As children become better able to put themselves in the place of another person, they can see things as the other person would. Adopting the other's perspective gives them two points of view, and, in turn, the likelihood that they will experience conflict. Which perspective is right? They can understand the reasons for the other person's actions and know that the other can understand theirs—that each of them can consider the intentions of the other. Children who reason at this level don't have to rely on others' reactions to evaluate behavior. They can look at the motives behind an action. Even though fairness is central to reasoning at this stage, morality is still preconventional because children consider only the actions and intentions of those they are with and not the rules or laws of the group, whether the school or community.

Conventional Moral Reasoning: Internalizing Standards   Children at the level of **conventional moral reasoning** want to live up to the standards of their group and are not motivated simply by the desire to avoid punishment. These standards have become their own and are no longer simply other people's rules.

preconventional moral reasoning Kohlberg's first level of moral reasoning, characterized by the absence of internalized standards.

conventional moral reasoning Kohlberg's second level of moral reasoning, in which moral thinking is guided by internalized social standards.

In the course of moral development, adolescents come to see themselves not only as members of the community but also as able to challenge community decisions that they feel are wrong. These high school students are attending a school board meeting to protest the dropping of a class.

Stage 3: Conformist, or "Good Boy, Nice Girl"   The self-reflection that comes with formal thought makes it possible for children, when they move into adolescence, to see themselves as they imagine others would. This third-person perspective forms the basis for taking the norms of their group, in the form of concern with what others think of them, into consideration. This concern about the opinions of others adds a new dimension to morality: the need to live up to the expectations of others. Kohlberg (1984) believes that Stage 3 reasoning is dominant during adolescence and is even common in adulthood. The prevalence of Stage 3 reasoning helps to explain adolescents' sensitivity to the approval of peers. Rather than thinking through a situation in terms of the claims of those involved, adolescents are likely to be swayed by the opinions of their friends. See the Research Focus, "The Dependent Variable: When Is a Stereotype Simply a Good Guess, and When Is It Bad Judgment?"

Stage 4: Social Accord, or "Law and Order"   As the ability to think more abstractly increases, adolescents begin to see themselves as members of an invisible but nonetheless real community. As such, they realize the need to evaluate actions by the community's standards. Kohlberg believes that reasoning at the fourth stage is frequently the highest that most people reach. Although Stage 4 reasoning is usually adequate for most situations, it breaks down when laws conflict with human values. When this occurs, individuals must develop a way to see their society in relation to the needs of others.

Postconventional Moral Reasoning: Questioning Values   Only at the level of **postconventional moral reasoning** does Kohlberg believe that individuals develop genuine inner controls over behavior; the principles by which they live are self-derived standards rather than the conventions of their community. Motives, as well, reflect a sense of obligation to live within a code that is determined by one's principles. Thus, Kohlberg distinguishes levels of moral development in terms of both a progressive internalization of standards for behavior and motives for living according to these standards (Hoffman, 1980; Kohlberg, 1984).

postconventional moral reasoning
Kohlberg's third level of moral reasoning, in which moral thinking is guided by self-derived principles.

Stage 5: Social Contract   Kohlberg believes that individuals move into Stage 5 only when they have been exposed to other value systems, usually in late adolescence.

Research Focus

The Dependent Variable: When Is a Stereotype Simply a Good Guess, and When Is It Bad Judgment?

We all know that it's wrong to react to others on the basis of stereotypes. Yet how often do we do so? Stereotypes lead us to expect one type of behavior or another in individuals, based simply on their group membership. Adolescents live in a world of well-defined social groups, each of which is associated with characteristic behaviors. "Jocks," for instance, are thought of as noisy and rowdy, "preppies" as well-to-do and college bound, and "techies" as spending more time with their computers than with peers. How likely are adolescents to make judgments about the behavior of other adolescents, in the absence of any other information, based on stereotypes such as these?

Stacey Horn, Melanie Killen, and Charles Stangor (1999) wanted to know as well. These investigators were interested in the way high school students would evaluate the appropriateness of punishing other students, in the absence of supporting evidence, when the actions of which they were accused were either consistent or inconsistent with stereotypes for their groups. Would adolescents' decision making, in other words, be affected by commonly held stereotypes about members of other groups?

Stacey Horn and her associates asked ninth-graders to read a scenario in which some students had too much to drink at a dance and committed an act of vandalism. The students subsequently were told by the student council that they must pay for the damages despite the absence of evidence indicating they were responsible. The students were described either as "jocks" (football players) or as "techies" (computer club members), and the vandalism they committed was either damaging the sound equipment at the party or breaking into the school computer system. Thus, the action could be consistent with students' stereotypes (for example, computer club members who broke into the computer system) or inconsistent (for example, football players who broke into the computer system). After reading the scenario, students were asked to evaluate the action of the student council, to give the reasons on which they based their evaluation, and then to indicate whether they believed the student council's behavior was justified.

Why did these investigators use more than one measure of stereotyping? If the measures don't all show the same relationships, how are we to evaluate which one is more accurate? The answer is that different measures pick up different aspects of behavior. Three criteria distinguish accurate measures: reliability, validity, and sensitivity.

The first consideration with any measure of behavior, or *dependent variable*, is its *reliability*. It should yield the same value for a person each time. If a student takes an intelligence test, for instance, and retakes it in 3 weeks, one expects the score to be about the same on both occasions. Differences in IQ from one testing to the next reflect factors other than intelligence—that is, *error*. Reliable measures have little error. Second, measures must have *validity*. They must measure what they are designed to measure. Some of the very first intelligence tests were highly reliable but not very valid. Some, for instance, measured how rapidly people could tap their fingers, something that can be measured with little error but that turns out to have little to do with actual intelligence. Third, *sensitivity* is a characteristic of good measures: They are able to detect even small differences where these exist. Current measures of intelligence do more than sort individuals into categories of, say, bright, average, and dull. They offer numerous distinctions within each.

Returning to adolescents' stereotypes and their decision making, let's consider what Horn and her associates found. They discovered that adolescents evaluated the actions of the student council as wrong, indicating that it would be unfair to punish a group simply because the type of damage that had been done fit the stereotype of the group. However, they also found that the types of reasons adolescents brought to bear in supporting this position differed depending on whether the actions were consistent with their stereotypes of either group. When their stereotypes were confirmed, they were less likely to bring moral arguments to bear, leading to fewer concerns about fairness in the absence of supporting evidence. Only by using several response measures could the investigators sort out these differing relationships.

Individuals who come to respect others' ways of life find it difficult to continue seeing their own as more valid. Once individuals recognize that their society's conventions are in some sense arbitrary, they are forced to look beyond the conventions themselves to the function they serve. When they do, they discover that laws derive their importance because they represent agreements among people who live together, not because they are right in and of themselves. Members of a society enter into a contract with others in the society in which they agree to live within its laws, forgoing some individual freedoms, for the mutual benefit of all.

Stage 6: Universal Principles This stage provides individuals with yet another perspective: seeing past the mutual agreements shared by members of a society to the values these agreements reflect. The social contracts we enter into reflect underlying values such as truth, justice, honor, and the value of life itself. The step that individuals take in order to gain a perspective on their society removes them from the claims of time and circumstance. Kohlberg (1984) asserts that all societies throughout history have recognized these values—that they are, in fact, universal ethical principles. Those who reason at this final stage understand that social conventions are imperfect reflections of these values and, consequently, individuals must look beyond conventions, and even laws, to their own principles when arriving at moral decisions.

Critique of Kohlberg's Theory Elliot Turiel (1983), a psychologist at the University of California, Berkeley, maintains that even very young children distinguish moral rules from conventional ones. Conventional rules reflect accepted ways of doing things. As these change, so do the rules. Standards of dress and speech reflect these flexible relationships. Rules relating moral concerns to behavior, however, are inflexible. Moral rules reflect a concern for the well-being of others and do not change with climates of opinion.

Charles Helwig, Carolyn Hildebrandt, and Elliot Turiel (1995) interviewed first-, third-, and fifth-graders and found that nearly all the children agreed that moral acts such as pushing someone down would not be all right even in the context of a game that legitimized such actions. The youngest children, however, were less clear about acts leading to psychological harm, such as name-calling as part of a game. Similarly, Larry Nucci, Cleanice Camino, and Clary Sapiro (1996), interviewing 9- and 15-year-olds in Brazil, found that children as well as adolescents distinguished moral from conventional issues, agreeing that if there were no rules against doing so, it would be all right not to wear a school uniform, but not to hit or steal. Thus, even children distinguish moral from conventional concerns.

Although even very young children distinguish moral acts from conventional ones on the basis of whether they involve harm, it is unclear whether this is because they have isolated harm itself as the issue of concern or because such actions are typically punished. Philip Zelazo, Charles Helwig, & Anna Lau (1996) told children stories in which an action that typically is harmful, such as hitting, has positive consequences. Thus, children were told a story in which parents who had gone on a trip brought back a strange animal that "gets hurt and cries" when petted and "feels good and smiles" when it is hit. The question of interest is whether children, when asked whether it was good or bad to hit the animal, would base their judgments on indications of whether harm had occurred (outcomes such as crying or smiling) or rely on known sanctions against hitting.

They found that at every age, from 3 through 5, children based their judgments as to whether an action was acceptable on whether the character appeared to have been harmed—that is, on the outcome of the action. Since this was true for both types of stories, these findings indicate that even young children take the welfare of another into consideration rather than relying on social sanctions against specific actions such as hitting. They also found that, with age, the complexity of children's judgments increased. Thus, the youngest preschoolers tended to base their evaluations on a single consideration, such as the outcome of the action *or* the intentions of the character, whereas by the age of 5, children could consider both when evaluating actions.

Lying and Truth Telling Not only do children distinguish moral issues from conventional concerns at an earlier age than Kohlberg assumed they could, but they also take intentions into consideration when evaluating the acceptability of various behaviors. One such behavior is lying versus truth telling.

Piaget (1965) was one of the first to look at children's understanding of what it means to lie. Adults consider people to have lied when they have misrepresented what they know to be so in order to deceive someone. Simply failing to report something accurately in the absence of intentional deception is not considered lying. Piaget found that, in making judgments about lying, children relied more heavily on whether a child had been believed than on whether that child had intended to deceive someone. Later research has found that children consider intention at a much earlier age than Piaget believed possible (Peterson, 1995; Wimmer, Gruber, & Perner, 1984).

In most cases, intentional deception involves an attempt to get away with something. However, what if misrepresentations of the truth, even though intentional, were motivated not by a desire to get away with something, but by respect for one's cultural values? Thus, children raised in collectivist cultures that emphasize not only honesty but also modesty as ways of promoting social harmony might consider it acceptable to lie about their achievements if asked to acknowledge these publicly. In comparison, children raised in individualistic cultures, in which behaviors that aggrandize the self are not considered wrong, should evaluate lying about a good deed as less acceptable.

Kang Lee, Catherine Cameron, Fen Xu, Genyao Fu, and Julie Board (1997) compared Canadian and Chinese children's evaluations of the goodness or badness of telling the truth or lying under different circumstances. Canadian children can be expected to reflect their culture's value of individualism and pride in personal accomplishments. Chinese children can be expected to reflect their culture's emphasis on collectivism and modesty in order to maintain social harmony. Thus, in China, doing a good deed is valued, but admitting to having done so violates cultural values of modesty and humility. These values raise the interesting question of how Chinese children would evaluate telling the truth versus lying about having done a good deed. A comparison of Chinese and Canadian children should show the effect of culture, whereas a similar comparison concerning lying about misdeeds would not be expected to find any differences.

Seven-, 9, and 11-year-olds evaluated stories about children as "naughty" or "good" in which the children had done a good deed or committed a misdeed and either told the truth about what they had done or lied. They found that Canadian children evaluated telling the truth equally positively at each age, whereas Chinese children's evaluations of telling the truth became less positive with age, increasingly reflecting the culture's value of modesty. Thus, 8% of 7-year-olds, 28% of 9-year-olds, and 48% of 11-year-olds evaluated telling the truth negatively. When asked why, they were likely to say the child was trying to get the teacher's praise, something that is actively discouraged in schools.

With respect to lying about doing a good deed, Canadian children considered telling a lie to be wrong, though older children tended less so than younger ones. Only the youngest Chinese children, however, considered it wrong to lie about a good deed. Older children evaluated this positively, as reflecting a value of modesty and humility. With respect to telling the truth about committing a misdeed, however, Canadian and Chinese children did not differ. Both evaluated telling the truth positively.

With respect to questioning values, long before children can read bumper stickers telling them to "Question Authority!" they do so. Even young children have been found to question the legitimacy of directives from authority figures such as parents and teachers when these could result in harm to others or are patently unfair. That is, children distinguish moral issues from conventional, or

In collectivist cultures where humility is highly valued, not speaking about one's accomplishments is regarded more positively than in individualist cultures where personal achievement is highly valued.

authority-based, ones at an early age (Laupa & Turiel, 1986). They also distinguish how much a person knows about a situation when evaluating who should be listened to, even when the more knowledgeable person is a child rather than an adult (Laupa, 1991).

But to what extent are children able to make such distinctions when the moral dimensions are less clear-cut, as when they are separated from issues of physical harm? And to what extent are judgments such as these affected by one's culture? Most Asian cultures, for instance, regard respect for one's elders and deference to those in positions of authority as virtues, elevating these above mere convention.

Korean children in first, third, and fifth grades listened to stories about moral dilemmas in which a child was told to do something that was morally right or not right, such as trying to find the person who had lost some money or keeping the money. Children indicated it was better to listen to those who encouraged the child to do the (morally) right thing, even when these directions ran counter to directions given by a person in authority, such as a principal or teacher. Thus, even in instances where no physical harm is involved, children distinguish moral issues from obedience to authority figures. This distinction is especially compelling in that it is made by children raised in a culture in which deference to those in authority is regarded as virtuous (Kim, 1998).

Kohlberg's theory, despite contradictory findings such as the above, enjoys wide support. His theory has an intrinsic elegance. Each of the six stages is a logical extension of the preceding one, and the progression is systematically related to new role-taking skills and cognitive maturity. But there may be another reason to account for the popularity of this theory. Kohlberg has given us a sympathetic view of human nature. He accounts for our ability to control our behavior in terms of the development of an inner sense of justice, rather than the carrot-and-stick approach of social-cognitive theory.

Carol Gilligan questions whether justice is the highest arbiter of moral issues. She finds that an ethic of care, rather than a morality of justice, is more characteristic of females. She points out that Kohlberg developed his theory based on interviews with males. Like many developmentalists before him, Kohlberg equated the male perspective with development in general (see Chapter 1).

Gilligan: An Ethic of Care

Carol Gilligan (1982, 1988a, 1988b, 1989a, 1989b), of Harvard University, offers a fresh perspective on moral development, one that balances male-oriented theories such as Kohlberg's and Freud's with insights gained from interviews with females. Gilligan finds that most females think of morality more personally than males do; they adopt an **ethic of care.** They speak of morality in terms of their responsibilities to others rather than as the rights of individuals. Their moral decisions are based on compassion as well as reason, and they stress care for others as well as fairness.

Gilligan traces these approaches to differences in the way females and males define themselves in relation to others. Whereas males tend to view themselves as separate from others, females see themselves in terms of their relationships with others. These themes of separation and connectedness translate into different approaches to morality. The assumption that one is separate from others highlights the need for rules to regulate the actions of each person with respect to the other; the assumption that one is connected to others emphasizes the responsibility each has to the other (Gilligan, 1982).

Gender differences also exist in the way individuals think of responsibility. Males tend to think of responsibility as *not* doing something that would infringe

ethic of care Gilligan's description of a morality based on responsiveness to and care for others.

on the rights of others, such as not hurting them. Females think of responsibility in terms of *meeting* the needs of others—that is, as something to be done. Both males and females are concerned with not hurting others, yet each sex thinks of this in a different way. Gilligan points out that, given differences such as these, attempts to chart moral development as a single sequence are bound to give us only half the picture.

Gilligan traces moral development in females through three levels, each of which reflects a different resolution to the conflict between responsibility to self and responsibility to others. Movement from one level to the next occurs in two transitional periods. At the first level, the primary concern is with oneself. Transition to the next level occurs when one sees caring only for oneself as selfish and at odds with responsibility to others. At the second level, females equate morality with goodness and self-sacrifice, or caring for others. Transition to the third level occurs when they experience problems in their relationships that result from excluding themselves from their own care. At the third level, they equate morality with care for both themselves and others.

Level 1: Caring for Self (Survival)   The primary concerns at this level of moral development are pragmatic: What's best for me? Actions are guided by self-interest. Gilligan notes that the issue of "rightness" is considered only when several of one's needs are in conflict and force the individual to consider which need is more important. Otherwise there is little conflict over making the right decision.

Why might individuals function at this level? Gilligan believes that a preoccupation with one's needs reflects feelings of helplessness and powerlessness. These feelings have their origin in being emotionally cut off, or *disconnected*, from others. The females she interviewed who were at this level had frequently been hurt by others and often chose to hold themselves apart from others rather than experience further pain. Feeling alone and cut off from others, they were left with the sense that they had to look to their own needs, because no one else would (Gilligan, 1982).

This first level is similar to Kohlberg's preconventional level of moral reasoning. In neither level do individuals consider others except for their possible reactions to what they do—-that is, except as potential consequences for their actions. Conflict is also absent in both levels and self-interest, rather than the need to make the right decision, dictates what one does.

Transition: From Selfishness to Responsibility   Individuals begin to move beyond the first level when they experience a discrepancy between the way they are and the way they feel they ought to be, between self-concern and responsible concern for others.

Level 2: Caring for Others (Goodness)   Gilligan assumes that females move to a second level of moral development when they internalize social conventions. The progression is similar to that described by Kohlberg for movement from preconventional to conventional reasoning. Gilligan (1982) notes that, in the first level,

> morality is a matter of sanctions imposed by a society of which one is more subject than citizen, [and in the second] moral judgment relies on shared norms and expectations. The woman at this point validates her claim to social membership through the adoption of societal values. Consensual judgment about goodness becomes the overriding concern as survival is now seen to depend on acceptance by others. (p. 79)

Transition: From Conformity to Choice   The equation of morality with conventional feminine goodness is a step toward repairing the failed relationships that led to a preoccupation with the self at the first level. But this equation creates a second imbalance that itself is in need of repair. Conventional images of feminine goodness center on the care of others. They also involve self-sacrifice. Females at the second level of morality purchase membership in the larger community at the cost of caring for themselves. The price of membership is costly and introduces tensions that, for some, will prompt movement to the third level. These individuals realize that excluding themselves from their own care creates as many problems as excluding others had done previously; in other words, goodness results in as much hurt as selfishness (Gilligan, 1986). This realization is an important step in moving to an ethic of care that includes themselves as well as others. Gilligan, like Kohlberg before her, believes that many females do not take this step and do not develop beyond conventional forms of thought.

Level 3: Caring for Self and Others (Truth)   To move into the third level, females must move beyond the conventional wisdom that tells them to put the needs of others above their own. In doing so, they must reformulate their definition of care to include themselves as well as others. As females reconsider their relationships with others, they once again must consider their own needs. Questions such as "Is this selfish?" again arise. Because these occur in the context of relationships with others, they also prompt a reexamination of the concept of responsibility.

When one moves beyond conventional forms of wisdom, one finds there is no one to turn to for answers but oneself. Females at this level cannot rely on what others might think; they must exercise their own judgment. This judgment requires that they be honest with themselves. Being responsible for themselves, as well as for others, means they must know what their needs actually are. As Gilligan (1982) asserts, "The criterion for judgment thus shifts from goodness to truth when the morality of action is assessed not on the basis of its appearance in the eyes of others, but in terms of the realities of its intention and consequence" (p. 83). The bottom line is simple: To care for oneself, one must first be honest with oneself and acknowledge the reasons behind one's actions.

Individuals at this level adopt an inclusive perspective that gives equal weight to their responsibility to themselves and to others. Care extends to all. To exclude the self would introduce pain that could otherwise be avoided, and their commitment to minimizing pain requires a new balance of concern for self with responsibility for others.

Although Gilligan and Kohlberg document developmental sequences that parallel each other in many respects, a critical difference separates these two accounts. Kohlberg believes that his sequence is a path universally trodden by all individuals as they move into adulthood. He assumes that this sequence takes the form it does because it reflects developments in cognitive maturity that have a strong biological component (see the discussion of Piaget in Chapter 1). Gilligan is not equally convinced that the sequence she documents in adolescent girls and young women is developmentally necessary. She does not believe the sequence to be "rooted in childhood," as does Kohlberg. She suggests, instead, that it is a response to a crisis and that the crisis is adolescence itself (Gilligan, 1989a).

Gilligan proposes that leaving childhood is problematic for girls in ways that it is not for boys. The problem lies with the culture each enters. Adolescence introduces the expectation that children will assume the conventions of their society, whether these be adult gender roles, the knowledge that forms the basis of cultural wisdom, or behaviors that fit prescribed definitions of "goodness" and "rightness." Why should this expectation present more problems for girls?

Gilligan's answer is powerful. The most visible figures populating the landscape of adulthood are males—whether plumbers, politicians, poets, or philosophers—and their collective experiences form its norms. Girls risk losing themselves as they relax the intimate bonds of childhood to embrace a larger world of experience. Gilligan (1989b) writes

> As the river of a girl's life flows into the sea of Western culture, she is in danger of drowning or disappearing. To take on the problem of her appearance, which is the problem of her development, and to connect her life with history on a cultural scale, she must enter—and by entering disrupt—a tradition in which "human" has for the most part meant male. Thus a struggle often breaks out in girls' lives at the edge of adolescence. (p. 4)

The problem is pervasive because it is woven into the very fabric of cultural thought. Even formal education, Gilligan suggests, presents a challenge to female identity: "In learning to think in the terms of the disciplines and thus to bring her thoughts and feelings into line with the traditions of Western culture, . . . she also learn[s] to dismiss her own experience" (p. 2).

Gilligan (1989a) traces the crisis of connection for girls to their ability to find a "voice" with which to speak and a context in which they will be heard. The culture they are entering has not been equally responsive to the voices of women and men, "or at least has not been up to the present. The wind of tradition blowing through women is a chill wind, because it brings a message of exclusion. . . . The message to women is: keep quiet and notice the absence of women and say nothing" (p. 26).

Critique of Gilligan's Theory   Gilligan has suggested that individuals are likely to function at Level 1 when they have been hurt by others, causing them to be preoccupied with their own needs. As a consequence, one might expect that children who have been maltreated would evaluate moral transgressions differently than those who had not been maltreated. Surprisingly, however, when such comparisons have been made, maltreated children do not differ from others in their evaluations of hypothetical moral situations (Smetana, Kelly, & Twentyman, 1984). One might still find differences, however, if they were evaluating actual transgressions.

Judith Smetana and her associates (1999) looked for such differences, comparing maltreated and nonmaltreated children's evaluations of actual transgressions in their classrooms, such as hitting or name-calling, as well as hypothetical transgressions. As might be expected, actual transgressions were judged to be more serious than hypothetical situations. However, maltreated children did not differ from those who were not maltreated in how seriously they evaluated moral transgressions (either hypothetical or actual) or in their reasons for why actions were permissible or wrong. Thus, their own maltreatment did not blunt their moral sensitivities. However, they did differ in their emotional reactions to mistreatment. Among those who had been abused, the ones who expressed most sadness also evaluated actual transgressions as more serious, thought they should be punished more severely, and were more likely to mention the intrinsic harmfulness of these actions. These findings suggest that the way children perceive and evaluate social relations is constructed from their own experiences and that those who have been physically harmed are, if anything, even more sensitive to the intrinsic harm to others in moral transgressions.

What evidence is there for gender differences in moral concerns? D. Kay Johnston (1988) asked 11- and 15-year-olds to generate solutions to two of Aesop's fables involving moral issues. Specifically, she wanted to know whether gender differences exist in the spontaneous use of justice and care orientations and whether both orientations are available to adolescents of each sex. Boys were much more likely to spontaneously adopt a justice than a care approach to both of the fables. Girls, however, were fairly evenly divided in their adoption of either approach. Judgments about the best solution showed that boys still strongly preferred (three to one) a justice solution to one of the fables; girls strongly favored a care solution as best to both of the fables.

Judy Daniels, Michael D'Andrea, and Ronald Heck (1995) replicated Johnston's experiment with adolescents in Hawaii and found no difference in the solutions spontaneously offered by girls and boys. Furthermore, when asked for the best solution to the dilemmas, all adolescents offered a care approach. Differences between their findings and those of Johnston might reflect cultural differences or simply changes in gender roles with time. In individualistic cultures such as the mainland United States, the rights of individuals tend to be emphasized, whereas in traditionally collectivistic cultures such as Hawaii, the good of the collective, or group, is emphasized (Markus & Kitayama, 1991).

It is also possible that differences between these studies may be due to changing gender roles (Sochting, Skoe, & Marcia, 1994). Rosemary Jadack and her associates (1995) found that females and males differed little in the extent to which they adopted a care or a justice orientation in reasoning about real-life types of dilemmas. In fact, individuals of either sex frequently used reasoning characteristic of both approaches, suggesting that these are not competing perspectives. Similarly, Gillian Wark and Dennis Krebs (1996) found that, although females did mention more care-based reasons than males, the difference was small and occurred only when they were reasoning about certain types of problems.

Gilligan views the developmental sequence that she catalogues as complementing that of Kohlberg, not as an alternative (Gilligan & Attanucci, 1988). She points out, however, that the care orientation would have been missed had she and others not studied females as systematically as Kohlberg studied males.

Freud: Morality and the Superego

Freud's theory of moral development derives from his more general theory of personality development. Like other organismic theorists, Freud looked to sources within the organism to explain certain developmental changes. Freud assumed that the strong biological forces he identified must be balanced by equally strong social constraints that develop only with age.

Freud believed that responsibility for moral behavior resides with the **superego,** the last of the three facets of the personality to develop (see Chapter 9). The superego embraces the cultural standards of right and wrong that make up the *conscience.* Prior to the development of the conscience (at about age 5), Freud assumed that children are governed only by the desire to win parental affections and the fear of being rejected for wrongdoing. Like social-cognitive theorists and Kohlberg, Freud believed that an internalized code or ethic is not present in early childhood.

Freud (1925b/1961) assumed that the libido—the life force within each individual—seeks genital expression in childhood, and that the object of the child's sexual desires is the very person who is closest in so many other ways. For the boy, this is the mother; for the girl, it will become the father. Sexual desire for the parent of the opposite sex makes the parent of the same sex a rival. The emotional triangle that results creates unbearable anxiety in the child. Freud believed that children repress their sexual desires to reduce the anxiety they experience and

superego The aspect of personality in Freudian theory that represents the internalized standards and values of society.

identify with the same-sex parent. **Identification** is the process by which the child internalizes or appropriates the values and behaviors of the parent. These values form the superego and serve as the basis for an internalized set of standards for behavior.

Freud assumed the situation differed for male and female children. Freud reasoned that girls are not as motivated as boys to resolve Oedipal tensions, because they have already suffered an incalculable loss: They were not born with a penis. Rather than fearing castration (castration anxiety), they long for a penis (penis envy). Because girls literally have less to lose than boys, they do not experience the same anxiety that motivates boys to identify with the same-sex parent. Also, the figure with whom the girl identifies, the mother, is not as powerful or threatening as the father. As a consequence, Freud believed that girls' superegos are not as strong or as demanding as those of boys.

The final step in moral development occurs in adolescence when puberty threatens the surface tranquility achieved through repression and identification. New sexual desires assail the fragile bulwark the child has erected against Oedipal turmoil. Freud assumed that adolescents' only defense against the onslaught of their own sexuality and the incestuous threat this poses is to emotionally distance themselves from their parents. In doing so, they have to toss out the parental figures they had internalized in childhood. Adolescence becomes a time for reworking the parental standards that have been uncritically accepted as part of these figures (Josselson, 1980, 1987).

Critique of Freud's Theory Freud's theory of personality development and his assumptions about moral development are widely accepted. His theory influences vast numbers of clinical practitioners and is taught in college courses around the world. Many of his concepts—such as the unconscious, projection, and repression—have entered the popular vocabulary. Nevertheless, the bulk of support for this theory comes from clinical evidence based on small numbers of individuals and is often heavily interpreted (Hoffman, 1980).

Carol Travis and Carole Wade (1984) point to the absence of systematic, objective support for Freud's twin concepts of castration anxiety and penis envy, concepts that are central to his explanation of moral development in males and females, respectively. Regarding the concept of penis envy, they note that females as well as males value the male role more highly, but point out that males have enjoyed more power, greater opportunities, and more privileges than females. Do females envy males for their penis? Or do they desire the social advantages that go with having one?

Freud believed that the absence of castration anxiety in females and the presence, in its stead, of penis envy resulted in a weaker superego in females and differences in their moral behavior.

These assumptions concerning the basis for gender differences in moral behavior have not received empirical support. Research on the internalization of moral standards does not find males to have stronger superegos than females. Nor do differences in behavior, when they occur, favor males. They are, if anything, as likely to favor females (Ford, Wentzel, Wood, Stevens, & Siesfeld, 1989; Lobel & Levanon, 1988).

Research has similarly failed to support other of Freud's assumptions related to the development of morality. For instance, adolescence is not a period of emotional turmoil for most teenagers. Also, large surveys of normal adolescents do not find they are preoccupied with sex or with controlling their impulses. Nor do most adolescents have weak egos, nor have they cut emotional ties with their parents (see Chapter 9).

identification The child's uncritical incorporation of parental ways and beliefs.

Internalizing Standards   How does Freud explain the facts that other theories of moral development have addressed? Like social-cognitive theorists (as well as Kohlberg and Gilligan for conventional standards of morality), Freud assumes that individuals acquire their values and their sense of right and wrong by internalizing society's norms. The conditions that prompt children to internalize parental standards differ for each theory, however. Freud traces internalization to resolution of the Oedipal complex and identification with the parent of the same sex. Social-cognitive theory speaks of the child's ability to reinforce itself, rather than having to receive praise or punishment at the hands of others. Both theories must address the central problem with internalization as an explanation for moral conduct: If one's culture is the ultimate source of moral authority in an individual's life, how does a person ever reach a level higher than that which characterizes the society? Gilligan and Kohlberg both view the internalization of social conventions as an intermediate step in moral development. Gilligan believes that females take this step when they experience a discrepancy between their self-concern and concern for others. Kohlberg traces this step to increases in cognitive maturity.

Considering Intentions   For Freud, the emergence of the superego explains the child's shift from evaluating behavior in terms of its consequences to the motives that underlie it. Social-cognitive theorists, in contrast, explain this shift in terms of the social-learning experiences of the child, but frequently fail to take into consideration the child's own motives and intentions or the expectation that adolescents will begin to think for themselves. Kohlberg attributes this shift to new levels of cognitive maturity and role-taking skills. Gilligan's analysis of morality begins with individuals who have already made this transition.

Questioning Values   And how might Freud explain the flexibility that characterizes the moral thought that develops in some with late adolescence? Rather than refer to changing social expectations, increasing cognitive maturity, or the need to repair relationships, psychoanalytic thought attributes flexibility in moral judgments to the work of the ego in balancing the demands of the id and superego. Individuals who remain relatively inflexible are those dominated by a threatening superego. The ability to evaluate a situation, to develop coping strategies, and to delay gratification of one's impulses are all functions of the ego and characterize mature moral functioning.

Children's Religious Beliefs

Do children think of God the same way adults do? Or does one find evidence of developmental changes in their understanding of God just as one does in their moral understanding? James Fowler (1981, 1991) suggests that such evidence exists. He has identified stages of religious belief that parallel the stages of moral development discussed earlier.

Schoolchildren's views of God, for instance, reflect the concrete nature of the way they think in general. To them, God is someone with a human form who sits celestially enthroned above them. They accept the teachings and stories of their religion literally and do not question them, other than to try to fit them into their current ways of understanding, such as wondering how God can be everywhere at the same time (Fowler, 1981).

Similarly, the ability to think in more abstract ways that comes with adolescence transforms children's religious beliefs. More abstract qualities of God, such

Children go through different stages of religious belief. This boy, at his bar mitzvah, may later question some of the dogma he has learned in preparation for this important Jewish rite.

as compassion, righteousness, and mercy, can be appreciated; and more sophisticated reasoning about religious practices is possible (Helwig, 1995). Adolescents also begin to question their religious beliefs, just as they question other values that they had previously taken for granted. For instance, adolescents are likely to wonder, "If God is all-powerful, why is there suffering and evil in the world?" The answers they arrive at reflect an increasingly personalized faith, much as Kohlberg's and Gilligan's final stages of morality reflect commitment to personally-arrived-at principles.

One of the first components to children's religious identity, just as with gender or ethnicity, consists in labeling, or identifying themselves in terms of a particular religious denomination. When children are asked what these labels mean, one sees evidence of a clear developmental trend to their understanding. In a series of studies, David Elkind (1961, 1962, 1963) asked Catholic, Jewish, and Protestant children how they could tell whether a person was of the same religion that they were. Irrespective of the particular religion, children's understanding of what distinguished one religion from another underwent the same developmental sequence. The youngest children, 5- to 6-year-olds, had not as yet distinguished what it meant to belong to a particular religion. For instance, when asked "What is a Protestant?" they were likely simply to answer "a person."

By middle childhood, however, children identified members of religious groups in terms of concrete behaviors and characteristics. Thus, one who is Catholic might be identified as someone who goes to Mass every Sunday, or one who is Jewish as a person who goes to temple and attends Hebrew School. Such an understanding, as Elkind points out, highlights the differences between religions. That is, if one is going to temple, one cannot also be attending Mass. One is either one religion or the other, and the two are noticeably different.

At a third stage, however, which children reach as they enter adolescence, they begin to appreciate the commonalities to different religions, understanding that one can worship God irrespective of whether one does this in a temple or a church. In this stage, children identify their religion in terms of abstract beliefs.

Thus, Jewish children might describe someone of their faith as "a person who believes in one God and doesn't believe in the New Testament," or a Protestant might describe another Protestant as "a person who believes in God and Christ and is loving to other people" (Elkind, 1961, 1962, 1963).

How important, one might ask *is* religion to children's sense of themselves? When asked to describe themselves, in other words, how likely are children to mention their religion? Rachel Royle, Martyn Barrett, and Eithne Buchanan-Barrow (1998) had children of various religions and nationalities, all of whom lived in London, sort cards into either of two boxes, one labeled "Me" and the other "Not Me." Each card identified some aspect of a single identity component, such as a child's gender, ethnicity, language, age, or religion. Once children had finished this initial sort, they were asked to go through the "Me" cards again and select the one that was most descriptive of themselves. This card was removed and they selected the next most descriptive card, continuing in this way until each of the terms had been ranked in terms of importance.

Religion emerged as a significant aspect of identity, being among those most likely to be selected as "Me." Furthermore, its importance to children's sense of themselves increased with age. Perhaps predictably, younger children (4–6 years) were more likely to identify themselves in terms of their gender. Middle children (7–8 years), on the other hand, were more likely to do so in terms of their nationality. But for older children (9–11), religion was more important, being mentioned more frequently than their sex, age, or nationality. Even so, some religions contributed to children's identity more heavily than did others, possibly reflecting the minority status they conferred. A similar trend has been found for ethnicity, in which individuals who are members of a minority are more aware of their ethnicity than are those belonging to the majority, the latter frequently not even having a sense of their own ethnicity (Phinney, 1989). So, too, with religion. For Muslims living in London, religion was more salient than it was for Christians.

When children think of religion, how do they think of God? Bradley Hertel and Michael Donahue (1995) analyzed the responses of fifth- through ninth-graders to nine descriptors of God. Two dimensions emerged. One described God in terms of love, and the second described God in terms of authority. Items related to the first of these, for instance, described God as loving someone irrespective of what that person had done, whereas those related to the second described God in terms of rules and punishing wrongdoers. Of these two dimensions, the image of God that predominated among these youth was overwhelmingly that of a loving God. This was true, by the way, for their parents as well.

Summary

The Self

In middle childhood, children develop a sense of industry, through which they come to know themselves by their accomplishments. They are ready to apprentice themselves as learners and willingly work alongside parents and teachers. A sense of inferiority can develop in those who do not persist at the things they attempt until mastery is achieved. Increases in reflectiveness, in combination with newly developing skills, lay a foundation for changes in their self-concept.

Self-Concept

Children's self-concept refers to the set of beliefs children hold about themselves. There are characteristic differences between the way older and younger children think of the self. Older children describe themselves in terms of general traits; younger children describe themselves in terms of specific behaviors. Older children describe themselves in terms of their relationships with others; younger children describe themselves in terms of their preferences and possessions. Older children's self-characterizations are more complex and tolerate inconsistencies, whereas those of younger children remain simple. Finally, children's self-concepts tend to become more realistic with age.

Self-Esteem

Self-esteem refers to children's overall positive or negative evaluation of themselves. Relationships with parents provide the foundation for self-esteem. When parents are loving, children feel lovable and develop feelings of self-worth. Children appear to first evaluate themselves in terms of overall self-worth at about the age of 8; prior to this, children differ in how they feel about themselves but do not articulate these feelings in relation to their concept of self.

Friendships

Friends are usually of the same sex, race, socioeconomic background, and grade in school, and they have the same social status with peers. The assistance children receive from each other as well as the fun they have together contribute to the quality of their relationships. Children are likely to have as many as eight or nine important friendships; different patterns of qualities characterize the relationships children have with different friends.

Peer Relations

Children's social status is fairly stable throughout the grade school years. A number of statuses can be distinguished in terms of their interactive styles. Both popular and average children are cooperative, take turns, and play well with others. Popular children tend to set the norms for their group and are able to maintain play with others for longer periods of time; others appear to have more fun when playing with them. Rejected children are more aggressive than others, both physically and verbally, are more likely to exclude others when playing, and engage in more inappropriate behavior. Neglected children, who spend most of their time in solitary play, also engage in inappropriate behavior but are not aggressive. Since these statuses appear to reflect genuine differences in skills, intervention programs need to focus on skill building.

Children who form friendships with aggressive children run the risk either of being the object of relational aggression or of being drawn into aggressive interactions with others. Victimization, just like aggression, is a relatively stable characteristic of children. Those who are likely to be victimized are children who cry easily, have poor social skills, and are submissive when attacked.

Cross-Ethnic Friendships

Interracial and interethnic friendships form when children live in integrated neighborhoods and attend integrated schools. Interracial friendships face challenges posed by different enculturation experiences. Children of different backgrounds can perceive and react to the same situation differently; misinterpretations and hurt feelings can result.

Families in Transition

Nearly half of all children will experience divorce. The impact of divorce depends on conditions in the child's life, such as age, gender, amount of marital conflict, support from family and friends, and economic stability. The effectiveness of parenting drops in the first several years following divorce, and both parental self-esteem and children's coping strategies suffer. Marital conflict, rather than divorce itself, contributes heavily to the stress children experience, but exposure to conflict need not always be negative.

Most children in single-parent families live with their mothers. Daughters fare better in single-parent families than do sons. With remarriage, daughters experience more problems than before, whereas sons experience fewer. Stepparents, usually stepfathers, report that most difficulties center on issues of authority and discipline. Role clarity facilitates interaction in stepparent families.

Children and Their Families

Even when the family structure remains stable, children's relationships with parents change in middle childhood; children and parents simply spend less time together. Not only the time parents and children spend together, but also the way they interact, changes. Parents spend less time in hands-on caretaking activities and more in monitoring activities at a distance, keeping track of where children are and whom they are with.

Several domains of authority exist within a family, and parental authority shifts in only some of them. Conflicts arise when parents and children do not agree about which issues should remain under parental authority and for how long.

The emotional climate within the family changes as emotions are transmitted from one person to another. Research on emotional transmission reveals a number of patterns. First, negative emotions are more easily transmitted than positive ones. Second, the emotions of men are more likely to affect their wives and children than vice versa. Third, emotions are more likely to flow from parents to children than from children to parents; and fourth, it is common for an emotion that is passed from one person to assume a different form in the next person.

Social-Cognitive Theory and Moral Development

Social-cognitive theory assumes that children eventually internalize controls that initially are effective only when enforced by others. In doing so, children acquire their community's standards. Age-related changes in moral thought are explained by referring to the experiences that make different forms of thought most likely at different ages. Research on variables predicting cheating supports social-cognitive theory.

Kohlberg and Moral Development: Morality as Justice

At the preconventional level of moral reasoning, individuals lack internalized standards of right and wrong; their motives are only to satisfy their needs without getting into trouble. At the conventional level of moral reasoning, individuals have internalized the standards of their community and are motivated to live according to the standards of their group. At the postconventional level of moral reasoning, individuals live according to self-derived principles rather than the conventions of their community.

Higher levels of reasoning increase with age. Although some studies find that many individuals reason at adjacent stages about different situations, critics of Kohlberg's theory argue that individuals can usually distinguish conventional from moral issues even as children.

Gilligan: An Ethic of Care

Gilligan asserts that most females think of morality more personally than do males. She finds that an ethic of care characterizes females' approach to moral decisions; this ethic emphasizes compassion and a sense of responsibility to others in contrast to the justice orientation of Kohlberg, which emphasizes reliance on reasoning and moral standards.

Gilligan traces gender differences in moral reasoning to differences in ways of viewing the self. Females define themselves in relation to others; from this comes a sense of responsibility of each to the other. Males define themselves as separate from others; the assumption of separateness highlights the need for rules to regulate the actions of each with respect to the other.

Gilligan traces moral development in females through three levels, each reflecting a different resolution to their conflict between responsibilities to themselves and to others. In Level 1 the primary concern is care for oneself. Females soon see this as selfish and move to Level 2, in which they equate morality with care of others. Only as they encounter problems that result from excluding themselves as legitimate recipients of their own care do females move on to Level 3, in which they equate morality with care both of themselves and of others.

Research finds that while a care orientation is not necessarily the approach adopted by all females it is somewhat more characteristic of females than males. Studies find that both females and males share concerns about justice and care and that individuals frequently use both orientations in thinking through a dilemma.

Freud: Morality and the Superego

Freud placed the responsibility for moral behavior in the superego, an aspect of the personality that embraces cultural standards of right and wrong. The superego develops when the young child identifies with the same-sex parent. Freud assumed the superego of females to be weaker than that of males because they are not as motivated to resolve Oedipal tensions and they identify with a less-threatening parental figure.

Despite the usefulness of Freud's theory to clinicians, his assumptions concerning gender differences in moral development have not been supported by research.

Children's Religious Beliefs

Schoolchildren's views of God reflect the concrete nature of the way they think in general. They accept the teachings and stories of their religion literally and do not question them. With age, intellectual changes make it possible for older children and adolescents to view God in new ways and to question beliefs they once accepted uncritically. As with identity status, processes of exploration and commitment determine the form beliefs will take. Religion remains important in children's lives across changes in age. One of the first components to children's religious identity, just as with gender or ethnicity, consists in labeling, or identifying themselves in terms of a particular religious denomination. By middle childhood, children identify members of religious groups in terms of distinctive behaviors and characteristics. By adolescence, they are able to appreciate the commonalities to different religions. Across all ages, children are most likely to describe God in terms of love.

Key Terms

active listening (p. 465)

conventional moral reasoning
(p. 477)

emotional transmission (p. 470)

enculturation (p. 460)

ethic of care (p. 482)

identification (p. 487)

I-message (p. 466)

industry (p. 448)

overt aggression (p. 458)

postconventional moral reasoning
(p. 478)

preconventional moral reasoning
(p. 477)

relational aggression (p. 458)

role clarity (p. 464)

superego (p. 486)

you-message (p. 466)

Appendix   CDC Growth Charts

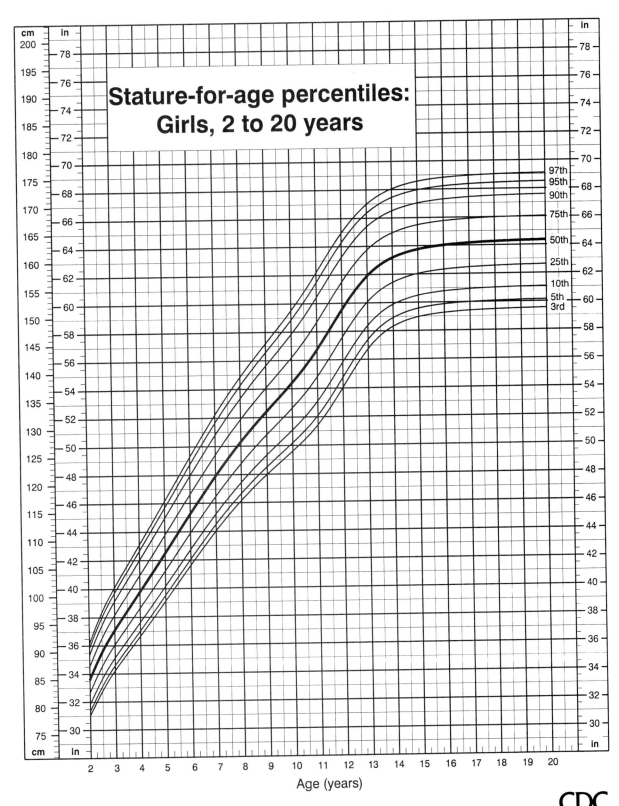

**Stature-for-age percentiles:
Girls, 2 to 20 years**

Age (years)

97th
95th
90th
75th
50th
25th
10th
5th
3rd

SOURCE: Developed by the National Center for Health Statistics in collaboration with
the National Center for Chronic Disease Prevention and Health Promotion (2000).

CDC
CENTERS FOR DISEASE CONTROL
AND PREVENTION

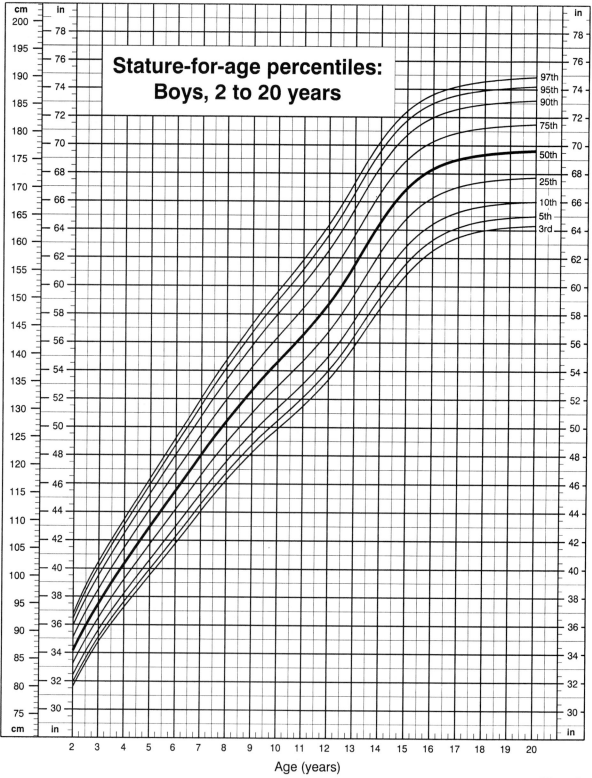

Stature-for-age percentiles:
Boys, 2 to 20 years

SOURCE: Developed by the National Center for Health Statistics in collaboration with
the National Center for Chronic Disease Prevention and Health Promotion (2000).

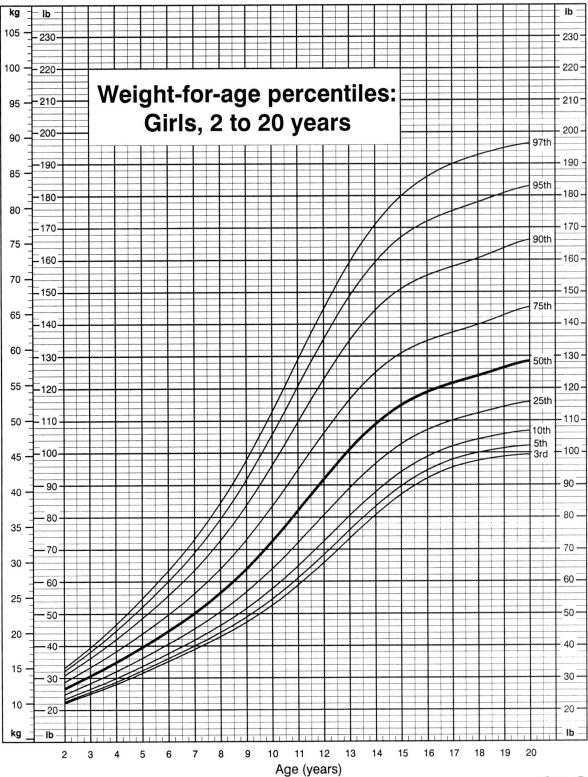

Weight-for-age percentiles: Girls, 2 to 20 years

Age (years)

SOURCE: Developed by the National Center for Health Statistics in collaboration with the National Center for Chronic Disease Prevention and Health Promotion (2000).

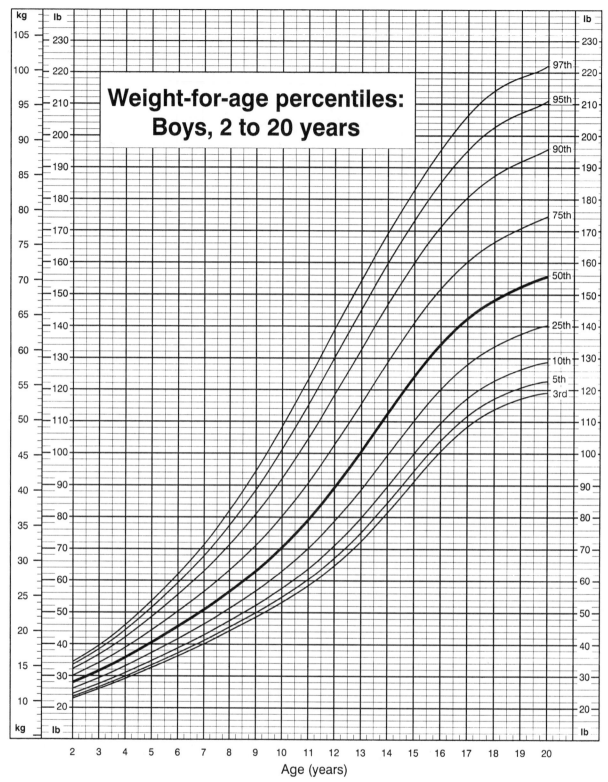

Weight-for-age percentiles:
Boys, 2 to 20 years

Age (years)

SOURCE: Developed by the National Center for Health Statistics in collaboration with
the National Center for Chronic Disease Prevention and Health Promotion (2000).

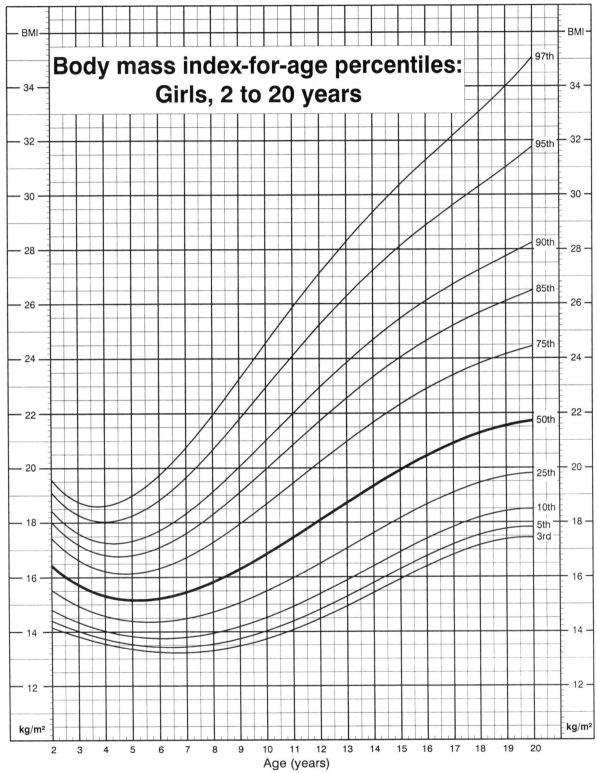

Body mass index-for-age percentiles: Girls, 2 to 20 years

Age (years)

BMI — kg/m²

SOURCE: Developed by the National Center for Health Statistics in collaboration with
the National Center for Chronic Disease Prevention and Health Promotion (2000).

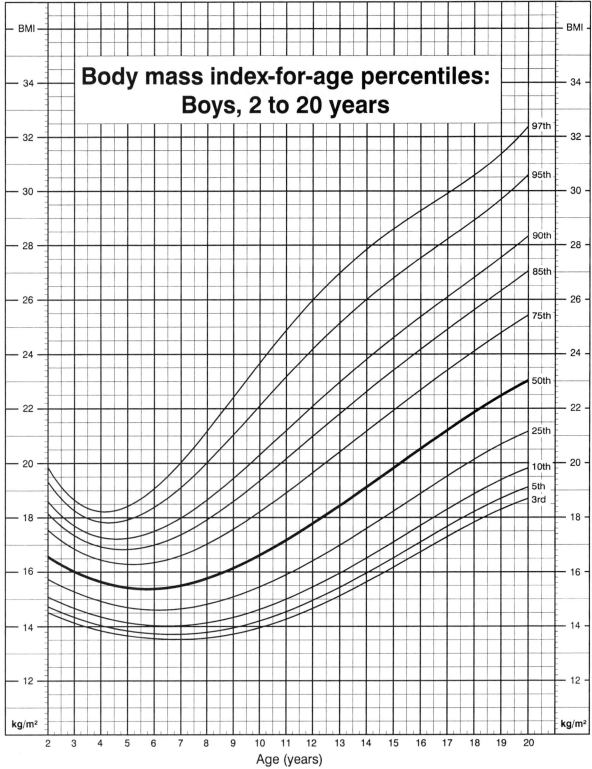

Body mass index-for-age percentiles:
Boys, 2 to 20 years

Age (years)

SOURCE: Developed by the National Center for Health Statistics in collaboration with
the National Center for Chronic Disease Prevention and Health Promotion (2000).

Glossary

academic tracking   The assignment of students to one of several courses of study in high school on the basis of criteria such as academic interests and goals, past achievement, and ability.

accommodation   Piaget's term for the process by which individuals alter cognitive structures to fit new experiences or events.

achieved ethnic identity   The final stage in ethnic identity formation; a clear sense of one's ethnicity that reflects feelings of belonging to and emotional identification with one's group.

acrosomal reaction   The release of the enzymes by the acrosome as a result of capacitation.

acrosome   The cap on the head of the sperm containing enzymes that digest the outer surface of the ovum.

activators   Proteins that facilitate the copying of DNA segments by picking up messages at regulatory sites along the DNA track and relaying them to coactivators.

active listening   A way of listening that reflects the message and feelings back to the speaker.

active sleep   A sleep state characterized by frequent body movement; also known as REM sleep because of the presence of rapid eye movements.

active wakefulness   A waking state characterized by frequent and vigorous movement.

affective disorders   Disorders whose primary symptoms reflect a disturbance of mood, such as depression.

afferent, or sensory, pathway   A series of neurons carrying impulses from the periphery (skin, muscles, joints, and internal organs) to the central nervous system.

agency   An aspect of mature functioning characterized by achievement and mastery; the complement of communion.

alleles   The complementary forms of a gene located at the same site on the autosomes that determine the expression of a particular trait.

allocentric representation   Representing the location of objects in relation to an abstract frame of reference, such as a map.

amniotic sac   A transparent, watertight membrane that develops around the embryo and is filled with amniotic fluid.

anorexia   An eating disorder characterized by severely limiting the intake of food; most common in females.

Apgar scale   A method of rating the physical state of a newborn in terms of appearance or color, heart rate, reflex irritability, muscle tone, and respiration.

ascending infections   Infections transmitted during birth; the most common are the herpes viruses and gonorrhea.

assimilation   Piaget's term for the process by which individuals fit new information into their present ways of understanding.

assumptive realities   Assumptions made on the basis of limited information.

asynchrony   Differences in the timing of pubertal changes within an adolescent, or from one adolescent to the next.

attachment   The affectional bonds that infants form with those who care for them; the ways in which infants organize their behavior around these caregivers, using them as a base from which to explore and to which to return for safety when stressed.

authoritarian parenting   A style of parenting that stresses obedience, respect for authority, and traditional values.

authoritative parenting   A style of parenting that stresses self-reliance and independence; parents are consistent, maintain an open dialogue, and give reasons when disciplining.

autobiographical memories   Memories that constitute the personal narrative that tells the story of oneself; emerges at about age 4.

automatization   Increases, with continued experience, in the efficiency with which children can engage in various mental activities.

autonomy   Being independent and responsible for one's actions.

autosomes   The 22 matching pairs of chromosomes that, together with the sex chromosomes of the 23rd pair, are found in the cell nucleus.

axioms   The unquestioned assumptions that form the basis of a theory.

axon   A long filament extending from a nerve cell, through which neural impulses are transmitted.

babbling   The production of vowel and consonant sounds by infants in the 2nd to 3rd month.

basal factors   Factors that communicate directly with RNA polymerase.

basic-skills approach   An approach to teaching reading that starts with teaching children the sounds of individual letters and how to sound out words.

bimanual coordination   The ability to use both hands simultaneously but to do different things, such as holding a paper with one hand and cutting with scissors with the other.

blastocyst   A thin-walled hollow sphere resulting from the differentiation of morula cells into the trophoblast and the inner cell mass.

body mass index (BMI)   Weight in kilograms divided by the square of a person's height in meters.

bootstrapping   A strategy children use to learn names for things through their knowledge of word classes and syntactic cues.

brain stem   The area at the base of the brain that contains the midbrain, the pons, and the medulla oblongata and controls basic functions such as breathing and heart rate.

bulimia   An eating disorder characterized by bingeing and then purging; most common in females.

capacitation   A change in the outer membrane of the sperm, triggered by chemicals in the female reproductive tract, that allows the acrosome's enzymes to be released.

cell proliferation   A brain growth process that consists of the overproduction of both neurons and their interconnections.

cell pruning   A brain growth process that consists of the selective elimination of excess cells and the cutting back of connections.

central nervous system   The brain and the spinal cord.

centration   Piaget's term for the tendency to focus on one aspect of an object to the exclusion of others; characterizes preoperational thinking.

cephalocaudal growth trend   The developmental pattern in which growth begins in the region of the head and proceeds downward.

cerebellum   A large structure located behind the cerebral cortex that coordinates sensory input and muscle responses.

cervix   The opening to the uterus.

chromosomes   Microscopic filaments within a cell nucleus carrying genetic information and composed of DNA and protein.

circumcision   Surgical removal of the prepuce covering the glans of the penis.

cleavage   The form of cell division initiated by fertilization; unlike ordinary mitosis, the cells do not double in size before dividing.

clique   A peer group made up of one's best friends, usually including no more than five or six members.

clitoris   That part of the external genitals in females that is the primary source of sexual stimulation.

coactivators   Molecules that integrate signals from activators and repressors and send them on to basal factors.

communion   An aspect of mature functioning characterized by empathy and friendship; the complement of agency.

conditional response (CR) In respondent conditioning, the reflex learned in response to a new stimulus.

conditional stimulus (CS) In respondent conditioning, the new environmental stimulus used to elicit a conditional, or reflexive, response.

connectedness A quality of family interactions thought to be important for individuation; it reflects openness to and respect for others' opinions.

conscience That part of the personality that is concerned with issues of right and wrong.

conservation The realization that something remains the same despite changes in its appearance.

constructive approach The theoretical perspective that individuals' expectations color their experiences of the world; that each individual constructs a particular reality from experience.

continuity-discontinuity issue The question of whether the same set of developmental laws applies to all stages of the life cycle and to all species (continuity assumption) or whether different laws apply to different stages and different species (discontinuity assumption).

conventional moral reasoning Kohlberg's second level of moral reasoning, in which moral thinking is guided by internalized social standards.

corpus luteum The ruptured ovarian follicle formed by the release of an ovum; important source of progesterone early in pregnancy.

Cowper's glands Glands in males that secrete a lubricating fluid that facilitates passage of sperm through the urethra.

crossing over During meiosis, the exchange of corresponding genes in homologous chromosomes; one of the sources of genetic diversity.

crowd A peer group, averaging 20 members and formed from several cliques of the same age group.

cytomegalovirus A member of the herpes family that has become the most common form of fetal viral infection.

deductive reasoning Reasoning from the general to the particular.

defining features Characteristics that identify items as members of a category.

dendrites Fibers extending from a neuron that receive input from neighboring neurons.

depression An affective disorder that may take any of three major forms, all of which are characterized by a disturbance of mood; the three forms are major depressive disorder, dysthymia, and adjustment disorder with depressed mood.

development The orderly set of changes that occur over the life span.

differentiation A developmental trend characterized by a progression from the general to the specific.

difficult infants Infants who tend to be negative in mood, irregular in their biological functioning (such as in patterns of sleeping and waking and becoming hungry), and slow to adapt to changes; a temperament type identified by Thomas and Chess.

dizygotic twins Twins who develop from two separate ova, fertilized at the same time by different sperm.

DNA Deoxyribonucleic acid, the double-stranded molecule in chromosomes that encodes genetic information.

dominant allele The gene of an allele pair that produces a particular trait.

donor insemination A fertility procedure in which sperm from a donor are injected into the birth mother's uterus at the time of ovulation.

Down syndrome A chromosomal disorder caused by an extra 21st chromosome (trisomy 21); characterized by distinctive facial features, slow motor development, and some degree of mental retardation.

drowsiness A state of either falling asleep or waking up when the body is relaxed, breathing is regular, and the eyes have a dreamy stare.

easy infants Infants who tend to be cheerful and playful, regular in their biological functioning (such as in patterns of sleeping and waking and becoming hungry), and able to adapt easily to changes; a temperament type identified by Thomas and Chess.

ecological self The self that is directly perceived in terms of one's ongoing actions.

ectoderm The outer layer of the inner cell mass, which will develop into the outer layer of skin, the nervous system, and the sensory organs.

efferent, or motor, pathway   A series of neurons carrying impulses from the central nervous system to the periphery (skin, muscles, joints, and internal organs).

egg and sperm donation   A fertility procedure in which donor sperm are used to fertilize donor ova, and the resulting embryo is inserted into the birth mother's uterus.

egg donation   A fertility procedure in which an ovum removed from a donor woman is fertilized with the father's sperm, and the resulting embryo is inserted into the birth mother's uterus.

ego   In psychoanalytic theory, the executive aspect of the personality that attempts to satisfy impulses in socially acceptable ways.

egocentric representation   Representing the location of objects in relation to oneself; typical of young children's subjective understanding of space.

egocentrism   The failure to realize that one's perspective is not shared by others.

Electra complex   A Freudian concept in which the young girl is sexually attracted to her father.

emotional transmission   Transference of emotions from one person to another, especially in a family, through daily interactions.

encoding   The formation of mental representations for one's experience.

enculturation   Acquiring the norms of one's social group.

endocrine system   The system of the body that includes the glands that produce hormones and those parts of the nervous system that activate, inhibit, and control hormone production.

endoderm   The inner layer of the inner cell mass, which will develop into the digestive and respiratory tracts and internal glands and organs.

endometrium   The inner lining of the uterus.

enuresis   Bed-wetting.

epididymis   A mass of coiled tubes near the top of each testis that receives the sperm produced by the testes.

epigenesis   At each stage of development, the emergence of new complexities that cannot be predicted from, or reduced to, earlier forms.

epigenetic principle   Erikson's assumption that an internal plan governs the timing or period of ascendance for each new development.

epiphyseal growth plates   In a child, areas near the ends of a bone that produce new cells.

episiotomy   An incision made in the mother's vaginal opening to prevent tearing of the tissue during delivery.

equilibration   Piaget's term for the balance between assimilation and accommodation that is responsible for the growth of thought.

estrogens   Sex hormones produced primarily by the ovaries.

ethic of care   Gilligan's description of a morality based on responsiveness to and care for others.

ethnic identity   An awareness of belonging to an ethnic group that shapes one's thoughts, feelings, and behavior.

ethnic identity search   The intermediate state in ethnic identity formation; exploration of the meaning of one's ethnicity.

ethnographic field study   Observational research conducted in natural settings that facilitates the study of the unique contributions of the social groups to which individuals belong.

experience-dependent mechanisms   Neural processes that enable the organism to establish new connections between neurons when exposed to unique experiences.

experience-expectant mechanisms   Neural processes, such as those specialized for language use or for pattern detection, that enable the organism to respond to common environmental stimuli.

extended self   The self that includes not only what one is doing at the present moment but also memories of one's past experiences and imaginings about one's future.

factor analysis   A statistical procedure designed to identify underlying dimensions, or factors, that account for the relationship among several variables.

Fallopian tubes   The tubes that feed into either side of the uterus from the ovaries; also called oviducts.

fast mapping   Children's ability to map the meaning of a new word onto a referent after hearing the word used in context just once.

female genital mutilation   Removal of the clitoris, the primary source of sexual stimulation in females, and of the inner labia, and sewing shut most of the outer labia (sometimes inaccurately referred to as female circumcision).

fetal alcohol effects (FAE)   A pattern of disabilities related to, but less severe than, fetal alcohol syndrome.

fetal alcohol syndrome (FAS)   A pattern of disabilities, including mental retardation, low birthweight, heart defects, and atypical facial features, resulting from consumption of alcohol during pregnancy.

flow   The experience of becoming totally absorbed in a challenging activity.

fontanels   In an infant, gaps between the bony plates of the skull.

formal operational thought   Piaget's fourth stage of intellectual development, assumed to characterize adolescence and adulthood, during which mental operations are extended to include thoughts in addition to concrete objects.

gametes   Sperm and ova, which, when mature, have 23 individual instead of 23 pairs of chromosomes.

gastrulation   The formation of three layers of embryonic cells: the ectoderm, the mesoderm, and the endoderm.

gender differences   Culturally determined differences in masculinity and femininity.

gender identity   Experience of oneself as male or female.

gender labeling   The ability to label oneself as a boy or girl; develops by about age 2.

gender schemas   Cognitive structures that direct the pickup of information about the self as it relates to one's gender.

gender stereotyping   Culturally based expectations of behaviors that are appropriate for each sex.

genes   Short segments of the DNA strand, responsible for transmission of particular traits; thousands of genes are carried within each chromosome.

genotype   The total set of genes inherited at conception.

glial cells   Cells that support and nourish neurons and produce myelin.

gonads   The sex glands; the ovaries in females and the testes in males.

gonorrhea   A sexually transmitted bacterial infection that can be transmitted to an infant during birth and can lead to blindness; damage can be averted with preventive measures at birth.

grasp reflex   Spontaneously grasping an object pressed against the palm of the hand.

growth   The result of metabolic processes in which proteins are broken down and used to make new cells.

growth spurt   A period of rapid growth that occurs during puberty.

guided participation   Rogoff's term for the shared activity of a novice and one who is more skilled, in which both participate to decrease the distance between their respective contributions to the activity; an extension of Vygotsky's zone of proximal development that assumes a more active role for the learner.

habituation   Decreased responsiveness to a stimulus with repeated exposure to it.

hand dominance   The superiority of one hand to the other for doing such things as throwing a ball, writing, or using a fork; occurs at the time of brain lateralization.

hand preference   The tendency to use one hand instead of the other to do such things as throw a ball, write, or use a fork, even when marked superiority is not apparent with the preferred hand.

hedgehog genes   Genes that direct the manufacture of morphogens.

hepatitis B   A virus that can cause liver failure, jaundice, and fever in infected infants.

herpes   A viral infection that can be transmitted during birth; can damage the central nervous system.

holophrase   A single word used to represent a phrase or sentence; typical of the first stage of language acquisition.

hormones   Chemical messengers that are secreted directly into the bloodstream and are regulated by the endocrine system.

human immunodeficiency virus (HIV)   Can be transmitted by an infected mother to her fetus; the risk of transmission can be reduced with drug therapy.

hypothalamus   A center within the brain that regulates hormonal activity and regulatory activities such as eating, drinking, and body temperature.

id   In psychoanalytic theory, the aspect of the personality that demands immediate gratification of biological impulses; operates according to the pleasure principle.

identification   The child's uncritical internalization of parental behaviors and attitudes.

identity achievement   The resolution of conflict over identity through the personal formulation of adult gender roles, occupational goals, and religious and political commitments.

identity diffusion   A failure to develop a strong sense of self coupled with a failure to experience much discomfort or conflict over the issues of identity resolution.

identity foreclosure   A resolution of the problem of identity through the assumption of traditional, conventional, or parentally chosen goals and values without the experience of crisis or conflict concerning identity issues.

identity formation   In adolescence, a synthesizing of elements of one's earlier identity into a new whole; involves individuation.

imaginary audience   The illusion of being the focus of attention; assumed to be due both to adolescents' ability to think about thought in others and to their confusing the concerns of others with their preoccupation with themselves.

I-message   A message that tells the listener how his or her actions make one feel.

individuality   A quality of family interactions thought to be important for individuation, reflecting the ability to express one's ideas and say how one differs from others.

individuation   The process of distinguishing one's attitudes and beliefs from those of one's parents.

inductive reasoning   Reasoning from the particular to the general.

indulgent parenting   A style of parenting characterized by warmth and nurturance but little supervision.

industry versus inferiority   Erikson's term for the sense of accomplishment that comes from being able to make things and that comes with doing things well.

in-hand manipulation   The ability to move an object around in one hand without the help of the other hand, such as moving a crayon from the palm of the hand to the fingertips.

initiative   The term used by Erik Erikson for a child's sense of purposefulness and effectiveness.

inner cell mass   The group of cells in the blastocyst from which the embryo is formed.

intelligence   The ability to profit from experience and adapt to one's surroundings; measured by intelligence tests.

intentionality model   Lois Bloom's model of language development, which assumes that the impetus for language development is the growth of the child's mind rather than the conversational skills of the adult.

in vitro fertilization   A fertility procedure in which ova are taken from the birth mother and fertilized in a laboratory with sperm from the father.

isolate   A term for adolescents who have few friends, either within a clique or outside it, and who have few links to other adolescents in the social network.

jargon babbling   Babbling that reproduces the intonation, rhythmic structure, and pitch of speech.

jigsaw classroom   A classroom organized into small, ethnically balanced working groups in which each student contributes a different part of the lesson.

Klinefelter's syndrome   A genetic disorder in males caused by an extra X chromosome; symptoms include small testes, insufficient production of testosterone, and infertility.

landmark representation   Representing the location of objects in relation to environmental landmarks.

lanugo   Fine, downy hair that covers the skin of the fetus.

lateralization   The process of specialization of the two halves of the cortex.

laws   Relationships that are derived from axioms and that can be proven to be true or false.

liaison   A term for adolescents who have friends in several cliques but who do not themselves belong to any one clique.

libido   In psychoanalytic theory, the psychic energy that is expressed through different zones of the body and motivates much of behavior.

long-term memory   The form of memory in which information is semantically encoded, or stored according to meaning, for later retrieval.

low birthweight   Weight of less than 5½ pounds, or 2,500 g, at birth.

male generic language   Use of the pronoun he to refer to an individual of either sex and use of words such as man or mankind to refer to all people.

maltreatment   Nonaccidental and avoidable harm done to children, whether from abuse or neglect.

mean length of utterance (MLU)   The average number of morphemes in a child's sentences.

meiosis   The process of cell division in which sex cells mature, reducing the number of chromosomes from 23 pairs to 23 individual chromosomes.

membrane depolarization   The neutralization of the surface polarity of the ovum after a sperm succeeds in fusing with the ovum's membrane; this change bars entrance by other sperm.

menarche   The occurrence of a girl's first menstrual period.

mental operations   Piaget's term for actions that can be carried out in one's head and then reversed or undone.

mesoderm   The middle layer of the inner cell mass; it will develop into the muscles, bones, and circulatory, excretory, and reproductive systems.

messenger RNA (mRNA)   The form of ribonucleic acid (RNA) that carries genetic codes from the DNA in the cell nucleus to the sites of protein synthesis in the cytoplasm.

metamemory   The awareness of one's memory and of those factors that affect it.

mitosis   The process of cell division in which body cells replicate; the chromosomes of each new cell are identical to those of the parent cell.

model   A set of assumptions about reality and human nature from which theories proceed.

monozygotic twins   Twins who develop from the same fertilized ovum, or zygote.

moratorium   The experience of conflict over the issues of identity formation prior to the establishment of firm goals and long-term commitments.

Moro reflex   A reflex in infants in response to a sudden loss of support or loud noise, in which they arch their back, throw their arms out, and quickly bring them in.

morphemes   The units of language that communicate meaning.

morphogens   Proteins that tag different embryonic cells for different functions.

morula   A solid cluster of cells resulting from the cleavage of a fertilized ovum.

multiple regression   A statistical technique designed to investigate the relationship between a set of predictor variables and an outcome variable.

multiply determined   Of characteristics that are the result of many contributing factors.

myelin   A fatty substance that coats axons and increases the speed of conduction of nerve impulses.

nature-nurture controversy   The controversy concerning whether heredity (nature) or the environment (nurture) is primarily responsible for development.

negative reinforcement   An event that increases the frequency of the behavior on which its removal is made contingent.

neglectful parenting   A style of parenting characterized by little warmth, nurturing, or supervision.

neurons   Brain cells responsible for the conduction of nerve impulses.

neurotransmitters   Chemicals released into the synapse that mediate the transmission of impulses.

nocturnal emission   A spontaneous ejaculation of seminal fluid during sleep; sometimes called a wet dream.

normally distributed   Frequency distributions in which most scores cluster around the middle, or the mean, in the shape of a bell curve.

nucleotides   Subunits of DNA consisting of a sugar molecule, a phosphate molecule, and a nitrogenous base.

obesity   A condition in which one weighs more than 30% above one's ideal body weight.

observational learning   In social-cognitive theory, learning by observing what others do and imitating what one sees.

Oedipal complex   A Freudian concept in which the young boy is sexually attracted to his mother.

operant conditioning   A simple form of learning in which the probability of a behavior is affected by its consequences.

outer cell mass   The outer layer of cells (the trophoblast) of the blastocyst that will develop into tissues supporting the developing organism.

ovaries   Structures within the female reproductive system flanking the uterus that house the ova and produce female sex hormones.

overextension   A child's use of a word to refer not only to all members of the group that the word labels for adults but also to other referents.

overt aggression   Hostility expressed in physical acts such as hitting, punching, and kicking.

overweight   A condition in which children are at or above the 85th percentile of weight for their height.

ovum (plural, ova)   The female sex cell, or gamete.

penis   The part of the external genitals in males that is the primary source of sexual stimulation.

penis envy   A Freudian concept in which the young girl longs for a penis.

peripheral nervous system   That part of the nervous system that connects the sensory receptors and muscles and glands and internal organs to the central nervous system.

personal fable   The feeling of being different and special; thought to derive from the imaginary audience.

phenotype   The observable or measurable characteristics of an organism, resulting from the interaction between the genotype and the environment.

phonemes   The smallest distinguishable units of sound in a language.

pituitary   An endocrine gland located beneath the hypothalamus that is part of a feedback system regulating the hormonal control of puberty.

placenta   A spongy mass of tissue attached to the uterine lining and connected to the embryo by the umbilical cord from which the fetus receives oxygen and nutrients and through which waste products are excreted.

plasticity   The degree to which one area of the brain can assume the functions governed by another area following injury to the latter.

positive reinforcement   An event that increases the frequency of the behavior on which its occurrence is made contingent.

postconventional moral reasoning   Kohlberg's third level of moral reasoning, in which moral thinking is guided by self-derived principles.

preconventional moral reasoning   Kohlberg's first level of moral reasoning, characterized by the absence of internalized standards.

preoperational thought   Piaget's second stage of intellectual development, thought to characterize toddlerhood and early childhood, during which experience is represented symbolically.

preterm   Infants born more than 3 weeks before the due date.

primary circular reactions   Substage 2 of Piaget's sensorimotor stage in which infants (1–4 months) repeat a physical behavior involving their own body.

primary motor cortex   The area of the cortex responsible for governing voluntary movement of discrete muscles.

primary sex characteristics   Sex differences in the reproductive system that develop during puberty.

prostate gland   A structure at the base of the urethra in males that is involved in producing sperm.

protective factors   Factors that counter risk factors and reduce the probability of undesirable developmental results.

proximity seeking   An infant's attempts to stay close to the mother and follow after her, asking to be picked up or attempting to crawl into her lap; a behavior seen during the clear-cut attachment phase.

proximodistal growth trend   The developmental pattern in which growth progresses outward from the center of the body to the extremities.

pseudostupidity   The inability to see the obvious by making a simple task more complicated than it is; believed to derive from the ability to think hypothetically and consider a problem from all possible perspectives.

quiet sleep   A sleep state characterized by relative inactivity except for brief startles; there are no rapid eye movements (REM); also known as NREM (non-REM) sleep.

quiet wakefulness   A waking state in which an infant is relaxed and attentive and moves its body little.

rapid eye movements (REM)   Rapid movements of the eyes beneath closed lids during certain sleep stages.

recessive allele   The gene of an allele pair that governs the expression of a trait only in the presence of another recessive allele.

reductionism   The explanation of complex behaviors by reducing them to their simpler components.

reflective abstraction   Piaget's term for the process in which features of actions become abstracted, turning the actions into thought.

regression   Movement from a more complex, differentiated state to one that is less so, with decreases in the adaptiveness of behavior.

regulatory genes   Genes in the DNA strand that regulate which genes are copied.

rehearsal   Repeating items to be memorized; a common strategy for retaining items in short-term memory

reinforcement   An event that, when it is made contingent on behavior, increases the frequency of that behavior.

relational aggression   Hostility expressed in acts manipulating the relationship, such as divulging secrets or spreading lies.

REM smiles   Early smiles in infants prompted by changes in brain-wave activity in the brain stem.

repression   A defense mechanism that operates by relegating distressful thoughts and feelings to the unconscious.

repressors   Proteins that inhibit the copying of DNA segments by picking up messages at regulatory sites along the DNA track and relaying them to coactivators.

resilient   Able to recover readily from illness, change, or misfortune.

respondent conditioning   A simple form of learning in which an involuntary reflex is brought under the control of another environmental stimulus.

risk factors   Factors associated with an increased rate of undesirable behavior or disease.

RNA polymerase   An enzyme that copies DNA into messenger RNA during the transcription process.

role clarity   An understanding among family members about each one's role.

rooting reflex   Turning the head and starting to suck in response to a brush on the cheek; an adaptive reflex in infants.

rubella   German measles; once a common cause of birth defects in the United States.

"rules" for scanning   Patterns of scanning used by infants to actively search for things in their visual field.

scaffolding model   A model of language development that assumes that the impetus for language development is adults' initiation of conversation and providing of a scaffold, or structure, to support the emergence of new language forms.

schemas   Piaget's term for the mental structures through which the child represents experience through actions.

scripts   Schematic representations of familiar routines used by young children to organize and recall everyday events.

scrotum   The sac that hangs just beneath the penis and houses the testes.

secondary circular reactions   Substage 3 of Piaget's sensorimotor stage in which infants (4–8 months) repeat behaviors affecting objects outside their body.

secondary motor cortex   The area of the cortex responsible for voluntary patterned movements of groups of muscles.

secondary sex characteristics   Differences between females and males in body structure and appearance, other than differences in the reproductive system; include differences in skeletal structure, hair distribution, and skin texture.

secular trend The earlier onset of puberty, faster growth, and the differences in size, both in height and in weight reached by adolescents today than in the past.

secure base The use of the caregiver by infants as a base from which to venture forth to explore and to periodically return for comfort and reassurance.

self-disclosure The sharing or exchange of personal information; considered a primary basis for the development of intimacy.

semen A milky white fluid in which sperm are suspended.

seminal vesicles Structures within the male reproductive system in which sperm are stored.

sensitivity The ability to accurately "read" an infant's signals; a behavior related to the attachment relationship.

sensorimotor stage Piaget's first stage of intellectual development, during which sensory experiences are coordinated with motor behaviors.

sensory memory A very brief form of memory, lasting for less than a second, that is used during the processing of information.

separation anxiety The evident distress infants experience when the mother or other caregiver is out of sight; a behavior seen during the clear-cut attachment phase.

sex chromosomes The 23rd pair of chromosomes that determine the sex of the child; females have two X chromosomes, and males have one X and one Y chromosome.

sex constancy The understanding that one's sex remains the same and will not change as a function of how one looks or dresses; also termed gender constancy.

sex differences Biological and physiological differences distinguishing the sexes.

short-term memory The form of memory used for immediate tasks; its capacity is about seven items at one time; also known as working memory.

slow-to-warm infants Infants who have low activity levels, give mild reactions, are slow to adapt to changes,

tend to withdraw from new situations, and react to situations in a mild way; a temperament type identified by Thomas and Chess.

small for gestational age (SGA) Low-birthweight infants who weigh less than 90% of the infants of the same gestational age.

smegma A thick secretion that collects around the glans in males and under the prepuce.

social capital The relationships, both within the family and the community, that contribute to resiliency in children.

social referencing Checking with a caregiver or other familiar figure for cues about how to respond to a new or ambiguous event.

social smiling Smiling in response to what is taking place around one; expression of emotion that begins between 4 and 6 weeks.

sperm The male sex cell, or gamete.

spermarche A boy's first ejaculation of seminal fluid.

stage A level of development that is assumed to be qualitatively different from the earlier level from which it evolves. Stages are assumed to occur in a fixed sequence and to occur universally within a species.

standard deviation A standardized unit that expresses the average variability among scores.

strange situation A procedure used by Mary Ainsworth to assess differences in attachment security: The mother sits with the infant in a comfortable room until a stranger enters; she and the stranger talk a while and she leaves when the infant is not looking, leaving the infant alone with the stranger.

strategy Any activity that is consciously used to improve one's performance or attain a goal.

structural genes Genes in the DNA strand that provide the codes for the construction of new proteins.

sucking reflex Sucking in response to a touch on the mouth; an adaptive reflex in infants.

sudden infant death syndrome (SIDS) Also called crib death, the principal cause of death in infants from the 1st month to the 1st year of life; smoking during pregnancy increases the risk.

superego In psychoanalytic theory, the aspect of the personality that represents the internalized standards and values of society and emerges when the child identifies with the parent of its own sex.

surfactant A substance that lines the air pockets in the lungs.

surrogate birth mother A woman who becomes pregnant usually by artificial insemination or surgical implantation of a fertilized egg for the purpose of carrying the fetus for another woman.

syphilis A sexually transmitted bacterial infection that can cause damage to the central nervous system and to developing organs and bones; easily treated with antibiotics.

temperament Underlying predispositions contributing to an infant's activity level, emotionality, and sociability.

teratogens Agents that interfere with normal prenatal development.

tertiary circular reactions Substage 5 of Piaget's sensorimotor stage in which infants (12–18 months) begin to experiment with different ways of accomplishing something; the beginning of problem solving.

testes Structures within the male reproductive system contained in the scrotum that produce sperm and male sex hormones.

testosterone A sex hormone produced by the testes.

theory A set of testable statements derived from the axioms of a model.

toxoplasmosis A parasitic disease, often transmitted in cat feces, that can cause birth defects if the mother is infected during the first trimester.

transfer RNA (tRNA) The form of ribonucleic acid (RNA) that carries amino acids to the cytoplasm, where proteins are assembled according to the genetic code carried by the messenger RNA.

transition The phase of labor when uterine contractions reach a peak and the cervix is nearly completely dilated.

transplacental infections Infections of the fetus due to organisms that initially infect the mother and then cross the placenta.

trophoblast The outer layer of blastocyst cells from which develop the tissues that support the developing organism.

Turner's syndrome A rare genetic disorder in females caused by the absence of one X chromosome; characterized by a distinctive physical appearance (such as webbing of the neck and drooping eyelids) and failure of the ovaries to develop.

umbilical cord The cord connecting the embryo to the placenta through which oxygenated blood and nutrients are carried to the organism, and waste products are removed.

unconditional response (UCR) In respondent conditioning, the reflexive response to a particular stimulus.

unconditional stimulus (UCS) In respondent conditioning, the stimulus that triggers a reflexive, or unconditional, response.

underextension A child's use of a word to refer to only some but not all of the instances for which it is used by adults.

unexamined ethnic identity The initial stage in ethnic identity formation; a lack of awareness of the issues related to one's ethnicity; a simple internalization of the values of the dominant culture.

urethra The urinary canal, leading from the bladder to the urethral opening.

uterus A muscular enclosure at the top of the vagina that holds the fetus during pregnancy.

vagina The muscular tube in females leading from the labia at its opening to the uterus.

vas deferens Long coiled tube that carries sperm to the seminal vesicles, where they are stored.

vernix A protective white, greasy coating that covers the skin of the fetus.

visual acuity Ability to see fine detail.

vocabulary explosion The rapid addition of new words to a toddler's vocabulary; usually occurs late in the 2nd year.

WAIS-R   An intelligence scale for adults that is individually administered.

whole-language approach   An approach to teaching reading that starts by exposing children to contexts where reading is important in order to engage their interest so that they will be motivated to attempt to read and discover the basic principles of reading.

XYY syndrome   A genetic disorder in males caused by an extra Y chromosome; symptoms may include above-average stature, speech delays, learning disabilities, some degree of mental retardation, and behavior disturbance; also known as polysome Y syndrome.

yolk sac   A sac outside the body of the embryo that produces blood cells until the embryo's liver, spleen, and bone marrow are sufficiently developed to take over this function.

you-message   A message communicating what you think of another person.

zona reaction   A release of granular particles and enzymes beneath the ovum's outer membrane, triggered by the sperm's fusion with the ovum's membrane, that affects the membrane's ability to bind with sperm.

zone of proximal development   Vygotsky's term for the closeness between a person's current performance and what it might optimally be; readiness to learn something new.

zygote   A single cell resulting from the union of the ovum and sperm at conception.

References

Aboud, F. E. (1987). The development of ethnic self-identification and attitudes. In J. S. Phinney & M. J. Rotheram (Eds.), *Children's ethnic socialization*. Beverly Hills, CA: Sage.

Acredolo, L. P. (1978). The development of spatial orientation in infancy. *Developmental Psychology, 14*, 224–234.

Acredolo, L. P., & Hake, J. L. (1982). Infant perception. In B. J. Wolman (Ed.), *Handbook of developmental psychology*. Englewood Cliffs, NJ: Prentice-Hall.

Adler, N., Smith, L., & Tschann, J. (1998). Abortion among adolescents. In L. Beckman & S. Harvey (Eds.), *The new Civil War*. Washington, DC: American Psychological Association.

Ahlsten, G., Cnattinguis, S., & Lindmark, G. (1993). Cessation of smoking during pregnancy improves fetal growth and reduces infant morbidity in the neonatal period: A population-based prospective study. *Acta Paediatrica, 82*, 177–181.

Aiken, L. R. (1987). *Assessment of intellectual functioning*. Boston: Allyn & Bacon.

Ainsworth, M. D. S. (1973). The development of infant-mother attachment. In B. M. Caldwell & H. N. Ricciuti (Eds.), *Review of child development research* (Vol. 3). Chicago: University of Chicago Press.

Ainsworth, M. D. S. (1985). Attachments across the lifespan. *Bulletin of the New York Academy of Medicine, 61*, 791–812.

Ainsworth, M. D. S. (1993). Attachment as related to mother-infant interaction. In C. Rovee-Collier & L. P. Lipsett (Eds.), *Advances in infancy research* (Vol. 8). Norwood, NJ: Ablex.

Ainsworth, M. D. S., & Bell, S. M. (1969). Some contemporary patterns of mother-infant interaction in the feeding situation. In A. Ambrose (Ed.), *Stimulation in early infancy*. New York: Academic Press.

Ainsworth, M. D. S., Blehar, M. C., Waters, E., & Wall, S. (1978). *Patterns of attachment: A psychological study of the strange situation*. Hillsdale, NJ: Erlbaum.

Ainsworth, M. D. S., & Marvin, R. S. (1995). On the shaping of attachment theory and research: An interview with Mary D. S. Ainsworth (Fall 1994). In E. Waters, B. E. Vaughn, G. Posada, & K. Kondo-Ikemura (Eds.), Caregiving, cultural, and cognitive perspectives on secure-base behavior and working models: New growing points of attachment theory and research. *Monographs of the Society for Research in Child Development*, Serial No. 244, 60, Nos. 2–3.

Aitken, D., & Chaplin, J. (1990). Sex miseducation. *Family Therapy Networker, 14*, 24–25.

Akers, J. F., Jones, R. M., & Coyl, D. D. (1998). Adolescent friendship pairs: Similarities in identity status development, behaviors, attitudes, and intentions. *Journal of Adolescent Research, 13*, 178–201.

Alibali, M. W. (1999). How children change their minds: Strategy change can be gradual or abrupt. *Developmental Psychology, 35*, 127–145.

Allen, K. E., & Marotz, L. (1989). *Developmental profiles: Birth to six*. Albany, NY: Delmar.

Almeida, D. M., Wethington, E., & Chandler, A. L. (1999). Daily transmission of tensions between marital dyads and parent-child dyads. *Journal of Marriage and the Family, 61*, 49–61.

Als, H. (1995). The preterm infant: A model for the study of fetal brain expectation. In J. P. Lecanuet, W. P. Fifer, N. A. Krasnegor, & W. P. Smotherman (Eds.), *Fetal development: A psychobiological perspective* (pp. 439–471). Hillsdale, NJ: Erlbaum.

Amato, P. R. (1993). Children's adjustment to divorce: Theories, hypotheses and empirical support. *Journal of Marriage and the Family, 55*, 23–38.

Amato, P. R., & Gilbreth, J. G. (1999). Nonresident fathers and children's well-being: A meta-analysis. *Journal of Marriage and the Family, 61*, 557–573.

Ambler, J. S. (1994). Who benefits from school choice: Some evidence from Europe. *Journal of Policy Analysis and Management, 13*, 454–476.

American Psychiatric Association. (1985). Functional enuresis. In *Diagnostic and statistical manual of mental disorders III-R*. Washington, DC: Author.

American Psychiatric Association. (1994). *Diagnostic and statistical manual of mental disorders* (4th ed.). Washington, DC: Author.

Ampofo-Boateng, K., Thomson, J. A., Grieve, R., Pitcairn, T., Lee, D. N., & Demetre, J. D. (1993). A developmental and training study of children's ability to find safe routes to cross the road. *British Journal of Developmental Psychology, 11*, 31–45.

Ansuini, C. G., Fiddler-Woite, J., & Woite, R. S. (1996). The source, accuracy, and impact of initial sexuality information on lifetime wellness. *Adolescence, 31*, 283–289.

Archer, S. L. (1985). Career and/or family: The identity process for adolescent girls. *Youth and Society, 16*, 289–314.

Archer, S. L. (1989a). Gender differences in identity development: Issues of process, domain, and timing. *Journal of Adolescence, 12*, 117–138.

Archer, S. L. (1989b). The status of identity: Reflections on the need for intervention. *Journal of Adolescence, 12*, 345–359.

Archer, S. L. (1992). A feminist's approach to identity research. In G. R. Adams, T. P. Gullotta, & R. Montemayor (Eds.), *Adolescent identity formation*. Newbury Park, CA: Sage.

Arduini, D., Rizzo, G., & Romanini, C. (1995). Fetal behavioral states and behavioral transitions in normal and compromised fetuses. In J. P. Lecanuet, W. P. Fifer, N. A. Krasnegor, & W. P. Smotherman (Eds.), *Fetal development: A psychobiological perspective* (pp. 83–99). Hillsdale, NJ: Erlbaum.

Arehart, D. M., & Smith, P. H. (1990). Identity in adolescence: Influences of dysfunction and psychosocial task issues. *Journal of Youth and Adolescence, 19*, 36–72.

Arey, L. B. (1954). *Developmental anatomy*. Philadelphia: W. B. Saunders.

Armstrong, D. F., Stokoe, W. C., & Wilcox, S. E. (1995). *Gesture and the nature of language*. Cambridge: Cambridge University Press.

Arnett, J. J., & Taber, S. (1994). Adolescence terminable and interminable: When does adolescence end? *Journal of Youth and Adolescence, 23*, 517–537.

Artman, L., & Cahan, S. (1993). Schooling and the development of transitive inference. *Developmental Psychology, 29*, 753–759.

Asher, S. R. (1983). Social competence and peer status: Recent advances and future directions. *Child Development, 54*, 1427–1434.

Asher, S. R., Markell, R. A., & Hymel, S. (1981). Identifying children at risk in peer relations: A critique of the rate-of-interaction approach to assessment. *Child Development, 52*, 1239–1245.

Bahrick, L. E., Walker, A. S., & Neisser, U. (1981). Selective looking by infants. *Cognitive Psychology, 13*, 877-890.

Baillargeon, R. (1987). Object permanence in 3½- and 4½-month-old infants. *Developmental Psychology, 23*, 655–664.

Bakan, D. (1966). *The duality of human existence: Isolation and communion in Western man*. Boston: Beacon Press.

Baldwin, D. A., Markman, E. M., Bill, B., Desjardins, N., Irwin, J. M., & Tidball, G. (1996). Infants' reliance on a social criterion for establishing word-object relations. *Child Development, 67*, 3135–3153.

Ball, E. W. (1997). Phonological awareness: Implications for whole language and emergent literacy programs. *Topics in Language Disorders, 17*, 14–26.

Bandura, A. (1977). *Social learning theory*. Englewood Cliffs, NJ: Prentice-Hall.

Bandura, A. (1980). Self-referent thought: A developmental analysis of self-efficacy. In J. H. Flavell & L. D. Ross (Eds.), *Cognitive social development: Frontiers and possible futures*. New York: Cambridge University Press.

Bandura, A., Ross, D., & Ross, S. A. (1963). Imitation of film-mediated aggressive models. *Journal of Abnormal and Social Psychology, 66*, 3–11.

Banks, C. A. McG. (1993). Restructuring schools for equity: What we have learned in two decades. *Phi Delta Kappan, 75*, 42–48.

Banks, J. A. (1993). Multicultural education: Development, dimensions, and challenges. *Phi Delta Kappan, 75*, 22–28.

Bardwick, J. M., & Douvan, E. (1971). Ambivalence: The socialization of women. In V. Gornick & B. K. Moran (Eds.), *Women in sexist society*. New York: Basic Books.

Barkley, R. A. (1990). *Attention deficit hyperactivity disorder: A handbook for diagnosis and treatment*. New York: Guilford Press.

Barnard, K. E., Morisset, C. E., & Spieker, S. (1993). Preventive interventions: Enhancing parent-infant relationships. In C. H. Zeanah, Jr. (Ed.), *Handbook of infant development*. New York: Guilford Press.

Barnett, W. S. (1992). Benefits of compensatory preschool education. *Journal of Human Resources, 27*, 279–312.

Barnett, W. S. (1995). Long-term effects of early childhood programs on cognitive and school outcomes. *The Future of Children, 5*, 25–50.

Baron, J. B., & Sternberg R. J. (1987). *Teaching thinking skills: Theory and practice*. New York: Freeman.

Barrera, M., Jr., Chassin, L., & Rogosch, F. (1993). Effects of social support and conflict on adolescent children of alcoholic and nonalcoholic fathers. *Journal of Personality and Social Psychology, 64*, 602–612.

Barrett, K. C. (1995). A functionalist approach to shame and guilt. In J. P. Tangney & K. W. Fischer, (Eds.), *Self-conscious emotions: The psychology of shame, guilt, embarrassment, and pride* (pp. 25–63). New York: Guilford Press.

Barrett, K. C., Zahn-Waxler, C., & Cole, P. M. (1993). Avoiders vs. amenders: Implications for the investigation of guilt and shame during toddlerhood? *Cognition and Emotion, 7*, 481–505.

Barrett, M. (1995). Early lexical development. In P. Fletcher & B. MacWhinney (Eds.), *The handbook of child language* (pp. 362–392). Oxford: Blackwell.

Barth, R. P., Fetro, J. V., Leland, N., & Volkan, K. (1992). Preventing adolescent pregnancy with social and cognitive skills. *Journal of Adolescent Research, 7*, 208–232.

Bartle, S. E., Anderson, S. A., & Sabatelli, R. M. (1989). A model of parenting style, adolescent individuation and adolescent self-esteem: Preliminary findings. *Journal of Adolescent Research, 4*, 283–298.

Bartsch, K. (1996). Between desires and beliefs: Young children's action predictions. *Child Development, 67*, 1671–1685.

Bartsch, K., & Wellman, H. M. (1995). *Children talk about the mind*. New York: Oxford University Press.

Bast, J., & Reitsma, P. (1998). Analyzing the development of individual differences in terms of Matthew effects in reading: Results from a Dutch longitudinal study. *Developmental Psychology, 34*, 1373–1399.

Bates, E., Camaioni, L., & Volterra, V. (1975). The acquisition of performatives prior to speech. *Merrill Palmer Quarterly, 2*, 205–226.

Bath, J. (1998). Dealing with nocturnal enuresis in children. *Community Nurse, 4*, 15–16.

Bauer, P. J., & Mandler, J. M. (1989). Taxonomies and triads: Conceptual organization in one- to two-year-olds. *Cognitive Psychology, 21*, 156–184.

Baugher, E., & Lamison-White, L. (1996). *Poverty in the United States: 1995* (U.S. Bureau of the Census Current population reports, Series P60-194). Washington, DC: U.S. Government Printing Office.

Baumeister, L. M., Flores, E., & Marin, B. V. (1995). Sex information given to Latina adolescents by parents. *Health Education Research, 10*, 233–239.

Baumrind, D. (1967). Child care practices anteceding three patterns of preschool behavior. *Genetic Psychology Monographs, 75*, 43–88.

Baumrind, D. (1971). Current patterns of parental authority. *Developmental Psychology Monographs, 4*, 1–103.

Baumrind, D. (1989). Rearing competent children. In W. Damon (Ed.), *Child development today and tomorrow* (pp. 349–378). San Francisco: Jossey-Bass.

Baumrind, D. (1991). Effective parenting during the early adolescent transition. In P. A. Cowan & E. M. Hetherington (Eds.), *Family transitions* (pp. 111–164). Hillsdale, NJ: Erlbaum.

Baumrind, D. (1993). The average expectable environment is not good enough: A response to Scarr. *Child Development, 64*, 1199–1217.

Baumrind, D. (1996). The discipline controversy revisited. *Family Relations, 45*, 405–414.

Baxter, C. (1999). Gryphon. In J. A. Stanford (Ed.), *Responding to literature* (3rd ed., pp. 908–920). Mountain View, CA: Mayfield. (Reprinted from *Through the safety net*, by C. Baxter, 1985, New York: Viking)

Beardsley, T. (1991). Smart genes. *Scientific American, 265*, 86–95.

Beckman, L., & Harvey, S. (1998). *The new Civil War: The psychology, culture, and politics of abortion*. Washington, DC: American Psychological Association.

Belenky, M. F., Clinchy, B. M., Goldberger, N. R., & Tarule, J. M. (1986). *Women's ways of knowing*. New York: Basic Books.

Belkin, L. (1999, July 25). "Getting the girl." *The New York Times Magazine*, 26–31, 38, 54.

Bell, R. Q. (1968). A reinterpretation of the direction of effects in studies of socialization. *Psychological Review, 75*, 81–85.

Belle, D. (1994). Social support issues for "latchkey" and supervised children. In F. Nestmann & K. Hurrelmann (Eds.), *Social networks and social support in childhood and adolescence* (pp. 293–304). New York: Walter de Gruyter.

Belsky, J. (1984). The determinants of parenting: A process model. *Child Development, 55*, 83–96.

Belsky, J. (1986). Infant day care: A cause for concern? *Zero to Three, 6*, 1–7.

Belsky, J. (1990). Parental and nonparental care and children's socio-emotional development: A decade in review. *Journal of Marriage and the Family, 52*, 885–903.

Belsky, J. (1996). Parent, infant, and social-contextual antecedents of father-son attachment security. *Developmental Psychology, 32*, 905–913.

Belsky, J., Campbell, S. B., Cohn, J. F., & Moore, G. (1996). Instability of infant-parent attachment security. *Developmental Psychology, 32*, 921–924.

Bem, S. L. (1981). Gender schema theory: A cognitive account of sex-typing. *Psychological Review, 88*, 354–364.

Bem, S. L. (1985). Androgyny and gender schema theory: A conceptual and empirical integration. In T. B. Sonderegger (Ed.), *Nebraska symposium on motivation, 1984: Psychology and gender* (pp. 179–226). Lincoln: University of Nebraska Press.

Benbow, C. P., & Stanley, J. C. (1980). Sex differences in mathematical ability: Fact or artifact? *Science, 210*, 1262–1264.

Benbow, C. P., & Stanley, J. C. (1982). Consequences in high school and college of sex differences in mathematical reasoning ability: A longitudinal perspective. *American Educational Research Journal, 19*, 598–622.

Benbow, C. P., & Stanley, J. C. (1983). Sex differences in mathematical reasoning ability: More facts. *Science, 222*, 1029–1031.

Benda, B. B., & DiBlasio, F. A. (1994). An integration of theory: Adolescent sexual contacts. *Journal of Youth and Adolescence, 23*, 403–420.

Bendersky, M., Alessandri, S. M., Sullivan, M. W., & Lewis, M. (1995). Measuring the effects of prenatal cocaine exposure. In M. Lewis & M. Bendersky (Eds.), *Mothers, babies, and cocaine: The role of toxins in development* (pp. 163–178). Hillsdale, NJ: Erlbaum.

Benedikt, R., Wertheim, E. H., & Lave, A. (1998). Eating attitudes and weight-loss attempts in female adolescents and their mothers. *Journal of Youth and Adolescence, 27,* 43–57.

Benenson, J. F., Apostoleris, N. H., & Parnass, J. (1997). Age and sex differences in dyadic and group interaction. *Developmental Psychology, 33,* 538–543.

Benoit, D., & Parker, K. C. H. (1994). Stability and transmission of attachment across three generations. *Child Development, 65,* 1444–1456.

Berezin, J. (1990). *The complete guide to choosing child care.* New York: Random House.

Berman, B. D., Winkleby, M., Chesterman, E., & Boyce, W. T. (1992). After-school child care and self-esteem in school-age children. *Pediatrics, 89,* 654–659.

Berndt, T. J. (1982). The features and effects of friendships in early adolescence. *Child Development, 53,* 1447–1461.

Bernstein, A., & Cowan, P. (1975). Children's concepts of how people get babies. *Child Development, 46,* 77–91.

Bertenthal, B. I., Campos, J. J., & Barrett, K. (1984). Self-produced locomotion: An organizer of emotional, cognitive, and social development in infancy. In R. Emde & R. Harmon. *Continuities and discontinuities in development* (pp. 174–210). New York: Plenum Press.

Bertenthal, B. I., & Fischer, K. W. (1978). Development of self-recognition in the infant. *Developmental Psychology, 14,* 44–50.

Best, C. T. (1988). The emergence of cerebral asymmetries in early human development: A literature review and a neuroembryological model. In D. L. Molfese & S. J. Segalowitz (Eds.), *Brain lateralization in children: Developmental implications* (pp. 5–34). New York: Guilford Press.

Betancourt, H., & Lopez, S. R. (1993). The study of culture, ethnicity, and race in American psychology. *American Psychologist, 48,* 629–637.

Bigler, R. S., Jones, L. C., & Lobliner, D. B. (1997). Social categorization and the formation of intergroup attitudes in children. *Child Development, 68,* 530–543.

Birch, L. L. (1980). Effects of poor models' food choices and eating behaviors on preschoolers' food preferences. *Child Development, 51,* 489–496.

Birch, L. L., & Deysher, M. (1986). Caloric compensation and sensory specific satiety: Evidence for self-regulation of food intake by young children. *Learning & Motivation, 16,* 341–355.

Birch, L. L., & Fisher, J. O. (1998). Development of eating behaviors among children and adolescents. *Pediatrics, 101,* 539–549.

Birch, L. L., Johnson, S. L., Andresen, G., Peters, J. C., & Schulte, M. C. (1991). The variability of young children's energy intake. *New England Journal of Medicine, 324,* 232–235.

Birch, L. L., McPhee, L., Shoba, B. C., Steinberg, L., &

Krehbiel, R. (1987). "Clean up your plate": Effects of child feeding practices on the conditioning of meal size. *Learning & Motivation, 18,* 301–317.

Bjorklund, D. F. (1989). *Children's thinking.* Pacific Grove, CA: Brooks/Cole.

Blader, J. C., Koplewicz, H. S., Abikoff, H., & Foley, C. (1997). Sleep problems of elementary school children. *Archive of Pediatric Adolescent Medicine, 151,* 473–480.

Bledsoe, E. (1996). "Out of a jam." From *Chicken soup for the soul: Home delivery.* An e-mail service from M. V. Hansen.

Bloom, L., Margulis, C., Tinker, E., & Fujita, N. (1996). Early conversations and word learning: Contributions from child and adult. *Child Development, 67,* 3154–3175.

Blumberg, M. S., & Lucas, D .E. (1996). A developmental and component analysis of active sleep. *Developmental Psychobiology, 29,* 1–22.

Blumenthal, S. J., & Kupfer, D. J. (1988). Overview of early detection and treatment strategies for suicidal behavior in young people. *Journal of Youth and Adolescence, 17,* 1–23.

Blyth, D. A., & Leffert, N. (1995). Communities as contexts for adolescent development: An empirical analysis. *Journal of Adolescent Research, 10,* 64–87.

Bolger, K. E., Patterson, C. J., & Kupersmidt, J. B. (1998). Peer relationships and self-esteem among children who have been maltreated. *Child Development, 69,* 1171–1191.

Bolton, I. M. (1989). Perspectives of youth on preventive intervention strategies. *Report of the Secretary's Task Force on Youth Suicide* (Vol. 3). Washington, DC: U.S. Government Printing Office.

Boone, R. T., & Cunningham, J. G. (1998). Children's decoding of emotion in expressive body movement: The development of cue attunement. *Developmental Psychology, 34,* 1007–1016.

Booth, J. R., Perfetti, C. A., MacWhinney, B. (1999). Quick, automatic, and general activation of orthographic and phonological representations in young readers. *Developmental Psychology, 35,* 3–19.

Bornstein, M. H., Haynes, O. M., O'Reilly, A. W., & Painter, K. M. (1996). Solitary and collaborative pretense play in early childhood: Sources of individual variation in the development of representational competence. *Child Development, 67,* 2910–2929.

Bosma, H. A., Jackson, S. E., Zijsling, D. H., Zani, B., Cicognani, E., Xerri, M. L., Honess, T. M., & Charman, L. (1996). Who has the final say? Decisions on adolescent behavior within the family. *Journal of Adolescence, 19,* 277–291.

Bouchard, C., Malina, R. M., & Perusse, L. (1997). *Genetics of fitness and physical performance.* Auckland, New Zealand: Human Kinetics.

Bourne, E. (1978a). The state of research on ego identity: A review and appraisal. Part I. *Journal of Youth and Adolescence, 7,* 223–257.

Bourne, E. (1978b). The state of research on ego identity: A review and appraisal. Part II. *Journal of Youth and Adolescence, 7,* 371–392.

Bower, T. G. R. (1982). *Development in infancy* (2nd ed.). San Francisco: W. H. Freeman.

Bower, T. G. R., Broughton, J. M., & Moore, M. K. (1971). The development of the object concept as manifested by changes in the tracking behavior of infants between 7 and 20 weeks of age. *Journal of Experimental Child Psychology, 11,* 182–193.

Bowlby, J. (1982). *Attachment: Attachment and loss* (Vol. 1). New York: Basic Books.

Boyce, W. T., & Jemerin, J. M. (1990). Psychobiological differences in childhood stress response: I. Patterns of illness and susceptibility. *Developmental and Behavioral Pediatrics, 11,* 86–93.

Boyes, M. C., & Chandler, M. (1992). Cognitive development, epistemic doubt, and identity formation in adolescence. *Journal of Youth and Adolescence, 21,* 277–304.

Bradbury, M. G., & Meadow, S. R. (1995). Combined treatment with enuresis alarm and desmopressin for nocturnal enuresis. *Acta Paediatrica, 84,* 1014–1018.

Bradley, R. H., Whiteside, L., Mundfrom, D. J., Casey, P. H., Kelleher, K. J., & Pope, S. K. (1994). Early indications of resilience and their relation to experiences in the home environments of low birthweight, premature children living in poverty. *Child Development, 65,* 346–360.

Braine, M. D. S. (1963). The ontogeny of English phrase structure: The first phase. *Language, 39,* 3–13.

Brazelton, T. B., & Cramer, B. G. (2000). Caring for a premature infant. In D. N. Sattler, G. P. Kramer, V. Shabatay, & D. A. Bernstein (Eds.), *Child development in context; Voices and perspectives* (pp. 16–20). Boston: Houghton Mifflin.

Brent, D. A., Perper, J. A., Goldstein, C. E., Kolko, D. J., Allan, M. J., Allman, C. J., & Zelenak, J. P. (1988). Risk factors for adolescent suicide: A comparison of adolescent suicide victims with suicidal in-patients. *Archives of General Psychiatry, 45,* 581–588.

Brice-Heath, S. (1982). Questioning at home and at school: A comparative study. In G. Spindler (Ed.), *The school achievement of minority children: New perspectives.* Hillsdale, NJ: Erlbaum.

Brinthaupt, T. M., & Lipka, R. P. (1985). Developmental differences in self-concept and self-esteem among kindergarten through twelfth grade students. *Child Study Journal, 15,* 207–221.

Brodinsky, D. M., Singer, L. M., & Braff, A. M. (1984). Children's understanding of adoption. *Child Development, 55,* 869–878.

Brody, G. H., Stoneman, Z., & Flor, D. (1996). Parental religiosity, family processes, and youth competence in rural, two-parent African American families. *Developmental Psychology, 32,* 696–706.

Brody, G. H., Stoneman, Z., & Gauger, K. (1996). Parent-child relationships, family problem-solving behavior, and sibling relationship quality: The moderating role of sibling temperaments. *Child Development, 67,* 1289–1300.

Brody, G. H., Stoneman, Z., & McCoy, J. K. (1994). Forecasting sibling relationships in early adolescence from child temperaments and family processes in middle childhood. *Child Development, 65,* 771–784.

Bronfenbrenner, U. (1979). *The ecology of human development.* Cambridge, MA: Harvard University Press.

Bronfenbrenner, U. (1990). Discovering what families need. In D. Blankenhorn, S. Bayme, & J. B. Elshtain (Eds.), *Rebuilding the nest* (pp. 27–38). Milwaukee, WI: Family Service American.

Bronson, G. W. (1974). The postnatal growth of visual capacity. *Child Development, 45,* 873–890.

Bronson, G. W. (1982). *The scanning patterns of human infants: Implications for visual learning.* Norwood, NJ: Ablex.

Bronson, G. W. (1994). Infants' transitions toward adult-like scanning. *Child Development, 65,* 1243–1261.

Brooks-Gunn, J. (1991). Consequences of maturational timing variations in adolescent girls. In R. M. Lerner, A. C. Petersen, & J. Brooks-Gunn (Eds.), *Encyclopedia of adolescence* (Vol. 2, pp. 614–618). New York: Garland.

Brooks-Gunn, J., & Duncan, G. J., (1997). The effects of poverty on children. *Children and Poverty, 7,* 55–71.

Brooks-Gunn, J., & Ruble, D. N. (1982). The development of menstrual-related beliefs and behaviors during early adolescence. *Child Development, 53,* 1557–1566.

Brooks-Gunn, J., & Ruble, D. N. (1986). Men's and women's attitudes and beliefs about the menstrual cycle. *Sex Roles, 14,* 287–299.

Brooks-Gunn, J., & Warren, M. P. (1985). Measuring physical status and timing in early adolescence: A developmental perspective. *Journal of Youth and Adolescence, 14,* 163–189.

Brown, J. L., & Pollitt, E. (1996). Malnutrition, poverty, and intellectual development. *Scientific American, 274*(2), 38–43.

Brown, J. R., Donelan-McCall, N., & Dunn, J. (1996). Why talk about mental states? The significance of children's conversations with friends, siblings, and mothers. *Child Development, 67,* 836–849.

Brown, R. (1957). Linguistic determinism and the part of speech. *Journal of Abnormal and Social Psychology, 55,* 1–5.

Brown, R. (1958). How shall a thing be called? *Psychological Review, 65,* 14–21.

Brown, R. (1965). *Social psychology.* New York: Free Press.

Brown, R. (1973). *A first language: The early stages.* London: Allen & Unwin.

Bruner, J. S. (1983). *Child's talk: Learning to use language.* Oxford: Oxford University Press.

Brunquell, D., Crichton, & L., Egeland, B. (1981). Maternal personality and attitude in disturbances of child rearing. *American Journal of Orthopsychiatry, 51,* 680–690.

Bryant, B. K. (1994). How does social support function in childhood? In F. Nestmann & K. Hurrelmann (Eds.), *Social networks and social support in childhood and adolescence* (pp. 23–36). New York: Walter de Gruyter.

Bryk, A. S., Lee, V., & Holland, P. B. (1993). *Catholic schools and the common good.* Cambridge, MA: Harvard University Press.

Buchanan, C. M., Maccoby, E. E., & Dornbusch, S. M. (1992). Adolescents and their families after divorce: Three residential arrangements compared. *Journal of Research on Adolescence, 2,* 261–291.

Bugental, D. B., Lyon, J. E., Lin, E. K., McGrath, E. P., & Bimbela, A. (1999). Children "tune out" in response to the ambiguous communication style of powerless adults. *Child Development, 70,* 214–230.

Burchinal, M. R., Campbell, F. A., Bryant, D. M., Wasik, B. H., & Ramey, C. T. (1997). Early intervention and mediating processes in cognitive performance of children of low-income African American families. *Child Development, 68,* 935–954.

Burchinal, M. R., Ramey, S. L., Reid, M. K., & Jaccard, J. (1995). Early child care experiences and their association with family and child characteristics during middle childhood. *Early Childhood Research Quarterly, 10,* 33–61.

Burhans, K. K., & Dweck, C. S. (1995). Helplessness in early childhood: The role of contingent worth. *Child Development, 66,* 1719–1738.

Butler, G. E., McKie, M., & Ratcliffe, S. G. (1990). The cyclical nature of prepubertal growth. *Annals of Human Biology, 17,* 177–190.

Butler, R. (1998). Age trends in the use of social and temporal comparison for self-evaluation: Examination of a novel developmental hypothesis. *Child Development, 69,* 1054–1073.

Cain, K. M., & Dweck, C. S. (1995). The relation between motivational patterns and achievement cognitions through the elementary school years. *Merrill-Palmer Quarterly, 41,* 25–52.

Cain, V. S., & Hofferth, S. L. (1989). Parental choice of self-care for school-age children. *Journal of Marriage and the Family, 51,* 65–77.

Camarena, P. M., Sarigiani, P. A., & Petersen, A. C. (1990). Gender-specific pathways to intimacy in early adolescence. *Journal of Youth and Adolescence, 19,* 19–32.

Campbell, F. A., Helms, R., Sparling, J. J., & Ramey, C. T. (1998). Early childhood programs and success in school: The Abecedarian study. In W. S. Barnett et al. (Eds.), *Early care and education for children in poverty: Promises, programs, and long-term results.* Albany: State University of New York Press.

Campione, J. C., & Brown, A. L. (1978). Toward a theory of intelligence: Contributions from research with retarded children. *Intelligence, 2,* 279–304.

Canobi, K. H., Reeve, R. A., & Pattison, P. E. (1998). The role of conceptual understanding in children's addition problem solving. *Developmental Psychology, 34,* 882–891.

Cantwell, D. P. (1996). Attention deficit disorder: A review of the past 10 years. *Journal of the American Academy of Child and Adolescent Psychiatry, 35,* 978–987.

Carey, S. (1978). The child as word learner. In M. Halle, J. Bresnan, & G. A. Miller (Eds.), *Linguistic theory and psychological reality* (pp. 264–293). Cambridge, MA: MIT Press.

Carter, D. B., & Levy, G. D. (1988). Cognitive aspects of early sex-role development: The influence of gender schemas on preschoolers' memories and preferences for sex-typed toys and activities. *Child Development, 59,* 782–792.

Casas, J. M., Wagenheim, B. R., Banchero, R., & Mendoza-Romero, J. (1994). Hispanic masculinity: Myth or psychological schema meriting clinical consideration? *Hispanic Journal of Behavioral Sciences, 16,* 315–331.

Casco, C., Tressoldi, P. E., & Dellantonio, A. (1998). Visual selective attention and reading efficiency are related in children. *Cortex, 34,* 531–546.

Case, R. (1992). The role of the frontal lobes in the regulation of cognitive development. *Brain and Cognition, 20,* 51–73.

Cash, T. F., & Henry, P. E. (1995). Women's body images: The results of a national survey in the USA. *Sex Roles, 33,* 19–28.

Caughy, M. O., DiPietro, J. A., & Strobino, D. M. (1994). Day-care participation as a protective factor in the cognitive development of low-income children. *Child Development, 65,* 457–471.

Caviness, V. S., Jr., Kennedy, D. N., Bates, J. F., & Makris, N. (1997). The developing human brain: A morphometric profile (pp. 3–14). In R. W. Thatcher, G. R. Lyon, J. Rumsey, & N. Krasnegor (Eds.), *Developmental neuroimaging: Mapping the development of brain and behavior.* San Diego: Academic Press.

Cech, D., & Martin, S. (1995). *Functional movement development across the life span.* Philadelphia: W. B. Saunders.

Center to Prevent Handgun Violence. (2000). *The school shootings . . . and beyond.* Retrieved March 8, 2000, from the World Wide Web: http://www.handguncontrol.org/chldgns.htm

Centers for Disease Control and Prevention. (1993). Recommendations of the International Task Force for Disease Eradication. *Morbidity and Mortality Weekly Report, 42,* 17.

Centers for Disease Control and Prevention. (1995a). Monthly immunization table. *Morbidity and Mortality Weekly Report, 44*(43), 823.

Centers for Disease Control and Prevention. (1995b). Symptoms of substance dependence associated with use of cigarettes, alcohol, and illicit drugs—United States, 1991–1992. *Morbidity and Mortality Weekly Reports, 44*(44), 830–831; 838–839.

Centers for Disease Control and Prevention. (1995c). Update: AIDS among women—United States, 1994. *Morbidity and Mortality Weekly Report, 44*(5), 81–84.

Centers for Disease Control and Prevention. (1995d). Vaccination coverage levels among children aged 19–35 months—United States, April–June 1994. *Morbidity and Mortality Weekly Report, 44*(20), 396–398.

Centers for Disease Control and Prevention. (1996a). CDC surveillance summaries, September 27, 1996. *Morbidity and Mortality Weekly Report, 45* (No. SS-4).

Centers for Disease Control and Prevention. (1996b). Youth risk behavior surveillance—United States, 1995. *Morbidity and Mortality Weekly Report, 45* (No. SS-4), 1–86.

Centers for Disease Control and Prevention. (1999). Prevalence of sedentary leisure-time behavior among adults in the United States. Retrieved October 4, 1999, from the World Wide Web: http://www.cdc.gov/nchswww/products/pubs/pubd/hestats/3and4/sedentary.htm

Centers for Disease Control and Prevention. (2000, Winter). Preventing obesity among children. *Chronic Disease Notes & Reports, 13*, 1–4.

Chandler, M. (1997). Rescuing magical thinking from the jaws of social determinism. *Child Development, 68*, 1021–1023.

Chandler, M. J., & Hala, S. M. (1994). The role of personal involvement in the assessment of early false-belief skills. In C. Lewis & P. Mitchell (Eds.), *Origins of an understanding of mind* (pp. 403–426). Hove: Erlbaum.

Changeux, J. P., & Danchin, A. (1976). Selective stabilisation of developing synapses as a mechanism for the specification of neuronal networks. *Nature, 264*, 705–712.

Chao, R. K. (1994). Beyond parental control and authoritarian parenting style: Understanding Chinese parenting through the cultural notion of training. *Child Development, 65*, 1111–1119.

Charpak, N., Ruiz-Pelaez, J. G., Figueroa de C., Z., & Charpak, Y. (1997). Kangaroo mother versus traditional care for newborn infants less than 2000 grams: A randomized, controlled trial. *Pediatrics, 100*, 682–688.

Chase-Lansdale, P. L., Gordon, R., Brooks-Gunn, J., & Klebanov, P. K. (1997). Neighborhood and family influences on the intellectual and behavioral competence of preschool and early school-age children. In J. Brooks-Gunn, G. Duncan, & J. L. Aber (Eds.), *Neighborhood poverty: Context and consequences for development* (pp. 79–118). New York: Russell Sage.

Chase-Lansdale, P. L., Wakschlag, L. S., & Brooks-Gunn, J. (1995). A psychological perspective on the development of caring in children and youth: The role of the family. *Journal of Adolescence, 18*, 515–556.

Chasnoff, I. J., Landress, H. J., & Barrett, M. E. (1990). The prevalence of illicit-drug or alcohol use during pregnancy and discrepancies in mandatory reporting in Pinellas County, Florida. *New England Journal of Medicine, 32*, 1202–1206.

Chen, X., Hastings, P. D., Rubin, K. H., Chen H., Cen, G., & Stewart, S. L. (1998). Child-rearing attitudes and behavioral inhibition in Chinese and Canadian toddlers: A cross-cultural study. *Developmental Psychology, 34*, 677–686.

Child Care Aware. (1999). Ways to measure quality. Retrieved August 27, 1999, from the World Wide Web: http://www.naccrra.net/childcareaware/quality.htm

Children's Defense Fund. (1994). *The state of America's children: Yearbook 1994*. Washington, DC: Author.

Chiu, M. L., Feldman, S. S., & Rosenthal, D. A. (1992). The influence of immigration on parental behavior and adolescent distress in Chinese families residing in two Western nations. *Journal of Research on Adolescence, 2*, 205–239.

Chodorow, N. (1978). *The reproduction of mothering*. Berkeley: University of California Press.

Chomsky, N. (1957). *Syntactic structures*. The Hague: Mouton.

Chomsky, N. (1965). *Aspects of the theory of syntax*. Cambridge, Mass: MIT Press.

Christoffel, K. K., & Arisa, A. (1998). Commentary. *Pediatrics, 101*, 103–105.

Christoffel, K. K., Spivak, H., & Witwer, M. (2000). Youth violence prevention: The physician's role. *MS JAMA, 283*, 1202-1203.

Chugani, H. T. (1997). Neuroimaging of developmental non-linearity and developmental pathologies (pp. 187–196). In R. W. Thatcher, G. R. Lyon, J. Rumsey, & N. Krasnegor (Eds.), *Developmental neuroimaging: Mapping the development of brain and behavior*. San Diego: Academic Press.

Church, J. (1961). *Language and the discovery of reality*. New York: Random House.

Cicchetti, D., & Lynch, M. (1995). Failures in the expectable environment and their impact on individual development: The case of child maltreatment. In D. Cicchetti & D. J. Cohen (Eds.), *Developmental psychopathology* (Vol. 2, pp. 32–71). New York: Wiley.

Cicchetti, D., & Rizley, R. (1981). Developmental perspectives on the etiology, intergenerational transmission and sequelae of child maltreatment. In *New directions for child development* (Vol. 11, pp. 31–56). San Francisco: Jossey-Bass.

Cisneros, S. (1993). *Woman hollering creek, and other stories*. New York: Random House.

Clark, B. (1988). *Growing up gifted* (3rd ed.). New York: Macmillan.

Clark, E. V. (1995). Later lexical development and word formation. In P. Fletcher & P. MacWhinney (Eds.), *The handbook of child language* (pp. 393–412). Oxford : Blackwell.

Clark, R., Hyde, J. S., Essex, M. J., & Klein, M. H. (1997). Length of maternity leave and quality of mother-infant interactions. *Child Development, 68,* 364–383.

Clausen, J. A. (1975). The social meaning of differential physical and sexual maturation. In S. E. Dragastin & G. H. Elder (Eds.), *Adolescence in the life cycle.* New York: Wiley.

Codori, A. M., Hanson, R., & Brandt, J. (1994). Self-selection in predictive testing for Huntington's disease. *American Journal of Medical Genetics, 54,* 167–173.

Cogswell, M. E. Scanlon, K. S., Fein, S. B., & Schieve, L. A. (1999). Medically advised, mother's personal target, and actual weight gain during pregnancy. *Obstetrics and Gynecology, 94,* 616–622.

Cohen, R. J., Swerdlik, M. E., & Phillips, S. M. (1996). *Psychological testing and assessment* (3rd ed.). Mountain View, CA: Mayfield.

Cohen, W. R. (1995). Maternal-fetal conflicts: Ethical and policy issues. In A. Goldworth, W. Silverman, D. K. Stevenson, E. W. D. Young, & R. Rivers (Eds.), *Ethics and perinatology* (pp. 10–28). New York: Oxford University Press.

Cohler, B. J., Stott, F. M., & Musick, J. S. (1995). Adversity, vulnerability, and resilience: Cultural and developmental perspectives. In D. Cicchetti & D. J. Cohen (Eds.), *Developmental psychopathology* (Vol. 2, pp. 753–800). New York: Wiley.

Coie, J. D., & Kupersmidt, J. B. (1983). A behavioral analysis of emerging social status in boys' groups. *Child Development, 54,* 1400–1416.

Cole, P. M., & Newcombe, N. (1983). Interference effects of verbal and imaginal strategies for resisting distraction on children's verbal and visual recognition memory. *Child Development, 54*(1), 42–50.

Coleman, J. S. (1988). Social capital in the creation of human capital. *American Journal of Sociology, 94,* 95–120.

Coles, R. (1970). *Erik Erikson: The growth of his work.* Boston: Little, Brown.

Coley, R., & Chase-Lansdale, P. (1999). Stability and change in paternal involvement among urban African American fathers. *Journal of Family Psychology, 13*(3), 416–435.

Comer, J. P. (1985). The Yale–New Haven Primary Prevention Project: A follow-up study. *Journal of the American Academy of Child Psychiatry, 24,* 154–160.

Comer, J. P. (1988). Educating poor minority children. *Scientific American, 259,* 42–48.

Comer, J. P., Haynes, N. M., Joyner, E. T., & Ben-Avie, M. (Eds.). (1996). *Rallying the whole village: The Comer process for reforming education.* New York: Teachers College Press.

Condon, W., & Sanders, L. (1974). Synchrony demonstrated between movements of the neonate and adult speech. *Child Development, 45,* 456–462.

Condry, J. C., & Ross, D. F. (1985). Sex and aggression: The influence of gender label on the perception of aggression in children. *Child Development, 56,* 225–238.

Cooper, R. P., & Aslin, R. N. (1990). Preference for infant directed speech in the first month after birth. *Child Development, 61,* 1584–1595.

Corcoran, M. E., & Chaudry, A. (1997). The dynamics of childhood poverty. *Children and Poverty, 7,* 40–54.

Corse, S. J., Schmid, K., & Trickett, P. K. (1990). Social network characteristics of mothers in abusing and nonabusing families and their relationships to parenting beliefs. *Journal of Community Psychology, 18,* 44–59.

Cotgrove, A., Zirinksy, L., Black, D., & Weston, D. (1995). Secondary prevention of attempted suicide in adolescence. *Journal of Adolescence, 18,* 569–577.

Coulton, C. J., Korbin, J. E., & Su, M. (1999). Neighborhoods and child maltreatment: A multi-level study. *Child Abuse & Neglect, 23,* 1019–1040.

Courage, M. L., & Adams, R. J. (1990). Visual acuity assessment from birth to three years using the acuity card procedures: Cross-sectional and longitudinal samples. *Optometry and Vision Science, 67,* 713–718.

Courtney, M. L., & Cohen, R. (1996). Behavior segmentation by boys as a function of aggressiveness and prior information. *Child Development, 67,* 1034–1047.

Coustan, D. R. (1995a). Fetal physiology. In D. R. Coustan, R. V. Haning, Jr., & D. B. Singer (Eds.), *Human reproduction: Growth and development* (pp. 139–160). New York: Little, Brown.

Coustan, D. R. (1995b). Maternal physiology. In D. R. Coustan, R. V. Haning, Jr., & D. B. Singer (Eds.), *Human reproduction: Growth and development* (pp. 161–181). New York: Little, Brown.

Cozby, P. C. (1997). *Methods in behavioral research* (6th ed.). Mountain View, CA: Mayfield.

Craighead, L. W., & Green, B, J. (1989). Relationship between depressed mood and sex-typed personality characteristics in adolescents. *Journal of Youth and Adolescence, 18,* 467–474.

Cramer, P., & Skidd, J. E. (1992). Correlates of self-worth in preschoolers: The role of gender-stereotyped styles of behavior. *Sex Roles, 26,* 369–390.

Crane, J. (1991). The epidemic theory of ghettos and neighborhood effects on dropping out and teenage childbearing. *American Journal of Sociology, 96,* 1126–1159.

Cratty, B. J. (1986). *Perceptual and motor development in infants and children* (3rd ed.). Englewood Cliffs, NJ: Prentice-Hall.

Crick, N. R., & Dodge, K. A. (1996). Social information-processing mechanisms in reactive and proactive aggression. *Child Development, 67,* 993–1002.

Crick, N. R., & Grotpeter, J. K. (1995). Relational aggression, gender, and social-psychological adjustment. *Child Development, 66,* 710–722.

Crnic, K. A., Greenberg, M. T., Ragozin, A., Robinson, N., & Basham, R. (1983). Effects of stress and social support on mothers and premature and full-term babies. *Child Development, 54,* 209–217.

Cronan, T. A., Cruz, S. G., Arriago, R. I., & Sarlom A. J. (1996). The effects of a community-based literacy program on young children's language and conceptual development. *American Journal of Community Psychology, 24,* 251–272.

Cross, W. E., Jr. (1980). Models of psychological nigrescence: A literature review. In R. L. Jones (Ed.), *Black psychology.* New York: Harper & Row.

Cross, W. E., Jr. (1987). A two-factor theory of black identity: Implications for the study of identity development in minority children. In J. S. Phinney & M. J. Rotheram (Eds.), *Children's ethnic socialization.* Beverly Hills: Sage.

Csikszentmihalyi, M. (1990). *Flow: The psychology of optimal experience.* New York: Harper & Row.

Csikszentmihalyi, M. (1997). *Finding flow.* New York: Basic Books.

Dahl, M., Tybjærg-Hansen, A., Wittrup, H., Lange, P., & Nordestgaard, B. (1998). Cystic fibrosis F508 heterozygotes, smoking and reproduction: Studies of 9141 individuals from a general population sample. *Genomics, 50*(1), 89–96.

Daniels, J., D'Andrea, M., & Heck, R. (1995). Moral development and Hawaiian youths: Does gender make a difference? *Journal of Counseling and Development, 74,* 90–93.

Darling, C. A., & Hicks, M. W. (1982). Parental influence on adolescent sexuality: Implications for parents as educators. *Journal of Youth and Adolescence, 11,* 231–245.

Davidson, E. H. (1990) How embryos work: A comparative view of diverse modes of cell fate specification. *Development, 108,* 365–389.

Dawson, G., & Fischer, K. W. (1994). *Human behavior and the developing brain.* New York: Guilford Press.

Day, J. C. (1996). *Population projections of the United States by age, sex, race, and Hispanic origin: 1995 to 2050* (U.S. Bureau of the Census Current Population Reports No. P25-1130). Washington, DC: U.S. Government Printing Office.

Deater-Deckard, K., Dodge, K. A., Bates, J. E., & Pettit, G. S. (1996). Physical discipline among African American and European American mothers: Links to children's externalizing behaviors. *Developmental Psychology, 32,* 1065–1072.

DeCasper, A. J., & Fifer, W. P. (1980). Of human bonding: Newborns prefer their mothers' voices. *Science, 208,* 1174–1176.

DeCasper, A. J., & Spence, M. J. (1986). Prenatal newborns' perception of speech sounds. *Infant Behavior and Development, 9,* 135–150.

de Gaston, J. F., Jensen, L., Weed, S. E., & Tanas, R. (1994). Teacher philosophy and program implementation and the impact on sex education outcomes. *Journal of Research and Development in Education, 27,* 265–270.

Dejin-Karlsson, E., Hanson, B. S., Oestergren, P. E., Sjoeberg, N-O., & Marsal, K. (1998). Does passive smoking in early pregnancy increase the risk of small-for-gestational age infants? *American Journal of Public Health, 88,* 1523–1527.

DeJong, W. (1999). Building the peace: The resolving conflict creatively program. *National Institute of Justice, Program Focus,* 2–16.

Dempster, F. N. (1981). Memory span: Sources of individual and developmental differences. *Psychological Bulletin, 89,* 63–100.

Denham, S. A., McKinley, M., Couchoud, E. A., & Holt, R. (1990). Emotional and behavioral predictors of preschool peer ratings. *Child Development, 61,* 1145–1152.

Devaney, B. L., Ellwood, M. R., & Love, J. M. (1997). Programs that mitigate the effects of poverty on children. *Children and Poverty, 7,* 88–112.

de Vries, J. I. P. (1992). The first trimester. In J. I. P. de Vries (Ed.), *Fetal behavior: Developmental and perinatal aspects* (pp. 3–16). New York: Oxford University Press.

Dewey, J. (1896). The concept of the reflex arc in psychology. *Psychological Bulletin, 3,* 357–370.

Diaz, R. M. (1983). Thought and two languages: The impact of bilingualism on cognitive development. *Review of Research in Education, 10,* 23–54.

Dietz, W. H., & Gortmaker, S. L. (1985). Do we fatten our children at the television set: Obesity and television viewing in children and adolescents. *Pediatrics, 75,* 807–812.

Dietz, W. H., & Stern, L. (Eds.). (1999). *American Academy of Pediatrics: Guide to your child's nutrition.* New York: Villard Books.

Dillard, A. (1974). *Pilgrim at Tinker Creek.* New York: Harper's Magazine Press.

Dillard, A. (1987). *An American childhood.* San Francisco: Harper & Row.

Dixon, J. P. (1997). The spatial child. In D. N. Sattler & V. Shabatay (Eds.), *Psychology in context: Voices and perspectives* (pp. 173–176). Boston: Houghton Mifflin.

Dobson, P. (1989). Easing childhood shame. *Nursing Times, 85,* 79–80.

Dodge, K. A. (1983). Behavioral antecedents of peer social status. *Child Development, 54*(6), 1386–1399.

Dodge, K. A., Pettit, G. S., McClaskey, C., & Brown, M. (1986). Social competence in children. *Monographs of the Society for Research in Child Development, 51* (2, Serial No. 213).

Doherty, W. J., Kouneski, E. F., & Erickson, M. F. (1998). Responsible fathering: An overview and conceptual framework. *Journal of Marriage and the Family, 60,* 277–292.

Donahue, M. J., & Benson, P. L. (1995). Religion and the well-being of adolescents. *Journal of Social Issues, 51,* 145–160.

Donaldson, M. (1978). *Children's minds.* New York: Norton.

Dornbusch, S. M., Ritter, P. L., Mont-Reynaud, R., & Chen, Z. (1990). Family decision making and academic performance in a diverse high school population. *Journal of Adolescent Research, 5,* 143–160.

Dorris, M. (1989). *The broken cord.* New York: Harper & Row.

Dovidio, J., & Gaertner, S. (1986). *Prejudice, discrimination, and racism.* Orlando, FL: Academic Press.

Downey, G., Lebolt, A., Rincon, C., & Freitas, A. L. (1998). Rejection sensitivity and children's interpersonal difficulties. *Child Development, 69,* 1074–1091.

Downey, G., Purdie, V., & Schaffer-Neitz, R. (1999). Anger transmission from mother to child: A comparison of mothers in chronic pain and well mothers. *Journal of Marriage and the Family, 61,* 62–73.

Downey, S., & McCormick, J. (2000, May 15). Razing the vertical ghettos. *Newsweek,* pp. 36–37.

Drumm, P., & Jackson, D. W. (1996). Developmental changes in questioning strategies during adolescence. *Journal of Adolescent Research, 11,* 285–305.

Dubois, D. L., & Hirsch, B. J. (1990). School and neighborhood friendship patterns of Blacks and Whites in early adolescence. *Child Development, 61,* 524–536.

Duke-Duncan, P. (1991). Body image. In R. M. Lerner, A. C. Petersen, & J. Brooks-Gunn (Eds.). *Encyclopedia of adolescence* (Vol. 2, pp. 90–94). New York: Garland.

Dunn, J., Brown, J., & Beardsall, L. (1991). Family talk about feeling states and children's later understanding of others' emotions. *Developmental Psychology, 27,* 448–455.

Dupper, D. (1995). Moving beyond a crime-focused perspective of school violence. *Social Work in Education, 17*(2), 71–72.

Dweck, C. S. (1986). Motivational processes affecting learning. *American Psychologist, 41,* 1040–1048.

Dweck, C. S. (1989). Motivation. In A. Lesgold & R. Glaser (Eds.), *Foundations for a psychology of education.* Hillsdale, NJ: Erlbaum.

Dweck, C. S., & Repucci, N. D. (1973). Learned helplessness and reinforcement responsibility in children. *Journal of Personality and Special Psychology, 25,* 109–116.

Early, L. A., Bhatt, R. S., & Rovee-Collier, C. (1995). Developmental changes in the contextual control of recognition. *Developmental Psychobiology, 28,* 27–43.

Ecklund-Flores, L., & Turkewitz, G. (1996). Asymmetric headturning to speech and nonspeech in human newborns. *Developmental Psychobiology, 29,* 205–217.

Eden, G. F., & Zeffiro, T. A. (1997). PET and MRI in the detection of task-related brain activity: Implications for the study of brain development (pp. 77–90). In R. W. Thatcher, G. R. Lyon, J. Rumsey, & N. Krasnegor (Eds.), *Developmental neuroimaging: Mapping the development of brain and behavior.* San Diego: Academic Press.

Eimas, P. D., & Quinn, P.C. (1994). Studies on the formation of perceptually based basic-level categories in young infants. *Child Development, 65,* 903–917.

Eisenberg, N. (1996). Meta-emotion and socialization of emotion in the family—a topic whose time has come: Comment on Gottman et al. (1996). *Journal of Family Psychology, 10,* 269–276.

Eisenman, R. (1994). Conservative sexual values: Effects of an abstinence program on student attitudes. *Journal of Sex Education and Therapy, 20,* 75–78.

Ekman, P. (1984). Expressions and the nature of emotion. In P. Ekman & K. Scherer (Eds.), *Approaches to emotion.* Hillsdale, NJ: Erlbaum.

Ekman, P. (1994). Strong evidence for universals in facial expressions: A reply to Russell's mistaken critique. *Psychological Bulletin, 115,* 268–287.

Elkind, D. (1961). The child's conception of his religious denomination I: The Jewish child. *Journal of Genetic Psychology, 99,* 209–225.

Elkind, D. (1962). The child's conception of his religious denomination II: The Catholic child. *Journal of Genetic Psychology, 101,* 185–193.

Elkind, D. (1963). The child's conception of his religious denomination III: The Protestant child. *Journal of Genetic Psychology, 103,* 291–304.

Elkind, D. (1967). Egocentrism in adolescence. *Child Development, 38,* 1025–1034.

Elkind, D. (1978a). *The child's reality: Three developmental themes.* Hillsdale, NJ: Erlbaum.

Elkind, D. (1978b). *A sympathetic understanding of the child: Birth to sixteen* (2nd ed.). Boston: Allyn & Bacon.

Elkind, D. (1980). Strategic interactions in early adolescence. In J. Adelson (Ed.), *Handbook of adolescence.* New York: Wiley.

Elkind, D. (1985). Egocentrism redux: Reply to D. Lapsley and M. Murphy's *Developmental Review* paper. *Developmental Review, 5,* 218–226.

Ellis, B. J., McFadyen-Ketchum, S., Dodge, K. A., Pettit, G. S., & Bates, J. E. (1999). Quality of early relationships and individual differences in the timing of pubertal maturation in girls: A longitudinal test of an evolutionary model. *Journal of Personality and Social Psychology, 77,* 387–401.

Ely, R., Melzi, G., Hadge, L., & McCabe, A. (1998). Being brave, being nice: Themes of agency and communion in children's narratives. *Journal of Personality, 66,* 257–284.

Emde, R. N., & Harmon, R. J. (1972). Endogenous and exogenous smiling systems in early infancy. *Journal of the American Academy of Child Psychiatry, 11,* 77–100.

Emde, R. N., Plomin, R., Robinson, J, Corley, R., DeFries, J., Fulker, D. W., Reznick, J. S., Campos, J., Kagan, J., & Zahn-Waxler, C. (1992). Temperament, emotion, and cognition at fourteen months: The MacArthur longitudinal twin study. *Child Development, 63,* 1437–1455.

Emde, R. N., & Robinson, J. (1979). The first two months: Recent research in developmental psychobiology and the changing view of the newborn. In J. Noshpitz & J. Call (Eds.), *Basic handbook of child psychiatry.* New York: Basic Books.

Engle, P. L., Gorman, K. S., Martorell, R., & Pollitt, E. (1992). The ORIENTE study: Infant and preschool psychological development. *Food & Nutrition Bulletin, 14,* 201–214.

Ennett, S. T., & Bauman, K. E. (1996). Adolescent social networks: School, demographic, and longitudinal considerations. *Journal of Adolescent Research, 11,* 194–215.

Enright, R. D., & Lapsley, D. K. (1981). Judging others who hold opposite beliefs: The development of belief-discrepancy reasoning. *Child Development, 52,* 1053–1063.

Ensher, G. L., & Clark, D. A. (1994). Newborns at risk: *Medical care and psychoeducational interventions* (2nd ed.). Gaithersburg, MD: Aspen.

Entwisle, D. R., Alexander, K. L., Olson, L. S., & Ross, K. (1999). Paid work in early adolescence: Developmental and ethnic patterns. *Journal of Early Adolescence, 19,* 363–388.

Ephron, N. (1972). *Crazy salad: Some things about women.* New York: Knopf.

Erdrich. L. (1996). *The blue jay's dance.* New York: HarperPerennial.

Erikson, E. H. (1954). Problems of infancy and early childhood. In G. Murphy & A. J. Bachrach (Eds.), *An outline of abnormal psychology.* New York: Modern Library.

Erikson, E. H. (1959). Identity and the life cycle: Selected papers. *Psychological Issues Monograph* (1, Series 1). New York: International Universities Press.

Erikson, E. H. (1963). *Childhood and society* (2nd ed.). New York: Norton.

Erikson, E. H. (1968). *Identity, youth and crisis.* New York: Norton.

Eskanazi, B., & Bergman, J. J. (1995). Passive and active maternal smoking during pregnancy, as measured by serum cotinine, and postnatal smoke exposure. I. Effects on physical growth at age 5 years. *American Journal of Epidemiology, 142,* 10–18.

Estes, D. (1998). Young children's awareness of their mental activity: The case of mental rotation. *Child Development, 69,* 1345–1360.

Estes, T. K. (1998). From birth to conception: Open or closed. *European Journal of Obstetrics, Gynecology, and Reproductive Biology, 78,* 169–177.

Evans, E. D., Craig, D., & Mietzel, G. (1993). Adolescents' cognitions and attributions for academic cheating: A cross-national study. *Journal of Psychology, 127,* 585–602.

Executive Summary. (1999, October). *The Carolina Abecedarian Project.* Chapel Hill, NC: Frank Porter Graham Child Development Center, University of North Carolina at Chapel Hill. Retrieved October 22, 1999, from the World Wide Web: http://www.fpg.unc.edu/~abc/embargoed/executive_summary.htm

Eysenck, H. J., & Eysenck, M. W. (1985). *Personality and individual differences: A natural science approach.* New York: Plenum.

Fabes, R. A., Eisenberg, N., Smith, M. C., & Murphy, B. C. (1996). Getting angry at peers: Associations with liking of the provocateur. *Child Development, 67,* 942–956.

Fabricius, W. V., & Wellman, H. M. (1983). Children's understanding of retrieval cue utilization. *Developmental Psychology, 19,* 15–21.

Farver, J. A., & Shin, Y. L. (1997). Social pretend play in Korean- and Anglo-American preschoolers. *Child Development, 68,* 544–556.

Fauber, R., Forehand, R., Thomas, A. M., & Wierson, M. (1990). A mediational model of the impact of marital conflict on adolescent adjustment in intact and divorced families. *Child Development, 61,* 1112–1123.

Faust, M. S. (1983). Alternative constructions of adolescent growth. In J. Brooks-Gunn & A. C. Petersen (Eds.), *Girls at puberty.* New York: Plenum.

Federal Interagency Forum on Child and Family Statistics. (1997). *America's children: Key national indicators of well-being.* Washington, DC: U.S. Government Printing Office.

Feiring, C., & Lewis, M. (1993). Do mothers know their teenagers' friends? Implications for individuation in early adolescence. *Journal of Youth and Adolescence, 22,* 337–354.

Feldman, C. F., Stone, A., & Renderer, B. (1990). Stage, transfer, and academic achievement in dialect-speaking Hawaiian adolescents. *Child Development, 61,* 472–484.

Feldman, S. S., Mont-Reynaud, R., & Rosenthal, D. A. (1992). When East moves West: The acculturation of values of Chinese adolescents in the U.S. and Australia. *Journal of Research on Adolescence, 2,* 147–173.

Fenson, L., Dale, P. S., Reznick, J. S., Bates, E., Thal, D., Bates, E., Hartung, J., Pethick, S., & Reilly, J. (1993). *The MacArthur communicative development inventories: User's guide and technical manual.* San Diego: Singular Publishing Group.

Fernald, A. (1985). Four-month-old infants prefer to listen to motherese. *Infant Behavior and Development, 8,* 181–195.

Fernald, A. (1993). Approval and disapproval: Infant responsiveness to vocal affect in familiar and unfamiliar languages. *Child Development, 64,* 657–674.

Field, A. E., Camargo, C. A., Taylor, C. B., Berkey, C. S., Frazier, L., & Gillman, M. W. (1999). Overweight, weight concerns, and bulimic behaviors among girls and boys. *Journal of the American Academy of Child and Adolescent Psychiatry, 38,* 754–760.

Field, T. M., Schanberg, S. M., Scafidi, F., Bauer, C. R., Vega-Lahr, N., Garcia, R., Nystrom, J., & Kuhn, C. M. (1986). Effects of tactile/kinesthetic stimulation on preterm neonates. *Pediatrics, 77,* 654-658.

Filer, L. J., Jr. (1995). Iron deficiency. In F. Lifshitz (Ed.), *Childhood nutrition* (pp. 53–60). Ann Arbor, MI: CRC Press.

Fillmore, C. J. (1982). A descriptive framework for spatial deixis. In R. Jarvella & W. Klein (Eds.), *Speech, place, and action: Studies in deixis and related topics.* New York: Wiley.

Finkelhor, D. (1990). Early and long-term effects of child sexual abuse: An update. *Professional Psychology: Research and Practice, 21,* 325–330.

Fisher, C., & Tokura, H. (1996). Acoustic cues to grammatical structure in infant-directed speech: Cross-linguistic evidence. *Child Development, 67,* 3192–3218.

Fisher, J. O., & Birch, L. L. (1996). Maternal restriction of young girls' food access is related to intake of those foods in an unrestricted setting. *FASEB Journal, 10,* A225.

Fisk, W. R. (1985). Responses to "neutral" pronoun presentations and the development of sex-biased responding. *Developmental Psychology, 21,* 481–485.

Flavell, J. H., Beach, D. R., & Chinsky, J. M. (1966). Spontaneous verbal rehearsal in a memory task as a function of age. *Child Development, 37,* 283–299.

Flavell, J. H., Flavell, E. R., & Green, F. L. (1983). Development of the appearance-reality distinction. *Cognitive Psychology, 15,* 95–120.

Flavell, J. H., Flavell, E. R., Green, F. L., & Korfmacher, J. E. (1990). Do young children think of television images as pictures or real objects? *Journal of Broadcasting & Electronic Media, 34,* 399–419.

Flavell, J. H., Green, F. L., & Flavell, E. R. (1993). Children's understanding of the stream of consciousness. *Child Development, 64,* 387–398.

Flavell, J. H., Green, F. L., & Flavell, E. R. (1995). Young children's knowledge about thinking. *Monographs of the Society for Research in Child Development, 60*(1, Serial No. 243).

Flavell, J. H., Green, F. L., & Flavell, E. R. (1998). The mind has a mind of its own: Developing knowledge about mental uncontrollability. *Cognitive Development, 13,* 127–138.

Flavell, J. H., Miller, P. H., & Miller, S. A. (1993). *Cognitive development* (3rd ed.). Englewood Cliffs, NJ: Prentice-Hall.

Fleming, P. J., Blair, P. S., Bacon, C., et al. (1996). Environment of infants during sleep and risk of the sudden infant death syndrome: Results from 1993–1995 case-control study for confidential inquiry into stillbirths and deaths in infancy. *British Medical Journal, 313,* 191–195.

Flieller, A. (1999). Comparison of the development of formal thought in adolescent cohorts aged 10 to 15 years (1967–1996 and 1972–1993). *Developmental Psychology, 35,* 1048–1058.

Flynn, J. R. (1984). The mean IQ of Americans: Massive gains 1932–1978. *Psychological Bulletin, 95,* 29–51.

Ford, M. E., Wentzel, K. R., Wood, D., Stevens, E., & Siesfeld, G. A. (1989). Processes associated with integrative social competence: Emotional and contextual influences on adolescent social responsibility. *Journal of Adolescent Research, 4,* 405–425.

Forehand, R., Thomas, A. M., Wierson, M., Brody, G., & Fauber, R. (1990). Role of maternal functioning and parenting skills in adolescent functioning following parental divorce. *Journal of Abnormal Psychology, 99,* 278–283.

Fouts, G., & Burggraf, K. (1999). Television situation comedies: Female body images and verbal reinforcements. *Sex Roles, 40,* 473–481.

Fowler, J. W. (1981). *Stages of faith: The psychology of human development and the question for meaning.* San Francisco: Harper & Row.

Fowler, J. W. (1991). Stages in faith consciousness. *New Directions for Child Development, 52,* 27–45.

Frankel, K. A. (1990). Girls' perceptions of peer relationship support and stress. *Journal of Early Adolescence, 10,* 69–88.

Freedman, D. G., & Freedman, M. (1969). Behavioral differences between Chinese-American and American newborns. *Nature, 224,* 1227.

Freedman, D. S., Srinivasan, S. R., Valdez, R. A., Williamson, D. F., & Berenson, G. S. (1997). Secular increases in relative weight and adiposity among children over two decades: The Bogalusa heart study. *Pediatrics, 99,* 420–426.

Fremon, C. (1995). *Father Greg and the homeboys.* New York: Hyperion.

French, S. A., Perry, C. L., Leon, G. R., & Fulkerson, J. A. (1995). Dieting behaviors and weight change history in female adolescents. *Health Psychology, 14,* 548–555.

Freud, A. (1937). *The ego and the mechanisms of defense.* London: Hogarth Press.

Freud, S. (1961). *Collected works, standard edition.* London: Hogarth Press.

Freud, S. (1961). New introductory lectures in psychoanalysis. In J. Strachey (Ed.), *The standard edition of the complete psychological works of Sigmund Freud.* New York: Norton. (Originally published 1933.)

Freud, S. (1961). Some psychical consequences of the anatomical distinction between the sexes. In J. Strachey (Ed.), *The standard edition of the complete psychological works of Sigmund Freud* (Vol. 19). London: Hogarth Press. (Original work published 1925b.)

Freud, S. (1961). The dissolution of the Oedipal complex. In J. Strachey (Ed.), *The standard edition of the complete psychological works of Sigmund Freud* (Vol.19). London: Hogarth Press. (Original work published 1925a.)

Freud, S. (1964). The neuro-psychoses of defense. In J. Strachey (Trans. and Ed.), *The standard edition of the complete psychological works of Sigmund Freud* (Vol. 3, pp. 45–61). London: Hogarth Press. (Original work published 1894.)

Frick, J. E., & Columbo, J. (1996). Individual differences in infant visual attention: Recognition of degraded visual forms by four-month-olds. *Child Development, 67,* 188–204.

Fried, P. A., O'Connell, C. M., & Watkinson, M. A. (1992). 60- and 72-month follow-up of children prenatally exposed to marijuana, cigarettes, and alcohol: Cognitive and language assessment. *Developmental and Behavioral Pediatrics, 13*, 383–391.

Fried, P. A., & Watkinson, B. (1990). 36- and 48-month neurobehavioral follow-up of children prenatally exposed to marijuana, cigarettes, and alcohol. *Journal of Developmental and Behavioral Pediatrics, 11*, 49–58.

Fried, V. M., Makuc, D. M., & Rooks, R. N. (1998). Ambulatory health care visits by children: Principal diagnosis and place of visit. *Vital Health Statistics, 13*(137).

Friedler, G. (1988). Effects on future generations of paternal exposure to alcohol and other drugs. *Alcohol Health & Research World, 12*, 126–129.

Friedler, G. (1996). Paternal exposures: Impact on reproductive and developmental outcome: An overview. *Pharmacology, Biochemistry and Behavior, 55*(4), 691–700.

Friedman, W. J. (1999, April 16). *Arrows of time in infancy: The representation of temporal invariances.* Electronic poster presented at the meetings of the Society for Research in Child Development. Albuquerque, NM.

Friedman, W. J. (1997, November 20). *The development of infants' perception of temporally undirected events.* Paper presented at the Fifth Annual Workshop on Object Perception and Memory, Philadelphia.

Frisch, R. E. (1983). Fatness, puberty, and fertility: The effects of nutrition and physical training on menarche and ovulation. In J. Brooks-Gunn & A. C. Petersen (Eds.), *Girls at puberty.* New York: Plenum.

Frisch, R. E. (1991). Puberty and body fat. In R. M. Lerner, A. C. Petersen, & J. Brooks-Gunn (Eds.), *Encyclopedia of adolescence* (Vol. 2, pp. 884–892). New York: Garland

Frye, D., Rawling, P., Moore, C., & Myers, I. (1983). Object-person discrimination and communication at 3 and 10 months. *Developmental Psychology, 19*, 303–309.

Furman, W., & Bierman, K. L. (1983). Developmental changes in young children's conceptions of friendship. *Child Development, 54*(3), 549–556.

Furman, W., & Buhrmester, D. (1992). Age and sex differences in perceptions of networks of personal relationships. *Child Development, 63*, 103–115.

Gaddis, A., & Brooks-Gunn, J. (1985). The male experience of pubertal change. *Journal of Youth and Adolescence, 14*, 61–69.

Galper, A., Wigfield, A., & Seefeldt, C. (1997). Head Start parents' beliefs about their children's abilities, task values, and performances on different activities. *Child Development, 68*, 897–907.

Gamoran, A., & Mare, R. D. (1989). Secondary school tracking and educational inequality: Compensation, reinforcement, or neutrality? *American Journal of Sociology, 94*, 1146–1183.

Garbarino, J. (1999). *Lost boys.* New York: Free Press.

Garbarino, J., & Sherman, D. (1980). High-risk neighborhoods and high-risk families: The human ecology of child maltreatment. *Child Development, 51*, 188–198.

Garcia, J. (1993). The changing image of ethnic groups in textbooks. *Phi Delta Kappan, 75*, 29–35.

Gardner, H. (1983). *Frames of mind.* New York: Basic Books.

Gardner, J. M. M., Grantham-McGregor, S. M., Chang, S. M., Himes, J. H., & Powell, C. A. (1995). Activity and behavioral development in stunted and nonstunted children and response to nutritional supplementation. *Child Development, 66*, 1785–1797.

Garfinkel, I., Miller, C., McLanahan, S., & Hanson, T. (1998). *Deadbeat dads or inept states: A comparison of child support enforcement systems.* New York: Russell Sage.

Garland, A. F., & Zigler, E. (1993). Adolescent suicide prevention: Current research and social policy implications. *American Psychologist, 48*, 169–182.

Garnica, O. (1977). Some prosodic and paralinguistic features of speech to young children. In D. E. Snow & C. A. Ferguson (Eds.), *Talking to children: Language input and acquisition.* Cambridge: Cambridge University Press.

Garrett, P., Ng'andu, N., & Ferron, J. (1994). Poverty experiences of young children and the quality of their home environments. *Child Development, 65*, 331–345.

Gavazzi, S. M., & Sabatelli, R. M. (1990). Family system dynamics, the individuation process, and psychosocial development. *Journal of Adolescent Research, 5*, 500–519.

Gavin, L. A., & Fuhrman, W. (1989). Age differences in adolescents' perceptions of their peer groups. *Developmental Psychology, 25*, 827–834.

Ge, X., Conger, R. D., Lorenz, F. O., Elder, G. H., Montague, R. B., & Simons, R. L. (1992). Linking family economic hardship to adolescent distress. *Journal of Research on Adolescence, 2*, 351–378.

Geary, D. C., Bow-Thomas, C. C., Fan, L., & Siegler, R. S. (1993). Even before formal instruction, Chinese children outperform American children in mental addition. *Cognitive Development, 8*, 517–529.

Geary, D. C., Bow-Thomas, C. C., Fan, L., & Siegler, R. S. (1996). Development of arithmetical competencies in Chinese and American children: Influence of age, language, and schooling. *Child Development, 67*, 2022–2044.

Geller, L. G. (1985). *Word play and language learning for children.* Urbana, IL: National Council of Teachers of English.

George, T. P., & Hartmann, D. P. (1996). Friendship networks of unpopular, average, and popular children. *Child Development, 67*, 2301–2316.

Gershkof-Stowe, Thal, D. J., Smith, L. B., & Namy, L. L. (1997). Categorization and its developmental relation to early language. *Child Development, 68*, 843-859.

Gesell, A. (1940). *The first five years of life: The preschool years.* New York: Harper.

Gewirtz, J. L. (1976). The attachment acquisition process as evidenced in the maternal conditioning of cued infant responding (particularly crying). *Human Development, 19,* 143–155.

Giardino, A. P., Christian, C. W., & Giardino, E. R. (1997). *A practical guide to the evaluation of child physical abuse and neglect.* Thousand Oaks, CA: Sage.

Gibbs, J. T. (1989). Black American adolescents. In J. T. Gibbs, L. N. Huang, & associates (Eds.), *Children of color.* San Francisco: Jossey-Bass.

Gibson, J. J. (1966). *The senses considered as perceptual systems.* Boston: Houghton Mifflin.

Gilbert, S. F. (1994). *Developmental biology* (4th ed.). Sunderland, MA: Sinauer Associates.

Giles-Sims, J., & Crosbie-Burnett, M. (1989). Stepfamily research: Implications for policy, clinical interventions, and further research. *Family Relations, 38,* 19–23.

Gilligan, C. (1982). *In a different voice: Psychological theory and women's development.* Cambridge, MA: Harvard University Press.

Gilligan, C. (1986). Exit-voice dilemmas in adolescent development. In A. Foxley, M. S. McPherson, & G. O'Donnell (Eds.). *Development, democracy, and the art of trespassing: Essays in honor of Albert O. Hirschman.* Notre Dame, IN: University of Notre Dame Press.

Gilligan, C. (1988a). Adolescent development reconsidered. In C. Gilligan, J. V. Ward, J. M. Taylor, & B. Bardige (Eds.), *Mapping the moral domain.* Cambridge, MA: Harvard University Press.

Gilligan, C. (1988b). Exit-voice dilemmas in adolescent development. In C. Gilligan, J. V. Ward, J. M. Taylor, & B. Bardige (Eds.), *Mapping the moral domain.* Cambridge, MA: Harvard University Press.

Gilligan, C. (1989a). Preface: Teaching Shakespeare's sister. In C. Gilligan, N. P. Lyons, & T. J. Hanmer (Eds.), *Making connections: The relational worlds of adolescent girls at Emma Willard School.* Cambridge, MA: Harvard University Press.

Gilligan, C. (1989b). Prologue. In C. Gilligan, N. P. Lyons, & T. J. Hanmer (Eds.), *Making connections: The relational worlds of adolescent girls at Emma Willard School.* Cambridge, MA: Harvard University Press.

Gilligan, C., & Attanucci, J. (1988). Two moral orientations: Gender differences and similarities. *Merrill-Palmer Quarterly, 34,* 223–237.

Ginsburg, H., & Opper, S. (1988). *Piaget's theory of intellectual development.* (3rd ed.). Englewood Cliffs, NJ: Prentice-Hall.

Glezerman, M. (1993). Artificial insemination. In V. Insler & B. Lunenfeld (Eds.), *Infertility: Male and female* (2nd ed.). New York: Churchill Livingstone.

Glick, P. C. (1989). Remarried families, stepfamilies, and stepchildren: A brief demographic profile. *Family Relations, 38,* 24–27.

Globus, A., Rosenzweig, E. L., Bennett, E. L., & Diamond, M. C. (1973). Effects of differential experience on dendritic spine counts in rat cerebral cortex. *Journal of Comparative and Physiological Psychology, 82,* 175–181.

Godwin, K. A., Kemerer, F., Martinez, V., & Ruderman, R. (1998). Liberal equity in education: A comparison of choice options. *Social Science Quarterly, 79,* 502–522.

Golding, J. M., & Baezconde-Garbanati, L. A. (1990). Ethnicity, culture, and social resources. *American Journal of Community Psychology, 18,* 465–486.

Goldman-Rakic, P. S. (1987). Development of cortical circuitry and cognitive function. *Child Development, 58,* 601–622.

Goldsmith, D. F., & Rogoff, B. (1997). Mothers' and toddlers' coordinated joint focus of attention: Variations with maternal dysphoric symptoms. *Developmental Psychology, 33,* 113–119.

Goldsmith, H. H., Buss, K. A., & Lemery, K. S. (1997). Toddler and childhood temperament: Expanded content, stronger genetic evidence, new evidence for the importance of environment. *Developmental Psychology, 33,* 891–905.

Goldsmith, H. H., Buss, A. H., Plomin, R., Rothbart, M. K., Thomas, A., Chess, S., Hinde, R. A., & McCall, R. B. (1987). Roundtable: What is temperament? Four approaches. *Child Development, 58,* 505–529.

Golinkoff, R. M., Jacquet, R. C., Hirsh-Pasek, K., & Nandakumar, R. (1996). Lexical principles may underlie the learning of verbs. *Child Development, 67,* 3101–3119.

Golombok, S., Cook, R., Bish, A., & Murray, C. (1995). Families created by the new reproductive technologies: Quality of parenting and social and emotional development of the children. *Child Development, 66,* 285–298.

Gomes-Schwartz, B., Horowitz, J., & Cardarelli, A. (1990). *Child sexual abuse: The initial effects.* Newbury Park, CA: Sage.

Gontard, von A., Eiberg, H., Hollmann, E., Rittig, S., & Lehmkuhl, G. (1998). Molecular genetics of nocturnal enuresis: Clinical and genetic heterogeneity. *Acta Paediatrica, 87,* 571–578.

Gorman, K. S., & Pollitt, E. (1992). Relationship between weight and body proportionality at birth, growth during the first year of life, and cognitive development at 36, 48, and 60 months. *Infant Behavior and Development, 15,* 279–296.

Goss, G. (1996, February). *Weaving girls into the curriculum.* Paper presented at the annual meeting of the American Association for Colleges for Teachers Education, Chicago.

Gottfried, A. E., Fleming, J. S., & Gottfried, A. W. (1998). Role of cognitively stimulating home environment in children's academic intrinsic motivation: A longitudinal study. *Child Development, 69,* 1448–1460.

Grandjean, A. C. (1988). Eating versus inactivity. In K. Clark, R. Parr, & W. Castelli (Eds.), *Evaluation and management of eating disorders.* Champaign, IL: Life Enhancement.

Greenberg, M. T., Lengua, L. J., Coie, J. D., Pinderhughes, E. E., Bierman, K., Dodge, K. A., Lochman, J. E., & McMahon, R. J. (1999). Predicting development of school outcomes using a multiple-risk model: Four American communities. *Developmental Psychology, 35,* 403–417.

Greenfield, P. M., & Smith, J. H. (1976). *The structure of communication in early language development.* New York: Academic Press.

Greenough, W. T., Black, J. E., & Wallace, C. S. (1987). Experience and brain development. *Child Development, 58,* 539–559.

Gregory, D., with Lipsyte, R. (1964). *Nigger: An autobiography.* New York: Dutton.

Groome, L., Bentz, L., & Singh, K. (1995). Behavioral state organization in normal human term fetuses: The relationship between periods of undefined state and other characteristics of state control. *Sleep, 18*(2), 77–81.

Grotevant, H. D., & Cooper, C. R. (1986). Individuation in family relationships. *Human Development, 29,* 82–100.

Grotpeter, J. K., & Crick, N. R. (1996). Relational aggression, overt aggression, and friendship. *Child Development, 67,* 2328–2338.

Gunnar, M. R., Brodersen, L., Nachmias, M., Buss, K., & Rigatuso, J. (1996). Stress reactivity and attachment security. *Developmental Psychobiology, 29,* 191–204.

Guntheroth, W. G. (1995). *Crib death: The sudden infant death syndrome* (3rd ed.). Armonk, NY: Futura.

Gustafson, G. E., & Harris, K. L. (1990). Women's responses to young infants' cries. *Developmental Psychology, 26,* 144–152.

Hagerman, R. J. (1999). Growth and development. In W. W. Hay, Jr., A. R. Hayward, M. J. Levin, & J. M. Sondheimer (Eds.). *Current pediatric diagnosis & treatment* (pp. 1–18). Stamford, CT: Appleton & Lange.

Haith, M. M. (1980). *Rules that infants look by.* Hillsdale, NJ: Erlbaum.

Haith, M. M. (1993). Future-oriented processes in infancy: The case of visual expectations. In C. Granrud (Ed.), *Visual perception and cognition in infancy* (pp. 235–264). Hillsdale, NJ: Erlbaum.

Haith, M. M., Bergman, T., & Moore, M. J. (1977). Eye contact and face scanning in early infancy. *Science, 198,* 853–855.

Haith, M. M., Hazan, C., & Goodman, G. S. (1988). Expectation and anticipation of dynamic visual events by 3.5-month-old babies. *Child Development, 59,* 467–479.

Haith, M. M., Wentworth, N., & Canfield, R. L. (1993). The formation of expectations in early infancy. In C. Rovee-Collier & L. P. Lipsitt (Eds.), *Advances in infancy research* (Vol. 8). Norwood, NJ: Ablex.

Hakuta, K. (1999). The debate on bilingual education. *Developmental and Behavioral Pediatrics, 20,* 36–37.

Hala, S., & Chandler, M. (1996). The role of strategic planning in accessing false-belief understanding. *Child Development, 67,* 2948–2966.

Hale, S. (1990). A global developmental trend in cognitive processing speed. *Child Development, 61,* 653–663.

Hall, C. S. (1954). *A primer of Freudian psychology.* Cleveland: World.

Hallinan, M. T., & Teixeira, R. A. (1987). Opportunities and constraints: Black-White differences in the formation of interracial relationships. *Child Development, 58,* 1358–1371.

Han, F J., Leichtman, M. D., & Wang, Q. (1998). Autobiographical memory in Korean, Chinese, and American children. *Developmental Psychology, 34,* 701–713.

Hanauer, D. (D. H.) (2000). Dying to be bigger. In D. N. Sattler, G. P. Kramer, V. Shabatay, & D. A. Bernstein (Eds.), *Child development in context: Voices and perspectives* (pp. 102–105). Boston: Houghton Mifflin.

Hanna, E. Z., Faden, V. B., & Dufour, M. C. (1997). The effects of substance use during gestation on birth outcome, infant and maternal health. *Journal of Substance Abuse, 9,* 111–125.

Harlow, H. F., & Zimmerman, R. (1959). Affectional responses in the infant monkey. *Science, 130,* 421–432.

Harper, L. V., & Sanders, K. M. (1975). The effect of adults' eating on young children's acceptance of unfamiliar foods. *Journal of Experimental Child Psychology, 20,* 206–214.

Harper, M. J. K. (1988). Gamete and zygote transport. In E. Knobil & J. Neill (Eds.), *The physiology of reproduction* (pp. 103-134). New York: Raven.

Harris, L. (1988). *Public attitudes toward teenage pregnancy, sex education, and birth control.* New York: Planned Parenthood of America.

Harris, P. L. (1997). The last of the magicians? Children, scientists, and the invocation of hidden causal powers. *Child Development, 68,* 1018–1020.

F, P. L., & Nunez, M. (1996). Understanding of permission rules by preschool children. *Child Development, 67,* 1572–1591.

Harsha, D. W. (1995). The benefits of physical activity in childhood. *American Journal of Medical Science, 310,* S109–S113.

Hart, C. H., Nelson, D. A., Robinson, C. C., Olsen, S. F., & McNeilly–Choque, M. K. (1998). Overt and relational aggression in Russian nursery-school-age children: Parenting style and marital linkages. *Developmental Psychology, 34,* 687–697.

Hart, D., & Fegley, S. (1995). Prosocial behavior and caring in adolescence: Relations to self-understanding and social judgment. *Child Development, 66,* 1346–1359.

Hart, S. N. (1991). From property to person status: Historical perspective on children's rights. *American Psychologist, 46,* 53–59.

Harter, S. (1996). Developmental changes in self-understanding across the 5 to 7 shift. In A. J. Sameroff & M. M. Haith (Eds.), *The five to seven year shift* (pp. 207–236). Chicago: University of Chicago Press.

Hartmann, T. (1995). *ADD success stories.* Grass Valley, CA: Underwood Books.

Hartup, W. W. (1992). Conflict and friendship relations. In C. U. Shantz & W. W. Hartup (Eds.), *Conflict in child and adolescent development* (pp. 186–215). New York: Cambridge University Press.

Hartup, W. W. (1996). The company they keep: Friendships and their developmental significance. *Child Development, 67,* 1–13.

Haselager, G. J. T., Hartup, W. W., van Lieshout, C. F. M., & Riksen-Walraven, J. M. A. (1998). Similarities between friends and nonfriends in middle childhood. *Child Development, 69,* 1198–1208.

Haslam, G. (1988). The horned toad. In G. Soto (Ed.), *California childhood* (pp. 138–145). Berkeley, CA: Creative Arts.

Hauser-Cram, P. (1996). Mastery motivation in toddlers with developmental disabilities. *Child Development, 67,* 236–248.

Hayes, C. D. (Ed.). (1987). *Risking the future: Adolescent sexuality, pregnancy, and childbearing.* (Vol. 1). Washington, DC: National Academy Press.

Heemskerk, J., & DiNardo, S. (1994). *Drosophila hedgehog* acts as a morphogen in cellular patterning. *Cell, 76,* 449–460.

Hegi, U. (1995). *Salt dancers.* New York: Simon & Schuster.

Helburn, S., Culkin, M. L., Morris, J., Mocan, N., Howes, C., Phillipsen, L., Bryant, D., Clifford, R., Cryer, D., Peisner, Feinberg, E., Burchinal, M., Kagan, L. L., & Rustici, J. (1995). *Cost, quality, and child outcomes in child-care centers.* Public report. Denver: Economics Department, University of Colorado.

Held, R., & Hein, A. (1963). Movement-produced stimulation and the development of visually guided behaviors. *Journal of Comparative and Physiological Psychology, 56,* 872–876.

Helwig, C. C. (1995). Adolescents' and young adults' conceptions of civil liberties: Freedom of speech and religion. *Child Development, 66*(1), 152–166.

Helwig, C. C., Hildebrandt, C., & Turiel, E. (1995). Children's judgments about psychological harm in social context. *Child Development, 66,* 1680–1693.

Henderson-Smart, D. J., Ponsonby, A-L, & Murphy, E. (1998). Reducing the risk of sudden-infant-death syndrome: A review of the scientific literature. *Journal of Paediatric Child Health, 34,* 213-219.

Henley, N. (1989). Molehill or mountain? What we do know and don't know about sex bias in language. In M. Craw-

ford & M. Gentry (Eds.), *Gender and thought.* New York: Springer-Verlag.

Hepper, D. G. (1992). Fetal psychology: An embryonic science. In J. G. Nijhuis (Ed.), *Fetal behaviour: Developmental and perinatal aspects* (pp. 129–156). New York: Oxford University Press.

Hermer, L., & Spelke, E. S. (1994). A geometric process for spatial reorientation in young children. *Nature, 370,* 57–59.

Herrera, R. S., & DelCampo, R. L. (1995). Beyond the superwoman syndrome: Work satisfaction and family functioning among working-class, Mexican-American women. *Hispanic Journal of Behavioral Sciences, 17,* 49–60.

Hersch, P. (1998). *A tribe apart; A journey into the heart of American adolescence.* New York: Fawcett Columbine.

Hertel, B. R., & Donahue, M. J. (1995). Parental influences on God images among children: Testing Durkheim's metaphoric parallelism. *Journal for the Scientific Study of Religion, 34,* 186–199.

Hervada, A. R., & Hervada-Page, M. (1995). Infant nutrition: The first two years. In F. Lifshitz (Ed.), *Childhood nutrition* (pp. 43–60). Ann Arbor, MI: CRC Press.

Hetherington, E. M. (1989). Coping with family transitions: Winners, losers, and survivors. *Child Development, 60,* 1–14.

Hetherington, E. M., & Clingempeel, W. G. (1992). Coping with marital transitions: A family systems perspective. *Monographs of the Society for Research in Child Development, 57*(2–3, Serial No. 227).

Hetherington, E. M., Cox, M., & Cox, R. (1982). Effects of divorce on children and parents. In M. E. Lamb (Ed.), *Nontraditional families.* Hillsdale, NJ: Erlbaum.

Hetherington, E. M., Hagan, M. S., & Anderson, E. R. (1989). Marital transitions: A child's perspective. *American Psychologist, 44,* 303–312.

Heyman, G. D., & Dweck, C. S. (1998). Children's thinking about traits: Implications for judgments of the self and others. *Child Development, 64,* 391–403.

Heymann, S. J., & Earle, A. (1999). The impact of welfare reform on parents' ability to care for their children's health. *American Journal of Public Health, 89,* 502–505.

Hill, J. O., & Trowbridge, F. L. (1998). Childhood obesity: Future directions and research priorities. *Pediatrics, 101,* 570–574.

Hirsch, R. H., Paolitto, D. P., & Reimer, J. (1979). *Promoting moral growth: From Piaget to Kohlberg.* New York: Longman.

Hjälmas, K. (1998). Nocturnal enuresis: Basic facts and new horizons. *European Urology, 33,* 53–57.

Hodges, E. V. E., Boivin, M., Vitaro, F., & Bukowski, W. M. (1999). The power of friendship: Protection against an escalating cycle of peer victimization. *Developmental Psychology, 35,* 94–101.

Hodges, E. V. E., Finnegan, R. A., & Perry, D. G. (1999). Skewed autonomy-relatedness in preadolescents' conceptions of their relationships with mother, father, and best friend. *Developmental Psychology, 35,* 737–748.

Hoffman, H. J., Damus, K., Hillman, L., & Krongrad, E. (1988). Risk factors for SIDS: Results of the NICHD SIDS cooperative epidemiological study. *Annal New York Academy of Sciences, 533,* 13–30.

Hoffman, M. (1991). How parents make their mark on genes. *Science, 252,* 1250–1251.

Hoffman, M. L. (1980). Moral development in adolescence. In J. Adelson (Ed.), *Handbook of adolescent psychology.* New York: Wiley.

Hogan, R. (1980). The gifted adolescent. In J. Adelson (Ed.), *Handbook of adolescence.* New York: Wiley.

Hogan, R., & Weiss, D. (1974). Personality correlates of superior academic achievement. *Journal of Counseling Psychology, 21,* 144–149.

Hogue, A., & Steinberg, L. (1995). Homophily of internalized distress in adolescent peer groups. *Developmental Psychology, 31,* 897–906.

Holt, J. (1969). *How children learn.* New York: Pitman.

Hooker, D. (1952). *The prenatal origin of behavior.* University of Kansas Press.

Horn, S., Killen, M., & Stangor, C. (1999). The influence of group stereotypes on adolescents' moral reasoning. *Journal of Early Adolescence, 19,* 98–113.

Horney, K. (1937). *The neurotic personality of our time.* New York: Norton

Horney, K. (1967). *Feminine psychology.* New York: Norton.

Hornik, R., Risenhoover, N., & Gunnar, M. (1987). The effects of maternal positive, neutral and negative affective communications on infant responses to new toys. *Child Development, 58,* 937–944.

Horowitz, F. D., & O'Brien, M. (1986). Gifted and talented children. *American Psychologist, 41,* 1147–1152.

Horta, B. L., Victora, C. G., Menezes, A. M., Halpern, R., & Barros, F. C. (1997). Low birthweight, preterm births, and intrauterine growth retardation in relation to maternal smoking. *Paediatr Perinat Epidemiol, 11,* 140–151.

Howard, G. R. (1993). Whites in multicultural education: Rethinking our role. *Phi Delta Kappan, 75,* 36–41.

Howes, C. (1983). Patterns of friendship. *Child Development, 54,* 1041–1053.

Howes, P., & Cicchetti, D. (1993). A family/relational perspective on maltreating families: Parallel processes across systems and social policy implications. In D. Cicchetti & S. L. Toth (Eds.), *Child abuse, child development, and social policy* (pp. 399–438). Norwood, NJ: Ablex.

Huang, L. N., & Yin, Y. (1989). Chinese American children and adolescents. In J. T. Gibbs, L. N. Huang, & associates (Eds.), *Children of color.* San Francisco: Jossey-Bass.

Hu-DeHart, E. (1993). The history, development, and future of ethnic studies. *Phi Delta Kappan, 75,* 50–54.

Hudspeth, W. J., & Pribram, K. H. (1992). Psychophysiological indices of cerebral maturation. *International Journal of Psychophysiology, 12,* 19–29.

Humphrey, G. K., & Humphrey, D .E. (1985). The use of binaural sensory aids by blind infants and children: Theoretical and applied issues. In F. Morrison & C. Lord (Eds.), *Applied developmental psychology* (Vol. 2). New York: Academic Press.

Humphrey, L. L. (1989). Observed family interactions among subtypes of eating disorders using structural analysis of social behavior. *Journal of Consulting and Clinical Psychology, 57,* 206–214.

Hunt, L., Fleming, P., & Golding, J., the ALSPAC Study Team. (in press). Does the supine sleeping position have any adverse effects on the child? I: Health in the first six months. *Pediatrics.*

Hur, Y., & Bourchard, T. J. (1995). Genetic influences on perceptions of childhood family environment: A reared apart twin study. *Child Development, 66,* 330-345.

Huston, A. C., McLoyd, V. C., & Coll, C. G. (1994). Children and poverty: Issues in contemporary research. *Child Development, 65,* 275-282.

Hwang, M. Y. (1999). Are you obese? *Journal of the American Medical Association, 282,* 1596.

Hyde, J. S. (1981). How large are cognitive gender differences? A meta-analysis using *w*2 and *d. American Psychologist, 36,* 892–901.

Hyde, J. S. (1984). Children's understanding of sexist language. *Developmental Psychology, 20,* 697–706.

Idjradinata, P., & Pollitt, E. (1993). Reversal of developmental delays in iron-deficient anaemic infants treated with iron. *Lancet, 341,* 1–4.

Irion, J. C., Coon, R. C., & Blanchard-Fields, F. (1988). The influence of divorce on coping in adolescence. *Journal of Youth and Adolescence, 17,* 135–145.

Irwin, J., & Austin, J. (1997). *It's about time: America's imprisonment binge.* Belmont, CA: Wadsworth.

Isabella, R. A. (1994). Origins of maternal role satisfaction and its influences upon maternal interactive behavior and infant-mother attachment. *Infant Behavior and Development, 17,* 381–388.

Iverson, J. M., & Goldin-Meadow, S. (1997). What's communication got to do with it? Gesture in children blind from birth. *Developmental Psychology, 33,* 458–467.

Izard, C. E. (1983). Emotions in personality and culture. *Ethos, 11,* 305–312.

Izard, C. E. (1994). Innate and universal facial expressions: Evidence from developmental and cross-cultural research. *Psychological Bulletin, 115,* 288–299.

Izard, C. E., & Maletesta, C. Z. (1987). Perspectives on emotional development I. In J. D. Osofsky (Ed.), *Handbook of infant development* (2nd ed.). New York: Wiley.

Jackson, J. F. (1993). Human behavioral genetics, Scarr's theory, and her views on interventions: A critical review and commentary on their implications for African American children. *Child Development, 64,* 1318–1332.

Jadack, R. A., Hyde, J. S., Moore, C. F., & Keller, M. L. (1995). Moral reasoning about sexually transmitted diseases. *Child Development, 66,* 167–177.

James, W. T. (1890). *The principles of psychology.* New York: Holt.

Jansen, R. P. S. (1978). Fallopian tube isthmic mucus and ovum transport. *Science, 201,* 349–351.

Jansen, R. P. S. (1984). Endocrine response in the fallopian tube. *Endocrine Review, 5,* 525–551.

Jarrett, R. L. (1995). Growing up poor: The family experiences of socially mobile youth in low-income African American neighborhoods. *Journal of Adolescent Research, 10,* 111–134.

Jensen, A. R. (1969). How much can we boost IQ and scholastic achievement? *Harvard Educational Review, 39,* 1–123.

Jensen, A. R. (1985). The nature of the Black-White difference on various psychometric tests: Spearman's hypothesis. *Behavioral and Brain Sciences, 8,* 193–263.

Joffe, M., & Ludwig, S. (1988). Stairway injuries in children. *Pediatrics, 82,* 457–461.

John, E. M., Savitz, D. A., & Sandler, D. P. (1991). Prenatal exposure to parents' smoking and childhood cancer. *American Journal of Epidemiology, 133,* 123–132.

Johnson, M. H. (1995). The inhibition of automatic saccades in early infancy. *Developmental Psychobiology, 28,* 281–291.

Johnson, M. L., Veldhuis, J. D., & Lampl, M. (1996). Is growth saltatory? The usefulness and limitations of frequency distributions in analyzing pulsatile data. *Endocrinology, 137,* 5197–5204.

Johnson, R. L., Laufer, E., Riddle, R. D., & Tabin, C. (1994). Ectopic expression of *Sonic hedgehog* alters dorsal-ventral patterning of somites. *Cell, 79*(7), 1165–1173.

Johnson, S. C., & Solomon, G. E. A. (1997). Why dogs have puppies and cats have kittens: The role of birth in young children's understanding of biological origins. *Child Development, 68,* 404–419.

Johnson, S. L., & Birch, L. L. (1994). Parents' and children's adiposity and eating style. *Pediatrics, 94,* 653–661.

Johnson, S. P., & Aslin, R. N. (1995). Perception of object unity in 2–month-old infants. *Developmental Psychology, 31,* 739–745.

Johnson, S. P., & Nanez, J. E. (1995). Young infants' perception of object unity in two-dimensional displays. *Infant Behavior and Development, 18,* 133–143.

Johnson, W., Emde, R. N., Pannebecker, B., Stenberg, C., & Davis, M. (1982). Maternal perception of infant emotion from birth through 18 months. *Infant Behavior and Development, 5,* 313–322.

Johnston, D. K. (1988). Adolescents' solutions to dilemmas in fables: Two moral orientations—two problem-solving strategies. In C. Gilligan, J. V. Ward, J. M. Taylor, & B. Bardige (Eds.), *Mapping the moral domain.* Cambridge, MA: Harvard University Press.

Jones, M. C. (1957). The late careers of boys who were early- or late-maturing. *Child Development, 28,* 113–128.

Jones, M. C. (1958). A study of socialization patterns at the high school level. *Journal of Genetic Psychology, 93,* 87–111.

Jones, M. C. (1965). Psychological correlates of somatic development. *Child Development, 36,* 899–911.

Jones, M. C., & Bayley, N. (1950). Physical maturing among boys as related to behavior. *Journal of Educational Psychology, 41,* 129–148.

Jones, M. C., & Mussen, P. H. (1958). Self-conceptions, motivations, and attitudes of early- and late-maturing girls. *Child Development, 29,* 491–501.

Joos, S. K., Pollitt, E., & Mueller, W. H. (1982). The Bacon Chow Study: Effects of maternal nutritional supplementation on infant mental and motor development. *Food & Nutrition Bulletin, 4,* 1–4.

Josselson, R. L. (1980). Ego development in adolescence. In J. Adelson (Ed.), *Handbook of adolescent psychology.* New York: Wiley.

Josselson, R. L. (1982). Personality structure and identity status in women as viewed through early memories. *Journal of Youth and Adolescence, 11,* 293–299.

Josselson, R. L. (1987). *Finding herself: Pathways to identity development in women.* San Francisco: Jossey-Bass.

Josselson, R. L. (1988). The embedded self: I and thou revisited. In D. K. Lapsley & F. C. Power (Eds.), *Self, ego, and identity.* New York: Springer-Verlag.

Josselson, R. L. (1992). *The space between us.* San Francisco: Jossey-Bass.

Jusczyk, P. W., Hirsh-Pasek, K., Kemler Nelson, D. G., Kennedy, L. J., Woodward, A., & Piwoz, J. (1992). Perception of acoustic correlates of major phrasal units by young infants. *Cognitive Psychology, 24,* 252–293.

Jusczyk, P. W., Johnson, S. P., Spelke, E. S., & Kennedy, L. J. (1999). Synchronous change and perception of object unity: Evidence from adults and infants. *Cognition, 71,* 257–288.

Just, E. E. (1919). The fertilization reaction in *Echinarachinus parma. Biological Bulletin, 36,* 1–10.

Justice Policy Institute. (1997, Fall). *Crime and justice trends in the District of Columbia.* Prepared by the National Council on Crime and Delinquency. Washington, DC: Office of Grants Management and Development, District of Columbia Government.

Kagan, J. (1981). *The second year.* Cambridge, MA: Harvard University Press.

Kagan, J. (1996). Three pleasing ideas. *American Psychologist, 51*, 901–908.

Kagan, J. (1997). Temperament and the reactions to unfamiliarity. *Child Development, 68*, 139–143.

Kagan, J., Arcus, D., Snidman, N., Feng, W. Y., Hendler, J., & Greene, S. (1994). Reactivity in infants: A cross-national comparison. *Developmental Psychology, 30*, 342–345.

Kagan, J., & Snidman, N. (1991). Temperamental factors in human development. *American Psychologist, 46*, 856–862.

Kail, R. (1991). Developmental changes in speed of processing during childhood and adolescence. *Psychological Bulletin, 109*, 490–501.

Kamii, M. (1991). Why Big Bird can't teach calculus: The case of place value and cognitive development in the middle years. In N. Lauter-Klatell (Ed.), *Readings in child development* (pp. 100–104). Mountain View, CA: Mayfield.

Kaufman, C., Grunebaum, H., Cohler, B., & Gamer, E. (1979). Superkids: Competent children of schizophrenic mothers. *American Journal of Psychiatry, 136*, 1398–1402.

Keating, D. P. (1980). Thinking processes in adolescence. In J. Adelson (Ed.), *Handbook of adolescent psychology*. New York: Wiley.

Keen, S. (1970). Reflections on a peach-seed monkey. In *To a dancing God* (pp. 100–101). New York: Harper & Row.

Kegan, R. (1982). *The evolving self: Problem and process in human development*. Cambridge, MA: Harvard University Press.

Kegan, R. (1994). *In over our heads*. Cambridge, MA: Harvard University Press.

Keirsey, D. (1999, January 25). The great A.D.D. hoax. Retrieved March 3, 2000, from the World Wide Web: http://keirsey.com/addhoax.html

Keith, L. G., & Luke, B. (1993). Multiple gestation. In F. R. Witter & L. G. Keith (Eds.), *Textbook of prematurity: Antecedents, treatment, and outcome* (pp. 115–126). Boston: Little, Brown.

Keller, M., & Wood, P. (1989). Development of friendship reasoning: A study of interindividual differences in intraindividual change. *Developmental Psychology, 25*, 820–826.

Kelley, M. L., Power, T. G., & Wimbush, D. D. (1992). Determinants of disciplinary practices in low-income Black mothers. *Child Development, 63*, 573–582.

Kenen, R. (1993). *Reproductive hazards in the workplace*. New York: Haworth Press.

Kennell, J., Klaus, M., McGrath, S., Robertson, S., & Hinkley, C. (1991). Continuous emotional support during labor in a U.S. hospital. *Journal of the American Medical Association, 265*, 2197–2201.

Kenny, A. M., Guardado, S., & Brown, L. (1989). Sex education and AIDS education in the schools: What states and large school districts are doing. *Family Planning Perspective, 21*, 56–64.

Kent, R. D., & Miolo, G. (1995). Phonetic abilities in the first year of life. In P. Fletcher & P. MacWhinney (Eds.), *The handbook of child language* (pp. 301–334). Oxford: Blackwell.

Kerfoot, M., Harrington, R., & Dyer, E. (1995). Brief home-based intervention with young suicide attempters and the families. *Journal of Adolescence, 18*, 557–568.

Kim, J. M. (1998). Korean children's concepts of adult and peer authority and moral reasoning. *Developmental Psychology, 34*, 947–955.

King, S. (1998). The body. In *Apt pupil* (pp. 293–436). New York: Signet.

King, T., & Fullard, W. (1982). Teenage mothers and their infants: New findings on the home environment. *Journal of Adolescence, 5*, 333–346.

Kingston, M. H. (1976). *Woman warrior: Memoirs of a girlhood among ghosts*. New York: Knopf.

Kipp, K., & Pope, S. (1997). The development of cognitive inhibition in streams-of-consciousness and directed speech. *Cognitive Development, 12*, 239–260.

Kirby, D. (1984). *Sexuality education: An evaluation of programs and their effect*. Santa Cruz, CA: Network Publications.

Klebanov, P. K., Brooks-Gunn, J., McCarton, C., & McCormick, M. C. (1998). The contribution of neighborhood and family income to developmental test scores over the first three years of life. *Child Development, 69*, 1420–1436.

Klesges, R. C., Shelton, M. L., & Klesges, L. M. (1993). Effects of television on metabolic rate: Potential implications for childhood obesity. *Pediatrics, 91*, 281–286.

Klonoff-Cohen, H. S., Edelstein, S. L., Lefkowitz, E. S., Srinivasen, I. P., Kaegi, D., Chang, J. C., & Wiley, K. J. (1995). The effect of passive smoking and tobacco exposure through breast milk on sudden infant death syndrome. *Journal of the American Medical Association, 273*, 795–798.

Knobil, E. (1980). The neuroendocrine control of the menstrual cycle. *Recent Progress in Hormone Research, 36*, 53–88.

Ko, Y. H., & Pedersen, P. L. (1997). Frontiers in research on cystic fibrosis: Understanding its molecular and chemical basis and relationship to the pathogenesis of the disease. *Journal of Bioenergetics and Biomembranes, 19*, 417–427.

Kobayashi-Winata, H., & Power, T. G. (1989). Child rearing and compliance: Japanese and American families in Houston. *Journal of Cross-Cultural Psychology, 20*, 333–356.

Kochanska, G., Casey, R. J., & Fukumoto, A. (1995). Toddlers' sensitivity to standard violations. *Child Development, 66*, 643–656.

Kochanska, G., Murray, K., & Coy, K. C. (1997). Inhibitory control as a contributor to conscience in childhood: From toddler to early school age. *Child Development, 68*, 263–277.

Kochman, T. (1987). The ethnic component in Black language and culture. In M. J. Rotheram & J. S. Phinney (Eds.), *Children's ethnic socialization: Pluralism and development* (pp. 219–238). Beverly Hills: Sage.

Kohl, H. W., III, & Hobbs, K. E. (1998). Development of physical activity behaviors among children and adolescents. *Pediatrics, 101,* 549–554.

Kohlberg, L. (1976). Moral stages and moralization: The cognitive developmental approach. In T. Lickona (Ed.), *Moral development and behavior.* New York: Holt, Rinehart & Winston.

Kohlberg, L. (1984). *The psychology of moral development.* New York: Harper & Row.

Kohlberg, L., & Kramer, R. (1969). Continuities and discontinuities in childhood and adult moral development. *Human Development, 12,* 93–120.

Kohler, I. (1962). Experiments with goggles. *Scientific American, 206,* 62–86.

Kontos, S., Howes, C., Shinn, M., & Galinsky, E. (1995). *Quality in family child care and relative care.* New York: Teachers College Press.

Koocher, G. P., & DeMaso, D. (1990). Children's competence to consent to medical procedures. *Pediatrician, 17,* 68–73.

Koplan, J. P., & Dietz, W. H. (1999). Caloric imbalance and public health policy. *Journal of the American Medical Association, 282,* 1579–1581.

Kopp, C. B. (1989). Regulation of distress and negative emotions: A developmental view. *Developmental Psychology, 25,* 343–354.

Korbin, J., & Coulton, C. (1995). *Neighborhood impact on child abuse and neglect: Final report on Grant # 90CA-1494.* Washington, DC: National Center on Child Abuse and Neglect.

Korenman, S., Miller, J. E., & Sjaastad, J. E. (1995). Long-term poverty and child development in the United States: Results from the NLSY. *Children and Youth Services Review, 17*(1–2), 127–155.

Kotlowitz, A. (1991). *There are no children here.* New York: Anchor/Doubleday.

Kovacs, D. M., Parker, J. G., & Hoffman, L. W. (1996). Behavioral, affective, and social correlates of involvement in cross-sex friendship in elementary school. *Child Development, 67,* 2269–2286.

Krasnoff, A. G. (1989). Early sex-linked activities and interests related to spatial abilities. *Personal and Individual Differences, 10,* 81–85.

Krebs-Smith, S. M., Cook, A., Subar, A. F., Cleveland, L., Friday, J., & Kahle, L. L. (1996). Fruit and vegetable intakes of children and adolescents in the United States. *Archives of Pediatric Adolescent Medicine, 150,* 81–86.

Kroger, J. (1986). The relative importance of identity status interview components: A replication and extension. *Journal of Adolescence, 9,* 337–354.

Kroger, J. (1988). A longitudinal study of ego identity status interview domains. *Journal of Adolescence, 11,* 49–64.

Kroger, J. (1995). The differentiation of "firm" and "developmental" foreclosure identity statuses: A longitudinal study. *Journal of Adolescent Research, 10,* 317–337.

Kroger, J. (1996). Identity, regression, and development. *Journal of Adolescence, 19,* 203–222.

Kroger, J., & Greene, K. E. (1996). Events associated with identity status change. *Journal of Adolescence, 19,* 477–490.

Krug, E. G., Dahlberg, L. L., & Powell, K. E. (1996). Childhood homicide, suicide, and firearm deaths: An international comparison. *World Health Statistics Quarterly, 49,* 230-235.

Kuhl, P. K., Andruski, J. E., Chistovich, I. A., Chistovich, L. A., Kozhevnikova, E. V., Ryskina, V. L., Stolyarova, E. I., Sundberg, U., & Lacerda. F. (1997). Cross–language analysis of phonetic units in language addressed to infants. *Science, 277,* 684–686.

Kuhn, T. S. (1962). *The structure of scientific revolutions.* Chicago: University of Chicago Press.

Kulin, H. E. (1991a). Puberty, hypothalamic-pituitary changes of. In R. M. Lerner, A. C. Petersen, & J. Brooks-Gunn (Eds.), *Encyclopedia of adolescence* (Vol. 2, pp. 900–907). New York: Garland.

Kulin, H. E. (1991b). Puberty, endocrine changes at. In R. M. Lerner, A. C. Petersen, & J. Brooks-Gunn (Eds.), *Encyclopedia of adolescence* (Vol. 2, pp. 897–899). New York: Garland.

LaFromboise, T. D., & Low, K. G. (1989). American Indian children and adolescents. In J. T. Gibbs, L. N. Huang, & associates (Eds.), *Children of color.* San Francisco: Jossey-Bass.

Lagattuta, K. H., Wellman, H. M., & Flavell, J. H. (1997). Preschoolers' understanding of the link between thinking and feeling: Cognitive cueing and emotional change. *Child Development, 68,* 1081–1104.

Laible, D. J., & Thompson, R. A. (1998). Attachment and emotional understanding in preschool children. *Developmental Psychology, 34,* 1038–1045.

Lakoff, G. (1987). *Women, fire and dangerous things.* Chicago: University of Chicago Press.

Lamb, M. E. (1977). The development of mother-infant and father-infant attachments in the second year of life. *Developmental Psychology, 13,* 637–648.

Lamb, M. E. (1981). The development of father-infant relationships. In M. E. Lamb (Ed.), *The role of the father in child development* (2nd ed., pp. 459–488). New York: Wiley.

Lamott, A. (1993). *Operating instructions: A journal of my son's first year.* San Francisco: Pantheon Books.

Lampinen, J. M., & Smith, V. L. (1995). The incredible (and sometimes credulous) child witness: Child eyewitnesses' sensitivity to source credibility cues. *Journal of Applied Psychology, 80,* 621–627.

Lampl, M., & Johnson, M. L. (1993). A case study of daily growth during adolescence: A single spurt or changes in the dynamics of saltatory growth? *Annals of Human Biology, 20,* 595–603.

Landau, S., Lorch, E. P., & Milich. (1992). Visual attention to and comprehension of television in attention-deficit hyperactivity disordered and normal boys. *Child Development, 63*, 928–937.

Lannfelt, L., Axelman, K., Lilius, L., & Basun, H. (1995). Genetic counseling in a Swedish Alzheimer family with amyloid precursor protein mutation (letter). *American Journal of Human Genetics, 56*, 332–335.

Lapsley, D. K., FitzGerald, D. P., Rice, K. G., & Jackson, S. (1989). Separation-individuation and the "new look" at the imaginary audience and personal fable: A test of an integrative model. *Journal of Adolescent Research, 4*, 483–505.

Larson, R. W., & Almeida, D. M. (1999). Emotional transmission in the daily lives of families: A new paradigm for studying family process. *Journal of Marriage and the Family, 61*, **5**–20.

Larson, R. W., & Gillman, S. (1999). Transmission of emotions in the daily interactions of single-mother families. *Journal of Marriage and the Family, 61*(1), 21–37.

Larson, R. W., Richards, M. H., Moneta, G., Holmbeck, G., & Duckett, E. (1996). Changes in adolescents' daily interactions with their families from ages 10 to 18: Disengagement and transformation. *Developmental Psychology, 32*, 744–754.

Larson, R., & Richards, M. H. (1994). *Divergent realities*. New York: Basic Books.

Lau, S., & Lau, W. (1996). Outlook on life: How adolescents and children view the life-style of parents, adults and self. *Journal of Adolescence, 19*, 293–296.

Laupa, M. (1991). Children's reasoning about three authority attributes: Adult status, knowledge, and social position. *Developmental Psychology, 27*, 321–329.

Laupa, M., & Turiel, E. (1986). Children's concepts of adult and peer authority. *Child Development, 57*, 405–412.

Laursen, R., Coy, K. C., & Collins, W. A. (1998). Reconsidering changes in parent-child conflict across adolescence: A meta-analysis. *Child Development, 69*, 817–832.

Lawrence, R. A. (1994). *Breastfeeding: A guide for the medical profession*. St. Louis: Mosby.

Lecours, A. R. (1982). Correlates of developmental behavior in brain maturation. In T. Bever (Ed.), *Regressions in mental development*. Hillsdale, NJ: Erlbaum.

Ledoux, S., Choquet, M., & Manfredi, R. (1993). Associated factors for self-reported binge eating among male and female adolescents. *Journal of Adolescence, 15*, 75–91.

Lee, K., Cameron, C.A., Xu, F., Fu, G., & Board, J. (1997). Chinese and Canadian children's evaluations of lying and truth telling: Similarities and differences in the context of pro- and antisocial behaviors. *Child Development, 68*, 924–934.

Leger, J., Limoni, C., & Czernichow, P. (1997). Prediction of the outcome of growth at 2 years of age in neonates with intra-uterine growth retardation. *Early Human Development, 48*, 211–223.

Leinbach, M. D., Hort, B. E., & Fagot, B. (1997). Bears are for boys: Metaphorical associations in young children's gender stereotypes. *Cognitive Development, 12*, 107–130.

Leland, N. L., & Barth, R. P. (1993). Characteristics of adolescents who have attempted to avoid HIV and who have communicated with parents about sex. *Journal of Adolescent Research, 8*, 58–76.

Leon, G. R., Perry, C. L., Mangelsdorf, C., & Tell, G. J. (1989). Adolescent nutritional and psychological patterns and risk for the development of an eating disorder. *Journal of Youth and Adolescence, 18*, 273–282.

Lerner, R. M. (1976). *Concepts and theories of human development*. Menlo Park, CA: Addison-Wesley.

Lerner, R. M. (1986). *Concepts and theories of human development* (2nd ed.). New York: Random House.

Leslie, A. M. (1982). The perception of causality in infants. *Perception, 11*, 173–186.

Leslie, A. M. (1986). The necessity of illusion: Perception and thought in infancy. In L. Weiskrantz (Ed.), *Thought without language* (pp. 185–210). Oxford: Clarendon.

Lester, B. M., Boukydis, C. F., & Zachariah, C. (1992). No language by a cry. In H. Papousek, J. Jurgens, & M. Papousek (Eds.), *Nonverbal vocal communications: Comparative and developmental approaches*. New York: Cambridge University Press.

Lester, B. M., Freier, K., & LaGasse, L. (1995). Prenatal cocaine exposure and child outcome: What do we really know? In M. Lewis & M. Bendersky (Eds.). *Mothers, babies, and cocaine: The role of toxins in development* (pp. 19–40). Hillsdale, NJ: Erlbaum.

Lever, J. (1976). Sex differences in the games children play. *Social Problems, 23*, 478–487.

Lever, J. (1978). Sex differences in the complexity of children's play and games. *American Sociological Review, 43*, 471–483.

Levine, L. E. (1983). Mine: Self-definition in 2-year-old boys. *Developmental Psychology, 19*, 544–549.

Levinson, R. A., Wan, C. K., & Beamer, L. J. (1998). The contraceptive self-efficacy scale: Analysis in four samples. *Journal of Youth and Adolescence, 27*, 773–793.

Levitt, M. J., Guacci-Franco, N., & Levitt, J. L. (1993). Convoys of social support in childhood and early adolescence: Structure and function. *Developmental Psychology, 29*, 811–818.

Levitt, R. A. (1981). *Physiological psychology*. New York: Holt, Rinehart & Winston.

Lewis, C., Freeman, N. H., Kyriakidou, C., Maridaki-Kassotaki, K., & Berridge, D. M. (1996). Social influences on false belief access: Specific sibling influences or general apprenticeship? *Child Development, 67*, 2930–2947.

Lewis, M. (1993). The emergence of emotions. In M. Lewis & J. Havilland (Eds.), *Handbook of emotions* (pp. 223–235). New York: Guilford Press.

Lewis, M. (1995). Embarrassment: The emotion of self-exposure and evaluation. In J. P. Tangney & K. W. Fischer (Eds.),. *Self-conscious emotions: The psychology of shame, guilt, embarrassment, and pride* (pp. 198–218). New York: Guilford Press.

Lewis, M., & Brooks-Gunn, J. (1979). *Social cognition and the acquisition of self.* New York: Plenum.

Lewis, M., & Michaelson, L. (1983). From emotional state to emotional expression: Emotional development from a person-environment perspective. In D. Magnusson & V. L. Allen (Eds.), *Human development: An interactional perspective* (pp. 261–275). New York: Academic Press.

Lewis, M., Ramsay, D. S., & Kawakami, K. (1993). Differences between Japanese infants and Causasian American infants in behavioral and cortisol response to inoculation. *Child Development, 64*, 1722–1731.

Lewis, S. (1996). *A totally alien life-form—Teenagers.* New York: New Press.

Lewkowicz, D. J. (1996). Infants' response to the audible and visible properties of the human face: 1. Role of lexical-syntactic content, temporal synchrony, gender, and manner of speech. *Developmental Psychology, 32*, 347–366.

Lewontin, R. (1982). *Human diversity.* New York: Scientific American Books.

Li, X., Sano, H., & Merwin, J. C. (1996). Perception and reasoning abilities among American, Japanese, and Chinese adolescents. *Journal of Adolescent Research, 11*, 173–193.

Lillard, A. S. (1993). Young children's conceptualization of pretense: Action or mental representational state? *Child Development, 64*, 372–386.

Lillard, A. S. (1996). Body or mind: Children's categorizing of pretense. *Child Development, 67*, 1717–1734.

Lindsey, E. W., Mize, J., & Pettit, G. S. (1997). Differential play patterns of mothers and fathers of sons and daughters: Implications for children's gender role development. *Sex Roles, 37*, 643–661.

Lips, H. M. (1997). *Sex and gender: An introduction* (3rd ed.). Mountain View, CA: Mayfield.

Little, R. E., & Sing, E. F. (1987). Father's drinking and infant birth weight: Report of an association. *Teratology, 36*, 59–65.

Livesley, W. J., & Bromley, D. B. (1973). *Person perception in childhood and adolescence.* London: Wiley.

Lobel, T., & Levanon, I. (1988). Self-esteem, need for approval, and cheating behavior in children. *Journal of Educational Psychology, 80*, 122–123.

Longo, F. J. (1987). *Fertilization.* New York: Chapman and Hall.

LoSciuto, L., Rajala, A. K., Townsend, T. N., & Taylor, A. S. (1996). An outcome evaluation of Across Ages: An intergenerational mentoring approach to drug prevention. *Journal of Adolescent Research, 11*, 116–129.

Lou, H. C., Hansen, D., Nordentoft, M., Pryds, O., Jensen, F.,

Nim, J., & Hemmingsen, R. (1994). Prenatal stressors of human life affect fetal brain development. *Developmental Medicine and Child Neurology, 36*, 826–832.

Lovitt, T. C. (1989). *Introduction to learning disabilities.* Boston: Allyn & Bacon.

Lucas, B. (1988). Family patterns and their relationship to obesity. In K. C. Clark, R. B. Parr, & W. P. Castelli (Eds.), *Evaluation and management of eating disorders.* Champaign, IL: Life Enhancement.

Luciana, M., & Nelson, C.A. (1998). The functional emergence of prefrontally-guided working memory systems in four- to eight-year-old children. *Neuropsychologia, 36*, 273–293.

Lund, R. D., & Chang, F. F. (1986). The normal and abnormal development of the mammalian visual system. In W. T. Greenough & J. M. Juraska (Eds.), *Developmental neuropsychobiology* (pp. 95–118). San Diego: Academic Press.

Lynch, S. R. (2000). The potential impact of iron supplementation during adolescence on iron status in pregnancy. *Journal of Nutrition, 130*, 448S–451S.

Maccoby, E. E. (1984). Socialization and developmental change. *Child Development, 55*(2), 317–328.

Maccoby, E. E. (1988). Gender as a social category. *Developmental Psychology, 26*, 755–765.

Maccoby, E. E. (1990). Gender and relationships. *American Psychologist, 45*, 513–520.

MacFarlane, J. (1975). Olfaction in the development of social preferences in the human neonate. In *Parent-infant interaction* (Ciba Foundation Symposium No. 33, pp. 103–117). Amsterdam: Elsevier.

Macfie, J., Toth, S. L., Rogosch, F. A., Robinson, J-A., Emde, R. N., & Cicchetti, D. (1999). Effect of maltreatment on preschoolers' narrative representations of responses to relieve distress and of role reversal. *Developmental Psychology, 35*, 460–465.

MacPhee, D., Fritz, J., & Miller-Heyl, J. (1996). Ethnic variations in personal social networks and parenting. *Child Development, 67*, 3278–3295.

Maletesta, C. Z., Culver, C., Tesman, J. R., & Shepard, B. (1989). The development of emotional expression during the first two years of life. *Monographs of the Society for Research in Child Development, 54* (Serial No. 219).

Malina, R. M. (1990). Physical growth and performance during the transitional years (9–16). In R. Montemayor, G. R. Adams, & T. P. Gullotta (Eds.), *From childhood to adolescence.* Newbury Park, CA: Sage.

Malina, R. M., & Bouchard, C. (1991). *Growth, maturation, and physical activity.* Champaign, IL: Human Kinetics Books.

Malloy, M. H., Kleinman, J. C., Land, G. H., & Schramm, W. F. (1988). The association of maternal smoking with age and cause of infant death. *American Journal of Epidemiology, 128*, 46–55.

Mandler, J. M. (1990). A new perspective on cognitive development in infancy. *American Scientist, 78*, 236–243.

Mandler, J. M. (1992). How to build a baby: II. Conceptual primitives. *Psychological Review, 99*, 587–604.

Mandler, J. M., Bauer, P. J., & McDonough, L. (1991). Separating the sheep from the goats: Differentiating global categories. *Cognitive Psychology, 23*, 263–298.

Mangelsdorf, S. C., Shapiro, J. R., & Marzolf, D. (1995). Developmental and temperamental differences in emotion regulation in infancy. *Child Development, 66*, 1817–1828.

Marcia, J. E. (1980). Identity in adolescence. In J. Adelson (Ed.), *Handbook of adolescent psychology*. New York: Wiley.

Marcia, J. E. (1988). Common processes underlying ego identity, cognitive/moral development, and individuation. In D. K. Lapsley & F. C. Power (Eds.), *Self, ego, and identity: Integrative approaches*. New York: Springer-Verlag.

Marcus, M., Silbergeld, E., Mattison, D., & the Research Needs Working Group. (1993). A reproductive hazards research agenda for the 1990s. *Environmental Health Perspectives Supplements, 101*, 175–180.

Marieb, E. N. (1992). *Human anatomy and physiology* (2nd ed.). Redwood City, CA: Benjamin/Cummings.

Markus, H. R., & Kitayama, S. (1991). Culture and the self: Implications for cognition, emotion, and motivation. *Psychological Review, 98*, 224–253.

Marsh, H. W., Craven, R., & Debus, R. (1998). Structure, stability and development of young children's self-concepts: A multicohort-multioccasion study. *Child Development, 69*, 1030–1053.

Martin, C. L., & Halverson, C. F. (1981). A schematic processing model of sex typing and stereotyping in children. *Child Development, 52*, 1119–1134.

Martin, C. L., & Halverson, C. F. (1983). The effects of sex-typing schemas on young children's memory. *Child Development, 61*, 1427–1439.

Martin, E. C. (1986). Being in junior high. In D. Cavitch (Ed.), *Life studies: A thematic reader* (2nd ed.). New York: St. Martin's.

Martorano, S. C. (1977). A developmental analysis of performance on Piaget's formal operations tasks. *Developmental Psychology, 13*, 666–672.

Mascolo, M. F., & Fischer, K. W. (1995). Developmental transformations in appraisals for pride, shame, and guilt. In J. P. Tangney & K. W. Fischer (Eds.), *Self-conscious emotions: The psychology of shame, guilt, embarrassment, and pride* (pp. 64–113). New York: Guilford Press.

Maugh, T. (1999, October 22). Study finds major benefits from quality day care. *Los Angeles Times*, pp. A3, A38.

Maurer, D., & Maurer, C. (1988). *The world of the newborn*. New York: Basic Books.

Mayes, L. C., & Bornstein, M. H. (1995). Developmental dilemmas for cocaine-abusing parents and their children. In M. Lewis & M. Bendersky (Eds.), *Mothers, babies, and cocaine: The role of toxins in development* (pp. 251–272). Hillsdale, NJ: Erlbaum.

Mayr, E. (1982). *Growth of biological thought: Diversity, evolution, and inheritance*. Cambridge, MA: Harvard University Press.

Mazor, A., & Enright, R. D. (1988). The development of the individuation process from a social-cognitive perspective. *Journal of Adolescence, 11*, 29–47.

McAdams, D. P., Hoffman, B. J., Mansfield, E. D., & Day, R. (1996). Themes of agency and communion in significant autobiographical scenes. *Journal of Personality, 64*, 339–377.

McCartney, K., Scarr, S., Phillips, D., & Grajek, S. (1985). Day care as intervention: Comparisons of varying quality programs. *Journal of Applied Developmental Psychology, 6*, 247–260.

McCary, J. L., & McCary, S. P. (1982). *McCary's human sexuality* (4th ed.). Belmont, CA: Wadsworth.

McCormick, L. K., Bartholomew, L. K., Lewis, M. J., Brown, M. W., & Hanson, I. C. (1997). Parental perceptions of barriers to childhood immunization: Results of focus groups conducted in an urban population. *Health Education Research, 12*, 355–362.

McFarlane, A. H., Bellissimo, A., Norman, G. R., & Lange, P. (1994). Adolescent depression in a school-based community sample: Preliminary findings on contributing social factors. *Journal of Youth and Adolescence, 23*, 601–620.

McGhee, P. E. (1979). *Humor: Its origin and development*. San Francisco: Freeman.

McGilly, K., & Siegler, R. S. (1989). How children choose among serial recall strategies. *Child Development, 60*, 172–182.

McHugh, P. R. (1999). How psychiatry lost its way. *Commentary, 108*(5), 32.

McLanahan, S. S., & Booth, K. (1989). Mother-only families: Problems, prospects, and politics. *Journal of Marriage and the Family, 51*, 557–580.

McLaughlin, D., & Whitfield, R. (1984). Adolescents and their experience of parental divorce. *Journal of Adolescence, 7*, 155–170.

McNeill, D. (1970). *The acquisition of language: The study of developmental psycholinguistics*. New York: Harper & Row.

Mechanic, D., & Hansell, S. (1989). Divorce, family conflict, and adolescents' well-being. *Journal of Health and Social Behavior, 30*, 105–116.

Meeks Gardner, J. M., Grantham-McGregor, S. M., Chang, S. M., Himes, J. H., & Powell, C. A. (1995). Activity and behavioral development in stunted and nonstunted children and response to nutritional supplementation. *Child Development, 66*, 1785–1797.

Meltzoff, A. N., & Borton, R. W. (1979). Intermodal matching by human neonates. *Nature, 282*, 403–404.

Menken, J., Trussell, J., & Larsen, U. (1986). Age and infertility. *Science, 233,* 1389–1394.

Menn, L., & Stoel-Gammon, C. (1995). Phonological development. In P. Fletcher & P. MacWhinney (Eds.), *The handbook of child language* (pp. 335–359). Oxford : Blackwell.

Menticoglou, S. M., Manning, F., Harman, C., & Morrison, I. (1995). Perinatal outcome in relation to second-stage duration. *American Journal of Obstetrics and Gynecology, 173,* 906–912.

Merriman, W. E., Evey-Burkey, J. A., Marazita, J. M., & Jarvis, L .H. (1996). Young two-year-olds' tendency to map novel verbs onto novel actions. *Journal of Experimental Child Psychology, 63,* 466–498.

Merriman, W. E., & Stevenson, C. M. (1997). Restricting a familiar name in response to learning a new one: Evidence for the mutual exclusivity bias in young two-year-olds. *Child Development, 68,* 211–228.

Mervis, C. B. (1987). Child-basic object categories and early development. In U. Neisser (Ed.), *Concepts and conceptual development* (pp. 201–235). Cambridge: Cambridge University Press.

Meryash, D. L. (1995). *Genetics.* In D. R. Coustan, R. V. Haning, Jr., & D. B. Singer (Eds.), *Human reproduction: Growth and development.* New York: Little, Brown.

Meyers, A. F., Simpson, A. E., Weitzman, M., et al. (1989). School breakfast program and school performance. *American Journal of Diseases of Children, 143,* 1234–1239.

Miller, C. T., & Downey, K. T. (1999). A meta-analysis of heavyweight and self-esteem. *Personality and Social Psychology Review, 3,* 68–84.

Miller, D. T., Weinstein, S. M., & Karniol, R. (1978). Effects of age and self-verbalization on children's ability to delay gratification. *Developmental Psychology, 14,* 569–570.

Miller, G. (1989). Foreword. In J. T. Gibbs, L. N. Huang, & associates (Eds.), *Children of color.* San Francisco: Jossey-Bass.

Miller, G. A., Galenter, E., & Pribram, K. H. (1960). *Plans and the structure of behavior.* New York: Holt, Rinehart & Winston.

Miller, J. (Ed.). (1973). *Psychoanalysis and women.* New York: Brunner/Mazel.

Miller, J. (1976). *Toward a new psychology of women.* Boston: Beacon Press.

Miller, L. A., Shaikh, T., Stanton, C., Montgomery, A., Rickard, R., Keefer, S., & Hoffman, R. (1995). Surveillance for fetal alcohol syndrome in Colorado. *Public Health Reports, 110,* 690–697.

Miller, P. J., Wiley, A. R., Fung, H., & Liang, C. (1997). Personal storytelling as a medium of socialization in Chinese and American families. *Child Development, 68,* 557–568.

Minuchin, S., Rosman, B., & Baker, L. (1978). *Psychosomatic families: Anorexia nervosa in context.* Cambridge, MA: Harvard University Press.

Mischel, H. N., & Mischel, W. (1983). The development of children's knowledge of self-control strategies. *Child Development, 54,* 603–619.

Mischel, W. & Mischel, H. N. (1976). A cognitive social-learning approach to morality and self-regulation. In T. Lickona (Ed.), *Moral development and behavior: Theory, research, and social issues.* New York: Holt, Rinehart & Winston.

Mischel, W., & Rodriguez, M. L. (1993). Psychological distance in self-imposed delay of gratification. In R. R. Cocking, K. A. Renninger, et al. (Eds.), *The development of meaning of psychological distance* (pp. 109–121). Hillsdale, NJ: Erlbaum.

Mischel, W., Shoda, Y., & Rodriguez, M. L. (1992). Delay of gratification in children. In G. Loewenstein, J. Elster, et al. (Eds.), *Choice over time* (pp. 147–164). New York: Russell Sage.

Mitchell, E. A., Scragg, R., Stewart, A. W., Becroft, D. M. O., Taylor, B. J., Ford, R. P. K., Hassall, I. B., Barry, D. M. J., Allen, E. M., & Roberts, A. P. (1991). Results from the first year of the New Zealand cot death study. *New Zealand Medical Journal, 104,* 71–76.

Mitchell, E. A., Touhy, P. G., Brunts, J. M., Thompson, J. M. D., Clements, M. S., Stewart, A. W., Ford, R. P. K., & Taylor, B. J. (1997). Risk factors for sudden infant death syndrome following the prevention campaign in New Zealand. *Pediatrics, 100,* 835–840.

Mitchell, J. J. (1990). *Human growth and development: The childhood years.* Calgary, Alberta: Detselig Enterprises.

Mix, K. S., Levine, S. C., & Huttenlocher, J. (1997). Numerical abstraction in infants: Another look. *Developmental Psychology, 33,* 423–428.

Mize, J., & Pettit, G. S. (1997). Mothers' social coaching, mother-child relationship style, and children's peer competence: Is the medium the message? *Child Development, 68,* 312–332.

Mokdad, A. H., Serdula, M. K., Dietz, W. H., Bowman, B. A., Marks, J. S., & Koplan, J. P. (1999). The spread of the obesity epidemic in the United States, 1991–1998. *Journal of the American Medical Association, 282,* 1519–1522.

Molina, B. S. G., & Chassin, L. (1996). The parent-adolescent relationship at puberty: Hispanic ethnicity and parent alcoholism as moderators. *Developmental Psychology, 32,* 675–686.

Moon, C., Cooper, R .P., & Fifer, W. P. (1993). Two-day-olds prefer their native language. *Infant Behavior and Development, 16,* 495–500.

Moore, K. A., & Glei, D. (1995). Taking the plunge: An examination of positive youth development. *Journal of Adolescent Research, 10,* 15–40.

Moore, K. L, & Persaud, T. V. N. (1993). *Before we are born* (4th ed.). Philadelphia: Saunders.

Moore, S. M. (1995). Girls' understanding and social constructions of menarche. *Journal of Adolescence, 18,* 87–104.

Morrison, T. (1973). *Sula*. New York: Plume.

Mounts, N. S., & Steinberg, L. (1995). An ecological analysis of peer influence on adolescent grade point average and drug use. *Developmental Psychology, 31,* 915–922.

Mueller, C. M., & Dweck, C. S. (1998). Praise for intelligence can undermine children's motivation and performance. *Journal of Personality and Social Psychology, 75,* 33–52.

Mumme, D. L., Fernald, A., & Herrera, C. (1996). Infants' responses to facial and vocal emotional signals in a social referencing paradigm. *Child Development, 67,* 3219–3237.

Munoz, K. A., Drebs-Smith, S. M., Ballard-Barbach, R., & Cleveland, L. E. (1997). Food intakes of U.S. children and adolescents compared with recommendations. *Pediatrics, 100,* 323–329.

Munroe, R. (1955). *Schools of psychoanalytic thought.* New York: Dryden Press.

Muscati, S. K., Koski, K. G., & Gray-Donald, K. (1996). Increased energy intake in pregnant smokers does not prevent human fetal growth retardation. *Journal of Nutrition, 126,* 2984–2989.

Musick, J., Stott, F., Spencer, K. K., Goldman, J., & Cohler, B. (1987). Maternal factors related to vulnerability and resiliency in young children at risk. In E. J. Anthony & J. J. Cohler (Eds.), *The invulnerable child* (pp. 229–252). New York: Guilford.

Mussen, P. H., & Jones, M. C. (1957). Self-conceptions, motivations, and interpersonal attitudes of late- and early-maturing boys. *Child Development, 28,* 243–256.

Muuss, R. E. (1990). *Adolescent behavior and society* (4th ed.). New York: Random House.

Nagata, D. K. (1989). Japanese American children and adolescents. In J. T. Gibbs, L. N. Huang, & associates (Eds.), *Children of color.* San Francisco: Jossey-Bass.

Narahara, M. (1998). *Gender bias in children's picture books: A look at teachers' choice of literature.* Unpublished master's thesis, University of California, Long Beach, Long Beach, California.

Nation, K., & Snowling, M. J. (1998). Individual differences in contextual facilitation: Evidence from dyslexia and poor reading comprehension. *Child Development, 69,* 996–1011.

National Center for Health Statistics. (1968–1991). *Vital statistics of the United States: Vol. 2. Mortality—Part A* [for 1966–1988]. Washington, DC: U.S. Government Printing Office.

National Center for Health Statistics. (1999). *Healthy people 2000 review, 1998–99.* Hyattsville, MD: Public Health Service.

National Head Start Association. (1990). *Head Start: The nation's pride, a nation's challenge.* Alexandria, VA: Author.

Needle, R. H., Su, S. S., & Doherty, W. J. (1990). Divorce, remarriage, and adolescent substance use: A prospective longitudinal study. *Journal of Marriage and the Family, 52,* 157–169.

Neisser, U. (1967). *Cognitive psychology.* New York: Appleton-Century-Crofts.

Neisser, U. (1976). *Cognition and reality.* San Francisco: Freeman.

Neisser, U. (1992). The development of consciousness and the acquisition of self. In F. S. Kessel, P. M. Cole, & D. L. Johnson (Eds.), *Self and consciousness: Multiple perspectives* (pp. 1–18). Hillsdale, NJ: Erlbaum.

Neisser, U., Boodoo, G., Bouchard, T. J., Boykin, A. W., Brody, N., Ceci, S. J., Halpern, D. F., Loehlink, J. C., Perloff, R., Steinberg, R., & Urbina, S. (1996). Intelligence: Knowns and unknowns. *American Psychologist, 51,* 77–101.

Nelson, K. (1992). Emergence of autobiographical memory at age 4. *Human Development, 35,* 172–177.

Nelson, K., Fivush, R., Hudson, J., & Lucariello, J. (1983). Scripts and the development of memory. In M. T. H. Chi (Ed.), *Trends in memory development: Contributions to human development* (Vol. 9, pp. 52–70). Basel, Switzerland: Karger.

Ness, R. B., Grisso, J. A., Hirschinger, N., Markovic, N., Shaw, L. M., Day, N. L., & Kline, J. (1999). Cocaine and tobacco use and the risk of spontaneous abortion. *New England Journal of Medicine, 340,* 333–339.

Netley, C. T. (1986). Summary overview of behavioral development in individuals with neonatally identified X and Y aneuploidy. *Birth Defects, 22,* 293–306

Newacheck, P. W., Hughes, D. C., & Stoddard, J. J. (1996). Children's access to primary care: Differences by race, income, and insurance status. *Pediatrics, 97,* 26–32.

Newman, D. L., Caspi, A., Moffitt, T. E., & Silva, P. A. (1997). Antecedents of adult interpersonal functioning: Effects of individual differences in age 3 temperament. *Developmental Psychology, 33,* 206–217.

NICHD Early Child Care Research Network. (1998). Relations between family predictors and child outcomes: Are they weaker for children in child care? *Developmental Psychology, 34,* 1119–1128.

Nicholls, R. D. (1993). Genomic imprinting and uniparental disomy in Angelman and Prader-Willi syndromes. *American Journal of Medical Genetics, 46,* 16–25.

Nicklas, T. A., Webber, L. S., Srinivasan, S. R., & Berenson, G. S. (1993). Secular trends in dietary intakes and cardiovascular risk factors of 10-year-old children: The Bogalusa Heart Study. *American Journal of Clinical Nutrition, 57,* 930–937.

Nieto, A., Matorras, R., Serra, M., Valenzuela, P., & Molera, J. (1994). Multivariate analysis of determinants of fetal growth retardation. *Eur J. Obstet Gynecol Reprod Biol, 53,* 107–113.

Nijhuis, J. (1995). Physiological and clinical consequences in relation to the development of fetal behavior and fetal behavioral states. In J.-P. Lecanuet, W. P. Fifer, N. A. Krasnegor, & W. P. Smotherman (Eds.), *Fetal development: A psychobiological perspective* (pp. 67–82). Hillsdale, NJ: Erlbaum.

Nilsson, L., & Hamberger, L. (1990). *A child is born*. New York: Delacorte.

Nørgaard, J. P., Pedersen, E. B., & Djurhuus, J. C. (1985). Diurnal anti-diuretic hormone levels in enuretics. *Journal of Urology, 134*, 1029–1031.

Norton, E. M., Durlak, J. A., & Richards, M. H. (1989). Peer knowledge of and reactions to adolescent suicide. *Journal of Youth and Adolescence, 18*, 427–437.

Nowakowski, R. S. (1987). Basic concepts of CNS development. *Child Development, 58*, 568–595.

Nucci, L., Camino, C., & Sapiro, C. M. (1996). Social class effects on northeastern Brazilian children's conceptions of areas of personal choice and social regulation. *Child Development, 67*, 1223–1242.

Nurmi, J.-E., Poole, M. E., & Kalakoski, V. (1996). Age differences in adolescent identity exploration and commitment in urban and rural environments. *Journal of Adolescence, 19*, 443–452.

O'Connell, A. N. (1976). The relationship between life-style and identity synthesis and re-synthesis in traditional, neotraditional, and nontraditional women. *Journal of Personality, 44*, 675–688.

O'Shea, P. A. (1995). The fetus as patient: Prenatal diagnosis and treatment. In D. R. Coustan, R. V. Haning, Jr., & D. B. Singer (Eds.). *Human reproduction: Growth and development* (pp. 247–264). New York: Little, Brown.

O'Sullivan, J. T., & Howe, M. L. (1995). Metamemory and memory construction. *Consciousness and Cognition: An International Journal, 4*(1), 104–110.

O'Sullivan, J. T., Howe, M. L., & Marche, T. A. (1996). Children's beliefs about long-term retention. *Child Development, 67*, 2989–3009.

Oakes, J. (1985). *Keeping track: How schools structure inequality*. New Haven, CT: Yale University Press.

Oakley, G. P., Jr. (1997). Doubling the number of women consuming vitamin supplement pills containing folic acid: An urgently needed birth defect prevention complement to the folic acid fortification of cereal grains. *Reproductive Toxicology, 11*, 579–581.

Ocampo, K. A., Knight, G. P., & Bernal, M. E. (1997). The development of cognitive abilities and social identities in children: The case of ethnic identity. *International Journal of Behavioral Development, 21*, 479–500.

Ogbu, J. U. (1981). Black education: A cultural-ecological perspective. In H. P. McAdoo (Ed.), *Black families*. Beverly Hills: Sage.

Ogbu, J. U. (1992). Understanding cultural diversity and learning. *Educational Researcher, 21*, 5–14.

Ogden, C. L., Troiano, R. P., Briefel, R. R., Kuczmarski, R. J., Flegal, K. M., & Johnson, C. L. (1997). Prevalence of overweight among preschool children in the United States, 1971 through 1994. *Pediatrics, 99*(4), E1.

Okun, A., Parker, J. G., & Levendosky, A. A. (1994). Distinct and interactive contributions of physical abuse, socioeconomic disadvantage and negative life events to children's social, cognitive, and affective adjustment. *Development and Psychopathology, 6*, 77–98.

Oller, D. K. (1999, August). *Bilingual infants show neither advantages nor disadvantages over monolingual infants*. Paper presented at the meeting of the Society for Research in Child Development, Kansas City.

Olsen, J. (1992). Cigarette smoking in pregnancy and fetal growth. Does the type of tobacco play a role? *International Journal of Epidemiology, 21*, 279–284.

Olshan, A. F., & Faustman, E. M. (1993). Male-mediated developmental toxicity. In *Annual Review of Public Health, 14*, 159–181.

Olshan, A. F., Teschke, K., & Baird, P. A. (1990). Birth defects among offspring of firemen. *American Journal of Epidemiology, 131*, 312–321.

Olson, H. C., Grant, T. M., Martin, J. C., & Streissguth, A. P. (1995). A cohort study of prenatal cocaine exposure: Addressing methodological concerns. In M. Lewis & M. Bendersky (Eds.), *Mothers, babies, and cocaine: The role of toxins in development* (pp. 129–162). Hillsdale, NJ: Erlbaum.

Olweus, D., Limber, S., & Mihalic, S. (1999). *Blueprints for violence prevention. Book 9: Bullying prevention program*. Boulder, CO: Center for the Study and Prevention of Violence.

Orfield, G. A. (1993). *The growth of segregation in American schools: Changing patterns of segregation and poverty since 1968*. Alexandria, VA: National School Boards Association.

Orlofsky, J., & Frank, M. (1986). Personality structure as viewed through early memories and identity status in college men and women. *Journal of Personality and Social Psychology, 5*, 580–586.

Osherson, D. N., & Markman, E. M. (1975). Language and the ability to evaluate contradictions and tautologies. *Cognition, 3*, 213–226.

Oswald, H., Krappmann, L., Uhlendorff, H., & Weiss, K. (1994). Social relationships and support among peers during middle childhood. In F. Nestmann & K. Hurrelmann (Eds.), *Social networks and social support in childhood and adolescence* (pp. 171–189). New York: Walter de Gruyter.

Overton, W. F., Ward, S. L., Noveck, I. A., Black, J., & O'Brien, D. P. (1987). Form and content in the development of deductive reasoning. *Developmental Psychology, 23*, 22–30.

Oyen, N., Markestad, T., Skjaerven, R., Irgens, L. M., Hel-weg-Larsen, K., Alm, B., Norvenius, G., & Wennergren, G. (1997). Combined effects of sleeping position and prenatal risk factors in sudden infant death syndrome: The Nordic epidemiological SIDS study. *Pediatrics, 100,* 613–621.

Padden, C., & Humphries, T. (1989). *Deaf in America: Voices from a culture.* Cambridge, MA: Harvard University Press.

Page, D. C., Fisher, E. M., McGillivray, B., & Brown, L. G. (1990). Additional deletion in sex-determining region of human Y chromosome resolves paradox of X, = (Y;22) fe-male. *Nature, 346,* 279–281.

Page, R. N. (1990). Games of chance: The lower-track cur-riculum in a college-preparatory high school. *Curriculum Inquiry, 20,* 249–281.

Paley, V. G. (1997). Mollie is three. In D. N. Sattler & V. Sha-batay (Eds.), *Psychology in context: Voices and perspectives* (pp. 139–143). Boston: Houghton Mifflin.

Palinscar, A. S., & Brown, A. L. (1984). Reciprocal teaching of comprehension-monitoring activities. *Cognition and In-struction, 1,* 117–175.

Papini, D. R., Farmer, F. L., Clark, S. M., & Snell, W. E., Jr. (1988). An evaluation of adolescent patterns of sexual self-disclosure to parents and friends. *Journal of Adolescent Re-search, 3,* 387–401.

Papini, D. R., Snell, W. E., Belk, S. S., & Clark, S. (1988, April). *Developmental correlates of women's and men's sexual self-disclosures.* Paper presented at the meeting of the South-western Psychological Association, Tulsa, OK.

Pardeck, J. A., & Pardeck, J. L. (1990). Family factors related to adolescent autonomy. *Adolescence, 25,* 31–319.

Parker, J. G., & Gottman, J. M. (1989). Social and emotional development in a relational context. In T. J. Berndt & G. W. Ladd (Eds.), *Peer relationships in child development.* New York: Wiley.

Parker, S., Nichter, M., Nichter, N., Vuckovic, N., Sims, C., & Ritenbaugh, C. (1995). Body image and weight concerns among Afro American and White adolescent females: Dif-ferences that make a difference. *Human Organization, 54,* 103–115.

Parks, G. (1990). *Voices in the mirror: An autobiography.* New York: Doubleday.

Parry, T. R. (1996). Will pursuit of higher quality sacrifice equal opportunity in education? An analysis of the educa-tion voucher system in Chile. *Social Science Quarterly, 77,* 821–841.

Pasley, B. K., & Ihenger-Tallman, M. (1989). Boundary ambi-guity in remarriage: Does ambiguity differentiate degree of marital adjustment and integration? *Family Relations, 38,* 46–52.

Patrikakou, E. N. (1996). Investigating the academic achieve-ments of adolescents with learning disabilities: A struc-tural modeling approach. *Journal of Educational Psychology, 88,* 435–450.

Patterson, S. J., Sochting, I., & Marcia, J. E. (1992). The inner space and beyond: Women and identity. In G. R. Adams, T. P. Gullotta, & R. Montemayor (Eds.), *Adolescent identity formation.* Newbury Park, CA: Sage.

Pavlov, I. P. (1927). *Conditioned reflexes.* London: Oxford Uni-versity Press.

Peck, S. (1995). *All-American boy: A memoir.* Los Angeles: Alyson.

Pederson, D. R., & Moran, G. (1995). A categorical descrip-tion of infant-mother relationships in the home and its re-lation to Q-sort measures of infant-mother interaction. In E. Waters, B. E. Vaughn, G. Posada, & K. Kondo-Ikemura (Eds.). Caregiving, cultural, and cognitive perspectives on secure-base behavior and working models: New growing points of attachment theory and research. *Monographs of the Society for Research in Child Development, 60* (2–3, Serial No. 244).

Pegg, J. E., Werker, J. F., & McLeod, P. J. (1992). Preference for infant-directed over adult-directed speech: Evidence from 7-week-old infants. *Infant Behavior and Development, 15,* 325–345.

Pehoski, C., Henderson, A., & Tickle-Degnen, L. (1996). In-hand manipulation in young children: Rotation of an ob-ject in the fingers. *American Journal of Occupational Therapy, 51,* 544–552.

Pehoski, C., Henderson, A., & Tickle-Degnen, L. (1997). In-hand manipulation in young children: Translation move-ments. *American Journal of Occupational Therapy, 51,* 719–728.

Perkins, D. N. (1987). Knowledge as design: Teaching think-ing through content. In J. B. Baron & R. J. Sternberg (Eds.), *Teaching thinking skills: Theory and practice.* New York: Freeman.

Peskin, H. (1967). Pubertal onset and ego functioning. *Journal of Abnormal Psychology, 72,* 1–15.

Peskin, H. (1973). Influence of the developmental schedule of puberty on learning and ego development. *Journal of Youth and Adolescence, 2,* 273–290.

Peskin, J. (1996). Guise and guile: Children's understanding of narratives in which the purpose of pretense is decep-tion. *Child Development, 67,* 1735–1751.

Petersen, A. C., Compas, B. E., Brooks-Gunn, J., Stemmler, M., Ey, S., & Grant, K. (1993). Depression in adolescence. *American Psychologist, 48,* 155–168.

Petersen, A. C., Crockett, L., Richards, M., & Boxer, A. (1988). A self-report measure of pubertal status: Reliability, valid-ity, and initial norms. *Journal of Youth and Adolescence, 17,* 117–134.

Petersen, A. C., & Taylor, B. (1980). The biological approach to adolescence. In J, Adelson (Ed.), *Handbook of adolescent psychology.* New York: Wiley.

Peterson, C. C. (1995). The role of perceived intention to de-ceive in children's and adults' concepts of lying. *British Journal of Developmental Psychology, 13,* 237–260.

Pettit, G. S., Bates, J. E., & Dodge, K. A. (1997). Supportive parenting, ecological context, and children's adjustment: A seven-year longitudinal study. *Child Development, 68,* 908–923.

Pettit, G. S., Dodge, K. A., & Brown, M. M. (1988). Early family experience, social problem solving patterns, and children's social competence. *Child Development, 59,* 107–120.

Phelps, K. E., & Woolley, J. D. (1994). The form and function of young children's magical beliefs. *Developmental Psychology, 30,* 385–394.

Phelps, L., Johnston, S. S., Jimenez, D. P., Wilczenski, F. L., Andrea, R. K., & Healy, R. W. (1993). Figure preference, body dissatisfaction, and body distortion in adolescence. *Journal of Adolescent Research, 8,* 297–310.

Phillips, D. A., Voran, M., Kisker, E., Howes, C., & Whitebook, M. (1994). Child care for children in poverty: Opportunity or inequity? *Child Development, 65,* 472–492.

Phillips, D. M., & Dryden, G. L. (1991). Comparative morphology of mammalian gametes. In B. S. Dunbar & M. G. O'Rand (Eds.). *A comparative overview of mammalian fertilization.* New York: Plenum Press.

Phinney, J. S. (1989). Stages of ethnic identity development in minority group adolescents. *Journal of Early Adolescence, 9,* 34–49.

Phinney, J. S. (1990). Ethnic identity in adolescents and adults: Review of research. *Psychological Bulletin, 108,* 499–514.

Phinney, J. S. (1993). A three-stage model of ethnic identity development. In M. Bernal & G. Knight (Eds.), *Ethnic identity: Formation and transmission among Hispanics and other minorities* (pp. 61–79). Albany: State University of New York Press.

Phinney, J. S. (1996). When we talk about American ethnic groups, what do we mean? *American Psychologist, 51,* 918–927.

Phinney, J. S., Ferguson, D. L., & Tate, J. D. (1997). Intergroup attitudes among ethnic minority adolescents: A causal model. *Child Development, 68,* 955–969.

Phinney, J. S., & Kohatsu, E. (1997). Ethnic and racial identity development and mental health. In J. Schulenberg, J. Maggs, & K. Hurrelmann (Eds.), *Health risks and developmental transitions during adolescence* (pp. 420–443). New York: Cambridge University Press.

Phinney, J. S., & Rosenthal, D. A. (1992). Ethnic identity in adolescence: Process, context, and outcome. In G. Adams, R. Montemayor, & T. Gullotta (Eds.), *Advances in adolescent development* (Vol. 4). Newbury Park, CA: Sage.

Phinney, J. S., & Rotheram, M. J. (1987). Childen's ethnic socialization: Themes and implications. In M. J. Rotheram & J. S. Phinney (Eds.), *Children's ethnic socialization: Pluralism and development.* Beverly Hills: Sage.

Phinney, J. S., & Tarver, S. (1988). Ethnic identity search and commitment in Black and White eighth graders. *Journal of Early Adolescence, 8,* 265–277.

Piaget, J. (1952). *The origins of intelligence in children.* New York: International Universities Press.

Piaget, J. (1954). *The construction of reality in the child.* New York: Basic Books.

Piaget, J. (1965). *The moral judgment of the child.* New York: Free Press.

Piaget, J. (1971). *Biology and knowledge.* Chicago: University of Chicago Press.

Piaget, J., & Inhelder, B. (1969). *The psychology of the child.* New York: Basic Books.

Pickles, A., Pickering, K., Simonoff, E., Silberg, J., Meyer, J., & Maes, H. (1998). Genetic "clocks" and "soft" events: A twin model for pubertal development and other recalled sequences of developmental milestones, transitions, or ages at onset. *Behavior Genetics, 28,* 243–253.

Pipp-Siegel, S., & Foltz, C. (1997). Toddlers' acquisition of self/other knowledge: Ecological and interpersonal aspects of self and other. *Child Development, 68,* 69–79.

Pleck, J. H., Sonenstein, F. L., & Ku, L. C. (1990). Contraceptive attitudes and intention to use condoms in sexually experienced and inexperienced adolescent males. *Journal of Family Issues, 11,* 294–312.

Pleck, J. H., Sonenstein, F. L., & Swain, S. O. (1988). Adolescent males' sexual behavior and contraceptive use: Implications for male responsibility. *Journal of Adolescent Research, 3,* 275–284.

Plomin, R., & Daniels, D. (1987). Why are children in the same family so different from one another? *Behavioral and Brain Sciences, 10,* 1–60.

Plomin, R., DeFries, J. C., & Fulker, D. W. (1988). *Nature and nurture during infancy and early childhood.* Cambridge, MA: Cambridge University Press.

Plomin, R., DeFries, J. C., & McClearn, G. E. (1990). *Behavioral genetics: A primer* (2nd ed.). New York: Freeman.

Plomin, R., Reiss, D., Hetherington, E. M., & Howe, G. W. (1994). Nature and nurture: Genetic contributions to measures of the family environment. *Developmental Psychology, 30,* 32–43.

Plummer, D. L. (1995). Patterns of racial identity development of African American adolescent males and females. *Journal of Black Psychology, 21,* 168–180.

Plummer, D. L. (1996). Black racial identity attitudes and stages of the life span: An exploratory investigation. *Journal of Black Psychology, 22,* 169–181.

Pollitt, E. (1994). Poverty and child development: Relevance of research in developing countries to the United States. *Child Development, 65,* 283–295.

Pollitt, E., Golub, M., Gorman, K., Grantham-McGregor, S., Levitsky, D., Schurch, B., Strupp, B., & Wachs, T. (1996). A reconceptualization of the effects of undernutrition on children's biological, psychosocial, and behavioral development. *Social Policy Report, 10*(5), 1–22.

Pollock, S., & Gilligan, C. (1982). Images of violence in Thematic Apperception Test stories. *Journal of Personality and Social Psychology, 42,* 159–167.

Porter, R .H., Makin, J. W., Davis, L. B., & Christensen, K. M. (1992). An assessment of the salient olfactory environment of formula-fed infants. *Physiology & Behavior, 50,* 907–911.

Posada, G., Gao, Y., Wu, F., Posada, R., Tascon, M., Schoelmerich, A., Savi, A., Kondo-Ikemura, K., Haaland, W., & Synnevaag, B. (1995). The secure-base phenomenon across cultures: Children's behavior, mothers' preferences, and experts' concepts. In E. Waters, B. E. Vaughn, G. Posada, & K. Kondo-Ikemura (Eds.), Caregiving, cultural, and cognitive perspectives on secure-base behavior and working models: New growing points of attachment theory and research. *Monographs of the Society for Research in Child Development, 60* (2–3, Serial No. 244).

Posner, J. K., & Vandell, D. L. (1999). After-school activities and the development of low-income urban children: A longitudinal study. *Developmental Psychology, 35,* 868–879.

Povinelli, D. J., Landau, K. R., & Perillous, H. K . (1996). Self-recognition in young children using delayed versus live feedback: Evidence of a developmental asynchrony. *Child Development, 67,* 1540–1554.

Povinelli, D. J., & Simon, B. B. (1998). Young children's understanding of briefly versus extremely delayed images of the self: Emergence of the autobiographical stance. *Developmental Psychology, 34,* 188–194.

Powell, G. J. (1985). Self-concepts among Afro-American students in racially isolated minority schools: Some regional differences. *Journal of the American Academy of Child Psychiatry, 24,* 142–149.

Powers, S. I., Hauser, S. T., Schwartz, J. M., Noam, G. G., & Jacobson, A. M. (1983). Adolescent ego development and family interaction: A structural-developmental perspective. In H. D. Grotevant & C. R. Cooper (Eds.), *Adolescent development in the family.* San Francisco: Jossey-Bass.

Pratt, M. W., Kerig, P., Cowan, P. A., & Cowan, C. P. (1988). Mothers and fathers teaching 3-year-olds: Authoritative parenting and adult scaffolding of young children's learning. *Developmental Psychology, 24,* 832–839.

Price, D. W. W., & Goodman, G. S. (1990). Visiting the wizard: Children's memory for a recurring event. *Child Development, 61,* 664–680.

Prislin, R., Dyer, J. A., Blakely, C. H., & Johnson, C. D. (1998). Immunization status and sociodemographic characteristics: The mediating role of beliefs, attitudes, and perceived control. *American Journal of Public Health, 88,* 1821–1826.

Pungello, E. P., & Kurtz-Costes, B. (1999). Why and how working women choose child care; A review with a focus on infancy. *Developmental Review, 19,* 31–96.

Purcell, P., & Stewart, L. (1990). Dick and Jane in 1989. *Sex Roles, 22,* 177–185.

Putallaz, M. (1983). Predicting children's sociometric status from their behavior. *Child Development, 54*(6), 1417–1426.

Putallaz, M., & Gottman, J. M. (1981). An interactional model of children's entry into peer groups. *Child Development, 52,* 986–994.

Quinn, P. C., & Eimas, P. D. (1996). Perceptual cues that permit categorical differentiation of animal species by infants. *Journal of Experimental Child Psychology, 63,* 189–211.

Ramirez, O. (1989). Mexican American children and adolescents. In J. T. Gibbs, L. N. Huang, & associates (Eds.), *Children of color.* San Francisco: Jossey-Bass.

Raudenbush, S. W., Rowan, B., & Cheong, Y. F. (1993). Higher order instructional goals in secondary schools: Class, teacher, and school influences. *American Educational Research Journal, 30,* 523–553.

Ray, W., & Ravizza, R. (1985). *Methods toward a science of behavior and experience* (2nd ed.). Belmont, CA: Wadsworth.

Reese, E., & Fivush, R. (1993). Parental styles of talking about the past. *Developmental Psychology, 29,* 596–606.

Reese, H. W., & Overton, W. F. (1970). Models of development and theories of development. In L. R. Goulet & P. B. Baltes (Eds.), *Life-span developmental psychology: Research and theory.* New York: Academic Press.

Reiss, A. L., Abrams, M. T., Singer, H. S., Ross, J. L., & Denckla, M. B. (1996). Brain development, gender and IQ in children: A volumetric imaging study. *Brain, 119,* 1763–1774.

Repacholi, B. M., & Gopnik, A. (1997). Early reasoning about desires: Evidence from 14- and 18-month-olds. *Developmental Psychology, 33,* 12–21.

Repetti, R. L. (1993). Short-term effects of occupational stressors on daily mood and health conditions. *Health Psychology, 12,* 125–131.

Repetti, R. L., & Wood, J. (1997). Families accommodating to chronic stress: Unintended and unnoticed processes. In B. H. Gottlieb (Ed.), *Coping with chronic stress* (pp. 191–220). New York: Plenum.

Report of the Secretary's Task Force on Youth Suicide (1989). *Vol. 1: Overview and recommendations* (DHHS Publication No. ADM 89-1621). Washington, DC: U.S. Government Printing Office.

Resnick, M., Harris, L., & Blum, R. (1993). The impact of caring and connectedness on adolescent health and well-being. *Journal of Pediatrics and Child Health, 29* (Suppl. 1), 3–9.

Restak, R. (1984, November). Master Clock of the brain and body. *Science Digest,* 54–104.

Reynolds, A. J., & Temple, J. A. (1998). Extended early childhood intervention and school achievement: Age thirteen findings from the Chicago longitudinal study. *Child Development, 69,* 231–246.

Rice, C., Koinis, D., Sullivan, K., Flusberg, H. T., & Winner, E. (1997). When 3-year-olds pass the appearance-reality test. *Developmental Psychology, 33,* 54–61.

Rice, K. G., Cole, D. A., & Lapsley, D. K. (1990). Separation-individuation, family cohesion, and adjustment to college: measurement validation and test of a theoretical model. *Journal of Counseling Psychology, 37,* 195–202.

Rieser, J. (1979). Spatial orientation of six-month-old infants. *Child Development, 50,* 1078–1087.

Rivara, F. P., & Grossman, D.C. (1996). Prevention of traumatic deaths to children in the United States: How far have we come and where do we need to go? *Pediatrics, 97,* 791–797.

Roberts, L. (1991) Does egg beckon sperm when the time is right? *Science, 252,* 214.

Roberts, W., & Strayer, J. (1996). Empathy, emotional expressiveness, and prosocial behavior. *Child Development, 67,* 449–470.

Robinson, J. A., McKenzie, B. E., & Day, R. H. (1996). Anticipatory reaching by infants and adults: The effect of object features and apertures in opaque and transparent screens. *Child Development, 67,* 2641–2656.

Rochat, P., & Morgan, R. (1995). Spatial determinants in the perception of self-produced leg movements by 3- to 5-month-old infants. *Developmental Psychology, 31,* 626–636.

Rockefeller, J. D. (1998, Fall). [Interview]. *Georgetown Public Policy Review.*

Rodriguez, R. (1982). *Hunger of memory: The education of Richard Rodriguez.* Boston: Godine.

Roggman, L. A., Langlois, J. H., Hubbs-Tait, L., & Rieser-Danner, L. A. (1994). Infant day-care, attachment, and the "file drawer problem." *Child Development, 65,* 1429–1443.

Rogoff, B. (1990). *Apprenticeship in thinking.* New York: Oxford University Press.

Rogoff, B. (1996). Developmental transitions in children's participation in sociocultural activities. In A. J. Sameroff & M. M. Haith (Eds). *The five to seven year shift* (pp. 273–294). Chicago: University of Chicago Press.

Rogow, A. M., Marcia, J. E., & Slugowski, B. R. (1983). The relative importance of identity status interview components. *Journal of Youth and Adolescence, 12,* 387–400.

Roquer, J. M., Figueras, J., Botet, F., & Jimenez, R. (1995). Influence on fetal growth of exposure to tobacco smoke during pregnancy. *Acta Paediatrica, 84,* 118–121.

Rosa, F. W., Wilk, A. L., & Kelsey, F. O. (1986). Teratogen update: Vitamin A congeners. *Teratology, 33,* 355–364.

Rosch, E., & Mervis, C. B. (1975). Family resemblances: Studies in the internal structure of categories. *Cognitive Psychology, 8,* 382–439.

Rosen, C. S., Schwebel, D. C., & Singer, J. L. (1997). Preschoolers' attributions of mental states in pretense. *Child Development, 68,* 1133–1142.

Rosenberg, M., Schooler, C., & Schoenbach, C. (1989). Self-esteem and adolescent problems: Modeling reciprocal effects. *American Sociological Review, 54,* 1004–1018.

Rosenblum, G. D., & Lewis, M. (1999). The relations among body image, physical attractiveness, and body mass in adolescence. *Child Development, 70,* 50–64.

Rosenthal, D. A., & Feldman, S. S. (1992). The nature and stability of ethnic identity in Chinese youth: Effects of length of residence in two cultural contexts. *Journal of Cross-Cultural Psychology, 23,* 213–227.

Rosenthal, D. A., & Hrynevich, C. (1985). Ethnicity and ethnic identity: A comparative study of Greek-, Italian-, and Anglo-Australian adolescents. *International Journal of Psychology, 20,* 723–742.

Rosenthal, E. (1990, February 4). When a pregnant woman drinks. *The New York Times Magazine, 30,* 49, 61.

Rosenthal, R., & Vandell, D. L. (1996). Quality of care at school-aged child-care programs: Regulatable features, observed experiences, child perspectives, and parent perspectives. *Child Development, 67,* 2434–2445.

Rosenzweig, M. R. (1984). Experience, memory, and the brain. *American Psychologist, 39,* 365–376.

Rosenzweig, M. R., Bennett, E. L., & Diamond, M. C. (1972). Brain changes in response to experience. *The nature and nurture of behavior: Developmental psychobiology.* New York: Freeman.

Rotenberg, K. J., & Eisenberg, N. (1997). Developmental differences in the understanding of and reaction to others' inhibition of emotional expression. *Developmental Psychology, 33,* 526–537.

Rothbart, M. K. (1986). Longitudinal observation of infant temperament. *Developmental Psychology, 22,* 356–365.

Rothbart, M. K., & Ahadi, S. A. (1994). Temperament and the development of personality. *Journal of Abnormal Psychology, 103,* 55–66.

Rothbaum, F., & Weisz, J. R. (1994). Parental caregiving and child externalizing behavior in nonclinical samples: A meta-analysis. *Psychological Bulletin, 116,* 55–74.

Rotheram, M. J., & Phinney, J. S. (1983). *Intercultural attitudes and behaviors of children.* Paper presented at the meeting of the Society for Intercultural Evaluation, Training and Research, San Gimignano, Italy.

F, M. J., & Phinney, J. S. (1987). Ethnic behavior patterns as an aspect of identity. In J. Phinney & M. Rotheram (Eds.), *Children's ethnic socialization: Pluralism and development.* Beverly Hills: Sage.

Rotheram-Borus, M. J., & Phinney, J. S. (1990). Patterns of social expectations among black and Mexican-American children. *Child Development, 61,* 542–556.

Rowe, D. C., Vazsonyi, A. T., & Flannery, D. J. (1994). No more than skin deep: Ethnic and racial similarities in developmental process. *Psychological Review, 101,* 396–413.

Royle, R., Barrett, M., & Buchanan-Barrow, E. (1998, July). *"Religion is the opiate of the masses" (Marx, 1876): An investigation of the salience of religion for children.* Paper presented at the XVth Biennial Meeting of the International Society for the Study of Behavioural Development, Berne, Switzerland.

Rubin, D. H., Krasnilnikoff, P. A., Leventhal, J. M., Weile, B., & Berget, A. (1986). Effect of passive smoking on birthweight. *Lancet, 2,* 415–417.

Rubin, J., Provenzano, F., & Luria, Z. (1974). The eye of the beholder: Parents' views on sex of newborns. *American Journal of Orthopsychiatry, 44,* 512–519.

Rubin, Z. (1980). *Children's friendships.* Cambridge, MA: Harvard University Press.

Ruble, D. N., & Brooks-Gunn, J. (1982). The experience of menarche. *Child Development, 53,* 1557–1566.

Ruck, M. D., Abramovitch, R., & Keating, D. P. (1998). Children's and adolescents' understanding of rights: Balancing nurturance and self-determination. *Child Development, 64,* 404–417.

Runyan, D. K., Hunter, W. M., Socolar, R. R. S., Amaya-Jackson, L., English, D., Landsverk, J., Dubowitz, H., Browne, D. H., Bangdiwala, S. I., & Mathew, R. M. (1998). Children who prosper in unfavorable environments: The relationship to social capital. *Pediatrics, 101,* 12–18.

Russell, A., & Finnie, V. (1990). Preschool children's social status and maternal instructions to assist group entry. *Developmental Psychology, 26,* 603–611.

Rutter, M. (1986). The developmental psychopathology of depression. In M. Rutter, C. E. Isard, & P. B. Read. (Eds.), *Depression in young people.* New York: Guilford Press.

Sadler, T. W. (1990). *Langman's medical embryology* (6th ed.). Baltimore: Williams & Wilkins.

Sahni, R., Schulze, K. F., Stefanski, M., Myers, M. M., & Fifer, W. P. (1995). Methodological issues in coding sleep states in immature infants. *Developmental Psychobiology, 28,* 85–101.

Salkovskis, P. M. & Rimes, K. A. (1997). Predictive genetic testing: Psychological factors. *Journal of Psychosomatic Research, 43,* 477–487.

Saltz, E., Campbell, S., & Skotko, D. (1983). Verbal control of behavior: The effects of shouting. *Developmental Psychology, 19*(3), 461–464.

Samalin, N. (with Whitney, C.). (2000). Sibling rivalry, sibling love. In D. N. Sattler, G. P. Kramer, V. Shabatay, & D. A. Bernstein (Eds.), *Child development in context* (pp. 70–75). Boston: Houghton Mifflin.

Sansavini, A., Bertoncini, J., & Giovanelli, G. (1997). Newborns discriminate the rhythm of multisyllabic stressed words. *Developmental Psychology, 33,* 3–11.

Savage, M. P., & Scott, L. B. (1996). Physical activity and rural middle school adolescents. *Journal of Youth and Adolescence, 27,* 245–253.

Savitz, D. A., & Chen, J. (1990). Parental occupation and childhood cancer: Review of epidemiologic studies. *Environmental Health Perspectives, 88,* 325–337.

Savitz, D. A., Schwingl, P. J., & Keels, M. A. (1991). Influence of paternal age, smoking and alcohol consumption on congenital anomalies. *Teratology, 44,* 429–440.

Savitz, D. A., Whelan, E. A., & Kleckner, R. C. (1989). Effect of parents' occupational exposures on risk of stillbirth, preterm delivery, and small-for-gestational-age infants. *American Journal of Epidemiology, 129,* 1201–1217.

Savitz, D. A., Zhang, J., Schwingl, P., & John, E. M. (1992). Association of paternal alcohol use with gestational age and birth weight. *Teratology, 46,* 465–471.

Scarr, S. (1992). Developmental theories for the 1990s: Development and individual differences. *Child Development, 63,* 1–19.

Scarr, S. (1993). Biological and cultural diversity: The legacy of Darwin for development. *Child Development, 64,* 1333–1353.

Scarr, S., & Weinberg, R. A. (1983). The Minnesota adoption studies: Malleability and genetic differences. *Child Development, 34,* 260–267.

Schaal, B., Orgeur, P., & Rognon, C. (1995). Odor sensing in the human fetus: Anatomical, functional, and chemoecological bases. In J. P. Lecanuet & W. P. Fifer (Eds.), *Fetal development: A psychobiological perspective.* Hillsdale, NJ: Erlbaum.

Schaie, K. W., & Willis, S. L. (1993). Age difference patterns in psychometric intelligence in adulthood: Generalizability within and across ability domains. *Psychology and Aging, 8,* 44–55.

Schanck, R., & Abelson, R. P. (1977). *Scripts, plans, goals, and understanding.* Hillsdale, NJ: Erlbaum.

Schneider, W., Korkel, J., & Weinert, F. E. (1989). Domain-specific knowledge and memory performance: A comparison of high- and low-aptitude children. *Journal of Educational Psychology, 81,* 306–312.

Scholer, S. J., Mitchel, E. F., Jr., & Ray, W. A. (1997). Predictors of injury mortality in early childhood. *Pediatrics, 100,* 342–347.

Schuckit, M. A., & Schuckit, J. J. (1989). Substance use and abuse: A risk factor in youth suicide. In *Report of the Secretary's Task Force on Youth Suicide. Vol. 2.* Washington, DC: U.S. Government Printing Office.

Schwartz, D., Dodge, K. A., Pettit, G. S., & Bates, J. E. (1997). The early socialization of aggressive victims of bullying. *Child Development, 68,* 665–675.

Schwartz, J. C., Schrager, J. B., & Lyons, A. E. (1983). Delay of gratification by preschoolers: Evidence for the validity of the choice paradigm. *Child Development, 54,* 620–625.

Scott-Jones, D., & Turner, S. L. (1988). Sex education, contraceptive and reproductive knowledge, and contraceptive use among black adolescent females. *Journal of Adolescent Research, 3,* 171–187.

Sedlak, A. J., & Broadhurst, D. D. (1996). *Third national incidence study of child abuse and neglect.* U.S. Department of Health and Human Services. Washington, DC: U.S. Government Printing Office.

Seiber, J. E. (1980). A social learning approach to morality. In M. Windmiller, N. Lambert, & E. Turiel (Eds.), *Moral development and socialization.* Boston: Allyn & Bacon.

Seifer R., & Schiller M., (1995). In E. Waters, B. E. Vaughn, G. Posada, & K. Kondo-Ikemura (Eds.), Caregiving, cultural, and cognitive perspectives on secure-base behavior and working models: New growing points of attachment theory and research. *Monographs of the Society for Research in Child Development,* Serial No. 244, 60, Nos. 2–3.

Seifer, R., Sameroff, A. J., Barrett, L.C., & Krafchuk, E. (1994). Infant temperament measured by multiple observations and mother report. *Child Development, 65,* 1478–1490.

Seixas, P. (1993). Historical understanding among adolescents in a multicultural setting. *Curriculum Inquiry, 23,* 301–327.

Shaw, G. M., O'Malley, C. D., Wasserman, C. R., Tolarova, M. M., & Lammer, E. J. (1995). Maternal periconceptional use of multivitamins and reduced risk for conotruncal heart defects and limb deficiencies among offspring. *American Journal of Medical Genetics, 59,* 536–545.

Sherman, J. A. (1978). *Sex-related cognitive differences: An essay on theory and evidence.* Springfield, IL: Thomas.

Shifflett-Simpson, K., & Cummings, E. M. (1996). Mixed message resolution and children's responses to interadult conflict. *Child Development, 67,* 437–448.

Short-DeGraff, M. (1988). Sensory and perceptual development and behavioral organization (pp. 337–410). In M. Short-DeGraf (Ed), *Human development for occupational and physical therapists.* Baltimore: Williams & Wilkins.

Shulman, S., Seiffge-Krenke, I., & Samat, J. (1987). Adolescent coping style as a function of perceived family climate. *Journal of Adolescent Research, 2,* 367–381.

Siegler, R. S. (1976). Three aspects of cognitive development. *Cognitive Psychology, 8,* 481–520.

Siegler, R. S. (1991). *Children's thinking* (2nd ed.). Englewood Cliffs, NJ: Prentice-Hall.

Siegler, R. S. (1996a). Unidimensional thinking, multidimensional thinking, and characteristic tendencies of thought. In A. J. Sameroff & M. M. Haith (Eds.), *The five to seven year shift: The age of reason and responsibility* (pp. 63–84). Chicago: University of Chicago Press.

Siegler, R. S. (1996b). *Emerging minds: The process of change in children's thinking.* New York: Oxford University Press.

Siegler, R. S. (1998). *Children's thinking* (3rd ed.). Upper Saddle River, NJ: Prentice-Hall.

Siegler, R. S., & Robinson, M. (1982). The development of numerical understandings. In H. W. Reese & L. P. Lipsitt (Eds.), *Advances in child development and behavior* (Vol. 16). New York: Academic Press.

Silverstein, B., Perdue, L., Peterson, B., & Kelly, E. (1986). The role of the mass media in promoting a thin standard of bodily attractiveness for women. *Sex Roles, 14,* 519–532.

Simmons, R. G., & Blyth, D. A. (1987). *Moving into adolescence.* New York: Aldine de Gruyter.

Simpson, G. E. & Yinger, J. M. (1985). *Racial and cultural minorities* (5th Edition). New York; Plenum Press.

Simpson, J. L. (1995). Pregnancy and the timing of intercourse. *New England Journal of Medicine, 333,* 1563–1565.

Sinclair, A. H., et al. (1990). A gene from the human sex-determining region encodes a protein with homology to a conserved DNA-binding motif. *Nature, 346,* 240–244.

Singer, D. B. (1995). Human embryogenesis. In D. R. Coustan, R. V. Haning, Jr., & D. B. Singer (Eds.), *Human reproduction: Growth and development* (pp. 27–37). New York: Little, Brown.

Singer, D. G., & Singer, J. L. (1990). *The house of make-believe.* Cambridge, MA: Harvard University Press.

Sitskoorn, M. M., & Smitsman, A. W. (1995). Infants' perception of dynamic relations between objects: Passing through or support? *Developmental Psychology, 31,* 437–447.

Sittenfeld, C. (1995). Your life as a girl. In B. Findlen (Ed.), *Listen up: Voices from the next feminist generation* (pp. 36–44). Seattle: Seal Press.

Skinner, B. F. (1938). *The behavior of organisms: An experimental analysis.* New York: Appleton-Century-Crofts.

Skinner, B. F. (1953). *Science and human behavior.* New York: Macmillan.

Skinner, B. F. (1961). *Cumulative record* (Rev. ed.). New York: Appleton-Century-Crofts.

Skoog, S. J. (1998). Editorial: Behavior modification in the treatment of enuresis. *Journal of Urology, 160,* 861–862.

Slaughter, V., & Gopnik, A. (1996). Conceptual coherence in the child's theory of mind: Training children to understand belief. *Child Development, 67,* 2967–2988.

Slaughter-Defoe, D. T., Nakagawa, K., Takanishi, R., & Johnson, D. J. (1990). Toward cultural/ecological perspectives on schooling and achievement in African- and Asian-American children. *Child Development, 61,* 363–383.

Slavin, R. E. (1985). Cooperative learning: Applying contact theory in desegregated schools. *Journal of Social Issues, 31,* 45–62.

Sloane, J., Kellerman, A., Reay, D., Ferris, J., Kospesell, T., Rivara, F., Rice, C., Gray, L., & LoGerfo, J. (1988). Handgun regulation, crime, assaults, and homicides. *New England Journal of Medicine, 319,* 1256–1262.

Smetana, J. G., & Asquith, P. (1994). Adolescents' and parents' conceptions of parental authority and personal autonomy. *Child Development, 65,* 1147–1162.

Smetana, J. G., & Berent, R. (1993). Adolescents' and mothers' evaluations of justification for disputes. *Journal of Adolescent Research, 8,* 252–273.

Smetana, J. G., Braeges, J. L., & Yau, J. (1991). Doing what you say and saying what you do: Reasoning about adolescent-parent conflict in interviews and interactions. *Journal of Adolescent Research, 6,* 276–295.

Smetana, J. G., & Gaines, C. (1999). Adolescent-parent conflict in middle-class African American families. *Child Development, 70,* 1447–1463.

Smetana, J. G., Kelly, M., & Twentyman, C. T. (1984). Abused, neglected, and nonmaltreated children's conceptions of moral and conventional transgressions. *Child Development, 55,* 277–287.

Smetana, J. G., Toth, S. L., Cicchetti, D., Bruce, J., Kane, P., & Daddis, C. (1999). Maltreated and nonmaltreated preschoolers' conceptions of hypothetical and actual moral transgressions. *Developmental Psychology, 35,* 269–281.

Smith, J. A., & Epstein, L. H. (1991). Behavioral economic analysis of food choice in obese children. *Appetite, 17,* 91–95.

Smith, J. C. (1994). Hedgehog, the floor plate, and the zone of polarizing activity. *Cell, 76,* 193–196.

Smith, L., & Rhodes, J. (1994, April). *Exploring female representation in current adolescent literature.* Paper presented at the annual meeting of the American Educational Research Association, New Orleans.

Smith, T. E. (1990). Parental separation and the academic self-concepts of adolescents: An effort to solve the puzzle of separation effects. *Journal of Marriage and the Family, 52,* 107–118.

Smolak, L., Levine, M. P., & Gralen, S. (1993). The impact of puberty and dating on eating problems among middle school girls. *Journal of Youth and Adolescence, 22,* 355–368.

Snow, C. E. (1995). Issues in the study of input: Finetuning, universality, individual and developmental differences, and necessary causes. In P. Fletcher & B. MacWhinney (Eds.), *The handbook of child language* (pp. 180–193). Oxford: Blackwell.

Snow, R. E. (1986). Individual differences and the design of educational programs. *American Psychologist, 41,* 1029–1039.

Sochting, I., Skoe, E. E., & Marcia, J. E. (1994). Care-oriented moral reasoning and prosocial behavior: A question of gender or sex role orientation. *Sex Roles, 31,* 131–147.

Sokolov, E. M. (1963). Higher nervous functions: The orienting reflex. *Annual Review of Physiology, 25,* 545–580.

Solomon, G. (1990). Using technology to reach at-risk students. *Electronic Learning, 9,* 14–15.

Solomon, G. E. A., Johnson, S. C., Zaitchik, D., & Carey, S. (1996). Like father, like son: Young children's understanding of how and why offspring resemble their parents. *Child Development, 67,* 151–171.

Sorel, N. C. (1984). *Ever since Eve: Personal reflections on childbirth.* New York: Oxford University Press.

Sorenson, R. C. (1973). *Adolescent sexuality in contemporary America: Personal values and sexual behavior, ages thirteen to nineteen.* New York: World.

Sowell, T. (1978). Race and IQ reconsidered. In T. Sowell (Ed.), *American ethnic groups.* Washington, DC: Urban Institute.

Speight, S. L., Vera, E. M., & Derrickson, K. B. (1996). Racial self-designation, racial identity, and self-esteem revisited. *Journal of Black Psychology, 22,* 37–52.

Spelke, E. S. (1988). Where perceiving ends and thinking begins: The apprehension of objects in infancy. In A. Yonas (Ed.), *Perceptual development in infancy: The Minnesota Symposia on Child Psychology,* Vol. 20. Hillsdale, NJ: Erlbaum.

Spencer, M. B. (1985). Racial variations in achievement prediction: The school as a conduit for macrostructural cultural tension. In H. McAdoo & J. McAdoo (Eds.), *Black children: Social, educational, and parental environments.* Beverly Hills: Sage.

Spires, H. A., Gallini, J., & Riggsbee, J. (1992). Effects of schema-based and text structure-based cues on expository prove comprehension in fourth graders. *Journal of Experimental Education, 60,* 307–320.

Spreen, O. (1988). *Learning disabled children growing up.* New York: Oxford University Press.

Springer, K. (1996). Young children's understanding of a biological basis for parent-offspring relations. *Child Development, 67,* 2841–2856.

Sroufe, L. A., Bennett, C., Englund, M., Urban, J., & Shulman, S. (1993). The significance of gender boundaries in preadolescence: Contemporary correlates and antecedents of boundary violations and maintenance. *Child Development, 64,* 455–466.

Stahl, S. A., McKenna, M. C., & Pagnucco, J. R. (1994). The effects of whole-language instruction: An update and a reappraisal. *Educational Psychologist, 29,* 175–185.

Starkey, P., Spelke, E. S., & Gelman, R. (1990). Numerical abstraction by human infants. *Cognition, 36,* 97-128.

Stein, J. A., & Newcomb, M. D. (1999). Adult outcomes of adolescent conventional and agentic orientations: A 20-year longitudinal study. *Journal of Early Adolescence, 19,* 39–65.

Stein, J. H., & Reiser, L. W. (1994). A study of white middle-class adolescent boys' responses to "semenarche" (the first ejaculation). *Journal of Youth and Adolescence, 23,* 373–384.

Stein, Z., Susser, M., Saenger, G., & Marolla, F. (1975). *Famine and development: The Dutch hunger winter of 1944–1945.* Oxford: Oxford University Press.

Steinberg, L. (1987). The impact of puberty on family relations: Effects of pubertal status and pubertal timing. *Developmental Psychology, 23,* 451–460.

Steinberg, L. (1989). Reciprocal relationship between parent-child distance and pubertal maturation. *Developmental Psychology, 24,* 122–128.

Steinberg, L., Brown, B. B., & Dornbusch, S. M. (1996). *Beyond the classroom.* New York: Simon & Schuster.

Steinberg, L., Lamborn, S. D., Darling, N., Mounts, N. S., & Dornbusch, S. M. (1994). Over–time changes in adjustment and competence among adolescents from authoritative, authoritarian, indulgent, and neglectful families. *Child Development, 65,* 754–770.

Stevenson-Hinde, J. (1998). Parenting in different cultures: Time to focus. *Developmental Psychology, 34,* 698–700.

Stigler, J. W., & Stevenson, H. W. (1991, Spring). How Asian teachers polish each lesson to perfection. *American Educator,* 12–20, 43–47.

Stiles, D. A., Gibbons, J. L., Hardardottir, S., & Schnellmann, J. (1987). The ideal man or woman as described by young adolescents in Iceland and the United States. *Sex Roles, 17,* 313–320.

Stipek, D. (1995). The development of pride and shame in toddlers. In J. P. Tangney & K. W. Fischer (Eds.), *Self-conscious emotions: The psychology of shame, guilt, embarrassment, and pride* (pp. 237–254). New York: Guilford Press.

Stipek, D., Recchia, S., & McClintic, S. (1992). Self-evaluation in young children. *Monographs of the Society for Research in Child Development, 57* (Serial No. 226).

Stoddart, T., & Turiel, E. (1985). Children's concepts of cross-gender activities. *Child Development, 56,* 1241–1252.

Straus, M. A., & Gelles, R. J. (1986). Societal change in family violence from 1975 to 1985 as revealed by two national surveys. *Journal of Marriage and the Family, 48,* 465–479.

Streissguth, A. P. (1994). A long-term perspective of FAS. *Alcohol Health & Research World, 18,* 74–81.

Streri, A., & Spelke, E. S. (1988). Haptic perception of objects in infancy. *Cognitive Psychology, 20,* 1–23.

Strong, B., & DeVault, C. (1999). *Human sexuality* (3rd ed.). Mountain View, CA: Mayfield.

Sue, S. (1991). Ethnicity and culture in psychological research and practice. In J. Goodchilds (Ed.), *Psychological perspectives on human diversity in America* (pp. 51–85). Washington, DC: American Psychological Association.

Super, C. M., Herrera, M. G., & Mora, J. O. (1990). Long-term effects of food supplementation and psychosocial intervention on the physical growth of Colombian infants at risk of malnutrition. *Child Development, 61,* 29–49.

Swanston, H. Y., Tebbutt, J. S., O'Toole, B. I., & Oates, R. K. (1997). Sexually abused children 5 years after presentation: A case-control study. *Pediatrics, 100,* 600–608.

Swarr, A. E., & Richards, M. H. (1996). Longitudinal effects of adolescent girls' pubertal development, perceptions of pubertal timing, and parental relations on eating problems. *Developmental Psychology, 32,* 636–646.

Switzer, J. Y. (1990). The impact of generic word choices: An empirical investigation of age- and sex-related differences. *Sex Roles, 22,* 69–82.

Szymczak, J. T., Jasinska, M., Pawlak, E., & Zwierzykowska, M. (1993). Annual and weekly changes in the sleep wake rhythm of school children. *Sleep, 16,* 433–435.

Tanaka, J. W., & Taylor, M. (1991). Object categories and expertise: Is the basic level in the eye of the beholder? *Cognitive Psychology, 23,* 457–482.

Tanner, J. M. (1974). Sequence and tempo in the somatic changes in puberty. In M. M. Grumbach, G. D. Grave, & F. E. Mayer (Eds.), *Control of the onset of puberty.* New York: Wiley.

Tanner, J. M. (1978). *Foetus into man: Physical growth from conception to maturity.* Cambridge, MA: Harvard University Press.

Tanner, J. M. (1991). Menarche, secular trend in age of. In R. M. Lerner, A. C. Petersen, & J. Brooks-Gunn (Eds.), *Encyclopedia of adolescence* (Vol. 2, pp. 637–641). New York: Garland.

Tavris, C., & Wade, C. (1984). *The longest war: Sex differences in perspective* (2nd ed.). San Diego: Harcourt Brace Jovanovich.

Taylor, M., & Carlson, S. M. (1997). The relation between individual differences in fantasy and theory of mind. *Child Development, 68,* 436–455.

Terman, L. M. (1925). *Genetic studies of genius. Vol. 1: Mental and physical traits of a thousand gifted children.* Stanford, CA: Stanford University Press.

Thatcher, R. W. (1994). Cyclic cortical reorganization. In G. Dawson & K. W. Fischer (Eds.), *Human behavior and the developing brain.* New York: Guilford.

Thatcher, R. W. (1997). Neuroimaging of cyclic cortical reorganization during human development. In R. W. Thatcher, G. R. Lyon, J. Rumsey, & N. Krasnegor (Eds.), *Developmental neuroimaging: Mapping the development of brain and behavior* (pp. 91–106). San Diego: Academic Press.

Thelen, E. (1995). Motor development. *American Psychologist, 50,* 79–95.

Thelen, E., & Fisher, D. (1982). Newborn stepping: An explanation for a "disappearing reflex." *Developmental Psychology, 18,* 760–775.

Thomas, A., & Chess, S. (1977). *Temperament and development.* New York: Brunner/Mazel.

Thomas, A., Chess, S., & Birch, H .G. (1963). *Behavioral individuality in early childhood.* New York: New York University Press.

Thomas, J. R., & French, K. E. (1985). Gender differences across age in motor performance: A meta-analysis. *Psychological Bulletin, 98,* 260–282.

Thomas, R. M. (1979). *Contemporary theories of child development.* Belmont, CA: Wadsworth.

Thompson, J. S., & Thompson, M. W. (1986). *Genetics in medicine* (4th ed.). Philadelphia: Saunders.

Thornton, M. C., Chatters, L. M., Taylor, R. J., & Allen, W. R. (1990). Sociodemographic and environmental correlates of racial socialization by Black parents. *Child Development, 61,* 401–409.

Thorpy, M. J., Korman, E., Spielman, A. J., Glovinsky, P. B. (1988). Delayed sleep phase syndrome in adolescents. *Journal of Adolescent Health Care, 9,* 22–27.

Tickle, C., Summerbell, D., & Wolpert, L. (1975). Positional signaling and specification of digits in chick limb morphogenesis. *Nature, 254,* 199–202.

Timmer, S. G., Eccles, J., & O'Brien, K. O. (1985). How children use time. In F. T. Juster & F. P. Stafford (Eds.), *Time, goods, and well-being* (pp. 353–381). Ann Arbor: University of Michigan.

Tittle, C. K. (1986). Gender research and education. *American Psychologist, 41,* 1161–1168.

Tjian, R. (1995). Molecular machines that control genes. *Scientific American, 272,* 54–61.

Tobias, A. L. (1988). Bulimia: An overview. In K. Clark, R. Parr, & W. Castelli (Eds.), *Evaluation and management of eating disorders.* Champaign, IL: Life Enhancement Publications.

Tobin-Richards, M. H., Boxer, A. M., & Petersen, A. C. (1983). The psychological significance of pubertal change: Sex differences in perceptions of self during early adolescence. In J. Brooks-Gunn & A. C. Petersen (Eds.), *Girls at puberty.* New York: Plenum Press.

Toth, S. A. (1986). The boyfriend. In *Life studies: A thematic reader* (2nd ed.). New York: St. Martin's.

Trautman, P. D., & Rotheram, M. J. (1986). Specific treatment modalities for adolescent suicide attempters. In *Report of the Secretary's Task Force. Vol. 3.* Washington, DC: U. S. Government Printing Office. Reported in Trautman, P. D. (1989).

Treiman, R., Tincoff, R., Rodriguez, K., Mouzaki, A., & Francis, D. J. (1998). The foundations of literacy: Learning the sounds of letters. *Child Development, 69,* 1524–1540.

Troiano, R. P., & Flegal, K. M. (1998). Overweight children and adolescents: Description, epidemiology, and demographics. *Pediatrics, 101,* 497–504.

Tschann, J. M., Adler, N. E., Irwin, C. E., & Millstein, S. G., et al. (1994). Initiation of substance use in early adolescence:

The roles of pubertal timing and emotional distress. *Health Psychology, 13,* 326–333.

Tudor, T. (1980). *The Tasha Tudor book of fairy tales.* New York: Platt & Munk.

Turiel, E. (1983). *The development of social knowledge: Morality and convention.* Cambridge, England: Cambridge University Press.

UNICEF. (1993). *The state of the world's children, 1993.* New York: Oxford University Press.

Urberg, K. A., Degirmencioglu, S. M., Tolson, J. M., & Halliday-Scher, K. (1995). The structure of adolescent peer networks. *Developmental Psychology, 31,* 540–547.

U.S. Bureau of the Census. (1992). *Current population reports, Series P-25, No. 1104a, Projections of the population of the United States by age, sex, and race: 1983–2080.* Washington, DC: U.S. Government Printing Office.

U.S. Bureau of the Census. (1996). *Statistical abstract of the United States, 1996* (116th ed.). Washington, DC: U.S. Government Printing Office.

U.S. Bureau of Labor Statistics. (1995). *Employment status of women: By marital status and presence and age of children: 1960–1994* (Bulletin 2340). Washington DC: U.S. Department of Labor, Bureau of Labor Statistics.

U.S. Bureau of Labor Statistics. (1999).*Employment characteristics of families in 1998.* Washington DC: U.S. Department of Labor, Bureau of Labor Statistics.

U.S. Department of Education. (1996a). *Digest of educational statistics 1996, NCES 96-133.* Washington, DC: U.S. Government Printing Office.

U.S. Department of Education. (1996b*). Eighteenth annual report to Congress on the implementation of the Individuals with Disabilities Education Act.* Washington, DC: OSERS.

U.S. Department of Health and Human Services, Children's Bureau. (1998). *Child maltreatment 1996: Reports from the states to the National Child Abuse and Neglect Data System.* Washington, DC: U.S. Government Printing Office.

U.S. Department of Justice. (1995). *Justice sourcebook, 1995.* Washington, DC: Bureau of Justice Statistics.

Van Ausdale, D., & Feagin, J. R. (1996). Using racial and ethnic concepts: The critical case of very young children. *American Sociological Review, 61,* 779–793.

Vandell, D. L., & Corasaniti, M. A. (1988). The relation between third graders' after-school care and social, academic, and emotional functioning. *Child Development, 59,* 868-875.

van den Boom, D. C. (1989). Neonatal irritability and the development of attachment. In G. A. Kohnstamm, J. E. Bates, & M. K. Rothbart (Eds.), *Temperament in childhood* (pp. 299–318). New York: Wiley.

van den Boom, D. C. (1994). The influence of temperament and mothering on attachment and exploration: An experimental manipulation of sensitive responsiveness among lower-class mothers with irritable infants. *Child Development, 65,* 1457–1477.

van den Boom, D. C. (1995). Do first-year intervention effects endure? Follow-up during toddlerhood of a sample of Dutch irritable infants. *Child Development, 66,* 1798–1816.

van den Broek, P. W. (1989). Causal reasoning and inference making in judging the importance of story statements. *Child Development, 60,* 286–297.

van den Broek, P. W., Lorch, E. P., & Thurlow, R. (1996). Children's and adults' memory for television stories: The role of causal factors, story-grammar categories, and hierarchical level. *Child Development, 67,* 3010–3028.

Van de Walle, G., & Spelke, E. S. (1996). Spatiotemporal integration and object perception in infancy: Perceiving unity versus form. *Child Development, 67,* 2621–2640.

Van Gool, W. A., & Mirmiran, M. (1986). Effects of aging and housing in an enriched environment on sleep-wake patterns in rats. *Sleep, 9*(2), 335–347.

Vansant, A. F. (1995). Development of posture. In D. Cech & S. Martin (Eds.), *Functional movement development across the life span.* (pp. 275–294). Philadelphia: Saunders.

Verschueren, K., Marcoen, A., & Schoefs, V. (1996). The internal working model of the self, attachment, and competence in five-year-olds. *Child Development, 67,* 2493–2511.

Viano, D. C. (1995). Restraint effectiveness, availability, and use in fatal crashes: Implications to injury control. *Journal of Trauma, 38,* 538–546.

Vikan, A., & Clausen, S. E. (1993). Freud, Piaget, or neither? Beliefs in controlling others by wishful thinking and magical behavior in young children. *Journal of Genetic Psychology, 154,* 297–314.

Visher, E. B., & Visher, J. S. (1989). Parenting coalitions after remarriage: Dynamics and therapeutic guidelines. *Family Relations, 38,* 65–70.

von Gontard, A., Eiberg, H., Hollmann, E., Rittig, S., & Lehmkuhl, G. (1998). Molecular genetics of nocturnal enuresis: Clinical and genetic heterogeneity. *Acta Paediatrica, 87*(5), 571–578.

von Hofsten, C. (1982). Eye-hand coordination in newborns. *Developmental Psychology, 18,* 450–461.

Vosniadou, S. (1994). Universal and culture-specific properties of children's mental models of the earth. In L. A. Hirschfeld & S. A. Gelman (Eds.), *Mapping the mind: Domain specificity in cognition and culture* (pp. 412–430). New York: Cambridge University Press.

Vosniadou, S., & Brewer, W. F. (1992). Mental models of the earth: A study of conceptual change in childhood. *Cognitive Psychology, 24,* 535–585.

Vuchinich, S., Angelelli, J., & Gatherum, A. (1996). Context and development in family problem solving with preadolescent children. *Child Development, 67,* 1276–1288.

Vygotsky, L. S. (1978). *Mind in society: The development of higher psychological processes.* Cambridge, MA: Harvard University Press.

Wagner, B. M., Cohen, P., & Brook, J. S. (1996). Parent/

adolescent relationships: Moderators of the effects of stressful life events. *Journal of Adolescent Research, 11,* 347–374.

Wainryb, C., Shaw, L. A., & Maianu, C. (1998). Tolerance and intolerance: Children's and adolescents' judgments of dissenting beliefs, speech, persons, and conduct. *Child Development, 69*(6), 1541–1555.

Waldman, I. D. (1996). Aggressive boys' hostile perceptual and response biases: The role of attention and impulsivity. *Child Development, 67,* 1015–1033.

Wallerstein, J. S. (1989). *Second change.* New York: Ticknor & Fields.

Wallerstein, J. S., Corbin, S. B., & Lewis, J. M. (1988). Children of divorce: A ten-year study. In E. M. Hetherington & J. D. Arasteh (Eds.), *Impact of divorce, single-parenting, and stepparenting on children.* Hillsdale, NJ: Erlbaum.

Ward, S. L., & Overton, W. F. (1990). Semantic familiarity, relevance, and the development of deductive reasoning. *Developmental Psychology, 26,* 488–493.

Wark, G. R., & Krebs, D. L. (1996). Gender and dilemma differences in real-life moral judgment. *Developmental Psychology, 32,* 220–230.

Wason, P. C., & Johnson-Laird, P. N. (1972). *Psychology of reasoning: Structure and content.* Cambridge, MA: Harvard University Press.

Wasserman, P. M. (1988) The mammalian ovum. In E. Knobil & J. Neill (Eds.), *The physiology of reproduction* (pp. 69–102). New York: Raven.

Waters, E. (1978). The reliability and stability of individual differences in infant-mother attachment. *Child Development, 49,* 483–494.

Waters, E., Vaughn, B. E., Posada, G., Kondo-Ikemura, K. (Eds.). (1995). Caregiving, cultural, and cognitive perspectives on secure-base behavior and working models: New growing points of attachment theory and research. *Monographs of the Society for Research in Child Development, 60* (2–3, Serial No. 244).

Watson, D., Clark, L. A., & Harkness, A. R. (1994). Structures of personality and their relevance to psychopathology. *Journal of Abnormal Psychology, 103,* 18–31.

Watson, J. D. (1968). *The double helix: A personal account of the discovery of the structure of DNA.* New York: Atheneum.

Waugh, R. F., Godfrey, J. R., Evans, E. D., & Craig, D. (1995). Measuring students' perceptions about cheating in six countries. *Australian Journal of Psychology, 47,* 73–80.

Webster, C. (1994). Effects of Hispanic ethnic identification on marital roles in the purchase decision process. *Journal of Consumer Research, 21,* 319–331.

Wechsler, D. (1981). *WAIS-R Manual: Weschler Adult Intelligence Scale – Revised.* San Antonio, TX: Psychological Corporation.

Weiner, I. B. (1980). Psychopathology in adolescence. In J. Adelson (Ed.), *Handbook of adolescent psychology.* New York: Wiley.

Welch-Ross, M. K. (1997). Mother-child participation in conversation about the past: Relationships to preschoolers' theory of mind. *Developmental Psychology, 33,* 618–629.

Wells, A. S. (1996). African-American students' view of school choice. In B. Fuller & R. Elmore (Eds.), *Who chooses? Who loses? Culture, institutions, and the unequal effects of choice.* New York: Teachers College Press.

Werner, E. (1989). High-risk children in young adulthood: A longitudinal study from birth to 32 years. *American Journal of Orthopsychiatry, 59,* 72–81.

Werner, E. (1994). Overcoming the odds. *Developmental and Behavioral Pediatrics, 15,* 131–136.

Werner, E., & Smith, R. (1982). *Vulnerable but invincible: A longitudinal study of resilient children and youth.* New York: McGraw-Hill.

Werner, E., & Smith, R. (1992). *Overcoming the odds: High risk children from birth to adulthood.* Ithaca, NY: Cornell University Press.

Wertz, D. C., Fletcher, J. C., & Berg, K. (1995). *Guidelines on ethical issues in medical genetics and the provision of genetic services.* Geneva: World Health Organization.

White, K. L., Speisman, J. C., & Costos, D. (1983). Young adults and their parents: Individuation to mutuality. In H. D. Grotevant & C. R. Cooper (Eds.), *Adolescent development in the family.* San Francisco: Jossey-Bass.

Wilcox, A. J., Weinberg, C. R., & Baird, D. D. (1995). Timing of sexual intercourse in relation to ovulation. *New England Journal of Medicine, 333,* 1517–1521.

Wilder, P. A. (1995). Muscle development and function. In D. Cech & S. Martin (Eds.), *Functional movement development across the life span* (pp. 137–157). Philadelphia: Saunders.

Wiley, A. R., Rose, A. J., Burger, L. K., & Miller, P. J. (1998). Constructing autonomous selves through narrative practices: A comparative study of working-class and middle-class families. *Child Development, 69,* 833–847.

Will, J., Self, P., & Datan, N. (1976). Maternal behavior and perceived sex of infant. *American Journal of Orthopsychiatry, 46,* 135–139.

Williams, M. (1983). *The velveteen rabbit.* New York: Knopf.

Wilson, R. S., & Matheny, A. P., Jr. (1986). Behavior-genetics research in infant temperament: The Louisville Twin Study. In R. Plomin & J. Dunn (Eds.), *The study of temperament: Changes, continuities and challenges* (pp. 81–98). Hillsdale, NJ: Erlbaum.

Wilson, W. J. (1993). *The ghetto underclass: Social science perspectives.* Newbury Park, CA: Sage.

Wimmer, H., Gruber, S., & Perner, J. (1984). Young children's conception of lying: Lexical realism—moral subjectivism. *Journal of Experimental Child Psychology, 37,* 1–30.

Winer, G. A., Craig, R. K., & Weinbaum, E. (1992). Adults' failure on misleading weight-conservation tests: A developmental analysis. *Developmental Psychology, 28,* 109–120.

Winer, G. A., & McGlone, C. (1993). On the uncertainty of conservation: Responses to misleading conservation questions. *Developmental Psychology, 29,* 760–769.

Wise, P., Chavkin, W., & Romero, D. (1999). Assessing the effects of welfare reform policies on reproductive and infant health. *American Journal of Public Health, 89,* 1514–1521.

Witte, J. F. (1996). School choice and student performance. In H. F. Ladd (Ed.), *Holding schools accountable: Performance-based reform in education.* Washington, DC: Brookings Institution.

Witte, J. F., Thorn, A. C. A., Pritchard, K., & Claibourn, M. (1994). *Fourth-year report: Milwaukee parental choice program.* Madison, WI: Robert LaFollette Institute of Public Affairs.

Witter, F. R., & Keith, L. G. (1993). *Textbook of prematurity: Antecedents, treatment, & outcome.* Boston: Little, Brown.

Wolf, W. S., & Campbell, C. C. (1993). Food pattern, diet quality, and related characteristics of school children in New York State. *Journal of the American Dietetic Association, 93,* 1280–1284.

Wolfson, A. R. (1996). Sleeping patterns of children and adolescents: Developmental trends, disruptions, and adaptations. *Child & Adolescent Psychiatric Clinics of North America, 5,* 549–568.

Women on Words and Images. ((1975). *Dick and Jane as victims: Sex stereotyping in children's readers* (Expanded ed.). Princeton, NJ: Author.

Wood, K. C., Becker, J. A., & Thompson, J. K. (1996). Body image dissatisfaction in preadolescent children. *Journal of Applied Developmental Psychology, 17,* 85–100.

Woolley, J. D. (1997). Thinking about fantasy: Are children fundamentally different thinkers and believers from adults? *Child Development, 68,* 991–1011.

Worden, P. E., & Boettcher, W. (1990). Young children's acquisition of alphabet knowledge. *Journal of Reading Behavior, 22,* 277–295.

Wright, L. S., Frost, C. J., & Wisecarver, S. J. (1993). Church attendance, meaningfulness of religion, and depressive symptomatology among adolescents. *Journal of Youth and Adolescence, 22,* 559–568.

Wrobel, G. M., Ayers-Lopez, S., Grotevant, H. D., McRoy, R. G., & Friedrick, M. (1996). Openness in adoption and the level of child participation. *Child Development, 67,* 2358–2374.

Wynn, K. (1992). Addition and subtraction by human infants. *Nature, 358,* 749–750.

Wynn, K. (1995). Infants possess a system of numerical knowledge. *Current Directions in Psychological Science, 4,* 172–177.

Wynn, K. (1996). Infants' individuation and enumeration of actions. *Psychological Science, 7,* 164–169

Yau, J., & Smetana, J. G. (1993). Chinese-American adolescents' reasoning about cultural conflicts. *Journal of Adolescent Research, 8,* 419–438.

Ying, Y. (1994). Chinese American adults' relationship with their parents. *International Journal of Social Psychology, 40,* 35–45.

Yip, R., Parvanta, I., Scanlon, K., Borland, E. W., Russell, C. M., & Trowbridge, F. L. (1992). Pediatric Nutrition Surveillance System—United States, 1980–1991. *Morbidity and Mortality Weekly Report, 41,* 1–24.

Yoder, J. D., & Kahn, A. S. (1993). Working toward an inclusive psychology of women. *American Psychologist, 48,* 846–850.

Youniss, J. (I994). Children's friendship and peer culture: Implications for theories of networks and support. In F. Nestmann & K. Hurrelmann (Eds.), *Social networks and social support in childhood and adolescence* (pp. 75–88). New York: Walter de Gruyter.

Youth Indicators. (1996). *Trends in the well-being of American youth.* Washington, DC: U.S. Government Printing Office.

Zahn-Waxler, C., Friedman, R. J., Cole, P. M., Mizuta, I., & Hiruma, N. (1996). Japanese and United States preschool children's responses to conflict and distress. *Child Development, 67,* 2462–2477.

Zelazo, P. D., Helwig, C. C., & Lau, A. (1996). Intention, act, and outcome in behavioral prediction and moral judgment. *Child Development, 67,* 2478–2492.

Zeskind, P. S., Klein, L., & Marshall, T. R. (1992). Adults' perceptions of experimental modifications of durations of pauses and expiratory sounds in infant crying. *Developmental Psychology, 28,* 1153–1162.

Zhang, J., Savitz, D. A., Schwingl, P. J., & Cai, W. (1992). *International Journal of Epidemiology, 21,* 273–278.

Zito, J. M., Safer, D. J., dosReis, S., Gardner, J. F., Boles, M., & Lynch, F. (2000). Trends in the prescribing of psychotropic medications to preschoolers. *Journal of the American Medical Association, 283,* 1025–1030.

Zollar, A. C. (1985). *A member of the family: Strategies for Black family continuity.* Chicago: Nelson-Hall.

Zuckerman, B. (1988). Marijuana and cigarette smoking during pregnancy. In I. J. Chasnoff (Ed.), *Drugs, alcohol, pregnancy, and parenting* (pp. 73–89). Hingham, MA: Kluwer Academic.

Zuckerman, M. (1990). Some dubious premises in research and theory on racial differences. *American Psychologist, 45,* 1297–1303.

Credits

Photo Credits

Contents p. vii, © Amy C. Etra/Photo Edit; p. viii, © Petit Format/Nestle/PhotoResearchers, Inc.; p. ix, © Mark Richards/PhotoEdit; p. x, © Laura Dwight/PhotoEdit; p. xi, © Michael Newman/PhotoEdit; p. xii, © Jose Carrillo/PhotoEdit; p. xiii, © Tom McCarthy/PhotoEdit; p. xiv, © Myrleen Cate/PhotoEdit; p. xv, © Dwayne Newton/PhotoEdit; p. xvi, © Shmuel Thaler, Jeroboam; p. xvii, © Jeff Greenberg/PhotoEdit; p. xviii, © David Young-Wolff/PhotoEdit; p. xix, © Tony Freeman/PhotoEdit **Chapter 1** p. 0, © Jonathan Meyers/FPG International; p. 2, © Myrleen Ferguson/PhotoEdit; p. 5, © Wm. Cochrane/Impact Visuals; p. 10, © Elizabeth Crews; p. 11, © Neil Ricklen/PhotoEdit; p. 12, © Amy C. Etra/PhotoEdit; p. 14, © Elizabeth Crews; p. 18, © AP/Wide World Photos; p. 25, Courtesy Professor Albert Bandura/Stanford University; p. 26, © Corbis; p. 27, © Ted Streshinsky/Corbis; p. 29, © Rachel E. Chodorow-Reich; p. 31, © Farrell Grehan/Corbis; p. 34, © David Young-Wolff/PhotoEdit; p. 36, © Jerry Bauer/Courtesy Carol Gilligan; p. 40, © Louis Goldman/Photo Researchers, Inc. **Chapter 2** p. 45, © Tom Levy/Photo 20–20; p. 49, Courtesy Carnegie Institution of Washington; p. 52, © Dr. Dennis Kunkel/Phototake; p. 56, © David M. Phillips/Science Source/Photo Researchers, Inc.; p. 57, Courtesy Marine Biological Laboratory; p. 67, © Jose Carrillo/PhotoEdit; p. 69, © SPL/Custom Medical Stock Photo; p. 73, © Joel Gordon **Chapter 3** p. 80, © Lee White/Corbis; p. 84L, Photo Lennart Nilsson/Albert Bonniers Forlag. *A Child is Born*. Dell Publishing Company; p. 84R, Photo Lennart Nilsson/Albert Bonniers Forlag. *A Child is Born*. Dell Publishing Company; p. 86, © Custom Medical Stock Photo; p. 87L, Photo Lennart Nilsson/Albert Bonniers Forlag. *A Child is Born*. Dell Publishing Company; p. 87R, © Petit Format/Nestle/Photo Researchers, Inc.; p. 90, Photo Lennart Nilsson/Albert Bonniers Forlag. *A Child is Born*. Dell Publishing Company; p. 95, Photo Lennart Nilsson/Albert Bonniers Forlag. *A Child is Born*. Dell Publishing Company; p. 99, © Index Stock Imagery; p. 105, © Spencer Grant/PhotoEdit; p. 106, © David Young-Wolff/PhotoEdit; p. 107L, Courtesy of Victor W. Swayze, MD, Associate Professor, University of Iowa, College of Medicine, and staff psychiatrist, Veterans Affairs Medical Center, Iowa City, IA; p. 107R, © Peter Berndt, M.D., P.A./Custom Medical Stock Photo; p. 116, © David Young-Wolff/PhotoEdit; p. 118, © Mark Richards/PhotoEdit; p. 121, © Jonathan Nourok/PhotoEdit **Chapter 4** p. 130, © David Young-Wolff/PhotoEdit; p. 133, © Myrleen Cate/PhotoEdit; p. 138TL, © Elizabeth Crews; p. 138TR, © Elizabeth Crews; p. 138BL, © Elizabeth Crews; p. 138BR, © Elizabeth Crews; p. 139, Courtesy Fels Research Institute; p. 143, © Myrleen Ferguson/PhotoEdit; p. 144, © Michael Newman/PhotoEdit; p. 147, © Amy C. Etra/PhotoEdit; p. 149, © Michael Newman/PhotoEdit; p. 153TL, © Elizabeth Crews; p. 153TR, © Elizabeth Crews; p. 153ML, © Michael Newman/PhotoEdit; p. 153MR, © Laura Dwight/PhotoEdit; p. 153BL, © Elizabeth Crews; p. 159, © Elizabeth Crews; p. 161, © Shmuel Thaler/Jeroboam **Chapter 5** p. 168, © David Young-Wolff/PhotoEdit; p. 170, © Laura Dwight/PhotoEdit; p. 174, © Elizabeth Crews; p. 176, © Elizabeth Crews; p. 185, © Michael Newman/PhotoEdit; p. 186, © Myrleen Cate/PhotoEdit; p. 189, © Mary M. Steinbacher/PhotoEdit; p. 192, © Amy C. Etra/PhotoEdit; p. 194, © Elizabeth Crews; p. 196, © Spencer Grant/PhotoEdit; p. 200, © Michael Newman/PhotoEdit; p. 202, © Michael Newman/PhotoEdit; p. 205, © D. Greco/The Image Works, Inc.; p. 209, © Index Stock Imagery **Chapter 6** p. 212, © Myrleen Cate/PhotoEdit; p. 214, © Myrleen Cate/PhotoEdit; p. 215, © Myrleen Cate/PhotoEdit; p. 216, Courtesy Harlow Primate Lab, University of Wisconsin, Madison; p. 217, © Mary Kate Denny/PhotoEdit; p. 220, © Michael Newman/PhotoEdit; p. 223, © Elizabeth Crews; p. 228, © Mark Richards/PhotoEdit; p. 229, © Tony Freeman/PhotoEdit; p. 231, © Logan Wallace/The Image Works; p. 235, © Index Stock Imagery; p. 237, © Elizabeth Crews; p. 241, © Myrleen Cate/PhotoEdit; p. 242, © Michael Newman/PhotoEdit; p. 243, © Elizabeth Crews **Chapter 7** p. 248, © Myrleen Cate/PhotoEdit; p. 250, © Myrleen Cate/PhotoEdit; p. 252, © Jose Carrillo/PhotoEdit; p. 254, © Clark Jones/Impact Visuals; p. 255, © Tony Freeman/PhotoEdit; p. 256, © Rachel Epstein/PhotoEdit; p. 262, © Elizabeth Crews; p. 263, © Elizabeth Crews; p. 265, © Mary Kate Denny/PhotoEdit; p. 269, © Spencer Grant/PhotoEdit; p. 273, © Mark Richards/PhotoEdit; p. 275, © Stephanie Rausser/FPG International; p. 280, © Cindy Charles/PhotoEdit; p. 288, © David Young-Wolff/PhotoEdit; p. 289, © Elizabeth Crews **Chapter 8** p. 294, © Laura Dwight/PhotoEdit; p. 298, © Elizabeth Crews; p. 299, © M. Bernsau/The Image Works; p. 301, © Michael Siluk/Jeroboam; p. 303, © Tom Prettyman/PhotoEdit; p. 305, © Barbara Stitzer/PhotoEdit; p. 311, © David Young-Wolff/PhotoEdit; p. 315, © Felicia Martinez/PhotoEdit; p. 318, © Laura Dwight/PhotoEdit; p. 319, © William Cochrane/Impact Visuals; p. 321, © Elizabeth Crews; p. 326, © Myrleen Cate/PhotoEdit **Chapter 9** p. 332, © Joel Gordon; p. 335, © Michael Newman/PhotoEdit; p. 337, © Elizabeth Crews; p. 339, © David Young-Wolff/PhotoEdit; p. 342, © Elizabeth Crews; p. 344, © Tony Freeman/PhotoEdit; p. 346, © Michael Newman/PhotoEdit; p. 349, © Phil Lauro/Index Stock Imagery; p. 350, © Tom McCarthy/PhotoEdit; p. 355, © Mary Kate Denny/PhotoEdit; p. 357, © Elizabeth Crews; p. 361, © Myrleen Cate/PhotoEdit; p. 364, © Elizabeth Crews **Chapter 10** p. 372, © Shmuel Thaler/Jeroboam; p. 375, © Elizabeth Crews; p. 377, © Rudi Von Briel/PhotoEdit; p. 381, © Rachel Epstein/PhotoEdit; p. 385, © R. Hutchings/PhotoEdit; p. 386, © Phil Schermeister/Corbis; p. 388, © Michael Newman/PhotoEdit; p. 390, © Elizabeth Crews; p. 396, © David Young-Wolff/PhotoEdit; p. 398, © A. Lichtenstein/The Image Works; p. 400, © Michael Newman/PhotoEdit; p. 402, © Zuzana Killam/Jacksonville Journal-Courier/The Image

Works **Chapter 11** p. 406, © James Wilson/
Woodfin Camp and Associates; p. 409,
© Elizabeth Crews; p. 412, © Tony
Freeman/PhotoEdit; p. 415, © Jonathan
Meyers/JAM Photography; p. 417,
© Michael Newman/PhotoEdit; p. 418,
© Jeff Greenberg/PhotoEdit; p. 422,
© Elizabeth Crews; p. 424, © David Young-
Wolff/PhotoEdit; p. 427, © Jonathan
Meyers/JAM Photography; p. 430,
© Elizabeth Crews; p. 434, © Myrleen
Cate/PhotoEdit; p. 438, © Dwayne
Newton/PhotoEdit; p. 440, © Tony
Freeman/PhotoEdit; p. 441, © Elizabeth
Crews **Chapter 12** p. 446, © Myrleen
Cate/PhotoEdit; p. 448, © John Hartman/
Stock Connection/PictureQuest; p. 450,
© Rudi Von Briel/PhotoEdit; p. 452,
© Jonathan Meyers/JAM Photography;
p. 455, © Cleo Photography/PhotoEdit;
p. 456, © David Young-Wolff/PhotoEdit;
p. 459, © Mary Kate Denny/PhotoEdit;
p. 463, © M. Bridwell/PhotoEdit; p. 465,
© Laura Dwight/PhotoEdit; p. 471, © Maria
Dumlao/Impact Visuals; p. 473, © Cleo
Photography/PhotoEdit; p. 478, Courtesy
Nancy Cobb; p. 481, © Eastcott/The Image
Works; p. 489, © Bill Aron/PhotoEdit
Chapter 13 p. 494, © Brian Phillips/The
Image Works; p. 499, © Michael Newman/
PhotoEdit; p. 501, © Spencer Grant/
PhotoEdit; p. 504, © David Young-Wolff/
PhotoEdit; p. 508, © Elizabeth Crews;
p. 513, © Bonnie Kamin/PhotoEdit; p. 515,
© Tony Freeman/PhotoEdit; p. 519, © 1993
B. Bodine/Custom Medical Stock Photo;
p. 522, © Syracuse Newspapers/Gary Walts/
The Image Works; p. 526, © Elizabeth
Crews **Chapter 14** p. 530, © Joel Gordon;
p. 533, © Robert Brenner/PhotoEdit; p. 536,
© Comstock Inc./M & C Werner; p. 537,
© Elizabeth Crews; p. 539, © Suzanne
Arms/Jeroboam; p. 540, © Ellen Sinisi/The
Image Works; p. 545, © Myrleen Cate/Tony
Stone Images; p. 546, © David Lassman/
The Image Works; p. 548, © Index Stock
Imagery; p. 552, © Michael Newman/
PhotoEdit; p. 556, © Jeff Greenberg/
PhotoEdit; p. 561, © Will Hart/PhotoEdit
Chapter 15 p. 568, © Index Stock Imagery;
p. 572, © Elizabeth Crews; p. 576, © Elizabeth
Crews; p. 578, © Bonnie Kamin/PhotoEdit;
p. 579, © David Young-Wolff/PhotoEdit;
p. 581, © Comstock Inc./T. Dickinson;
p. 582, © Robert Eckert/Index Stock
Imagery; p. 585, © Jeff Greenberg/Photo-
Edit; p. 588, © John Eastcott/Yva
Momatiuk/The Image Works; p. 591,
© Skjold Photographs; p. 595, © Elizabeth
Crews; p. 599, © Tom Carter/Index Stock
Imagery; p. 602, © Mark Constantini/SF
Examiner; p. 605, © A. Ramey/PhotoEdit;
p. 608, © Mary Kate Denny/PhotoEdit;
p. 610, © PhotoEdit

Text and Illustration Credits

Chapter 1 Fig. 1.6 From Steven Schwartz, *Abnormal Psychology: A Discovery Approach*, Mayfield Publishing Company, 2000. Box 1.1, Box 1.2 Reprinted by permission of the publisher from *In a Different Voice* by Carol Gilligan, Cambridge, Mass.: Harvard University Press. Copyright © 1982 by Carol Gilligan. **Chapter 2** P. 75 From *The Blue Jay's Dance* by Louise Erdrich. Copyright © 1995 by Louise Erdrich. Reprinted by permission of HarperCollins Publishers, Inc. Box 2.1 From *Choices, Not Chances* by Aubray Milunsky. Copyright © 1977, 1989 by Aubrey Milunsky, M. D. By permission of Little, Brown and Company, Inc. **Chapter 3** Pp. 109, 113 From *The Blue Jay's Dance* by Louise Erdrich. Copyright © 1995 by Louise Erdrich. Reprinted by permission of HarperCollins Publishers, Inc. Fig. 3.7 From *Mothers, Babies, and Cocaine: The Role of Toxins in Development*, edited by Margaret Bendersky and Michael Lewis. Reprinted by permission of Lawrence Erlbaum Associates. Fig. 3.10 *Scientific American*, September 1979, p. 116. Illustration by Tom Prentiss. Reprinted with permission from Nelson H. Prentiss. P. 118 From *The Earliest Relationship* by T. Berry Brazelton and Bertrand Cramer. Copyright © 1990 by T. Berry Brazelton, M. D. and Bertrand G. Cramer, M. D. Reprinted by permission of Perseus Books Publishers, a member of Perseus Books, L. L. C. Fig. 3.11 From *Fetal Development: A Psychobiological Perspective*, edited by Jean-Pier Lecanuet, William P. Fifer, Norman A. Krasnegor and William P. Smotherman. Reprinted by permission of Lawrence Erlbaum Associates. **Chapter 4** Pp. 136, 164 From *Operating Instructions* by Anne Lamott. Copyright © 1993 by Anne Lamott. Reprinted by permission of Pantheon Books, a division of Random House, Inc. P. 159 From *The Blue Jay's Dance* by Louise Erdrich. Copyright © 1995 by Louise Erdrich. Reprinted by permission of HarperCollins Publishers, Inc. Fig. 4.8 Reprinted by permission of the publisher from *The Postnatal Development of the Human Cerebral Cortex, Vol. I-VIII* by Jesse LeRoy Conel, Cambridge, Mass.: Harvard University Press. Copyright © 1939-1975 by the President and Fellows of Harvard College. Fig. 4.9 Adapted from "Pattern Perception in Early Infancy" by P. Salapatek in *Infant Perception: From Sensation to Cognition, Basic Visual Processes, Volume I*, edited by Leslie B. Cohen and Philip Salapatek. Copyright © 1975 by Academic Press. Reproduced by permission of the publisher. Fig. 4.11 From *Cognition and Reality: Principles and Implications of Cognitive Psychology* by Ulric Neisser. Copyright © 1976 by W. H. Freeman and

Company. Used by permission. Fig. 4.12 From *Development in Infancy* by T. G. R. Bower. Copyright © 1982 by W. H. Freeman and Company. Used by permission. P. 154 Graphs in Research Focus Box Reprinted with permission from Dimitry Schidlovsky, the illustrator. P. 165 Chart in Social Policy Box From "Malnutrition, Poverty, and Intellectual Development" by J. Larry Brown and Ernesto Pollitt, *Scientific American*, February 1996. Copyright © 1996 by Scientific American, Inc. All rights reserved. Fig. 4.14 From *The Cerebral Cortex of Man* by Penfield and Rasmussen, Macmillan, 1950. Reprinted by permission of The Gale Group. **Chapter 5** Pp. 174, 176 From *Operating Instructions* by Anne Lamott. Copyright © 1993 by Anne Lamott. Reprinted by permission of Pantheon Books, a division of Random House, Inc. Fig. 5.1 From A. N. Meltzoff and R. W. Borton, "Intermodal Matching by Human Neonates," *Nature*, November 1979, Vol. 282, p. 403. Reprinted with permission from the publisher and the author. Fig. 5.2 From E. S. Spelke, "Where Perceiving Ends and Thinking Begins: The Apprehension of Objects in Infancy," *Perceptual Development in Infancy: The Minnesota Symposia on Child Psychology*, Vol. 20, p. 200. With permission from Lawrence Erlbaum Associates, Inc. and the author. Fig. 5.4 From R. Baillargeon, 1987, "Object Permanence in 3 1/2 and 4/12 month old infants," *Developmental Psychology*, Vol. 23, pp. 655–664. Copyright © 1987 by the American Psychological Association. Adapted with permission. Fig. 5.5 From *Development in Infancy* by T. G. R. Bower. Copyright © 1982 by W. H. Freeman and Company. Used by permission. Fig. 5.6 From Karen Wynn, "Addition and Subtraction by Human Infants," *Nature*, Vol. 358, p. 749. With permission from the publisher and the author. T 5.2 From *Speech and Language Handouts* by Mary Brooks and Deedra Engmann-Hartung, 1976, Austin, TX: PRO-ED, Inc. Adapted with permission. **Chapter 6** Pp. 238 From *Operating Instructions* by Anne Lamott. Copyright © 1993 by Anne Lamott. Reprinted by permission of Pantheon Books, a division of Random House, Inc. Fig. 6.1 From J. Belsky, 1996, "Parent, Infant, and Social-Contextual Antecedents of the Father-Son Attachment Security," *Developmental Psychology*, Vol. 32, pp. 905-913. Copyright © 1996 by the American Psychological Association. Adapted with permission. Box 6.1 With permission from Child Care Aware, a project of the National Association of Child Care Resource and Referral Agencies (NACCRRA), Washington, D.C. Fig. 6.2 From D. L. Newman, A. Caspi, T. E. Moffitt and P. A. Silva, 1997, "Antecedents of Adult

Interpersonal Functioning: Effects of Individual Differences in Age 3 Temperament," *Developmental Psychology*, 33, p. 213. Copyright © 1997 by the American Psychological Association. Adapted with permission. Fig. 6.3 From M. R. Gunnar, L. Brodersen, M. Nachmias, K. Buss and J. Rigatuso, "Stress Reactivity and Attachment Security," *Developmental Psychobiology*, Vol. 29, pp. 191-204. Reprinted by permission of John Wiley & Sons, Inc. T 6.1 From D. Stipek, S. Recchia and S. McClintic, 1992, "Self-Evaluation in Young Children," *Monographs of the Society for Research in Child Development*, Vol. 57, 1, Serial No. 226. With permission from Society for Research in Child Development. **Chapter 7** Box 7.1, 7.2 From K. E. Allen and L. Marotz, 1989, *Developmental Profiles: Birth to 6*, First Edition. Reprinted with permission of Delmar, a division of Thomson Learning. Fax 800 730-2215. T 7.1, 7.2, 7.4, 7.5 From *American Academy of Pediatrics: Guide to Child's Nutrition* by W. H. Dietz and L. Stern. Copyright © 1999 by W. H. Dietz and L. Stern. Reprinted by permission of Villard Books, a Division of Random House, Inc. Box 7.4 From *A Practical Guide to the Evaluation of Child Physical Abuse and Neglect* by A. P. Giardino, C. W. Christian, and E. R. Giardino, 1997. Reprinted by permission of Sage Publications, Inc. **Chapter 8** Fig. 8.2 From C. S. Rosen, D. C. Schwebel and J. L. Singer, 1997, "Preschoolers' Attributions of Mental States in Pretense," *Child Development*, Vol. 68, 1133–1142. With permission from Society for Research in Child Development. Fig. 8.3 From R. Kai, 1991, "Developmental Changes in Speed of Processing During Childhood and Adolescence," *Psychological Bulletin*, Vol. 109, 490-501. Copyright © 1991 by the American Psychological Association. Reprinted with permission. Fig. 8.4 From F. N. Dempster, 1981, "Memory Span: Sources of Individual and Developmental Differences," *Psychological Bulletin*, Vol. 89, pp. 63–100. Copyright © 1981 by the American Psychological Association. Reprinted with permission. T 8.1 From K. McGilly and R. S. Siegler, 1989, "How Childen Choose Among Serial Recall Strategies," *Child Development*, Vol. 60, pp. 172–182. With permission from Society for Research in Child Development. **Chapter 9** Box 9.1 From P. J. Miller, A. R. Wiley, H. Fung and C. Liang, 1997, "Personal Storytelling as a Medium of Socialization in Chinese and American Families," *Child Development*, Vol. 68, 557–568. With permission from Society for Research in Child Development. Fig. 9.2 From T. Stoddart and E. Turiel, 1985, "Children's Concepts of Cross-Gender Activities," *Child Development*, Vol. 56, pp.

1241–1252. With permission from Society for Research in Child Development. T 9.1 From D. Baumrind, 1989, "Rearing Competent Children," in W. Damon, ed., *New Directions for Child Development: Adolescent Health and Human Behavior*, pp. 349–378. Reprinted by permission of Jossey-Bass, Inc., a subsidiary of John Wiley & Sons, Inc. P. 368 Graph in Social Policy Box from *Journal of Applied Psychology*, 1995, Vol. 80, pp. 621–627. **Chapter 10** Fig. 10.2 From K. Ampofo-Boateng, J. A. Thompson, R. Grieve, T. Pitcairns, D. N. Lee and J. D. Demetre, "A Developmental and Training Study of Children's Ability To Find Safe Routes To Cross the Road," *British Journal of Developmental Psychology*, March 1993, Vol. 11, Part 1, pp. 31–46. Copyright © 1993 British Journal of Developmental Psychology. Reproduced with permission of the publisher. P. 387 From "Gryphon" in *Through the Safety Net* by Charles Baxter, p. 909. With permission from Darhansoff and Verill Literary Agency. Fig. 10.4 From A. F. Vansant, 1995, "Development of Posture," *Functional Movement Across the Life Span* by D. Cech and S. Martin, pp. 275–294. With permission from W. B. Saunders. Fig. 10.7 From "The role of the Frontal Lobes in the Regulation of Cognitive Development," *Brain and Cognition*, Vol. 20, pp. 51–73, 1992 by R. Case. Copyright © 1992 by Academic Press. Reproduced by permission of the publisher. Box 10.1 From *American Academy of Pediatrics: Guide to Your Child's Nutrition* by W. H. Dietz and L. Stern. Copyright © 1999 by W. H. Dietz and L. Stern. Reprinted by permission of Villard Books, a Division of Random House, Inc. **Chapter 11** Fig. 11.1 From *Life-Span Human Development*, First Edition by C. Sigelman and D. Shaffer. Copyright © 1991 by Wadsworth. Reprinted with permission of Wadsworth, a division of Thomson Learning. Fax 800 730–2215. Fig. 11.2 From R. S. Siegler, 1976, "Three Aspects of Cognitive Development," *Cognitive Psychology*, Vol. 8, pp. 481–520. Copyright © 1976 by Academic Press. Reproduced by permission of the publisher. Fig. 11.3 From R. S. Siegler, *Children's Thinking*, Third Edition. Copyright © 1997 Prentice-Hall, Inc. Reprinted by permission of Prentice-Hall, Inc., Upper Saddle River, NJ. Fig. 11.4 From D. C. Geary, C. C. Bow-Thomas, L. Fan and R. S. Siegler, 1996. "Development of Arithmetic Competencies in Chinese and American Children's Influence of Age, Language, and Schooling," *Child Development*, Vol. 67, pp. 2022–2044. With permission from Society for Research in Child Development. Fig. 11.5 From J. W. Stigler and H. W. Stevenson, 1991, "How Asian Teachers Polish Each Lesson to Perfection," *American Educator* (Spring), pp.

12–20, 43–47. Reprinted with permission from the Spring 1991 issue of the American Educator, the quarterly journal of the American Federation of Teachers. P. 436 From *The Spatial Child* by John Dixon, pp. 174–175. Courtesy of Charles C. Thomas, Publisher, Ltd., Springfield, Illinois. Fig. 11.6 From C. S. Mueller and C. S. Dweck, 1998. "Praise for Intelligence Can Undermine Children's Motivation and Performance," *Journal of Personality and Social Psychology*, Vol. 75, pp. 33–52. Copyright © 1998 by the American Psychological Association. Reprinted with permission. **Chapter 12** P. 455 From "Gryphon" in *Through the Safety Net* by Charles Baxter, p. 918. With permission from Darhansoff and Verill Literary Agency. T 12.1 From J. G. Smetana and R. Berent, 1983, "Adolescents' and Mothers' Evaluation of Justifications for Disputes," *Journal of Adolescent Research*, vol. 8, pp. 252–273. Reprinted by permission of Sage Publications, Inc. Box 12.1 Adapted from J. G. Smetana and P. Asquith, 1994, "Adolescents' and Parents' Conceptions of Parental Authority and Personal Autonomy," *Child Development*, Vol. 65, pp. 1147–1162. With permission from Society for Research in Child Development. **Chapter 13** Table 13.2 From B. Goldstein, 1976, *Introduction to Human Sexuality*, 1976, p. 80, Star Publishing Company, Belmont, CA. Used with permission from the publisher. Fig. 13.3 Adapted from D. B. Cheek, 1974, "Body Composition, Hormones, Nutrition, and Adolescent Growth," in M. M. Grumbach, G. D. Grave and F. E. Mayer, eds., *Control of the Onset of Puberty*. Reprinted by permission of John Wiley & Sons, Inc. Fig. 13.6 From J. M. Tanner, "Earlier Maturation in Man," *Scientific American*, January 1968, p. 26. Copyright © 1968 by Scientific American, Inc. All rights reserved. **Chapter 14** Fig. 14.1 From J. M. Hunt, *Intelligence and Experience*, Ronald Press, 1960. Used with permission of John Wiley & Sons, Inc. Fig. 14.2 From *The Growth of Logical Thinking: From Childhood to Adolescence* by Jean Piaget and Barbel Inhelder. Copyright © 1958 by Basic Books, Inc. Reprinted by permission of Basic Books, a member of Perseus Books, L. L. C. Fig. 14.3 Reprinted by permission of the publisher from *Psychology of Reasoning: Structure and Content* by P. C. Watson and P. N. Johnson-Laird, Cambridge, Mass.: Harvard University Press. Copyright © 1972 by P. C. Watson and P. N. Johnson-Laird. P. 553 Graph in Research Focus Box from G. Downey, A. Lebolt, C. Rincon and A. L. Freitas, 1988, "Rejection, Sensitivity and Children's Interpersonal Difficulties," *Child Development*, Vol. 69, pp. 1074, 1091. With permission from Society for Research in Child Development. Box 14.2 Adapted from S. L. Ward and W. F. Overton, 1990, "Semantic Familiarity, Relevance, and the Development of Deductive Reasoning," *Developmental Psychology*, Vol. 26, pp. 488–493. Copyright © 1990 by the American Psychological Association. Adapted with permission. Box 14.3 From D. N. Perkins, 1987, "Knowledge as Design: Teaching Thinking Through Content," in *Teaching Thinking Skills: Theory and Practice* by J. B. Baron and R. J. Sternberg. With

permission from David Perkins. **Chapter 15** Pp. 577–578 From *Identity: Youth and Crisis* by Erik H. Erikson. Copyright © 1968 by W. W. Norton & Company, Inc. Used by permission of W. W. Norton & Company, Inc. P. 588 From *Voices in the Mirror* by Gordon Parks. Copyright © 1990 by Gordon Parks. Used by permission of Doubleday, a division of Random House, Inc. Fig. 15.1 From S. T. Ennett and K. E. Bauman, 1996, "Adolescent Social Networks: School, Demographic, and

Longitudinal Considerations," *Journal of Adolescent Research*, vol. 11, pp. 194–215. Reprinted by permission of Sage Publications, Inc. Fig. 15.2 Adapted from S. J. Blumenthal and D. J. Kupfer, 1986, "Generalizable Treatment Strategies for Suicidal Behavior" in *Psychobiology of Suicidal Behavior, Annals of the New York Academy of Sciences, Volume 487*, edited by J. J. Mann and M. Stanley, New York Academy of Sciences, New York, 1986, pp. 327–340. Used with permission.

Author Index

Author Index **I-9**

Pope, S. K., 290, 367
Porter, R. H., 143
Posada, G., 215, 218
Posada, R., 218
Posner, J. K., 378–379
Povinelli, D. J., 334, 336, 450
Powell, C. A., 164, 166
Powell, G. J., 587
Powell, K. E., 611
Power, T. G., 361, 364
Powers, S. I., 577
Pratt, M. W., 364
Pribram, K. H., 19, 258
Price, D. W. W., 329
Prislin, R., 279
Pritchard, K., 443
Provenzano, F., 9
Pryds, O., 101
Pungello, E. P., 224, 225
Purcell, P., 428
Purdie, V., 470
Putallaz, M., 458

Queen, P. M., 165
Quinn, P. C., 192, 193

Ragozin, A., 362
Rajala, A. K., 382–383
Ramey, C. T., 201, 440
Ramey, S. L., 224, 227
Ramirez, O., 472
Ramsay, D. S., 230
Ratcliffe, S. G., 388
Raudenbush, S. W., 562
Ravizza, R., 308
Rawling, P., 194
Ray, W., 308
Ray, W. A., 280, 281
Reay, D., 601
Recchia, S., 239, 240
Reese, E., 338
Reese, H. W., 14, 17, 18
Reeve, R. A., 413
Reid, M. K., 227
Reilly, J., 197
Reimer, J., 551
Reiser, L. W., 508
Reiss, A. L., 258
Reiss, D., 73
Reitsma, P., 427
Renderer, B., 431
Repacholi, B. M., 193
Repetti, R. L., 470
Repucci, N. D., 438
Resnick, M., 607
Restak, R., 498
Reynolds, A. J., 201, 441
Reznick, J. S., 197, 228, 229
Rhodes, J., 428
Rice, C., 306, 310, 601
Rice, K. G., 525, 575
Richards, M., 499
Richards, M. H., 464, 472, 510, 511, 517, 519, 604

Rickard, R., 106
Riddle, R. D., 84
Rieser, J., 187
Rieser-Danner, L. A., 224
Rigatuso, J., 234
Riggsbee, J., 557
Riksen-Walraven, J. M. A., 455
Rimes, K. A., 68
Rincon, C., 455, 550
Risenhoover, N., 193
Ritenbaugh, C., 516, 518
Ritter, P. L., 572
Rittig, S., 396, 397
Rivara, F., 601
Rivara, F. P., 280
Rizzo, G., 93
Roberts, A. P., 105
Roberts, L., 56
Roberts, W., 354
Robertson, S., 116
Robinson, C. C., 361
Robinson, J., 228, 229, 237
Robinson, J.-A., 283
Robinson, J. A., 186, 187
Robinson, M., 421, 422
Robinson, N., 362
Rochat, P., 150
Roche, T., 601
Rockefeller, J. D., 222
Rodriguez, K., 426
Rodriguez, M. L., 267
Rodriguez, R., 419, 430
Roggman, L. A., 224
Rognon, C., 93
Rogoff, B., 33–34, 35–36, 193, 385, 386
Rogosch, F., 577
Rogosch, F. A., 283
Rogow, A. M., 583
Romanini, C., 93
Romero, D., 30
Rooks, R. N., 279
Roquer, J. M., 104
Rosa, F. W., 100
Rosch, E., 190
Rose, A. J., 244–246
Rosen, C. S., 312
Rosenberg, M., 602
Rosenblum, G. D., 515, 516–517
Rosenthal, D. A., 587, 589
Rosenthal, E., 105
Rosenthal, R., 380
Rosenzweig, E. L., 142
Rosenzweig, M. R., 142
Rosman, B., 519
Ross, D., 24
Ross, D. F., 7
Ross, J. L., 258
Ross, K., 387
Ross, S. A., 24
Rotenberg, K. J., 353
Roth, W. T., 102, 110
Rothbart, M. K., 227, 230, 232, 237
Rothbaum, F., 361
Rotheram, M. J., 350, 431, 432, 459, 460, 605

Rotheram-Borus, M. J., 460
Rovee-Collier, C., 146
Rowan, B., 562
Rowe, D. C., 348
Royle, R., 490
Rubin, D. H., 104
Rubin, J., 9
Rubin, K. H., 361
Rubin, Z., 355, 356
Ruble, D. N., 508, 509
Ruck, M. D., 469
Ruderman, R., 442–443
Ruiz-Pelaez, J. G., 124–125
Runyan, D. K., 288, 368
Russell, A., 358
Russell, C. M., 164
Rustici, J., 225
Rutter, M., 602
Ryskina, V. L., 198

Sabatelli, R. M., 572, 573
Sadler, T. W., 82–83, 86, 88, 91, 98, 100, 140
Saenger, G., 100
Safer, D. J., 395
Sahni, R., 132
Salkovskis, P. M., 68
Saltz, E., 264, 265
Samalin, N., 474
Samat, J., 577
Sameroff, A. J., 230
Sanders, K. M., 277
Sanders, L., 148
Sandler, D. P., 111
Sano, H., 545
Sansavini, A., 195
Sapiro, C. M., 480
Sarigiani, P. A., 596
Sarlom, A. J., 440
Savage, M. P., 515
Savi, A., 218
Savitz, D. A., 104, 105, 110, 111
Scafidi, F., 126
Scanlon, K., 164
Scanlon, K. S., 100
Scarr, S., 71, 72, 225, 235
Schaal, B., 93
Schaffer-Neitz, R., 470
Schaie, K. W., 546
Schanberg, S. M., 126
Schanck, R., 329
Schieve, L. A., 100
Schiller, 215
Schmid, K., 362
Schneider, W., 327
Schnellmann, J., 515
Schoeffs, V., 353
Schoelmerich, A., 218
Schoenbach, C., 602
Scholer, S. J., 280, 281
Schooler, C., 602
Schrager, J. B., 267
Schramm, W. F., 105
Schulte, M. C., 278

Subject Index

remarriage, 463–464
role clarity, 464
siblings, 472–474
single-parent, 462–463
as social capital, 288–291
suicide, 606
in transition, 460–474
See also fathers; mothers; parenting
FAS (fetal alcohol syndrome), 106–109, *107, 110*
fast mapping, 202, 210
fathers
attachment patterns, *221,* 221–222
divorce, 461
noncustodial, 365
smoking by, 105
toxicity from, 110–113
fatigue, 603
fearfulness, 230, 232–233, 256
Federal Family and Medical Leave (1993), 222
female genital mutilation, 507
females. *See* girls
fertile period, 57–58
fertilization, 52–58, 74–76, 78, 82–83, *83*
fetal alcohol effects (FAE), 107, *110*
fetal alcohol syndrome (FAS), 106–109, *107, 110*
"file drawer problem," 224
fine motor skills, 259–262
firearms, 611
firefighters, 110
five-year-olds
controllability of thoughts, 416
increased control, 251–252, 265
memory, *327*
pedestrian safety, 383–384
self-care, *257*
sex roles, 347
skill development, *259*
understanding by, 316
See also early childhood
Fleming, Alexander, 555–556
flow, in infants, 158–160
folic acid, 99–100
follicle-stimulating hormone (FSH), 50, *497,* 498
fontanels, 139–140, *140*
Food Stamp Program, 400, 404–405
foreskin, 507
formal operational thought, 537–539
four-year-olds
delay of gratification, 267
expectations, 256
individuation, 251–252
racial constancy, 352
self-care, *257*
self-recognition, 335
skill development, *259*
understanding by, 311–312, 315, 317
See also early childhood
free-response data, 469
Freud, Anna, 26–27

Freud, Sigmund
drive reduction, 216, 246
moral development, 486–488, 492
Oedipal/Electra complexes, 345–346, 369
psychodynamic theory, 16, 20–21, 25–26, 42–43
friendships
adolescence, 591–599, 612–613
aggressive children, 458
constructive interpretation, 570–571, 612
cross-ethnic, 459–460, 491, 596, 613
early childhood, 355–359, 370
intergenerational, 382–383
middle childhood, 380, 454–460, 491
parental authority over, 467–470
peer groups, 596–599, 613
popularity, 455–457
preadolescence, 593–595
self-concept and, 452–454
suicide and, 604
Frisbee analysis, 558–559
FSH (follicle-stimulating hormone), 50, 498
F-tests, 261

gametes, 50–53
gangs, 356–357, 564, 602
Gardner, Howard, 433
gastrulation, 87
gender differences
after-school hours, 378–379
body image, 515–517
cognitive primacy, 347
constructive approach, 347–348, 369
definition, 342
expectations, 7
height and weight, 388
identity formation, 583–586
intelligence, 545–547
in language, 428–429
morality, 482–487
play, 358–359
psychoanalytic approach, 345–347, 369
response to rejection, 455–456
role transgressions, 343, *343*
sex differences and, 341–342, 369
social learning approach, 343–345, 369
in teaching materials, 428–429, 444–445
See also sex differences
gender identity, 342
gender labeling, 341
gender schemas, 347, 370
gender stereotyping, 342–343, 347, 369, 428–429, 444–445, 524–525
generative interviews, 420–421
generosity, 359
genes, 47–49, 78, 84–85
genetic counseling, 67–68, 70
genetics
chromosomal disorders, 66–67
environmental contributions, 71–77
exceptions to Mendel's laws, 63–65
genetic disorders, 65–66
inherited traits, 60–61
mode of action, 58–59

multiple determinancy, 62–63
sex-linked inheritance, 62–64
temperament and, 228–229
genetic testing, 67–68
genitals
boys, 505–507, *506*
girls, 504–505, *505*
prenatal development, *89,* 89–90
genital stage, 21
genotypes, 59, 71–72, 123
gifted children, 433–435, 445
Gilligan, Carol, 33, 36–39, 41–43, 482–486, 492
girls
depression, 602
early and late maturing, 514
genital mutilation, 507
growth spurt, 503
identity formation, 583–586
importance of body image, 514–516, *518*
masturbation, 508
mathematics, 547
menarche, 500–501, *502,* 503, 507–508, *509*
moral development, 482–486
physical changes of puberty, *500, 502, 503, 630*
recollection of puberty, 500–501
reproductive system, 504–505, *505*
sexual activity, *523*
glans, 505
glial cells, 140
GnRH (gonadotropin-releasing hormone), 497–498, *498*
gonadostat, 498–499
gonadotrophic hormones, *497, 498*
gonadotropin-releasing hormone (GnRH), 497–498, *498*
gonads, *497*
gonorrhea, *102,* 103
gossip, 593–594
grasp reflex, *153,* 155
gross motor skills, 258–259
group identity, 28–29
growth
adolescence, 500–504
behavioral consequences, 254–257, 291
charts, *253, 389*
definition, 11
early childhood, 252–258, 291
middle childhood, 387–389, 398–399, 404
poverty and, 398–404
psychological implications, 263–270, 292
secular trends, 388
stunting, 399
growth hormone, 256, *497*
growth spurt, 503–504
Gryphon (Baxter), 387
guided participation, 36, 386
guilt, 244–245
gunshot deaths, 611
Guthrie, Marjorie, 66
gynosperm, 52

habituation, 19, 180, *180, 182*
Haith, Marshall, 144, 170–171
hand dominance, 262

Kingston, Maxine Hong, 451
kitten carousel, 160, *161*
Klinefelter's syndrome, 66–67
Kohlberg, Lawrence, 476–482, 492
Kohler, Ivo, 186
Korean children, 338, 482. *See also* Asian
    American children; Asian children
Kotlowitz, Alex, 356–357, 368

labia, *505*
labor, childbirth, 114–117, *115*
La Leche League, 163
Lamaze method, 116
Lamott, Anne, 136, 164, 174–176, 187, 238
landmark representation, 187
language development
    bilingualism, 322–323, 419–420, 430–431,
        445
    communication patterns, 430
    environmental risks, *114*
    first sentences, 203–205
    first sounds, 195–197
    first words, 197–200
    gender stereotypes, 428–429, 444–445, 524
    infants, 148, 195–205, 210–211
    milestones, *206–207*
    naming things, 200–203
    parent-talk, 198
    personal narrative, 337–338
    theories of, 205–209, 211
lanugo, 94
latchkey children, 377–381, 403
latency stage, 21
lateralization, 393, 404
laughter, 237–238. *See also* humor
Lau v. Nichols, 322–323
laws, 15
lead intake, *110*
learning disabilities, 435–437, 445
letter recognition, 6–7
LH (luteinizing hormone), 50, 498
liaisons, 597–598, *598*
libido, 20, 26, 486–487
lightening, 95–96
listening, active, 465
lithium intake, *110*
longitudinal design, 178–179, 516–517
long-term memory, 414–415, 444
Louisville Twin Study, 229
love, 611
low birthweight, 100, *104,* 112, 118–119,
    124–125, 128
luteinizing hormone (LH), 50, *497,* 498
lying, 480–482

machine metaphor, 17
magic, 303–305
magnet schools, 442–443
mainstreaming, 437
male generic language, 428–429
males. *See* boys
malnutrition
    during early childhood, 272
    during infancy, 165–166

during pregnancy, 100
    supplemental food programs, 164–165,
        273–274
maltreatment
    bullies and, 458–459
    cues to, 287
    definition, 281
    effects of, 286–287
    evaluations of transgressions, 485
    prevalence of, 282, 286
    risk factors, 283–286, 293
    sexual abuse, 286–288
Mandler, Jean, 192–195, 208–209
Marcia, James, 580–582, 584–586, 589
marijuana, during pregnancy, *110*
masked depression, 603
masochism, in women, 346
masturbation, 345, 508
maternity leave, 221–222
mathematics
    academic tracking, 561–562
    counting strategies, 421–422, *422*
    gender differences, 546–547
    place value, 410, 422
    preschool, 321–322
    teaching methods, 423–424
maturation, 31–32, 383
mean length of utterance (MLU), 204, 210
Medicaid, 402–403, 405
medical insurance, 30
medications, 395, 397
meiosis, 50–51, 53
membrane depolarization, 57
memory
    autobiographical, 337–338
    for causal connections in stories, 328–329
    of childhood, 2–4
    length of, 414–417, 444
    metamemory, 325, 330, 415–416
    reliability of, 260–261
    strategies, 322–327, 330
menarche, 500–501, *502,* 503, 507–508, *509*
Mendel, Gregor, 58–59, 63
menstruation onset, 500–501, *502,* 503,
    507–508, *509*
Mental Development Index (MDI), 163
mental operations, 299–300, 408–410
mental representation substage, *172,* 175
mental retardation, 63
mental uncontrollability, 416
mentoring, 381–383
mercury intake, *110*
mesoderm, 87
mesomorphs, 514
messenger RNA (mRNA), 47–48
meta-analysis, 365
metamemory, 325, 330, 415–416
metaphors, 557–559
Mexican American children. *See* Hispanic
    children
middle childhood
    after-school hours, 377–381, 403
    arithmetic, 420–425
    brain maturation, 391–393

concrete operational thought stage,
    408–410, 443–444
developmental profiles, 374–387, 403
discretionary time, 375–376, 403
friendships, 380, 454–460, 491
growth, 387–389, 398–399, 404
humor, 418–419, 444
information processing, 411–419, 444
limitations of thought, 417–418, 444
memory, 414–417
mentoring, 381–383
morality, 474–488
motor skills, 390–391, 404
new responsibilities, 385–387, 404
parental relationship, 439–442, 464–470
pedestrian safety, 381–385, 404
reading, 425–427
school, 419–439
self-esteem, 451–452, 491
sense of self, 448–454, 490–491
siblings, 472–474
sleep problems, 394–398, 404
Mind in Society (Vygotsky), 34
minority status, 350, 586. *See also* ethnicity
mirrors, 241–242
mitosis, 50
modeling behavior, 277, 292
models
    comparison of, 19
    definition, 13–15, 42
    environmental, 17–19, 21–24, 42, 170–171,
        343–345
    organismic, 16, 18–20, 30–42, 345–348
    psychodynamic, 16, 20–21, 25–30, 42–43
monozygotic twins, 53–54
morality
    behavior, 475–476
    cheating, 476
    conscience, 245–246, 476, 486
    critique of Kohlberg's theory, 480–482
    Freud's theory of, 486–488, 492
    gender differences, 483–486
    Gilligan's ethic of care, 482–486, 492
    internalizing standards, 474–475,
        477–478, 483, 488
    Kohlberg's theory of moral reasoning,
        476–482, 492
    lying, 480–482
    parental authority in, 467
    religious beliefs, 488–490, 492
    stereotypes, 479
    universal principles, 480
moratorium, 580–581, 589
morning sickness, 95–96
Moro reflex, 153, *153,* 155
morphemes, 204
morphogens, 84
Morrison, Toni, 3
morula, 82, *84*
mothers
    attachment patterns, 219–220
    bond with child, 124–125
    differentiation from, 29–30
    emotional understanding, 354–355